Hugo Black of Alabama

Bred to a harder thing than triumph . . .

—WILLIAM BUTLER YEATS

HUGO BLACK OF ALABAMA

*How His Roots and Early Career
Shaped the Great Champion
of the Constitution*

STEVE SUITTS

NewSouth Books
Montgomery

NewSouth Books
P.O. Box 1588
Montgomery, AL 36102

Library of Congress Cataloging-in-Publication Data

Suitts, Steve.
Hugo Black of Alabama : how his roots and early career shaped the
great champion of the constitution / Steve Suitts.
p. cm.
ISBN 1-58838-144-7
1. Black, Hugo LaFayette, 1886-1971. 2. United States. Supreme
Court—Biography. 3. Judges—Alabama—Biography. 4. Judges—
United States—Biography. I. Title.
KF8745.B55S85 2005
347.73'2634—dc22

2004029510

Design by Randall Williams
Printed in the United States of America

TO

CAMILLE AND CHUCK

FOR

MOM, GINNY, DAVID, & PHILLIP

AND IN TRIBUTE TO

PEOPLE OF GOOD WILL EVERYWHERE

WHO LOVE THE SOUTH SO MUCH THEY WANT TO MAKE IT BETTER.

Contents

Acknowledgments

While it bears my name as author, this book depended over a long time upon the good will, support, knowledge, and assistance of many people whom I wish to recognize. As a young man, I began studying the life and times of Hugo Black as a research assistant to Charles Morgan, Jr., who started a Black biography in 1970. The biography languished because, as one of Alabama's great civil rights lawyers, Chuck was too busy helping to bring the U.S. Constitution to the South and, later, to lead a national movement to impeach President Richard M. Nixon.

In the early 1980s, Chuck invited me to become a co-author of the Black biography, but neither of us had adequate time to complete the necessary research, writing, and reflection. Ten years later, because of Chuck's declining health and his faith in an erstwhile research assistant from Alabama, the biography became mine to write. Anyone who examines this book's endnotes will see the enormous importance of Chuck's interviews. What the sources cannot evidence is his boundless intellect, which helped to shape my own knowledge and perspectives. As Chuck said to me once, and I should say to readers, this is not the book he would have written. Everyone also should know that it could not have been written without him.

I do not know the names of countless persons who undoubtedly helped with this book. For one thing, Chuck had a way of enlisting almost everyone he met in any project he undertook. More broadly, books of scholarship depend upon the men and women who quietly operate libraries and archives, one of America's truly important democratic institutions. To all librarians in the reading rooms, stacks, references desks, back offices, and cubbyholes, I offer my genuine appreciation for the assistance and courtesies shown me during the hundreds of hours I spent in your buildings. Also, I want to recognize the people who took the time to recall Hugo Black and the other people and events in their lives. Many of their names are listed in the book's references. Most deserve their own biographies.

A large number of other people helped in my research. Some friends may have forgotten by now. While I did not keep a little black book, as did Judge Black, I do remember my friends' assistance. Cathy Wright and Henry Agee helped with research on specific questions of fact. Mike Mobbs shared his home and ear during several of my research trips to Washington. Jim Looney transported files from Washington to Atlanta. Emily Carsow researched Alabama cases before computers made it as easy as my typing two words into the computer. Neil Bradley also assisted in case research. Tim Pace, Jim Montgomery, Mark Mandell, J. L. Chestnut, Marvin Whiting, John England, and Francis Walter took the time to help track down leads for research and interviews. Tom Gordon, Steve Franklin, and Guin Robinson helped locate photographs.

John Egerton helped in many ways but none more vital than never allowing me to forget the importance of finishing this book. Decades ago, Leslie Dunbar enabled financial support for Chuck Morgan and me to do research. Over the years, Paul Gaston, Raymond Wheeler, Gwen Cherry, Jack Murrah, Mary Frances Derfner, Rick Montague, John A. Griffin, Lottie Shackelford, and Harry Ashmore constituted a Greek chorus of encouragement. I only wish all were here to read the book. Alexis Barrett, Frances Self Drennen, Johnny Greene, Dot Hughley, and Pat Williams spent hours reading my chicken-scratch or listening to my Alabama twang in producing manuscripts and transcripts. All provided useful comments on the work.

I am indebted to Jeff Norrell and David Chalmers for reading parts of earlier manuscripts. Their comments helped me avoid some of my mistakes. My old friends Ralph and Marjorie Knowles have helped over the years with friendly counsel and support. My longtime partner in the work to move societies beyond poverty and racism, Lynn Jones Huntley, read parts of my manuscript and assisted me in thinking deeply about my subject. Larry Yackle is the brave soul who first read all of my early manuscript, produced research materials, and gave me insightful comments on style and substance.

Randall Williams is my friend and editor. He understood and edited this book better than anyone else could. I am also thankful to Suzanne La Rosa, who proves that "steel magnolias" can grow up in New York. Also very supportive at NewSouth Books were Brian Seidman, Mildred Wakefield, and Lisa Emerson. Others who assisted with important detail work were Janet Keene, Jenelle Mason, Horace Williams, and Joyce Alarcón.

Allen Tullos has accompanied me on this intellectual journey since the start. In early days, late at night, he would find me in the University of Alabama Library basement (where old newspapers were stored) and stay an extra hour to help read. In 1971, he and I spent weeks researching and copying newspapers and public records together in the Clay County courthouse. Over the decades, he has helped with interviews, research, reading parts of the manuscript, and long, thoughtful conversations about Alabama and Black. Peter Buttenwieser is one of my best friends who was invaluable to this book. Over the years, he critiqued chapters, responded to my occasional flood of thoughts, and supported my work as a Yankee who understands and loves the good of the South. As Yeats said, "Friends that have been friends indeed."

Finally, I owe a public expression of appreciation to my family in Alabama and in Georgia. The first time I met my wife, Ginny, over thirty years ago, we talked primarily about Hugo Black and Alabama. And, we have continued the conversations over these many years. My sons, David and Phillip, who are certainly "city boys," have come to the conclusion that their "dad can turn any conversation to Alabama and Hugo Black"—and for good reason.

Together these named and unnamed persons have made essential contributions to this book. I truly appreciate each one and hope the book is worthy of their cooperation and support.

STEVE SUITTS

Preamble

'. . . I am a Southerner . . .'

HOMECOMING—1970

Amid persisting, thunderous applause, the old man's head protruded slightly above the podium as he smiled mischievously at one moment, innocently at another. His hazel eyes twinkled brightly, as if they retained a deep, devilish secret which he had no intention of divulging, while from a distance his wrinkled, happy face seemed baby-smooth, almost angelic, brightly lit by the banquet lights that shone about his white hair, white shirt, and white, formal dinner jacket. "I am delighted to be down here," he murmured with a touch of practiced shyness as the audience's noises slowly quieted. "It's always delightful for me to come back to Alabama."

At eighty-four, Hugo L. Black—senior member of the United States Supreme Court—stood before an overflowing crowd of lawyers, politicians, judges, friends, and family who had assembled in Birmingham to welcome him home, to celebrate his remarkable public career which began in this city at a time when most of the audience had not been born. It was July 1970, a sultry, intolerant time in Alabama, and ironically the venue was the Alabama Bar Association's annual convention, a meeting that Black rarely, if ever, attended earlier during his twenty-two years as one of the state's practicing attorneys. Now Judge Black was making the first publicized appearance in his old home since *Brown v. Board of Education of Topeka, Kansas*, the 1954 decision outlawing public school segregation. That case, more than any other single act or event, had propelled America away from government-sanctioned racial discrimination and estranged Black from his homeland.

Black began with a strong, clear voice, trained long before the public use of microphones and honeycombed with an agreeable, distinctively rural accent. The old man had not lived in Alabama for more than forty years, but he sounded more Southern than most of his audience who still lived in the heart of Dixie. "I recall very vividly," he said, "a few years ago, *our* state legislature, that I love very much, passed a resolution suggesting that they would probably purchase a cemetery lot for me in some *other* state." He paused to let the humor take effect, but ripples of nervous, embarrassed laughter were not loud enough to muffle Dorothy Thomas, wife of a Mobile federal district court judge who sat at a table in front of the dais within earshot of the speaker and across from Black's family.

"That's right, Hugo," Mrs. Thomas hissed. "That's where you need to be, Hugo. *In a cemetery lot.*"

"Needless to say," Black continued, "I did not accept."

"We don't want you here, Hugo. *We don't want you!*" Mrs. Thomas muttered loudly. Three years earlier, Judge Daniel Holcombe Thomas had informed Black that he was "one of Alabama's most distinguished sons" and later would tell one of Black's relatives about the "warm reception" that his "friend" Hugo had received at the bar association. Now, however, Thomas sat stone silent allowing his wife's indiscretion, which he usually hushed, to have full range.[1]

"I had a telegram from some people *down* in one of the Southern states," Black remembered. After sixteen years of self-imposed exile, Black was at long last telling one of his favorite stories publicly "*down*" in one of the Southern states, in his own beloved Alabama. "At my home [in suburban Washington] there was at one time a colored family that lived right behind my house. As a matter of fact, they were in speaking distance. More than speaking distance. They *were on part of the original lot* on which my house is occupied," Black said. The telegram was from a group "down in the neighboring state of Florida—their 'affection' for me had extended all the way down to the state of Florida." The group wanted Judge Black to live with the "horrible" racial integration that *Brown* mandated. So, they "had taken up a collection in order to buy" a house and "put a colored family close to me."

"I wrote them," the Judge continued, "and told them I appreciated the favor, but I'd rather they just send me the money . . . because I already had a colored neighbor right behind me!"

Laughter and applause erupted from the audience, including a handful of African Americans who appeared unconcerned that during this time of America's black power and black pride movements the Judge spoke about the "colored," a term of identity replaced two decades earlier by "Negro" and more recently by "black" in respectful public discourse. In Washington, Black's law clerks had changed his draft opinions more than once over the years by writing "Negro" in place of their judge's references to "colored." And, when remembering his Alabama years in court chambers across from the nation's Capitol, Black occasionally had been heard praising a friend for his "Anglo-Saxon courage."

If Judge Black seemed woefully unaware of his outdated patterns of speech after more than three decades closeted within the small circle of the nation's highest court, he did know—without benefit of Dorothy Thomas' outbursts—that his role in placing constitutional law behind the principle of equal rights for all people, regardless of race or color, had earned him the undying hatred of many of the South's white people and their leaders. Since 1954, tons of mail had told him so. "Come down, Hugo, to Alabama," taunted one anonymous letter, "you s.o.b." Another informed Black that white Southerners wanted to "beat your damn brains out" and warned: "should you make a 'return trip' to Alabama, it will be your last trip on earth."

Most Alabama editors were less threatening, but equally hostile. Years after the *Brown* decision, for instance, the *Greensboro Watchman* still fumed: "Hugo Black is a great lawyer," its editor admitted, "but he is more than that. He is an apostate, a turncoat, a quisling. He is any other thing as long as it is an opprobrious term meant to describe a man who used his people—his benefactors—for all they are worth and then turned on them."

In past years, Judge Black had worried that this hatred might endanger the safety and welfare of his law clerks, who were mostly from Alabama and the South, if they returned home to practice law. Black's own son, Hugo Jr., was a lawyer who left Alabama after years of enduring anonymous phone calls condemning his daddy as a "nigger-lover." Massive, white anger made it impossible for anyone named Hugo Black to win a jury verdict before Birmingham's all-white juries. In turn, Black's law clerks and family had dreaded invitations for him to appear publicly in Alabama or the Deep South. To their relief, Black refused all invitations after 1954 because he knew that either danger or embarrassment would befall him and his Court if he made a publicized visit in Dixie.

Though the intervening years had dampened the hostility, Judge Black remained a man who inspired vitriolic hatred among whites of every rank. "I wouldn't walk two steps to see that old scalawag," proclaimed a taxi driver as he ferried guests from the airport to the Parliament House, then Birmingham's poshest, modern hotel where the marquee openly welcomed Justice Black. Many whites in Alabama—from judges and their spouses to rural editors to working people on the margin—remained unwilling to forgive or forget, as if their own sense of Southern honor, perhaps their own identity depended on a lingering loathing. "He's done more to tear down white men," proclaimed the cabbie, "than any other white man in the world."[2]

By the summer of 1970, after years of resistance, white Alabama had been forced by the Supreme Court to live with the end of legal segregation: integrated lunch counters, blacks on civil and criminal juries, and the votes of thousands of African American citizens. In fact, the growing presence of black voters had produced an emerging, fragile style of biracial, statewide politics for the first time since the 1890s. This development accounted for the fact that among the hundreds of lawyers and dignitaries standing to applaud Judge Black were Governor Albert P. Brewer and Alabama Supreme Court Chief Justice Howell Heflin.

A month earlier, the state's senior U.S. Senator, John J. Sparkman, had conspired with Black's former clerks to assure that the Judge would attend the event. The senator asked Black to accompany him personally in a meeting with the nation's new chief justice on the pretext that Sparkman needed Black's help in convincing Warren E. Burger to travel to the Alabama Bar Association's meeting. For Black it was a puzzling, rare request, the first time since 1954 that an Alabama member of Congress had sought his counsel and assistance. Sparkman had entered politics supporting an incumbent Senator Hugo Black in the 1930s, but he and every other Alabama politician had kept their political distance after *Brown*. Until now.

Overshadowing this remarkable public endorsement was the harsh, complex reality of Alabama and its politics. Despite promises of change, Alabama was obsessed and manipulated by massive racial fears and hatred. A month before the bar meeting, white Alabama voters had defeated Albert Brewer, a New South moderate, and once more elected George Wallace who employed a simple run-off campaign: "Promise them the moon and holler nigger," Wallace said.

Needing the governor's chair to sustain a planned run for president in 1972, Wallace had attacked Brewer as a "sissy" and the "tool of black militants." Earlier in the summer, Wallace's radio ads had asked white men to suppose "your wife is driving home at eleven o'clock at night. She is stopped by a highway patrolman. He turns out to be black. Think about it . . . Elect George C. Wallace."

His campaign flyers showed an innocent, unsuspecting little white girl in her bathing suit surrounded closely by seven gleeful, half-clad black youth. "This Could Be Alabama Four Years From Now," the ad warned, "BLACKS VOW TO TAKE OVER ALABAMA." As Wallace said to a local white official, "If I don't win, niggers are going to control this state." Conjuring up the sullen, awesome powers of a long racialist tradition, Wallace won.

Now, within the campaign's echoes, Hugo Black had returned home to a state that still could not accept his Court's principle of simple justice and to the welcoming admiration of a coterie of public officials who, for the most part, were victims of Wallaceism. Howell Heflin, an oversized, beguiling judge with a courtly, grandfatherly manner, followed in time Hugo Black and his own fanatically racist uncle, "Cotton Tom" Heflin, to serve cautiously, but honorably, in the U.S. Senate; however, the other state politicians involved in Black's homecoming were Alabama's walking wounded—moderate, timid leaders bludgeoned by the revival of racist demagoguery and now congregating like baleful Irishmen whose memory of a victorious time long ago offered the only solace.

To deflect public criticism or embarrassment, this homecoming had been publicized as an occasion for Alabama lawyers to meet Warren Burger, who had not visited the state since becoming U.S. chief justice. This ruse, too, had complications. Burger had been appointed by President Richard M. Nixon—whom Black greatly distrusted—in hopes that the Midwestern jurist would lead the Supreme Court to curtail many of the judicial decisions which Black had written or joined. Yet, Justice Black loved his Court more than anything else—other than the U.S. Constitution, the South, and Alabama—and he readily agreed to accompany the chief justice to the state. Until "about five minutes before" he entered the hotel's banquet hall, Black did not realize the occasion's true purpose.[3]

Black's former clerks had kept the event's true purpose a secret because they feared that, without a pretext, Black would decline another invitation to appear publicly in the state. They knew that while the risk of embarrassment, misunderstandings, and danger lingered, this convocation might be the last opportunity to celebrate their judge in his own home as one of Alabama's few living prophets.

Even without knowing he would be guest of honor, Justice Black was deeply affected by the prospects of any type of public appearance in the state that twice elected him to the U.S. Senate. Weeks before the trip, he awoke in the middle of the night, worried about how to manage a public reunion with friends, politicians, former clerks, and family. Now, however, as he stood before the huge crowd in Birmingham, Hugo Black glowed with confidence, ebullience, and genuine, boundless joy.

"I do want to just say this," Black stated after promising to be brief, "it is a great pleasure to be back in Alabama." Like a lost survivor unable to realize that he had returned to the Promised Land, Black dwelled on what was obvious to everyone around him. "I love Alabama. I love the South . . . So far as I know not a single ancestor that I ever had settled north of the Mason & Dixon line. They were all Southerners. And so, *I am a Southerner.*"

It was, of course, this very fact that had unleashed the deep, widespread hatred of Judge Black. Many white Southerners believed Black had betrayed his own people, his own friends by forcing the South to dismantle its social customs and, in the words of innumerable Alabama politicians, by destroying "the very foundation of Southern civilization." In truth, he had done a great deal more. Hugo Black stands among a small number of Southerners who had a profound influence in shaping America and American government in the twentieth century. Beginning in the 1930s in Washington as a U.S. senator, he helped the nation out of the Great Depression, prompted a vast reorganization of the nation's airline and utility industries, developed the first federal statute limiting Congressional lobbying, and authored America's first minimum wage law.

As a member of the U.S. Supreme Court, Black was the earliest prophet of America's judicial revolution that radically transformed the nation's governing system, requiring by the 1960s that all agents of government respect an individual citizen's basic liberties regardless of race, religion, region, or income. Because of Justice Black's rulings, American citizens on both sides of the Mason & Dixon line, for the first time in the nation's history, enjoyed entitlements of the Bill of Rights—individual freedoms specifically mentioned in the Constitution that no government official at any level, in any county or hamlet, could lawfully ignore. Judge Black had written hundreds of opinions—many now the law of the land—expanding the rights of free speech to those whom society considered unpopular, weak, poor, zealous, or hated. During the bleak years of McCarthyism, few, if any, Americans provided a steadier moral force to fight against the nation's self-consuming hysteria about disloyalty and communism than Judge Black. In the 1960s he authored the Court's decree giving every poor American facing serious imprisonment a right to a lawyer. He joined his brethren in forcing the South to grant the right to vote to black citizens and in requiring all state legislatures to reapportion fairly. In addition, he wrote the Court's opinion that banned religious prayers from the nation's public schools.

These contributions to American life and law were unique for a white Southerner and prompted people of good will throughout the nation (primarily outside the South) to admire and honor him. But, no less impressive and fascinating was Hugo Black's own mysterious, personal journey from obscure, rural Alabama in the nineteenth century to a rare national prominence in the late twentieth century. Indeed, few public figures in modern American history and among the South's own in national political life appear by modern standards to embody so many contradictions and ironies, as rich and poignant as any cultivated in Southern literature. Some of Black's contradictions were known by legal scholars, critics, and many of the people before whom Black now stood. Some were within memory of only a few friends who, like Black, had survived from another century. Others Hugo Black had kept to himself or his family out of shame.

Together, these incongruities seemed legion—between Black's early days in Alabama and later years on the Supreme Court; between his national, judicial pronouncements and his Southern, political role; between his public persona and his actual person. Often they arose as a natural, innocent consequence of his having endured with a strong, vivid personality through the different fashions and fickleness of several eras, but in other cases the differences appeared on their face as products of purely opportunistic or morally indefensible conduct.

Here, for example, stood a man who never completed high school, never attended a liberal arts college, but who became one of the leading intellectuals of American jurisprudence. The son of a deeply conservative, rural merchant who opposed the Populist movement in the nineteenth century, Hugo Black became one of the first U.S. senators from the South in the twentieth century to propose radical economic reform in America. As a practicing lawyer, Black never wanted to try a case in federal court, although once on the federal bench he became one of the nation's earliest advocates for the federal courts' duty to protect any and all citizens from violations of fundamental Constitutional rights.

In Washington, Black was the author of the U.S. Supreme Court's opinion banning Christian prayers in America's public schools, and in Birmingham he was for twenty years a Baptist Sunday school teacher whose Bible classes in the 1920s were larger than most preachers' congregations. In the course of one lifetime, few people seemingly exceeded Hugo Black in his distrust of most newspapers and news media. And no one outranked him in America as the judicial defender of the press to print whatever they pleased, without restraint whatsoever. A man of strict, prudish morals—a genuine "juris-prude"—Black stood virtually alone in the history of the American judiciary in his constitutional belief that pornography could never be censored.

On the Court, Hugo Black made it particularly more difficult to arrest and convict people of crimes, while in Alabama he worked tirelessly as an aggressive prosecutor who complained often about too many rights for criminal defendants. One of the U.S. Senate's most aggressive and successful investigators, often accused of overriding sacred liberties in the 1930s, Justice Black became the century's foremost judicial critic of unchecked, damaging Senate investigations in the 1950s. On the Supreme Court, Black was the steady advocate for equal rights and an opponent of racial injustice, but as a lawyer in Alabama he was a card-carrying member of the Ku Klux Klan. And, finally, no one loved the South and its white people more deeply and was hated by them more vehemently than Hugo Black.[4]

Almost all in the crowd at the Parliament House on July 17, 1970, were eager on this occasion to forego any recognition of the enigmas and problems of their prophet's past, but, as an old man whose life held many yesterdays and few tomorrows, Hugo Black seemed bound by his own internal compass to return to that mysterious past, as if he could not speak of the present without searching backward. "My mother's people came from the state of South Carolina . . . Others of her people came from Virginia . . . Our people . . . were Irish," recalled the Judge vaguely. "As a matter of fact, the family tradition says that they left that country of Ireland in order to escape being hung," the Judge declared. "They were said to be related to Robert Emmet who was executed in Ireland" for attempting to overthrow English rule. "As a boy I was brought up on Robert Emmet's speech on the gallows and it was magnificent—magnificent then and magnificent now," Black proclaimed.

"My friend Frank Johnson here, I don't know if he is Irish," Black wondered aloud, as he looked across to the federal district judge from Montgomery, "but he does have some of the same traits that made Robert Emmet famous." Since his appointment to the federal bench by President Dwight Eisenhower, Frank M. Johnson had faithfully followed the sentiments and direction of Black's Supreme Court and now rivaled Hugo Black for distinction as the most hated white man of Alabama. After years of publicly criticizing the district judge as an "integrating, scalawagging, carpet-bagging, race-mixing bald-faced liar," George Wallace later suggested that Johnson deserved not a hanging, but a "barbed wire enema." His old friend Frank, Black now observed, was "a fighter for the things he believes in. And that was true of Robert Emmet." And, of course, that was true of Hugo Black.

Reminiscences now cascaded through Black's mind, as he remembered past decades. "This is very familiar ground to me," he continued, "because I had an accident right out in front of this Parliament House back in nineteen hundred and three. At that time, I was a student at the Birmingham Medical College," he recalled. Although his young hands and head were studying medicine, Black's heart was captured by the law, and he had been on his way downtown to the Metropolitan Hotel's lobby to listen to Birmingham lawyers swap stories of their courtroom triumphs.

Rambling through flashes of memory, as the audience sat in complete silence, Black seemed caught in a turnstile of time. Over the decades, Black's personal memory of his Alabama years had become very selective, often recalling the best and forgetting the worst. It was the natural habits of old age—and self-protection. If depicted without context or content, Black's worst moments in Birmingham easily would portray him as godfather to George Wallace, an egotistical demagogue gladly using bigotry to advance personal ambitions. The images that no one in July 1970 would recall included:

- Black standing before an all white jury ridiculing a "crazy nigger woman" and "nigger" men who traveled on a train from Chicago to Birmingham as news boys' screamed "Read All About Race Riot" outside the Birmingham courthouse.

- Black standing in another Birmingham courtroom adjusting window blinds to assure that an all-white jury saw a hostile Puerto Rican witness as a black-skinned "negro" or "dago" in an effort to free a fundamentalist Protestant preacher who killed an unarmed Catholic priest.

- Black parading solemnly in a white hood and full, flowing regalia with other masked members of Birmingham's Ku Klux Klan as they formed a massive human symbol of the fiery cross crackling before them.

- Black standing next to the Ku Klux grand dragon as he smiled at the packed assembly of Klansmen indulgently cheering his acceptance of a lifetime, gold membership card in the brotherhood whose members recently had helped elect him as Alabama's newest U.S. senator.[5]

NOW SPEAKING WITHIN TEN BLOCKS of that erstwhile Klan hall where he accepted the gold Kluxer card, recalling the years of an innocent, young medical student's arrival in Birmingham, Black betrayed no outward signs of envisioning his own worst images. In truth, it did not matter. Disappearing years and contemporary symbols of popular culture had surpassed the meaning of his past choices and conduct. A full, honest portrait of this complex man, his nature, and his living principles, one surviving throughout three tenses of time, would require a detailed accounting of the events, currents, and human choices of each era through which he lived.

Black's complicated past in Alabama, including both his best and worst moments, involved far more than one person's journey in one Southern state. By birthright, Black seemed destined to navigate his life along the lodestars of America's struggles for freedom, prosperity, justice, citizenship, diversity, and unity. In 1886, when Hugo Black's father christened his arrival on earth with a curse, distant events and voices across America were foreshadowing the persistent, pivotal themes that would shape his life and the life of his nation.

After immigrant families contributed thousands of pennies for its construction near Ellis Island, the Statue of Liberty arose in New York's harbor in 1886. The statute became the nation's premiere beacon of hope as Americans fought over the ideals and reality of democratic inclusion. In the same year, union leaders established the nation's largest, enduring labor organization, the American Federation of Labor (AFL), and in Chicago suffered one of its deepest historic tragedies, the Haymarket Trials of 1886, where eight editors of a union newspaper were convicted of murder and, afterwards, four were hung entirely because of their words and association—not their actions or deeds. The evidence at trial proved only that the union editors advocated in writing "armed resistance against capitalistic aggression" and spoke on the day of a deadly bombing about the need for workers to arm themselves. In law, the Haymarket Trials stand perhaps as the American legal system's deadliest punishment of the exercise of free speech and association, and, in labor history, they mark the beginning of America's onerous struggle to create an industrial, democratic society.

In 1886 in the nation's capitol, the U.S. Supreme Court issued a landmark case on American citizenship. Three years after striking down federal laws prohibiting racial discrimination—effectively removing freed slaves and their descendants from the practical protections of the U.S. Constitution—the nation's highest court held that the American corporation (a relatively new creature) was a "person" under the Constitution and entitled to the full protections of due process of law. Thereafter, for three-quarters of a century, the Supreme Court barred the federal government from protecting African American citizens against rabid racialism while, in effect, vigorously requiring state and federal governments to protect corporations as full citizens.

In the same year, two decades after the end of the Civil War, *Atlanta Constitution* editor Henry Grady proclaimed the arrival of a "New South," as he recalled before Northern capitalists the words of a born-again Southern secessionist: "There was a South of slavery and secession —that South is dead. There is a South of union and freedom—that South, thank God, is living, breathing, growing every hour." Grady's notion of a region where everyone puts "business above politics" captivated the imagination of the nation's businessmen and politicians who used the South's oppressive white supremacy and biracial poverty to expand Northern industry, while creating a social mirage of a New South. Into the twenty-first century, the New South would persist as both the hope and a myth of racial progress and define the vague ambitions of a region and nation too busy creating the future to reconcile the past.[6]

Yes, from birth Hugo Black seemed marked by the currents of destiny to chronicle America's struggles for democracy in a new, modern world. Yet, destiny is only the future once interred to the past. Only in reference to that past, only by remembering his own history, could Hugo Black speak of himself in the present tense. And only there—in those past years that had disappeared largely from public memory and recognition—would anyone find the true measure of Black's achievements and, finally, discover the rhyme and reasoning of his riddled life.

1

'Til Death Does Us Part'

The W. L. Black Family of Clay County

At age twenty, shortly before Christmas 1868, Martha Ardellah Street Toland stood encircled by friends before the Rev. M. M. Driver and swore before her Baptist God that she would love and cherish William Lafayette Black, in sickness and in health, for the rest of her life. She made her holy vow in her father's house in Bluff Springs, Alabama, near Hillabee Creek running between Jet Mountain and Mount Ararat, where within living memory Andrew Jackson's soldiers had massacred the Muskogee Indians. If "Della" did not know at that moment, two years after her solemn baptism and eighteen years before the birth of her last child, Hugo, that she would break her vow during a lifetime of tribulation, both she and her new husband understood that theirs was a marriage of ambition and tragedy far more than of passion and love. A tall, stout young man, slightly younger than his bride, with a winning manner and a large, handsome face seemingly unruffled by toil or trouble, "Fayette" Black's features masked a relentless, overriding desire to get beyond the hardscrabble life of his father and family. Fayette and everyone else along Hillabee Creek knew that he had won the hand of an attractive, petite woman from a more substantial family, a manly prize in the poor Southern backwoods of a dispirited nation recently at war with itself. They also realized that her heart truly belonged to Fayette's older brother, Columbus, killed five years earlier on the battlefield which Abraham Lincoln memorialized "as the final resting place of those who here gave their lives that our nation might live."

Columbus Black left home to enlist in the Confederate Army shortly after his seventeenth birthday in 1861, only a few months after Fort Sumter. He had added a year to his age when he signed with Alabama's Fourteenth Infantry Regiment. Typical of many of the twenty-seven thousand young Alabamians who enlisted in that first, innocent year of wartime, "Lum" left a family and a small farm—worked without slaves or profit—for the excitement of battle in defense of the South, the only homeland he could imagine or ever know. And he left Della Street Toland who, like other girls of thirteen at the edge of America's interior wilderness, was approaching an acceptable age for marriage.

Fayette and Della may have been brought together first as teenagers in a shared vigil, awaiting the news of battle and the safe return of her sweetheart and his brother. Southern newspapers reported with enthusiasm Confederate triumphs and heroism in the early years of war, but victories for the South often had heavy losses, and news of the dead and wounded traveled home much more slowly. In the summer of 1862, as General Robert E. Lee frustrated the Union armies around Richmond, the Confederates charged the bluecoats near Frayser's Farm, south of the rebel capital, where fighting deteriorated into confused, hand-to-hand combat. "The Fourteenth Alabama . . . was nearly annihilated," reported the commanding general. More than three hundred men were wounded, missing, or dead. With the grace of Della's prayers, Lum survived, although his regiment continued with only a ghost of its original, youthful strength.

A year later, Lum died on the second day of Gettysburg, a battle which foreshadowed the end of a dream for the Confederacy and for young Della. Filtered through time and religiosity, family legend tells that Lum cried, "Lordy, Lordy . . ." as he and other Southerners fell during General George Pickett's disastrous charge from Seminary Ridge. Military records suggest that Columbus may have been wounded in a rearguard action after Confederate General Ladmus Wilcox moved his men forward to divert the assault on the survivors of Pickett's charge, in a series of maneuvers that could not prevent General Lee's first major defeat.

Wherever Lum died, whatever his last words, his death was a profound, enduring sadness for Della. The War always marked her memory of grief without glory (a sentiment her first children would keenly feel) and her initiation into a world of faith where God's word filled the space usually occupied by a young woman's playful joy and passion. When news of Lum's death reached Fayette, around his fifteenth birthday, he sought honor and vengeance as best he knew how. He ran away to join the rebel army, to take up where his brother had fallen. George Walker Black, however, did not intend to lose another son—at that moment his only boy old enough to help work the fields. The elder Black went after Fayette and returned him to their farm near Pinckneyville, not far down Hillabee Creek from Bluff Springs.

Little survives to tell of Della's courtship with her loved one's brother, after the shock of Lum's death receded, although local customs would have had Fayette approach Della with a formality that governed all relations of life and death blessed by the rural Primitive Baptist church. The young couple may have attended worship services together or sat on the Toland porch within the sound of her father's voice. Their conversation may have been gay and lively at times, although just as likely it was punctuated with long periods of silence, moments of sorrow or meditation for her, times when his words could not avoid the remembrance of how death had brought them together. Fayette's act of youthful valor, attempting to take his brother's place on the battlefield, endeared him to Della who, like her own mother, treasured fidelity. Yet while Lum's death brought the couple together, his memory also sat between them, assuring a romance without the ripe sweetness of passion or temptation.

In an age and place where a woman's role was to procreate a large family and nurture children to work the fields, Della aspired for slightly more. She took a grammar school education, rare for a girl in an area where almost everyone of both sexes worked at hard labor with their hands and backs from the age of seven to death, which often came before a person's fiftieth birthday. Della's uncle Merit Street, who briefly had been a schoolteacher, may have taught Della to read and write from the Bible. Unlike the vast majority of women (and men) in Alabama during these years, Della's literacy gave her the only available means to traverse worlds and ideas far different and removed from the eighty square miles of backwoods that mapped the territory of her entire life.

Yet, when her mother died two years before the Civil War, Ardellah at the age of eleven was awakened from all childhood dreams and ambitions. She stopped schooling and took up the duties of the oldest child in a household without a woman and with two younger brothers. Her mother's last words were the Biblical psalmist's, "Bless the Lord, O my soul, and all that is within me, bless His holy name!" Chiseled on Mildred Street Toland's tombstone atop Mount Ararat, the verse stood as a testimonial to holy faith, allowing a mother to die in peace with her young children on earth, and teaching her oldest daughter how to cope with a stolen youth, Lum's tragic death, and, afterwards, years of quiet suffering.

Fayette, too, was relatively well educated, beyond the necessities of his time and place. He received at least a tenth-grade education, considered useful only for a boy who did not plan to spend the rest of his life behind a mule and plow. The Black family had been small farmers, backwoods merchants, or itinerant laborers as far back as the family tree records. For at least three generations, they had been working uncultivated soil and moving whenever free land or more opportunity beckoned from the other hillside. A man of limited resources, George Black moved to Alabama from Georgia on his wedding day in 1835. He endowed the names of national heroes on his boys—"Washington," "Columbus," and "Lafayette" (the last after the French nobleman who became a general in the service of George Washington to free the American colonies; the General passed through Georgia and Alabama in 1825 when George Black was a boy). Yet, the harshness of rural life quickly demeaned these birthrights, and common speech ground the expectations of "Columbus" down to the monosyllable "Lum." Fayette was the one Black son whose common name needed two syllables and whose ambitions would not be worn down by death, farming, or a young man's infatuations.

Fayette seemed to want all that George Black did not possess. The boy wanted off the farm to see the world. He wanted an easier life, without rural boredom and strenuous work. He wanted the excitement and pleasures that money—not youthful lust or real love—seemed to buy. Any day that he could slip away from his father's farm chores, Fayette walked ten miles to and from school. He was not seduced by the pleasures of learning, but education gave him the means to locate his future. School was far better than working the farm, and it was the only place, other than church, where he might regularly associate with the daughters of more prosperous families. By design or instinct, Fayette rejected the example set by his own parents, whose passions led them to conceive their first child three months before marriage. He acted as if far less interested in the impulses of amour than the promise of a useful relationship, one that could free him of the backwoods' hardships and drudgery.

Della Street Toland was Fayette's best opportunity for advancement. In east central Alabama, the Tolands and especially the Streets were locally prominent and relatively prosperous families. Della's grandfather Toland, who witnessed the first years of the Civil War, had been born in Ireland and was brought with his family to the United States as they escaped the gallows for their involvement in the misfired rebellion that Robert Emmet led against the "tyranny of English rule" at the start of the nineteenth century. The Tolands arrived at Charleston and settled inland around Laurens County, South Carolina, where, according to family legend, they bought the area's first cotton gin.

In a plantation area where black slaves outnumbered free whites, several Tolands became tradesmen, mechanics, and cabinetmakers, and others became professionals—doctors and lawyers who spread across the state and beyond. The Tolands lived in Laurens in 1824 when a young tailor, Andrew Johnson, opened a small shop thirty-one years before he would succeed President Lincoln. Later, Dr. H. H. Toland was celebrated locally for unending devotion to his wife, whom he embalmed and kept within an office cabinet for many years after her early death. Some Tolands moved to California. Della's father graduated from Transylvania College in Kentucky in 1828 and moved to Alabama after Andrew Jackson's defeat of the Creek Nation opened up lands for white settlement. The Tolands carried with them education, acquired skills, ambition, and often a tidy sum of money with which to build a new life.

The Streets, Della's maternal family, were from Virginia where her great-grandfather, a Baptist preacher, had fought in the Revolutionary War. Della's grandfather, Hezekiah Street, moved to Alabama around the late 1820s and established a small plantation in the shallow valley of Bluff Springs, a strip of unusual flat land that supported large cotton farms between the foothills and lakes of east central Alabama. Situated almost equal distance from a railroad line and Talladega, the area's commercial center, Street's plantation prospered. His descendants reported that he had more slaves than anyone else in the area, although county records suggest that the actual number might have been around ten. Street served in the Alabama legislature in the 1830s and was an important civic leader. He died in 1865, after witnessing the death of his daughter, Mildred. His son, Merit, took his father's place as head of his family and of Bluff Springs.

Della's Uncle Merit was a shrewd businessman even before he inherited his father's mantle. Five years before the beginning of the war that freed his father's slaves, at age thirty-two, Merit started the Street store about a mile from the family plantation. He was not only a merchant for the community but also its banker—"a note shaver & money maker" as representatives of the New York-based credit agency, Bradstreet & Co., called him. They immediately saw his business promise.

They found him prudent, industrious, thrifty, keen, and a close and tight trader of good habits. By their standards, St. Peter could not have given them a better client; Merit was as good as "Shylock," Bradstreet reported.

After the Civil War, Uncle Merit was among the few Alabamians not devastated by the South's defeat. He had served the Confederacy as the local justice of the peace, a safe, routine position of responsibility that he also held before the war. Merit's two sons were born during secession and thus saved from the war's casualty lists. At the time of Lee's surrender, the state was destitute, without plentiful crops and with a worthless Confederate currency, but Merit Street possessed land, plentiful store goods, and eighty-five bales of cotton which he held until they could be sold for a princely sum of U.S. dollars.

When Della prepared to consummate her half-hearted courtship, she was a woman of twenty who held a special place in her uncle's heart. She was a vivid reflection of his dead sister—her mother—in body, mind, and soul. Only a year before the wedding, Street had christened his own newborn girl "Mildred Ardellah Street," in loving tribute to his dead sister and his young niece, only to watch his baby die ten days later. Through these ordeals of death, neither Merit Street nor Della questioned the love and wisdom of their Almighty, a shared devotion that all the more caused Uncle Merit to prize Della like a daughter.

When Fayette Black repeated his vows of matrimony with Della in the presence of the Tolands, the Streets, and others, he knew the marriage did more than join together two young people for the sake of love within the grace of God, family, and community. It was the union of her families with his future. It was as close as Fayette Black could get, by any means, to Merit Street and his growing fortune. Nothing on his wedding day or night could have excited Fayette Black more.[1]

TWO YEARS INTO THEIR MARRIAGE, Fayette and Della faced the realities of living in a poor section of Alabama in the aftermath of a lost war fought primarily on Southern soil. While Della was occupied with the care of their first-born, diplomatically named "Robert Lee" for Lum's commander-in-chief, Fayette remained where he did not want to be, facing the backside of a mule. In a tiny community called Harlan, not far from the intersection of two old Indian trails, the Blacks had built a modest timber and mud house on land that no white man had wanted before the War. Della's relatives on the Toland side were nearby, and the house was about five miles from Uncle Merit's store. Yet, the land was uncultivated and had to be cleared of trees and underbrush to permit farming. Fayette had broken only a few acres, and all his worldly possessions and money did not exceed two hundred dollars. He had discovered that, while Merit Street dearly loved his niece, he also loved his own money, which he managed frugally, reverently, as if it measured not only man's industry but his sacrifice and devotion to God—all qualities Street expected of himself and others.

Despite his eagerness to leave his father's house, Fayette had moved into an even more modest existence: George Black's farm in Pinckneyville, with the labor of one of Fayette's younger brothers, was worth in 1870 three times as much as Fayette's homestead, and several former slaves in Clay County were as well off as Fayette. For an ambitious white man, this was a humble status.

Throughout post-War Alabama and the South, conditions remained mercilessly difficult. Near Talladega, white families were living in the woods in makeshift huts. Former slaves were often the victims of want, neglect, and rank racialism, as the system of labor after slavery became chaotic and often brutal. No one could offer regular employment outside of government, which was under the rule of black and white Republicans, none of whom were beholden to the families of Confederate soldiers now disfranchised in large numbers. As one partisan historian stated of the era: "No means of livelihood, however humiliating, could be overlooked. The Roman adage that necessity has no law became a living principle in the struggle for bread."

The period of Reconstruction, more often called "radical or carpet-bag rule" by planters and past Democratic leaders, was inevitably a time of widespread suffering, the result of economic devastation after waging an unsuccessful, deadly war. Most Southern whites blamed the misery and disorder on the Republicans who ruled in Washington and Montgomery, the state capital. The new government was attempting to establish a new society in the South against the will of the white population. Its motives and actions were often anything but pure, as Republicans pumped large public investments into favored, private railroad construction. But the fundamental breach between the government in Montgomery (maintained by a standing federal army) and white citizens across the state was a bitter disagreement over whether the end of slavery should require legal, political, or social equality with former slaves. In the mind of white society, Yankee carpetbaggers, Southern scalawags, and ignorant blacks were responsible for the whole of Southern defeat, indignity, and misery foretold at Gettysburg and persisting into the 1870s.

In parts of Alabama, local white leaders abandoned the rule of law as much for power as bread. Reinventing the role of the justice of the peace, who once had the duty to select respectable men to patrol the local community for the protection of civil order and moral standards, whites organized private, secret societies to reestablish a white man's rule through bluff, intimidation, and violence. The Ku Klux Klan was the more common order, although others such as the White Camellias used the same techniques of nightriding, anonymous circulars, and whippings to frighten blacks and whites who supported Reconstruction. Secret societies existed in counties surrounding Clay (Talladega and Randolph), but they weren't active in Fayette Black's community. In fact, during the War numerous white men had fled Confederate conscription into Clay's rough mountainous terrain. Unwilling to fight a war they did not support or understand, these renegades lived in exile until General Lee's surrender. As in several other counties in the Alabama hill country (especially Winston, which had seceded from Alabama when Alabama seceded from the Union), Clay's white citizens never had been entirely of one mind about which was worse—freed blacks or the old white society which the secret organizations were attempting to restore.

Amid limited opportunities and desperate conditions, Fayette remained trapped for eight long years on his farm in Harlan, as he slowly cleared more land and planted more crops. In 1872 he and Della had their first girl, Mildred, named after Della's late mother, Uncle Merit's sister. Within three years another boy was added, named Orlando after Della's Toland uncle who had become a successful doctor in California. Meanwhile, instead of toiling to clear more ground, Fayette tried to establish a herd of cattle which the law permitted to roam freely on unfenced land. This practice required little or no sustained effort for much of the year, especially in unpopulated areas like Harlan where cows with free range weren't likely to disturb others. Yet, nothing seemed to improve circumstances greatly for the Black family or anyone else in the area.[2]

The end of Fayette Black's life of subsistence came, finally, when Reconstruction was overturned in Alabama. In 1874 a white Democrat was elected governor for the first time since the end of the War, primarily due to a divided Republican party and a momentary coalition of white voters from both north and south Alabama. The election returned the machinery and patronage of state government to the white men who had believed in the cause of secession. As part of the self-styled Redeemers' reform, Alabama's legislature reestablished the elective position of justice of the peace, two for every precinct in every county. In August 1877, Fayette Black was elected justice of the peace for a three-year term in Clay's Wickers beat.

By 1877, the Democratic and Conservative Party of Alabama had restored many former Confederate leaders and followers to the voting rolls. And to help guarantee that only the right class of citizens held office, state law required local elected officials to post an assurance bond in an amount far beyond the means of almost all citizens. In the case of a local justice of the peace, one thousand dollars of property or cash was needed. With total assets of around $250, about the Alabama household average, Fayette Black had to rely on the sponsorship of the far wealthier Merit Street.

Everyone else in Clay County seemed to have suffered decline or stagnation during Reconstruction, but Street had enlarged his wealth as a merchant and expanded his business as a silent partner in at least three other dry goods stores in surrounding communities. By 1873, the last year of Alabama Reconstruction, New York mercantile agents were referring to Uncle Merit as the wealthiest person in Clay County, with a net worth of at least fifty thousand dollars. Adding to future prosperity, Street's store in 1875 became the location for the Bluff Springs post office, where everyone in the community had to come to pick up their mail. Also, Street now sat on the Democratic party's county executive committee, a body of approximately fifteen men who set the rules and qualifications for elections.

Along with Street, Joseph Allen White also signed as a surety on Fayette's justice of the peace bond. White had been elected a JP in 1875 and two years later was elected county sheriff. Street was also on White's bond. Both Black and White lived in the Wickers precinct and had been active Democrats even before "Redemption." Both had been a part of a county slate nominated at convention by the executive committee on which Street sat. Of the three men, only Street was worth at least one thousand dollars, and he alone made possible the right of the other two to hold office. Fayette's fourth child who arrived a few months after the JP election was usefully named Merit Vernon Black.

As local judge, Fayette Black settled disputes about contracts, property, or "any wrong or injury, except slander . . ." He was the "conservator of the peace" with broad powers to jail or fine anyone who committed a criminal offense or disturbed the peace of his community. For compensation, Fayette received a fee for each official act. On the theory that government should pay for itself, most county officials of the era earned their pay through fees. Fayette received fifteen cents for issuing a subpoena, a quarter for administering an oath, a dime for docketing each case in his record book, and fifty cents for producing a summary transcript of a hearing—all duties made possible by Fayette's earlier education. Trials were more lucrative, earning a two-dollar fee from the losing party; performing the rites of matrimony was a one-dollar duty, which Fayette did once or twice a year. Corralling loose stallions and jackasses that were mating with others' animals was also a solemn JP duty, costing the stud's owner one dollar per occurrence.

The rewards of public office didn't free Black from farming, but the income was a welcome supplement in a cash-poor economy. Some families were surviving an entire year by borrowing as little as twenty-five to thirty dollars from merchants like Merit Street in return for handing over part of their crops of corn or cotton at harvest. By these standards, Judge Black's few fees each month were significant; equally important, his election placed him within the circle of no more than one hundred men who ran the affairs of Clay County in the name of the Democratic and Conservative Party of Alabama and in the cause of white supremacy.

Clay's politics seemed ordained by its origins. The county was formed after the Civil War from parts of three existing counties, primarily Talladega where Merit Street lived. In December 1866, under the leadership of Whig politicians, the provisional Alabama legislature created Clay County on the same day it refused to approve the proposed Fourteenth Amendment to the U.S. Constitution promising equal treatment under law for African Americans. The refusal was less an act of rebel defiance than a momentary evasion, but it was responsible for the decision of the U.S. Congress to set up Reconstruction's military rule in Alabama.

Reflecting their own heritage, the Whig governor and legislature named the county for Henry Clay and the county seat as "Ashland" in honor of Clay's Kentucky plantation. Clay was also a Whig whose legislative compromises had held slaveholding and free states in the union for several years. He believed in a business-like approach to government and distrusted the common man's democracy. His prime political opponent was Andrew Jackson, perhaps the greatest hero of Alabama's frontier people, including many of Clay's settlers. It was thus ironic that only a few decades after General Jackson made Clay's land safe for white settlements, Alabama's Whig legislature named the county for his political rival.

Clay's Whig founders and the conservative Democratic leaders who took control after Reconstruction hoped to establish a local political system protecting property and stability amid a predominantly white population struggling for survival. Yet, this was political alchemy. Clay's poor white farmers may have voted in 1874 to end biracial political rule in the state, but they had not endorsed the dominance of politics by large planters, merchants, and camp followers—lawyers, doctors, newspapermen, and men like Fayette Black seeking to leave their farms and become a part of the ruling local ring.[3]

"The contest in this county seems to be getting warm," observed the editor of the *Ashland News* after planting season in 1878, one year after Fayette's JP election, "and the issue seems to be between the farmers and professional men—or rather a blind attack on the professional men by the farmers." Lamenting this "movement gotten up by a few designing men, probably of the radical stripe," the *News* insisted that this "great cry" violated sacred Democratic principles by making class distinctions. A few weeks later, the editor renewed attacks upon the "Disorganizers" of local politics for their lack of loyalty. "If a convention fails to nominate the man of our choice," wrote the editor, "we feel bound by our party fealty and by our love for the grand old party . . . to accept the man that is nominated."

Democratic hegemony was threatened at a county convention when delegates refused to nominate any of the announced candidates for the position of state representative. Presided over by Merit Street, the convention nominated a man who refused to serve. Delegates from county precincts then placed in nomination several names, including Street and Fayette Black. In the end, both withdrew, and an inexperienced young teacher and farmer won—handpicked by Democratic leaders so they could claim the nomination of a farmer. The insurgents claimed "fraud." "We have some political 'hags' in this county who cannot get office themselves," complained an independent supporter, "and they let their prejudices overbalance their judgment, and even their veracity."

While not mentioned by name, the major "hag" was Asbury S. Stockdale, a mediocre lawyer and facile backroom politician who headed the county's Democratic party. Stockdale maintained an office in the Ashland courthouse although he held no elective county office. He was an Ashland councilman and unofficial source of all political news. Whenever pony riders brought the mail, including weeks-old newspapers from Montgomery and Atlanta, Stockdale stood at the town square and read aloud the most important stories.

The governor also had appointed him county school superintendent. In this capacity, Stockdale administered funds for setting up and operating schools and paying teachers whom he personally certified. Apparently, political insurgents were not surprised that a deal had been made at the deadlocked convention to nominate one whose livelihood as a teacher depended on Superintendent A. S. Stockdale.

Faced with instability, Stockdale maneuvered to assure a local victory in the fall. He appointed Fayette and other loyal Democrats as "impartial" election inspectors, responsible for regulating voting in each precinct at a time when chicanery was a growing practice. Only a few weeks before the election, the *Ashland News* observed suggestively that elsewhere some independent candidates had dropped out, since they knew that on election day "the Democrats would 'count' them out"—the operative term for stealing an election. "A very wise decision," knowingly crowed the local Democratic paper.

Fearing that the independent movement also would hurt the Democratic Congressional nominee, whom Merit Street and Fayette Black helped to nominate at a second party convention, Stockdale invoked the white man's duty. "Clay and other counties with their Democratic majorities must come in full force to offset the negro vote in the black belt," he warned. In 1875, to dilute the voting power of former slaves, the Democratic legislature had broken up Alabama's majority-black counties into several congressional districts, including Clay's. Stockdale's echo, the *News,* charged that white voters must stay within the party of "General Jackson," or black voters would send "Radicals" to Washington to represent the county.

Clay did its Democratic duty. None of the insurgents won, although five of the county's fourteen precincts voted for independents. No less foreboding, a grand jury composed of a diversity of citizens, including the Rev. M. M. Driver who had married Fayette and Della, reported that too many county officials' assurance bonds were unwisely guaranteed by only one person's wealth. The jury declared that one "man's name on too many bonds is improper." No one had to guess who the one person was. The county's richest citizen, Merit Street, was the only man who could afford to be on "too many bonds" and the only name that appeared repeatedly in the county bond records.[4]

After the 1878 election, Clay's probate judge died unexpectedly, leaving his widow to operate Ashland's only boardinghouse, pretentiously called the Ashland Hotel by town promoters. The governor appointed Professor Hiram

Evans, headmaster and teacher at the Ashland school, to serve the remainder of the term. A small man overdressed in a Prince Albert coat with tails, Evans was one of the county's leading educators, who often beseeched both Greek gods and his Baptist Almighty in educating students and citizens. He was always "full of high sentence, but a bit obtuse," a doctrinaire Democrat enthralled by his own opinions. As a certified teacher, Evans was beholden to Superintendent Stockdale, who was probably responsible for the appointment—a fact not lost on independents. Afterwards, farmers accused Stockdale of being a one-man government of local patronage and control.

Over the next two years, Stockdale and Evans schemed to control poor farmers within the Democratic party. Yet independents persisted in attacking the party's use of a nominating convention as rigged politics. The *Ashland News* dismissed such "independent scuffle for office" as the reckless ambitions of unprincipled men. "Harmony in our ranks is essentially necessary at this time," the editor pleaded.

In June 1880, an independent revolt broke out at the county convention. Delegates refused to select party nominees and insisted that candidates go before voters in a direct primary election. "This day will hereafter be known . . . as the Black Saturday in Clay County," the *News* proclaimed. In reply, one reader charged that the stalemate should be blamed on Stockdale's trickery and his "Ashland Clique."

At issue was simply who would control local government, by what methods, and for whose benefit. A nominating convention gave local Democratic leaders the maximum opportunity to handpick nominees. Stockdale, Street, and camp followers like Fayette Black often controlled nominations by negotiation. When the young teacher/farmer was selected for the legislature in 1878, for instance, the leading candidate had a majority of the votes on the initial ballot at the convention. But, with a longstanding Democratic party rule requiring a two-thirds vote for nomination, Stockdale blocked the leading independent by parlaying with delegates in a locked convention until he found one of his own people acceptable to two-thirds of the convention. Now, two years later, a majority of delegates refused to nominate anyone by convention.

The *News* warned voters that direct democracy could lead to biracial Republicanism. The newspaper argued that Democratic votes would splinter among several Democratic candidates in an open election while independents could vote as a bloc and win with little more than a sixth of the total vote.

"The Democratic party of Clay is not six times stronger than the Republican!!" the editor declared.

When pleas for unity failed, Democratic leaders tried to respond to charges against Stockdale's "cesspools of corruption"—without losing control. By hook or crook, they strictly limited the field of Democratic candidates in an open election and erected a phantasm of reform. Only Hiram Evans and two other Democratic incumbents ran for reelection. Stockdale stepped down as chairman of the local party, and his brother was not reappointed as register of the chancery court. Finally, to assure a "correct" count from direct democracy, Sheriff White appointed Black and other loyal Democrats as both inspectors and special deputies to oversee the voting and counting of ballots.

The schemes worked. Conservative Democrats won. Stockdale retreated only as far as the local newspaper and retained his appointive post as head of the local public schools. The county Democratic party's new chairman was none other than Merit Street. His personal reputation and his address outside of Ashland seemed to outweigh concerns about his role as moneylender and local political financier.[5]

For four years, Street kept the local party in harmony. With an official address marked "Bluff Springs," the Democratic party cancelled the "Ashland Clique"—a simple, symbolic fact that silenced some past suspicions. Farmers seemed to think that the new Democratic chairman, the county's richest man, unlike Stockdale, had no reason to manipulate politics for his own personal gain.

Parsimonious in habits and speech, Street was a shrewd businessman with a relentless desire for money that was softened by a cordial personality and a forgetful, forgiving manner. He treated all farmers and their families with honest respect and was genuinely fond of children. A former teacher, he believed in the virtues of education. He had a sharp mind for figures, but at night he often left his store's doors open or his safe unlocked until his dutiful wife returned with the certainty that they needed closing. Street strictly avoided liquor and other earthly sins. He was regarded as correct, fair, and sober in all matters of personal and public conduct, despite the fact that he often used the local circuit court to dispossess farmers of their land or property whenever they reneged in a mercantile contract.

In politics, like business, Street's style and opinions appeared vaguely agreeable to most citizens, although his actions borrowed far more heavily from

Henry Clay's Whig philosophy than Andrew Jackson's faith in the common people's wisdom. In essence, Uncle Merit articulated an emerging creed of the New South, an outlook selectively respectful of the regional past but equally solicitous of national triumphalism. Discussing the "War of Secession," for example, Street lavishly praised the South's Confederate icons. Unlike some embittered Southerners, Street did not blame the South's defeat on Jeff Davis: "with the means commanded, the odds and powers against him, . . . no man could have succeeded better," Street stated. As to General Robert E. Lee, Clay's party leader declared, "*America* in my judgment has never produced a greater genius." As an American, Merit Street also acknowledged that General U. S. Grant had saved the Union.

On the broader, sensitive questions of the Civil War's causes and effects, rights and wrongs, Street spoke in parochial, religious terms, masterfully crediting victory to no side, other than the troops of righteousness. Here again, Street's philosophy presaged the secular version of a New South creed which *Atlanta Constitution* editor Henry Grady would proclaim a few years later. Street observed: "the only hope for the South was to have educated and elevated the negro more, making him a more refined and cultured slave . . . The Confederacy was powerful, but the Union more powerful . . . [T]here was divine intervention: slavery was not right . . . the Bible was more mighty than either the Union or Confederacy."

Despite his absolute faith, Merit Street did not often leave Clay's politics to divine intervention. Although too few records exist to ascribe an exact cause and effect, one curious scenario in 1882 may tell something about the ways by which Street kept the peace amid Clay's political wars. An anonymous letter to the editor in Ashland during the spring of 1882 recommended I. A. J. Nelson for state representative as "a zealous worker in the Democratic ranks." On cue, Nelson replied with transparent expressions of surprise and false modesty. "Should the people of Clay see fit to nominate me, I am, indeed surprised to receive such unmerited flattery," stated the independent candidate. This development was probably entirely un-"Merit"-ed. By June, as the local party convention neared, Nelson had abandoned politics to join an Ashland merchant in business and was on his way to Atlanta to purchase supplies with newly visible credit. Perhaps, he swapped business for politics without inducement. Yet, Street had both motive and means to offer inducements. Nelson's independent candidacy threatened a resurgence of trouble for Street's local party, and, in a county where money for a new commercial venture was extremely scarce, Street could use his wealth to safeguard the harmony of local politics.

Another possible example of Street's leadership began as a matter of public record. The county let a contract to a local Ashland merchant, H. A. Manning, a loyal, conservative Democrat, to make bricks for the construction of a new county jail in 1882. Shortly afterwards, reports circulated that the county treasurer had loaned Manning more than two thousand dollars in public funds to enable the project, an allegation prompted by the common belief that Manning didn't have the deep pockets for financing such construction. The treasurer dismissed the rumor as someone's "tongue in full practice of guile," and nothing in the county's surviving records support the charge. It is far more likely that Manning received funds from Street, who was at the time a silent partner in Manning's business. Street was the only person in the county who could have afforded such a loan, which kept local patronage within a small circle of local Democratic leaders and possibly returned a nice profit to the Democratic chairman.

Whatever mix of money and politics, in 1882 Clay's Democrats held a relatively peaceful nomination, for the first time since the end of Reconstruction. Independent candidates ran, but they did not muster a rebellion. On the party ticket headed by former Confederate general Edward A. O'Neal, a candidate for governor, Democrats nominated Merit Street for state senator to represent Clay and Talladega counties. Street would follow his father's path. "This action . . . was generally anticipated," wrote the *Ashland Banner* editor who had purchased the local paper from Stockdale and renamed it. At the party convention, Street almost won the necessary two-thirds vote on the first ballot—a ringing endorsement of his leadership. Calling Merit Street an "old land mark," Democrats praised their nominee as, "a well informed gentleman, a good citizen, a staunch Democrat . . . We predict for Mr. Street such an endorsement by the people . . . will put a quietus to malcontents and disorganizers."

Confident of finally making good on a Whig-like control of Clay's politics, A. S. Stockdale quietly resumed the local Democratic chairmanship. To endorse Stockdale's return, Edward O'Neal came to Clay County to speak. He was the first Democratic nominee for governor to appear in Clay. With Confederate credentials ever-evident, "General O'Neal" was introduced at an Ashland rally by an obsequious Stockdale, who evidenced "pent up feelings of patriotism and admiration." More likely his emotions arose from enormous relief. Stockdale had been born-again in politics. Riding the coattails of a Confederate general and Merit Street's political money and popularity, Stockdale presided over a large, sweet victory in November.[6]

Along the path of Uncle Merit's remarkable political career, not far behind, traveled Fayette Black. He had joined Street as a convention delegate who helped to nominate their Democratic Congressman and to reelect him in 1880. Less than two months later, Black received notification from Washington that the U.S. post office for the Harlan community was being transferred to his home. Since fetching mail was a favorite pastime of farmers wanting to get off the homestead to talk gossip and politics, especially during fallow seasons, the post office was a sinecure valuable far beyond its yearly five-dollar compensation. The post office allowed Fayette to start the "Black Store," a modest assortment of dry goods and farming supplies kept with the mail in a small building near Della's house. Fayette's initial finances for the store may have come from Della's uncle.

Whatever Street's exact role, Fayette was ready to use family and politics in as many ways as possible for material advancement. It apparently did not matter to Black as a faithful Democrat that his appointment came from a Republican Postmaster in Washington and that the true depth of his loyalty to the Democratic party might have been somehow understated to a Washington administration seeking Southern support—or at least political neutrality—through federal patronage. Nor is there evidence that Fayette was disturbed that, like Uncle Merit, he was eligible for a federal appointment only because he had not fought in the Confederate Army. Black's ambitions in politics and in life overpowered any misgivings about benefiting from the "Radical Republican Rule" that he and other local Democrats so often damned publicly.

During the time of Merit Street's political influence, Fayette also began to appear almost yearly as one of the relatively few men serving on the county's juries. While criminal jury trials were often the best source of excitement and entertainment in isolated rural counties, jury service was important to the community for achieving both justice and honest government. Juries assured that judicial decisions about guilt and innocence, right and wrong reflected democratic ideals, and Alabama's grand juries not only preferred criminal indictments but also served as a citizens' check on the conduct of local public officials.

Jury service could also be profitable. By local standards of the time, jurors were paid a handsome sum—a dollar and a half a day and five cents per mile for travel from and to their homes. In a dirt-poor place like Clay, one or two weeks as a juror—selected from registered voters through a drawing of names by the circuit clerk, probate judge, and sheriff—paid almost half what some farmers had to borrow from local merchants to survive for a whole year.

With one child old enough to help in the fields and two others able to do household chores, Fayette and Della were procreating a small workforce to sustain the farm as Fayette devoted more time to make politics pay. Black also expanded his land holdings and the value of his personal property. By 1883 (three years after getting the post office patronage), Fayette had tripled his net worth. An inventory of the Black household around this time included gold and silver watches and clocks, products of advantageous loans and bartering at the Black store.

If the names of his newborns continued to reflect his mood and motives, Fayette was beginning to feel wistful and roguish. His fifth child was christened Pelham, after the Alabama Confederate officer known for his charm among ladies as much as his gallantry on the battlefield. Since Lum Black hadn't served with John Pelham, the title wasn't in his honor or for anyone else in the extended family. The name probably captured the growing sense of independence and the longings of a father who, with only a third of his life remaining, pined for the missed thrills of a passionate youth and the comfort of riches.

In 1884, Fayette decided to take full advantage of Uncle Merit's political influence. When Street stood for reelection in the state senate, Black sought to succeed his old friend Joseph White as county tax collector. The position would involve a move to Ashland where the older children could get more than a grammar school education and Fayette might be able to set up a dry goods store.

Black also may have wanted to run in 1884 because his name would appear on the same ticket with the man he considered America's greatest president, Grover Cleveland.

Voters, however, were unwilling to transfer their respect for Merit Street to his nephew by marriage. Fayette was defeated, although family legend tells proudly of his hard work and credible showing at the polls. In retrospect, success might have separated further Della and Fayette, and, sixteen years into their marriage, they could have ended the growth of their family without the birth of their last son. As it was, their eighth child was to be born at Harlan within two years—amid disappointment, tumult, and death.[7]

"Hugo is all right," announced the father looking over the wrapped newborn, still damp from the womb. In a bitter, cold February, the words were as frosty as the air. "Hugo is all right," the father repeated, "but . . . damn the Lafayette!"

Lafayette Hugo Black's father was protesting the name that his children had fastened onto the new child. Fayette disliked giving his newborn the same fancy, useless title his father had bestowed on him. The irony was rich, perhaps enjoyed by the two oldest children, including Mildred Lenora who proposed Hugo as a substitute for the common Toland name of Hugh. Her conservative father, a backwoods merchant with patrician aspirations and values, endorsed the name of Victor Hugo, the poet and writer of *Les Miserables,* who had died a year earlier as a French icon of radical republican values, while he scorned a name honoring the princely French General Lafayette.

Increasingly a man of harsh words, unyielding opinions, and open contradictions, Fayette Black was in a dark, baleful mood. In recent weeks in Harlan, death seemed more common than life. At the start of the New Year, a deadening cold front had dropped the temperature more than forty degrees within a few hours and then held the mercury at zero. Two-year old "Ardellah" took sick as the weather oscillated between bitter cold and icy rain. Usually the doctor was at least a couple of hours away in Bluff Springs in the best of conditions, and now thawing ice and rains turned roads into muddy molasses, making them impassable. The child's mother was also in danger. Small in frame, at thirty-seven well past safe childbearing age, Della was carrying their eighth child, due any day, while attempting to nurse "Little Della" to health.

Monday, February 22, 1886, was a day that no member of the Black family ever forgot. It was as if God's wrath was visited upon the household in a test of Della's faith and Fayette's sanity. Little Della died, a probable victim of inadequate medicine and distant professional care. Two days earlier, she had spent her second birthday in bed, too feeble and weak to count the candles on a cake or to delight her father with a smiling hug and kiss. Now, as the dead child lay in a small, wooden bed, made by her grandfather Toland, a violent storm besieged Harlan. It may have been a tornado, although the family was too saddened and distracted with little Della's passing to see it approach. Houses were lifted from the earth and crashed, and others were shaken off their foundations. A part of the roof at the Black house was swept away. Robert Lee, the oldest sibling at fifteen, understood the destructive power most clearly as it rampaged their house, and for the rest of his life he feared a darkening cloud more than any evil on earth. While the tiny body lay inside, men worked into the night repairing the roof.

A few days afterwards, Little Della was taken to Bluff Springs and on Mount Ararat, within the sight of Uncle Merit's store, laid into the ground not far from the remains of her grandmother and her cousin bearing the same name. Like her namesake, Little Della had died prematurely, yet, the surviving Ardellah may have been the one truly cursed. As a child, Martha Ardellah had seen her mother interred here. Within a year of her own marriage, she had watched her aunt give birth to another Mildred Ardellah, only to see her die within ten days. Now as a mother, ready to give birth once more, Della witnessed the death and funeral procession of her youngest child. Under such incredible torment it was perhaps a little of God's grace that gave her another child, fragile, quite small, but healthy, on the twenty-seventh day of February, within hours of Little Della's burial. If Della Black rejoiced in the moment, women of lesser faith, believing in a lesser God, might have wished for their own death.[8]

OVERTAKEN BY PAIN AND TURMOIL, after eighteen years of indifferent relations, the adults in the Black household offered no solace to one another. Della relied on her church and faith as well as little Hugo's needs, while Fayette sought escape in whiskey, occasionally in vast quantities. The other children, ranging in age from fifteen to five, may have hoped that naming the last two newborns after their mother and father would bond their parents, but names could not restore an intimacy that never really existed. Della had performed her wifely duties in bed in order to assume her proper, desired role as mother. She dedicated her life to giving her children a mother's affection and guidance, which death had denied her as a child. Fayette found the bottle as his best lover for life.

Despite their distance and tribulations, Fayette and Della continued steadily to increase their family's material fortunes. The farm and store in Harlan were profiting, while others were quagmired in a "crop lien" economy built on debts to merchants, low prices for cotton, distant, costly rail transport, and poor land. Black's place in 1886 was an impressive spread by standards of the semi-frontier east of the Mississippi River: twenty hogs, ten sheep, three cows, and a horse and buggy. Most of the 280 acres were worked now by four boys and two tenants, who lived a few hundred feet from Fayette's own five-room house. True indications of his improved material status were Black's money bonds worth $10 and outstanding loans of $75 to local farmers.

Fayette was still advancing in the business of politics by continuing to follow Merit Street. Uncle Merit had entered local politics as a justice of the peace. With Street's help, Fayette did likewise in 1877. Uncle Merit had secured a political appointment for a local post office to bolster his position as merchant. With Street's help, Fayette received a similar appointment at Harlan and used the post to open his local store. Now, Street decided to step down from the state senate and the county Democratic executive committee. He was growing old and was easily tired by rigors of travel, business, and politics. He may have sensed that it was time for another step in the long succession of family and marriage. Three months after Hugo's birth, Fayette became Uncle Merit's heir on the local Democratic governing body. No longer a camp follower, "W. L. Black," as Fayette identified himself in public, sat now with A. S. Stockdale as one of a small number of men of business and influence leading the local Democratic and Conservative Party.[9]

Like recent stormy moments at the Black home, Clay's politics quickly became tumultuous. A new insurgency was on the political horizon and, without Merit Street's guidance, Stockdale and the Democratic committee blundered badly in 1886. "Keep negroes, independents, and republicans out of the beat meetings for they would work destruction in the Democratic party if they could," warned the *Watchman*, the new Democratic voice in the county. At the county convention, delegates from two precincts were unseated when they could not prove their Democratic credentials. Good riddance, mocked the newspaper, for those delegates were "notorious republicans, blind and lame negroes, and so-called independents" who from the bottoms of "their insignificant souls," piously parade about crying, "Oh! . . . we are disfranchised, right here in a free country." Democrats elected a slate of candidates including incumbent Hiram Evans as probate judge and W. J. L. Hood, the *Watchman* proprietor, for state legislator.

The insurgents' response was dramatic. Attacking the "Ashland Clique" and a "wired convention," independents held a people's meeting where they nominated their own candidates. They chose for state representative Professor Henry Clay Simmons, whose politics were a jumbled inheritance from both his namesake and Andrew Jackson. With a dark beard reaching to his waist, Simmons appeared like an Old Testament prophet condemning local Democrats with a stone tablet of marvelous, purple prose.

Far more than party loyalty and grandiloquence were in conflict. Simmons ran on a theme of "more schools, more money, and more teachers," a substantive program attacking the practices of limiting education and teaching posts to a privileged few. He cursed local merchants for charging high interest rates and seeking farmers' homes in mortgages for crop loans. The profits and practices of Asbury Stockdale, W. L. Black, and Merit Street were the issues that Henry Clay Simmons raised before large crowds.

In response, editor Hood pleaded with voters that more schools and teachers meant more taxes and lower standards. "My position," he beseeched, "is solely in the interest of the laboring class, and not of merchants." Since their candidate could not, Hood's supporters tried to match Simmons's oratory, accusing him of "deviltry and corruption enough to upturn creation."

Voters upturned only the Democrats' creations in Clay when they elected Simmons to the state legislature, along with another independent candidate from Talladega to succeed Merit Street as state senator. Hiram Evans and other conservative Democrats returned to the Ashland courthouse, but the county now was represented in the statehouse by the "disorganizers." The election results announced that farmers wanted their lawmakers to alter oppressive conditions. If the disastrous weather of early 1886 and a ruinous summer dry spell weren't the blame of politics, limited education and merchants' usurious loan rates also weren't acts of God. They were man's machinations, which Clay's farmers wanted a legislature to undo.[10]

According to official records, however, Clay County's new Montgomery delegation was stymied in every effort to undo what the Democrats had created. In an age when more local laws were passed than statewide statutes, not one new piece of legislation for the county was enacted during the insurgents' term. In a Democrat-controlled state legislature, the independents were virtually helpless, a situation which Clay's Democrats used at home to discredit the insurgency. Leaving his family to maintain the post office/store and the farm, W. L. Black routinely joined other local party leaders in traveling to shore up Democratic support.

In February 1888, shortly before Hugo Black celebrated his second birthday, Fayette was reelected to the Democratic executive committee. At the same meeting, Democratic leaders rejected a proposal for a direct primary election where voters would select the party's local nominees. With four years left on his term, Hiram Evans made an appeal against "prejudice," the conservatives' favorite term for the anger of farmers against the ruling class of merchants and professionals.

In a response led by Baptist minister M. M. Driver, independents became adventuresome and disruptive. They declared *themselves* the Clay County Democratic Party (leaving off "Conservative") and conducted their own primary election. Afterwards, they announced their slate of elected nominees, including Henry Clay Simmons, the Rev. Driver, and a renegade lawyer, C. A. Steed. Defections and disputes among regular Democrats abetted the political rebellion. A lawyer who briefly practiced with Stockdale bolted the old party when his partner and other Democratic leaders refused to nominate him or any other professional man from Ashland. "All the locks and keys in America," the lawyer angrily sputtered, "could not keep me" a Democrat.

In addition, in a serious charge of corruption, the incumbent circuit clerk accused Hiram Evans and the sheriff of colluding to keep independents off the juries. Judge Evans blasted the clerk as a "traitor to the party that had elected him" and dismissed his "falsehoods" as a petty attempt to "gain a little political notoriety." Clerk E. A. Phillips replied that the old professor "considers himself a modern Solomon, sitting high upon a pinnacle of official and social preferment above the people . . ." A new independent newspaper, *The Advance*, emerged briefly to urge middle ground between political desertion and "political tricksters, wire workers, and 'bosses' . . ." The conservatives sneered and undertook an unprecedented speaking tour of the county while shying away from debates with the independents who harped against the trickery of an "oligarchal party."

Perhaps no one was more surprised than Fayette Black's colleagues in the "oligarchal party" when they prevailed in every race in August 1888, although the margin of victory was uniformly close. Allen White's victory as sheriff was by a margin of only sixty votes, and no Democrat won by more than 250 votes. Party stalwarts, nonetheless, were indulgently self-congratulatory, with no pretense of a victor's grace. They accused the defeated independents of having appealed vainly to the "prejudice and passions of men." The local newspaper sounded as if it were reporting Democratic victory to General Robert E. Lee: "our representative elect, with the able and freely offered assistance of

A. S. Stockdale, Esq., Judge H. M. Evans, and Mr. M. W. Whatley . . . has carried war into the enemy's camps and demolished his stronghold . . . Mr. Whatley will be long and well remembered for his fearless and direct attack on the opposition."

M. Wilburn Whatley was one of the new, decorated officers in Clay's conservative army. A farmer and teacher who organized a local chapter of the Farmers' Alliance in 1886, Whatley was a trusted, new leader of the independent's constituency who had kept faith with the old party. The Alliance was strictly nonpartisan and promoted self-help for farmers by teaching modern methods of agriculture and by setting up farming cooperatives across the nation. As a local Alliance leader, Whatley spoke often at farmers' meetings and basket suppers. In the summer, he was recruited for the Democratic campaign, and, far more interested in politics than farming, Wilburn Whatley gladly launched an assault on the independent enemies of Democracy. Now, he shared its victory.[11]

Fayette Black did not join the Democratic revelry in Ashland. Rising quite early, soberly on the day after the election, he bundled Hugo onto a wagon seat with Della and traveled the long, hard dirt roads southeast toward Alex City, a station crossing of the Georgia Railroad. Along the way he had hours to consider the election since he and Della seldom chatted freely. The journey's purpose was ostensibly to purchase supplies for the Black store, but Alex City was "wet" (the sale of liquor was legal), and Fayette could renew his supply of whiskey while Della purchased books of arithmetic and strips of leather for repairing shoes. The town also had results of state elections since telegraph lines along the railroad tracks brought news more quickly.

The trip was an omen for the Black family, one of those occasions when the future reveals its hand through a coincidence of commonplace events. For the youngest member of the family it was a moment to feel the exciting, noisy nature of change moving across the American continent. Most children and adults in Clay County had only heard stories of such creatures, but at the age of two and a half L. Hugo Black saw his first steam locomotive. Standing on the porch of Frohsin's general store, no more than twenty yards from the rail tracks running down the heart of town, Hugo heard the train's arrival before it came into sight around the bend, just east of the commercial houses. The engine bellowed and smoked as the little boy ran forward screaming and clapping in furious delight. Here was the enormous, wondrous machine that seemed to possess more power, speed, and awe than anything living. It was America's vehicle for fast-moving economic progress in the late nineteenth century and would be the emerging literary symbol of a twentieth century America's "I think I can" spirit. It also would be a primary means for Hugo Black's future advancement and struggle in manhood. The little boy had met the future, and, by his own account, he never forgot the moment.

On the same trip, Hugo's father also may have glimpsed into the future—one that, without radical change, would soon deadend far short of his ambitions and dreams. Despite Clay's recent Democratic victories, Fayette's primary engine of advancement, politics as business, was approaching a sudden, abrupt derailment in Harlan. It was a future as overwhelming as a bellowing locomotive.

Rather than winning the war, Clay's recent campaign foretold that there would be no political peace. With almost two thousand votes cast, the Democrats had defeated Henry Clay Simmons by less than two hundred votes. Most contests were much closer. In his own beat, as party captain, Black had failed to carry a majority of votes for conservative candidates. These returns followed the 1886 elections when Fayette's precinct gave independents a slim majority. And the neighboring precinct of Millersville, where Uncle Merit lived, was now the stronghold for independents.

No longer could the county's party bosses maintain political control on the basis of favors for friends, as Stockdale's former law partner recently discovered. A beat politician in Clay could not win favors or office in the future if he did not have the support of his own friends and neighbors. And by 1888 Fayette did not have their support. In addition, farmers might begin to make local purchases and loans at someone else's store, if at all possible. Already, Clay was buzzing with talk about the Alliance setting up buying co-ops. If the Republicans defeated Grover Cleveland in November 1888 (as they did in the electoral college), post office appointments could go to independents who now had national Republican support. Without the mail stop, Black's store would wither.

Since Lafayette Hugo's birth, his father's every move for dramatic advancement had met with criticism or exposure at the hands of independents. W. L. Black regularly served on jury panels, but now the circuit clerk and independents were charging that the selection was rigged. Black was a member of the Democratic governing committee whose convention rules in 1886 had driven independents out of the party and into victory for the first time with candidates like Henry Clay Simmons who attacked money-shaving merchants like Fayette.

When independents attacked the practice of limiting schools and teaching jobs for a few professional families, they were attacking W. L. Black almost as much as A. S. Stockdale. In 1887, Stockdale appointed Fayette Black and a few other loyal Democrats as township superintendents. Fayette's daughter, Daisy, observed later in life: "Daddy was a great believer in education"—especially for his conservative friends and family. As Harlan's appointed education leader, Black established schools wherever he believed they should be located. He had approximately $80 in tax money each year to spend for educating white children in the Wickers beat. (There were no black children of school age in the area.) A large part of this money went to pay schoolteachers whom Black hired from lists that Stockdale certified. Among these teachers was Robert Lee Black, Fayette's oldest son, who taught in the Harlan area.

In the '88 campaign, Della's preacher, the Rev. M. M. Driver, and other insurgents accused conservative Democrats of "double dealing and corruption" in education. Among other things, they alleged that Stockdale, as "chairman of the Executive committee, together with other prominent men . . . holding official positions under the prestige of said party, did interfere in the passage of a Bill in the last Legislature of Ala. to render elective the office of county superintendents of education for Clay County by mis-stating facts to the last General Assembly." W. L. Black was only one of four men in the county who was both a party official and a township superintendent, and he was clearly one of the "other prominent men" accused of dishonestly defeating the bill for democratic control of local schools.

"Now our question is," wrote an anonymous newspaper correspondent in early 1888, "who is entitled to the largest credit of the public funds" for the schools? According to this citizen, township superintendents were distributing funds inequitably, and Stockdale sanctioned the practice. The rising tide for "more schools, more money, and more teachers" for all children simply would not ebb. In Millersville, where insurgents were gaining momentum, Stockdale had to remove the township superintendent within a year of Fayette Black's appointment, in an unsuccessful effort to quiet charges about partisan misuse of school monies.

In a semi-frontier society, these political disputes represented profound differences about wealth and opportunity, survival and prosperity that could not be confined to the stages of formal speeches and anonymous, cryptic exchanges in dried printer's ink. Many of Clay's families, including the Blacks, painfully realized how political differences in a small community breed divisiveness and acrimony amid kin, friends, and church. One of Della's nephews, William Toland, as well as other members of the Toland clan, had become local leaders in the independent movement in Millersville. Della's family preacher, M. M. Driver, was now leading the county's political insurgence. These political divisions created personal stress and social gaps in the webs of life that supported Della, and they came home to her and the Black family in a dramatic, painful episode.

Della and her family watched as Fayette Black was purged from the Primitive Baptist Church where she was baptized and had worshiped most of her life. Baptist deacons decided that Fayette must repent for his bouts of heavy drunkenness by appearing before the entire congregation, which would decide if he was deserving of forgiveness. Local legislation sponsored by Merit Street had made the sale of liquor in Clay a matter of criminal law, but the Baptist church believed that the abundant consumption of liquor also could be a matter of church law. Although Primitive Baptist preachers were known to take a swig of whiskey to fortify themselves during long, exhaustive revivals, church elders were empowered to punish a member who was guilty of regular public drunkenness as an injury to the morals of the community and the church.

A proud man with a high opinion of his own character, Fayette flatly refused to humble himself before his Baptist neighbors in accordance with church customs, and he was "withdrawn" from the church by the congregation's vote.

The church acted in keeping with its religious orthodoxy, but it also mirrored secular, political considerations. Fayette had invited their judgment on his worldly ways after he became a moneylender and a conservative political leader who used his party's rule for his personal benefit. Baptist farmers must have been particularly offended by Fayette's open hypocrisy. During a recent circuit court session, with W. L. Black as foreman and spokesman, the grand jury reported to Clay's citizens: "We regret that the making and selling of whiskey and other intoxicants is alarmingly on the increase in our county and from the testimony before us we think the results therefrom are deplorable." The grand jury report announced that crime and liquor were linked in the county since "where there have been no making or selling intoxicants there have been but few violations of the law." The grand jury report, bearing W.

L. Black's own signature, concluded: "We call upon the good citizens of the County to aid in the suppression of these crimes."

For independent, Primitive Baptist farmers who paid Black and other local merchants a "criminal" interest rate on crop loans and for Baptist preachers like M. M. Driver who represented the insurgent political movement, this official report was an audacious, double-faced outrage. Fayette Black had been paid about $15 of their tax money—more cash than many saw in half a year's time—through a rigged jury selection to lecture good, sober citizens on the "deplorable" problems of whiskey which Black enjoyed and abetted with his own excessive habits. In effect, therefore, the democratic process of the Baptist church punished Fayette Black, in keeping with the spirit of his own public words, since the democratic process at the courthouse had been corrupted by Black's own deeds.[12]

No, the narrow Democrats' victories in 1888 were not a cause for celebration for W. L. Black. Instead, they signaled sure defeat. There was no future for Black in the business of politics in Harlan. It was time to take his family to the county's center of commerce, politics, and faithful Democrats. It was time for W. L. Black to move up in the world—to Ashland.

A LITTLE MORE THAN A YEAR after the trip to Alex City, on a cold, inhospitable day in December, W. L. Black and his boys hitched their bulging wagon and began a slow, noisy journey to Ashland. Fayette was ready to leave Harlan as far behind as possible, although Della had good reason to be half-hearted.

Ashland was attractive to Della because it promised her children a better education, a prime concern that began in her house with reading the Bible and *Pilgrim's Progress.* Della's oldest two already had completed high school, and now Robert Lee and Ora wanted to attend college courses at the new Ashland Academy. Most of the other children also needed to attend higher grades not available at the Harlan school. And, there was Hugo. Soon he would be of school age, and his mother wanted only the very best education for him.

Yet, leaving the community where she had lived all her life was difficult for a woman whose strength was sustained in the memory of her mother's faith and the love of her extended family. Estranged from her husband, Della relied upon the Streets and Tolands living around Harlan and Bluff Springs for daily support and interaction and frequently visited Mount Ararat cemetery, where her mother and her baby daughter were buried. In 1889, sixteen miles to

Ashland was a world away for Della. She would dearly miss her uncles, aunts, and siblings—including her brother "Brack" Toland.

John Breckenridge Toland was Della's half-brother who at thirty-six possessed blazing red hair and almost as sweet a disposition as a man could possess. He loved children, reading, storytelling, women, and whiskey—in no particular order. Della's children often had sat listening to Uncle Brack tell stories of the ancestral Tolands' battles alongside the Irish rebel Robert Emmet at the start of the nineteenth century. After the British disbanded the Irish Parliament, Emmet led an incipient rebellion of tradesmen and laborers who, after months of clandestine planning, attempted to storm Dublin Castle, the English seat of government in Ireland. Emmet's followers piked to death the country's chief justice, who happened along in his carriage at the wrong moment, but the rebellion fizzled. The British Parliament considered suspending civil liberties for all Irish citizens, and, according to Uncle Brack, the Tolands narrowly escaped execution as they fled to American shores.

Robert Emmet was captured as he bid farewell to the woman he loved. He was tried for treason by a jury that did not deliberate in order to reach a guilty verdict. Within twenty-four hours, Emmet was hanged and beheaded within sight of Dublin Castle. The executioner lifted Emmet's severed head by its hair before a large crowd and chanted: "This is the head of a traitor, Robert Emmet." Afterwards, women stealthily dipped their handkerchiefs in the dark pools of Emmet's blood under the gaol planking. He was buried in an unmarked pauper's grave.

At trial, Emmet had spoken words repeated for generations by Irish Protestants, poets, and their descendents fighting for independence. His speech survives in a dozen variations. Uncle Brack probably rehearsed one of the American-oriented versions: "My lord, you are impatient for my sacrifice . . . Be yet patient! I have parted with everything that was dear to me in this life for my country's cause . . . I wished to procure for my country the guarantee which Washington procured for America. Let no man write my epitaph; let me repose in obscurity and peace, and my tomb remain uninscribed, until other times and other men can do justice to my character. When my country takes her place among the nations of the earth, then, and not until then, let my epitaph be written."

Emmet's "magnificent" words stirred the Black children and may have touched their mother who had memories of her youthful love for another rebel whose body was reposed in an unmarked grave, without epitaph, at a place where he fought for his community's independence.

There were some memories and situations Della would be glad to leave. True to her faith, Della had accompanied her children to every Sunday service at her Baptist church, but it was a painful experience after Fayette's expulsion. He refused to enter a Baptist church for the rest of his life, and his children never were comfortable in a congregation that banned their father.

Also, Della herself had become something of a heretic—at least on one contentious point of church dogma. Primitive Baptists did not countenance Sunday school, which they considered an interference with the holy words of God as conveyed directly by the Bible and Hardshell ministers, men called by the Divine to preach. This sect of the Baptist church believed that lay people had no business instructing other Baptists on what the Scriptures mean, but "moderates" believed Sunday schools were a valuable aid to religious worship in a county where churches couldn't afford a full-time minister to preach every week. Valuing education in all things, Della supported Sunday schools in opposition to the majority views of her old congregation.[13]

All things considered, Della was probably ready to follow Fayette to Ashland. Yet, in all likelihood, a third person had to agree to the family's move. As in the past, Uncle Merit Street was the only person with both the means and interest to help Fayette Black and his family advance.

According to county documents, Fayette did not have the necessary resources to move to Ashland, where he was purchasing half interest in the H. A. Manning store. In 1889, Black had approximately $500 of value in both the merchandise at his Harlan store and his improved farm. Fayette's new Ashland house, however, cost almost as much as his entire Harlan farm, and he was buying a business interest worth more than twice the value of his country store. To make up the difference, only one man in the county had the cash or credit to bankroll Fayette's new purchases. Only one man held a silent, financial interest in the Manning store. Only one man of wealth cared enough about Della and her family to invest in Fayette's new venture.

There is no surviving record to show if Merit Street extended a private loan or sought as collateral a pledge from Fayette Black to pursue a new devotion to sobriety, but Black certainly did not forsake the value of politics for enlarging his fortunes. He simply was changing roles and venues. As ample proof, W. L. Black was selected conveniently one last time to serve on a jury from the

Wickers precinct in 1889. He was paid a dollar and a half a day and five cents per mile for his travel to and from the county seat, during a time he needed to be back and forth to Ashland arranging details for his move. It was his last civic duty as a citizen of Harlan and a fitting transition for a man who had progressed in life through the business of local politics.[14]

As THE BLACKS SETTLED into their house on Church Street, Ashland seemed an exciting place for a family whose members had seen nothing else of the world. Ten years before a new century, new technologies—railroad locomotives, steam boats, telegraphs, and a device called the "telephone"—were binding together much of America's northeastern coast as an emerging marketplace for the worldwide exchange of ideas, goods, and capital. But those wonders had not yet reached Ashland, Clay County's seat of government, population 635. The town sat slightly beyond the slopes and hillsides that extended towards Talladega from the Appalachian Mountains that gave the county claim to the state's highest elevation. Not far from total isolation or desolation, the community connected to life beyond only through the dirt ruts leading into town and the people who came along them with goods, services, troubles, and news.

Ashland was built on three sides facing at its center a planked courthouse, now with a new bricked jail beyond the town square. A few hundred feet away from the square was a gully that served as community privy, maintained and cleaned only by nature. The stores were crude barnlike structures where merchandise from local farms and distant manufacturers were stacked, kept in large kegs, or displayed on rough shelves. The stores' uneven facades had awnings of protruding planks to shade pine benches where Confederate veterans idled until their next state government check arrived by pony riders at the probate judge's office. Beyond the square, houses were built on large lots, primarily in the two directions leading out of town, north and south. No one had more than oil lamps that blackened the ceilings for light and fireplaces and pot-bellied stoves for heat. Almost no windows had glass or screens, and only a few held wooden shutters.

Without a railroad or rich ores in the nearby hills, Ashland was a destination only for folk who had nowhere better to go. As the site of government in a county of fifteen thousand people (90 percent white), the town drew citizens to pay taxes, do business with the law, visit relatives in town or jail, serve on a jury, or purchase supplies. Farmers and their families also came to the courthouse's criminal trials, one of their few sources of public entertainment, or to hear news beyond their neck of the woods from friends and neighbors who gathered on Saturdays, if weather and crops permitted. Since its incorporation, the town had been "dry" (without legal alcohol), a condition of law not entirely observed. Yet, without the law and order of the courthouse, the six hundred people who lived within sight of town square, including its newest residents on Church Street, would have had little business or livelihood.

Every Black child except Hugo started school in the first week of January 1890, and their father took to his new business with rediscovered purpose and enthusiasm. "Manning & Black" was one of a half-dozen stores on the square competing for the patronage of farmers who soon would seek loans for planting next year's crops and merchandise for next month's needs. The new firm advertised straw hats and perfumes for women, but Fayette and other merchants attracted business largely because they functioned as the county's bankers/money lenders. Most customers were bound to them by credit, not consumer choice, through a "crop lien" system.

Farmers approached W. L. Black and H. A. Manning, as they did Merit Street, seeking a line of credit to purchase store supplies and goods they would need over the next year in exchange for a promise that, after the harvest in October or November, they would repay merchants from the sale of cash crops. To assure full payment, merchants took liens on prospective crops and the farmers' valuables. A lien gave a merchant the legal right to take possession and sell everything except a farmer's house if he failed to repay the loan on time. Under this system, backed by the force of the local sheriff, farmers did business with the merchants who offered the best supplies with the best credit terms, and the storekeepers loaned to farmers they trusted to produce a good crop of cotton or corn which could repay the loan with interest in full. Without local banks, merchants were the farmers' only sources of capital.

From the beginning of this system of finance, established after the Civil War, small black and white farmers in the South had struggled with high interest rates, low prices for cotton (the only crop that annually sold on the market for cash), poor land, and long spells of disagreeable weather. As a result, over two decades following the War, the value of Alabama farms stagnated, and by 1890 the number of small family farms in both Clay and the state was declining. The number of Clay County farms in debt was twice the state's rate, and Clay's farmers were paying one of the state's highest rates for mercantile interest, on average 11.4 percent in contrast to a state average of 8.7 percent. A national depression arising in 1890 worsened prospects of improvement and accelerated local farmers' collective search for fundamental change.

Nationally, the Farmers Alliance, a chapter of which Wilburn Whatley had organized in Clay, was looking to the federal government to change economic conditions. Like others who found self-help an ineffective cure for the harshness of a national economic system, the Alliance had begun to support federal policies to bolster the price of cotton and to make money easily available. With other groups, they called for a silver standard for U.S. currency instead the gold standard. This change, they argued, would pump more money into the economy and would, in effect, lower farmers' existing debt by increasing inflation. The proposal sparked a decade of national debate between "Gold Bugs" and "Silverites," and it reflected an economic division that was as real as farmers' growing indebtedness to merchants like W. L. Black.

Locally in this mutually dependent, often parasitic economy, farmers attacked the "professional men" and the "Ashland Ring" because they believed merchants and lawyers were profiting at their expense by controlling local government and the local economy. While the courthouse could not mint silver dollars nor set the price of cotton, public officials in Ashland made critical decisions about who received tax monies, jobs, and education; how citizens' land and personal property were valued and taxed; and when or how to foreclose on liened property and crops. At the statehouse, Clay's representatives alone could decide which officials would be elected locally by the people, rather than appointed by Montgomery's state officials; what were the rules, terms, and limits of lien laws and "stock" laws for grazing cattle; and how the state department of agriculture would assist farmers. Even before moving to Ashland, Black understood that the national debate about gold and silver and local issues of government power and privilege came home every time a farmer entered his store with the burden of negotiating another season's lien.[15]

With children to educate and a business to grow, W. L. Black sharply reduced his direct political involvement. Upon leaving Harlan, he gave up his seat on the county Democratic Executive Committee and did not seek another visible, political role. His friendship with Democratic chief Asbury Stockdale grew, but as an Ashland merchant Black operated exclusively behind the scenes in Clay's politics.

As party boss, Stockdale continued to try to project democratic change while maintaining his clique's control. In 1890, he led Democrats to experiment with the politics of inclusion in a year when only three elective posts were at stake. Conservatives gave the independent party two-fifths of the delegates at the local Democratic convention that nominated a state senator and held a primary election for state representative and school superintendent, which by state law had become an elective office. These concessions, Stockdale hoped, would quiet growing discontent.

His plan succeeded with all the wrong results. Wilburn Whatley lost his bid to be state senator at the "2/5 convention." Independents and Alliance men supporting Whatley charged that the convention was rigged when it nominated conservative attorney Martin Lackey, although Whatley's own brother accused him of buying votes. Republicans nominated their own county candidates for the first time since Reconstruction and tried unsuccessfully to attract independents in the general election. With their opponents split, conservative Democrats prevailed, and Stockdale retained his post as head of the local schools.

It was at best an accidental triumph. At worst, it galvanized the opposition. Many farmers believed in 1890 that their man, Wilburn Whatley, had been cheated of victory. As a result, Democrats won the election but lost the future loyalty of many farmers and of the Alliance leader who had helped them prevail in 1888. Also, Reuben Kolb (pronounced "Cobb"), Alabama's secretary of agriculture and a state Alliance leader, was defeated for governor in what many Clay farmers considered another rigged state Democratic convention; the chief lawyer for the Louisville & Nashville railroad, Thomas Goode Jones, became governor at a brokered convention.

In 1892, four months after Della sent Hugo to Ashland Academy's first form, Clay's sweltering political revolution erupted. In April, independents held a mass meeting at the courthouse to form the People's Party of Clay, "to labor and vote for *equal rights for all and special privileges for none.*" Wilburn Whatley and Henry Clay Simmons were elected to attend a statewide People's Party convention, and, blessed by the Rev. M. M. Driver's prayers, the new People's Party set a primary election for late May.

Freed of the necessity to please independent farmers, local conservative Democrats did not seem to know how to act. Hiram Evans abruptly gave up his post as probate judge and moved to Texas, but two prominent conservatives clashed bitterly for the nomination to succeed him. Stockdale entered the probate judge's race late, only to be reminded that elections cannot be brokered.

Stockdale's opponents got a combined total of more than eight hundred votes, while he received only eighty-nine. In every other Democratic race, at least four candidates bid for the nomination. Sheriff Allen White stepped down, but one of his deputies trying to succeed him received barely a hundred votes. The deputy proclaimed angrily that nine out of ten Democrats were liars since exactly 950 men had promised to vote for him.

The campaign in the general election began before crops were harvested, and the People's Party leaders commenced a whirlwind of activity and speeches. They echoed the platform of the national People's Party or "Populists" who had met earlier in Omaha, Nebraska. Declaring that "wealth belongs to him who created it," Populists supported a graduated income tax, government ownership of railroads and telegraphs, and the issuance of more money for the economy. They also accused "Bourbon Democrats" of chicanery at the polls.

Joseph Manning, son of Fayette's business partner, returned to Clay to tend to an ailing father and to assist the new political movement. Young, articulate, and energetic, Manning joined independent leaders whose forensic talents drew envious protests from Democrats. "If you'll give me Simmons to speak, Driver to pray," complained a local Democrat, "I can hold an enthusiastic meeting at the North Pole on any subject."

Conservative Democrats—"agonized Democrats," Simmons liked to call them—mounted a credible counterattack. The party of Jefferson and Jackson proclaimed support for government regulation, not public ownership of railroads; more freedom for private banks to lend money; "more efficient public schools"; the end of government subsidies to private companies; and lower tariffs on exporting farm goods. Democrats reminded voters that Alabama's Populists were the first party since Reconstruction to accept a Negro as a convention delegate and that it had a "Negro plank" designed to "arouse the Negro against white supremacy." The *Advance* editor summed it up: "The People's Party shows a Republican fatherhood and Independent motherhood and degeneration is evident throughout the offspring."

In 1892 Grover Cleveland attempted to return to the White House as only the second Democratic president since the Civil War, and Thomas Goode Jones, former L&N railroad lawyer, sought reelection as Democratic governor against Reuben Kolb's redoubled Populist campaign. The incumbent Democratic congressman was also fighting a challenge against Wilburn Whatley, now a boundless Populist. Across the South and the West, Populism had become a national, agrarian movement of poor whites, in alliance occasionally with blacks, to gain political power in order to redistribute economic opportunities and resources.

W. L. Black was an avid, boisterous partisan for Grover Cleveland, and his every word of praise was echoed during the campaign by his youngest son who, like his father, talked for Cleveland, argued for Cleveland, and shouted for Cleveland. At the age of six, Hugo Black also wanted to vote for Cleveland, although Clay's election practices were not quite that generous to Democratic causes. Whenever one of Fayette's conservative friends wanted a laugh, he would remind Hugo that his relatives in Millersville were Populists and, therefore, "You are a Populist, a third party-ite."

"I am *not*," the tiny boy protested in a pitched, shrill voice. "I am not a tird (sic) party—I a Democrat."

Asbury Stockdale was confidant that others of voting age would declare the same loyalty on election day. "As the campaign comes to a close, we see light," Stockdale wrote Governor Jones. "The great fight in Clay has been Jones vs. Kolb. In June it looked as if Kolb would have beaten you in Clay 700-800, but now the prospects are good for you to carry the County. I *think you will*." After recounting his own, personal sacrifices on Jones's behalf, Stockdale was ebullient about Democratic prospects across the state: "Looking for,—hoping for 40,000 majority in the state."

The election proved another of Stockdale's vain hopes. Kolb won Clay. Had it not been for fraudulent voting in Black Belt counties, where Democrats manipulated the votes of former slaves, Governor Jones would not have been reelected. Grover Cleveland also was not the clear choice of Clay's voters, although the nation did return him to the White House. One of the newest Populists, Wilburn Whatley, won a majority in Clay but lost the Congressional race in the district's two Black Belt counties because of questionable polling practices. Despite razor-thin margins, the People's Party candidates won all of Clay's county races. For the first time, Clay's entire courthouse belonged to farmers and the Populists.[16]

BEGINNING IN LATE 1892, the Black household focused much more on Ashland's schoolhouse than its courthouse. Della's youngest child started in Miss Lizzie Patterson's first form class. Inheriting his mother's small, almost fragile features, Hugo was well-groomed and closely inspected each day by Della before he left home. His clothes were both handsomely homemade and store-bought, in comparison with the worn, patched apparel of country kids. Hugo already knew how to read and write, due to the help of his sisters and mother, and, with a new piano in the house, he had just begun to play a few simple tunes by ear. With this head start, Della's boy moved rapidly through the beginner's reader and on to more challenging books.

Hugo was one of the best students in his section, but he shone no brighter than the rest of Della's children who were Ashland Academy's honor roll students and acknowledged speakers. Attending the college division, Ora was in the women's literary society, ambitiously named Sappho after the lyrical female poet of ancient Greece. She lectured on suitable topics such as "Heaven from all creatures hides the book of fate." Robert Lee also attended college classes and acted as his father's son. In a school debate, for instance, Lee opposed electing the president by popular vote. Merit Vernon was eight years older than Hugo and considered the smartest, most talented of all the high-achieving Black children. In a community with deep oral traditions, Vernon's speaking ability was remarkable. Perhaps his most memorable speech at the Academy was a dramatic rendition of "The Little Martyr," the story of a boy whose life is ruined by the effects of whiskey.

At home, each of Della's children was treated with the same high expectations. She rigidly enforced rules against rowdiness and foul language, although she endured her husband's occasional profane behavior and words. When Hugo came home from school with signs of a scuffle, it didn't matter that he was Della's precious little boy. She whipped him—a sore punishment for a boy who lost most schoolyard fights. During the week, Della required her children to read the Bible at home, although they could read other respectable literature. On weekends, her children went to Ashland's First Baptist Church for Sunday school and for worship services on the third Sunday of every month when the circuit-riding minister came to town. To please his mother and to entertain himself, Hugo attended the Baptist Sunday school on Sunday mornings and Methodist Sunday school in the afternoon.

Ashland's Sunday schools were the primary places outside the home where the town's women could create and project their own vision and values for society. Segregated from business, politics, the pulpit, and the law, Clay's women prevailed for a couple of hours each week to speak about matters of the Christian heart. On the seventh day, Della and other women retold New

Testament stories, such as that of the Good Samaritan, as lessons of good will, good deeds, and human goodness, so that the town's children might find love, hope, and charity more often than had the last generation. Men like Hiram Evans always headed the county's Sunday school association, but Clay's women shaped the moral content of the children's sessions.

Freed of farming's many daily, mundane chores, the wives of Ashland's professional men (virtually all conservative Democrats) organized and ran the town's Sunday schools and related church societies. Della and other members of the Ashland's Ladies Aid Society, for instance, tried to bring to life, in small portions, their own moral vision by caring for the county's sick and afflicted and by maintaining the church buildings and grounds. These works did not challenge the governing terms of the community their husbands tried to rule, but they represented a more contemplative, at times transcendent, perspective of humanity.

When Della gathered with other women to sweep gravesites, their work was filled with tears and shared memories of passed loved ones and unrealized possibilities. They did not mourn the loss of any grand sectional past—increasingly the animating force in the South's Confederate memorials—but instead the sacrifices of the living, the constant demands of a time and place where joy and sorrow, life and death were never far apart. When women prepared the sanctuary at Ashland's First Baptist Church, with its pyramid-shaped doors, sharply pitched, angular roof line, and its tall, pointed bell tower—each tier successively directing all eyes towards the heavens—Ashland's white women joined in a unique communion where the modest rituals of service to others symbolically brought to earth religious postulates of kindness and human interdependence. These deeds did not, could not, reshape the direction of Southern white society, but they were habits of survival and symbols of personal meaning that differed from the self-centered morality in play among the broader society of men.

The moral life that Della worked to instill in her own children was reinforced at the schoolhouse. Small, delicate, and strict like Della, Lizzie Patterson was one of only a few women holding teaching jobs in the county. "Miss Lizzie" had a facility for making students avoid doing anything which she might disapprove of, and her one simple commandment, enforced with a disappointing glance or in rare instances with a wooden ruler, seemed clear and unmistakable to Hugo and his classmates. In an elegant handwriting, Miss Lizzie wrote two words on the blackboard at the beginning of each day: "Do Right." That was enough instruction.

The whole school day explicated Miss Lizzie's injunction. The day usually began with a Christian prayer and Scripture reading. Lessons were taken from the Webster speller and *McGuffey Reader*, both conveying messages of righteous living as much as correct English. In one of Hugo's early lessons, the *Reader* admonished: "As for boys and girls that mind not their books, and love not the church and school, but . . . tell lies, curse, swear, and steal, they will come to some bad end and must be whipt till they mend their ways." *McGuffey* also stressed: "if you are not diligent in the improvement of your time, it is one of the surest evidences that your heart is not right with God. You are placed in this world to improve your time."[17]

Despite the Academy's ethos of righteous self-improvement, Robert H. Fisher, Clay's newly elected Populist superintendent, considered Ashland's newest school incorrigible. In 1893, Fisher announced a new *public* school in Ashland for the education of *all* children. The public funds which supported the Academy's elementary and secondary sections under Stockdale's term were to be redistributed to a new "Ashland Preparatory School," constructed by local Populist leaders on land less than half a mile from the Academy.

As stockholders and officers of the private, profit-making Academy, the town's leading conservatives were outraged. In late 1893, Stockdale, W. L. Black, and Allen White unsuccessfully asked local citizens to overturn Fisher's plans and, afterwards, petitioned the Democratic state superintendent to remove Fisher from office.

Black and company claimed that the new school was unnecessary and would create "discord and strife and . . . animosity between pupils of the respective schools." Two schools in so small a town "will have the inevitable tendency and effect to tear down, instead of to build up, permanent schools in the County." The Academy's patrons also charged Fisher with "making up a school for his own benefit" since Fisher planned to become the new school's salaried principal.

Robert Fisher's self-dealing was a conspicuous misuse of office which reflected a larger pattern in which he was dismantling Stockdale's old system of patronage to build his own. Yet, the movement for a new "common school" had broader support and more honorable motives. "I have seen the necessity for another school for years," observed a Populist school trustee, "that all the children in the community might have an equal showing . . . Our lands are poor, our people hard pressed and in debt and getting worse every year. We need a reformation," proclaimed the trustee. "Shall we hold up the college [Ashland Academy] at her own fixed prices and . . . let one-half of the children go uneducated?" he asked. "I am not looking so much to the education of the classes as I am to the education of the masses."

The central issue was how to use public dollars for education, and it reverberated with Henry Clay Simmons's earlier slogan of "more schools, more teachers, more money." According to Populist Joe Manning, only a third of the white children were attending schools and most in Clay were enrolled for only three summer months. Yet, Alabama's Democratic leaders begrudged even this minimal public schooling for white children. In Montgomery, Democratic Governor Thomas Jones withheld revenues from county superintendents in the fall of 1893 due to Alabama's sagging tax receipts. His lawful authority appears dubious, although he was strongly supported by the *Montgomery Advertiser,* Alabama's voice of Democratic conservatism, which dismissed public education as a dubious state function. For weeks, Jones left the state's public school teachers without pay because he diverted school funds to pay the interest on state debts which should have been covered by other revenues, including overdue taxes from the L&N railroad, Jones's old employer. One of Clay's new teachers sarcastically asked: "I wonder if the railroad is needing its money worse than us poor teachers who have paid our taxes twice and the railroad not at all?"

While they could do nothing about the governor's mischief, Ashland's Populists now had the political power to take public monies away from an independent school under the control of conservative Democrats and to create a common, publicly controlled school with a lower tuition and a mission to educate all children, including those who "have to plow and hoe for a living." Populists claimed the new school would stop using tax dollars to assure that "the apt and highest pupils succeed, but the dull and indifferent are sure to suffer."

Ashland Academy became a major political issue in Clay's 1894 campaign when Robert Fisher sought reelection. Once it opened, the new common school competed with the Academy for enrollment, after Fisher reluctantly appointed another Populist as the public school principal. In a telling moment, the conservative Democratic Executive Committee met for the first time outside the courthouse, at the Academy, to map the party's rules and campaign strategies.

Like rivaling candidates, the schools advertised their own competitive virtues in large ads in the *People's Party Advocate,* the new, local Populist newspaper. Now boasting itself as "A School For All," Ashland's Academy claimed: "Expenses as LOW as can be had in any first grade school in the State." The Academy also stressed its teachers' experience and competence, qualities it inferred were missing a half-mile away. The private school assured all parents that "Only Moral . . . Literature allowed." It published a new catalog promising no child would be barred due to a lack of money.

In response, the new Populist-created school advertised itself as one of the state's most desirable with "a new and commodious building" and "good stoves and heating apparatus" for winter sessions. "NO SCHOOL IN ALABAMA," it boldly bragged, "offers better inducements to those seeking a practical education. . . One-half the price usually charged."

In an excessively hot summer campaign, the Academy held graduation exercises which included Ora and Robert Lee Black, one of Uncle Merit Street's grandsons (who had been boarding with the Blacks). In an obvious political maneuver, the college gave honorary degrees to four local men, including John R. Graves Toland, Della's half brother. As a former, dedicated teacher, Uncle Graves may have been a deserving recipient. (The family boasted later that Toland taught Admiral Chester M. Nimitz, the commander who developed America's first nuclear-powered naval submarine, in grammar school.) But, in honoring a prominent Populist, Black and the other Democrats who owned the Academy were trying to recast their private school as an inclusive institution. And, of course, if an honorary degree helped one member of the Academy's board of directors improve his own domestic relations, all the better.[18]

In the broader, political campaign, Democrats handpicked candidates at a county convention. They also put their own professional and educational advantages to use. After the last election, the Democratic state legislature enacted a law introduced by Montgomery's Anthony D. Sayre that required all Alabama voters to reregister within a period of two and a half weeks in May 1894, a time of active farming. Touted as a reform for good government, the Sayre Law required ballots to list candidates alphabetically for each position and eliminated political party columns. Leaving almost nothing to chance, the Sayre Act annulled the vote of any person who stayed longer than five minutes in the voting booth and permitted the voter to seek assistance only from appointed polling officials.

In effect, unless he was coached before entering the voting booth, a Clay County farmer in 1894 had to be able to read in order to find and vote for a Populist candidate on the ballot. And he had only five minutes to figure it out. If confused, he could seek assistance solely from local Democratic party officials who in Clay were appointed by Asbury Stockdale. Through these methods, Democratic leaders hoped to use white farmers' illiteracy, perpetuated by Democratic education policies, and their own control of the voting apparatus, to discourage, disfranchise, disable, or steal Populist votes.

One Populist newspaper retitled the Sayre Act as "an Act to Perpetuate . . . Frauds," and Clay's Populist leaders protested loudly. At an earlier rally in Ashland during January's fallow days in 1894, Rueben Kolb and Joe Manning had delighted farmers with the apocryphal words of Governor Jones. "Give me the Sayre election law and let me sign it quick, lest my arm be paralyzed, for it forever wipes out Kolbism, Third partyism, and Negroism," they mocked. Afterwards, while it was still too wet and cold to work in the fields, Manning and Wilburn Whatley held a series of public speeches attacking "Black Belt Bourbonism," and demanding a free vote and a fair count. "It is liberty vs. slavery," shouted the Populists.

W. L. Black's beloved Grover Cleveland was also a prime political target among Clay's Populists. In a flash of doggerel, a third party-ite proclaimed: "Grover . . . called aloud, 'If yet my task be done? Free silver have we busted up, Gold basis for Shylock won.'" John T. Hudson, known as a "mongrel" among Democratic opponents, tried to preempt accusations about Populists' black support by accusing Cleveland of appointing an African American, "black enough to make ink," to a government post in the District of Columbia: "you can't fool the people any longer with your 'nigger racket'—It's all rot," Hudson told conservatives, "too rotten for anyone except an agonized democrat to fool with . . . I leave the subject to the people . . . who are the ones that stink of negro?"

The campaign was as vitriolic as it was racist with a melee of words, flags, guns, eggs, and fists. Clay's Democratic newspaper attacked its Populist counterpart with a breath-taking string of vituperative adjectives: "The . . . false, obnoxious, spiteful, repulsive, offensive, invectious, abominable and malicious thrust at the *Advance* in the sappy, scurrilous slime slinger of last week is characteristic of the little, dirty, scabby, sneaking, groveling, perfidious, unscrupulous, double-tongued, time-serving sheet in which it was published . . . what magniloquent prevaricators are these vainglorious braggarts."

The Democrats wrapped themselves with the Confederate flag since William Oates, the one-armed Confederate officer who assisted General Lee at Gettysburg, was their nominee for governor. Henry Clay Simmons, the county's "most eloquent political speaker" according to W. L. Black's youngest son, returned to the "agonized" party since apparently he could not abide the national alliance of Populists with blacks and Republicans. In an about-face, Simmons took to the stump now praising the party of the old Confederacy, which he had served.

A Populist nominee for the state legislature, Joe Manning, showed little respect for the South's sacred past. Concerning one opponent, he said: ". . . you have spoken about your forefathers fighting and dying for Democracy. It is a pity all of your sort didn't die when they did." At a speech outside of Clay, Manning was pelted with eggs until he gave up the platform. He quickly boarded an outbound train when his supporters feared he would be "egged, stoned, or shot to death." In Clay, Wilburn Whatley kept a pistol in his pocket as he campaigned for the Populist ticket, and, after cutting a man with a knife, Whatley warned that anyone trying to interfere with his speeches would prematurely meet his Maker.

On election day, in Black's old Wickers precinct, young farmers paraded a mule bedecked with a crown of colorful corncobs, signifying the heady victory which they expected for their gubernatorial candidate Reuben Kolb. The animal also had a tail of "Oates" swishing across its backside, placing the Democratic candidate just about where they thought his character was best defined. At several polling places, including Merit Street's store, men broke into a brawl after sharing illegal whiskey. In a couple of locations, Populists set up a procedure whereby one of the county's few black men was introduced to a Democrat as he came out of the voting place. The white Populists mocked that the Negro was going into the polls to cast a Populist ballot—"to kill" the Democrat's vote. White Populists thought it was riotous, revengeful fun, a fitting insult to Democrats for their party's fraudulent use of black voters in Alabama's Black Belt, but an angry white Baptist preacher fetched his rifle and tried the old-fashioned way of killing Populist votes.

When the tallies were done, Democrats failed to regain the county's political control, although the People's Party won most races by less than one hundred votes. Joe Manning became the new state legislator. Superintendent Robert Fisher was the only Populist defeated in the county. He lost by thirteen votes, a thin margin tipped by his own greed. The eight-year-old Hugo Black was at the courthouse watching the count until the last votes were tallied.

Democratic fraud in the Black Belt was so evident in the narrow victory of William Oates as governor that Joe Manning helped to organize a rally in Montgomery where a few hundred Populists, marching on the state capitol, demanded Reuben Kolb ascend to the governor's chair. After Oates took his oath of office on the spot where Jeff Davis became Confederate president, outgoing Governor Jones defied the Populist crowd by sending out an armed state militia whose guns and bayonets had left several dead and wounded in a recent Birmingham miners' strike. When Kolb hesitated in the face of loaded guns, Manning shouted: "Go ahead, Captain, they may kill you, but you will go down in history as a martyr to the Populist cause." Kolb declined immortality. In absence of a state law for challenging a fraudulent election, Alabama's Populists settled for one-third of Alabama's legislators, elected mostly from north Alabama counties.[19]

With a local Democratic school superintendent, W. L. Black and other conservative leaders took Ashland Academy out of politics by agreeing to share the Academy's control. Populist Probate Judge E. A. Phillips became secretary of the private school's board, which hired a new principal acceptable to both political camps, and both Democrats and Populists were hired later as teachers. In turn, public funds supported the private Academy, where Hugo now began his third grade. No other school for white children operated in the town. (As in the past, black children went to school in Ashland's local black church with hardly any public funds.)

Like other rare moments of political harmony in Clay, this settlement may have been perfected with the wealth of Merit Street, although this time through an ironic, dishonest twist of his last earthly wish. During a long, slow period of disability, Street had informed local citizens that he was leaving $15,000 in his will for a common school in Bluff Springs. At that time, this amount was a fabulous sum that could have endowed a state's university, much less a local school in the heart of Clay's most Populist section.

Uncle Merit had died in May 1891, only three months after A. S. Stockdale, Allen White, and W. L. Black arranged for public funds to support the private academy they owned for educating conservative Democrats' sons and daughters. The original of Street's will was lost, but it was redrawn from the memory and notes of Street's lawyer, a longtime Democrat from nearby Lineville. "In the name of Almighty God, Amen," the document began in characteristic style, "I, Merit Street . . . will and bequeath my soul to God who gave it, and that my body be interred in the old family grave yard [on Mount Ararat] near where I now live, and that a neat, substantial enclosure and tomb be placed over the same, not an extravagant, costly one . . ." After assuring that his wife would have all she needed to live comfortably, Street ordained four hundred acres of land and $15,000 for the establishment of "an Industrial School for Girls and Boys" within sight of his grave. The will described how to construct adequate buildings, including a "chapel of good size" for use by "all Christian denominations," and how to invest funds so that earnings could pay teachers in perpetuity.

"I direct that all children who may attend said school," continued Street's will, and "who live close enough to come from home should be charged no tuition." Street provided that "male scholars" work the school's farm as a part of their education and that "female pupils . . . be taught and required to do . . . such things as will be beneficial to them in after life." All products of student work were to generate funds for the school's ongoing operation. Street named his oldest son, Jay, Judge Hiram Evans, and J. L. M. Curry, a nationally known educator who began his career in Talladega, as school trustees. Most of Street's remaining wealth was divided equally between his two sons—with one condition. Street named his first son, a good, sober Democrat, as sole executor of his estate and required his youngest son, Robert, to quit drinking liquor for three consecutive years before he could receive the bulk of his legacy.

In June 1891, Hiram Evans had appointed a special judge to probate Street's will, ostensibly since Evans was a named party in the document. He appointed Asbury Stockdale, Clay's superintendent of schools and the major stockholder in the Ashland Academy. After a hearing with Street's family and lawyer at the Ashland courthouse on June 13, Stockdale approved terms of the reconstructed will, which was laid out in probate records. By the end of the month, Evans issued a decree approving Stockdale's order and judgment.

No school was ever built in Bluff Springs.

Merit Street's son apparently never assembled the school's trustees nor did he as executor of his father's will set aside any money or land for the school.

There was evidently no contact with the proposed school's most distinguished trustee, Dr. Curry, who had recently returned to America after serving as U.S. Ambassador to Spain. Another trustee of the proposed school, Hiram Evans, unexpectedly decided in early 1892 not seek reelection. Before a new probate judge took office, Evans moved to Texas, a common place of refuge at that time for Alabama men fleeing the law or a pregnant girl's irate father. Street's lawyer who had reconstructed the will moved to Birmingham and afterwards to parts unknown. Stockdale attempted in 1892 to succeed Evans as probate judge where he could control access to probate records—rather than remain as public school superintendent. Merit Street's wife and two sons, who also knew the terms of the will, remained silent throughout their lives, as did every professional man who participated in probating the will of their righteous friend.

When the conspiracy of silence developed and how it was sustained over time are mysteries whose solutions are long buried. It is curious that the endowment for a school in the original, misplaced will was included in the reconstructed document that Stockdale approved and recorded in probate journals. It would have been much easier to collude against Merit Street's last wishes had those terms simply been left out of the recomposed document. In fact, many years later, after Street's youngest son committed suicide and his oldest son mismanaged the family fortune, the original will was discovered by children exploring Street's old rolltop desk. The provisions for the school were there for all to read, but the money had been wastefully spent.

Street's descendants and his neighbors had assumed that the community had been cheated because Street's lawyer left the school out of the will when he rewrote it for probate. In fact, the treachery was more complicated and more profound, and its discovery could have been much simpler. Because the recorded will included the school endowment, the complicity probably began after the document was probated, during a time when a rich family's shock and grief can wane and selfish greed betrays old loyalties and truth. Yet, as the entanglements, inactions, and silence grew, Merit Street's true intentions were available to anyone with access to the handwritten, public journals in the probate judge's office.

During this time, the shadows of unusual private transactions prompted Populist leaders Wilburn Whatley and Robert Fisher to accuse Evans and Stockdale of personally receiving large sums of money from the county treasury through a series of devious, illegal, but undefined means. In addition, Populists charged that Judge Evans attempted to stage a theft of public records from his own office to cover up an unspecified crime. There were, however, no missing public monies or records, and allegations of misconduct were never seriously pursued. No one suspected that officials might be paid for a coverup with Street's own money. The old man's personal integrity apparently shielded his own family from any suspicion of wrongdoing. Ironically, Street's lifelong example of hard work, correctness, and parsimony as worshipful deeds to honor his Almighty was handed down to his sons and surviving wife as nothing more than a love of money which, in the end, proved more puissant than a stern father's last will, the needs of a poor white community's children, or standing law.

Whatever were the particular, private inducements for omissions and convenient departures, Asbury Stockdale and Ashland Academy's other primary stockholders had a clear self-interest for colluding with Street's family. They had invested substantial sums of their own monies in developing Ashland's private school that now depended on both public monies and student fees in the higher sections. As county superintendent, Stockdale had assured government support, but Street's new school, innovative and inexpensive, would have pulled away students and fees from across Clay County. In a few years, such a remarkable free educational institution also could have shifted the center of learning from Ashland to Bluff Springs. That development would have created real political pressure to invest more public monies in schools outside of Ashland. At stake for Stockdale, Black, and White were their own money and the best local education for their own children.

Stockdale's belated decision to give up his post as school superintendent to seek the post of probate judge in 1892 underscores the men's probable motives. Stockdale risked losing control of public monies supporting the Academy, but something more ominous loomed on the horizon. A new probate judge might easily discover Street's will in reviewing past records and raise the question of why the executor had not established the school endowment or why Stockdale as the special probate judge had not required observance of the will. The new probate judge could reopen the case and order the executor to create the endowed school or remove Street's son as executor of the entire estate. As it turned out, Stockdale embarrassed himself by receiving fewer than one hundred votes in his race for probate judge.

No record or memory survives to tell how much W. L. Black knew or participated in the conspiracy. He was in a position to know everything and to be paid for keeping his own counsel. In fact, according to tax records, Black's own wealth rose sharply after Street's death. Equally mysterious is why the new Populist probate judge, E. A. Phillips, did not discover Street's last will soon after he took office in 1893 and decree the formation of the free school for the county's Populist stronghold. A few years earlier, as court clerk, Phillips had accused Evans and White of rigging juror selection to protect Democratic interests. He and Evans were bitter political enemies, not a relationship of forgiveness. Perhaps Judge Phillips simply did not notice the exact terms of Street's will—at least for a few years.

This much is public record. After the 1894 election, the county's Populist probate judge joined conservative Democrats as an officer and primary stockholder of the Ashland Academy, and, in a terribly divided county, the school became the only semi-public institution where Populists and Democrats worked together. After 1894, Merit Street's rural grandchildren boarded in Ashland with the W. L. Black family while attending the Academy. By 1895, Judge E. A. Phillips had a taxable wealth rivaling that of W. L. Black, although Phillips's office afforded him an annual salary of only $500. Phillips did not seek reelection in 1898 but opened a large mercantile business in Ashland where he prospered.[20]

By whatever mix of private, public, and political motives, by whatever acts of betrayal, inducements and perfidy, both Democratic and Populist leaders left Bluff Springs and Clay County without a new, free, and well-endowed school for its poor white children. Ironically, Ashland Academy survived as the defilement of a rich man's last wish, and it became Merit Street's most enduring, if unintended, legacy.

AFTER THE 1894 ELECTION, W. L. Black began to establish his own living legacy. His oldest son, Robert Lee, was now twenty-five and a mirror of his father's physical traits—a large man whose long, handsome head was defined by wavy brown hair, a trimmed mustache grown slightly beyond the ends of his upper lip, and a right ear lobe tilting forward as if eager to hear a conversation. Yet, Lee had none of his father's character: no driving ambition, no strong animosities, no opinionated stubbornness, and no consuming taste for whiskey. Lee took life in its own good, sweet time. He much preferred lounging with a book instead of pushing Democratic dogma or negotiating a store lien. Lee reincarnated his father's body without his soul. Dutifully, however, as eldest son, Lee became

W. L. Black's heir in business and politics. He was, in effect, manager of the store, now owned solely by Fayette Black. Lee had joined Ashland's young men's Democratic Club and now, like his father before him, was elected to the local Democratic Executive Committee. Soon he became its secretary.

After six years in Ashland, W. L. Black had attained a long-sought prosperity. By 1896, he owned two houses and two "business houses" in town. His store supplies were valued at $1,200, according to the tax assessor. The crop liens that Fayette registered in courthouse records added up to more than $3,000 in loans. While promoting Lee as a local Democratic leader, W. L. joined the Ashland city council, an honorary post shared among the town's Democratic men.

Black wore his success with style and relish. His conservative friends praised him as a "leading merchant and enterprising citizen." Increasingly, he left Lee to mind the store while he went to Talladega, Goodwater, Montgomery, Alex City, and other centers of commerce in nineteenth-century Alabama. The local Democratic editor delighted in ribbing Black about his penchant for a foppy appearance: "With a comely form and faultless apparel, he will be the Beau Brummel of Clay."

Black's family was now a part of Ashland "society," modest as it was in comparison to New York, St. Louis, or Montgomery. Lee's courtship and marriage to a local girl was newsworthy for both conservative and Populist weekly papers. Since competition for printer's ink was slim in the backwoods, especially when politics wasn't stirring, a business trip by W. L. Black or the movement of the older Black children around the county was never too insignificant for a sociable comment by the local weeklies.

Black's children also were provided enviable opportunities in a place where most children were illiterate and bound for life to a profitless farm. Orlando secured a teaching job in north Alabama, where Fayette's father and other kin had moved. Pelham was grooming to be a lawyer. With a new Democrat as school superintendent, Ora received a teaching job in the Spring Hill community, despite the fact that it was a stronghold for Populists like Wilburn Whatley. Described as "one of Clay's most accomplished daughters," Ora married another schoolteacher at the Black home in the "social event of the season."

Like their father, the Black boys went about the county almost as dandies, clothed often in rare, store-bought apparel. When Hugo proudly wore a store-bought cap on a visit to Ora's classroom in Spring Hill, he was the envy and taunt of local boys who had bare heads and bare feet most of the year.

Age and comfort made W. L. more indulgent of his own vices and more intolerant of others. His alcoholism deepened into a subject of public ridicule and private torment. Without Uncle Merit to please and with Lee behind his store counter, Fayette's binges with whiskey apparently became more frequent, longer, and more public, in a town too small to hide foibles. When Robert Lee married, the local Democratic newspaper seemed obliged to assure readers that W. L. Black's son was "a honest, *sober*, intelligent young man." The Populist paper was not so circumspect. "W. L. Black, " reported the *People's Party Advocate* after New Years Day in 1894, "is suffering from la grippe . . . Did you 'swear off' last Monday morning?" it asked Black and others who were victims of holiday libations in a dry county.

The only lawful exceptions to prohibition in Clay were for use in "family circles," the one place Della could prevent her husband's drinking, and for "sacramental purposes," a use that hardly applied to a man expelled from his church for public drunkenness. Under the circumstances, dry Primitive Baptists and Populists had good reason to wonder how one of Ashland's city fathers could "get religion" every time he needed a sacramental drink in order to keep from breaking the law, which as a city council member he was sworn to uphold.

Unable to relinquish liquor and blind to most of his own shortcomings, Black concocted his own moments of mischief and embarrassment for Baptist teetotalers and preachers, whose piety he considered as counterfeit as the Populist position on silver. When the Shiloh Baptist Church at Hatchet Creek held a drive to build a new structure, for example, W. L. Black was among a list of prominent Populists and teetotalers as a financial supporter, acknowledged publicly as one of the "brethren and friends" of the church. For thirty cents, the lowest contribution on the list, Black bedeviled the dry Baptists who considered him as an unfit, sinning outcast in one church but as one of the Baptist "brethren" in another, if they needed a little of his cash for a building fund.

Della regularly invited the Baptist minister to dinner after his Sunday sermons, in keeping with her rotating duty as a churchwoman, but W. L. Black usually stayed on the porch, away from the preacher until food was served. On at least one occasion, while waiting alone, Black espied another "outsider" whose sinful ways had banished him from the church. The man was a well-known "sinner" and may have been slightly drunk. With exaggerated gestures of friendship, the elder Black prevailed upon the drunkard to join the family and the Baptist minister for Sunday dinner. Black relished demonstrating his version of the Good Samaritan to wife and guest.

Black stubbornly kept up his war with the Baptist church regardless of its emotional cost to his family. For example, Ora's wedding in November 1894, might have been the "social event" of Ashland's fall season, as the *Advance* wrote, but it did not include a Baptist ceremony. Despite the natural wishes of a devout mother and faithful daughter, Fayette would not attend a Baptist church nor did a Baptist minister get the opportunity to officiate a ceremony in his house. Ora and Della had to settle for a civil ceremony by a Justice of the Peace and a lavish "social event." By design or luck, Lee married a Methodist woman in her church.

Fayette's acts of mischief and spite were a continuing embarrassment to his wife, leaving emotional wounds that Della salved with her devotion to God, family, and church. These episodes, however, paled when compared with the pain that Fayette inflicted at another moment of death in the family.

In the fall of '95, Hugo's youngest sister Daisy took ill with a severe fever. It may have been the real "la grippe"—deathly influenza. While she was nursed to recovery, Merit Vernon became sick with the same symptoms. The boy was feverish for weeks, but by early November the danger seemed to have passed. With his father's blessing, Lee went to the Cotton States Exposition in Atlanta to see Grover Cleveland, and Orlando returned to north Alabama to teach. Yet, Merit Vernon's recovery proved false. At seventeen, "one of the brightest boys in Ashland College," the brother Hugo most emulated, died on Friday afternoon, November 15.

It was the third weekend of the month, and the Rev. J. D. Upshaw was in Ashland, as scheduled, to preach on Sunday at the First Baptist Church where he always saw Della, Merit Vernon, Hugo, and the other Black children. Upshaw was a moderate Baptist who believed in the virtues of Sunday school and ministerial training, but he was a Baptist minister who held worship services in a Baptist church, a place W. L. Black refused to enter.

In keeping with local customs, Vernon's body was laid out in the parlor of Black's home, where men and boys sat with it around the clock until the day of the funeral. Amid condolences and piteous reminders that "it is not all of life to have nor all of death to die," Della endured immeasurable grief from the loss of another child and from her husband's refusal ever again to step inside a Baptist church. Not even the disposition of his son's immortal soul changed Fayette Black. By Sunday morning, after untold negotiations, trauma, and recriminations, Merit Vernon Black's funeral was held with the only preacher in town, the Baptist Reverend Upshaw, presiding in the only religious building W. L. Black would enter, the Methodist church. Luckily for Della and her surviving children, Ashland's cemetery was considered nondenominational.

Within three weeks of his son's death, W. L. Black traveled to Atlanta's Cotton States Exposition to forget his misery. Whiskey was plentiful, and the attractions included the Hall of Confederate States, a giant Ferris wheel, Middle Eastern camels, and the first silent movies or "living pictures." Black returned to Atlanta after Christmas to bring in the new year, without local Populists' taunts about drinking himself sick. W. L. apparently intended on having the time of his life. As Black left town, Clay's *Advance* newspaper jokingly warned: "Atlanta and all of China will shake from one side of the earth to the other."

And Atlanta did. With Black among the gigantic crowds, the Gate City celebrated as if entering a new millennium in a wild, citywide party that closed the World Exposition and launched Atlanta anew as the brave city of Henry Grady's born-again New South. Downtown trains on New Year's Eve were overloaded with passengers who quickly joined strangers dancing in the streets, as peddlers sold cups of whiskey punch for a dime. In smoke-filled theaters, men stared hungrily as women revealed as much flesh and hip movement as public morals would brook. At Piedmont Park, massive crowds assembled in the last hours of the Exposition, while men, like boys fighting over a treasured copy of *National Geographic*, pushed for a glimpse of the exotic, foreign belly dancers. In the wake of his second child's death, W. L. Black finally was somewhere he wanted to be. It was as much of the wide world as he would ever see.

Back in Ashland, where W. L. did not want to be, Hugo Black was nearing the age of ten, a time when children begin to see cause and effect, to assign right and wrong to what they once witnessed simply as unrelated or inevitable events in a world of magic, fun, sorrow, and danger. As a boy exploring and watching the world around him, beginning to find his own identity and place, Hugo attached himself to individuals whom he respected. And, increasingly, Hugo was looking for guidance and role models away from the man whose seed gave him birth. The boy was beginning to develop a cold indifference towards his father, an emotional detachment shaped between the competing polarities of hate and love, something he probably first recognized as the terms of truce in his parents' own relations. These were early moments in the rites of passage from childhood and represented an unmarked, gradual shift in perspective and attitude that can be even more significant in a boy than the awakening of puberty, although a great deal less noticeable.

From a very early age, Hugo had understood the dangers of whiskey as he watched what it did to his father and how it contributed to his mother's deepest pain. Ashland's doctor had diagnosed Hugo at the age of five with catarrhal fever and prescribed medicinal whiskey to help save the boy's life. Because he came into the world so little and frail under death's wings, Della always considered Hugo a sickly child and feared that, like Little Della, he would die young. Of course, Hugo considered himself vulnerable. But, his reaction to whiskey was so strong even at the age of five that, entirely on his own, Hugo refused to take one drop of the evil liquid that he blamed for ruining his father's goodness. At five, Black couldn't spell the word "whiskey," but he knew by smell and observation that it was a ruinous substance that no human lips should ever touch. Della feared for her son's life, but she also feared what whiskey did to one's life. Together, mother and child prayed and disobeyed the doctor's orders.

W. L. Black's worsening alcoholism may have been one of the reasons Ora took Hugo with her to Spring Hill during the summers when she taught school. The boy enjoyed meeting and playing with new friends like Wilburn Whatley's youngest son, Barney, but an absence from home also spared Hugo from sad, inevitable moments when Della worked to sober or calm her drunken husband. Hugo's frequent trips to Millersville to visit the Tolands provided the same sort of shield. Except for the gentle waywardness of Uncle Brack, who also was expelled from the church for drinking, the Tolands were prohibitionists. Little wonder that Hugo spent many summers of his early youth fishing for catfish and eel in Hatchet Creek and playing with cousins miles away from Ashland.

Merit Vernon's death, however, marked a specific, turning point, a vague but certain period when a perceptive boy like Hugo sees over the shields that adults use to protect him and remembers not only death's sorrow but also man's misdeeds. It was a time when Hugo could no longer see the dangers and destruction of alcohol without also seeing the failures of his father. If at five a boy could face death and muster the free will to forego whiskey, against the advice of a doctor, at the age of ten he could wonder seriously why his father could not gather the same will to stop drinking and to end the tragic misery he unleashed on his family with every binge and every act of revenge against his old church. Self-discipline so painfully lacking in the father's habits was becoming the cardinal virtue so eagerly sought by his youngest son.

In the weeks following the new year, after W. L. Black had returned soberly from Atlanta, life continued in Ashland without Merit Vernon and without any other visible change in the Black household. The most disciplined of the older Black boys, Orlando decided to abandon teaching in north Alabama for medical school. He wanted to become a healer and an opponent of death. [21] At ten, Hugo could not make so dramatic a statement about his future. Yet, while he never forgot that W. L. Black was his father who provided well for his family, never again was Lafayette Hugo deliberately the echo of William Lafayette, as was that little boy of six who campaigned for Grover Cleveland simply because he was his father's son.

FOLLOWING HIS OLDER BROTHER PELHAM's interest in the law, Hugo began to discover inside Clay's courthouse a world of excitement and entertainment that was the province of men who were lawyers, judges, and politicians. During each circuit court session, attorneys from Ashland and surrounding counties commanded the courtroom on the second floor as they stood before a jury of twelve men—and often one small boy in the audience—to address questions of guilt and innocence. Civil cases were usually arid and uninteresting, but criminal trials could possess high drama and conflict, when attorneys with limited formal education could appear larger than life.

Martin Lackey, Esquire, literally fit the bill. He weighed 350 pounds and had the movements of a beached whale, as he made his slow, arduous journey up creaking steps to the courthouse's second floor. Except when the lawyer was leaning back in his special, oversized cane-bottom chair whittling wood as witnesses spoke, Hugo was never sure Lackey was awake, or even alive, during a trial. The lawyer sat immovably in the courtroom. In most cases, he associated a younger attorney to examine witnesses, as if the act of asking questions was simply more exercise than Lackey could possibly muster. Lackey's closing statements, however, could be volcanic, often providing a summation that molded the jury's understanding of the facts into an unstoppable, local logic that overcame his opponent's case.

Once, in a case that Hugo remembered for decades, a rape victim's family hired Lackey to help prosecute a Talladega man. The trial was a swearing contest between the victim and defendant, but Lackey permitted a series of character witnesses to testify for the accused without cross-examination. During summation to the jury, however, Lackey declared: "Ain't much to this case. This fella don't say much 'cept what a good fella he is over yonder in Talladega . . . brought plenty of Talladega county folks to swear to his character . . . But . . . I for one am sick and tired of these Talladega boys coming over here to Clay County to raise all their hell. Now you men go out there and send the Talladega boys that message." And they did.

Another of Hugo's favorites in the courthouse crowd was Charlie Steed, the only Ashland lawyer affiliated with the Populist movement. With a purple growth hanging under his chin like a turkey's wattle, Steed was all noise and animation, often portraying an unintended imitation of the frightened bird he resembled. Like most other self-described "lawmen," Steed did not have a full set of the *Code of Alabama* laws, although he did have a couple of volumes which he brought to the courtroom whenever his case required reinforcement. Oddly enough, these two volumes always gave Steed a helpful statute or citation to quote, no matter what issue was before the jury. Equally coincidental, whenever Steed read the *Code's* text in the courtroom, it usually was a section written in language that murdered the King's English. When a young opposing attorney suspiciously demanded to see for himself his opponent's quoted legal authority, Steed sneered, "You get your own book," as he slammed his shut.

At times, defendants staged their own drama. In one trial, a defendant slipped off an unlaced brogan and threw it at a hostile lawyer. Apparently, the witness' aim was as poor as his veracity. In murder cases, Hugo and other town boys hung around the jailhouse to steal a glimpse of the defendant through barred windows, to size up his character before they had the macabre thrill of watching him tried for his life.

In every case, Hugo Black sized up not only the facts and verdict but also the lawyers' performance. Hugo quickly became opinionated about how a case should be tried. He delighted in practitioners' triumphs when they "pulled one over on the other side" or quietly moaned when he thought they began "throwing away their cases by making stupid mistakes." After only a few trials, this young man deferred to no one in his opinion about how a witness should be examined or a case presented to a jury. Never, perhaps, did Hugo Black consider himself a better lawyer than did the boy sitting on a wooden bench in the Ashland courtroom.

Most local lawyers maintained offices around the town square, where the courthouse sat in the center, but only a few attorneys handled criminal cases. A majority were involved in civil cases, which seldom included juries but often involved enforcing and collecting judgments against farmers unable to repay merchants. The civil and criminal practices of law were not compatible once jury selection became more open to people across Clay's social and class divisions. An attorney who represented a merchant in taking a farmer's wagon, horse, and crops wasn't very persuasive before a jury of farmers later in a criminal trial. It may have been this problem that convinced Martin Lackey to move to an adjoining county where he could do collection work while continuing to practice criminal law in Clay.

Despite being "professional men," most of Ashland's attorneys did not make an easy living. Apart from merchants, their clients had little money to pay a lawyer, no matter how well Hugo rated their courtroom performance. Several local lawyers had second jobs or, like the *Ashland Advance* editor, moved fluidly from one profession to another. Some like Charlie Steed, became themselves the victims of court judgments when they failed to repay loans from W. L. Black or other merchants whose money helped them survive hard times.[22]

Most lawyers in Ashland were conservative Democrats, but in 1896 Populists controlled the courthouse, which in an election year became the center of politics as much as law. Now venturing beyond his father's own orbit, Hugo visited courtrooms as often for Populist speeches as for criminal trials. His cousin Bill Toland regularly attended the People's Party functions as a member of its local governing board, but Joe Manning and Wilburn Whatley were the speakers whose rhetoric enlivened a crowd. "The appeal for education that comes from the innocent faces of Alabama's mountaineers' children," Manning declared at one Populist rally, "as they caress a mother's care-worn face is coming to carry more force of persuasion with our voters than the bluster of Bourbons in their feigned warnings of 'Negro domination' . . . and fathers in Alabama begin to look to some other movement than the regime now cursing the state with ignorance . . . that they may hand down to their children and their children's children the Americanism of common schools—the magic wand that dispels lawlessness with greater surety than any other force."

Equally lively and entertaining were the local Populist editor's counterat-

tacks on his Democratic competitor, the "insinuative, flagrant . . . howl of
. . . Cleveland Banditts," and its doggerel about the "Dimmycratic prayer."
Before packed courtroom crowds, Populist leaders claimed for themselves the
"principles of Thomas Jefferson and Andrew Jackson," as they announced:
"The universal suffrage of Jefferson is the very foundation of our liberties and
the glorious heritage of freemen . . . the ballot is the only defense the weak and
the poor have of their rights, their liberties, and their earnings."

Clay was destined in 1896 for an acrimonious campaign, but across Alabama and the nation sharp political differences were fading. Joseph Forney
Johnston, an ambitious Birmingham banker dissatisfied with the life of a
local industrialist, emerged as a reform-minded Democratic candidate for
governor. Johnston represented the party's progressive wing, supporting the
Populists on the virtues of silver, fair elections, and Thomas Jefferson. He also
openly courted Populist voters. At the same time, the national Democratic
party nominated for president William Jennings Bryan of Nebraska who also
became the national Populist nominee. Bryan was the nation's most effective
advocate for the silver standard of American money.

This marriage between parties, principles, and people disturbed a small
number of local Democrats, including W. L. Black and A. S. Stockdale. They
had staked their fortunes on the philosophy of the gold standard and considered Johnston and Bryan as Populist wolves in Democratic sheepskins. In the
general election, Black and Stockdale swallowed their principles and voted for
Johnston, but not for Bryan, the Great Commoner. W. L. Black supported an
independent candidate running on the gold standard and, for the first time in
his life, did not vote a straight Democratic ticket. As their father's sons, Pelham,
Robert Lee, and Orlando also supported the Gold Bug ticket. The Black men
supplied four of fewer than four thousand votes that the independent ticket
received in Alabama.

It was a good election for Clay's Democrats. All statewide Democratic
candidates, including Johnston, carried the county, and Populists lost the local posts of tax assessor, tax collector, and school superintendent. They kept
the sheriff's job but by only fifty-five votes. While many Populists left the
courthouse discouraged by early returns, ten-year-old Hugo Black evaded his
mother's calls to stay until the last votes of the last precinct were counted. The
election proved to be a significant Democratic comeback.[23]

In the aftermath of 1896, W. L. Black withdrew largely from public life, although his fondnesses for immovable opinions and strong drink did not shrink. Robert Lee took his father's honorary place on the Ashland city council and was recognized by his own rights as a businessman "interested in matters affecting the welfare of the *church* and state." Both Lee and Orlando also represented the family as charter members of the county's first "True Blue Lodge of the Knights of Pythias," a growing national fraternal order.

Lee had his own family and house, Orlando was in medical school, and Pelham was often away studying for the law. Hugo was the only other male left under W. L. Black's roof, a circumstance cementing the wall of indifference between father and son. Pleasing his mother, Hugo spent a summer reading the Bible on the family's front porch and accompanied Della on visits with the Populist Tolands. Hugo enjoyed his own father's bewilderment when Uncle Merit's descendants put on their family tree the name of William Jennings Bryan, the "Great Commoner," who at the Democratic convention of 1896 had accused "the money-owning and the money-changing classes" like Street and Black of hoodwinking democracy with the gold standard. It was one connection by marriage that W. L. Black rejected.

In many of Clay's communities, politics continued to divide bloodlines. In 1898, when Populist E. A. Phillips stepped down as probate judge, several Democrats sought the post. Among them were brothers of Populists Joe Manning and Wilburn Whatley. In a rancorous convention, where a third Whatley brother was chairman, Democrats selected Matt Whatley as their brokered candidate over Wilburn. Afterwards, Wilburn Whatley became the Populist nominee, and in the summer of 1898 two Whatley brothers fought bitterly for the county's highest public office.

Wilburn Whatley had been a biennial candidate and political speaker for the last ten years. An unsuccessful candidate for state representative, state senator, probate judge, and twice for Congress, Wilburn was restless at all things, in all times. He had been a farmer, ferryboat operator, teacher, and manager of a busted gold mine. Once he supervised his boys in an extended project of building a new toll road with bridges not far from their home so that travelers could get up the nearby mountain in the winter. The business proved to be a rewarding enterprise—until the first hard rain washed away the makeshift bridges and left the new road impassable.

During the 1898 campaign, Wilburn walked from farm to farm since the family had no horse or mule to spare while his boys worked the fields. Early one Sunday morning, Whatley asked a cousin for the loan of a horse to go to a Sunday meeting. His cousin did not see the animal again for two weeks since Whatley conveniently failed to mention which Sunday he had in mind. Beset by wildly changing moods, Whatley was as dangerous as he was peripatetic. In fits of political rage, he had severely lashed one cousin with a buggy whip and knifed badly an old friend. At home, more than once Whatley's wife had stood behind a locked, solid door protecting her children and herself from his flashes of violent anger.

The Whatley brothers' feud remained largely nonviolent but very ugly. Matt accused Wilburn of brotherly betrayal, sacrificing family bonds for political ambition. Yet, it was bad blood in a fractured Democratic party that permitted Wilburn Whatley to win by forty-two votes. Democrats carried the county for all statewide races and three other local posts, but Populists held onto the positions of state representative and probate judge.[24] To the considerable chagrin of W. L. Black, A. S. Stockdale, and about half the Whatley clan, Wilburn Whatley moved his family to Ashland in early 1899 and became the county's leading public official.

GROWING UP IN ASHLAND SINCE THE AGE OF FOUR, Hugo at thirteen had constant opportunities to befriend the sons of his father's Democratic cronies, Allen White, Asbury Stockdale, or even Hiram Evans who had returned with his family recently to Clay. Yet, in his awakening years of adolescence, Hugo chose as his best friend Barney Whatley, the boy he had met years earlier at Spring Hill school who was now the son of the county's Populist probate judge.

A year apart in age, the older Barney and younger Hugo quickly became inseparable, as united in friendship as their fathers were divided in politics. At Ashland Academy, now occupied by children of Populists and Democrats, the two boys were in the same section, sitting next to one another in classes taught by former Probate Judge Hiram Evans, who had reappeared as mysteriously as he had left six years earlier. Apparently, the "Judge," as he was habitually called, believed he had nothing to fear in Ashland now that political leaders had settled the school issues. Still attired in a Prince Albert coat and no less full of himself and his own opinions, Judge Evans marched across a little platform in the front section of the all-boys classroom so that, standing or sitting, the teacher might tower above pupils. He was fond of quoting Greek philosophers, Confederate generals, and Biblical prophets.

"Young gentlemen," declared the judge in a sudden, prosecutorial tone, "do you know the difference between fame and notoriety?" After a long silence no boy dared to trespass, Evans proclaimed: "Well, I'm going to tell you. Robert E. Lee had fame. Jesse James had notoriety!" The teacher conveniently did not ask students to locate a term for a public official who secretly conspired to rob poor children of a free education and an old friend of his legacy of civic kindness.

Each week, Evans divided boys into debating teams, the Parliamentarians, Websterians, and others to improve speaking and thinking skills. Barney and Hugo usually joined as a team and practiced together after school. They argued the questions of Greek and Roman philosophers as often as modern public issues. Yet, the boys endured many hours of monotonous, rote teaching which they tried to enliven with secret classroom games of tag or "spy," including secret glimpses into the girls' classroom through a hidden peephole.

Barney and Hugo started their own secret society, the Buffaloes, a name echoing Evans's stories of Texas's Wild West. Imitating their elders' secret societies, the boys established an elaborate initiation ceremony. After a good bit of rigmarole, their candidate was placed over a large barrel so that his pants were tightened. Then, the chief Buffaloes raked a comb down his britches—creating a noise and sensation that convinced the newcomer that his pants had been ripped apart. Fearing certain punishment at home for ruining perhaps his only pair of everyday pants, the recruit inevitably screamed in horror only to learn from laughter that he had been "buffaloed."

Like most boys in an age of innocence and isolation, Hugo and Barney often had to make their own entertainment. They pitched pennies, played burn-out with hot sauce, threw horseshoes, tried a relatively new game called baseball, and played checkers with old Confederate veterans encamped on the courthouse lawn. Stirred by new urges of puberty, the boys coveted every scrap of explicit sex literature they could find and delighted privately in retelling dirty jokes they overheard from older boys and men. On Hugo's front porch, however, they read more acceptable literature like Nick Carter magazines, and they horsed around with Hugo's pet billy goat in the front yard—until the night it butted a drunken W. L. Black who later killed the animal.

Hugo and Barney were in Ashland when the first telephone was installed at the probate judge's office. The town had virtually missed the era of the telegraph, and up to now the only telephone in the county belonged to a mining company. Ashland's new telephone was to be used like a "911" number as a connection to the outside world for emergencies. Barney's adventurous father responded to one "emergency" as probate judge, marrying a couple in the county's mining area by telephone from his office in Ashland. The event secured Wilburn Whatley another peculiar spot in Clay's official history, but at the time it didn't strike the teenagers as anything to remember.

Both boys had to earn their spending money. Barney's daddy had no extra change to spare, and W. L. Black thought his son should appreciate the value of money by earning it. Judge Whatley employed his older sons and other relatives in every position under his control, and there were no odd jobs left in his office for the younger boys. Briefly, Barney and Hugo become drivers in a livery stable, Whatley's newest business venture. The boys enjoyed driving visitors like the head of the Anti-Saloon League from Ashland to Goodwater or Talladega, but, like all of Whatley's schemes, the business quickly went bust. The teenagers resorted to picking "bumble bee" cotton, hauling heavy items for the town's women, and performing almost any chore that promised a penny. One job they never sought or received was working at Black's store. Fayette's alcoholism was known to everyone in Ashland, including Hugo's playmates, and, in an unspoken agreement, Hugo never offered—and Barney never asked—to work or linger at the store.[25]

The boys' most rewarding job was as the "printer's devil" at competing local newspapers. Because of their literacy, the boys qualified to set type, letter by letter, creating the galleys of hand-driven presses. It also helped that they were the sons of Ashland's leading merchant and public official, who spent scarce advertising dollars. At the *Clay County Standard*, the latest name of the local conservative paper, the boys set type and occasionally wrote a short "news" brief about someone's visit to town or an event at the courthouse. The declining health of Dave Castleberry, a former Texas cowboy who now ran the Populist newspaper, gave Barney and Hugo more regular work in setting type and writing local copy. The *People's Party Advocate* was filled with canned pieces on the sweeping principles of Populism, supporting government ownership of utilities, railroads, and coal mines; a graduated national income tax; the direct popular election of the president, federal judges, and U.S. senators; and unlimited coinage of silver, gold, and paper money.

These articles of Populist faith were usually dense and awkwardly written, not the exciting stuff of Joe Manning's stump speech, but they were

Castleberry's steady effort to keep alive the notion of a larger governmental role in solving the problems that farmers and others faced. Like most weekly papers of that era, the *Advocate* had a generous supply of incorrect spelling and syntax, errors that both editor and his young typesetters shared, although seldom did the mistakes distract from the paper's central message of change through government action.

The boys discovered that Castleberry was a better Populist advocate than businessman. On the counter of his tiny office, Castleberry always had two or three wire baskets of eggs, a sign of Clay's barter economy. When Barney asked him one day why the trays were priced differently, the owner explained carefully that he had traded a newspaper subscription for a dozen eggs last week, when the price of eggs was higher. In all fairness, he explained, the week-old eggs should be sold for a higher price than the two baskets of fresh eggs, which arrived yesterday when prices were lower.

While their friendship was unaffected by foibles and divisions in Clay's adult life, Barney and Hugo had differences shaped by heredity and early experiences. Barney was a large, bulky boy at least four inches taller than Hugo, whose thinness and narrow face made him seem smaller than he was. Barney was always agreeable, but had little of his own father's restless energy. Hugo was a merchant's son, selling used magazines and books to other kids, starting a soda pop stand on the Fourth of July, and maintaining the town's exclusive franchise for *Grit* magazine until Barney and other boys realized that they could pass around a single copy before the next issue arrived. Like his father, Barney was pugnacious. Wilburn's boy was always getting into scraps with others, but Della's boy avoided scuffling whenever possible. His size and sickly self-image convinced Hugo that he could not win most arguments with his fists, nor did he find any reward for winning a fight when he arrived home. By habit, Hugo was more studious than his best friend—and all other boys of his age in Ashland. Hugo's love of reading was genuine after years of motherly encouragement.

According to Barney, the most striking difference between the two boys was the fact that he was a "country boy" and Hugo was a "town boy." In a town of only six hundred, this was a distinction of a few degrees in style and mannerisms, but a real source of occasional envy and friction. Not unlike his estranged father, Hugo could show off as a tiresome smart aleck and an unabashed fop in his fashionable store-bought clothes. Often sporting a Scotsman's cap, seen by bareheaded country boys as an enviable symbol of privilege, Hugo sometimes paraded his fancy clothes and precocious knowledge in a teenaged "oneupsmanship." Barney and other kids had no insight about how W. L. Black had manipulated politics and government to give his child more goods and a better education, but they did find at least one occasion to teach the town boy that the sons of country farmers know a thing or two.

Their plan was simple. After dark, a group of boys walked quietly to the outskirts of town to the farm of old man Rascoe, Ashland's blacksmith, where watermelons were turning ripe. Each boy was to steal one and run like the dickens to a predetermined place in the woods where all would enjoy the fruits of their labor. Unknown to Hugo, Barney and the other boys arranged to steer the town boy to the side of the patch where Rascoe grew a few citrons, used as fillers for canning preserves and pickles. Citrons grew on a vine and to an inexperienced eye looked much like watermelons although the insides were much more rubbery. The boys didn't think Hugo would know the difference.

They were right. Creeping into the field, the boys steered Hugo to a citron, which he hurriedly picked. When a boy began shooting his cap pistol, Della's son didn't mistake the sound for a farmer's gun, but he ran with the others like a fox holding onto its prized catch. In the woods, short of breath, boys began busting open their melons on the ground and scooping out the juicy, sweet fruit. Hugo dropped his stolen goods, but it bounced without cracking. Again, he copied the technique of more experienced boys, and again the citron only bounced. Again, again, and again, he tried. By this time, the other boys were rolling in laughter, tickled that Hugo could not tell the difference between a rubbery citron and a juicy watermelon. That night, a rare night, the town boy wasn't so smart after all.[26]

All pranks were forgiven and forgotten when criminal court convened in Ashland. Now accompanied by Barney, Hugo raced up the courthouse steps each day during court term to get his preferred seat for watching and assessing attorneys. Gone was Charlie Steed. He had eloped in the wee hours of the night with the local milliner whose unknown nocturnal romance was made possible by a secret trap door between their stores on the town square. Appearing for the first time in Clay was a Talladega lawyer, Borden Burr, whose compact stature and scrappy behavior gave him the reputation of a junkyard bulldog.

The criminal docket was cluttered with cases involving a banal spectrum of human wrongs, often misdeeds between friends and family consumed in the flames of passing anger, avarice, or false pride. Yet, one trial in these last moments of the nineteenth century represented the worst of Southern society's commonplace ways and a morality play which two teenage boys never forgot. The trial of Jim White, a white man accused of killing a black man, confirmed the tragic, emerging truth expressed by W. E. B. DuBois that the "problem of the twentieth century is the problem of the color line."

The basic facts of the case were undisputed. Twenty-year-old Jim White, whose rebelliousness exceeded adolescence, had a violent argument one night with twenty-two-year-old Eli Sims. No one knew exactly what Sims said to offend White, but it led to a scuffle that others stopped. At that point, White called Sims outside where he shot and killed him. White claimed Sims attacked him with a knife and that he then shot in self-defense. No knife or other weapon was found. Clay's sheriff arrested White, who stood trial in Ashland.

The case became a question of politics and justice within the white community. The black victim was the son of a woman who was a single parent and field hand. The white defendant was the son of Allen White, W. L. Black's oldest friend and a former sheriff. The elder White was now chairman of Clay's Democratic and Conservative Party, since Asbury Stockdale's local clout had suffered after his disastrous showing earlier at the polls. Some local Democrats accused the Populist sheriff of playing politics with a cardinal rule of Southern life by giving too little sanction to the word of a white man in a matter concerning a black man. They said that Jim was arrested and charged with murder to malign his father and their party. Others believed that Jim was guilty because he had no reason to lead Sims to a secluded spot except to shoot him. No knife was found. Murder was murder. At trial, however, Jim White was acquitted, although rumors suggested that eyewitnesses were bribed never to appear in court.

It was a poignant, painful crucible for county residents, especially the one out of ten who were African American and who remained publicly silent by necessity. The local white community followed Southern racial etiquette by keeping their doubts and shortcomings out of public view and the local newspaper. It was a ritual of silence that helped to perpetuate the social acceptance of such an evil, although it did not always quiet private conscience. Barney and Hugo were old enough to understand on their own terms for the first time how Southern justice was cruelly blinded by skin color, a reality made more vivid by the fact that the boys knew both young men. In fact, when younger,

Eli had been one of Hugo's preferred playmates around the town square.

W. L. Black was deeply troubled by the case. Privately, he broke with conservative colleagues and with his old friend, Allen White, by insisting that Jim White should have been convicted and imprisoned. Not hung, but imprisoned. Regardless of friendship, W. L. had a stern standard for others' conduct, and he feared a breakdown of law and order among the white community. "If one murderer can escape, none of us will be safe," he instructed his children. In time, Fayette Black's fears were borne out, for Jim White killed others over the years until he met his own violent death. But in 1899, Jim White went free, and the Sims case was the beginning of messy, lifelong lessons for Hugo Black about the disastrous, seemingly immovable nature of racialism and racial injustice in the century of a New South.

Before Eli Sims's death, Hugo had grown up largely within a grace of absence, a unique crossing of a particular time and place in the South where children were not inculcated with prevailing views about the ordained superiority of the white "race" and the base savagery of people of African descent. Because so few blacks lived in the county, many of Clay's adults did not perform the Southern rite of passage when, during white children's early reproductive years, they were taught the rules of racialism and the necessity to separate from their black playmates who suddenly had become too inferior, too vile, too dangerous despite several earlier years of innocent childhood relations.

Clay was not free of racialism, as its political discourse proved over the years. Populists like Joe Manning tried to deflate racial issues by claiming that accusations of "Negro domination" were designed to distract white farmers from the real issue of illegitimate power and wealth among Democrats. Yet resentment of African Americans was deeply ingrained within most small, white farmers. Many believed that former slaves, even more than the Black Belt's former slaveowners, were largely to blame for the region's hard times during the ravages of Civil War, Reconstruction, and now the decline of their local Populist movement. How so battered a group of people, largely without land or money, only twenty years free from slavery, could be responsible for such societal calamities was a question that no white person seriously raised in Clay County—or most other places. The illogic essentially borrowed from a prohibitionist view of whiskey: liquor's existence caused white men to do evil. Ban the evil. Likewise, white folk decided blacks caused whites to do evil. Ban them.

Like virtually any community in the South, racial fears and superstitions in Clay could create an insane, monstrous force, stronger than law or decency, whenever the white imagination and morality were jointly outraged by the appearance of evil in blacks' suspected or proven deeds. Five years before Hugo was born, fifteen miles from Harlan, hundreds of whites hunted down and lynched a black man accused of raping and brutally killing a white woman. No one doubted that, if he had stood trial, the black man would have been convicted and hung by Clay's white men. Yet, the collective desire for a social act of revenging violence led white men, women, and their children to erect a gallows from a corn crib door and twice hang the black man in a picnic atmosphere. For more than a century, white families near Cragford would keep the lynching chain, crib door, and even the dead white woman's dress like rare souvenirs of a religious experience worth remembering.

No, the unschooled nature of race relations in Clay did not create a more tolerant society or any liberating force for blacks or whites to avoid some of the worst moments of Southern history. It provided merely a small, fragile psychological space through which a young person might see other possible terms for human relations, before such options were rendered unthinkable. In this little bit of grace, limited as it was, what was *not* said to white children at this time and place in the South's obscure, rural areas was just as powerful in developing future race relations as what was said and done among opinionated white adults.

Hugo's own early experiences with people of African descent mixed elemental respect with damaging stereotypes, in part reflecting the world around him. In Harlan, white kids had taunted Hugo at the age of three with the chant of "nigger" because he was the only child looked after by a black woman, named Vic. Little Hugo vainly protested to his playmates that "Vit ain't no nitter!" In Ashland, shortly after arrival, Della gently corrected her son when he carried a plate of food to the back porch for "Uncle Dan," an elderly black handyman. His mom told Hugo that the Negro should be invited to eat his lunch alone at their kitchen table, not on the back porch.

Inspired by a boys' magazine, Hugo and Barney as teenagers set up a "detective agency" to investigate an old black man who had just moved to Ashland from Millersville where a mysterious fire had recently occurred. The boys camped out "around that poor Negro's house to see if we could hear anything that might lead us to catch the criminal who had set the building afire down in Millersville." After a couple of long, boring hours when nothing happened, the sleepy sleuths decided their baseless suspicion of the black man was no fun. Around the Ashland square, however, a retarded black boy unwittingly served as town clown for many white citizens. Apparently, the child's disabled mannerisms, slurred speech, and willingness to be the butt of practical jokes were a source of continued white amusement.

Common among all of Hugo's early encounters with racial customs was the universal assumption that African Americans by nature held a lower place in the world than did "Anglo Saxons." Whites in Clay considered blacks to be white people's servants, nannies, yardmen, and town clowns, whatever the different levels of respect and protection afforded them. As Hugo's lifelong friend observed, remembering those years in Clay County: "Nobody . . . hated the Negro, but they insisted he had his place and he belonged in it. And that his place was virtually that of a servant."[27]

In fact, within Alabama at the turn of the century, the paramount public issue was how and which of the competing white parties would control blacks as their political servants. For almost a decade, Populists had accused Democrats of manipulating black votes in the state's Black Belt to defeat Reuben Kolb as governor and Populist Congressional candidates like Wilburn Whatley. At various times, each party had claimed the other wanted to elevate blacks to the level of white society.

Now, with Populism fading, many white Democratic leaders, especially in the Black Belt, proposed amending the state constitution to remove virtually all blacks from the voting rolls through a series of indirect changes that they believed the U.S. Supreme Court would uphold. Democrats argued that by requiring all voters to have qualifications such as literacy or property—which almost all former slaves had been denied—federal courts would allow disfranchisement since the state constitutional amendments would speak nothing of "race."

The political reasoning behind this Democratic proposal sounded like a confession of human fallibility: unless blacks were entirely and permanently disfranchised, Democrats argued, white men will always fight among themselves, abandoning sacred principles of fairness and goodness towards one another to manipulate black votes for each's own white gain. In essence, the argument stated that the presence of powerless black folk made powerful white folk do evil to one another.

Many Populists were unconvinced of Democrats' motives. They charged that the proposed amendment also would disfranchise poor white farmers so that neither blacks nor whites could interfere with the vested interests of railroads, industrialists, and Black Belt planters. Ironically, leading the opposition to disfranchisement was the ambitious former industrialist, Governor Joseph Forney Johnston, who reversed his support of the proposal in an effort to unseat the incumbent U.S. Senator John T. Morgan, who had represented Alabama since Reconstruction. Johnston led Populists and some Democrats in a campaign against corporate oligarchy and false attempts at "white supremacy peace." The state's conservative Democrats were stunned. Black Belt newspapers called Johnston a "Judas," "chief trickster," who "knows that the people . . . of this section of the state ask to be relieved of the burden of the black man."

In truth, Black Belt leaders wanted it both ways. They wanted black men disfranchised, but they also wanted all black bodies in their counties to count for redistricting to exaggerate the seats their section of the state could receive in the U.S. Congress and the state legislature. It was a grand scheme. In the past, blacks were not counted fully, if at all, in reapportionment. In the U.S. Constitution, the founders had allowed states to count a slave as three-fifths of a person for purposes of dividing up white representation in the Congress. Before Reconstruction, representation in Alabama's legislature had been divided on the basis of only white inhabitants. Now, in the name of guaranteeing honest elections and harmonious white supremacy, conservative Democrats campaigned for a new constitution eliminating many poor, white voters who created the Populist revolution and ending most black voting—while at the same time counting blacks to exaggerate white political power in the Black Belt. In one document, Black Belt planters were attempting to gain permanent hegemony in Alabama politics.

Clay's Democratic stalwarts were solidly behind disfranchisement. They assured citizens that "white men will not be disfranchised." Clay's *Standard* recruited supporters by asking white farmers, "Will you fall in with the great army of white men of the state who favor honest government or enlist with the crowd that stands for negro domination?" Clay did not join the great white army, but, by a narrow margin, the state as a whole did. And, apparently not convinced of his purpose or sincerity, Alabama voters turned back Johnston's campaign for the U.S. Senate by a lopsided vote.

W. L. Black would have supported the conservatives' call for disfranchisement, had he not been too feeble to engage in public debate. As a new century hovered, Hugo's father was dying, resigned to the fact that he would escape the backwoods no further than Ashland. As if feeling the nearness of death, old man Black had put his worldly possessions in order during the previous year. The Black store circulated special notices demanding that customers settle all debts. W. L. pushed existing merchandise with a series of newspaper ads showing his keen insight about future consumer trends. "Buy Yourself Rich," he advertised. Even without new sales, Black had achieved the status of Ashland's leading merchant. Black's store sold more goods and loaned more money than any other business in the county, and his tangible assets approached $20,000, an impressive sum in dirt-poor Clay County at the end of the 1800s.

By their father's measure, the Black children were accomplished and settled in their own lives, although not without scars. After her first child died at birth in 1895, Ora had given birth to two more children, both girls. And both had died before age two. As if recognizing a plague on the Toland women, Ora gave up on becoming a mother and concentrated on being a devoted wife. Lee was now a father and shopkeeper in his own right. Orlando was finishing medical college. Carefree and careless, Pelham somehow had passed the bar exam in Montgomery and was now satisfactorily located as a member of the new law firm of "Stockdale and Black." Daisy was blossoming into an attractive, young woman with the sons of local merchants and professionals as suitors. And Hugo . . . well, everyone knew that Hugo was following Pelham into law.

With finances and family set, W. L. Black met death as he had endured life. After months of declining health, he died in September 1900 from cirrhosis of the liver. Hugo simply concluded that his father "drank himself to death." In a final act of ironic independence, the man who prized the Democratic party above all other secular or sacred institutions, who valued law and order even at the cost of an old friendship, whose son and friend were lawyers, W. L. Black died without a will and left his estate to be probated by Populist Judge Wilburn Whatley.

Black's curious failing may have been simply his last spiteful act, although it is difficult to see which old enemy he snubbed by dying without a will. Perhaps, merely perhaps, after the betrayal of Merit Street's last will, Black did not trust friend, foe, or family to honor his specific wishes after death. Had W. L. realized, in his last year, the enduring societal effects of governing all relations among friends, allies, and enemies largely by personal gain or greed? Or had he decided, in retrospect, that the defilement of Street's legacy was a breakdown of law and order that he would not tempt anyone to commit? Neither speculation fits Black's character and style. Official records tell no more than that by deliberate inaction, W. L. Black arranged for a Populist probate judge whom he politically opposed to distribute his lifelong accumulation of material goods.

W. L. Black had little else to leave. He had severed almost every loyalty a man could enjoy in the rural South. He had alienated or forsaken his wife, family, community, church, and almost all his friends. Near the end, claiming principle, he had even deserted his beloved Democratic party. If Hugo's father saw himself as Ashland's wealthiest merchant, a man of consistent, conservative business principles, his son easily could see a father unfailingly loyal only to money and demon whiskey. Surrounded by his family, W. L. Black died otherwise alone, within only a thin shell of dutiful love, outside the eternal grace of a Baptist God, and without the comforts of many friendships. In keeping with his wife's wishes, Black was buried in the cemetery of the First Baptist Church, a sanctuary he never entered while alive. In accordance with Alabama law, Judge Whatley's order distributing Black's assets to his wife and children is the last accounting of W. L. Black, and the last document to acknowledge the existence of Lafayette Hugo Black. Soon after the estate was settled, the youngest son of William Lafayette rearranged his name to place Hugo in front; for the rest of his life, he was Hugo L. Black.[28]

W. L. BLACK'S DEATH RELEASED HIS GROWN BOYS from their father's yoke, and they quickly set out with new directions and priorities for the first time in their lives. With his share of W. L.'s estate, Orlando moved to the southern edge of the county, set up a medical practice, and later married a Baptist woman in a Baptist church. Pelham moved into a house of his own and began a solo practice without his father's old friend as senior partner. After hiring an assistant to run the store he inherited, Lee traveled extensively around the South and paid the Talladega newspaper to publish his book, *The Deserter*, "the only novel ever written by a Clay County author and published in bookstores." With a plot that W. L. Black would never have tolerated, Lee's book tells of a Southerner who deserts the Confederate Army and hides in the county's northern mountains. It was published under an assumed name, a fashionable and prudent precaution in a region where reverence for the Confederate past had become idolatrous.

Not all past patterns and allegiances were broken. As Alabama voters narrowly ratified disfranchising amendments along the lines proposed by conservative Democrats, Lee and Pelham continued as leaders of their father's local party. Also, each son remained a faithful Baptist. Keeping with their father's party and their mother's church, once an obligation of childhood, was now the brothers' free choice.

Pelham also continued enjoying his father's vice, the demon drink. Endowed with his father's large features and his mother's elegant proportions, Pelham was strikingly handsome, a naturally gifted athlete, and a ladies' man whose sad, small eyes, like those of all W. L. Black's boys, were the only outward signs belying a happy childhood. In the late summer of 1902, within a few weeks of his speech at the county's Baptist convention on Sunday school literature, Pelham traveled in the family's Columbian buggy to a dance in Talladega, where young, eligible women and hard liquor were plentiful. On his way home, in a drunken condition, Pelham fell asleep with reins in hand. His horse shied to the right, off the road, and into a millpond where the buggy overturned. Next day, Pelham was discovered dead in the pond.

Lee sold the buggy to ease his mother's sad memories, but at sixteen, completing his junior year at the Academy, Hugo was stunned and disoriented by Pelham's death. Liquor had now robbed Hugo of a father he could not love or respect and a brother he idolized and followed. Hugo was no longer certain he wanted to be lawyer, and his last year in high school was not the halcyon days that every teenager seeks. With both surviving brothers already married, Hugo considered himself the new male head of what was left of the household of W. L. Black.

Pelham's tragedy led Hugo to select the evils of liquor as his topic at the Academy's annual elocution competition, an event as important then in school and community in the rural South as Friday night football would be decades later. It was the contest which Hugo's dead brother Merit Vernon had won after delivering very much the same speech about the "Little Martyr," whose life had been ruined by alcohol. No subject carried more genuine meaning and emotion with Hugo at that moment. Thirteen years his senior, Hugo's sister Ora envisioned an audience reacting emotionally to her little brother, just as it had to Merit Vernon whose own alcoholic father gave power and reality to his presentation.

On the Academy's stage before a packed auditorium, Hugo concluded his memorized rendition of a boy wasting his life in lawlessness and liquor with this lament:

> Oh Heavens, can such things be?
> Almighty power, send forth thy dart
> And strike me where I lie!

While speaking with skill and true passion, Hugo lost the contest. Another young man repeated a version of *Atlanta Constitution* editor Henry Grady's popular speech on the New South. The boy proclaimed:

> There was a South of slavery and secession;
> That South, thank God, is dead;
> There is a South of freedom and Union;
> That South, thank God, is living, breathing, growing every hour.

Stunned that his masterfully delivered speech took second place, Hugo concluded that "what is said can be far more important than how it is said." In fact, Black did not understand the more significant point. The Academy was now a different place than when Merit Vernon gave his speech on the personal tragedy of whiskey. It was no longer a school for the conservative Democrats' children. The Academy now represented all segments of the community—Democrats and Populists, Baptists and Methodists, Hardshells and moderates, dry and wet. All shared ownership, operations, and seats in what was becoming a common school. To this more diverse audience, the Black family's tragedy was far less compelling than when Merit Vernon spoke to an audience of mothers, fathers, and contest judges who were his parents' personal friends.

At the beginning of a new century, after five decades of war, destitution, and political divisions that tore open families, churches, and communities, Clay's white residents longed to put the past and their own collective tragedies behind them. The county had opposed Democratic disfranchisement, but its citizens yearned for a new time not ruled entirely by old hatreds and burdens. Henry Grady's speech captured this fundamental urge to be free, united, and prosperous in a New South. Coming to manhood in this era, Hugo Black never forgot his loss in elocution and, soon afterwards, memorized for use throughout his life Grady's hopeful words that had carried the day.[29]

In February, estrangement followed disappointment. At school, Hugo objected when a new professor punished his older sister Daisy by requiring her to stand on one foot in the corner of the girl's classroom. Hugo argued with the male teacher and eventually fought with both Daisy's teacher and his own new professor. Della arrived and left with her two children. Hugo never returned.

Without a high school degree, Black considered his options over the balance of the year. In the wake of Pelham's death, law school no longer appealed to him as he gravitated in search for a role model towards Orlando and the pursuit of the healing arts. Two sets of events in late 1903 probably shaped Hugo's direction. First, Barney Whatley's father became a fugitive from justice after a state examiner discovered that the probate judge had embezzled more than $2,000 in Confederate pension funds. Whatley had claimed pensions for dead veterans and had pocketed funds due widows who were told that the state money had not been received. Wilburn Whatley fled, leaving Barney and his family to bear the community's opprobrium and to survive on their own. The tragedy seemed to foreclose all prospects for Barney and Hugo to go to law school together. Barney's immediate need was to find any paying job that would help support his mother and himself; he had no inheritance.

Also, death returned to the Black family with a vengeance. Within a span of four months, Sister Ora's husband died, as did Lee's little boy. Born and reared in the long shadows of death, Hugo decided he would follow Orlando and heal the sick.

In the fall of 1903, Hugo took a buggy and train ride to Birmingham Medical College with every intention of hurrying back to practice medicine. Away from home for the first time, in an oversized mining town of forty thousand people, Hugo worked like a monk to complete three years of courses in two. Taking a small room near the college building, adjoining the newly built Hillman Hospital, Black studied seven days a week with regular time out only for Sunday school and worship services in the nearby Southside Baptist Church. Black did succumb to one indulgence. Almost despite himself, he was drawn to local hotels where he listened to lawyers exaggerate their victories and forget their defeats. On one such occasion, Black almost killed himself trying to hop a free ride on a moving trolley.

One of his medical teachers fortified Hugo's resolve to succeed with an oft-repeated quotation that rang true in the ears of the young student: "He who seeks one thing in life—and but one \ May hope to achieve it before life is done." Black needed one-mindedness to endure the distasteful aspects of medical education. Dismembering cadavers and working frequently in blood was very bothersome to a boy who considered himself sickly and for whom blood was a sign of approaching death. His sensitive, Roman nose was especially offended. The lab smells often made Black gag for fresher air. Still, sure that hard work would allow him to excel, Hugo passed the written exams for the first two years of medical study at the end of his first term, and he returned to Clay where he spent the summer helping his brother practice medicine.

Hugo's hard work continued at Wilsonville. Orlando worked night and day as he responded to an endless stream of disease and illness plaguing the backwoods of south Clay. If there was a single night during that summer when Dr. Black and his young assistant were not awakened for an emergency, it was forgotten over time. A man with a small, gentle face, like Della's, Orlando served all people in need regardless of their ability to pay. Hugo was inspired by his brother's dedication and managed to sustain long hours, but he could not escape a physical reaction to the blood, smells, and crude nature of the healing arts. His inability to cope with doctoring became clear on a night the two brothers visited a black woman in labor. Orlando discovered the baby was badly twisted in the womb, and, despite hours of effort, he could not save the infant without assuring the death of the mother. Before the night ended, the doctor lost both mother and child. With Hugo's assistance, Orlando removed the dead child, piece by piece, from the dead woman's womb.

Hugo was physically sick and emotionally exhausted by the experience. It proved to both brothers that the youngest was not a doctor by nature. Perhaps Orlando realized why Hugo was pursuing medicine instead of law. After a long talk, the elder brother insisted Hugo go to law school and become the lawyer he always wanted to be. As if relieved of a tremendous burden, Hugo readily agreed, making his brother a solemn pledge that he would help even more people as a lawyer than he would have as a doctor.[30]

In September 1904 Hugo Black boarded a train at Goodwater with Cleve Allen, another young man from Ashland, on the way to Tuscaloosa and the campus of the University of Alabama. When they arrived, Della's boy was impressed by his first visit to Alabama's Old South. Amid a canopy of oaks in bright, fall colors lining University Avenue, Hugo saw several stately mansions, including the governor's home from the early days of statehood when the town was Alabama's capital. After a night in a modest room at the McLester Hotel, Hugo and Cleve rented a room from a University professor and were ready to enroll.

Lodging proved easier than admission. Hugo wanted to enter the sophomore class since he considered his education at Ashland Academy equivalent to that of a freshman. Because he had no high school degree, however, University officials told Black that he could enter the sophomore class only if he passed a written exam. Fearing he might fail the test without added study, Black refused and appealed to the University president who luckily had been a former headmaster in Clay County. To Hugo's great surprise, the president turned him down. With a stubbornness befitting W. L. Black's son, Hugo decided to forego an undergraduate degree and enter law school for two years of training that automatically entitled him to practice law in the state.

Why, without a high school diploma, Black expected to be admitted as a sophomore at the University or why he was willing to give up entirely a liberal arts education because he wanted to spend only three years there, instead of four, are questions answered only in the mind of an eighteen-year-old who had oscillated between complete independence and total emulation of his brothers for several years. Still, it was another example of Black's complete lack of deference to established authority. At the age of five, he defied a doctor's life-or-death order. At ten, he critiqued the courtroom performance of experienced lawyers. As a teenager, he tackled two teachers and mastered two years of medical school in one. In each instance, Hugo Black evidenced an independent mind and spirit that he achieved through a self-discipline he thought was so desperately lacking in his own father.

The law school Black entered had fewer than forty-five students, one student librarian, and two instructors who presided in classrooms that were among the least desirable on campus. The entering class of 1904 had fewer than two dozen young men who like Black came mostly from the state's small towns. In the first year, Black took classes in the "law of persons" (personal property and domestic relations), contracts, torts, mercantile law, and constitutional and international law. In the second year, he would study evidence, "law of corporations," real estate, jurisdiction and procedure, and criminal law. In addition, Black took courses on basic economics, history, and Greek classics in the undergraduate school. He joined the law school's debating society and became class secretary after another student, Morris Allen, resigned the elective post.

Black's first year was little more than half-complete when his mother fell ill with pneumonia. In a cold, wet February, not unlike the one when Hugo was born and Little Della was buried, Ardellah Street Toland Black died in Ashland with her youngest son at her bedside, ten days before his nineteenth birthday. The local editor remembered "Mrs. W. L. Black" as she would have wanted, as "a member of the Baptist Church and a devoted Christian." Della's death left Hugo, a minor by law, without parents or a home. Clay's probate judge granted Hugo's motion to waive the "disability of age" so he could represent himself in settling his mother's estate, but the distress of death was not so easily managed.

No one could recall Della's life without remembering her hardships. The Ladies Aid Society remembered their "beloved sister Ardellah Black who has crossed death's mysterious river to join the loved ones who have preceded her," but their tribute revealed equally the daily tortured life of a woman enduring a drunken, irreverent husband and death's frequent grief. Sister Black was "not a leader yet always ready to follow to every good work," recalled her church sisters. "She lived a *consistent* Christian life, was patient in tribulation, meekly bearing the heavy burdens of sorrow which so frequently fell to her lot, and in a gentle unassuming, modest way, letting her light shine, manifesting a sweet spirit of trust and resignation."

Since his birth into a large family of a small community, Hugo had faced a relentless parade of death. He had mourned the passing of two brothers, two parents, one uncle, two little nephews, and two baby nieces. All had died since he was nine years old, and five of the nine had died in the last four and a half years. During the years when many young people can feel closest to human immortality, Hugo was heckled by death and now endured the loss of his deeply loved, almost enshrined mother. At nineteen, Hugo believed, as he always did, that "no mother was ever a greater inspiration to her child than mine was to me."

Hugo returned to Tuscaloosa a week after Della's funeral to the only room he could call home, to prepare for final exams. During the six weeks between his mother's death and late March, the end of the academic year, Hugo exercised incredible self-discipline. He scored high on the comprehensive law exams, placing himself on the honor rolls. Yet, his energetic spirit flagged. For once in his life, men around him decided Hugo was "one of those gentle souls that will use the devil himself with courtesy."[31]

During a long summer before the next academic year, Hugo kept busy with every diversion that his remaining family, friends, and neighbors could devise. A railroad came to Ashland in 1905. It was only a spur from Talladega, going through the county's unpromising mining area and no further than the town's borders, but Ashland celebrated the rail line as if the New South itself was coming down the tracks. Hugo joined a small party to celebrate the train's arrival and was among the first to ride. While staying with Lee's family, Hugo attended parties and dances, and, with his sister Daisy, he went to Millersville to fish in Hatchet Creek and visit relatives. Lee took him to Lookout Mountain, and Hugo stayed in the area for a visit with members of the Black family who had moved to that corner of north Alabama.

In the fall, Hugo returned to Tuscaloosa. Now he seemed willing to postpone adulthood's responsibilities and he took a room in the law school barracks with a student from the Black Belt. He threw himself into his studies and campus life. Somewhere in the year after his mother's death, Hugo began to loosen slightly the tight grip he always held on his own conduct. By no means did he consider touching a drop of liquor, but he did try smoking. It was not a flippant decision. Black was now on his own without his father's vice and his mother piety to define his choices. "I began smoking with the promise to myself," Black remembered, "that I would quit at any time that I believed it would be difficult for me to do so. I kept that resolution." Having lived between opposite forces in his family, church, and community—between Della and Fayette, Democrats and Populists, abstinence and excess, Sunday school Baptists and Primitive Baptists, merchants and farmers—Hugo experimented timidly after his mother's death with his own capacity to moderate a life of simple pleasures and discipline. As the Greeks whom he studied in a literature course suggested: "All things in moderation."

Moderation for Black was in fact conservative by popular standards. He began to play tennis, but not the more popular sports like football. He enjoyed the steam room of the men's bathhouse and inherited the post of senior class secretary. Yet, he did not join a fraternity or social club (including one known as the "K.K.K."). Active in the debate society, he won an argument about the need for additional anti-liquor legislation but lost a debate to a former salesman when Black supported the proposition that "the Legislature should repeal the law making highway robbery" punishable by death.

In class, Black was bored stiff by one professor but captivated by the other,

Professor Ormond Somerville, who accented his shy, scholarly demeanor with dry, mischievous wit. Somerville challenged students to think for themselves about the law, rather than mindlessly recite precedents. In a year after the U.S. Supreme Court had declared a state law limiting the bakery industry's hours of work as unconstitutional, Somerville reminded students that legislators, not judges, should make laws.

With an enigmatic smile, Somerville would note later that "never had a student . . . made greater progress" in his class than had Hugo Black. The young man who had judged the performance of Ashland's practicing lawyers at the age of ten apparently had a bit more to learn than he originally thought as he progressed through law school.

With hard work and singlemindedness, Black graduated from law school in the spring of 1906 in the top one-third of his twenty-two-member class and was awarded a Phi Beta Kappa key, although he did not receive it since he returned home before graduation ceremonies. "This fella seems to possess but one idea," Hugo's law school yearbook observed about him, "and that is a wrong one." The class historian, a fraternity fellow, predicted that he could find "at least six supreme court judges amongst us." Hugo Black was not listed.[32]

BLACK RETURNED DIRECTLY TO ASHLAND to set up a law office on the second floor of a wooden building, above E. A. Phillips's grocery, on the southeast corner of the town square, but he had no intention of staying there very long. Keeping his own counsel, Black had an ambitious, grand plan for advancement. For four or five years he would practice in the county, in competition with five other attorneys. Then, he would run for the state legislature. While in Montgomery, he would make contacts that allowed him to move to Birmingham to practice law. After five years there, he would run for Congress and from Washington go on to New York to practice law for the rest of his life. That was the plan.

With the remaining share of his parents' estate, Hugo furnished his office and purchased a substantial law library that would have left old Charlie Steed in disbelief. The books weren't necessary for a local practice, but they represented the huge ambitions of a young man who had no doubt that he would soon be moving to a wider world. Black paid six dollars a month to live with Lee's family, now in the house where he grew up, and erected a fancy, seven-dollar sign proclaiming, "Hugo L. Black, Attorney and Counselor at Law," at the street entrance to his upstairs office. Afterwards, he sat back and waited for his first client.

And he waited. Behind five other Ashland lawyers, including classmate Cleve Allen, Hugo was the newest, youngest, and most inexperienced attorney in a town that could not easily support two. In addition, men and women who had watched Hugo grow up had difficulty perceiving him as anyone but Della's little boy. Short, thin, and slight in stature, weighing less than 120 pounds, with a youthful face of delicately carved features, dressed in well-pressed attire, Hugo Black, counselor at law, appeared a lot like Hugo Black, Della's boy. To remake his image, Black tried strolling repeatedly to the drug store to purchase a cigar, which he chewed or smoked vigorously on his way back to his office, in hopes of appearing older and more experienced to the passing public.

Like its youngest lawyer, Ashland in late 1906 had more aspiration than prosperity. Fearing the town was being left behind, Ashland Democratic leaders were in the final stages of constructing a new, yellow brick courthouse with the lady of justice balancing her scales atop the cupola clock. City fathers hailed it as "one of the handsomest buildings in the state," marking the dawn of an new era of prosperous stores and pretty residences. In reality, without fertile, flat soil, rich mining ores, or developing industries, the county and its seat of government had reached the zenith of its small growth for decades to come. In a fitting, but embarrassing moment, the town celebrated the laying of the new courthouse's cornerstone in August 1906 with festive music and a parade. A hundred members of the Grand Order of the Masons, including one of its newer local members, Hugo Black, were led by Allen White, the local senior grand warden. But a gang of rowdy drunks sullied the event when they propositioned several women and staggered lewdly behind the entire procession.

Waiting for a trickle of clients, Black began "collection work" on the old accounts that had never been paid to his father's estate, probably because Lee didn't have the energy or temperament to pursue them. Some customers were willing to pay even past the statute of limitations out of respect for Black's father as a fair businessman. It revealed the upright character of his rural community and a side of Fayette Black that surprised his youngest son. Hugo also prepared reports for an Atlanta-based credit agency that qualified individuals for life insurance. It was pedestrian work that had almost nothing to do with the practice of law, but it paid the rent.

In keeping with Southern tradition, Black's law license earned him the title of "Colonel," which the *Standard* obligingly used whenever reporting on the social movements of "Col. H. L. Black." The rank did not enlist additional clients, however, and Hugo was left with large swaths of time in which he continued a self-imposed regimen of reading history, literature, and other subjects that a liberal arts education would have given him. When visiting his sister Daisy, who had married and moved to Hatchet Creek, Hugo practiced his elocution on the creek bank, often attempting to convince a jury of fish and eels of the innocence of his imagined client.

On his own, Black joined the First Baptist Church shortly after returning to Ashland, since it was what his mother would have wanted, and he became a church clerk and Sunday school teacher. Playing by ear, the only way he knew, Black performed as church organist on occasional Sundays. He spoke at the county Sunday school convention in March 1907, on "the Christian attitude towards Sunday school," reverberating the last speech that his brother Pelham gave before his death. Black also kept busy attending weddings, including that of Allen White's daughter where Black joined groomsmen festooned in black suits, white vests, and suede gloves. Yet, Hugo showed no serious interest in any of Clay's young women.

By early summer in 1907, Black had become a collections man and a very part-time lawyer. The Atlanta credit company now needed reports regularly, and Black's reputation for collecting bad debts had generated an increased business. That reputation and his family's loyalty to the Democratic party, now governing Clay's politics without rancor, were most likely why Hugo was appointed as the county's first tax commissioner under a new state law.

In a campaign against railroad control of state politics, Alabama's new progressive governor B. B. Comer and a sympathetic state legislature had established tax commissioners in each county to aid "revenue officers of the state in the collection of escaped, delinquent, and back taxes . . . , in discovering and prosecuting . . . all evasions and violations of the revenue laws." Appointed by the state tax commission with the approval of the governor, Black earned compensation only from the delinquent taxes he collected. Echoing Populist sentiment, the new law was aimed at forcing railroads and other out-of-state corporations to pay their fair share of state and local taxes.

Like Populist Reuben Kolb, B. B. Comer was from a planter's family of Barbour County, where George Wallace would emerge fifty years later. Comer was now a local manufacturer and mill owner burdened by the unfair shipping rates of Northern railroads. He supported effective regulation of railroads, not state ownership, a middle ground that attracted broad support. A Talladega merchant and Democratic activist, G. T. McElderry, captured Comer's appeal when he advised the governor: "Keep this fact always before the folks: 'we make no attack on invested capital, but wage always warfare against unfairness.'"

Black's appointment was a mixed blessing. The tax commissioner's role was far different in Clay than in Jefferson and Montgomery counties where railroads had large standing assets that were generally undervalued and undertaxed. In places where railroads paid more taxes, the county's people could pay less. In Clay, however, the only railroad line was locally owned, and it had little value beyond local pride. Although out-of-state corporations owned large tracts of land in the county's mountains, mining efforts were never substantial. There were no vast holdings of wealth by large, distant corporations in poor Clay, and the only people whose taxes could be raised and collected anew by the tax commissioner were the farmers and merchants who supported Comer's movement—and who would decide whether to send a young, ambitious man to Montgomery's state legislature.

On May 14, the day Governor Comer signed Black's new commission, shortly after the stroke of midnight, Ashland's church bells rang out suddenly, followed by the firing of shots. Recognizing a fire alarm, Black rushed to the new courthouse where he saw his law office and half the town ablaze. The fire was omnivorous, consuming all the buildings on the east side of the square and sparing nothing, not even Black's seven-dollar street sign. To keep the entire square from burning, city leaders dynamited a restaurant to create a fire break.

Like Hamlet's ghost, Ashland's fire haunted Hugo with the reality that something was amiss in himself or the stars. Without insurance, his office and prized law library were lost and, except for unsold land and uncollected debts, his inheritance was gone. Black realized, too, that he wasn't practicing law so much as collecting money, nor was he "helping even more people" as a lawyer—his promise when he quit medical school. Hugo's new appointment could not promote his future political chances. His detailed plans for success had proven unrealistic.

Over several weeks, Black explored options with friends, including Barney Whatley, who visited Clay from Birmingham where he now worked. By the fall, Black had decided to forgo more years in Clay and Montgomery. He would move instead to Birmingham where he would begin a new law practice from scratch.

Decades later, Black told Barney's brother that "many of the beliefs implicit in the opinions . . . [I have written on the U.S. Supreme Court] could be traced back to the times I spent with the plain, sturdy people of our birthplace." Yet, by 1907 these were the people of Black's past, not his future.

"Col. H. L. Black, one of the leading young lawyers of east Ala., has decided to leave Ashland and locate in Birmingham," announced the *Standard* on Friday, September 6, 1907. "He is a young man fully prepared and qualified to compete for his share of the practice even in the magic city and we are sure he will do well . . ." Not quite as self-assured, Black arranged to be inducted into the Ashland lodge of the Knights of Pythias on the same night he packed his bags.[33] He wanted to attend lodge meetings in Birmingham as a member as soon as possible to seek out prospective clients.

On the following day, with less than fifty dollars and knowing fewer than three dozen people at his destination, Hugo Black boarded the train in Ashland for the short trip to the crossroads of Birmingham and his future.

2

'Hugo-to-Hell'

BLACK GOES BACK TO BIRMINGHAM

At the start of a new century, Birmingham, Alabama was a Southern city uniquely beholden to the conflict of America's basic, binary forces—black and white, North and South, enslaved and free, patriarchal and communal, foreign and native, rural and urban, "wet" and "dry," honest and corrupt, democratic and aristocratic, Protestant and Catholic, capital and labor, heaven and hell. The clash of so many opposites in one location in the South was partly due to Birmingham's creation during the messy, conflicted aftermath of the Civil War and partly because of the geological accident that buried in the surrounding hills and mountains the rich ingredients for building a new nation upward and outward on coal, iron, and steel. In fewer than forty years, Birmingham had become the South's fastest growing city, on its way to overtake momentarily its rival Atlanta. Yet, more decisive for its enduring nature, Birmingham also had become an important new frontier town for America's twentieth century where conflict begat conflict as people and institutions attempted to shift the boundaries defining the South and the nation in pursuit of wealth, power, privilege, rights, and opportunities.

The signs of Birmingham's warring nature and industrial promise were evident from the platform of the L&N terminal where Hugo Black surveyed his new hometown on September 7, 1907. Northward along Birmingham's Twentieth Street rose the finished and partially finished, steel-ribbed monuments of current and future industrial empires, competing to stand tallest in the sky and housing managers, professionals, and speculators of the city's corporations and Northern capital.

More distant in the same direction were the county courthouse, city hall, and places of worship whose angular steeples, partially visible from the rail station, fractured the dull symmetry of rectangular buildings and rising iron skeletons of what were being called skyscrapers—the twenty-five story City Federal Building would be the tallest building in the Southeastern U.S. when it was completed a few years after Black's arrival. The city's retail shops, professional offices, and restaurants filled in Birmingham's northside, although a distinct Negro business section abutted on the west and a patchwork of Negro residences crowded the city's northern boundaries. Southward, the city spread with modest row houses and random shacks, a medical school, and, more distant, the luxurious homes sitting amid the foliage on Red Mountain where by local standards elevation measured privilege.

East and west were the basic industries whose rapid rise gave Birmingham its nickname of "the Magic City" and whose steelmaking dominance made it "the Pittsburgh of the South." Gigantic fires from open hearth furnaces lit up the night horizon and spewed out smoke and pollution that drifted across the city. Beyond the nearest pits, mostly on the west side, were more furnaces and plants of the Tennessee Coal, Iron, and Railroad Company (T.C.I.), the city's largest corporation. Still more iron and steel companies thrived in the outlying communities of Pratt City, Ensley, Fairfield, and Bessemer. On the eastern outskirts stood a few textile plants, including Avondale Mills, owned by Alabama Governor B. B. Comer. The houses of a white, working class population formed the emerging suburbs of Woodlawn and East Lake.

Close to the L&N platform, the surrounding railyard and warehouses also captured elements of the city's basic nature. This spot, where land speculators had merged interests with railroad promoters in the 1870s, marked the original tract from which the city had grown into a metropolitan area of more than one hundred thousand people. Railroads ran east and west from the heart of the city to the furnaces and plants. There, rail spurs abruptly turned northward as the essential routes to and from Alabama's rich mines of industrial ores and coal. In warehouses bordering the terminal, white tradesmen and merchants using hired black hands stored goods for distribution to an ever-increasing number of shops and businesses catering to a small number of managers and an army of meagerly paid workers. Interspersed around the rail station were several saloons where hard liquor was served legally six days a week—and often available seven. Slightly further towards the southeast was the district where the city fathers attempted to confine legal prostitution and its pimp, illegal gambling. In everyday life beyond the train station, in factories and stores, churches and saloons, corporate offices and government buildings, Birmingham's antagonistic forces melded into a mosaic of commonplace events, tragic behavior patterns, and bizarre habits of thought which the apostles of a New South proclaimed as proper and natural as the rules of plantation life fifty years earlier.

At the turn of the century, the *Age-Herald* editor had declared that "Birmingham . . . is one of the . . . most religious communities in America . . . No city in the South has more church-seating capacity compared to inhabitants—none has better preachers—and none has better filled churches." Yet, during the two decades leading up to 1907, the city had earned a reputation as "Bad Birmingham," where crime, violence, and vice were considered inevitable byproducts of the South's only fast-growing industrial city. On average, Birmingham police made enough arrests each year to jail a third of the city's entire population and, according to one local minister, there were more murders in one year in Jefferson County—with fewer than two hundred thousand people—than in all of England with its forty million residents. In addition, by 1907 the city's saloons outnumbered its churches; the city directory listed 120 saloons, not counting the more numerous illegal "blind tigers" and juke joints.[1]

The standard explanation for the city's bad behavior in the midst of one of America's "most religious communities" was as old as Southern slavery: African Americans comprised 40 percent of the city's population. "Hundreds of idle negroes can be seen on the streets every day," complained the *Birmingham News* in 1906. "They can all get work, but they don't want to work. The result is that they sooner or later get into mischief or commit crimes of one sort or another." Sixty percent of Birmingham's arrests involved blacks, and the vast majority of victims of violence were also African American.

Birmingham's system of law and order operated to belittle blacks, enrich a few whites, and serve the needs of local, expanding industries. Seldom did the system seek the ends of justice. Every arrest of an African American in Birmingham generated income for the county sheriff, deputies, justices of the peace, and court clerk, all of whom were paid only on the basis of the number of people accused, arrested, jailed, or tried for crimes. The "fee system" had abuses throughout Alabama, but it was pernicious in Birmingham where it provided local government revenues in lieu of taxes and supplied labor-hungry mining companies with forced, cheap labor.

A black man arrested in Jefferson County was bound over for trial, placed in the sheriff's jail, and ushered into court—generating income for a public official each step of the way. Then he was usually convicted and leased for a monthly rate to the local mines where the convict worked on demand until he served out his time or died. This merger of racism, industrial profit, and good government had resulted from the efforts of white planters and Southern industrialists to replace state-enforced slavery with state-imposed forced labor.

This system prompted historian W. E. B. DuBois to observe that in "no part of the modern world has there been so open and conscious a traffic in crime for deliberate social degradation and private profit as in the South since slavery." After Birmingham led Alabama in the 1880s to the all-white primary as a means to eliminate black political influence, few restraints remained. The fee system and other systematic tricks of racial exploitation went unchecked, vocally opposed only by a black weekly newspaper and a handful of white reformers. "There were 'Lane, the lawyer, Park, the doctor, and Samuel Ullman [a Jewish educator],' . . . the three men who were wont to show up in lonesome isolation at meetings attended only by women who wanted 'to get something done'" about Birmingham's abuses of democracy.

And there were Birmingham's labor unions, a mixed-up band of black and white workers who at differing moments were their own strongest allies or bitterest enemies. Whites dominated the craft and trade unions, and many members had migrated to Birmingham in hopes of creating a "white democracy" where white industrialists and white craftsmen could work as social equals. African Americans simply had not been figured into the equation and were mostly restricted to unskilled jobs. Mining was an exception, and underground both blacks and whites worked in all categories of labor. Miners' unions had organized across racial lines since the end of Reconstruction, but their efforts, like those of the city's social reformers, had proven too little. In Birmingham, sustaining black "crime" and maintaining white supremacy had become essential tools for the growth of both city government and local industry. "We could not do without the negroes," declared an engineer for the city's first mining company.

Yet systematic black subordination did not establish a white republic of equals. In Birmingham, the class lines were as real as the color line. "There are men here," warned the Knights of Labor fifteen years after the city's founding, "who could to-day enslave the negro and also the poor white man." And the poor white woman. "I wouldn't be without negro servants," observed a voluble Southern lady discussing her own problems of capital and labor in early Birmingham. "But as to these poor whites . . . they are the most hope-less, helpless, trifling set of people in the entire South . . . I don't know but one thing could be done with the women of that race to make them work and that is to employ them in factories."[2]

If Birmingham was one of America's "most religious communities," as the *Age-Herald* claimed, its residents did not seem to worship the same God in the same heaven. Thousands of African Americans were members of all-black Baptist and Methodist churches. Among the twenty thousand white church members, 59 percent were Protestant, 33 percent were Roman Catholic, and the rest were Jewish or Greek Orthodox. Among Protestants, Methodists were the city's largest denomination, 22 percent of all white church members; Pres-byterians were 14 percent; Baptists only 10 percent; and Episcopalians merely 2 percent. Although Baptists and Methodists were dominant in surrounding Jefferson County, Catholics were Birmingham's prevailing religious group in 1907, largely because almost a fifth of Birmingham's white residents were im-migrants, primarily Italians, who worked in the coal mines and metal plants.

Birmingham's diversity was exceptional for Alabama where native whites and Baptists were a large majority. It also was more a source of conflict than a sign of tolerance. Almost every public issue uncovered differences of religion, heritage, language, or tradition—often volatile differences within a mixture of race, place, gender, and class in a young, violent city on the South's industrial frontier.

In the fall of 1907, whiskey was the pressing civic concern. Baptists, Methodists, and a few key Presbyterians had lobbied successfully in Jefferson County—where their members were a majority of the white voters—for a referendum that would prohibit the sale of liquor in Birmingham, where anti-liquor supporters were a minority. The Anti-Saloon League had secured a vote on countywide prohibition on October 28.

Many "dry" Protestants believed that alcohol was an evil, but even more citizens considered it an important cause of Birmingham's lawlessness. They warned voters that whiskey inflamed the Negro into menacing, immoral be-havior and pointed to Birmingham dives and saloons where black men and white women mingled. Earlier, the *Alabama Baptist* had explained the nexus between banning liquor and controlling the black man: "Let's protect him from the men who want to sell him the damnable stuff that sets him crazy and makes him a demon and a terror to our women."

Opponents of prohibition were primarily immigrants (especially Italian and Irish Catholics), liquor wholesalers, retailers, distillers, and brewers (local businesses where Catholics and Jews had made notable inroads), and industrialists, several of whom were also Catholic. Managers of Birmingham's major industries, including T.C.I., described prohibition as a labor problem with unique racial implications. They warned "if a sweeping prohibition law should be enforced in this district, our *best* workmen will leave." In this racialized context, "best" meant "white." In other words, if county voters drove away the city's white immigrants by enacting prohibition, additional black workers, including convict laborers, would come to the city to work—"a most serious blow to the community, industrially, commercially, and morally."[3]

INTO THIS CAULDRON OF DIVERSITY and dispute stepped Hugo L. Black on a Saturday in early September 1907, adding to the city census a twenty-one-year-old, single, white, male, Baptist, prohibitionist attorney, with fifty dollars to his name and no influential connections. During the next twenty years, Black would be at home in Birmingham. With new friends and neighbors, he would negotiate human differences that had destroyed past ideals and empires and already had corrupted America's noble experiment in life, liberty, and law. In these formative decades, Black would face the historical forces of conflict and change clashing within the South's youngest industrial city.

From the L&N station, Black walked north along Twenty-first Street to find a Clay County man he had known while attending Birmingham's medical college four years earlier. Woodson Duke, a collection agent for a furniture store, lived with his brother and David J. Davis, a recent graduate of Yale Law School, in a small room at Mrs. G. S. Crim's boardinghouse on Fifth Avenue North. For twenty dollars a month, Mrs. Crim added a plate at her table and allowed Black to join the other three bachelors in sharing one room with two cramped double beds.

On his second day in the city, Black attended Birmingham's First Baptist Church, a stone-faced, unpretentious building only a few blocks away. The "Baraca Class" for young men was taught by an elderly public school teacher, a self-described spinster, whose sweet nature reminded Black of his mother. A leader of the church's Sunday school was Frank S. White, an elderly, bombastic attorney. At different times, White had represented both the state labor unions and the state governor. He had managed the last campaigns of Governor Comer

and incumbent U.S. Senator John T. Morgan, whose Senate tenure since Reconstruction had given him the stature of a Confederate patrician.

The severe figure of the Reverend Alfred J. Dickinson stood in the First
Baptist pulpit. He was a scholarly man whose sermons, filled with poetic and
complex prose, seemed to escape most of his congregation. Dickinson was an
iconoclastic Baptist who believed the Bible was open to criticism and interpretation. He was an officer in the local municipal ownership league, promoting
government ownership of all utilities, and an advocate of organized labor.
Personally, the preacher was an aloof, almost arrogant man who had great
difficulty relating to common folk.

Dickinson was of course a prohibitionist. In addition, he held a strong
antipathy for the Catholic church, which he believed had persecuted Baptists in
Europe for centuries, and he was a whole-hearted white supremacist. In 1905,
he told Baptists that "the Southern white man has decided that his greatest
heritage is the Anglo-Saxon blood in his veins . . ." These were not matters of
Baptist doctrine, but they were perspectives most Alabama Baptists shared.
"There are three things any of us can speak on," observed a contemporary
Alabama Baptist, "swinging loose and going to the zenith—whiskey, Catholics,
and niggers." In many white Baptist minds, including Dickinson's, apparently,
these seemed to be three stanzas of the same verse.

Dickinson and many Alabama Baptists also considered their church's
democratic principles, including the right of individuals and congregations
to control their own faiths, as a source for many American ideals. "Among
the contributions that Baptists have been largely instrumental in making to
civilization," observed one Birmingham Baptist minister, "may be . . . religious
liberty, the separation of church and state, the ideal of a spiritual democracy,
. . . and the public school system."

In the company of this eclectic, intellectual preacher, of a gentle, kindly
spinster, and of a prominent union lawyer, Hugo Black located a spiritual
home. Within a few weeks, he became a registered member of Birmingham's
First Baptist Church.[4]

Hurrying to make his fortune, Black rented an office on the second floor
of 1905½ Second Avenue, two blocks from both city hall and the county
courthouse and four blocks from Mrs. Crim's boarding house. Down the hall
were an elderly dentist, an absent-minded photographer, and an oversized
beautician. After only three days in Birmingham, Black had recreated himself

in circumstances resembling his setup in Ashland. Now, he sat back and waited for his first Birmingham client.

And, as in Ashland, he waited and waited. For more than a month, not one soul climbed the stairs at 1905½ to consult an attorney. "Had I searched the city over I could hardly have found an office where a prospective litigant was less likely to come looking for a lawyer," Black would later recall. Nearing panic, with most of his fifty dollars gone, Black moved across from the courthouse to a "desk" in the law offices of Shugart and Comstock, on the second floor of an ugly little building overpopulated with lawyers. For seven dollars a month, paid in advance, Black rented the right to sit at a desk in a large, open room and wait for someone to walk into the building and approach him directly. If a prospective client appeared, Black was obliged to take the person to his lawyer-landlord, who decided if he would take the case himself, in which case Black had to wait for another client. If Black as an "attorney-in-rent" did get to handle the case, he paid the landlord-lawyer a third of his fee. As Shugart explained, "They come in to see me. It's my office."

In a moment of poetic justice, the first Birmingham case for the lawyer from the backwoods of Clay County was a dispute over a litter of pigs. The case was in Republic, an outlying mining community where the company of the same name owned the entire town, except for personal property such as pigs. It was not a case that Black's lawyer-landlord deemed worthy of his personal attention. Recreating a scene that could have been played out decades earlier before Justice of the Peace W. L. Black, Hugo appeared at the appointed hour before a JP at the coal company's commissary. Several rifle-wielding men greeted him. Black's client confirmed that the men were friends and witnesses of the opposing party. Black's own client had no witnesses or guns.

Witness after witness offered an ironclad case proving the sow belonged to his client's adversary. As Black recalled, they "slaughtered" us on the facts. Common law clearly awarded all offspring to the owner of the sow, but Black argued that the judge should follow his conscience—not the law—when it came to a pigsty. With a straight face, Black reminded the JP that "awarding the claimant all the pigs would necessarily remove them from their hog father who up to that time had, most likely with their mother, watched over them." In the end, the judge returned the sow but allowed Black's client to keep half the litter. Black gladly left Republic alive with his first victory and a fee of ten dollars, minus train fare and three dollars to his lawyer-landlord.[5]

It was not what Southerners meant by "hog heaven," but Black's maiden victory gave him enough spare change to return to Clay County in late October as a big-city lawyer. "Hugo Black of Birmingham," noted the *Standard,* "visited in Ashland this week." Black sorely needed brother Lee to redouble efforts to produce cash from their father's lingering estate but was vague about his own financial jeopardy. "Have been pretty busy," Hugo volunteered, ". . . but have not made so much."

When Black returned to Birmingham, Jefferson's voters had approved countywide prohibition despite opposition from most Birmingham residents. (Black had not lived in the city long enough to vote.) As dry supporters rejoiced, the city was rocked by a national financial panic. Local stocks plummeted, and, with President Teddy Roosevelt's approval, New York financier J. P. Morgan arranged the sale of Birmingham's T.C.I. to the United States Steel Corporation, its primary competitor. U.S. Steel's chief executive assured the President that the giant steel company could not benefit from the purchase and was only preventing a "general industrial smash-up." According to scholars who later reviewed the transaction, T.C.I. had assets of nearly one billion dollars and was sold to its competitor for just over thirty-five million dollars, paid almost entirely in U.S. Steel bonds. "If they checked the panic by this transaction," observed one analyst, "they did it by taking a few dollars out of one pocket and putting millions into another."

The sale gave city promoters intoxicating visions of a second economic coming. With its Northern financing and ownership, the *Age-Herald* proclaimed, U.S. Steel would make the city hum like heavenly angels on earth. The rival *News* thought that vision too humdrum; it saw Birmingham fast becoming "the largest steel manufacturing center *in the universe.*" No one said so, but over two decades J. P. Morgan had become Alabama's high priest of industry and finance, first establishing the L&N Railroad and now U.S. Steel as the state's prevailing industries.

A week after the T.C.I. sale, Black could see little of this glorious advent from his rented desk. "This panic seems to have struck Birmingham with a full force," he observed, "and there is not much money floating around." For a struggling attorney, prosperity was unforeseeable; survival was a challenge.[6]

At Mrs. Crim's each night, Black carefully laid out his pants between the bedsprings and the mattress to get the creased look of a prospering lawyer. His roommate Woodson Duke steered a little collections work to him, and

Black attended regular meetings of Masons and Pythians. He also began joining virtually any organization that met within walking distance of Crim's boarding house. "While by no means skilled at building a practice," Black remembered with wry understatement, "I was of the opinion that the only ethical way was to meet people and make as many friends as possible." On his first night at the Jefferson Valley Lodge of the Knights of Pythias, Black met Herman Beck, owner of a candy and grocery distribution company. A man who crossed Birmingham's religious and economic boundaries, Beck had been an early, key supporter of B. B. Comer's political career and was now the state Pythias' vice chancellor. Also present was "Lane the lawyer," one of the three legendary figures who had stood for simple justice in early Birmingham. A. O. Lane was a courtly, white-haired Southern gentleman who had practiced law with Frank White before being appointed circuit judge by Governor Comer. Prior to the turn of the century, Lane had twice been Birmingham's mayor with support from both black and white voters.

As weeks and months passed, Hugo Black's income inched upward. The retail credit agency in Atlanta began using Black to check out applicants in Birmingham, and Woodson Duke's collection referrals increased. Luckily, the owner of the Republic pigs returned with a land problem that Black settled for $1,000 and his largest fee to date—$250. Black promptly moved across the hall to share an office with only one other lawyer, Bonner Miller, a shy, awkward attorney from the Black Belt.

During these months of Black's difficult struggle, Barney Whatley was in Birmingham, studying law books as he traveled back and forth on the trolley to a bookkeeping job in East Lake. With Hugo's permission, Barney registered Hugo's rented desk as the site of his legal training, although he seldom had time to come downtown. In 1908, Whatley passed the state bar exam, and the Clay County boys recaptured a lost dream. They joined together as the law firm of "Black and Whatley."[7]

THAT 1908 SUMMER, Birmingham was at the precipice of a gigantic, splintering clash between labor and capital. The number of free, foreign, and native miners around Birmingham had increased in recent years as coal stoked the city's enormous, hell-hot furnaces where machines and men reshaped nature's minerals. Birmingham had become a major source for the slabs of iron and steel upon which urban America and its factories were being built. Yet, seven months after the vaunted arrival of U.S. Steel, Birmingham prepared for a miners' strike that promised to disrupt the local economy and electrify the city's stormy social environment.

Labor relations in Birmingham's mining industries had always been rancorous and violent. In 1894, coal operators imported massive numbers of new black workers to break an interracial union, and Governor Thomas Jones had used Pinkerton agents and the state militia to crush Alabama's first major miners' strike. During the conflict, dozens were wounded or died from gunshots and dynamite, and thousands of workers afterwards went jobless. Since the turn of the century, the United Mine Workers' (UMW) black and white organizers had endured floggings and harassment but had signed thousands of new members. By 1904, despite a large union membership, Alabama coal companies like T.C.I., Sloss, and Republic refused to bargain with the UMW. These companies' furnaces were fueled with coal from their own mines worked in large part by convict labor.

Now, in 1908, UMW contracts with smaller commercial mines were expiring, and the Alabama Coal Operators Association, including U.S. Steel, prepared to break the union. The companies proposed to cut the free miners' pay. On July 6, the international UMW pledged support for a strike in Alabama's mines.[8]

Within two weeks, more than seven thousand miners left their jobs. In response, mining companies amassed a legion of private guards, and the Jefferson County sheriff enlisted more than one hundred armed deputies, paid for by the mining companies, to clamp down on agitators, including out-of-town organizers who were arrested for "preaching social equality." The coal operators shipped trainloads of black and immigrant workers ("scabs," the union called them) into the district to replace strikers, and the companies evicted hundreds of miners' families from company-owned houses. In response, the union rented farmlands where it set up tents and commissaries for evicted strikers and their families.

By July 15, violence had spread throughout the mining district. The UMW described a "reign of terror" where sheriff's deputies and private guards were "breaking up meetings and taking our men by force." The union accused coal companies of violent tactics designed to provoke violent responses. In one incident, company-paid deputies arrested thirteen black strikers and one white UMW member after an exchange of gunfire. The strikers were accused of "hooting" workers on their way to the mines, but the UMW objected that peaceful ridicule was not unlawful. Over five weeks, armed conflict and violence escalated into the semblance of warfare. Gunshots greeted trains arriving with scab labor. The home of a nonunion miner was burned to the ground. A mine shaft was dynamited. A black union man was lynched in broad daylight by a vigilance committee. Deputies and miners exchanged gunfire like soldiers at war. After one crossfire, a frightened reporter called it a "battle, which knows few equals in Alabama since the civil war."

When hundreds of black and white miners were arrested for trespass, inciting violence, and similar offenses, UMW attorney Frank White enlisted the assistance of other local lawyers, including a new attorney from Clay County who attended White's church. This legal work was grueling and hectic, although important for keeping up the union members' spirit of resistance. Miners expected union lawyers to defend them in court for what they had done in the support of the strike; the stakes were raised because striking miners who were convicted and sentenced by local courts could be returned to the mines as convict labor to help break their own strike.

In one case, Hugo Black defended a miner charged with trespassing at Republic, the company-owned town where Black had tried his pig case. After a warning to UMW members not to come back on the company's property for union organizing, company guards had arrested union men in the home of a miner. Black argued that the warning was not legally sufficient. The crime of "trespass after warning," Black insisted, only prohibited his client from returning to Republic for the same purpose, and, in this case, there was no evidence showing the purpose of his client's second visit. The trial judge was unimpressed by Black precise points of law and convicted the miner, although months later the Alabama Supreme Court reversed the conviction.[9]

The legal work was at best a rearguard action, unable to influence the power and tactics shaping the fate of the UMW action. Governor B. B. Comer was in Birmingham at his textile mills when the strike began and he stayed in the city to direct state actions until the strike ended. "I regard the strike situation as very serious," Comer informed his administrative aide, William E. Fort. When violence escalated, Comer summoned Alabama's Adjutant General Bibb Graves and state troops from the Confederate battleground of Chickamauga where they were in annual drill. Railroads transported the state troops without charge to Birmingham where they were stationed in groups of forty or fifty soldiers throughout company towns, mines, and rail junctions. The troops slept and ate in company towns at the expense of mining operators.

Despite his close relations with Frank White, Comer turned for advice in the strike to another Birmingham attorney, Samuel Weakley, a former chief justice of the state supreme court and the governor's lawyer in several cases against the L&N Railroad. Comer wanted to stop strikers from rabble-rousing at union meetings. Birmingham's industrialists had come to the conclusion, in the words of the *Birmingham News*, that "not all the soldiers of Alabama, not every man in the state available for military duty or qualified for the work of deputy sheriffs can stop this disturbance and this devilment unless authority be given them to disperse assemblies."

As soon as Judge Weakley advised that "any meeting *calculated to excite alarm* is an unlawful assembly and can be dispersed," Comer instructed Jefferson's sheriff to ban all assemblies near the mines, to stop any marching along public highways, and to disperse any gathering when a speaker incited "alarm." In a public proclamation, the governor threatened to authorize citizens to form a "posse comitatus" if necessary to assure that scabs were not prevented from working.

After deputizing hundreds more men at the mining companies' expense, Jefferson's sheriff enforced the new decree. The Reverend W. A. Lewis, a UMW Local official, was arrested on stage at an outdoor barbecue as soon as he "alarmed" his audience by referring to the sheriff's "dirty deputies." At another meeting, a black leader recounted the lynching of a black union member and the recent death of a handcuffed black prisoner who was shot in the back while attempting to flee. "The men who did this shooting are still in the employ of the sheriff," declared the speaker, who was promptly arrested by sheriff's deputies. UMW lawyers protested but were helpless against the state's blatant denial of free speech. Union leader W. R. Fairley charged that "every principle underlying the constitution of the United States is being violated by the corporations of Alabama" with the state government's assistance.[10]

While union supporters were dispersed and silenced, Birmingham's business leaders met to speak out for Governor Comer's decree and the right of "every man who wants to work." A resolution passed at the meeting impartially condemned all "murderers, assassins, lynchers, and dynamiters," but the leading citizens who spoke attacked the union and strikers. The *Birmingham News* publisher proclaimed to thunderous applause that "We have our constitutional rights" to be free of labor-restricting unions, "the foes of man." In the amen corner, developer Robert Jemison, Sr., attacked the union as "blood-thirsty instigators." These remarks, unlike those of the Reverend Lewis, apparently did not alarm anyone. Presiding at the meeting, A. O. Lane was the only city leader who did not blame solely the union "instigators" for lawlessness.

A thousand soldiers stood guard of the property of the coal operators. More than five hundred special deputies traveled the mining area to enforce the governor's decree. Hundreds of private guards patrolled mining companies. Coal companies castigated the UMW as the "Blood Stained Organization" and refused all union proposals for arbitration. Denied free speech and assembly, surviving with their families in tents, striking miners still refused to surrender. Some UMW chapters evaded the governor's decree by meeting daily to conduct "open air exercises, with prayer—and that good old song . . .'We Will Overcome.'"

On August 22, the *Birmingham Age-Herald* mustered powerful reinforcements when its first page proclaimed, "Social Equality Talk, Evil Feature Of Strike." Deploying the white South's ultimate weapon of social warfare, the paper reported on "white leaders of this coal strike, who are daily instilling into the minds of the blacks ideas of social equality, which if they do take root soon will result in a worse condition . . . of bloodshed and absolute annihilation. A worse page will be written in history than . . . when political carpetbaggers came among us."

The article described the "dangerous picture" of white and black women organizing into auxiliary unions, a development that "the caucasian blood of this state would rebel against." The reporter also supplied his own eyewitness account. "I have seen a negro place his arms around the neck of a white speaker in the presence of fair white women and children," Frank V. Evans wrote, "and apparently prompt him in secret what next to say to fire up the hearts of the ignorant blacks."

Over the next five days, Birmingham's daily newspapers repeated charges of social equality against strikers in columns, letters to the editor, and other news articles. "It is a lamentable condition that incites and permits ignorant negro leaders to address assemblies of white women and children as social equals," wrote Evans in a subsequent story, "advising as to moral and social questions . . . which can only be discussed properly with fair women in the private home by husband and father. It was a third of a century ago," Evans continued, "that the people of Alabama by rigid force and even the shedding of blood stopped . . . the idea of social equality . . . has it again come to this?" After reading Evans's articles, one citizen replied: if "Fairley and his black co-conspirators would have invaded southern Alabama and perpetuated the same damnable deeds he has inflicted on the people of Jefferson County, nothing further would be needed but the coroner."[11]

As the South's only interracial organizations, labor unions—primarily the United Mine Workers—faced constant race-baiting. In the Birmingham district, at least half of UMW members were African Americans, and both races shared positions of leadership. The elected vice president of the Alabama district was a black man as were three of eight elected members of the state executive board. The district president was white. In several local chapters with large black membership, African Americans were elected president. While the union was careful never to allow blacks' full voting strength, nowhere else in the Alabama and rarely in the South in 1908 did African Americans share any leadership or semblance of power in any kind of organization with white members.

UMW officials understood the potential danger of interracial work and went out of their way to deflect or return racial accusations. "They say the state is overridden with hordes of negroes carrying guns with murder in their hearts," observed W. R. Fairley, a white UMW official. "I would like to ask, if we have hordes in the coal mines of Alabama, who brought them here? Not the miners, but the operators . . . Why? To reduce the wages of the decent miners." Birmingham's *Labor Advocate* was extremely sensitive to accusations of the union's race mixing and strained at times to accuse the other side of a worse wrongdoing. It charged, for example, that state troops were forcing "undesirable negroes" into the Birmingham area and accused the local sheriff of hiring of armed, black deputies to patrol the mining areas. "The miners organized the negro in self-defense," pleaded the *Advocate*, "knowing full well the operators would use them to keep down the earnings of white miners."

These efforts to shift and explain the burden of race proved impotent when industrialists parlayed the strike into an issue of social equality. Within three days of the *Age-Herald's* article, Governor Comer ordered Adjutant General Bibb Graves to rout the miners' encampment to preserve public health. Brandishing bayonets and swords, a line of troops swept through the strikers' camp, slashing down tents and moving out families. Union leaders had volunteered to build any and all necessary sanitary facilities, under the militia's supervision, but the governor refused. "You know what it means to have eight or nine thousand niggers idle in the state of Alabama," Comer exploded, "and I am not going to stand for it."

In the late 1870s, as a young man in Barbour County, Comer had joined a gang of white men in attacking an unarmed local leader of biracial Reconstruction politics; the man's fifteen-year-old son died from the attackers' gunshots. No one was arrested for the murder. A third of a century later, Governor Comer had not altered his understanding of what constituted imminent danger to a Southern community's "health" and the justifiable means to suppress it.

Two days after destroying the miners' camp, Comer summoned white UMW officials, without his old friend Frank White, to deliver an ultimatum. If the miners' strike did not end immediately, the governor would call the legislature into special session to pass new vagrancy laws allowing the sheriff to arrest every idle miner. State legislators from rural Alabama were "outraged at the attempts to establish social equality between white and black miners," the governor declared, and were ready to legislate an immediate end to the miners' strike. Without the right to assemble or speak in the mining areas, without tents and commissaries for strikers' families, and without freedom from arrest for the act of striking, union officials knew that miners were doomed. The strike was over.

In the aftermath, many miners relocated to other sections of the country, while Black, White, and other UMW lawyers mopped up by appealing convictions and settling criminal cases. Union officials reported at their national convention that the Alabama strike failed because the union violated "the principles the South holds near and dear." Within months, UMW membership in Alabama collapsed to fewer than seven hundred, and Birmingham businessmen incorporated a Citizens Protective League to prevent future labor agitation. The coal operators association paid Frank Evans, the reporter who detailed the "facts" about "social equality," $500 for "his services rendered as newspaper correspondent" after he compiled his stories into a report. Mining companies discontinued payments for special deputies and disbanded troops of private guards, but, unbeknownst to the United Mine Workers, U.S. Steel continued to receive clandestine reports from at least one undercover informant within the local union leadership.[12] Having won the day, Birmingham's industrial leaders were secretly vigilant about the future, understanding clearly the enduring hostilities they had helped to create in the Magic City.

IN A CITY AT WAR WITH ITSELF, Black and Whatley were in contrast remark-
ably well suited as law partners even if their meager bank account always was
troublesome. Like his father, Barney enjoyed meeting people, exactly the talent
the new law firm needed to generate a steady stream of half-dollars for each
dossier filed on insurance applicants for the Retail Credit Agency in Atlanta.
On good days, Whatley completed fifteen or twenty reports from conversations with applicants' neighbors and co-workers; the firm received as much
$50 each month from Whatley's investigations.

Another source of regular income came from the Pythias Lodge. Herman
Beck had become the first Jew to serve as Alabama's grand chancellor. To keep
his lodge duties from burdening his business (and perhaps to project a more
traditional image), the grocery distributor engaged two young Baptists, Black
and Harwell Davis, to appear as his personal representatives at Pythian functions and ceremonies across the rural state. Black jumped at the chance to
have a monthly stipend of $50–100, as Whatley remembered, "just to make
a speech."

Apart from these sources, each unrelated to practicing law, the firm waited
for cases and income until someone walked up the stairs of the lawyers' building to the second floor, selected the door leading to office #7, and approached
one of the two young lawyers at the far end of the room instead of the older
man sitting nearby. In exactly this manner, Black and Whatley's first client, an
elderly black woman, surveyed her options before walking directly to Whatley.
She told him the story of how rocks had fallen and killed her son in a local
coal mine. "I took down the whole story . . . and naturally Hugo soon took
over the case," Whatley recalled. "I was glad for him to do it because I didn't
know enough about how to try the case." Not long afterwards, however, the
client returned.

"Mr. Whatley, I knows Mr. Black is a mighty good man and I likes him,"
the woman stated. "But I want *you* to handle my case."

"Why?" Whatley inquired.

"His face," the woman replied. "His face is too pleasant. I wants a lawyer
with a mean face like yours."

Beyond appearances, there was a clear division of labor in the new firm.
Black handled all litigation, including their first case which settled before trial.
Whatley handled credit reports and office work. In other words, Hugo made
the important decisions and handled the important cases. The partners worked

wonderfully together on these terms. "Now and then, though, I could get my way," Barney remembered. "I would just refer to Clay County . . . and mutter, 'That's just what you'd expect from a fella who don't know the difference between a citron and a watermelon.'"

Black's domineering style was not limited to his law office. At the age of twenty-three, he assumed the role of family patriarch in Clay County. Like an ancient chieftain, Black returned to Ashland to prosecute a man accused of killing a distant Toland cousin. When visiting Lee's family, Black disciplined his brother's children in front of their own parents, in their house, and by his standards of good punishment. Once, when his four-year-old niece Hazel annoyed him at the breakfast table, Hugo lifted her from a chair, and, without a word to her parents, he took the girl to the barn where he plopped her down with an invitation: "Now, you can moo as loud as you please."

Black also interrogated his brother, sixteen years his elder, about family planning and finances. "Lee, how are you going to educate all these children? It takes money, you know," Hugo insisted. "Big families are wonderful, if they can have a chance at education . . . You're going to send them to college, aren't you!" Black scolded, "Higher education is a must these days!" Black was equally self-assuming in other ways. Rail thin, he was repulsed by obesity and freely lectured anyone of any age with too much fat on why and how to lose weight. With a showman's flair, he also instructed Ashland children on the virtues and techniques of consuming a saucer of raw eggs as a daily dietary supplement.[13]

In Birmingham, Black was becoming more confident about his own future. He moved his law firm to the second floor of the new Farley Building, a block from the courthouse, and transferred his residence to the city's southside amid fashionable homes on Red Mountain's slopes. Black shared a spacious upstairs apartment with five or six other bachelors, including David J. Davis. Another roommate, Harry Yockey, was a salesman for West Publishing Company, and Black persuaded him to locate a full set of *Alabama Reports* in the new offices of Black and Whatley as a showcase where prospective customers could examine the books. Once more, Black had a full law library—this time without spending an inheritance.

As in the days in Clay County, Hugo and Barney became inseparable. Keeping long hours at the office, they often ate pork chops and potatoes together in Joe Wheeler's cafe near the L&N station or at Cooper Brothers' where the menu included "Clay County vitals"—turnip greens, sow belly, cornbread, and buttermilk. They dined at such places because plentiful plates of food there cost less than fifteen cents. They also continued to join lodges of any stripe, including Elks, Masons, Odd Fellows, and Woodmen of the World. Both taught young men's Sunday school classes at the city's prominent Baptist churches, Hugo at First Baptist, Barney at Southside Baptist. And they never refused invitations to speak on any subject to any crowd. Once when invited to East Lake for a speech, Black found only three men assembled in the lodge hall. When the "assembly" implored him to speak, Black stood up and gave a lecture as forceful as his address on the "Little Martyr" at Ashland Academy.

Due to finances, the men restricted their social life to church, lodges, or someone else's parties. At one masquerade party, unable to afford costumes, Barney and Hugo went in street clothes as the self-proclaiming "Rivals," the protagonists in a popular contemporary pulp fiction. Staying in character at the party, whenever one of the pair began talking to a young woman, the other tried to win away her interest. "Taking opposite sides just for the fun of it" was great, cheap amusement for these boyhood rivals, although an argumentative persona was hardly a disguise of Black's true identity.[14]

In their law office, the pair whiled away the hours waiting for new clients by creating a mock courtroom with Barney as opposing counsel. The young men "raised hell with each other" about procedural questions or substantive issues to prepare Black for the real courtroom. Unfortunately, in the beginning, they did not practice or consult the supplements of their free law books quite enough.

Black's first case in circuit court was filed on behalf of Mrs. S. P. Beecher, a widow who owned a small shop. Four men, one claiming to be a constable, had entered her store during the lawless days of the UMW strike. "Under color of his office," Black asserted, the lawman and his underlings rudely evicted Beecher's customers, closed her shop, and confiscated a medicine box, a candy jar, three lamps, and other property without replacement or explanation.

According to Black's complaint, his client "was humiliated, her credit impaired, her business injured, and customers driven off." She sued for damages claiming the men had no legal authority or no legal cause for their high-handed actions. Before Judge A. O. Lane on the first day of trial, Black asked the court to amend his original complaint to eliminate one of the defendants who had died after the lawsuit was filed.

Like a fox trapping its prey, the defendant's lawyer twice asked Judge Lane, "Is the amendment allowed?" When assured that it had been, Black's opponent moved that the suit be dismissed. Citing a recent appeals court decision on Alabama's senseless maze of procedural rules, the lawyer argued that the "effect of the amendment was to discontinue the case . . . The parties were thereby out of court." After studying case law overnight, Judge Lane concluded that, while disagreeing with the higher court's opinion, he had to dismiss the suit. Black had removed one of four "joint defendants" from his original complaint without showing just cause, without first proving that the defendant was dead. According to Alabama's civil procedures, this mistake forever "discontinued the entire action" against all defendants.

In a handwritten appeal—customary for an Alabama lawyer's work in 1909—Black feebly claimed that his amendment was not on record because he had handed his written motion to Judge Lane, not to the clerk who records court documents. Actually, Black's argument was as sensible as the technical procedure he failed to observe, but it was not as persuasive for one simple reason: Alabama's legislature and higher courts had established arcane, nonsensical procedures to eliminate legitimate lawsuits by poor citizens challenging corporations with inexperienced lawyers. Plaintiffs' lawyers had to avoid a maze of procedural traps to keep their clients in court, regardless of a case's merit. In this case, because Black was outfoxed in Alabama's arcane labyrinth of civil procedures, his client lost her chance in court. Worse, Mrs. Beecher had to pay the court costs of the men who ransacked her business.

Within weeks, Black appeared in Judge Lane's courtroom again. This time the case involved Willie Morton, a black convict miner who had been kept at forced labor two weeks beyond his prison term by Sloss Iron and Coal Company during the miners' strike. Representing Sloss was William Grubb, one of the city's most respected corporate lawyers. Stung once by an opponent's greater mastery of civil procedures, Black had prepared for the Morton case as if his own liberty was in jeopardy.

For more than a day and a half, Grubb and Black swapped pleadings, arguments, and strategies on complex procedural motions designed by Sloss's attorney to remove Black's client from court on technical grounds. It was not unusual in Alabama's legal system to spend more time arguing technical rules than presenting a case's merits. In this instance, however, Judge Lane finally told his old friend, "Billy, it seems plain you cannot plead this young man out of court, so I suggest you simply join issue and go to trial." Afterwards, an all-white jury awarded Morton $137.50, plus court costs. The award brought less than $40 to Black and Whatley after the fee was divided with attorney Bonner Miller, who had referred it to them. It was, nevertheless, Black's first jury verdict in a civil trial, a victory that he and others would remember far longer than his first, botched case in circuit court.

Most of Black's legal work was much more routine. Often his clients were African Americans arrested for petty crimes, and Black or Whatley had "to go down to police court now and then and defend some Negro for five dollars." Their white clients usually were coal miners or manual laborers with small claims or problems without legal remedies. "We made enough to live on and get by . . . but no big fees," Whatley recalled.

Competition among Birmingham lawyers was fierce. The city had a few large law firms who represented corporations, a host of small practitioners who tried to sue them, and a fair number of "ne'er-do-wells" who survived in ragged subsistence. Like the forces in conflict within Birmingham society, the city's lawyers were in a symbiotic relationship where one could not exist without the hostility of the other. Due in part to the law's limits, shaped by a Black Belt-controlled state legislature and a conservative Alabama Supreme Court, opportunities for plaintiffs' lawyers to generate big fees in the courts were rare in 1909. Survival for both the earnest small practitioners and the profession's mountebanks often depended on the commonplace mistreatment and misery of blacks brought into the criminal courts by a wicked fee system.

One charlatan, a drunken Confederate veteran, hung about the Farley building pestering Hugo and Barney with stories of imagined achievements on battle fields and in courtrooms. The old soldier represented Negroes in the inferior courts just enough to keep himself in liquor. Without an office, he picked up clients in the building's lobby as they searched for a lawyer. While he was polar opposite of the sober, disciplined Hugo Black, the old veteran understood that the bonds of hostility united all lawyers. Whenever leaving Black and Whatley for a change of venue, the old man yelled, "Now boys, remember, if you love me, sue my clients."

Despite shared hardships, Black and Whatley had only one point of personal disagreement—whiskey. Barney drank moderately, but his consumption of any liquor deeply worried Fayette Black's son. Hugo was absolutely sure drinking any amount of liquor would lead to personal destruction, and he campaigned relentlessly for Barney to quit. He pleaded, scolded, and advocated the sure virtue of total abstinence to protect his best friend from the horrors of his own past.

Whatley wasn't the only one Black tried to save. In late 1909, prohibitionists campaigned for a state constitutional amendment to outlaw liquor throughout Alabama. It had support from Governor Comer, many Methodists, Judge Samuel Weakley (prohibition's chief legal strategist), and most Baptists, including Black who spoke for the amendment wherever he had a platform. Black believed in one absolute solution for everyone, and, like America's abortion opponents decades later, he saw himself upholding an undeniable moral imperative—saving people from killing themselves or others. Alabama voters were far less certain of these moral and practical questions; they overwhelmingly rejected the amendment. Still, the vote did not disturb prohibition in Jefferson County nor settle the disagreement between the wet and dry halves of the Black and Whatley firm.

Prohibition's defeat started a year of disappointment. In 1910 Black suffered from a complicated appendectomy. Fourteen days in the hospital wiped out his meager savings. Soon afterwards, Barney discovered he had tuberculosis. Birmingham's industrial furnaces had badly polluted the air and endowed the city with one of the nation's highest TB rates. Whatley's doctor suggested he move to Colorado where high altitudes, little industry, and dry air might be natural tonics to extend his life for a few years. "I'm going," he informed Hugo. "What else can I do?" David J. Davis agreed to buy Barney's interest in the firm's pending cases with future payments of $50 a month. With no more than a trunk of clothes, an IOU, and his Alabama lawyer's license, Whatley left Birmingham on a westbound train.

Black and Davis operated much as Black and Whatley had. Davis ran the office and did the paperwork. Black made all big decisions and tried all big cases. The new partner was patient, kind, careful, talented, and loyal—qualities that endeared him as a friend. "There was never a time after I got to know David J. that I would not have entrusted him with my life," Black remembered. Yet, Davis was inept at bringing business into the firm or doing half-dollar credit investigations. He lacked Barney's natural ease with people and Hugo's boundless energy. From the start, David J. functioned as a junior associate, not a partner.[15]

Davis's limits didn't matter when Black began developing enough legal business for both men. Building on new friendships and emerging courtroom triumphs, Black steered his practice towards personal injury cases where workers were harmed on the job due to their employers' negligence. He stopped appearing in civil cases as a defense attorney and decided that his skills before a local jury on behalf of men injured by Birmingham's major industries was his ticket to a future beyond subsistence.

In a suit against U.S. Steel, for instance, Black represented a furnace worker injured when a foreman instructed the "tipper" to unload a vat of mixed ores. Before Judge A. O. Lane, Black's case swung on whether the jury believed that a company witness was telling the truth. The firm of Percy, Benners, and Burr represented U.S. Steel. Born to a prominent plantation family in the Mississippi Delta, Walker Percy [grandfather of the famous novelist of the same name] was Birmingham's leading corporate attorney, who had married the daughter of the city's first coal and steel operator, Henry F. DeBardeleben. Borden Burr was a Talladega lawyer who had practiced in the Clay County courthouse when Hugo was a teenager. In this case, Black won a cash judgment because, over Percy's objections, he convinced a jury that the defendant's chief witness was a liar who could not be trusted.

In another case, Black won an award against several railroads for overcharging his local Masonic lodge for shipping freight. When the L&N failed to pay promptly, Black secured an order from a justice of the peace to confiscate all typewriters in the company's freight office as payment. The maneuver stalled the railroad's entire local shipping business for a brief time and delighted many of Black's fellow Masons who seldom had seen railroads scurry so. "They paid us quick," smirked a lodge officer.

The rising trend in personal injury lawsuits worried Birmingham's industrial leaders who complained bitterly about the misuse of the jury system. They claimed most cases were "fake, trivial, and fool damage suits." According to railroad and industrial managers, a "reign of the shyster lawyer" plagued Birmingham. Statistics showed that in November 1910, more than one thousand lawsuits, seeking damages of $11.5 million against corporations, were pending in local courts. Corporate managers argued that these lawsuits were a direct result of unscrupulous citizens who faked injuries and their "lawyers who are the scum of the earth."

Regaling the public about dishonest, shiftless Negroes pretending injuries from chauffeur-driven automobiles (Birmingham's latest badge of social status), industrialists contended that honest workers were the real victims. "Owing to the hazards of modern industry, and *frequently* to the ignorance or negligence of the employee," not the company, a corporate spokesman observed, "accidents . . . occur daily here in the Birmingham district . . . there is much unprofessional soliciting and very often trivial or fake suits are brought to the great detriment of the workman, who loses his job, of course."

Yet, defendants in most of Birmingham's damage suits were railroads or iron and coal companies. Very few smaller companies were sued. By the industrialists' own data, more than eight hundred cases—almost four out of five—were against companies in these two industries. Fifteen railroad companies were defendants in 463 lawsuits, more than 40 percent of all cases. Rather than "one of the great present-day problems" of Birmingham, personal injury litigation was a direct challenge to a small number of companies—the city's largest industries, who at times were attempting to limit their labor costs by avoiding safety expenses.

During this publicity campaign, Judge A. O. Lane was the only public voice suggesting that corporations had created many of their own problems. "Much of the prejudice that exists today against companies and corporations in the public mind," Lane asserted, "has been created to large degree by the corporations themselves . . . The spirit of some corporations is simply 'to get out of everything.'" Because many companies did "right" only when forced by lawsuits, Lane believed that corporations had created a "spirit of antagonism and a habitual attitude of distrust" among the people.

A courtly man in manner and speech, with the face of a cuddly teddy bear whose bushy white eyebrows framed dark, sympathetic eyes, Judge Lane was disturbed that corporations had emerged as legal instruments for organizing Alabama's land, labor, and capital in a new industrial age without countervailing human values. "Individuals in control of great companies will frequently do certain unjust things for the company that they would not do as individuals," Lane sadly observed. "Their code of ethics for themselves, strange to say, is often entirely different . . . when it comes to meting out justice."

Judge Lane's sense of justice and fairness made him "the kind of man people not merely liked but loved," Black remembered. Lane had served Birmingham for more than three decades, first as mayor before the turn of the century and more recently as circuit judge.[16] In a divided city, Lane was one of a handful of leaders who had won respect across the community's warring factions and sections. This rare stature made him the natural choice to lead a revised city government that Birmingham implemented in the spring of 1911. The change was a reform born in the fight to permit local liquor, led by the city's industrialists, and ironically it gave a devout prohibitionist—a young, aggressive damage suit lawyer—his first official title of "Judge."

DURING THE 1907 LIQUOR REFERENDUM, U.S. Steel's attorney Walker Percy had suggested that Birmingham's problems of whiskey could be controlled if city hall changed. "The aldermanic position is one of minor importance; the honor does not, as a rule, appeal to the best class of our citizens," observed Percy in explaining the shortcomings of current officials. To stop liquor abuses, Percy urged the city to change from a board of aldermen, elected in different city districts, to a commission of three members elected by all city voters.

After Jefferson's voters adopted county prohibition, Percy's reform stayed alive through efforts of the *Birmingham News*, whose publisher agreed that three "strong, high class businessmen" should run the city like "a business corporation in which the taxpayers are stockholders." Yet many small merchants, the *Labor Advocate*, and incumbent aldermen opposed the reform, fearing a change would diminish their own ability to elect candidates from neighborhood districts.

Despite A. O. Lane's misgivings, the corporation was now a popular, seductive model for democratic government. It represented orderliness and efficiency in a city where shifting factions swung public policies like a pendulum after each election. Of course, a corporate model of governance had been completely adopted in Birmingham's coal mining areas. U.S. Steel and other corporations had built "company towns" where workers toiled in company mines, lived with their families in company houses, shopped at company commissaries, met in company lodges, worshiped in company churches, and obeyed the laws enforced by company guards.

In the beginning, these company-created communities were necessary because housing was unavailable near the mines in isolated, hilly terrain. But company towns had proved extremely helpful in controlling workers in the 1908 miners' strike. Walker Percy's proposal also served Birmingham's corporate interests. Percy sought a commission of businessmen who would strictly regulate liquor, not ban it. He wanted a local government that would regulate, not disrupt, the city's supply of black industrial labor. And he hoped business-oriented city commissioners would be more sympathetic to local industrialists' longstanding efforts to escape the city's corporate taxes.

In 1911, as a state legislator, Percy pushed the enactment of a bill creating a three-member commission, which the governor initially appointed. A. O. Lane was almost everyone's first choice for the new commission, and the governor also appointed an incumbent alderman and a local corporation attorney.[17] All three were "local optionists," those who supported regulation, not prohibition of liquor.

As commissioner for public justice responsible for police and courts, Judge Lane assembled Birmingham's 168 police officers in the city courtroom within a week of his taking office. "The prohibition laws of the city of Birmingham must be and shall be enforced," Lane declared. "If you can't do it, then we will get men who can. . . . It may well be," Lane continued, "that the sale of liquor will again be legalized in the city. It will then be the duty of the police to see that the sale of liquor is kept within lawful bounds, but until the change is made it is essential that the law be enforced."

Lane had other concerns. Early in his term, he insisted the city remove iron shackles at night from the legs of city convicts—almost all African Americans. "It does not matter what is done in Atlanta!" snapped Lane, when told by a city bureaucrat that the "Gate City" kept its convicts in irons throughout their sentence. With the acquiescence of Birmingham's other commissioners, Lane ended the "outrageous practice" the following day. Lane also discovered that two black boys, eight and ten years old, had been sentenced by a city judge to 280 days on the city's chain gang for "stealing trifles"—"no sin committed against society." Responding to a mother's appeal, Lane rescued the boys. They were taken home and given a thrashing in front of their families by an "officer of discretion and feeling" who was given "unconditional instructions to permit no brutality." Lane assured the white public that "these boys will never come back again."[18]

Even before this incident, Lane knew he had to transform the city's courts. Facing a staggering debt of half a million dollars, Birmingham commissioners needed to slash the city payroll. In 1910, the city had annexed a large part of the suburbs (excluding most industrial plants), and city expenses had increased more than tax revenues. Police courts had grown to four salaried judges, including an old Confederate veteran who bragged that the "negro offender was an open book" which he read at leisure. During the last year, city courts had handled more than ten thousand misdemeanor cases and almost seven hundred preliminary hearings for felonies. Lane's challenge seemed impossible: slash the courts' expenses, handle the current docket, and restore the impartial rule of justice. To accomplish this feat, astonishing virtually everyone, Lane asked Hugo Black to become the city's sole "police court" judge on a part-time basis.

Lane needed an aggressive, competent, and fair lawyer with a modest income who would see the appointment as an advance of his career. While maintaining a part-time court in Ensley, Lane could offer a salary of $1,500 a year for a judge to do the work of three full-time judges, each of whom had been paid $3,600. Lane also needed a new judge who would enforce all laws fairly and the prohibition laws with gusto. By all counts, Black was his man.

Black, however, was chary to give up his law practice just as it was becoming rewarding. He suggested his law partner David J. Davis, who wanted to be a judge. But, Black, not Davis, had the driving, dominating personality the job required. To sweeten his offer, Lane promised to remove all preliminary hearings from police court and authorized Black to continue a private practice in circuit court.

On Wednesday, April 12, 1911, Judge Hugo Black assumed his duties in Birmingham's "recorders court" and quickly disposed of fifty-five cases. The judge announced that the court henceforth would convene at 8:30 AM and dispense with afternoon sessions. In wooden, legal prose, he also plugged his law firm. "The firm of Black & Davis will continue to serve its clientage with no interference between my duties at the recorder's court and my private business," announced Judge Black.

Each weekday morning, and often on Saturdays, Black presided over the city's ordinary misery and misdeeds in a courtroom possessing the trappings of an livestock auction house. In a windowless room on the ground floor at the rear of city hall, Judge Black sat at an elevated desk with his back to the wall. His bench was bordered by tables for the court clerk and bailiff. There was no witness box. The clerk maintained a blackboard where he wrote the names of the accused and the amount of their fines and imprisonment, if any, after each case. At the other end of the room was a large iron cage, commonly called the "monkey cage," where dozens of prisoners stood together, one mass of humanity. A bailiff fetched prisoners to stand before the judge as their cases were called. The remaining cramped space was occupied by crowds of family members and witnesses, lawyers, bystanders, and as many as twenty-five policemen, who referred to themselves as "bulls." The poorly lit, often damp room where Judge Black ruled supreme for a day smelled of unwashed, pressed flesh and hummed with a vulgar, monotonous volume of noise and disorder.

A majority of the police court cases arose among the black and white poor, whose frustrations and personal misfortune led to incidental violence, rowdiness, or the mischief of idle hands. Half the cases in a typical month were for disorderly conduct, assault and battery among family or friends, shooting craps, vagrancy, and loitering. Other common offenses were petit larcenies such as the theft of chickens and carrying concealed weapons. Although local news reports indicated that only African Americans were in the city's "monkey cage" for misbehaving, the accused in Judge Black's court often included at least four whites for every six blacks. But, no more than four of every hundred prisoners were white women.

The court's clerk was an Irishman with a brogue as thick as Birmingham's smog. He gave the judge a new title during an early session of court. When a defendant asked the name of this new judge, the Irishman whispered Black's Christian name. "Hugh-Go-L," the Irishman exclaimed. Offended, the accused man replied, "You go to hell, yourself!" Thus Black became Judge "Hugo-to-Hell." The title stuck, perhaps because at least two of every three defendants during Black's tenure were sent to work in chain gangs on city streets.

Black's judicial tenure coincided with a flood of prohibition cases. A. O. Lane's orders to enforce the liquor law or leave the police force prompted Birmingham officers to increase the number of "probi" arrests from 31 to more than 150 within a month. After four months, the number of prohibition cases reached 326 in July 1911; with arrests for drunkenness, they were a fourth of the total docket.[19]

With a true believer's tenacity, Judge Black became the chief lawgiver for a bone-dry Birmingham. "90/90" was the usual notation on his docket book in prohibition cases: $90 in fines and ninety days in jail. For owners of "blind tigers," the makeshift barrooms in houses and huts that served dangerous bootleg whiskey, Black usually stiffened the fines to the maximum: $500 and ninety days in jail. In the case of a young Negro couple operating a blind tiger for less than a day before their arrest, Black levied fines of $100 each. "Two hundred dollars a day is going some!" protested their lawyer, habituated to token fines. Judge Black also worked hard to find guilt beyond a reasonable doubt. When the police recovered nothing more than an empty glass and flask smelling of whiskey, Judge Black didn't hesitate to conclude that its owners were guilty not only of consuming, but also of selling illegal liquor.

Many of the accused realized this new jeopardy and began enlisting attorneys. Defense lawyers were especially fond of quashing liquor charges by proving that the policeman did not know that the substance sold at the time of arrest was, in fact, alcoholic. If a police officer went by the appearance of a confiscated bottle, a defense lawyer showed that there was no real evidence of possession since his client could have placed anything in a used liquor bottle. "I must have evidence to convict," Judge Black scolded policemen. Because the court had no prosecuting attorneys, Black was part prosecutor and part judge in these cases, and in both roles he was frustrated by the new defense strategies. "When you make an arrest," Black told the police, "be sure you sample the stuff."

"Why, judge, you don't mean for us to drink some of it?" responded an officer who protested that everything from embalming fluid, furniture polish, and red paint was being sold and consumed as whiskey.

"I did not mean," Black explained, "for you to drink it all; just sample it."

"Suppose a policeman is a prohibitionist, what should he do?" another asked.

"I admit having a strong imagination," Judge Black responded, "but some things are beyond my conception . . . smell it. A man does not have to make a hog of himself to determine what a bottle contains."

More than individual convictions were at stake. In early July, the city's local optionists petitioned to hold a new referendum to repeal countywide prohibition, and the election was set for August 24. Labor lawyer C. P. Beddow, the First Baptist Church's Reverend Alfred Dickinson, and Borden Burr, one of Birmingham's few corporate lawyers in favor of prohibition, led the opposition. The Saloon Opposition League dispatched speakers, held "dry dollar dinners," and rallied Protestant voters.

Even before the campaign emerged, however, anti-prohibition leaders had orchestrated a winning strategy, one in which Hugo Black unwittingly played a pivotal role. As Judge Black enforced county prohibition in the city, Birmingham's wets used his convictions to prove that prohibition was a failure. Declaring that regulated saloons were the only hope for a return to law and order, local optionists argued that aggressive law enforcement did not curtail liquor consumption and often turned otherwise innocent young men into liars and criminals. Judge Lane issued reports showing that police officers and the police court could not create a dry environment, no matter how many arrests and convictions they obtained. Citing figures covering Black's judgeship, Lane noted that 559 of Judge Black's 668 guilty verdicts in prohibition cases were appealed to the circuit court where they waited on the docket for months or years. In addition, only 109 cases in recent years had resulted in final convictions after jury trials.

"The reason why blind tigers will never be suppressed is the indifference of the jurors," Lane stated. "I have made an earnest and sincere effort . . . to eradicate the blind tigers . . . but I am of the opinion that they will never be . . . until whiskey is placed where men can get it without violating the laws." Each of Birmingham's new commissioners endorsed Lane's call for regulated saloons as did Chief of Police George Bodeker.

Because of Judge Black's court, the dry camp no longer could argue that the city simply needed honest enforcement to make prohibition work. Their oldest, best argument for why prohibition wasn't working—a failure of good faith law enforcement—had been emasculated in large part by the work of a young, sincere, prohibitionist judge.

Black did not endorse Lane's views. In late July, as the campaign intensified, he stiffened penalties in liquor cases. According to a local reporter, fines in his court increased "daily at a greater rate than the interest on an advanced loan by a money shark." Yet, Judge Black was atypically silent on the referendum, and in August, the crucial period of the dry campaign, Black left Birmingham for a month of vacation.

Black's decision to skip town may have been motivated by a sense of loyalty to Judge Lane, although friends and associates in Alabama often differed publicly on the liquor question. Walker Percy, for example, was an outspoken "wet" while his law partner, Borden Burr, was a rabid dry leader. Therefore, it is likely that a mix of both personal loyalty and awakening political ambition motivated Black's absence. Three weeks before the referendum, from Barney Whatley's new home in Colorado, Black wrote an open letter to the *Birmingham Age-Herald,* a leading voice for regulated saloons. He made no mention of prohibition. Instead, Black reported on the popularity of Birmingham's own U.S. Congressman Oscar W. Underwood among Colorado Democrats. Black called for a national conference in Birmingham to plan the nomination of Underwood for president. Underwood was chairman of the powerful House Ways and Means Committee and a self-proclaimed local optionist. His friends were promoting him in the upcoming 1912 presidential campaign as the first serious Democratic candidate from the South since Reconstruction. In effect, at a moment when Birmingham grappled with its most divisive political issue, one that had ruled his own life, Judge Black chose to evade the pending controversy. Instead, he allied himself publicly with a popular movement to nominate a local optionist for president. On election day, voters reopened Birmingham's licensed saloons, while Hugo Black was in Breckenridge, Colorado, visiting his old friend Barney who was alive, well, and still enjoying an occasional drink.[20]

After Black returned home in early September, without bone-dry prohibition to enforce, he continued to receive frequent, favorable coverage from the *Age-Herald,* whose court reporter was captivated by how the judge handled black folks' misfortunes. Two or three times weekly, Judge Black was featured in news stories, often accompanied by small sketches of scenes from his courtroom. The reporter found great humor in ignorance, pathos, and misery among Birmingham's black poor and rendered his stories with a novelist's imagination, a racist's ear for dialect, and a careful cataloguing of the different hues of black skin, which the reporter described as "yellow," "saffron-colored," "ebony," "chocolate-colored," "printer's ink" and "son of midnight."

In a society where wealth, health, and education were denied to almost half the local population on account of race, stories of Judge Black's court blended folk humor and prevailing racist perspectives, an ordinary mixture in the everyday experience of early twentieth century America. In one article, "A Study In Black," John Adams was accused of using a billiard stick to assault "a gingercake 'complected person.'" The defendant admitted the assault, but insisted that the victim had "personified" him.

"Jedge, ah doesn't deny lambastin' dat yaller pusson," Adams reportedly testified, "but, jedge, ah was jest 'bliged der do hit, 'cause he cast recollections on ma color dat no gemmen could pos'bly stand . . . he called me a eight rock."

"An eight rock: what in the name of the Seven Sunderland Sisters do you mean?" Judge Black demanded.

"Why, jedge, ain't you' neveh played pool . . . Da eight rock, jedge, is de black ball."

"Well of all the—," Black muttered. "Well, John, much as I realize the proneness of human beings to resent untrue remarks about their personal appearance, I am of the opinion that so far as your color . . . [the victim] was about correct . . . Unless I am color blind, your complexion puts to shame the raven's wing, or Egypt's darkness, polished ebony, or carved jet . . ." The defendant was sentenced to $100 in fines and one hundred days at hard labor in the mines "during which time you will have ample opportunities to carry out any scheme you may devise to preserve the darkling hues of your coal black frontispiece."

In dealing with the black community's multitude of problems, Judge Black was often practical, paternalistic, and even-handed, even if published reports suggest that he always seemed to be speaking to the *Age-Herald's* white readers as much as to the black defendants. Judge Black took seriously black-on-black assaults, which usually prompted one of his harshest penalties. He surprised the courtroom and a reporter when he released eleven African Americans after deciding that white police officers' testimony was insufficient to prove disorderly conduct beyond a reasonable doubt. The case did not involve life or death, but Black's decision broached a danger considered equally grave in Southern society. "With all due respect," the reporter reminded Judge Black, "a negro's testimony does not go very far against that of a white man, especially if he happens to be an officer" of the court. Yet, in Black's courtroom it went far enough at times to free the accused, regardless of color, under color-blind standards of justice.

Domestic disputes tested Judge Black's tolerance. "That's just the way with you people," the Judge scolded a black woman, "you have your man arrested and put the officers and court to all kinds of trouble and then try to shield him when brought to trial." The woman had denied the charges she made when her husband was arrested. Bachelor Black also lectured black lovers on the proper terms of "connubial happiness" before issuing fines of $10 for disorderly behavior. Shysters and folk healers met a particularly harsh fate in the police court. Judge "Hugo-to-Hell" gave fines of $140 and 130 days of hard labor to a black man dressed as a woman caught in a game of bait and fleece. He dismissed the eyewitness testimony of a black man after learning that he was a "digger of roots" trying to cure disappointed lovemaking. "I would not convict a poodle dog on your testimony," the former medical student told the man. "If you are brought before me on a charge of hoodooing any of your race out of their hard earnings," the judge continued, "you will be given an opportunity . . . not in digging roots but that strata of geological formation that has made this district famous"—coal.

In another case, when the judge learned that a white "Dr. Frenchy" had sold three-cent healing charms for $7.50, Black lectured the defendant on selling "this trash to ignorant negroes" and gave the white man a sentence of $75 and ninety days of hard labor. In a case where more than a hundred blacks appeared in court to vouch for the curative powers of a black faith healer, the judge threw up his hands in disgust: "If you negroes want to be flim-flammed out of your money by this faith healer, it suits me. He is dismissed."[21]

Judge Black often enforced white society's law against idle black hands. The common wisdom in white society was articulated by Police Chief George Bodeker: "The negro vagrants cause more trouble in a city than all the other criminal classes combined . . . From this class are drawn the sneak thieves . . . the purse snatchers, and other petty criminals." Periodically, Birmingham's police rounded up idle men on the streets during a workday or late at night when workingmen should be at home. In court, if an African American or white male did not demonstrate that he had a steady job, Black gave him "two months of employment" on the city's chain gang.

When a white man's self-described past employment of "light lifting" turned out to be pick-pocketing, the judge gave him sixty days on the chain gang so he could make "a daily tour of the city with a broom" cleaning streets. When hobos were arrested in camp at the rail tracks, Black gave them sixty days of forced work on the city's roads if they couldn't show that they had a local job lined up. Black pressed jobless men into city work so often that the *Age-Herald* referred to the police court as "Judge Black's employment agency" where "jobs are always open."

The police court clerk's blackboard also listed, on average, thirty to forty cases against white women arrested for prostitution although the local reporter never discovered anything newsworthy in these cases. In Birmingham, sex for hire was legal within designated establishments of the "red light district," just south of the railroad tracks. Women who operated too late at night, solicited on the streets, or opened houses outside the district were arrested and brought before Judge Black, who found most guilty.

Black was something of a "juris prude" on and off the court, in large part because he measured all white women by his mother's examples of simple correctness, self-restraint, and Biblical goodness. In a locally celebrated case,

Judge Black fined a young white couple for kissing in a public park, although he allowed the woman to pay a smaller fine since a kiss was "naturally worth less to her." Black assured the public that he didn't want to outlaw romance or kissing, for his own sake, but he was obliged to enforce the local ordinance against such a public display of affection. Black applied the laws of prudery to all. The young man Black fined may have been a distant nephew of Hugo's friend, Herman Beck.

As a bachelor, Judge Black complained about the modern woman's fashions. Her hats were so large that they could serve as umbrellas during a rain shower and her gigantic hairpins could impale male companions like harpooned whales, Black insisted. Yet, when a mother appealed to the mercy of the court or a son justified his conduct as necessary to care for his sick mother, Black was always forgiving and uncharacteristically lenient.[22]

By the middle of 1912, at age twenty-six with only a year on the bench, Judge Black had become one of Birmingham's emerging, visible civic leaders. His breezy humor and fashionable speech cut a youthful, modern image, but it was his combining of public relations with public justice, comic dicta with common sense, that made good copy. The *Age-Herald* now called him "the presiding genius of the recorder's court." Unknown and ignored by the press and public leaders months earlier, Black's presence at public functions was now sought after. He was among the men who gathered to select a slate of delegates to support Oscar Underwood at the Democratic National Convention during the summer. He joined the Country Club where men of influence congregated. In Clay County, local citizens beseeched him as a celebrity to umpire the annual Fourth of July baseball game. After friend Harry Yockey and Black barely escaped food poisoning at a local diner, the *Age-Herald* treated its readers to a glimpse of the injudicious, sickened disposition of their "eminent jurist."

Black's standing in the fraternity of men also began to rise visibly. Along with William E. Fort, a new circuit judge appointed by his old boss, Governor Comer, Black was one of the "prominent men" on the program for a local Pythians' banquet. As a noted bachelor, Black spoke on the issue of "the Ladies." Judge Black represented all Birmingham members at the Masons' regional meeting.

At home, Black's roommates lampooned their new celebrity, the only prohibitionist among them, by elevating him to supreme court judge in a "death penalty" case against one of their own charged with drinking milk in their presence. The defendant must have pleaded that his mother taught him to drink cow's milk, since Judge Black spared his life.[23]

In truth, Black's court established a new local standard of performance that pleased both local reformers, including industrial leaders, and Birmingham's commissioners struggling with the city's budget. No longer did defendants, including black industrial workers, languish in the city jail for weeks awaiting trial on misdemeanor charges. Judge Black gave every accused person a chance for a hearing usually within twenty-four hours. Justice in the police court was swift and efficient. Judge Black was proving that local governments could dispose of cases fairly and much faster at a savings of at least $12,000 a year. Black also gave the city a more just system since defendants who were declared not guilty—usually one out of every four in police court—did not have to spend several weeks in forced labor awaiting trial.

Judge Black showed how well local courts could do without a fee system at exactly the right moment, as Birmingham business leaders spearheaded a renewed effort to end Jefferson County's system. Leading the charge, U.S. Steel's Walker Percy said the fee system had made the Jefferson sheriff the richest public official in the South. No longer fearing labor unions, the local Chamber of Commerce supported dismantling fee practices, which disrupted the control of an essential workforce. "As a result of these practices," observed Sloss-Sheffield Steel and Iron Company's vice president, "the larger industries are handicapped often for help." It had become common practice for corporations to buy "protection" for their black workers by paying constables not to arrest African Americans for petty offenses or to pay an "on-the-spot cash bond," a term invented to hide the reality of a bribe given to arresting officers who failed to take the suspect into custody. In other instances, corporations paid fines and court costs for employees and later docked their pay.

In early 1912, a local grand jury issued a special report condemning the backlog of thousands of cases in the circuit courts due to "the iniquitous evil of the grasping fee system." Jurors recommended the impeachment of a justice of the peace who showed "a most shameless abuse of the fee system," and sharply criticized H. P. Heflin, county solicitor: "only 25 percent of the cases disposed of resulted in convictions," in Heflin's office, and Heflin had convicted only six of forty-four persons indicted for murder in 1911.

The grand jury also criticized Judge Black. Jurors believed he was soft on vagrants, whom they considered "loafing leeches upon the community" and the prime cause of the city's petty crimes. "We . . . urge the police department to inaugurate a ruthless campaign against the vagrants and that Judge Black impose a sentence instead of a fine, which is tantamount to a license to carry on their nefarious practices."

The fee system's beneficiaries saw an opportunity and joined the attack on Black. They charged that Judge Black had achieved efficiency and haste at the expense of an accused person's right to a fair hearing. They noted that in a recent session Black disposed of 150 cases in 150 minutes. Both Lane and the *Age-Herald*, Black's new public relations agent, rushed to his defense. They noted that Judge "Hugo-to-Hell" presided over a large number of guilty pleas, which were quick and routine, and heard testimony in only about fifteen cases each day. They argued Black's swift justice was far better than the fee system's delayed injustice.

In the fall of 1912, as Birmingham's reformers gained the upper hand on issues of money and justice, Black decided to resign. "Judge Lane finally agreed that the wisest thing for me to do at that time would be . . . to devote more time and attention to my law practice," Black recalled. After a year and a half of adulatory publicity, Black's image as a remarkable local judge had greatly enhanced his public reputation. Now, he wanted to build a prosperous law practice on the basis of his talent and his elevated community standing.

On October 22, Black's last day in the police court, the bailiff announced the arrest of "Hugo-to-Hell" on the charge of "abandonment." Chief of Police Bodeker presented the "case" against Black. "Judge, the police department and other friends in the city hall have decided to 'watch' you as you leave . . . and as a mark of the high esteem in which you are held by the police department," the chief stated, "I present on their behalf this watch." It was an open-faced pocket watch encased in solid gold, a gift that Black treasured. Decades later, the timepiece helped Judge Black recall days when he was revered, rather than despised, by the police over whose conduct he ruled. It was also a keepsake for remembering a key period in his career when he emerged from obscure, uncertain subsistence.

Usually given to exaggeration, Chief Bodeker was unknowingly prescient this day when he told Black: "We wish you every success and some day to see you in a much higher judicial position than that which you have so ably filled."[24]

3

'A Dern Sight More Snakes Than You Can Kill'

FIGHTING FOR FAIRNESS

After eighteen months in the dank courtroom at the rear of city hall, Judge Black (as his clients and colleagues continued to call him) was now completely at home in Birmingham. At one with the city's restless, contentious nature, Black had a natural love for the excitement and profits of warring with words, and as both a young bachelor and an aggressive lawyer he used every opportunity to argue, especially if the disagreement could lead to advancing his station and emerging ideals.

Given back his weekday mornings, Black joined thirty young men in early 1913 to organize the city's debating and literary society. Like the group in Ashland Black had attended, this society promoted "self-improvement through the study and debate of questions of a practical nature." At the group's charter meeting at the YMCA building, Judge Black was elected chairman. Later, when politics took hold, Black debated the question of whom Alabama should elect the coming year to the U.S. Senate: Spanish American War hero and prohibitionist Richmond Hobson or Birmingham's own Congressman Oscar W. Underwood. Black argued for Hobson's candidacy. And in a mock trial at Woodlawn city hall, Judge Black represented a young lady who modestly claimed an injury of $50,000 for breach of the most important promise a bachelor could make to an eligible woman in those days. The pretend jury gave Black's client full damages, but the verdict was overturned by popular demand. The case was retried several times before Sunday schools in local Methodist churches.

On Sunday mornings when not arguing before Methodists, Black rose around five o'clock to prepare a discussion for the Barraca Sunday school class at the First Baptist Church. Seldom did he prepare a full lecture. His role was to present a topic, offer a forceful, often unconventional perspective, and spark a spirited discussion among Baptist men who were free to make their own decisions. Sunday school instruction was Black's tribute to his mother's religious devotion and his own contribution to a "moral and spiritual force that builds up the moral fiber of community life." His classes were topical and lively, and they often drew more adults than did Dr. Dickinson's lofty sermons.

On Sunday afternoons, Black joined a parade of bachelors, including his new friend Albert Lee Smith, to Woodlawn, East Lake, and other Birmingham suburbs, as the city's young men went courting. In spacious parlors of new suburban homes, with carefully trimmed lawns, the mothers of young, unmarried women stacked plates high with delicious cakes, snacks, and other nonalcoholic refreshments for eligible men who called unannounced, usually in pairs or triplicates. Conversations were silly and teasing but proper fun. In this venue, Judge Black was as vain and foolish as any young man of twenty-seven—and sometimes more so. One young lady thought Black had no sense at all because he was always so silly and carefree. Yet, even in these surroundings, Hugo could not resist his first love. Time and again, Black entertained hostesses by debating Albert Lee or another friend on such pressing topics as who was the greater man, Twiddledee or Twiddledum.[1]

Albert Lee Smith was from a family of college presidents. His father had served as president of Howard College, a Baptist school in East Lake. Black met Smith at church, and the two quickly became buddies. Like Barney Whatley, Albert Lee was a "mixer" by nature. He sold business insurance and had as many reasons as Black to go to parlors, lodges, and the country club. Both men were habitually underweight and together might not have weighed 250 pounds. They also shared a fancy for stylish clothes, expensive automobiles, and long cigars. Despite the noxious smoke often encircling them, the two bachelors were known at country club dances as "visitors' delight," always available as dates for young women from out of town. Neither had a serious romance. One young lady who visited, before she married the budding young writer F. Scott Fitzgerald, was Zelda Sayre from Montgomery, daughter of a state supreme court justice and, according to Black's memory, the "raciest woman I ever met."

Both Albert Lee and Hugo were ambitious, hard-working, and smart. They understood that they could help one another in their separate professions. With acumen about property, Albert Lee helped Black invest in local real estate as his bank account grew. In turn, Black helped Smith sell policies. On a Christmas trip to Clay County, for example, Hugo told Albert Lee: "Take your rate book. We'll sell some insurance." Black introduced Albert Lee to every businessman around the Ashland square. It must have been a powerful introduction from the young lawyer who lost everything because he had *no* insurance after the great fire of 1907. "Finally wound up that I could brag there wasn't a store on the square that I didn't have on one or more policies," recalled Smith.

As this new friendship prospered, Black's law partnership dissolved due to incompatibility. David J. Davis no longer could stay in a practice where the other partner was responsible for generating virtually all the business and trying all the cases. Before his recent marriage, David J. had enjoyed occasional quiet nights with Hugo in their bachelor apartment, taking turns reading aloud Gibbon's *Rise and Fall of the Roman Empire* and other serious works. But Black's domineering role at the office, despite its financial advantages for a new Davis family, was too much for this proud, reserved man whose own ambitions and self-respect were being overwhelmed. In Black's words, because of his partner's "eminent sense of fairness," Davis wanted out. The men remained devoted friends, mutually helpful and admiring, but Davis apparently understood that his friendship with Black needed more space and independence than a law partnership permitted.[2]

From new offices a block west of the courthouse, Black engaged a young lawyer, one of many over the years, as an associate to handle office paperwork while Black tried cases. Black's growing success before local juries had begun to have a multiplying effect, generating more income and more clients. Yet, his new clients were usually like his old ones—poor and poorly paid workers. Many were African Americans. Most endured problems, injuries, or the death of loved ones involving railroads, insurance companies, or coal and mining companies. In each case he won, Black received a third to one-half of the jury award. But, success at trial did not translate into immediate cash. In many cases, corporate lawyers appealed to higher courts, suspending or eventually overturning the jury's decision. As a result, Black traveled frequently to Montgomery to argue that the Alabama Supreme Court should uphold decisions of a Birmingham trial judge and jury.

One particular case illuminates both Black's talents before a jury and his formidable difficulties with the state's conservative highest court. Black represented a young white couple in Gracies, a small mining village south of the

Birmingham area. On a bitterly cold, windy night, the day after Christmas 1909, the couple traveled home with their baby on the L&N train after visiting relatives, only to watch their station pass in the dark. "The train stopped at Gracies," Black's client testified, "what might be called a quarter of a minute," far too little time for a miner, his wife, and their one-year-old child to exit. To reach home from the next stop near Birmingham, W. F. Cornelius walked five miles with wife and child wrapped only in his thin coat in "very cold, high wind" across Red Mountain. He could not afford $6.50 to rent a horse and buggy. No one suffered permanent injury, but the mother was "sick and sore" for a few weeks. Black asked a jury to order the railroad to pay his clients $1,999 for damages both actual and "exemplary"—for wrongs done to his clients due to wanton or evil acts by the defendant. Twelve white male jurors in Birmingham deliberated and awarded the Cornelius family more than $1,000.

Stunned, attorney Hugh Morrow appealed on the railroad's behalf, and the Alabama Supreme Court reversed the award. "It does not matter how skillfully a plaintiff may state, in his complaint, a case of action for simple negligence," the Court lectured, "he can recover nothing . . . unless . . . he offers some evidence of the negligence." The Court declared that there was not one scintilla of evidence upon which a jury could justify awarding exemplary damages.

Black retried the case before a second Birmingham jury. This time, Black's client was only Nannie, W. F. Cornelius's wife. A Southern working class woman, the white plaintiff sought only actual damages for the inconvenience and anguish of her ordeal at the hands of the railroad. Black amended his complaint to enlarge his request for damages to $2,999.

At trial, both a female passenger (a second miner's wife) and a local miner who met the train at Gracies vouched for Cornelius's story. The train did not come to a full halt at the Gracies/Calera. In defense, Hugh Morrow called three witnesses. The L&N flagman testified that the train stopped for at least forty-five seconds at the Gracies/Calera depot. Under cross-examination, the witness denied that it was "custom" for the train to skip a stop at Gracies and other smaller depots whenever it needed to restore its schedule. Black asked the witness why he did not put a stepping stool on the ground at Gracies/Calera for his client and other ladies getting off the train. "We would put one there at a lady's request or put one there for an older person," the flagman replied. But, he added, "I never use one at Calera."

A male passenger traveling to Montgomery testified the train definitely came to a full stop at the depot, but under Black's questioning he admitted that he "may" have been talking to his wife at the time and, no, he could not say how long the train actually stopped. The conductor was the defense's final witness. He asserted that the train stopped an ample time for exiting, at least a minute and a half, and recalled that other passengers in another train car easily got off at Calera. Yet, in answering Black's questions, the conductor acknowledged that the "others" were a white straw boss and his "section negroes, a floating gang of negroes" who repaired rail lines. Yes, the conductor confessed, "Some negroes might have gotten up before the train stopped" although he stubbornly denied that railroad men were able to exit trains faster than women with children. Finally, the conductor admitted the train was late for its scheduled arrival in Montgomery.

Before final arguments, Black asked the court to instruct jurors to disregard the testimony he elicited from defense witnesses about the railroad's "custom" whenever it was running late. This was a plaintiffs' attorney's cunning for having it both ways, for both making a suggestive point to a jury about what really was going on in a case and later removing it from the record to guard against grounds for appellate reversal. The jurymen got Black's meaning and awarded his client an even larger judgment of $1,250—more than four times W. F. Cornelius's yearly pay.

For a second time Hugh Morrow appealed and Black's verdict was overturned. The Alabama Supreme Court ruled that the trial court admitted improper hearsay testimony. At trial, the circuit judge allowed Mr. Cornelius to repeat his conversation with the railroad's flagman after the train moved away. "I asked him why he did not stop the train long enough for me to get off," Cornelius had testified, "and he said he did, and I told him we did not have time to get off." This part of the testimony, declared Justice Anthony D. Sayre, "was a narrative by the parties to the conversation, and from their respective viewpoints of a transaction then past was hearsay and should not have been allowed."

Justice Sayre's holding is an example of how tortured prose and inexplicable logic were dressed up as complex legal doctrine so that an appeals court could have grounds to reverse a jury verdict it simply did not like. Legalistic nonsense about hearsay testimony often was used for this purpose. In this case, both the flagman and Cornelius testified, although with different stories, about the same conversation in response to probing questions from both lawyers.

Without testimony as "narrative" about past conversations, almost no plaintiff could carry the burden of proof.

The real reason for Sayre's reversal is found in his opinion's dicta. Exasperated by the very existence of this case, Sayre lectured Black, the lower court, and Birmingham juries about the legal and practical duty of a railroad serving the general public. The L&N is not obligated to "hold its train at its stopping place," Justice Sayre wrote, "while plaintiff slept, chatted with other passengers, or loitered on the way, before exercising herself to get off." Nothing at trial or in the record submitted to the high court suggested these facts as a part of this case. They were fabricated entirely by the conceit of a judge who assumed a great deal more about the irresponsible, indolent character of Nannie Cornelius and other lower-class white women than the record before him revealed. Justice Sayre clearly agreed with the L&N flagman when he testified, in effect, that he never put down a stepping stool at the Gracies/Calera stop since a Southern "lady" never got off there.

This scorn for poor, working whites had a long history in Sayre's public career. Two decades earlier, as a state legislator he authored the Sayre Election Act which disfranchised many poor, illiterate white voters during the Populist revolt, and, now as an emerging intellectual leader of the state's highest court, Sayre was forever vigilant in preserving Old South notions of honor, conservatism, and justice as the governing framework for interpreting Alabama law. Like Clay County's Hiram Evans, Sayre wore striped, diplomatic trousers and a black Prince Albert jacket, signets of his identity as a true Southern man of the old order. His family tree blossomed with Confederate tradition. His wife's father served in the Confederate Congress, and his own uncle built the Confederate White House in Montgomery. His sister was married to Senator John Tyler Morgan, a former Confederate general and Alabama's U.S. senator since Reconstruction.

While his young rebellious daughter, Zelda, was already making herself into a dazzling icon of the modern woman, Justice Sayre had little interest in anyone or anything except his duty to embody and uphold the old South's patriarchal notions of justice. Even his wife addressed him in private only as "Judge." Sayre did not own a house since he refused to be indebted to anyone, and he declined to campaign for election, leaving that chore to political friends—mostly corporate lawyers. Apparently, Sayre resisted any direct contact with or overt obligation to common white people. By all accounts, Sayre was a "living fortress" against the winds of a new, more democratic white South. Six days a week, sitting across from a wall map of Alabama's railroad lines in a Spartan-like office at the Alabama Supreme Court, on the second floor of the state capitol where Confederate President Jefferson Davis took his oath of office, Sayre was Alabama's premiere guardian and giver of Old South law. In 1913, and later, Justice Sayre had no intention of allowing a jury of common white men, a wily attorney named Hugo Black, and a poor white woman feigning to be a "Southern lady" to corrupt the old virtues which ruled his holdings, much of Alabama law, and by his lights all of "Southern civilization."

Yet the state's highest court made oblique exceptions to Old South customs if the issues endangered current privileges of property. In another case, Black represented a free black miner, Sam Bradford, who was injured when a roof caved on top of him. An all-white jury awarded Bradford damages, but Walker Percy's firm appealed on behalf of the mining company to the Alabama Supreme Court which struck down the award because the trial judge had charged the jury in error on the law. The evidence at trial showed that Bradford's white supervisor ignored the black man's concern about the mine's unsafe roof, but the Court held that the trial judge should have instructed jurors that Bradford as a miner was partially responsible for his own injury since he knowingly continued to work in a dangerous area.

Alabama's highest court put Bradford literally between a falling rock and a hard place. His real-life choices were: disobey a white supervisor's instructions—and face certain dismissal for violating a longstanding custom of Southern race relations—or bear partial responsibility for his own injury in a rock slide.[3]

Perhaps the Court's reasoning was formed by its own dismay that white jurors in segregated Birmingham disregarded another sacred Southern custom. To render Bradford a cash award, white jurors had to decide, in part, that they believed a black miner's testimony over that of his white foreman. This was no mean achievement, and it reflected the developing talents of Bradford's lawyer. Hugo Black's ability at times to get a white jury to abandon Southern customs seemed to come from a second sense, an innate understanding about how to express the real meaning of a case through examining witnesses and final arguments. Black often expanded issues beyond the circumstances of his client, and over the course of a trial he convinced white men that they and their white neighbors had a stake in the fate of his black client. It was their white self-interest in "equal justice for all and special privilege for none" that was at issue in favorable verdicts for many of his clients.

In the Nannie Cornelius case, Black knew that the jury would be suspicious of L&N railroad agents in a case involving train stops since small communities throughout the county had been fighting railroads' attempts to cut down the number of train stops. In the mining case, Black seemed to recognize that some jurors would believe what UMW officials recently had preached in Birmingham—that in local mines the perils of the black worker set the standards of law and fairness visited upon the white worker. No lawyer or observer who knew Alabama's courtrooms has ever articulated exactly how Black employed his second sense for guiding jurors' impressions and views to win cases, but both mounting awards in Birmingham courtrooms and repeated reversals in Montgomery were differing but indisputable proof that this talent existed in gathering abundance. Judge Black's earnings from his law practice in 1913 were more than $7,000, even after most of the largest awards were reversed. It was an impressive income at a time when the city's L&N trainmen took home around $300 a year.

The most intriguing proof of Black's sizable abilities came on a day in late 1913 when Hugh Morrow came to Black's office to offer him a full partnership in his corporate firm, the largest in the state. Representing a long list of corporations, Morrow and his partners who faced Black in the Cornelius case wanted his talents on their side. The offer convinced Black that "I had actually arrived as a lawyer," although he graciously declined the offer. "I expressed some doubt as to whether I could enjoy a practice limited to that kind of trial work," Black recalled. He also informed Morrow that he was seriously considering giving up private practice to run for county solicitor.

The idea of becoming county prosecutor may have evolved out of several sources. The solicitor's post was a natural political step after a police court judgeship during which newspapers lavished praise on Black for his approach to law and order. The position would keep Black in the courtroom where he enjoyed the challenge of matching wits and skills with an opponent. In addition, Black's old friend, Barney Whatley, had been elected in late 1912 as a reform-minded district attorney for three rural counties in Colorado, and the success of one of the old "Rivals" may have sparked a thought with the other. Black also received encouragement from Judge William E. Fort, one of two circuit judges in Jefferson County's criminal division. A protégé of Governor

B. B. Comer, Fort believed that the county solicitor had to change if the mal-functioning local courts were to improve.

Black's interest in the job had nothing to do with money. Although the position paid $4,500 per year, Black would lose substantial income as county solicitor. State law permitted solicitors to conduct a private practice, but Black knew Jefferson's job would require all his energy and time. His best hope was to supplement his income from past jury awards, if some were settled or sustained by appeals courts throughout his four-year tenure. In any event, Black knew now that he could make a large income in Birmingham's courtrooms, and that knowledge seemed to free him from the immediate necessity to do so. By the end of 1913, Black decided to run.[4]

Daily headlines revealed the campaign's central issue: how to curtail the greed, inefficiencies, and unfairness that clogged the county's criminal courts. The fee system lingered like a parasite. Compounding its evils, deputy sheriffs and JPs had begun to pay Negro "spotters" to start card games or dice throwing on Sundays (the day after pay day) in order to set up arrests. Deputies defended the practice by claiming that spotters promoted law and order since they helped to arrest men who were prone to gamble illegally elsewhere.

"The fee system is the worst evil that we have to combat in this county," remarked Birmingham's Chief of Police George Bodeker, who tested public opinion for a race for sheriff. "It has always seemed preposterous to me," he said, "that the office of sheriff of Jefferson County should pay approximately the same as the office of the President of the United States." Judge Fort pointed out another insidious effect of the fee system. "I refer to the astonishing fact that witnesses, who are summoned and required to attend the criminal courts of this county are not paid in cash for their daily attendance," he stated, "but are forced to accept county script, payable out of the 'fine and forfeiture fund'" which was usually depleted since the fee system leeched onto numerous arrests and long imprisonment, not fines. Claims against the fund went back five years, Fort charged, and most witnesses sold their script to local speculators for as little as ten cents on the dollar. "How can we expect prompt trials for criminal cases when there is every inducement for a witness to avoid service?"

A month later, a grand jury in Judge Fort's court attacked the fee and script systems as "a great injustice" and complained that wholesale liquor dealers were dispatching wagons to the county's small mining and industrial towns where they illegally sold liquor. Jurors also repeated complaints about the city's vagrants. "85 or 90 percent of the six hundred or more cases investigated by us," they reported, "is due to the large number of worthless, loafing, able-bodied white men and negroes who will not work and who are permitted to idle their time away in the pool rooms, saloons, and public places." The grand jury charged that convict leasing was a primary cause of so many vagrants since many prisoners stayed in Jefferson without jobs after performing hard labor without pay in local mines.

The *Birmingham News* agreed. "Much has been said about convicts being dumped into Birmingham . . . and this has long been recognized as one of the elements entering into the increase of lawlessness." Urging tougher law and order, the paper concluded, "With the right kind of effort, Jefferson County can be made a place where respect for law is wholesome, and where violence is the exception rather the rule."[5]

Judge Black believed that the "right kind of effort" began by removing county solicitor Harrington Heflin, who had served in the post since before the century's beginning. Brother to U.S. Congressman Tom Heflin, a loquacious rabble-rouser representing east Alabama (including Clay County), Harrington was a large, slow man who shared none of Tom's raw charisma or devout opposition to liquor. As solicitor, Heflin had shown little interest in prohibition laws and scant energy in prosecuting a voluminous criminal docket despite stinging criticism from grand juries. The solicitor continued to leave much of the courtroom work to assistants and wasn't always at the courthouse when major criminal trials were tried.

The 1914 elections promised to be a baptism of fire for all incumbents in law enforcement. The sheriff declined to run for reelection, apparently believing that he and the fee system would be defeated. On the eve of the campaign, candidate George Bodeker was removed from office after Deputy Sheriff Conrad Austin charged that the police chief had received personal favors from owners of the city's bordellos and professional gamblers. Bodeker claimed prohibition opponents set him up, but City Commissioner George Ward declared that the community needed a new standard of conduct from all leaders. Candidates for the state legislature divided between wet and dry camps, but almost all supported dramatic reform in local courts.

Black's announcement of candidacy, which Judge Fort helped to write, tried to capture this spirit of reform. In a large newspaper ad entitled "To The People," Black declared that recent investigations, grand jury reports, "and public utterances of the Senior Judge of the criminal court [Judge Fort] have caused people to realize the conditions of our county and desire an improvement . . . The criminal records of this county demonstrate beyond doubt that the criminal element of Jefferson County does not fear the law." Black accused Heflin of claiming "the right to a life tenure of this office" contrary to democratic principles. "I challenge him," Black continued, "to tell the people why he has not convicted a sufficient number of murderers to decrease the frightful number of killings . . . The people should know," Black insisted.

A few weeks later, as Heflin's campaign posters appeared across the city, Black published another large, wordy ad entitled, "Black Challenges Heflin." "Our county has been advertised to the world as being a notorious resort of criminals," Black noted. "Our records show that there are more unlawful homicides in this country alone than in all of England, Ireland, and Scotland . . . Mr. Heflin states on his posters that he is seeking reelection . . . on his '**splendid record**.' I challenge him to meet me at any time and place he names to discuss that '**splendid record**'. . . The innocent defendant wants a trial," Black concluded, "and the guilty defendant should have a trial."

Black abandoned his law practice for six months and canvassed the county to shake hands and talk to people on the streets, in office buildings, and at country stores. His campaign involved one basic strategy: to meet and make enough new friends, one person at a time, to win. The solicitor's position was not important enough to draw much attention, much less a crowd for a rally. Therefore, Black's public speaking was often restricted to nonpolitical issues.

The literary society let Black show off his forensic abilities. Sunday school classes around the county helped him explain his moral positions to Baptists and Methodists. His service on the legal committee of the Boys Club put him in touch with active men and women concerned about homeless youth. His attendance and speeches at fraternal halls—Masons, Elks, Woodsmen, and even the "Dramatic Order of the Knights of Khorassan"—gave him a chance to add to his list of brethren and friends. Most useful were the Knights of Pythias, who had elected him to an office in the local lodge. Chapter meetings around the county and a district meeting in Birmingham in early 1914 kept Judge Black in contact with many active, influential men.

Two other candidates also qualified to oppose Heflin. F. D. McArthur was a young lawyer who practiced in criminal courts and had the support of local labor leaders. The other candidate, Z. T. Rudolph, was a seasoned attorney with twenty years experience and the support of many prestigious families. The handsome, stylish McArthur also campaigned against Heflin's record which, he claimed, showed less than a 20 percent conviction rate. But, he distanced himself from Judge Black. "I am making no effort," McArthur proclaimed, "to ride into office on my fraternal or lodge connections," which, nonetheless, he listed in his ads.[6]

By March, the campaign was in full blast for an April 6 primary election. Black peppered newspaper pages with four-inch ads showing his name, portrait, and a pithy phrase in small letters underneath. "HUGO BLACK" the ads shouted below a stern, youthful face whose sad eyes looked directly into the camera and whose brow seemed extraordinarily high due to his swept-back hair, parted almost squarely in the middle above a straight-lined nose. "Hugo Black can be found at the courthouse when he is elected solicitor . . . He believes the salary should be EARNED." Another small ad stated below his photograph: "The Gamblers Are Against This Man for Solicitor."

Heflin recoiled from the harsh criticism. In a quarter-page ad with tiny type, the solicitor rambled for a few thousand words in his own defense. "Some men seem willing to give Jefferson County a bad name here and abroad in an effort to get themselves elected to office," Heflin complained. He admitted that his conviction rate was not good, but he was helpless since the fee system prompted "so many worthless cases to prosecute." The blame for the county's problems lay with the sheriff's office, Heflin pleaded. "I am striving to do that which is best for the human family in Jefferson County."

Black's old law partner and friend Barney Whatley returned in good health to Birmingham to help campaign in the last month. Barney had moved to a rural mining section of Colorado after he read in the Denver newspapers that its entire bar association—one elderly man—had died. Now he was district attorney of three counties and maintaining a growing private practice. Whatley joined Albert Lee Smith, David J. Davis, and a few others as a campaign caucus to develop and implement final strategies for Hugo's election.

Black's friends knew that all three challengers to Heflin were running on a platform of reform. What, then, were Hugo's comparative advantages and strategies? Judge Black alone was an ardent prohibitionist with a public record on the issue, even if he quietly avoided the last referendum. Now, Black could count on most citizens who cast a "dry" ballot. In addition, Black's fraternal brothers and clients were a source of support. But, spread around the county, his working class clients were not always registered to vote, and a large number of them were in fact useless since "the hell of it was the colored people couldn't vote," Whatley complained. "If they could, he would have had . . . an almost unanimous election" in black precincts.

The important, uncertain voters were businessmen, professionals, shop-keepers, and merchants—spiritual descendants of W. L. Black, conservative men who supported an orderly, peaceful community in which to do business from the streets and office buildings. Some might tend towards Rudolph with his Birmingham lineage and family connections, but, if Black showed himself as qualified and capable by their standards, his youth and vigor might attract them. Finally, the candidate and his friends recognized that a vote for anyone except Hugo Black amounted to a vote for Heflin. Unlike statewide elections, county elections had no runoff. In Jefferson's local races, the candidate with the highest number of votes on April 6 would win, whether or not the total was a majority of votes. Black had to convince voters that Heflin would win if they split their votes too widely among three opponents.

At the end of March, Black's campaign appealed to conservative voters with a series of published endorsements from prominent citizens under Black's ever-present photograph. A. O. Lane, who had given Black his title of "Judge," declared: "I do not hesitate to recommend him to voters of this county." Another endorsement came from W. I. Grubb, formerly U.S. Steel's local counsel and now a U.S. district court judge by appointment of Republican President William Howard Taft. Judge Grubb affirmed that Black was "fully qualified and competent to fill the office."

Black and his friends also organized the Hugo Black Club. The "benefits of membership" were prosecution of the guilty and protection of the innocent. Club members collected petitions for Black and distributed campaign literature. By April 2, Black advertised that more than two thousand people, including prominent lodge leaders, were his club members.[7] In the week before the election, tens of thousands of small colored cards were printed and distributed. On both sides they stated in bold type: "**Black or Heflin—Which?**" Black ran the same question in small, bold ads throughout local papers.

In response, Rudolph published large newspaper ads with a long list of his local advisory committee, sparkling with prominent citizens like investors Robert Jemison and Hill Ferguson as well as several corporate lawyers, including one of Walker Percy's partners. The outgoing sheriff, a long-time beneficiary of the fee system, was also on Rudolph's committee of "reformers." Rudolph attacked Black as much as Heflin. "We promise you that if you elect Mr. Rudolph to this office, it will have dignity," the ad stated. On the following day, Black took up Rudolph's challenge. "Do not be deceived into thinking the results of an election can be changed in a day by long advertisements," Black assured supporters. "We will pile up a majority . . . This is your campaign, not mine. I am not backed by any monied interests, but by you."

Birmingham newspapers did not back Black's campaign. "For solicitor it appears to the *News* that the best fitted man is Mr. Z. T. Rudolph." The *Birmingham Ledger* agreed, while the *Age-Herald* endorsed no one. In response, Black issued a stinging Sunday sermon in an ad to "His Friends." "We have fought a good fight; we have kept faith with the people; and victory is ours . . . My campaign committee is not composed of a few capitalists or ring politicians but of hundreds of men in every walk of life . . . The time has passed when the result of an election can be changed by the mere stroke of an editor's pen," Black insisted. "I have not sought the endorsement of any newspaper, monied interest or lawless element . . . Mr. Heflin is still my only real opponent." On election eve, with the aid of the city's night watchmen, Black supporters entered every major office building in downtown and placed on every desk a second version of the little colored cards: **"Black or Heflin—Which?"**

While calling for a campaign on a "gentlemanly plane," Rudolph's large, expensive advertisements attacked Black by name on election day. "Mr. Hugo Black, in his wail of defeat in Sunday's paper, indefinitely insinuates that 'a few capitalists or ring politicians' have furnished the 'means' for the campaign . . ." These were "pitiable appeals and astounding claims" from a man rudely disappointed by not receiving the papers' endorsements, Rudolph claimed. "Only prejudice or *egotism* could ignore or be blind to the weight, influence, and propriety of these expressions of our press." In this way, Rudolph's committee members indirectly reminded Birmingham's voters of the street talk about "Ego" Black, as detractors called him. The ad also described Black as a man who ran both a law office and a campaign of "prejudice" (the term of Hiram Evans's attack on Populists thirty years earlier), trying to rally the masses against Birmingham's classes.

In his final campaign statement, the incumbent tried to copy Black's appeal. Heflin claimed that the "bitter and unfair fight" against him had failed because "men who earn their living by the sweat of their faces" knew that he "dared to prosecute the big criminals" and show "mercy to the poor and unfortunate."

Black won the primary election with 41 percent of the 16,576 total votes. Fewer than 7,000 voters had elected the new prosecutor. "Ego" led Heflin by more than 2,000 votes and Rudolph by more than 3,500 votes. "I want my friends to know that I more than appreciate their loyal support and influence," Black triumphantly stated. "I accept the result of the election as a protest of the people against existing conditions in the county . . . and I call upon the good citizens to cooperate with me in my efforts," concluded Black, as he and Barney Whatley retreated to the old home place in Ashland.[8]

SIX MONTHS AFTER HIS APRIL VICTORY, Democrat Black ran unopposed in the general election. The "other party" no longer offered local candidates in Jefferson, and its statewide slate had failed miserably in every election since W. L. Black was elected a conservative justice of the peace in 1878. Yet, joining Hugo Black on the ballot in the Democratic column, under the symbol of a banty rooster perched atop a banner proclaiming "White Supremacy," were politicians who held sharply differing views, philosophies, and interests on current issues—especially on "booze and business."

Charles Henderson, a local optionist, was a south Alabama member of the state railroad commission who became governor by defeating former Governor B. B. Comer. Although Comer led in the primary, he lost in a run-off election, a system recently adopted with wet-corporate support. In the same run-off, businessman Thomas E. Kilby was elected lieutenant governor, favoring prohibition, as did the newly elected attorney general William Logan Martin. The Alabama Anti-Saloon League also claimed it had helped elect enough dry Democratic legislators to pass statewide prohibition over any Henderson veto.

In the primary, Alabama voters had also nominated two opposing Democrats for the same seat in the U.S. Senate. Former governor Joseph F. Johnston had served as a U.S. senator from 1906 until he died in 1913, and oddly the Alabama legislature set up two elections to replace him. One was to fill the seat for the remainder of the current term, and the other was to elect a person for a full six-year term. To fill Johnston's "short shoes," Alabama elected Frank S. White, the old Comer confidante, union attorney, and Baptist prohibitionist. For a full term, voters elected U.S. Rep. Oscar W. Underwood, an opponent of strict prohibition and increasingly a friend of industrialists.

Forney Johnston, the late senator's son, managed Underwood's campaign.

Forney's peculiar stances in 1914 captured the shifting, befuddled character of Alabama politics. A brilliant, belligerent corporate lawyer with a wicked tongue, Johnston orchestrated virtually every statement and maneuver in Underwood's campaign against U.S. Rep. Richmond Hobson, a Spanish-American War hero and sponsor of national prohibition. Congressman Underwood was a boring public speaker who stayed on the job as Democratic majority leader in Washington. Forney Johnston became the campaign's protagonist—the virtual candidate. He authored the campaign book defining Underwood's issues and attacking Hobson's weaknesses. "Nothing finer as for its language, nothing more logical in its conclusions has ever been written in Alabama," praised one newspaper. Whenever Hobson attacked Underwood, Johnston responded. Whenever Hobson made a mistake, Johnston attacked. The majority leader stood as silent as a maiden in waiting while his shinning knight went to battle.

The Senate campaign quickly fell from any pretense of a "gentlemanly plane." Guided by his campaign manager, L. B. Musgrove, Representative Hobson called Underwood a "tool of Wall Street" and a stooge for the nation's liquor industry. Hobson's supporters whispered among Baptists and Methodists that Oscar, a confirmed Protestant, was really a Roman Catholic. In turn, Johnston attacked Hobson as an absentee Congressman who violated sacred principles of white supremacy. Johnston chronicled Hobson's votes to prevent discrimination against anyone wearing a soldier's uniform, including Negro soldiers; to allow Filipinos to go to West Point, a precedent Johnston said would allow "bushmen, stranglers, fast-backs, and Chinese mixtures" into America's armed forces; and to instigate an inquiry into whether white military commanders had wrongfully discharged a group of black soldiers. According to Johnston, Hobson also scandalously betrayed Southern society when he referred to African American jubilee dancers in Washington as "ladies and gentlemen of culture."

After Underwood's primary victory, Forney Johnston announced that "on personal grounds" he would vote for B. B. Comer in the run-off, even though Comer bitterly opposed the railroads and liquor clients whom Johnston represented. Comer had enabled the appointment of Forney's father to the U.S. Senate, and Johnston felt he was duty-bound by family honor to support the old prohibitionist. The political irony was especially poignant since Forney also represented the same interests his own father had opposed at the turn of the century. After Henderson defeated Comer, however, Johnston was free to join the governor-elect in an unsuccessful effort to have Forney's brother elected the legislature's speaker of the house over a prohibitionist candidate.[9]

It was a muddled moment in Alabama politics, as a new generation of diverse leaders with conflicting ideals emerged in the wake of bearers of past reform. Like Forney Johnston, Alabama voters seemed momentarily pulled in different directions by obligations to the past and ambitions for the future. Yet the 1914 election marked a point of passage, with the departure of three major leaders who had fought to reform Alabama politics since the end of Reconstruction. The governor's campaign had included Reuben Kolb who mysteriously reappeared after almost twenty years. Twice denied the governor's chair as a Populist by the hook and crook of W. L. Black's Democratic and Conservative Party, Kolb stood like a ghost of elections past, calling vainly for "peace after turmoil" and "a square deal for all people." Gone too was Joseph F. Johnston, the Alabama industrialist-banker who brought Populists back into the Democratic party and became the leading voice of protest against the constitutional convention of 1901.

B. B. Comer's political career also ended in 1914. Businessman Comer had led the state's progressive movement by bringing several white constituencies, divided during the Populist era, under one political tent against unfair railroad rates and for dry laws. Many prevailing candidates in 1914, including Charles Henderson, Frank White, Thomas Kilby, William Logan Martin, and even Hugo Black had begun their public careers in the Comer movement. Now, one of Comer's disciples had defeated him with the support of the railroads, his arch political enemy.

Although the leaders of past reform were ushered off stage, no one among the new generation of politicians was yet able to name the new age. At an earlier meeting, the state Democratic Executive Committee had argued endlessly about how a run-off election might affect Comer and shape Alabama politics. Almost everyone failed to understand that Comer did not create the political movement he led and that a run-off could end only his career—the political movement that often bore his name had deeper roots and gathered vitality from unmet human needs. Yet, one person from Hugo Black's past did understand. Martin Lackey, the whale-sized lawyer whom young Hugo had watched in amazement in the Clay County courthouse, spoke at the Democratic meeting like an Ancient Mariner. "Beware," Lackey cackled. In adopting a run-off, anti-progressive Democrats could defeat Comer, but in doing so they would stir up "a dern sight more snakes than you can kill" in Alabama politics.

As a candidate, Black stayed out of other races in 1914, but he too had divided loyalties within the privacy of the voting booth. Despite his absolutism on prohibition, Black voted for Oscar W. Underwood, opponent of prohibition and Hobson's "tool of Wall Street." [10] Like Forney Johnston and many Alabama voters, Black was pulled in different directions. Despite a growing reputation as the cocksure, domineering "Ego," Black held only a general notion of political leadership and public ideals in 1914. Running for solicitor, his position for "aggressive but fair and effective enforcement of the law" was almost self-revealing in the presence of a languishing Harrington Heflin and the overt evils of a fee system. In many respects, Black's opposition to a corrupt system defined at that moment all that a good solicitor should be.

Black voted for Underwood because he considered him the "best man for the job," a description that measured the politician by more than his positions on prohibition and corporations. At this juncture in his career, Black saw Underwood as a leader exercising honest independence—a central quality in Black's own evolving notion of statesmanship. Since childhood, in fact, these personal properties had moored Black's own ethical growth. Read. Think for yourself, Black's mother and sisters instructed him as a little boy. Be your own judge of the Bible and God's word, his Baptist church taught. "Do Right!" his teacher Lizzie Patterson commanded. Even W. L. Black, whose inability to live by his own words left a permanent scar on his last son, had shown Hugo the virtues of financial independence.

In Birmingham, A. O. Lane best embodied the attributes Black admired in politics. Lane had never been the workingman's candidate or the industrialist's voice. Lane stood as an independent judge amid Birmingham's warring factions. A man with "full sympathy for the weak and suffering," Lane lived among the wealthy. He was an opponent of prohibition, but an advocate for strictly enforcing prohibition laws when they existed. He was a friend of many powerful industrialists, but also the most articulate critic of Birmingham's increasingly corporate nature. Lane's personal independence, informed by a rooted sense of fairness, earned respect from most of the city's conflicting white communities and the gratitude of many poor African Americans. More than any other person, Lane inspired and embodied Black's sense of political leadership as "unselfish public service."

Measuring himself by this model, Judge Black served in the police court as A. O. Lane might have done when he was mayor and ex officio judge. In his law practice, Black turned down a prestigious corporate firm because he could not represent corporate clients who claimed that a Negro miner was responsible for his own injuries after he obeyed his white boss's orders to work an unsafe mine. As Judge Lane said in 1911, "The spirit of some corporations is simply 'to get out of everything.'" That was not fairness to Lane or to Black. Like his mentor, Black also enjoyed Birmingham's fashionable Southside society and belonged to its country club. His friends included successful professional men and those striving to be the next generation of managers of Birmingham capitalism—as well as common laborers, craftsmen, shopkeepers, and farmers. Black had come to believe that the only ethical way to build a political career was to win votes by winning people's friendship—to attract people's loyalty, respect, and support based on his honesty, talent, fairness, and independence which they could measure by his public and private life.

To try to stand astride different communities of interest in Birmingham seemed a natural and proper posture in 1914 for a man who in boyhood weaved in and out of both sides of his politically divided family and community, who attended services for every different church in town, who declared "I a Democrat" at the age of six but who found his best friend amid the family of a leading Populist at the age of twelve. To prize independence of thought came honestly to a lawyer who as a boy sat in judgment of the performance of opposing attorneys thrice his age.

Of course, issues mattered. For Black, whiskey was a plain evil. Fighting the injustices of corporations was an honorable livelihood. "Equal rights for all and special privileges for none" was a slogan with real meaning echoing the animating political message of his past and present. Comerism had been the political movement of his coming of age. But, the defining virtues Black sought in life, law, and politics were not so much opposition to booze and business, not really opposition to a corrupt fee system, and not even support for the basic notions of Populism or progressivism. Instead, Black sought the certainty of independence, honesty, and fairness as defining traits that he pursued with friends and neighbors in Sunday schools, courtrooms, campaigns, and now elective office. As Black stated after his election victory, "I shall go into the office absolutely free from . . . any trade, combination, or promise, except the promise to do my full duty."

Following a self-described "summer vacation" of reading criminal law, Black appointed three young attorneys and inherited two others to work in his office. He selected Walter Brower and William Welch as assistant solicitors. Brower had lost a close race for the state legislature, while Welch was elected as a legislator with the endorsement of local prohibitionists. Black chose his law school classmate Morris Allen as his assistant and stenographer. The other two assistant solicitors were Ben Perry of Bessemer and Joseph Tate, solicitor of the circuit court.

By peculiar statute and custom, Perry and Tate were Black's assistants in criminal cases although both were elected officials. Perry represented suburban Bessemer that had been given a quasi-autonomous county government with special deputies and an assistant solicitor who handled cases arising only in that area. Tate held an elective position that gave him co-equal authority with the county solicitor in civil cases but assigned him to work under Black's authority in criminal cases. Since Jefferson County constituted one discrete circuit, the county solicitor and the circuit solicitor were officers of the same jurisdiction. This legal arrangement was eccentric, but Black's new stationery made his view of the situation crystal clear. Listed among members of Black's staff was "Joseph Tate, circuit solicitor and ex officio *assistant* county solicitor."

Judge Black took office on December 1 and quickly realized that dramatic changes, far exceeding the hard work of five prosecutors, were necessary to set right Harrington Heflin's old criminal docket. More than three thousand cases were docketed for trial. Almost one hundred were murder cases. More than three hundred men sat in the county jail awaiting trial. Almost five thousand arrests were made yearly, and the grand juries usually indicted as many as seven hundred people every year. Black and Will Welch drafted bills that Welch would introduce in the legislature to authorize investigators and additional stenographers for the prosecutor's office. But the county solicitor boldly acted on his own. He recommended that Judge Fort dismiss almost five hundred cases immediately. "The greater number of these cases are against negroes charged with gambling or abusive language, who have been confined in jail for a period of time which constitutes adequate punishment," Black stated. He noted that two deputies, spurred by the fee system, had been responsible for most of the arrests.

By early 1915, Black's plan to clean up the jail, the docket, and Birmingham's crime took shape. The solicitor steered his first grand jury towards examining cases of serious crime—murder, assault with intent to kill, and burglary—to lessen the crowded docket of petty offenses. In an unusual interim report, Black's first grand jury recommended that the state legislature and governor abolish all positions of justices of the peace in Jefferson and replace them with one additional circuit judge. Black wanted to end the office his father once held since it generated petty "arrests for revenue only." In its final report, the grand jury also recommended ending convict leasing and the sheriff's practice of skimping on prisoners' upkeep so he could pocket left-over funds. "The sheriff is not entitled to any profit on feeding prisoners," Black wrote in the report.

To restore citizens' confidence in the safety of public streets, Black made pickpockets a prime target; he arrested and tried them as if they were murder suspects. To reduce overcrowding, Black and his assistants walked through the jail gathering two dozen plea bargains with sentences ranging from three months for petit larceny to five years for burglary. On one tour, Black discovered an African American who had been in jail for four months on the so-called charge of "suspicion." The solicitor filed an immediate *habeas corpus* petition securing the man's release.[11]

While trying to slow down insignificant arrests and shorten jail time, Black sped up the trial of important cases. Each weekday, five major criminal cases—usually dealing with murder, criminal assault, or robbery—were set for trial. Most defendants were convicted. The obstacle to an even faster pace was the lack of enough judges, a problem solved only partially when Governor Charles Henderson appointed none other than Harrington Heflin to fill a vacant judgeship. However Black might have felt standing before the man he had defeated, he knew that Judge Heflin was at least more active than the bed-ridden jurist he replaced (although Heflin's energy and speed were no more impressive on the bench than when he had been solicitor).

At Will Welch's urging, the legislature passed a law providing for a new trial judge, and Black filed a brief in support of it before the governor. Black recited figures on backlogged cases and jail population. Another judge would unclog the criminal docket and the local jail, Black argued, and save the state about $36,000 a year in the cost of maintaining jail inmates. "In the meantime prisoners are being confined at the expenses of the people, without a trial, and deprived of their constitutional right to a speedy trial, while the professional criminal, who makes bond, is reveling in interminable delays . . . Time is the best criminal lawyer, and the delay of trials has done more than any other one cause to create a spirit of lawlessness in the county," Black pleaded. Unimpressed, Governor Henderson vetoed the legislation.

Henderson wasn't the only one who disagreed with Black's approach to reform. Joseph Tate claimed publicly that his office of circuit solicitor should proceed independently of Black to try criminal cases. He accused Black of being leader of an "alliance which works together indirectly to keep the jail and dockets of Jefferson overcrowded." The charges confirmed Tate's own alliance with the status quo, but Black silenced his ex officio assistant by pointing out that the civil docket, for which Tate was primarily responsible, had more than four thousand pending cases.[12]

Black challenged lawlessness at what he considered its source. He used the courts' injunctive powers to frustrate gambling tables and liquor suppliers. At the Gaiety Hotel where gambling rooms operated on the upper floors, behind barricaded doors wired with electric bells to warn of approaching officers, Black discovered roulette wheels, cards, dice, and other gambling paraphernalia which he confiscated by court order. Black filed mandamus petitions to block the parole of men whom earlier he had convicted of professional gambling. Yet, Governor Henderson paroled offenders almost as fast as Black could convict them.

With new state prohibition laws, passed over Henderson's veto, Black became the first Alabama solicitor to enforce a statute prohibiting liquor advertising—even before liquor became illegal. Black sought injunctions against the owners of local billboards and news agencies who sold out-of-town newspapers containing liquor ads. With deputies in tow, he toured the city's saloons and wholesale liquor dealers (which he could not close until July 1, the first day of statewide prohibition) and ordered the immediate removal of all advertisement, including the firm's name if it included words like "liquor," "whiskey," "beer," or "saloon."

On Second Avenue, Black found a wholesale dealer who advertised that he would ship whiskey into Alabama from another state *after* prohibition—a perfectly legal evasion since the upcoming state prohibition law had no authority to unduly interfere with interstate commerce. The sign, if not the practice, came down. Black caught sight of another evasion, a display window with a whiskbroom bearing the label "whisk" placed side by side with a metal object labeled "key." Black banned the double entendre with a restraining order. Such zealous enforcement of the "dry ad" law prompted local reporters to worry aloud if red noses and potbelly stomachs on Birmingham citizens might also be declared liquor ads under Judge Black's strict construction. Surely, one reporter observed, "red noses are prima facie evidence of tampering with the wine cup . . . and an extended girth is more often due to a love of creature comforts supplied by the . . . brewer and distiller." The solicitor was not amused.

Black enlisted former state supreme court justice Samuel Weakley, author of the state's prohibition laws, to resist a suit challenging the ad act. A city court judge sided partially with the challengers when he ruled that the law could not prohibit a local news agency from selling out-of-state newspapers, such as the *Cincinnati Inquirer,* because it contained liquor ads. The paper was an article of interstate commerce, the judge declared, and the U.S. Constitution kept states from interfering unduly with commerce among states. "This very plainly appears," the judge wrote, "not only from the debates in the convention, but in those masterful letters . . . written by Hamilton, Jay, and Madison and which composed the federalist." Black read a different meaning in the founders' words and appealed to the Alabama Supreme Court.[13]

Black's crusade to end lawlessness applied to north Birmingham as much as south. Beyond limiting petty arrests of black citizens, the solicitor worked to convict blacks for crimes against other blacks. African Americans were often subject to harsher penalties for crimes against whites, but black-on-black crime was usually treated in the courthouse as an understandable mishap. Many whites expected blacks to shoot craps and to shoot one another. Judge Black, however, did not accept serious crime anywhere in his jurisdiction and pushed the all-white grand juries to indict black defendants with maximum charges whether victims were white or black.

"The best men of the county" were also subject to Black's aggressive pursuit of law and order. Entirely on circumstantial evidence, Black indicted Louis Walton, a respected, elderly businessman who had fallen into bankruptcy. A man "of birth and breeding," Walton was accused of murdering his "partner," a poor white clerk named Moses Barton who had worked for Walton years earlier at a mine commissary. While struggling with bankruptcy, "old man Walton" created a dummy corporation with three shareholders, himself, his wife, and Barton. The company had no assets. Nor did Barton. On the night of his murder, Barton told his girl friend that he was down to his exactly last nickel, "all I have between me and Heaven." It was not enough. Barton died from two bullet shots to the head at close range. Walton claimed he never met Barton that night, as originally planned, and offered proof that someone else took the old man home. A few months earlier, however, Walton had taken out insurance policies worth $30,000 on both himself and Barton as "partners" and personally had paid all premiums, including a payment on the day Barton was killed.

Many of Birmingham's social and business leaders were horrified that Black would indict Walton for first-degree murder without solid, physical evidence. Some also were angered when Black insisted the court deny Walton bail, fearing the defendant's flight. After several hearings and appeals, the courts set a bond of $25,000, and Walton was released after a large department store owner and a local hotel magnate posted bond.

By summer 1915, Black's reforms had noticeable effects. The number of jail inmates in late May was less than half the earlier three hundred. Deputies no longer made regular, wholesale raids "on working negroes" for crap shooting on Saturdays and Sundays. The cost of maintaining prisoners in Jefferson County had fallen by a third. And the backlog on the criminal docket was reduced by almost eight hundred cases during seven months. These reforms were accompanied by dogged prosecution of current serious crimes. More than 250 indictments for felonies had been returned. Almost twelve hundred cases had been processed, and the solicitor's office secured convictions in most of four hundred jury trials for serious offenses. Swift trials were followed by certain, visible punishment for all serious crimes. As dramatic proof of this new day, on Friday morning June 25, under the angular shadows of St. Paul's Catholic Church, standing east of the county jail yard, the Church's assistant priest administered last rites for two black prisoners before they were hung in open view.[14] The black men had been convicted of killing other African Americans.

After seven months of intense, arduous reform, Hugo Black took a real vacation to the West, visiting Barney Whatley in Colorado and his maternal uncle, Thomas Orlando Toland, in California. With criminal court adjourned until the fall, Black's assistant, Will Welch, was also free to join colleagues in the state legislature as they rushed to enact a series of their own urgent reforms for Alabama. Already, over Governor Henderson's veto, legislators had enacted a systemic regime of prohibition laws that became effective July 1. Now other systematic issues were in the hopper.

As chairman of the House elections committee, Welch sponsored the law eliminating the runoff election that had defeated B. B. Comer. In late 1914, the new state Democratic Executive Committee chairman, former Adjutant General Bibb Graves, had appointed corporate attorney Borden Burr to head a group to examine the runoff election. The state committee could have implemented Burr's proposals without legislative action, but anti-liquor leaders wanted to remove the runoff by state law so that the change could not easily be reversed.

Welch incorporated Burr's reforms into the legislation he steered to passage. The new law eliminated the runoff election in statewide Democratic primaries and in turn gave voters a chance to mark first and second choices on ballots for each office. In any race where no candidate received a majority of first votes, the "second choice" votes were added to the tallies. In this case, the candidate with the largest number of first and second votes was the winner.

Reform also included legislating honesty and access to the ballot. Welch sponsored a new Corrupt Practices Act limiting the amounts of money that could be legally spent for any one candidate and requiring public reports on campaign expenditures. The new law aimed not only to curtail corporate influence in politics but also to stop candidates from purchasing public office. The current secretary of state, for example, had eliminated his runoff opponent in the last election by giving an inducement of $1,000 for his opponent to retire from the race. The elected agriculture commissioner gave good state jobs to his political opponents once they withdrew.

Welch also sponsored a new voter registration law overturning sections of the 1893 Sayre law. The new legislation provided that three state officials—not simply the governor—would appoint county voter registrars who were obligated to travel into every precinct for several months each year to register voters. The law also gave a citizen the right to a jury trial to contest any actions of the local registrars.

Finally, with Welch's involvement, the legislature restructured the state's judicial system. Dry legislators wanted a state court system that functioned effectively to enforce the law, especially prohibition, and some lawmakers were equally concerned about limiting corporate and wet influence on local solicitors who were often on private retainer with regulated corporations, primarily railroads. As a result, the legislature passed a consolidated judiciary bill trying to streamline court cases and a statewide act providing a uniform system for circuit solicitors who would have to obey stricter limits on corporate retainers.

By the end of a brief 1915 session, Alabama's legislature had enacted a new election law, an anti-corrupt practices act, a voter registration law, and judicial reform. It was a sweeping moment of structural change for Alabama's white democratic government. As Martin Lackey had prophesied, it was a "dern sight more snakes" than dry, corporate, and anti-progressive politicians could handle.

One law among the reforms stirred considerable excitement in Birmingham. "Hugo Black Doomed," proclaimed a newspaper after passage of the new circuit solicitors bill. "The indications are that nothing can preserve the office of Hugo Black, county solicitor," remarked a reporter. "The members of the committee, despite the fact that the great majority of them are prohibitionists, declared that they could not play politics in the interest of any individual. Under their plan Solicitor Tate will do the prosecuting in Jefferson when their bills become effective."

Local reporters met Black when he returned to Birmingham on August 10. In the face of adversity, he was in a pleasant, almost flippant mood—a sure sign that Black was enjoying a delicious little secret. He talked about San Francisco's great world fair, which he said made "Coney Island look like a one-horse street carnival." When pressed to comment on his own doomed fate, Black stoically assured reporters he would live with the new law that made circuit solicitors the chief criminal prosecutors throughout Alabama in 1916, only two years into Black's four-year term. Black declared that he was looking no farther than the upcoming September term of the grand jury.

The county solicitor knew more than he cared to say. As chairman of the key legislative committee, assistant solicitor Will Welch had hovered over the drafting of the circuit solicitors bill. No exceptions had been made for Jefferson County or for Hugo Black, but the law did provide that current county solicitors should continue in their present jobs until their full terms expired in those "circuits of one county having more than three judges and having a county solicitor." Only one such county existed in Alabama,[15] and its county solicitor was Hugo Black.

4

Bessemer Blues

The Ends of Justice

On the western border of the Magic City, Birmingham's first industrialist, Henry DeBardeleben, had built Bessemer thirty years earlier
as an ideal community for iron and steel production. Named after
the Englishman who invented the modern steel-making system, the town's
original buildings were a curious assortment of facades that DeBardeleben had
transported from the New Orleans Cotton Exposition of 1884 to satisfy his
fancy for a little suburban showcase. The town's first large structure, christened
"Montezuma Hotel," had been the exhibition hall for Mexico, and part of the
city's rolling mill came from the Exposition's Jamaica building.

The industrialist's need for profits, however, quickly overtook personal
whim. Soon after the turn of the century, Bessemer had become the metropolitan area's junkyard, a souring mix of consumptive, dirty metal industries
with an abundance of misused and misdirected people. By 1915, town promoters swelled with pride when they read a curling tribute from a New York
ad agency: "Bessemer, with their smoke-belching foundries and coke-pits,
red-eyed with sleepless fires,—grim children of the iron age." The town's
population was almost 60 percent black, unskilled, and generally as poor as
sin on Holy Sunday.[1]

Bessemer was the industrial Black Belt of the state, and in the safety of race
relations of the early twentieth century, whites took advantage as often as possible for their own financial and social gain. Many Bessemer residents made a
small living in dangerous pig iron mills and related industries or by exploiting
others' ignorance and dependency. The basic terms of race relations in Bessemer
were not unique, but it was an urban community where the routine and often

official use of racial terror had become so common, in such a relatively short time, that it seemed unremarkable.

In September 1915, when Bessemer police officer A. D. Maddox arrived at the grand jury room on the second floor of the Jefferson County courthouse, he seemed perfectly willing to talk about the common ways of law enforcement in his town, initially incapable of imagining that racial violence was outside the grace of law or white morality. Maddox was not an articulate or thoughtful man, but he was an experienced, well-connected law officer with an uncanny ability to wiggle out of trouble that was often caused by his own violent temper. Like a man prattling among friends, Maddox showed no reluctance in answering the county prosecutor's questions about his treatment of suspects whose skin color was black.

"I have not hit, or beat, any negroes *lately* to get any confessions," Maddox told Hugo Black and the other white men of the grand jury. "I don't remember their names, but I have hit them to get the confessions from some of them.

"That is the way . . . we get the confessions," Officer Maddox continued. ". . . I did that to the negro who broke in Jeff Davison's store. I slapped him in the face several times. I hit him with my hand—I did not hit him with anything else. I think his name was Dickson, alias Chicken. Bob Childers was with me then. I think he hit him with his hand, too . . . He had not said anything out of the way to us, and had not offered to hit us, and he had not cursed us. He was sitting down and I slapped him over on the chair and he told us where the goods were," Maddox recounted. "He never did ask us *not* to hit him."

When Judge Black pressed for names of others he had beaten, Maddox was unhelpful; racial brutality had become too habitual for vivid memory. "I don't remember any names, but I have slapped a good many . . . When we get the real dope on them we have to get the information the best way we can."[2]

Officer Maddox's testimony raised a matter of old business. A year earlier the grand jury had learned that Bessemer policemen extorted money from African Americans after random arrests. A black man had appeared before the grand jury to testify, but a few days afterwards he signed an affidavit stating that he lied about the police. Black's predecessor took no further action. Black learned that the African American witness had been beaten and maimed by Bessemer police officers after his grand jury appearance. One of Black's assistants approached the black man about testifying again, but he refused to "talk about any white man. All this negro wants is to be left alone," the assistant reported. "He knows what it means to appear before a grand jury against a Bessemer officer."

Assistant Ben Perry of the Bessemer division was assigned to investigate. Perry spoke to a large number of African Americans, local lawyers, and friends of the town's board of aldermen. By September 1915, statements from both black and white citizens implicated several Bessemer police officers. Yet, legal action was very unlikely.

Evidence of actual brutality and mistreatment depended primarily on the statements of African Americans, many of whom refused to appear in the courthouse for fear of retaliation. Also, many blacks were not credible witnesses in the eyes of white jurors since they had records of prior arrests or convictions often relating to drunkenness, gambling, or petty larceny. Faced with the word of black ex-convicts against that of white policemen, without corroboration of misdeeds from other whites, a white jury—even a grand jury under Hugo Black's careful guidance—would likely balk. Unfortunately, damaging information from white citizens was largely impermissible hearsay, told to them by policemen or third parties. Few whites were eyewitnesses to any specific beating by the Bessemer blue.

Under the circumstances, a civil suit would be an easier route than a criminal case because of a lower standard of proof, but county prosecutors were not authorized by state statute to bring a civil lawsuit on behalf of private citizens for claims of damages. Alabama law also blocked the only other possible civil action, impeachment from office: county grand juries could not prefer impeachment proceedings against city police officers or elected officials, only against county and state officers.

Black's plan to dodge these obstacles was far from foolproof. It ran the risk of adding to the county solicitor's growing list of political enemies and of rendering no convictions, no one out of office, and no change. In essence, the plan called for the grand jury to summon the policemen, town fathers, and others who had personal knowledge of police mischief. Black would question them about their conduct and their knowledge of events. Black, however, would not warn any police officer that his testimony before the grand jury could indict and convict him of a crime. Since Black was not going to use the testimony for a criminal prosecution, he had no legal obligation to inform subpoenaed witnesses of their constitutional right against self-incrimination. After gathering evidence, without disclosing sources, the grand jury would make a special report to Judge Fort—naming names if possible—and call upon the city of Bessemer to take appropriate action. The plan just might work. But it might not.

Black and Perry moved quickly to find out. An early witness was the Bessemer agent for the Frisco Railroad, which had experienced a steady loss of cash and materials without any clear signs of forcible entry. With the aid of two Bessemer policemen, Frisco agents caught the burglar. He was a third Bessemer police officer. The errant officer was set free without charges.[3]

Tobe McCoy, a black man, gave brief testimony. "I was passing by there Sunday when they raided the crap game. I didn't have any pistol. I ran from them. I didn't hear him say to stop. He shot at me and hit me in the leg . . . I wasn't in the game atall . . . I didn't have any weapon of any kind. I never owned a pistol. I was running when he shot me."

Before calling Officer Maddox, Black sought testimony from three other law officers, each with the surname of "Houston." They appeared like a chorus of innocent monkeys from childhood mythology. They saw no evil, heard no evil, and spoke no evil—at least, no evil they could recognize.

George Houston: "I helped make a raid on a crap game Sunday at Raymond mines . . . and the negroes all broke to run . . . The negro who got shot was named Tobe McCoy . . . He was shot in the back part of the hip . . . It was about three or four months ago that Parker shot another negro . . . He shot his finger off. He has killed two or three negroes in the last five or six years."

C. M. Houston: "I was on the police force but I resigned . . . It has been the custom down there that if a man arrests a negro with a pistol, he would give the pistol to the man making the arrest. [The Chief] gave it to the man to keep, just like it was his own property . . . We got seventy-five or one hundred pistols in eight months."

Ellis Houston (a current Bessemer officer): "I have slapped one or two myself, to make them tell me where the goods were. I have slapped some of them pretty hard, making . . . nose bleeds . . . I slapped them because you can slap harder,—and you don't hurt your fist. No," he continued, "the negro couldn't do much to defend himself. I never hit any with a pistol. I don't remember using a leather strap on any of them. We haven't got any electric contrivances. If there is anything you can do to them but hit them I don't know what it is."

Another Bessemer officer—not a "Houston"—appeared: "I have seen negroes after they were beat up . . . Maddox and some others had these negroes down there about stealing, and they strapped them," the officer testified. "I don't know who the negroes were. There was a big strap there that they beat them with. It was a belly-band strap. It had a buckle at one end and a strap, or 'cracker,' on the other. They usually had that at hand, I think."

Members of Bessemer's governing board also appeared. They too acted like the city's three blind mice when asked by Black to remember things that they were morally unable to notice. "I don't know anything of my own knowledge about any of the negroes being beat up to get confessions—not of a serious nature," testified the first aldermen. "I expect I have seen a dozen or more—just carry them through pretty rough treatment to get information . . . I don't think of anything that the Grand Jury ought to investigate," he concluded.

"I haven't heard anything," the second alderman repeatedly stated in response to virtually all of Black's questions. "I am not exactly on the inside," he confessed. "I am chairman of the market committee,—but we have no market." The third member was on three active committees of the Bessemer board of aldermen—finance, sanitation, and police. But he knew little more. "I don't know anything about the dispositions of the pistols . . . I never heard that the detectives were getting negroes in a room and beating them up to make them confess," he swore. "I have never heard that at all."

Bessemer's city clerk, another of the prolific Houston clan in city employment, relayed innocently his own knowledge of standard procedures.

"A negro who does not pay his fine is put in jail and serves a sentence?" Black asked.

"Yes," replied the clerk. "If the mayor will let him off on open account, it is up to him."

Dr. J. S. Winters, chairman of the police committee, also testified. "Did you know that Maddox had been constantly in the practice of beating prisoners, and didn't deny it?" Black asked.

"No, sir," the elderly physician indignantly replied, ". . . I can't find out anything."

Winters had appointed Maddox acting police chief earlier for reasons he could not explain to the grand jury. He admitted that there were "loads of whiskey" in the police department, but he did not know where it came from. "I think we have a pretty good body of men," the police committee chairman sputtered, "and I don't think they would be bought up *that cheap*."

Bessemer Mayor I. A. Lewis was one of the last witnesses. He admitted there had been beatings. "How many members of the police force of Bessemer are there that you would believe on oath?" Black asked.

"I don't know," the mayor pondered. "I would have to figure."[4]

Armed with both affidavits and testimony, Black quickly wrote a special grand jury report. As drafts were being prepared, word leaked to newspapers that "charges of a sensational nature" were included in a special grand jury report. "Solicitor Hugo L. Black when approached discounted the rumor and . . . laughed at the suggestion that a partial report of any particular impact was forthcoming," reported the Friday morning paper. At four-thirty that afternoon, the jury foreman submitted a special report on Bessemer police practices to presiding Judge William E. Fort. "We have made diligent inquiry into criminal conditions and find that in certain portions of the county the officials of the law, who are solemnly charged with the duty of its just execution, have transgressed the fundamental rights and constitutional privileges of its citizens."

In words that Judge Black wrote, jurors reported with regret that they could not impeach police officers but remained silent on why they did not indict them. They called Bessemer's police practices dishonorable, tyrannical, despotic, and cowardly. They found "a uniform practice has been made of taking helpless prisoners, in the late hours of night, into a secluded room . . . and there beat them until they were red with their own blood, in the efforts to obtain confessions . . . We find that this cowardly practice in which four big officers with pistols safely strapped on their bodies would thus take advantage of ignorance and helplessness, has been continuously in operation for a long number of years," continued Black's report. "A leather strap with a buckle on one end, and a big flap on the other was invested for this purpose. . . In this room were none present but the officers and the helpless prisoner, often innocent of the crime of which he was charged, arrested without a warrant, on the vague suspicion."

The grand jury recommended that the city remove three policemen, A. D. Maddox, Ellis Houston, and a brother of city council president George Ross. The report said Maddox and Houston had admitted regularly using the "third degree" in a "manner so cruel that it would bring discredit and shame upon the most uncivilized and barbarous community."

The report declared police officers have a solemn duty in "protecting the weak, unfortunate, and humble, as well as the rich and powerful," but it carefully avoided mentioning that most victims of official violence were African American. Nowhere does the word "Negro," "colored," or even a more commonplace substitute appear in the report. The document refers to the "race" of only one person, "a white man" whom Officer Maddox struck in a fit of rage at city court. Yet, everyone knew the color of the issues Black raised. In covering the grand jury report, Birmingham's black newspaper announced in bold headlines on its front page: "Negro Should Have Justice Under the Law."

Bessemer politicians reacted to Black's words with masculine white fury. Mayor Lewis apparently had figured out, after all, how many of his men he would believe under oath. "It would have been more manly. . ." the mayor insisted, "had the grand jury reported the good they saw . . . I know there is much more good than bad in every officer." One alderman called Black's report contemptible, and another complained that Black went further in his use of "the third degree" than Bessemer police, although no grand jury witness could show markings from a leather strap. "There are ways . . . to ask a white man questions," protested the alderman, "and I never talked to a negro working for me in the manner that Black spoke to me." Despite their objections, city council members adopted a resolution authorizing the city attorney, mayor, and police committee to meet with Black.

During the following two weeks, Black and the Bessemer city attorney worked out an agreement to establish an investigative committee with members appointed equally by the city and Black's assistant, Ben Perry, an elected official of the Bessemer division. In addition, the inquiry and testimony would be open. Bessemer police would not be allowed to bully anyone who appeared, and Perry would present the solicitor's case. Before hearings began, Black received "droves" of new information about Bessemer police's misdeeds. Black's strategy prompted an unforeseen benefit, an opportunity to build a public case as he went along.

During the first evening of hearings, Perry called a string of black and white witnesses who endured, observed, or heard about beatings from Bessemer policemen. A black man testified that Officers Ross and Maddox had beaten him in a bathtub until he confessed falsely to stealing a white woman's purse. Most witnesses were white. Perry also offered a stack of citizens' affidavits (race unmentioned) who swore to police beatings or other misconduct. After a similar, second night of testimony, the solicitor rested his case. In defense, the policemen's lawyer called the city physician who swore he had never given medical assistance to any man in jail as a result of a police beating. On cross-examination, the doctor admitted that it was possible for officers to beat up men without calling him to repair them. Several white witnesses testified that Maddox and other policemen had retrieved their stolen property from Negro criminals, although they had no knowledge of the official techniques of recovery.

In keeping with an old custom, the defense attacked the police officers' victims. The police chief called Bessemer Negroes a "bad lot" and reminded the committee that the portraits of white police officers "who had been killed by bad negroes" were hanging on the surrounding walls of the city council chambers. A county deputy sheriff from Birmingham, a beneficiary of the fee system, testified that Bessemer was a "tough district" for handling bad Negroes and that he had found it necessary in Bessemer "to thrash negroes" in the line of duty. After hearing brief closing arguments, the investigative committee recessed until it could reach a majority opinion.[5]

Black's efforts to publicize Bessemer's transgressions of "fundamental rights and constitutional privileges" of all citizens did not obscure the issue of "race," and his political opponents quickly tried to portray Black's defense of the Negro as a betrayal of the white man. Less than two weeks after the Bessemer report, Jefferson County's ambitious Deputy Sheriff Conrad Austin accused solicitor Black of "freeing negro gamblers" while prosecuting innocent white men. A year earlier, Austin's testimony had brought the downfall of Birmingham Police Chief George Bodeker.

"As every man in town knows," Deputy Austin stated, "the negro crooks hang around negro gambling games. There have been a number of murders committed by negroes as a direct result of negro gambling." Yet, Hugo Black and his assistants "are not prosecuting the negroes of Jefferson County." Even worse, Austin charged, the county prosecutor was indicting innocent whites and arranging for "white men to remain in jail several weeks" while "negroes have been released on their own recognizance." In effect, Austin accused Black of freeing dangerous, murderous blacks and jailing innocent, harmless whites.

Black's assistant Walter Brower promptly responded: "It is the natural tendency that where a pernicious fee system exists deputy sheriffs would resent the freeing of a few negroes." Brower assured white citizens that Black's office had released only "hard working negroes whose only offense consisted in throwing dice on Sunday. They were not professional gamblers." Professional gamblers of any skin shade would be locked up as long as possible, Brower promised.

Shadows of Bessemer extended into the courtroom as others questioned Black's integrity and judgment. In a trial of a white man accused of wrecking a train, killing three and injuring several, the defendant accused city detectives and railroad investigators of coercing his confession before the grand jury. He swore at trial that officials threatened to break his neck if he did not confess. In fact, grand jury minutes show that the county solicitor warned the defendant that any of his statement could be used to convict him. The documents also reveal the defendant informed Black and the grand jury that "nobody has offered me anything" or threatened him. The trial jury convicted the defendant but, as if pulled by uncertainty, fixed his punishment at only ten years in prison.

In another case, in return for a ten-year sentence, a black teenager pled guilty as an accomplice in the murder of a white man. When Black presented the plea bargain to a jury, already empanelled to try the case, he explained that the young man was nothing more than a bystander in a brutal crime. After a half-hour of deliberation, the jury returned and asked the judge if they could impose a heavier sentence. When denied that power, the jurors reluctantly accepted Black's deal. "We had the wrong boy," the solicitor explained to reporters. "This boy only convicted himself through his own confession, and his account shows that he tried to prevent the killing. If the real murderer . . . is ever captured by the police," Black stated, "we will do our best to hang him."

Black seemed undaunted by these incidents. He continued to clear the criminal dockets and the county jail of old cases involving black defendants. In early October, he asked Judge Fort to dismiss more than one hundred additional "petty cases of Sunday gambling and dice throwing" against African American defendants. None of the freed men was a professional gambler or vagrant.

Meanwhile, political developments also raised serious questions about the viability of Black's impartial style of public service. The grand old man of independence and fairness in Birmingham's politics, A. O. Lane, was in a fight for his political life with a quirky suburban druggist, Arlie Barber, a self-proclaimed socialist.

On election eve, Black presided at a Lane rally on the courthouse steps where he joined Walker Percy, industrialists, and others who spoke of Lane's superior qualities and virtues. "Judge Lane's bitterest enemy could be confident of fair treatment at his hands as a public official," Percy declared. "His most intimate friend . . . could not swerve him a hair's breadth from what he believed to be the path of duty. The poor and friendless can receive from him an audience as quickly as the most influential man in the community."

In his turn at the podium, Black admitted that he agreed and disagreed on issues with both candidates, but the more important consideration was the fact that Judge Lane was not a politician who shifted with the temper of the times. He was an honest public servant who had been fighting for the things he believed were right in Birmingham for three decades. He was a good citizen and a good friend to people from all segments of the community. "When the time comes when I must repudiate friendship," declared Black, "such as existed between Judge Lane and myself and prove myself unworthy of gratitude, I am willing to resign every claim upon the friendship of any city or any community. So long as I believe my friend honest," Black said of his old mentor, "I am for him."

Others speakers attacked Arlie Barber as a fool, preaching socialistic propaganda while covertly representing liquor interests. The voters disagreed or didn't care. By almost a two-to-one margin, on Monday, October 18, Barber carried suburban Birmingham in a landslide victory. The city had its first socialist commissioner, ironically its first voice of suburban politics, and Black lost his prime mentor and exemplar of public service. Within six months of defeat, Judge Lane died of a heart attack.[6]

Two days after the election, the Bessemer investigation committee released its unanimous findings vindicating Black's grand jury report. The committee found Maddox and other policemen "guilty of cruel and inhumane treatment to defenseless, weak, and unprotected prisoners" and recommended their discharge. The committee also asked Mayor Lewis, City Board President George Ross, and the head of the police committee, Dr. Winters, to resign since they had been "derelict in the performance of duties." Dr. Winters acceded, but President Ross scoffed: "I was elected by the people of Bessemer . . . I am guilty of no wrong . . . I will not resign."

Once Judge Black's publicity agent, the *Birmingham Age-Herald* now defended Bessemer and Ross. "There is more in the Bessemer situation than appears on the surface," the paper suggested. It charged that the grand jury was "engineered" by Ross's political opponents as a part of a wider effort to run him out of office. Besides, the editors observed, Bessemer's police practices "are prevalent in every other city."

Inspired by newspaper support, Bessemer's aldermen staged a political farce. First, the Board refused to accept the citizens' committee report or the resignation of any board member. It did accept the resignation of five police officers charged with wrongdoing in the report. Two weeks later, however, the Board received applications for vacancies in the police department and quickly appointed three "new" officers who were three of the five who had resigned. Only Maddox and Ellis Houston were not rehired, although Maddox later returned to Bessemer's blue. The three "new" officers were also given a 10 percent raise in pay.[7]

Frustrated in Bessemer, Black refused to retreat one millimeter in challenging Birmingham's white officials who practiced and profited from racial terror. In fact, ignoring political trends, Black redoubled his efforts. In a mining community west of the city, Black discovered a justice of the peace arresting blacks on charges of gambling, drunkenness, and cursing. Negroes were convicted without a hearing. Mine operators often paid these fines since they preferred advancing wages to losing industrious workers. The JP habitually failed to document convictions and pocketed most fines. In short order, after personally reviewing the JP's books, Black acted as both prosecutor and witness in a successful impeachment trial.

In another case, two Birmingham policemen fatally shot a young black man. The county solicitor tried valiantly to make a case of first-degree murder against the officers, although he could summon only African Americans as eyewitnesses. Testimony in the case showed that the slain Negro had failed to hold his tongue when an officer's remarks offended him. "This negro said, 'Well I don't care any more about a white man that I do about a negro.'" In reply, a policeman said, "Mind how you speak nigger!" and "slapped him two or three times." The black man ran but another "negro, Big Tooth, outrun him and knocked him down in the tracks." The officer approached the fallen Negro, "hit him across the head with his pistol, and . . . shot him in the back." A second policeman arrived. Looking up into the face of the officer, the injured black man pleaded, "Lordy, Lordy," before the second police officer aimed and "shot him in the head."

Five blacks testified as eyewitnesses to the murder before a grand jury of white clerks, salesmen, mechanics, and shopkeepers. Every black witness saw the same incident: the murder of an unarmed man whose only infraction was his failure to show fear and submissive deference to a white police officer. The two white policemen apparently were unworried that half a dozen black citizens saw them kill a black man in cold blood. The officers could not imagine that Birmingham courts would hold them accountable. After all, white men were the law.

The minute books from the grand jury's secret proceedings fail to reveal Black's mood as he presented this string of witnesses. Nothing tells whether he shuddered slightly when he heard repeated the legendary last words of his mother's first love, Columbus Black, in the victim's dying declaration of "Lordy, Lordy." No record illuminates whether Black recalled Eli Sims' murder from boyhood days in Clay. Then, as later, he never divulged whether personal experience helped nurture the taproots of his resolve to attack brutal practices, to challenge racialist standards of law and order. As an exercise of his own self-discipline, his own approach to law and justice, Black strove to place his actions for fairness in a system of written laws, not individual human experiences, and in the wisdom of a historical truth that literally commanded "equal rights to all, special privileges for none."

Yet, what is evident from the grand jury minutes is the fierce determination of a county solicitor who painstakingly built a mountain of consistent testimony from Negro witnesses, all employed and "credible" in the narrow sight of white society, in order to elevate eighteen ordinary white men to a peak of moral clarity from which they could see, beyond the blinding wrong of old customs and routine practices, a human decency that insisted two white police officers stand trial for the cold-blooded murder of another human being. The grand jury indicted the police officers.

With the same intense resolve, Black reached into the past to prosecute another murder case. He sought to indict a white police officer for murdering an elderly Negro man in April 1913, more than a year before Black became solicitor. The case had languished in Harrington Heflin's grand jury records, without an indictment, forgotten by everyone but the county prosecutor. Black decided the white officer had to be brought before the bar of justice. Capital offenses had no statute of limitations.

In the case, rookie cop T. J. Pierce accused Ernest Whitaker, an elderly black man, of running a "blind tiger" from the rear of his home. According to Whitaker's friend, "Mr. Pierce jerked out a pistol and jabbed him three times . . . Mr. Pierce made one shot" that hit Whitaker's house. "Ernest throwed Mr. Pierce down and took his pistol away from him." Veteran police officer W. H.

Propst then arrived and retrieved his colleague's gun. "Boss," Whitaker explained, "I did take his gun from him . . . I thought he was going to shoot me."

In careful, just-the-facts language, Propst told the grand jury what happened next. "Pierce had his gun in his hand and he said to the old negro, 'You do know where my hat is' and he hit the negro across the head . . . I grabbed Pierce by the right shoulder and Whitaker by the left . . . Pierce struck the negro with his gun and said, 'God damn you, you take another gun away from me . . .' He seemed to be very much excited and mad . . . and he just shot Whitaker . . . it was four shots . . . Whitaker died almost instantly . . . he didn't have any weapon."[8]

Black pursued these cases of "defenseless murder" with consummate skill and religious devotion, but he was not naive about the difficulties of winning convictions at trial. Little wonder that the first police brutality case Black brought to trial after the Bessemer investigation had a different racial complexion. It was a case where a white constable of Pinkney City, a crossroads in the county's northern sections, murdered Gus Goolsby, an eighteen-year-old local white boy. The trial continued Black's challenge to official, senseless lawlessness without the element of "race." The case tested the willingness of a trial jury to punish unprovoked police violence without blinking. Equally useful, it also demonstrated the county prosecutor wanted to protect poor, vulnerable whites as well as poor blacks.

The case's facts were simple. Pinkney's mayor, an ex officio justice of the peace, had sentenced the slain young man to twenty days of labor on the town's streets after he was caught as a minor in the local pool hall. Leaving court, the boy broke and ran. He was shot in the back by the city constable, an appointee of the town mayor whose nearby honky-tonk offered black hookers and whiskey by the buckets to boys of any age and race. Several local white men and women with good reputations were eyewitnesses who saw Constable Albert Box gun down the boy. In fact, one witness's account had Box dead-to-right: "Goolsby started to run . . . Box . . . shot at him, and he shot the second time and hit him. He drew up his gun, the second time, like this [demonstrating the use of two hands to steady and aim the pistol]. I told him when he turned around that he didn't have any right to shoot that boy."

On October 20, Black opened the Box prosecution by telling the jury that an officer of the law had committed "cold blooded murder." The constable's attorney claimed that the death was accidental; the gun had gone off by mistake. Black and Walter Brower produced eight white eyewitnesses. All stated that Box drew his pistol and fired once directly at the fleeing boy. Then, "Box deliberately aimed and steadied his pistol with both hands and fired" the fatal shot. In his defense, Box told the jury his first shot went into the air and he "stumbled over a ditch which discharged the pistol again" killing the boy. On cross-examination, Black won an admission that Box was an experienced gunman, easily able to shoot off a chicken's head at ten paces.

In the middle of cross-examining Box, Black was forced to leave the courtroom. He raced down the hall to Judge Harrington Heflin's court. The solicitor discovered Joseph Tate asking the court to dismiss a case involving the pickax murder of a black man because the indictment read the white defendant's name as "B. W. Richardson" when the court minutes stated he was "B. W. R. Richardson." Black was furious. The technicality was the latest in a series of errors undertaken by his opponents in law enforcement. Earlier in the week, sheriff's deputies had made conspicuous errors in delivering notices to citizens on the jury venire. Many deputies opposed the solicitor's prosecution of white policemen and his dismissal of fee-generating cases against black suspects. Their mistakes had postponed all criminal cases, including the Box and Pierce cases, for a few days. Now, Black discovered Tate attempting to dismiss the Richardson case because of what Black described as "merely a clerical error."

Black told Judge Heflin that the extra initial in the defendant's name "meant nothing in the eyes of the law." Black said he, not Tate, was the county's chief prosecutor, and Black was prepared immediately to try the case. Judge Heflin demurred. He left the case of the missing initial alone but decided the defects in serving the jury venire had not been cured. He dismissed all prospective jurors and postponed until next year all pending cases, except the Box trial in Judge Fort's courtroom.

Later in the evening, reporters asked Black to comment on the postponements. "I have *absolutely* nothing to say at the present time," he remarked. In private, Black was furious. Joseph Tate would no longer be permitted to prosecute cases involving black victims, he declared. This incident was not the first time Tate had used typographical errors to quash or postpone prosecution of cases involving black victims and white defendants. In fact, Black found Tate's "attitude in regard to helpless minorities" repugnant and unacceptable. Black remembered that in earlier years Tate had pleaded with a jury to give two young blacks the death penalty for allegedly stealing tools from a farmer.

If the county's chief prosecutor could do nothing about the conduct of his old predecessor, Judge Heflin, he could—and did—keep Tate away from future criminal trials involving Negroes.

The Box trial ended with a theatrical quality. In closing arguments, Walter Brower (substituting for a preoccupied boss) brought the jury to tears recalling the tragedy of a fallen boy and a heartsick mother. With his own small son on his knee, his wife and other children at his side, Box listened earnestly to his lawyer's pleas that the shooting was a tragic accident. After hours of deliberation, the jury decided Box was guilty of second-degree murder and sentenced him to twenty-five years in prison. Judge Heflin's ruling, however, gave the defense a chance for a credible challenge to the legality of the jury.

The grand jury had to conclude its work prematurely. They had been in session for twenty-one days and had heard 1,511 witnesses in 391 cases, each and every one presented by Black. They said nothing in their final report about Bessemer. In a routine statement, the eighteen white jurymen thanked the county solicitor for his consideration and courtesy "in our efforts to carry out the ends of justice."[9]

Within two intense months of late 1915, Hugo Black had broken new ground and old customs in the law and order of Birmingham, but he had not reached the ends of justice he sought. By trumpeting a different standard of fairness, by insisting that white policemen uphold written law, blind to skin color or ancestry, Black's words and deeds projected a new, untried vision of the solemn duty of government. It was a moral concept of law and order that many white citizens of all classes could not imagine, much less accept. Yet, Black did not propose a system for racial justice. That notion summoned a linguistic memory of Reconstruction that virtually no white Southerner in the early twentieth century, including Black, wanted to reenact. Black's concept was a system of laws that protected "the weak, unfortunate, and humble," whomever they happened to be, "as well as the rich and powerful." Twenty-five years later, Judge Black would invoke this vision again, with far greater authority and success, as he commanded the nation's law officers to protect the "helpless, weak, and outnumbered."[10] Indeed, not until that distant and as yet unexpected time and place were the ends of justice which Hugo Black faithfully pursued in Bessemer actually accomplished in any real measure of law or fact.

5

Haughty Warriors

Battling for Civic Righteousness

Almost everyone in Birmingham had something to commemorate with the arrival of 1916. On the fifty-third anniversary of the Emancipation Proclamation, Senator Frank White—one of the last Confederate veterans to sit in the U.S. Senate from Alabama—stood before more than a thousand African Americans overcrowding the Sixteenth Street Baptist Church. "You might suppose that I fought to keep you in slavery," White bluntly informed his listeners, "but not at all. The institution never did appeal to me. My companion in boyhood was a negro and he followed me to the war. I never knew him to fail to prove his loyalty on any occasion. Slavery was objectionable, but you must not forget that you are not the only people ever held as slaves."

Remembering lessons from Biblical bondage and Ireland's St. Patrick, the former "short-shoe" senator insisted that past hardships could be a blessing and the foundation of future progress. White's South was a place where racial paternalism often masqueraded as interracial friendship, but that was also a more benign form of Southern race relations. His South was a place where slave and slaveholder, black and white citizens shaped one another. "You have made the Southern people the greatest people that ever lived," the elderly Anglo lawyer declared. "You should realize it, we should appreciate it. Don't forget, however, we made you. We gave you your religion . . . language . . . your civilization."

White paid tribute to Tuskegee's Booker T. Washington, who had died two months earlier. The senator described the black educator as "my Washington," who "did not work for one race, but all the races." Yet, White saved his greatest praise for the Emancipator. "Lincoln, a *Southern* man, brought about your freedom," he argued, generously recasting standard sectional history. "He was a Southern man, born just sixty miles from where Jefferson Davis was born. We must remember him; we must erect a statue to him, and I want to have the honor of being the first to contribute to its erection in Birmingham."

Despite Senator White's warm endorsement, no plans were subsequently undertaken in the city to build a monument to Lincoln, but Birmingham had begun in early 1916 to honor others within the South's sacred past and to search noisily among conflicting segments for the heroes of tomorrow and the terms of their rule. A few weeks before Emancipation Day, large crowds of white citizens attended the Jefferson Theater for the city's first showing of D. W. Griffith's photoplay, *Birth of a Nation.* With a native Alabamian in a leading role, this "supreme motion picture of the South" aroused enthusiasm and deep, emotional responses to its portrayal of Reconstruction history and heroes. "Particularly thrilling," observed a local reviewer, "are the scenes showing the inception of the Ku Klux Klan" of the 1870s and "their work of vengeance at a time when no other help was at hand." Veterans like Senator White could attend the matinee without charge when they showed a Confederate cross of honor.

The film arrived at a propitious moment. Birmingham was preparing to host the twenty-sixth annual convention of the United Confederate Veterans. A regional reunion of all who fought in gray, this celebratory event was scheduled to commence in May, and the chamber of commerce already had raised a large part of $25,000 for the occasion, as a planning committee of businessmen regularly met to work out details.

Griffith's film ran several weeks and contributed to excitement about the upcoming celebration and its honored past. The city commission president, a lawyer and businessman elected in 1913 from Old Birmingham, encouraged people to see the film for both its silent drama and as "a force for historical study." George B. Ward thought the movie "has a distinct value towards harmonizing the relations of the white and colored races." Editor Oscar Adams of the *Birmingham Reporter*, a black newspaper, strongly disagreed. "The white people will come out less friendly towards the Negro than he was when he went in," Adams warned. "This begins a new prejudice of race feeling which neither race can afford."

Local daily newspapers ran photographs and stories about the film's production and the origins of the Klan that it gallantly portrayed. Organized fifty years earlier and subsequently headed by the last Confederate general to surrender, Nathan Bedford Forrest, the South's old secret society was "an institution of chivalry, humanity, and patriotism," according to the *Age-Herald*. "The Klan devoted their efforts to putting down disorder among the bad negroes . . . It was the brave deeds of the Ku Klux Klan that saved the South," the paper stated.[1]

Some Birmingham homes also celebrated the anniversary of Alabama's bone-dry prohibition. A statewide ban of liquor in January 1915—passed over the veto of Governor Charles Henderson and four years ahead of national prohibition—provided what some saw as an opportunity to restore a new humanity and morality befitting the nation's Bible Belt and a state with one of the highest numbers of Baptists. This moral cause was no less sacred to its true believers than the hallowed grounds of Chickamauga and Gettysburg, although battlefields for prohibition were often in the legislature, voting booths, blind tigers, courtrooms, and jails—places of daily conflict where dry forces had made modest inroads during the last year. Temperance councils, Baptist preachers, and others who strove for a "moral Alabama" gladly reenlisted in the war against whiskey's wickedness and for "civic righteousness."

Hugo Black was an important soldier in this new moral conflict. As chief prosecutor in the state's largest county, Black originated almost one-third of all the state's liquor cases during the first year of prohibition. Despite protests from newspaper publishers, Black had convinced the Alabama Supreme Court that the state could ban liquor advertisements since they were merely "solicitations for business," transactions which the state had the police powers to regulate. Now, in early 1916, Black attacked Birmingham's liquor shippers and dealers. He sought a temporary injunction against the Southern Express Company, which shipped liquor through Jefferson County to other states. Black argued that the company was violating the anti-advertising law since the bottles and boxes of liquor had labels that "advertised its content" and the company maintained price lists and purchase orders that described or "advertised" liquor.

Those finely printed words were prohibited, Black claimed, by state statute that expressly mentioned "price lists" as an illegal ad. Black also argued that another state law authorized confiscation since the whiskey was in quart bottles. Alabama now presumed that any liquor shipped into the state in quarts was intended for consumption in Alabama. Black believed that a court injunction would halve the liquor coming into Jefferson, but a city court judge denied his petition. Again, Black appealed.

Stopped on one front, Black persisted along another. For the second time in less than a year, Black prosecuted a white man, E. M. Gibson, for distributing leaflets advertising liquor. Earlier Gibson had been convicted on the same offense and sentenced to three months in jail and $250 in fines. Governor Henderson, however, paroled Gibson immediately and reduced his fine to $25. On the second conviction, Judge William Fort sentenced Gibson to three months and a $500 fine. Temperance supporters were so impressed by Judge Black's use of anti-advertising laws that they pushed the U.S. Congress to pass national legislation making it unlawful to advertise liquor if it traveled by U.S. Mail through a dry state. Members of the Alabama congressional delegation sponsored the proposal, but it got nowhere.

Closer to home, prohibition leaders prepared a full slate of candidates for the May Democratic primary. Their leaders were an assorted lot. Among them was Captain Richmond Hobson, running for reelection to the Congress in the mining areas outside of Birmingham after his earlier defeat by Senator Underwood. Black's former law partner, David J. Davis, announced his candidacy against Judge Harrington Heflin, and Borden Burr sought to become Alabama's dry representative on the national Democratic party's governing board.

Burr was in politics for one issue and one issue only: prohibition. He was a fighter by nature and attacked any and all public officials when he thought they were backsliding on prohibition. Schooled in the courtrooms and politics of Talladega and Clay counties, Burr saw only good or evil, with no gray between. He was merciless when he charged his opponents, whether they were striking miners, injured workers, or liquor optionists. In the current campaign, Burr condemned Senator Underwood for supporting legislation to permit the District of Columbia to vote on prohibition. Such a referendum unfairly stacked the deck against a dry law, Burr charged, "when thirty thousand negro voters would be allowed to participate. I want a dry district," Burr stated, "and I know from experience that the vast majority of negroes vote wet."

Burr also traveled to Washington to oppose the nomination of Louis Brandeis to the U.S. Supreme Court. U.S. Steel's Birmingham lawyer disliked Brandeis's hostility to big business, but Burr traveled a thousand miles to oppose the Court's first Jewish nominee because Brandeis was a *local optionist* who failed to rid Boston of whiskey.[2]

Alabama's anti-prohibitionists were aware of the importance of May elections and the need for new, effective strategies. In late February, to develop a ticket of wet candidates, Forney Johnston as "head of the slate makers" called together corporate lawyers and businessman who had helped engineer Senator Underwood's last campaign. Slate-making had become a political necessity. Alabama's recent elections reforms, which Burr and Black's assistant Will Welch had shepherded, now restricted corporate contributions in campaigns and eliminated runoffs, even when no candidate received a majority of votes. As a result, local optionists had a good chance to win only if they joined their money and support behind one candidate before the campaign began.

In Jefferson County, wet candidates in 1916 attempted to steer away from prohibition as the central issue. Judge Heflin, for example, campaigned against David J. Davis on the issue of Hugo Black. He charged that the courtrooms could not be fair and impartial if two law partners ran the courthouse as prosecutor and judge. Davis ignored the charge while assuring voters that he could clean out liquor interests, court delays, and corruption.

Black kept out of Davis's race, in part because of a bulging docket and relentless grand jury sessions. In addition, Black was no longer the universally admired magistrate of police court or a widely popular prosecutor. Black had been making enemies faster than winning friends.

Ignoring political consequences, Black continued to follow his independent sense of justice and fairness wherever it took him. He fueled animosities among lawmen by indicting a Bessemer deputy sheriff for bribery, based solely on the grand jury testimony of black citizens. He summoned a railroad company's top officials before the grand jury to question them about improper train headlights in the city. And, despite persistent objections from prominent citizens, Black personally conducted the high-profile trial of Louis Walton.

Opening Walton's trial, Black called the businessman a calculating, cold-blooded murderer who killed for money. The prosecutor produced fifty witnesses who established circumstantial evidence indicating that one of Birmingham's "best citizens" had killed Moses Barton, whom Walton promised to treat as his "son." Black showed how, in a business that did not exist, Walton took out insurance policies on his "partner," whose family had to borrow money to bury him. In his own defense, Walton called dozens of character witnesses, many listed in Birmingham's social directory. Walton insisted the crime "was a regular negro job . . . it must have been negroes who did it." According to this socially constructed argument, Birmingham's "regular" order of human relations naturally involved poor blacks and poor whites killing one another without motive. In the end, jurors hopelessly deadlocked, with four members refusing to convict. Black stubbornly persisted. To the disbelief of the defendant and his friends, the county solicitor announced he would set a new trial in order to convict and hang Louis Walton.

In late April, Black faced the rabid anger of a suburban white community itching for a mob lynching. In Ensley, a young white woman had been raped at an outlying mining operation near Cat Mountain, and a young African American, Percy Fox, was apprehended and taken immediately before the victim. "I'm positive that is the same . . . There can be no mistake," she sobbed. Armed white men lingered near the Ensley jail and threatened vigilante action. Real and imagined, sordid details of the victim's ordeal spread like brush fire. In truth, the victim had told a rather guarded story. "He pulled my clothes up," the white woman told Hugo Black and the grand jury. "He was choking me, and he said he was going to do that to me, 'god damn you.' I don't know how long it took," she concluded.

While Fox was in custody under special precautions, Black tried calmly, speedily to determine the facts in the grand jury room. A large number of white eyewitnesses placed the seventeen-year-old African American at or near the scene of the rape. Black also called Negro witnesses, all swearing that Fox was not the young man near the mining area that day. The grand jury indicted Fox, and Black quickly brought the case to trial. The judge cleared the courtroom, and after one day of testimony, including the victim's, a jury returned a guilty verdict with life imprisonment. Apparently, the young black man was relieved not to be hanged and decided not to appeal. Some local whites, however, were outraged that Black had let the defendant escape the gallows. Within hours of the verdict, Black secretly transported Fox "for safe keeping" to the state penitentiary in south Alabama by way of a L&N baggage car.[3]

Black's handling of Percy Fox left anger and outrage simmering within Ensley's white community, adding to a growing list of the prosecutor's detractors. But at this moment most of white Birmingham was distracted by collective nostalgia for the ways of the "Gray Fox" in the glorified days of secession. As May arrived, surviving Civil War officers who had served under Nathan Bedford Forrest gathered early, before the official proceedings of the Confederate reunion. They included local men such as Judge Samuel Weakley, eminent prohibitionist, and U.S. Steel lawyer Walker Percy, local optionist. In a business session, reunion leaders considered a motion to build a monument in honor of the slaves of the Confederacy, but they referred it to a committee for indefinite study. *Birth of a Nation* returned for its third engagement at local theaters, and hundreds crowded under the new electric fans at both matinee and evening showings. Birmingham's mothers and maids busily pressed special uniforms for Boy Scouts assigned to carry the bags of arriving aged soldiers.

Because of prohibition, this public celebration would have to survive with nothing stronger than barrels of cool rainwater, placed around Birmingham's streets to refresh the old warriors as they strolled about the city. May's primary elections, however, intoxicated local optionists. Prohibition opponent Will Bankhead, the son of a U.S. senator, defeated Richmond Hobson in the Tenth Congressional District. A wet corporate lawyer defeated the irascible Borden Burr, and Judge Heflin narrowly won over David J. Davis. In these and other races, "civic righteousness" was left high and dry at the polls. Still, for a little time, it did not really matter. The Old South's valor and virtue was the order of the day.

The consoling, jubilant worshiping of the Lost Cause and its born-again Southern patriotism truly was embraced by almost every Southern white, wet or dry, Protestant or Catholic, corporate manager or common laborer, old or new Birmingham. This Confederate celebration represented more than a communion of those living and dead who fought for a chivalrous white South. It had become the universal duty of Southern white citizenship. As General Bennett Young, commander-in-chief of the United Confederate Veterans, stated upon his arrival in Birmingham: "A Southern man would be a miscreant and a coward who failed to keep alive the memories of the Confederate Army."

By the middle of May, Birmingham proved conclusively that no such ignominy befitted its citizens. "The Magic City of the South has capitulated without a struggle to the soldiers of the Confederacy . . . accompanied by fife and drum corps and the martial strains of the bands playing 'Dixie'," reported one observer. "Stooped in shoulder and bowed of heads, the haughty warriors of the sixties came, but they were as proud in spirit and erect of head as in the day when they answered the call of the southland to fight an invading force."

As many as one hundred thousand people, more than half the population of metro Birmingham, turned out to cheer wildly the triumphant march of veterans and their supporters. Blessed by cool May weather, the parade of six

thousand gray veterans and almost twenty thousand other marchers from across
the South lasted two and one-half hours as Birmingham greeted them with
shouts, applause, and tears of respect and longing. Hearing the bands strike up
an antebellum tune, the old veterans danced the Virginia Reel in enthusiastic,
if not quite masterful style.

The crowds along the streets warmly received more than fifty "old-time"
Negroes, several with roosters for cockfighting tucked under their arms, as they
followed their old masters dressed in gray. Henry Walthall, the Birmingham
native who played a Confederate star in *Birth of a Nation*, wore a slouch hat
in the style of an old Southern gentleman. He rode a dark bay horse alongside
the actual officers of the old Confederacy as they paraded before the sitting
governors of Alabama and Georgia. Hundreds of "beautiful, charming, gracious,
and good" Southern white women threw kisses, danced, and flirted with the
old men parading through Birmingham streets gaily bedecked with the "Stars
and Bars" as well as other flags of the Old South. The Confederate navy, an
orphans' brigade, and robed members of the newly revived Knights of the Ku
Klux Klan also received loud applause as they passed through the streets.

As in all great pageantry, there were moments of sadness. "Each year their
parade shall grow smaller," one reporter noted, "each month the grim reaper
pauses long enough to sound the last call of Taps. As they fought, so shall they
die, bravely, honorably . . . And their memory shall be wafted gently throughout
this broad universe . . . never to die."

As self-made heirs of the Old South's legacy, Klansmen attended *en banc*
the evening performance of *Birth of a Nation*. William J. Simmons, the salesman who had been inspired by the D. W. Griffith film to revive the KKK,
came from Atlanta to inaugurate a Birmingham chapter. With robes flutter-
ing under the electric fans of the Jefferson Theater, twenty-five Klansmen
watched gallant white figures, like themselves, returning from another era to
protect their families from "bad negroes" and to uphold the region's tenacious
notion of righteousness in secret brotherhood. "A Klan has been organized in
Birmingham," noted a reporter, "and they seek only the best citizens, who are
closely affiliated with the Confederacy."[4]

WHILE THE SPECIAL TRAINS pulled into the Birmingham rail terminal, bringing old veterans and an assortment of state dignitaries to the Confederate
reunion, twenty-two men had begun to assemble in a passenger car attached

to an idling L&N engine a hundred miles south in the Montgomery rail yard. These armed confederates were also brought together by a secret order and were preparing for a civic battle that would unexpectedly prompt newspapers and newsreels to project Hugo Black's words, deeds, and image across Alabama and America for the first time.

The rail car's shades were drawn in a seemingly unoccupied compartment although inside there was a slight murmur of restrained voices. Near midnight, a restless local reporter working the depot for stories of petty crimes happened to notice shadows and furtive movements along the rail yard. When he investigated, the assembled men unceremoniously dragged him into the car where he was held incommunicado.

Shortly after 2:00 AM on this Wednesday, the train began an unscheduled journey ninety miles to the east across the state line. The one-car train passed through pastures, crossroads, and small towns such as Girard, a little cotton mill community on the Alabama border. Across the Chattahoochee River into Columbus, a growing Georgia town on the river's other side, the train slowed, and passengers swung off the back steps in pairs, walking casually in different directions. When the train reached the Columbus terminal, it was practically empty.

The Montgomery passengers drifted about the Georgia town, as inconspicuously as possible, and some took breakfast at local restaurants. By 7:00 AM, Alabama time, they had rendezvoused at the Rankin Hotel located at the river's edge. In a mezzanine room, men checked their guns, maps, and papers. A former detective for Atlanta's Southern Railway, M. S. Baughn reviewed the movements he had assigned each group of four or five men. One group also commandeered a telephone booth on the hotel's second floor. As the Girard town clock struck eight times, the Montgomery lawmen quickened their pace across the two bridges connecting Alabama and Georgia. At this hour, Alabama law permitted the execution of search warrants. As the lawmen arrived in Girard, the aroma of whiskey was so pervasive that the special deputies could smell the locations of liquor from the streets. Their warrants already identified prime locations.

At the first building near the riverfront, an officer attempted to open the door. "Is the key to the door in keeping of anyone in the sound of my voice?" he shouted. No answer. Promptly, he kicked open the door and discovered small quantities of beer—and more stoutly locked doors. After two officers arrived from a blacksmith shop with sledgehammers, the doors fell, revealing stacks and stacks of hard liquor.

As the search spread, storerooms and blind tigers yielded hundreds of cases of whiskey and rum. In other places, such as the Metropolitan Club, smaller quantities were in open view. By late morning, twenty deputies from a nearby dry county had joined in, and the fruits of the massive search filled almost two boxcars. The contraband was to be transported forty miles northwest to dry Opelika for safekeeping.

The Montgomery lawmen also met resistance. Girard's mayor deputized friends and neighbors to protect the property of local citizens against the invading force. Two owners of seized liquor were disarmed of Winchesters. The local sheriff moved ahead of the state lawmen with his own search warrants claiming that he, not they, would examine buildings. When confronted by state deputies, the sheriff grudgingly stepped aside.[5]

In Montgomery, Attorney General William Logan Martin, responsible for the entire operation, waited in his office for frequent reports from his special assistant, Mr. Baughn, sitting in the Columbus hotel phone booth. Although Baughn's local informants—mostly Baptist and Methodist preachers—had worked with Martin for months in gathering detailed information, the raid's final plans had been made hurriedly. Only five days earlier, on Friday afternoon, Martin had met with Governor Henderson at the governor's insistence. Weeks before, Henderson had approved expenses for Martin to pay Baughn as a "spy" to gather information on Girard's liquor, and Henderson wanted to know Martin's information and plans. The attorney general had no intention of being completely open and frank with the governor, the state's chief opponent of prohibition.

Through inheritance, the two men were political enemies. From south Alabama's Black Belt, "wet" in habit and business, Henderson was a self-described local optionist. Earlier, Henderson had been appointed by Governor B. B. Comer as the president of the State Railroad Commission, an opportunity Henderson used to join political forces with the corporations he regulated in order to defeat Comer in 1914. By family tradition, Logan Martin was a Comer man. His father came from the politically dry hills of northeast Alabama and had been attorney general in the 1890s. Comer picked the senior Martin in 1903 as Alabama's Speaker of the House, although Martin died the same year. Logan followed his father's footsteps to run for attorney general in

1914 on a political dry platform. He received key support from his father's old allies, men like Birmingham's Frank White and Samuel Weakley, and from corporate attorneys who were friends of his older brother Thomas Martin, vice president of the Alabama Power Company. Short and thin-boned, with black bean-shaped eyes slightly too large for his slender, delicate face, Logan Martin was hampered by Henderson almost from inauguration day. During this era, Alabama's governor had no paid legal advisors on his staff, and the attorney general was considered the governor's lawyer. Therefore, Henderson controlled practically all funds for the attorney general—outside of salaries for Martin, a stenographer, and two other lawyers. The prohibitionist legislature attempted to evade Henderson's control by providing Martin's office with an adequate budget for enforcing prohibition, but the governor vetoed the bill claiming it violated a constitutional relationship between the two offices. A legislative compromise permitted Martin to employ special personnel for enforcing prohibition, *with* the governor's prior approval, and authorized the attorney general to enlist any of the state's locally elected solicitors to assist him. Martin also had used private funds from Alabama citizens to do prohibition work, but the money proved inadequate.

Suspicious of Martin, Henderson used the powers of the purse to try to find out how much Martin knew and what he was doing to enforce prohibition. The meeting on Friday afternoon—five days before the raid—was for this purpose. It had been a terse, acrimonious exchange. Martin presented Henderson with only a rough sketch of his information about Girard, although the governor forced him to supply the names of some actual locations where illegal liquor had been discovered before he would approve vouchers for Baughn's past work. The attorney general asked Henderson to make the state militia available for a future Girard raid, but the bearish Henderson flatly refused. The governor said he had no authority to call out the militia for such purposes, although he did agree to cover the expenses of thirty special deputies to go to Girard if and when circumstances justified a liquor raid.

The governor and his assistants left for Birmingham's Confederate reunion under the impression that his office would get advance knowledge of any Girard raid since he had to approve specific expenses. With Henderson's general commitment, however, Martin quickly hired special deputies from Montgomery and Opelika for the secret dawn raid.

Now, five days later, as cases of liquor were stacking up in Girard, Martin received ominous reports from his special assistant. With so few men to serve warrants and guard the contraband in a town of six thousand, Baughn feared local hostility would escalate into violence, especially after mill hands left their shifts in the middle of the afternoon. The situation called for the state militia. Faced with no other choice, Martin reached Governor Henderson by telephone in Birmingham and asked him to call out the militia to quell a potential civil outbreak in Girard.

Henderson was furious. He shouted into the phone that the attorney general had created this crisis on his own. Now, he was asking the governor to take steps he had earlier said were outside his powers. After a heated, bitter exchange, the governor reluctantly agreed to Martin's request. With the advice of others at the reunion, including railroad lawyers and Judge J. S. Williams, a circuit judge from the Girard area, Henderson fashioned an executive order giving Martin the militia but stalling other parts of Martin's plans. The governor instructed the militia to take charge of the confiscated liquor and to store it in one of Girard's vacant buildings. The rail cars in which Martin had planned to transport the liquor to the safety of a politically dry county were now useless.[6]

The governor's order did not impede the seizure of liquor, which continued over several days. Lawmen discovered trapdoors leading to concrete storerooms containing hundreds of whiskey cases. Liquor was found in wells, open fields, high bushes, tall grass, potato patches, an abandoned church, and an outhouse. A second visit to the Manhattan Club revealed forty-five barrels beneath the cellar. Dozens of large corks floating down the muddy Chattahoochee turned out to be more than fishing lines. Bubbles tipped officers to the fact that the corks were the tops of one-gallon bottles of whiskey strung together. Further investigation located several cases of whiskey floating downstream.

The concealment of illegal substances was so universal that the county's two banks felt duty-bound to request publicly a search of their premises to get an official clean bill of health. Local public officials were not so lucky. State lawmen uncovered more than a hundred bottles of beer and several quarts of whiskey on Russell County Sheriff Pal Daniel's property. A state legislator's land held several stacks of liquor, and most members of the Girard city council expressed surprise when state deputies confiscated large quantities of liquor at their homes or businesses. Lawmen discovered six wagonloads of whiskey, stacked neatly in an old stable behind the residence of Girard Mayor Ed Morgan.

The mayor's own problems frustrated a second counter-tactic that local politicians had initiated for their own protection. As ex officio justice of the peace, Morgan was issuing arrest warrants against local townspeople for violating prohibition laws. While he appeared to join the cleanup, the mayor was allowing local men to plead guilty so that he could give them light fines and no imprisonment for their transgressions, thus shielding friends from jail and heavy fines at the hands of more impartial, law-enforcing judges. If the state later attempted to move against the already-convicted defendants, they could claim a violation of double jeopardy. But when the mayor became preoccupied with protecting his own liberty and property, this stratagem fell apart, and most liquor owners fled across the state line.

For weeks, lawmen continued to uncover new caches of whiskey as martial law was declared in Girard. Soldiers were posted throughout the town and especially at the bridges leading to Georgia. No one was permitted to loiter during the first week, and anyone found sitting on public property was required to walk or go to jail. All cars and wagons crossing between Girard and Columbus were stopped and searched. If "drivers do not stop and allow the militia to look through the cars, the tires will be punctured by shooting into them," warned the military captain. The movement of people and possessions underground also concerned lawmen. The city was "honeycombed with subterranean passages leading to gambling dens and storage places as deep as thirty-five feet under ground."

Estimated values of the contraband ranged from $300,000 to $1 million, a sum larger in 1916 than the state government's balance sheet at the end of the year. Never in Southern prohibition had lawmen seized such a large quantity of illegal liquor. The little mill town of Girard had been the shipping yard of whiskey for both Alabama and Georgia, or, as Governor Henderson reluctantly admitted, "the concentration camp of the immoral element of two States."[7] In Montgomery, Henderson explained his position to the press: "I have concluded that the liquor at Girard should be . . . held there until disposed of by an order of the court." The governor's decision worried the attorney general. Although he had no way to foresee all the governor's maneuvering, Martin did understand that his entire work could be gutted easily if Sheriff Pal Daniel remained in office in Russell County.

If the governor gave Daniel custody of the illegal liquor in Girard, the foxes would be guarding the hen house. While the sheriff claimed that he enforced prohibition laws, he had done little more than arrest itinerant peddlers who competed with local saloons and liquor dealers. Martin worried that the illegal contraband might disappear if Daniel took over its protection.

Accusing the sheriff of high crimes of omission, Martin asked Henderson to authorize impeachment proceedings in the Alabama Supreme Court. The governor refused. Instead, he called upon his friend, Judge J. S. Williams, to convene a special Russell County grand jury to consider impeaching the sheriff. The attorney general knew this approach would take months in trial and appeals, while the sheriff remained in office. It was also risky since Judge Williams was a wet.

Martin snubbed the governor's wishes and filed impeachment proceedings on behalf of more than fifty Russell County prohibitionists before the Supreme Court, whose opinions over the last year had begun to show strict adherence to the legislature's prohibitionist intent. Promptly after hearing the case, the Supreme Court found Sheriff Daniel guilty of neglect of duty and removed him from office.[8]

Next, Martin moved to litigate the legality of the massive seizure so that the last appeals could be exhausted before the governor sent the state militia home. The new sheriff was friendly to prohibition, but his handful of deputies was no match for scores of liquor owners and their agents who would be constantly looking for the opportunity to steal back their contraband. Martin was equally eager to indict and convict the whiskey owners in criminal court and to impeach local officials.

Yet Martin's plans weren't easily implemented. In the first session of circuit court called in July 1916, Judge Williams charged the grand jury to indict the guilty as "the eyes of the nation look on," but he did not charge them to investigate the misconduct of local officials or allow Martin to question prospective jurors on their willingness to convict for violations of prohibition laws. Unable to assure a favorable jury or to go after local officials, the attorney general declined to proceed. The special session ended a week after it began.

The attorney general conferred with Chief Justice John Anderson to develop a new strategy. Anderson had pledged to enforce strict prohibition according to the dry legislature's exact intent, in part as penance for drunkenly falling into his predecessor's grave during burial services several months earlier. The judge explained after his fall from grace that he drank whiskey to sooth his deep sorrow over the passing of an old friend on the court, and, unaccustomed to liquor's vile effects, he lost his balance and fell on top of the casket of the former chief justice. Now, literally having arisen from the dead, Anderson was eager to prove that he would faithfully uphold Alabama's dry laws. Martin requested the chief justice to use his authority, recently provided by the prohibitionist legislature, to order a special session of court in Russell County with a special judge who would help enforce dry laws.

Martin also needed extra lawyers. His two assistants were overloaded with providing everyday opinions to the different state departments and handling appeals from local circuits. Governor Henderson would not authorize Martin to hire private lawyers. That battle had been fought and lost. Martin's only option was to use a new state statute to order—or, realistically, to convince—one or two local solicitors to help. His choices were limited. Perhaps as many as half of the state's local solicitors were wet. Others were Martin's political enemies. In addition, state law be damned, many solicitors simply would not take an assignment that encroached on their private practice of law. Girard's work carried no extra pay and no assurance even that the governor would approve basic expenses.

Martin's first choice was predictable. Centerville Circuit Solicitor Fritz Thompson was a prohibitionist, a friend, and an experienced criminal lawyer. The second choice was far more doubtful: Hugo Black of Birmingham. True, no Alabama solicitor had been more aggressive in enforcing prohibition laws, and Birmingham men whom Martin trusted admired Black's abilities and devotion to prohibition. Black also was available since he was a full-time prosecutor without a private practice. On the other hand, Black's past private practice and public positions were hostile to regulated corporations like Thomas Martin's Alabama Power Company. And, Black had a reputation as egotistical, ambitious, and independent.

In announcing the special criminal court for Russell County, by order of the chief justice, the attorney general stated that Judge A. H. Alston had been assigned as presiding officer and Fritz Thompson and Hugo Black were to act as special assistant attorneys general. In the announcement, Black was erroneously referred to as "solicitor for the Birmingham *City* Court"—an unintended slight that indicated his secondary role in Girard. Martin and Thompson were to handle the grand jury, where the important work would be undertaken, and Black was to try criminal cases when and if any defendants could be found.[9]

HUGO BLACK HAD AMPLE REASON to doubt the wisdom of accepting his new assignment. Despite some reductions, Birmingham's backlog of criminal cases remained large and demanding. The controversial Walton case was docketed for trial again in September, and Judge Fort wanted the next grand jury to investigate continuing problems at Jefferson's jail. Also, Black had to forego his usual month-long trip to the West at a time when he needed rest and an old friend needed him.

In late June, Black had rushed to Colorado with a tragic mission. His old friend Barney Whatley had shot and killed his own father. On a cool June night at his Breckenridge ranch, Whatley intervened when his father threatened to whip a grandchild. The old man erupted in a violent rage, pulled a gun, and ran cursing his son. Shots were fired, and on the back porch Wilburn Whatley lay dead from a bullet of his son's gun. Barney was arrested and tried for the killing. Without being asked, Black went immediately to Colorado and took charge of the defense. He helped to persuade a coroner's inquest to find his friend's actions justifiable, and at trial Black's "eloquent address" in closing arguments overcame a local judge's hostile jury charge. Barney was found not guilty. Yet local newspaper headlines proclaimed, "Curtain Lifted on Family Skeleton." At trial, Barney and his family had to recount in open court the details of Wilburn Whatley's long history of erratic, violent behavior. The Whatleys and their attorney were careful not to mention one word about Wilburn's shameful theft of Confederate pensions, which had made him an Alabama fugitive.

Now almost thirty years old, after eighteen years of devoted friendship, Hugo and Barney did not talk to one another—or to anyone else—about the agony that their fathers had caused them and their families. Both knew, but it was not a subject for discussion. They were not men given to self-doubt or self-analysis. Yet, these men's lives were woven together by shared experiences, tragedies, and ambitions. Starting from the same small town, both wanted to be lawyers. Both were now local prosecutors. Both by nature were joiners who genuinely enjoyed the company of other men. And both equipped their lives through hard work and personal optimism.

In addition, both men were shaped often by the sins of their fathers. Just as Hugo's father's cardinal vice, whiskey, had killed W. L. Black, Wilburn Whatley's chief character flaw, a penchant for violence, had led to his own death. Hugo and Barney were their families' youngest boys, but both had taken their fathers' places in front of older brothers. From boyhood, both had observed the unspoken terms of their shared notion of friendship: be there for your friend in time of need whenever it came. "He came when I needed him," Barney said of his old friend.

Less than two months after he pulled the trigger killing his father, Whatley now faced a tough campaign for reelection as district attorney amid "unworthy" rumors springing from the tragedy of that June night. In 1914, Barney had returned to Alabama to help Hugo win his election as prosecutor. He came without being asked. Now, Black was *not* on his way to Colorado. Instead, he was on a train traveling for prohibition to lower Alabama. It was the journey of a man who had more than one good reason to be elsewhere.

Accompanied by assistant Morris Allen, Black arrived late at Seale, a community the size of Ashland where the Russell County courthouse stood on a commanding hill overlooking the railroad station. By mid-afternoon, Judge A. H. Alston had charged the grand jury in open court: "The enormity of the amounts of liquor seized at Girard, Alabama, leads to the reports of complicity of officials," the judge stated in a unwavering voice. "Gentlemen, investigate these matters. If an official has violated his duty, the law gives you the means to remove him . . . hew the line and let the chips fall where they may."

Every seat in the courtroom was taken, with "the aisles jammed and many standing around the walls and in the ante-chambers . . . balancing forward to catch every word that was spoken," according to a reporter. Judge Alston also told the jury to investigate reports of election fraud, gambling, and general lawlessness. In the opinion of local old-timers, "it was the strongest, most unusual charge ever delivered in the county." Promptly, the grand jury was escorted to a corner room of the courthouse's second floor where it heard evidence presented by the attorney general late into the evening.[10]

On the following day, Black conducted the first criminal trials. In most cases, Black declared the state ready for trial, and no defendant appeared. Judge Alston afterwards ordered a forfeiture of the defendant's appearance bond and his arrest, if possible. The new sheriff found it difficult and finally impossible to locate any criminal defendants. A certain "fine of $2,500 with a pen sentence staring them in the face . . . proved too strong a dose for those indicted," observed a reporter. Defendants were reportedly away on fishing trips, bird-watching expeditions, and extended vacations in Georgia and Florida.

By Wednesday night, August 9, Logan Martin departed for Montgomery to ask the governor to extradite a host of missing defendants and to request the chief justice to extend the special session. Fritz Thompson was left in charge of the grand jury, and Black was left to call the cases of missing defendants.[11] In a routine review of pending appeals, Black discovered no evidence that an appeal bond had been posted in six civil cases that had been tried in the first special session before Judge Williams. The defendants had filed notices of appeal but no appeal bonds, according to the circuit clerk.

The meaning of this discovery quickly dawned on the solicitor. Until September 1915, the law did not require defendants in civil suits to post a bond covering the costs of an appeal from circuit court; however, as Black knew, the state legislature decided to require bonds to make it more difficult for liquor owners to postpone the destruction of their contraband simply by appealing.

That night in Seale, Black dined with Fritz Thompson and Morris Allen. By 9:00 PM, Black had a plan. He instructed the circuit clerk to contact Frank DeGraffenried, who represented most defendants, and to ask the lawyer for copies of all official documents filed in circuit court on behalf of his six clients who did not show up for their criminal trials during the last three days. Next, Black and his old classmate retired to Hugo's room in the Dudley Hotel where Black drafted a motion.

"Comes the State of Alabama by Hugo L. Black . . . and shows the Court that . . . on the 13th day of July, 1916 an order was made by the Honorable J. S. Williams . . . condemning and forfeiting to the State of Alabama all prohibited liquors . . . and that . . . the Sheriff of Russell County . . . should publicly destroy the said prohibited liquor." Black's motion claimed that each defendant was a "fugitive from justice, and . . . cannot be found, and that as such . . . he is in contempt of this Court and has no standing in this Court, nor any right to be heard by himself or counsel." Therefore, the motion asked the court to "issue an order commanding the Sheriff to destroy all of said prohibited liquors."

With document in hand, Black and Allen transformed the modest hotel room into the Russell County courtroom. The bed served as judge. For three hours the two men went over the imagined proceedings. "Each point to destroy the liquor was made by the solicitor and his assistant, taking the part of the defendant attorney, attempted to stop the order." Black also rehearsed the timing and wording of his arguments and responses, just as he had on those occasions when he and Barney Whatley had practiced in their office. In the hotel room, the two men simulated the case all the way through appeals to the Alabama Supreme Court. Long after midnight, the mock trial ended. Black had won. In a few hours, he would discover if he could achieve the same result in a real courtroom.[12]

At 8:30 next morning, August 10, Black entered a courtroom sparsely occupied by the "unescorted ladies" wearing small white ribbons on their shirtwaists, badges of the local Women's Christian Temperance Union. They sat in the same seats each day "to see for one of the first times in Alabama the liquor traffic getting what they have wanted it to get all the time." Black stepped to the bench and handed Judge Alston his one-page motion. As it was read aloud, the audience literally gasped with surprise. Black explained that Judge Williams's orders to destroy the liquor could only be stayed by an appeal bond but that no such bonds had been posted. Therefore, Black had filed his motion against six defendants who had not shown up for their criminal trials. Black made it clear that he was not filing a motion against any liquor owners who were sitting in the Russell County jail. Only the six owners who had failed to show up for trial were the subject of this motion to destroy confiscated liquor.

In solemn tones and melodramatic gestures, Black declared the six were "fugitives from justice . . . in contempt of this Court" with "no standing in this Court . . . nor any right to be heard by themselves or counsel." The liquor of these fugitives can and must be destroyed *now*, Black insisted.

Judge Alston glanced inquiringly at Frank DeGraffenried who had walked forward from the back of the courtroom. Black's plan hung in the balance, but when DeGraffenried launched into a broadside against the solicitor's motion, Black smiled and settled back in his chair. Fritz Thompson came from the grand jury room and chuckled. Growing by the minute, the audience seemed confused. Appearing "as general counsel for the said defendant claimants," DeGraffenried proclaimed that his clients were fully entitled to be heard by the Court—despite Mr. Black's claims to the contrary—and that he wished to speak to the motion. Judge Alston replied, "The Court would be glad to hear you."

The attorney argued that no appeal bonds were necessary since the appeals had not yet been perfected. He also said that the court had no jurisdiction in the matter since the chief justice had authorized it only for criminal cases and the cases in question were civil in nature. By now, the courtroom was packed as townspeople gathered, and the grand jury recessed to observe Black's dramatic offensive.

Noting that counsel adequately represented the defendants, Black stated that he wanted to argue fully the merits of his motion. A "light dawned and Mr. DeGraffenried urgently requested that everything he'd said be withdrawn and expunged" from the record. "Mr. Black moved that this not be granted. Judge Alston ruled with him," observed a reporter.

The circuit clerk verified that, after the six defendants had lost their civil cases in July, Judge Williams had ordered their liquor destroyed and the defendants had failed to file appeal bonds. The sheriff testified that he was unable to find any of these defendants to stand trial on pending criminal charges, and, when Black asked the sheriff if Mr. DeGraffenried had been seen in Girard recently, he replied "Yes."

DeGraffenried was furious, demanding to know what Black implied by such a question. Black replied that he simply wanted to evidence that the defendants' attorney had an opportunity to inform his clients that their criminal cases had been called for trial. DeGraffenried assured the court that he did not know where his clients were and, had he known, he would have done his duty to bring them before the court. The liquor lawyer asked for a recess so that he could prepare a full response to the pending motion. The court agreed and adjourned until one-thirty in the afternoon.

With a clearer head, DeGraffenried might have pressed the court on the issue of jurisdiction. For all his careful, cagey planning, Black had failed to realize the importance of the jurisdictional questions. Judge Alston's jurisdiction was exclusively over criminal cases, and the condemnation of illegal liquor had occurred in civil court.[13] During recess, Black met with Judge Alston and Logan Martin, who arrived from Montgomery as surprised as everyone else by the swift turn of events. Black discovered that the attorney general had an order from the chief justice extending the jurisdiction of Judge Alston's court, but it did not alter the Court's exclusively criminal jurisdiction. By telephone, Martin apparently reached the chief justice and outlined developments. Judge Anderson agreed to alter his recent order and to provide Judge Alston's court with authority for "all orders civil or *quasi* civil as may be executive to the enforcement of the criminal laws." He dated his letter of amendment "August 10th, 1:00 P.M." and mailed it to the attorney general. Black assigned Morris Allen to type Judge Anderson's revised order as an original document.

Thirty minutes later, DeGraffenried returned to the courtroom with a copy of Judge Anderson's original order prescribing the court's authority only over criminal cases. He argued that Black's motion addressed a civil matter which was beyond Judge Alston's powers. In response, Black handed the judge a copy of the chief justice's second order, composed by phone minutes earlier, and Judge Alston overruled the defendants' motion to quash. Next, DeGraffenried offered to file appeal bonds for his clients, but Black quickly, loudly objected. "It's too late. Your clients are not before the court. They are fugitives from justice," Black protested. Judge Alston observed that DeGraffenried could not file appeal bonds on behalf of fugitives from justice whose whereabouts were unknown to him.

The magnitude of the proposed destruction was worth a good fight. From only one of the six defendants, the seized liquor had totaled 1,000 cases, 37 barrels, 5 drums, 110 loose gallons, 1,300 quarts, as well as 2,591 loose pints. The liquor of all six clients probably represented more than half of Girard's entire seized whiskey, beer, and wine, a fabulous supply exceeding the combined contraband of all other liquor raids in Alabama since the start of state prohibition. Shortly after 2 PM, DeGraffenried exhausted his pleas, and Judge Alston ordered the sheriff to destroy the six defendants' liquor. The Court adjourned, and the state's lawyers rushed to waiting automobiles, already hand-cranked, and sped away towards the whiskey warehouse.[14]

The intoxicating news crossed the county and the Chattahoochee River like a tidal wave. Within a few hours, more than four thousand people arrived by foot, wagon, and automobile at the state-controlled warehouse. Within the hour, the state's lawyers and the sheriff gathered in front of the first stack of liquor for photographs by newspapermen. Black stood in the middle between Logan Martin and the sheriff. Fixing a large satisfied smile on his face, Black pushed back a fashionable white flat-brimmed straw hat that would resemble a halo when many of the state's prohibitionists saw the picture on the front pages. The sheriff christened the new era by removing and breaking a bottle of Magnolia beer. Logan Martin destroyed a bottle of whiskey with exaggerated style, and then it was Black's turn. "Black was on the job for some time," noted one reporter. "His specialty was cracking E. W. Harper. He had a good swing, and seemed to understand what he was about."

For the rest of the day, liquor destruction became a melodrama of religious worship and pagan ritual, as gallons upon gallons of flowing liquids, rich in color, foam, and odor were offered in sacrifice to a vengeful Protestant dry God. Among thousands who assembled were church groups clicking their Kodaks to preserve the moment for posterity and other congregations of true believers who wished to behold the sight of this miraculous, righteous triumph. Finally, Lord, finally, it was good over evil.

Seventy-plus black laborers were hired to bring out barrels and cases of liquor, as the white sheriff, deputies, and militiamen hammered open spewing, gurgling liquor. When the contents of five thousand emptied bottles created pools of liquor that trickled down the streets, the sheriff moved the destruction to the banks of a ravine leading into the Chattahoochee. Soon there was a crowd of blacks "who like many whites were thirsting amazedly at the wholesale waste of the fiery fluid for which some of them might have given . . . their last pennies over bread for the families," wrote a local reporter.

Someone touched a match to the meandering whiskey, and it burst into "an almost invisible and treacherous blue flame . . . giving off an unbearable heat and odor." The fire was extinguished, and the ritual continued until nightfall.

Next morning, when the destruction began again, attorney Frank De-Graffenried was frantically seeking a court order to save the remainder of his clients' property. After Judge Alston's order, he had gone directly to Judge Williams in Union Springs. The anti-prohibitionist judge was sympathetic but unhelpful. He had no judicial power to stop the destruction. DeGraffenried returned to Seale and requested Judge Alston to enjoin his own order. The judge refused. By telephone, the attorney tried to reach Chief Justice Anderson. Near midnight, he spoke to another state Supreme Court justice who said he could not give advice. DeGraffenried must file a proper petition before the court before a justice could consider the matter.

Thursday morning, the Russell County lawyer was on his way to Montgomery in search of any judge who would listen. He visited a federal judge who declined to consider the issues. DeGraffenried waited, to no avail, for the chief justice's return from an out-of-town funeral (where Anderson was sober and upright). The lawyer then departed Montgomery on a fifty-mile trip to Tuskegee to see Oscar Lewis, chancellery court judge. Lewis was an ardent anti-prohibitionist. As a legislator, he had been Governor Henderson's unsuccessful candidate for state senate president *pro tempore* in a bold maneuver to take the power to appoint all committees from prohibitionist Lieutenant

Governor Thomas E. Kilby. After the plot failed, Henderson appointed Lewis as chancellor judge.

Reaching Tuskegee, DeGraffenried found Lewis was in Montgomery. The lawyer turned around and returned to the state capital. By 11:00 PM, DeGraffenried reached the city to discover that Chief Justice Anderson was at home. The justice, however, refused to sign an order stopping the liquor's destruction on grounds that the Supreme Court acts only by appeal from a lower court.[15] At 6:00 AM on the following day, a rumpled DeGraffenried pounded on the door of a guest room in Montgomery's fashionable Gay Teague Hotel. Judge Lewis opened the door and soon gave DeGraffenried what he wanted—an injunction to stop the liquor's destruction. The order was telegraphed to Sheriff Lindsey in Girard, and the Russell County lawyer drove home with a sigh of relief.

After arriving in Girard, DeGraffenried learned that demolition had not stopped. At Seale, he demanded that Judge Alston and Hugo Black cease the liquor destruction. Alston reminded the liquor lawyer that the chancellor court had no authority to overturn a decision of a circuit court in civil matters. Only a higher court could reverse Judge Alston's ruling.

Beleaguered and confused, DeGraffenried returned to Montgomery and Chief Justice Anderson with an appeal. In a written order, Anderson stated that no injunction was necessary or proper since DeGraffenried's clients had an adequate, available remedy in the circuit court—by filing appeal bonds properly signed and executed by his clients.

DeGraffenried must have been paralyzed momentarily. For two and a half days he had traveled hundreds of miles with little sleep in order to end the liquor's destruction. Now, Anderson told him that he had an easy remedy: file proper appeal bonds with the signatures of your clients in circuit court. It was that simple. By next morning, the attorney-in-travel had located two clients and hurriedly filed signed appeal bonds. Black was at the courthouse to greet him. The solicitor served the circuit clerk with an injunction requiring DeGraffenried to prove the bonds were valid. At a hearing, Black questioned each signature's authenticity. In fact, one bond had not been signed by the defendant but, according to the liquor lawyer, by a manager of his client's property. The other signature belonged to the second defendant, but neither had risked arrest to appear in person to sign the bonds.

Black launched an extensive debate with DeGraffenried over the validity of the manager's signature. The solicitor was incredibly long winded. Finally,

Judge Alston telephoned the manager to determine if it truly was his signature on the bond. Suddenly, Black agreed to an order stopping the destruction of the two defendants' whiskey. When the order reached Girard, however, all liquor belonging to the two defendants had been poured out. Their whiskey had become top priority as of Saturday morning, and Black's courtroom filibuster had given lawmen just enough time to break the last bottle before the stop order arrived.[16]

Throughout the weekend, workers continued to build large mounds of broken glass and wooden fragments from other whiskey owners' smashed liquor. The ravine of alcohol remained a local tourist attraction, although some spectators fainted from the stench. One wag suggested that the stream of whiskey flowing into the Chattahoochee would create a peculiar world of sober men and drunken fish. Another proposed a sign for the ravine: "For Sale—sand and gravel, pickled in alcohol. Fine for club house plaster." Cameramen from Universal Pictures captured newsreel scenes for silent screens around the country as Alabama whiskey became national news.

On Monday, five days after Black had joined in destroying the first liquor bottles, Frank DeGraffenried filed appeal bonds for his four remaining clients. It now appeared the moment of prohibition's triumph was over. Not so, protested Black. The solicitor summoned to the grand jury a young lawyer who had produced one of the bonds. "You are a lawyer and you know you don't have to answer" a self-incriminating question, Black stated. But the prosecutor wanted to know how the young lawyer knew where to find DeGraffenried's client, a fugitive from justice, to secure a signature. "I was told he was there," vaguely sputtered the lawyer. The witness could not swear that the person who signed the document was, in fact, an owner of the confiscated whiskey.

Black persisted, but by late morning, without any startling revelations, Judge Alston signed an order stopping destruction of the liquor until higher courts had acted. Black's grand jury probe had given deputies two or three extra hours to swing the axes of dry vengeance, but the massive, glorious destruction of the demon liquor had now ended.

Cleaning up began. The liquor ravine dried out, and the grand jury issued more than thirty-five additional indictments. Judge Alston gave maximum jail terms to the three men convicted on the first day of trial. Girard's police chief resigned, as did the entire city council after agreeing to the appointment of a slate of prohibitionists in their place.

SITTING IN A COLUMBUS HOTEL THE NEXT DAY, "the father of the moment for the destruction of the liquors," Hugo Black talked to reporters about recent events. "The birds have flown, and it now appears that Russell County has a nice collection of non-residents," Black cattily observed. The solicitor predicted similar clean-up efforts elsewhere in Alabama following what reporters now called "one of the greatest legal battles ever won" for prohibition. When asked about the direction of the prohibition movement, Black became blunt and evangelical. "We believe in putting the liquor in the gutters rather than the people," Black declared. "The state of Alabama is going to enforce its laws."[17]

Birmingham newspapers extensively covered Black's adventures at Girard, and on his first day back in his office, Saturday, August 19, Jefferson's county solicitor gave another interview to local reporters about his self-styled "vacation." "Oh, we had a great deal of fun down there," Black asserted. "Many of the prominent citizens of Girard are now in jail or fugitives from justice . . . Nearly all the confiscated liquor was destroyed," he said. "It was estimated that about $500,000 worth of liquor was thrown into the Chattahoochee River."

A reporter wanted to know how Black managed to pull off such a coup. "That's a very funny thing," smiled Black. "The first day I got there we tried three, and the juries gave them the limit. That scared the other culprits . . . the other defendants decamped for friendlier climates. We fooled around . . . and then it came to my ears that the fugitives had not filed appeal bonds on the confiscated liquor." Warming to his own story, Black explained, "It seems the attorney for the defendants had slipped up."

"I made a motion to destroy the liquors at once and orated at length on the fact that defendants were fugitives of justice, which did not have a thing to do with the case except to deceive the opposition," Black laughed. "Well, it deceived the enemy, I guess, for instead of filing immediate appeal bonds which could have been done in about two hours, the attorney of the defendants hurried about the state seeking injunctions while we went merrily on our task of throwing the confiscated liquor in the sewers."[18]

Now Alabamians knew. Prohibition's greatest victory had been achieved by a bit of legal acumen and a lot of courtroom bluff. More than legal talent, Black's histrionics and bravado had carried the day.

Of course, Black conveniently failed to outline for reporters the essential role of two friendly judges. His strategy would have collapsed if the chief justice had been unwilling to postdate his revised order. Without a change in Judge

Alston's jurisdiction, accomplished over the phone during court recess, Black would have failed. Nor did Black remember for reporters the crucial moment in the Russell County courtroom when DeGraffenried, exhausted of all other arguments, offered to post appeal bonds immediately for his clients. It was, in fact, exactly what he had a right to do to prevent the whiskey's destruction. Carefully, cunningly, Black had shouted, "It's too late." He proclaimed that DeGraffenried's clients were "fugitives from justice." He orated at length in order to give the impression that the defendants had no right to file a bond *because* they were fugitives from justice. In literal truth, he stated that because "you don't know where they are," it was too late for DeGraffenried's clients to sign a bond.

It was a subtle, deceitful, and critical difference of meaning in plain words. Judge Alston also was an essential accomplice in this ruse. His response to DeGraffenried's offer to post the bonds was equally deceptive. In essence, Judge Alston stated that DeGraffenried could not file signed appeal bonds on behalf of clients whose whereabouts were unknown. Distracted by Black's bombast, DeGraffenried thought the judge's statement sustained what he thought Black was arguing—that his clients, as fugitives, had no legal right to file an appeal bond.

Theatrical talent, luck, and like-minded judges were necessary for Black to take simple words with ordinary meaning and use them deceptively to allow the greatest legal moment that dry Alabama had ever enjoyed. And, in a lawyer's delight, Black achieved this prohibitionist glory by enforcing the original order of Judge Williams, Governor Henderson's friend and ardent anti-prohibitionist.

Concluding the reporters' interview, doused in abundant self-satisfaction, Black turned to his desk and plans for a demanding September criminal docket. In the excitement of the last three weeks, Black probably did not notice a small report out of Montgomery, announced on the same day as his courtroom victory in Girard. Governor Henderson had once again paroled E. M. Gibson, the fellow Black had convicted twice for handing out liquor leaflets. Claiming once more that Gibson had converted to bone-dry law and order, Henderson paroled him a second time.[19] Jefferson's county solicitor wasn't the only one who could get results by using simple words with duplicity. For Black, this little twist of justice would prove to be a more accurate omen of the events to come than was the sweet aftertaste of his celebrated, dry victory at Girard.

BIRMINGHAM REPORTERS APPARENTLY EXPECTED to find the county solicitor in his office on a Saturday afternoon. Black's entire life was focused on his job of fighting serious crime and illegal liquor, and he worked late at the courthouse almost every night and most weekends. His furnished apartment on the seventh floor of the new Ridgely was conveniently within six blocks of his office, as was the First Baptist Church where he continued to teach the men's Sunday school class. Many fraternal lodge halls, like the Pythians, were almost as near. Other than occasional business trips to Montgomery or Russell County, Black seldom moved outside his small orbit of work, lodges, and church. It was an existence reproducing the scale of daily living that Black had sustained since his boyhood when he seldom went beyond sight of Ashland's county courthouse.

What little time Black took from the solicitor's job was more often spent in self-education than on a social life. Although the Ridgely was occupied by singles, including a large number of female teachers, Black often stayed in his rooms reading books of history, economics, or politics—always nonfiction, never fiction—while roommate Walter Brower and other bachelors went downstairs to weekly dances and other social events in the courtyard gardens.

Black occasionally joined Albert Lee Smith and a regular group of bachelors for dinner at a restaurant atop one of the city's tallest buildings across from the courthouse. On these occasions, Black relaxed in a friendly, manly atmosphere of rivalry and practical jokes. One common prank was, in the language of a solicitor, theft by taking. "Damn fellows would swipe the other fellows' pie," recalled Smith, delighting in the memory of old days. When another man wasn't looking, somebody would "reach over and cut a piece" of his desert and proclaim, "Just kidding!" as he gulped down the stolen bite. Black was far more often a victim rather than a perpetrator of this crime.

Even in relaxation Black proved his shrewdness. One night, puzzling everyone at the table, the solicitor ordered his dessert to be brought first. When his cake arrived, Black leaned over, took a deep breath, and—"bluuuuuuuuuuuuuu"—blew his wet breath all over the dessert. No one wanted to get near it. While nearby diners might have questioned the table manners of their county's thirty-year-old chief prosecutor, Hugo's male friends weren't surprised. They knew Black always tried to have his cake and eat it too.

On a few free weekends, Albert Lee and Hugo escaped for a quick visit to Atlanta or the country club for golf or tennis. Unlike his performances in the courtroom, Black was usually patient and workmanlike on the tennis court.

He seldom went for a slam but tried to keep the ball in play until the other player made a mistake. Yet, Black's personal motto of "all things [except liquor] in moderation" did not govern his days as prosecutor. None of his other Alabama years was as busy, demanding, and pressure-cooked. A long-undiagnosed thyroid problem gave Black a vast store of restless energy and a slim physique that suggested good health, but the solicitor often pushed himself to the point of exhaustion. Because of his aggressive prosecutions, Black received death threats. Someone fired gunshots into his apartment.[20]

But Black would not be deterred or slowed. His time, emotions, and energies were entirely devoted to achieving law, order, and civic righteousness in his own city and home state.

In Greek mythology "ambrosia" was the nourishment of Zeus and other gods about whom Black read during quiet evenings at Ridgely Apartments, but Jefferson's county prosecutor was hell-bent on preventing its consumption by mere mortals in Birmingham. From the beginning of his solicitor's term, Black had been vexed by the sale of "near beers," nonalcoholic drinks that looked, smelled, and tasted like real beer. As consumption of liquor slowed, sales of near-beer and especially a beverage known as "Fehr's Ambrosia" began to boom. Prohibitionists, including Black, considered the substance as threatening as the real stuff since near beer made it difficult for police to identify real, illegal beer. For this reason, Alabama's prohibition law specifically outlawed "near beer," and Hugo Black intended to enforce the law.

Before departing earlier to Girard, Black had authorized a raid on Birmingham's L&N depot, which was storing almost a thousand gallons of ambrosia from a Kentucky brewery, and enlisted Judge Samuel Weakley to defend the sheriff's confiscation in the face of strenuous objections from railroad lawyers. "The sale of such beverages is objectionable," argued Weakley, "because . . . it affords for subterfuge and evasion." If ambrosia is sold, the author of Alabama's prohibition laws stated, the police would not be able to enforce the state's dry laws.

This seizure was problematic, however. The railroad's lawyers, former Governor Emmet O'Neal and Senator Oscar Underwood's chief advisor Forney Johnston, argued that the state had no evidence that Fehr's products were intended for sale in Alabama and the U.S. Constitution barred the local prosecutor from interfering with their interstate shipments. For more than a month, Johnston had urged the circuit court to bring the case to trial, and Black's assistants were equally persistent in postponing it. Now, the chief prosecutor was back from his Girard "vacation," and the controversy over near beer came to a head.[21]

On Tuesday morning, September 5, the ambrosia case was called again for trial. Answering for the railroads was Johnston, but no one appeared for the state. The circuit judge sent for circuit solicitor Joseph Tate and the deputy sheriff who had seized the liquor. The deputy proved unavailable since he was in another courtroom—on trial himself for illegally possessing real liquor. Finally, Black appeared to ask the judge to hold the case over again. He suggested disingenuously that he could not proceed on the county's behalf since the case was a civil matter and he was in charge of only criminal cases.

Johnston sneered. Feigning great surprise that "Ego" Black would admit to any limitation of authority or ability, the corporate lawyer reiterated that his witnesses had been assembled for the fourth time and that the county's solicitor was now present. Johnston insisted that the case go to trial immediately.

Black's evasion quickly fell apart. Joseph Tate arrived to inform the judge that he was conducting a criminal prosecution under Black's direction. Besides, Tate confessed, he was totally unfamiliar with the ambrosia case. Johnston was delighted. "It seems to me that the state's attorneys do not contemplate this case as a serious affair and are playful with the court," he contended. The judge agreed and granted Johnston's motion to dismiss the case due to a lack of good faith prosecution.

"I object to that," Black shouted. "I am here as sufficient security that there is no want of prosecution." Overruled, Black persevered. "I desire to make the statement that this disposition of this particular hearing does not mean that ambrosia will be sold in Birmingham."

"Such braggadocio statements," snorted Johnston, "are too puerile for us."

"Order!" the judge demanded, but Black persisted. "Well, there will be no Ambrosia sold, I'll tell you that now!" shouted the county solicitor as he left the courtroom.

Four days later, Black repeated his pledge to reporters: "Ambrosia will not be sold in Jefferson County." When served with the judge's order to return the ambrosia to the railroad *"instanter,"* the sheriff tarried. "I don't know just how long *instanter* means," pondered the sheriff, telling reporters about his difficulties both with understanding Latin and in getting drays to move the bottles from the county vault. "I'm preparing to do so tomorrow morning. I believe that will be *instanter* enough," he mused. Behind the scenes, Black was finishing legal papers to seize the beverages once more.

All of these public statements delighted the railroad lawyer. "Well, those fellows are making too much of a good thing," said Johnston. He immediately went to federal court, and Judge W. I. Grubb issued a temporary order requiring Black and the sheriff to deposit the ambrosia at the railroad depot. "We did not oppose the petition for temporary relief," Black explained as he worked late one Saturday night, "but we will fight the final injunction to the last notch . . . and if any attempts are made to sell the beverage it will be at the risk of the dealer, as Judge Grubb did not give them that relief."

Within a week, Black made good on his threat. Deputies arrested a local shopkeeper for selling ambrosia, and Black swore out a warrant for the arrest of Johnston's clients whom the shopkeeper identified as his dealer. Black also prosecuted a second shopkeeper for selling "Brother Wiser," another brand of near beer drink. The defense futilely claimed that the beverage was harmless and nonalcoholic. "It looks like beer," Black concluded, "and that is clearly a violation of the law."[22]

Black's words and work in Birmingham and Girard brought him a moment of celebrity status among the state's prohibitionists and a stack of mail from other Alabama communities pleading for assistance in stopping illegal liquor and its profiteering "immoral elements." In Mobile, the state's only port city on the Gulf of Mexico, a local temperance group had hired private detectives to gather evidence. The group claimed Mobile was another, key point of entry for illegal liquor in amounts that dwarfed Girard's contraband. Attorney General Logan Martin and Black agreed in late 1916 to visit Mobile to discuss the situation.

Departing Birmingham by train at 10:35 in the evening, Jefferson's indefatigable solicitor was initially coy with reporters, who remembered an earlier, sensational liquor story that also began with a late-night train ride. "I'm going to Mobile and will be gone several days," Black stated vaguely. When pressed about Alabama problems with whiskey rings, Black was more forthcoming. "There can be no open violation of the prohibition law . . . without the connivance or utter indifference of the constituted authorities," Black stated. "If in Jefferson County the juries were so indifferent to law enforcement that they brought in verdicts of not guilty on prohibition cases, I would still be able to enforce the laws through the use of injunctions."[23]

Despite Black's haughty proclamation, problems for Alabama prohibition were more fundamental and complex than merely public officials' failure to "do their sworn duty." Black and other teetotalers were often blind to the practical difficulties that many people had with prohibition. Perhaps, in dealing with alcoholism's ruined lives and "immoral elements," Black and prohibition's other absolutists were unable to see liquor's strong seduction as an accessible, personal agent of change in a world where misery, boredom, and uncertainty could be too much to humanly bear without moments of escape and even irresponsibility. After all, Adam did bite the apple.

Prohibition's opponents, including amoral men like Governor Henderson, acknowledged that whiskey defined the reigning morality of the day, but they seemed to understand better than dry absolutists the practical difficulties of banning all liquor. Since the earliest days of statehood, many citizens ranging from Primitive Baptist preachers to Italian newcomers had moderately consumed the demon rum for its mood-changing effects. Some men profited extravagantly only because beer and whiskey were illegal, and others used liquor as a tool for exploiting the poor and vulnerable. But, honorable opponents like A. O. Lane also believed absolute prohibition was impossible and fostered disrespect for law.

In the aftermath of the 1916 elections, when most dry candidates were defeated, prohibition leaders realized they had to rally their troops. Former Governor B. B. Comer called Governor Henderson's conduct in Girard "the shame of the state" and declared that the "fight in the next campaign is . . . whether we want the return of liquor again." Two years in advance, Lieutenant Governor Thomas Kilby announced he would run for governor in 1918 in the Comer tradition, as a businessman "uncompromising and unequivocal in his championship of the present state prohibition laws." The Anti-Saloon League organized members in an early plan to win a hard political struggle to keep Alabama dry.[24]

Yet, in 1916, Alabama's dry leaders were having problems maintaining whiskey as their supporters' singular focus. Some prohibitionists, especially in Birmingham, had begun to turn towards earlier issues that once glued together a battered coalition of the state's progressive movement. These dry activists were not retreating one inch on prohibition, but they were addressing a broader set of economic and social problems that they believed, along with the evils of liquor, destroyed the good life.

Black's own minister, Dr. A. J. Dickinson led in 1915-16 a campaign for government ownership of city services such as electricity, gas, and water despite strong opposition from Birmingham's industrial managers. An Alabama Power Company official accused Dickinson's group of trying to make Birmingham the "most socialistic city" in America. "Well, what of it?" snapped the Baptist minister. If socialism "considers the interest of society above . . . corporations," Dickinson asserted he was all for a socialistic city.

Convict leasing was also an economic-moral issue receiving added attention from leaders of civic righteousness. After Jefferson County stopped leasing its convicts, Frank White and Alabama's labor unions joined with advocates for improving public roads to establish the Alabama Convict Improvement Association to end the state's "immoral practice." In 1915 the Association renewed its attempt to persuade Alabama's dry legislature to stop convict leasing, despite opposition from Governor Henderson, mining operators, and Black Belt landowners.

Another emerging issue broadening the moral agenda was observance of the Sabbath. Birmingham's suburban Protestant ministers were organizing to close silent movie houses on Sunday since they feared "movies merchants" were trying to desecrate the holy day merely for profit. In addition, Arlie Barber, the city's new socialist police commissioner, had issued arrest warrants for movie operators showing films he considered unwholesome. He also proposed to close all pool halls on Sunday and to outlaw dominoes in public places every day of the week since the game could lead to gambling.[25]

These issues reflected and rekindled ancient, smoldering antagonisms between Protestant and Catholic churches, which many fundamentalist Baptist and Methodist ministers continued to see as the "arch enemy of American institutions." In 1916, amid public attacks on Catholics and their "Dago pontiff" for "debauching and destroying" the American Sabbath, nightriders burned a suburban Catholic church and school. Over the years, religious differences had come to embody other differences. Baptists and Methodists were usually of Germanic or Anglo heritages. Union leaders and common workers often occupied those church pews. Catholics included many immigrant Italians brought to the city by industrialists—at times to help bust unions—and family members of industrialist leaders such as Walker Percy and Henry DeBardeleben. Baptists and most Protestants supported state-controlled public schools. Catholics sponsored church schools. Baptists and Methodists were prime constituencies for banning whiskey and public amusements on Sundays while Catholics usually opposed prohibition and favored a more secular Sunday.[26]

The South's increasing worship of its Confederate past also unlashed many whites from sole devotion to prohibition. Birmingham's Confederate reunion aroused a new nostalgia for the Lost Cause's mythic virtues, and repeated engagements of D. W. Griffith's motion picture at local theaters seduced white Birmingham with honorific images of old-time white supremacy. The Ku Kluxers continued organizing locally, seeking to be heirs to this legacy by mirroring its imagery. At the Alabama State Fair, thousands of adults and children congregated for evening performances, where "more than one hundred descendants of the original Ku Klux Klan, dressed in the garb that so terrorized the negroes and carpetbaggers just after the civil war" marched at night with blazing torches before the grandstands. By the end of the year, the national Klan leader announced that there were 175 members in Birmingham and a new chapter of fifty members in Bessemer. KKK Imperial Wizard W. J. Simmons of Atlanta predicted that there was no limit to Birmingham's growing interest in reviving the South's old ways.

Yet, Simmons's secret order remained inept and small-minded as it tried to hitch a ride on the revived, romanticized rescue of the Old South. In late 1916, the Wizard appeared before Hugo Black and the grand jury with allegations of embezzlement. Simmons swore that his chief organizer had collected $800—$10 each from eighty members—around Birmingham. (This total was far below the 225 members announced publicly.) The Ku Klux organizer refused to turn over $160, all that was due the organization from its initial dues, but Black and the grand jury took no action. They could easily figure that, by maintaining "solicitors" who could pocket 80 percent of each membership fee, the Klan itself might be considered a vehicle as much as a victim of petty larceny.[27]

Despite the Klan's paltry ways, Old South traditions were gathering force in various venues in Birmingham. Jefferson's white male jurors, for instance, showed renewed reluctance to convict black defendants in cases arising in segregated black communities—including liquor cases. In October, Will Welch became exasperated after several juries acquitted African Americans for selling liquor to other blacks. "You can excuse them all . . . !" Welch barked after a judge asked if one potential juror could be excused. In another case, a white jury took only ten minutes to find a Negro innocent, although police had arrested him as he sold two quarts of whiskey in the city's black section. "Why that is flying in the teeth of the judge's charge," Welch protested. Exasperated, the assistant solicitor bemoaned: "What is the use of laws?"

Condoning lawlessness among descendants of African slaves, when misbehaving within their own segregated lives, was an old custom that had hampered Black's agenda of law and order from the start. Except for white-on-black crime, nothing was more difficult than black-on-black crime for securing convictions. To counter this tradition, prohibitionists had argued over decades that banning liquor in the black community was necessary to assure the safety of white women. Now, this dry white logic seemed less virile than another version of white supremacy, one pictured in the last scenes of *Birth of a Nation* where Southern white men castrated "bad negroes." It was as if a growing number of Birmingham's white men were swaggering with imagined ancestral supremacy, itching for a chance to have whiskey fire up some "bad negroes" whom they could overcome in glorious white triumph.

Black never reached Mobile's port in his late-night journey for prohibition. He had to turn back when a mild earthquake rocked Alabama, toppling chimneys and breaking dishes across the Deep South, and a hurricane with torrential rains and winds of 110 miles an hour blew across Mobile Bay, destroying parts of the county courthouse.[28] Yet, amid Alabama's political cross currents, Hugo Black needed to go no farther than his own city to see that "connivance" and "indifference" among elected officials were but one manifest of a more profound, complicated set of conditions hampering Alabama's prohibition movement—and endangering the frayed remnants of Alabama's partially progressive movement.

AT HOME, BLACK SOON FACED his own political squall. Rumors circulated that Joseph Tate would try to oust Black, by claiming that the 1915 circuit solicitor bill made Tate chief prosecutor as of January 1917, not at the end of Black's term. "Of course, I will contest these proceedings," Black told reporters.

Three months before President Woodrow Wilson asked Congress for a declaration of war against Germany, Black's squall line became a battle line. News reports reaching the county solicitor on January 6 reported that five hundred gallons of whiskey were stolen from Girard warehouses, now under the protection of an outmatched local sheriff. On the same day, news boys hawked headlines announcing that Louis Walton, a few days away from retrial, had killed himself and other passengers in a train explosion. And, at a press conference, Joseph Tate announced he was appointing assistants to replace Black's staff in accord with Alabama law.

News from Girard meant Governor Henderson had arranged for whiskey owners to steal back their existing confiscated liquor. A few months earlier, the governor withdrew state militiamen and refused to remove the liquor to a safer location. He also had emptied Logan Martin's official purse by refusing to authorize payments for many past Girard expenses and for any future prosecutions. Relying entirely on private money, Martin sued Henderson in a dispute that grew nastier each week. Unless the courts freed the attorney general, Henderson's purse strings were tying up prohibition enforcement across Alabama.

Louis Walton's death shocked the city. He was returning from Atlanta where he took out a $30,000 life insurance policy that paid double premiums to his wife in the event he died in a train accident. Walton's homemade bomb killed four people and injured dozens when it exploded in his face in the men's room of a smoker car, minutes before the train arrived at the Birmingham terminal. Driven by homicidal honor and social privilege, Walton's death was declared a suicide by a coroner's jury. Walton's friends, however, told a different story: a decent man was driven to a desperate, dishonorable end by Black's senseless prosecution.[29]

The last item of news on January 6, Tate's attempt to replace Black's assistants, defined the immediate battleground. Within ten days, Tate's friends filed a *quo warranto* action to remove Black from office. After it failed, Tate appeared before Judge Fort's criminal court on January 22 to declare the state was not ready to proceed. Black stood at his side and announced the state was ready. After considering written briefs, Judge Fort ruled that Black was the county's lawful chief prosecutor in criminal cases until his term expired in late 1919. Tate filed an appeal and announced that attorney Forney Johnston would represent him. Now, it was open warfare between Black and the best lawyer the state's railroads and liquor interests had to muster.

Johnston was a short, physically unimpressive man, possessing none of the clear, handsome features that gave his father a commanding persona. Yet, Forney's unfocused countenance and poorly fitting clothes hid a formidable intellect, a poet's turn of phrase, prodigious talent, and a flaring temper. In many ways, Johnston was driven by the same demons as Black. Throughout his life, Johnston worked to distance himself from his father's politics. The son enriched and endeared himself with corporate and political interests that his father betrayed or abandoned. Chief advisor to Senator Underwood and trusted counsel for Governor Henderson's administration, Forney Johnston represented railroads, Northern financiers, liquor interests, and banks in both politics and the courtroom. Now, after an inconclusive fight over ambrosia, Johnston appeared pleased and determined to rid Birmingham of its zealous, pious prosecutor.

The Alabama Supreme Court quickly decided Tate's appeal. In mid-February, in an unsigned opinion, the court held that Black was the county's chief prosecutor in criminal cases until his term expired but that Tate had authority to appoint his own assistants. "Whether this is wise or unwise legislation," the court disclaimed, "Whether the . . . county will have too many . . . assistant solicitors is . . . left to the discretion of the appointing authority, as well as the . . . character and efficiency of the appointees. Upon the propriety of such legislation the Court cannot and does not pass."

The court opinion sparked a long series of local battles with stratagems and verbal sorties as complicated and intricate as any played out in the deadly theaters of real war. Both Johnston and Black now fought on ground they would not surrender. Five days after the Supreme Court opinion, the county board of revenue refused to pay Black's assistants. The board acted on the basis of a legal opinion stating that Black's staff cost the county treasury almost $20,000, while the state government paid Tate's new assistants. Black protested, but the board stood by the opinion of its special attorney, Forney Johnston.

Black sued the board and instructed the county treasurer, the official who actually signed county checks, that "the Board of Revenue of Jefferson County has no power to employ attorneys to represent it." Black contended the board must by law get its legal opinions only from the county solicitor. A bizarre comedy ensued over several weeks. Tate's three assistants, ready to try cases, appeared each day at Black's office on the fourth floor of the county courthouse. Like naughty schoolboys, they sat in the hall until the courts adjourned. They went home and next day repeated the ritual. These assistants who did no work received paychecks from the state treasury. Black's assistants who tried cases inside the courtrooms worked without pay.

In a counterattack, Black reappeared before the Board of Revenue showing that, as of January 1917, his office had generated $16,000 over expenses. His assistants were more than paying their own way. Black insisted they should be paid. In March, for a brief moment, Black gained momentum. The circuit court granted his petition ordering the county board to pay his assistants, and the board did not to appeal. Afterwards, however, the county treasurer refused to sign checks for Black's assistants on the advice of his new attorney, Forney Johnston.[30]

At this point, even veteran reporters had to keep a scorecard to understand the affair. Joseph Tate remained Hugo Black's assistant in criminal cases. Tate also had assistants who sat in the courthouse hallway with pay while Black's assistants tried cases without pay. On behalf of the county treasurer, Black had sued the Board of Revenue to keep them from using Forney Johnston as legal counsel. Now, representing the Board of Revenue, Black sued the county treasurer because he followed the advice of his new lawyer, Forney Johnston. Utterly confusing, the situation revealed one unmistakable fact: the battle between Black and Tate was, in reality, a legal and political war between Hugo Black and Forney Johnston. Short men with big egos, both were haughty warriors battling in words and legal strategies for the essential power of law, tenets of civic righteousness, and the personal satisfaction of besting a sworn enemy.

Near mid-March, Johnston met with Governor Henderson at Birmingham's Tutwiler Hotel. Within three weeks, Henderson charged Jefferson's sheriff with malfeasance, although the sheriff claimed his only crime was working cooperatively with Hugo Black in enforcing prohibition laws. The governor instructed Attorney General Logan Martin to commence an impeachment trial before the Alabama Supreme Court, although in Girard the governor had insisted that only a local grand jury should consider impeaching a local sheriff.

Defending the sheriff and prohibition as a special defense attorney, Borden Burr spoke as if both his client and Black were on trial. Yes, Burr argued, felons were used as cooks in the jail, as alleged, but it was necessary because the sheriff and Black did not allow anyone convicted of a misdemeanor "to stay in jail long enough to unpack their gripes." Yes, the jail was shorthanded, Burr admitted, but it was because the sheriff and the county prosecutor did not profit from arresting people for petty or manufactured offenses. The state called the sheriff's work malfeasance. Burr called it aggressive law enforcement and honest prohibition. After only fifteen minutes of deliberation, the Supreme

Court unanimously acquitted the sheriff and, in effect, Hugo Black.

Amid the political ruckus, Black suffered a personal tragedy. On March 13, his brother Orlando died from "working himself to death" after fifteen years of tending to the sick and feeble around Wilsonville. Orlando had been Hugo's earliest model of conscience and public service. At the gravesite, near the town's shortening row of stores, Black's eulogy of "Lander" brought family and friends to tears as he remembered his brother's selfless dedication to others. For an overworked, embattled solicitor, the funeral was a sad retreat from his own battlefield and a troubling signal that the Black men could be mortally wounded by excess of virtue as well as sin.

Back in Birmingham, Black's friends rallied to his side. Led by Herman Beck, the Alabama Knights of Pythias honored the county solicitor as their "grand outer guard" for promoting lodge principles outside the brotherhood's realm. On May 11, a Jefferson grand jury praised the county solicitor's hard work and demanded that Tate discharge his assistants or face ouster. The jury's special report also sharply attacked the county treasurer for personally receiving more than $600 from the bank where he deposited the county's money (a balance of $400,000) in a non-interest bearing account.

Responses were swift, direct, and personal. The county treasurer accused Black of manipulating a grand jury to bully him into paying his assistants. "Amen," shouted Tate's assistants who reminded reporters that Will Welch, Black's assistant, was responsible for the law Black claimed as authority for paying his assistants. Who was really misusing public office? Full of triumph's grace, Black told reporters that he had no reason to threaten the county treasurer, "even though he is represented by Forney Johnston, the attorney for Mr. Tate and his assistants."

Tate also appeared conciliatory. He proposed that all assistant solicitors be dismissed and that he and Black alone divide up the duties of prosecuting criminal cases. To "Joseph R. Tate, Assistant Solicitor," Black responded in an open letter. Essentially, Black charged that Tate's suggestion was impractical, and that Tate was ignorant of the cases that need to be tried since he failed to show up for work during the past two months. "My office is at 410 Courthouse," Black wrote Tate. "Your services are needed, and I demand that you give them to the county in return for the salary you receive."[31]

On June 15, Black and Johnston argued before the state Supreme Court on whether Alabama's new solicitor's law required the county treasurer to pay

Black's assistants. On the same day, the Court sustained the confiscation of Girard liquor with illegal search warrants on the grounds that a discovery of illegal whiskey "cured" the illegal search. Less than a month later, the court cured Black's problems. It held that Joe Tate—not Hugo Black—had the legal authority to name all assistant solicitors, including Black's staff. "Why the legislature should have made the county solicitor, and not the circuit solicitor, the chief prosecuting officer of the circuit, or why the circuit solicitor, and not the county solicitor, was given the authority to name the assistants, we are not concerned," the court stated on the general principle that the Alabama legislature often defied reason. Concluding that ours is not to reason why, the court handed Forney Johnston the final victory.

On July 12, Black announced his resignation since he was unable to live with the court's "Solomon-like opinion" (the old Populist phrase once used to attack the arrogance of Clay's conservative Democrats). Black thanked the county's people for allowing him to do his duties "honestly and impartially." Governor Henderson accepted the solicitor's resignation without comment on the following day.[32]

ALTHOUGH BLACK WAS RARELY INTROSPECTIVE, he observed later in life that his term as county solicitor was the most demanding period of his entire public career, including his subsequent years as U.S. senator during the Great Depression and his thirty-four years on the U.S. Supreme Court. Statistics from his prosecutor's tenure, luckily available, add some detail to this conclusion and sketch a portrait of the various sides of Black's developing philosophy of fairness, independence, and law.

During almost two years as Jefferson's chief prosecutor, Black had been responsible for one-third of all criminal cases throughout Alabama and for six remarkable cases in Girard. He presented as many as ten thousand cases to the local grand jury, and his office tried almost thirty-five hundred serious criminal defendants, a third of whom were convicted. At the same time, after investigating each person's record to avoid political repercussions, Black dismissed almost four thousand cases, one third for charges relating to prohibition and about nine hundred relating to charges for "gaming" or shooting craps. Virtually all dismissals involved African American defendants. As solicitor, Black was chary to prosecute cases of wrongful speech. He dismissed all nine inherited cases for "boycotting" charged against striking workers. He dismissed twenty-three of twenty-eight indictments for "defamation," and 158 of 241 charges against citizens for use of "abusive language." Although his office tried the remaining anti-speech cases, jurors were not very receptive. Black's office lost more than half. During his term, ten men were sentenced to death upon Black's recommendation, including two for armed robbery. Thirty-nine men were convicted of first-degree murder, but forty-two were acquitted, in some degree due to Black's insistence that a jury ignore the race of a victim and killer when considering guilt or innocence.

The solicitor's prosecutions for second-degree murder were much more successful: only four of fifty-seven defendants were acquitted. Black attempted to convict fifteen men for rape, but all-male juries rendered only five convictions. While dismissing one case of miscegenation and forty of fifty-four cases of adultery, Black tried seven men for carnal knowledge of girls under twelve, but convicted only three. One woman was convicted for prostitution and another person for an "abortion."

As the primary person who defined the prevailing terms of law and order in Birmingham, Black's work reflected a sense of Old Testament justice in a city where high church rolls failed to restrain an abundance of public and private misdeeds. Black did not enforce each of Moses's commandments with equal vigor, but he tried to uphold a basic respect for life, regardless of skin color or social standing. That fact alone separated Black from the men who came before and from those who followed him as prosecutor. Black also refused to punish speech as often as most other Alabama prosecutors and preferred to focus primarily on forbidden, harmful conduct, for which he often demanded a judicial version of an eye-for-an-eye.

While he stressed the importance of individual responsibility, a basic assumption in democratic, Baptist tradition and the temperance movement, Solicitor Black was far more concerned about misdeeds of the powerful than the weak. This concern led him often to prosecute white men during an era when city leaders blamed lawlessness on black crime (which officials manufactured for profit). Dismissing a few thousand gambling *and* prohibition cases against African Americans, Black spent much of his energy trying to prosecute the white men who profited from putting people "in the gutters" by the sale and distribution of whiskey and professional gambling, white men who bludgeoned defenseless black suspects for the rewards of their arrest and coerced confessions, white men who enriched themselves by manufacturing crimes and convicts in the black community, and white men in white collars who tried to defraud insurance policies, kite commercial transactions, or murder the innocent in hopes that their social status could elevate them above the law. This approach to law enforcement is summed up in one stark, peculiar, historical fact. Hugo Black sent the last white man to the gallows in the history of Jefferson County.

This notion of law and order alienated many segments of Birmingham's white communities, including many of Southside's elite—but not all, not always. Heartened by Black's intolerance for manufactured, petty crimes, U.S. Steel's Walker Percy declared during the middle of Black tenure that the prosecutor's real worth "would be cheap at $25,000 a year," six times his public salary.[33] In addition, during the sheriff's impeachment trial, Percy's partner Borden Burr defended Black's record as a paragon of law enforcement. Throughout his term, Black's friends, like Herman Beck and other lodge brothers, came to his public defense whenever needed.

Black's tenure was less a product of any specific political agenda than it was the continuation of a political tradition where public service was a solemn duty to be fair-minded, honest, and independent. This tradition placed Black locally near the middle ground of politics, between the heavy-handed socialism of Arlie Barber and the complete corporatism of Forney Johnston, amid politicians like A. O. Lane and, more recently, Circuit Judge William Fort who carried on the basic, unifying sympathies of earlier progressivism.

In keeping with this heritage, Black's own definitions of law, order, and justice as county solicitor won approval, at different times, among some members of both the Baptist church and the country club, both union officials and corporate managers, both old Birmingham and suburbs, both the white and the black Pythian lodges. Yet, A. O. Lane's recent political defeat demonstrated that Birmingham's shifting, warring factions increasingly demanded fealty to specific issues and agendas, much more than to honesty and independence.

During his years as prosecutor, Black distinguished his public service with a rare, remarkable tolerance on race and an unyielding intolerance on prohibition. These were not commandments in Moses's laws, but they involved enduring historical issues that on his own Black chose to tackle. Racism was the overarching, moral question of daily Southern living, although habits of racial terror and profit had become so commonplace that most white Southerners were blind to the fact. Surrendering to the economic and social functions of racialism, whites had lost the imagination to comprehend the deep immorality of their own way of life. Instead, most whites recognized whiskey as the day's prevailing moral question, and, more than any other issue, it defined the conscious terms of white morality during Black's service.

Black fought energetically on both moral issues because his own background had given him the necessary discipline, will, and understanding to act according to his own moral compass. Long before Black called Bessemer police officers to the courthouse's fourth floor, a young man in Clay County had been freed from the strict teaching of racialist hatred. The South had made its bargain with the devil to sustain a few decades of legal, human slavery amid Black Belt plantations for a seemingly eternal legacy of distorted, torturous human relations, but Black had not. He fought for a rudimentary sense of colorblind justice and a system of "equal rights for all" that included the black man, although in no way did he fight on behalf of the black man.

Long before Black prosecuted men for carrying signs advertising liquor, a father's alcoholism and his brothers' deaths had shaped a little boy's lasting notion of what on God's earth could destroy love, respect, and human life as much as pulling a gun's trigger. Like the original forbidden fruit, liquor offered to enslave capacity or expand experience. But, Black wanted no such choice for himself or others. He summoned the elective powers of the law and his generous supply of energy and intelligence to rid his community of a demon that he believed man could never tame or befriend.

Over a bottle of nonalcoholic beverage, Black's rule of Old Testament law against the Old South morality came to an abrupt end. Through the persistence and talent of an opponent at least his equal, Black was ousted. Yet, as war in Europe—now with American troops—propelled the entire nation into a new era, with a growing sense of national patriotism and democratic aspirations, the triumph of America and its ideals was becoming the arching moral and practical imperative. It also would become a common battle cry among citizens continuing to fight in Birmingham and elsewhere for the right and might to define prevailing concepts of law, morality, and justice.

6

Home at War

FIGHTING FOR OLD GLORY

F our months into World War I, as American boys arrived at European
trenches to "protect world freedom from the German menace," Birmingham was strafed with noisy bursts of expansive patriotism and
nativist fears. The Jefferson Volunteers, who had fought in every war since the
Mexican War of 1846, were reactivated with bulging muster rolls of young
recruits and modern marching songs. Applications for officer training camps,
one with the name of Hugo L. Black, were closed in July 1917, because overwhelming numbers of young Alabamians were ready to fight for their country.
Throughout the city, citizens of every stripe and station volunteered for their
patriotic duty as all "moral, mental, and physical resources of the State were
mobilized for war."

Across Alabama, thousands of young men left their homes for the first time
towards distant and dangerous places. Each day's mail brought draft notices and
assignment orders which parents, wives, and girl friends knew could presage,
within a matter of months, the War Department's subsequent telegrams about
casualties of war. These fears proved painfully real for families of more than five
thousand Alabama men who never returned from America's first world war,
but many citizens seemed unable to envision any concept of wartime duty,
at home or abroad, in military or civilian life, that did not involve a real and
present danger from an imminent enemy. "I go suddenly away because of not
only an international. . . national but . . . a tragically individual crisis for every
true American," proclaimed the president of Birmingham-Southern College,
after he was called for service at Washington's State Department. "We may
arrive safely at our destination, or we may not," he warned.[1]

Many true Americans staying at home in Alabama, not even risking a journey across the Mason & Dixon line to looming dangers at a Washington desk job, saw exaggerated threats as near as the other side of town, a local coal mine, or another's church. Even before America's formal declaration of war, rumors circulated in Birmingham that Germans were establishing a network for intrigue and sabotage among Negroes. To evidence their patriotism, black leaders quickly organized a flag-waving rally at the courthouse and pushed enlistment in colored regiments. The local police, nonetheless, clamped down on suspicious activities among African Americans, including the selling of "subversive newspapers" such as the black-owned *Chicago Defender*.

In mines surrounding Birmingham, coal operators warned that renewed union organizing among black and white workers could create "the greatest hell ever known in Alabama" with labor strikes and slowdowns at a time when the war effort demanded self-sacrifice and discipline. Admitting he had no "real positive proof" of traitorous connections, Pratt Consolidated Coal's president complained in Washington and Montgomery that union members were ready to "commit crimes or violence," under possible "German influence."

Some Protestant leaders now considered the Catholic Church an un-American influence, alleging that because Catholics worshiped in the foreign Pope's sanctuary, they could not give full allegiance and support to the United States. In the minds of many Protestants, Catholics had become traitors in time of war.

LED BY THE FIRST BAPTIST CHURCH's Dr. Alfred Dickinson, the Society of True Americans (TAs) emerged in Birmingham in the summer of 1917 as an organization working to remove all Catholics and their "apologists" from public positions of influence. Dickinson's secret society published an official platform, demanding complete separation of church and state, government support for public schools only, a Bible in every school, freedom of speech and press, and "respect for Old Glory as the highest emblem of authority in the land." The statement read a great deal like the Baptist Church's historical social agenda, but now it was a call to arms against a church that challenged these principles and, by TA standards, jeopardized America. Was it not true that the Knights of Columbus were a platoon of the Catholic army, which required each member to take an oath of allegiance *to* the Pope while standing *on* the American flag?

The first casualty in Birmingham's religious war was the county's health officer, whose nomination to the city post was blocked because he was a Catholic. George Ward, an incumbent city commissioner, became the True Americans' second target as a Catholic "apologist." Ward had allowed Martin Eagan, a Catholic, to become Birmingham's police chief. Ward was a Protestant and a small businessman who, like A. O. Lane, tried to keep support among both the city's industrialists and labor leaders. But he, too, was a leader of Old Birmingham, disconnected from the Protestant moral issues—prohibition, public dancing, Sunday movies, and now anti-Catholicism—raging in the city's suburbs. Ward's opponent, a physician who served as East Lake's mayor before it was annexed into the city, had the support of Dickinson's group. After a quiet beginning, Ward's bid for reelection became a vitriolic referendum on the "principles of true Americanism."[2]

As THE FIRST SHOTS WERE FIRED in this war at home, Hugo Black was packing his clothes and books, preparing to leave Ridgely's furnished rooms. With Walter Brower and other courthouse buddies, Black had finished a quick training course conducted by Crampton Harris, a lawyer and an officer in the state militia. Now ordered to report to Tuscaloosa in late August for the Army's official testing and training, Black expected to be on the French battlefields within a few months.

While eager to serve his country, Black had opposed the United States entering the war. Like those of many rural north Alabamians, Black's views matched the opinion of the grand old man of American politics, William Jennings Bryan, who resigned as President Woodrow Wilson's Secretary of State because European nations were "fighting over questions which do not affect our welfare or destiny." Yet once America formally declared war, Black's views "were quite different." He was ready to risk all for his country.

After a crowded train ride to Tuscaloosa, Black was introduced to the realities of becoming a war hero. The Army's training facility was closed. He was instructed to report to Fort McPherson in Atlanta. There, he was informed that "Hugo L. Black" was assigned for Army training at Fort Oglethorpe, where Alabama's state militia often trained, near Chattanooga, Tennessee. Upon arrival at Oglethorpe, Black was assigned to field artillery, not to the foot soldiers' infantry that he had requested, and he discovered that his commanding officer was Major Crampton Harris.

Harris was a tall, erect figure who spoke in a measured, theatrical baritone

voice. His domineering manner rivaled Hugo's own self-confidence, he had
an extravagant opinion of his own prowess, and he outranked Black. Harris
had transferred his former pupil to artillery since anyone smart enough to pass
Harris's own military training course could "get a school trigonometry book
and learn everything about angles that a Field Officer needs to know" to command the firing of long-range missiles. Black pleaded that his "knowledge of
mathematics was inadequate" and requested a transfer to infantry, but Harris
dismissed lawyerish arguments. "You are in the army now," he told the former
solicitor, "and you will go where you are assigned."

As an artillery officer in training, Black had to master more than thetas
and secants in school books. Preparing for combat, where he would ride up
and down the line of fire amid blinding smoke and deafening artillery blasts,
officer candidates often rode bareback, sometimes while blindfolded to simulate
the worst battle conditions. Hugo Black had been a cautious boy, a studious
teenager, and a self-assured lawyer. Never had he put himself in such physically
demanding, hazardous circumstances. Besides, being thin and small, Black had
little natural padding for the Army's bony old horses that he felt were "equipped
with a razor" where they should have possessed a saddle.

Yet, it was not the Army mares nor the stable sergeants who earned Black's
undying contempt. No one better personified the inane, mulish, and bureaucratic nature of a large governmental operation such as the U.S. Army than
the second lieutenants who plagued Black's military career from start to finish.
The Army met its immediate need for trainers and unit officers to lead the
flood of volunteers by commissioning recent college graduates as "so called
provisional Second Lieutenants, which meant they, after several months of
special training, were accepted, like West Point graduates, as members of the
regular Army."

During the three months in officer training school, Black—a thirty-one-
year-old lawyer who had grown up around horses in Clay—was under the
supervision of a twenty-year-old second lieutenant who had three months of
training and had not met a horse before joining the Army. For their first lessons,
Black and other candidates met the second lieutenant to receive instructions
on how an Army officer properly mounts a horse with a saddle. Black's instructor "had memorized the ritual to perfection. There was no doubt in his mind
about how our feet should be raised, how it should be gracefully placed in the
stirrup while one's hand clung in proper fashion to the bridle. He completed

the instructions of the manual without deviating a hair's breath, even taking into account commas and periods. He illustrated the mount as he went along. The end result, however, was a little short of perfect." The lieutenant was mounted, facing the horse's wagging tail.

Compared to such leadership, Black easily impressed the Army with his horse sense. He was commissioned an Artillery Captain despite his own grave misgivings. With three months' training from second lieutenants, Captain Black's first assignment was to train a regiment of cavalrymen to become field artillery men. To lead the first drill, bareback riding, Black had studied carefully the hand signals of command so that he wouldn't appear like a second lieutenant to the experienced cavalrymen. Black, however, did not count on the stable sergeant delivering him a horse whose name, Black later learned, was "Old Von Hindenburg."

Once mounted at the parade grounds, Captain Black quickly realized he was sitting on a horse that gives his own orders. Despite Black's wishes to the contrary, the horse decided it preferred the stable yard over the parade ground and began a full gallop in that direction. The Captain's only recourse was to give his men a signal to follow. When the horse turned right, the Captain signaled a right turn. When the horse went left, he gave a left turn signal. Thankfully, after a full gallop the horse stopped outside the stable, where Black signaled his men to halt after they had followed him through a patch of thick woods, the horse's shortest route home. "Captain Black, I feel we are ready to ride right under enemy fire," a soldier told him after dismounting. "You are a bold and daring captain." Actually, the only thing that Captain Black dared was to wonder what he had done to offend the stable sergeant who assigned him "Old Von Hindenburg."[3]

In November 1917, assigned to the 81st Field Artillery Unit, Captain Black endured another month under the command of the Army's second lieutenants who, in the wisdom of military bureaucracy, were best qualified to act as interim commanders until a career colonel arrived. This experience convinced Black of the universal truth of an old Army adage: soldiers need not worry about saluting a general but "for God's sake never make that mistake with a second lieutenant."

Colonel William T. Littebrandt finally arrived at the 81st, and in this unkempt, profane soldier Black discovered a model commander who loved vulgarity, efficiency, the Army, and his country. Naturally, he also hated second lieutenants. "Read these endless pages of a Second Lieutenant's response to the short, simple questions I asked," bellowed the Colonel, after spitting out a few obscenities when he first met Black. The Colonel's troops called him "Jesse James," a man of notoriety, not fame, as Professor Hiram Evans had instructed Black. Yet Littebrandt was a man with Fayette Black's wicked tongue and Uncle "Brack" Toland's lovable nature. The Colonel promptly made Black his adjutant to help run the unit.

From Chattanooga, the 81st shipped by train to Camp Tremount near Palo Alto, California. As adjutant, Black's primary duties included keeping the War Department's Washington bureaucrats from interfering with the Colonel's job of making capable soldiers out of inexperienced recruits. The work allowed Black to escape a good deal of the monotony and boredom of the regular Army, but he made up for it by having to deal with the Army's Inspector General's Office. It was filled with men who were or had been second lieutenants. Black formerly had dealt with a Birmingham police department of 160 men, the city's largest bureaucracy. Now, every day, someone different in Washington's bureaucracy, three thousand miles away, tried to tell him and the Colonel how to run a regiment of a few hundred men in a camp of several thousand soldiers. The "Inspector General Department . . . could think up more criticism than any institution that ever existed," Captain Black concluded.

The Army's bureaucracy, near or far, played no favorites. It seemed inefficient at any time for anyone. On a warm California day, for instance, Captain Black returned from a shower to discover that his tent and possessions had burnt to the ground. The towel wrapped around his waist was his only stitch of clothing. Yet, try as he might, the regiment's adjutant could not get an immediate issue of new clothes. Only after completing a stack of paperwork and borrowing the pants of an enlisted man did Black get new uniforms. On another occasion, Black pulled money out of his own pocket to settle a dispute about a soldier's pay since it was the only way to avoid the Army's bureaucratic, administrative procedures. The twenty bucks Black forked over was more than his own soldier's pay, but he considered it well spent.[4]

Camp Tremount's location offered Black an occasional opportunity for sightseeing and a periodic visit with his uncle, Thomas Orlando Toland, a Los Angeles lawyer who had betrayed his father's wishes for him to be a doctor. Dr. Hugh Toland, Black's great-uncle, had moved to California and helped to establish the University of California's medical school. He generously supported his son's studies until the young man's treasonous announcement that he intended to pursue law. Thomas Toland was now a successful lawyer with ambitions for statewide political office, and he recognized both talent and a kindred spirit in his nephew. Toland asked Hugo to join his practice. Surprised and flattered, Black begged off and promised to consider the offer after he returned from European battlefields.

Living by the Army rule to "hurry up and wait," the 81st Regiment shipped to Fort Sill, Oklahoma, where they drilled and waited for additional orders. At the request of Colonel Littebrandt, Black practiced a little military law at Fort Sill when the regiment's best sergeant, "Old Nokomis," was court-martialed in a dispute between the Colonel and his new commanding officer. It was a petty charge, Littebrandt insisted, although the sergeant was guilty as sin.

Black quickly realized that his client had only one defense—creating enough bombast, confusion, and nonsense to keep the prosecuting attorney away from the real issue. At the hearing, as one soldier remembered, Black distracted "the prosecuting officer's attention from the circumstantial evidence by getting him to concentrate on a ridiculously absurd line of defense . . . which made him forget the evidence itself on which the man was likely to have been convicted." In the end, the prosecuting attorney, another second lieutenant, never recovered his case, and the tribunal found Black's client not guilty.

Despite the Army's comic trivialities and aimless bureaucracy, by the middle of 1918, war in Europe was real, tragic, and deadly for American boys. Almost fifty thousand had died, and one hundred thousand were wounded or missing. Yet, when the 81st Regiment's orders finally came, all soldiers—from colonel to adjutant to private, and perhaps even a few second lieutenants—were eager to fight for America. Black's first response was to set in motion a plan he had developed with Albert Lee Smith, who was stationed in Kentucky, to transfer Smith to the 81st. Both had sworn earlier that whenever one went to battle, if humanly possible the other would go, too. Black also used his connections as adjutant to arrange a furlough for himself. He planned to meet the regiment at port side before they shipped overseas, but first he returned to Alabama.[5] He wanted to set right his own world at home before the long voyage to the killing fields of France.

THE BIRMINGHAM TO WHICH Captain Black returned in late June 1918 was still at war with itself. Commissioner George Ward had lost his race for reelection after directly challenging the Society of True Americans. The *Birmingham News* had attacked the TAs as a "secret political society drawing a religious line" in the community, and Ward called it "un-Christian, un-Godly, un-American, and unfair." The election split many citizens along lines of Protestant intolerance, but it also blurred momentarily the basic economic differences that had fractured Birmingham. The *News* and many industrialists, for instance, were joined by the *Labor Advocate* in support of Ward, while Dr. Alfred Dickinson's candidate received endorsements from an incumbent commissioner, one of the city's earliest corporate attorneys, and a vice president of the city's large bank.

The TAs did not necessarily create an enduring political transformation in Birmingham, since war often creates exceptional, temporary circumstances. Nonetheless, they set a clear precedent for the open use of religious faith and sympathies as a political issue and exposed how deep were the unhealed wounds from a European past. After he took office, the first official act of Dickinson's candidate was to remove Martin Eagan, the Catholic police chief, and to install a faithful Protestant.[6]

The TAs also changed the rules about fraternal brotherhoods in politics. Until True Americans undertook to oust George Ward, fraternal lodges, men's secret societies, and male clubs in Birmingham had kept out of politics and direct social action. They were, of course, important forums for men like Black to make connections and friendships that could be used outside the lodge. Also, members of a secret order—be they Masons, Pythians, or Knights of Columbus—had always been free to defend the character and good name of a brother, even if attacked in politics. But, fraternal lodges and brotherly societies seldom allowed politics to be discussed as a matter of lodge business, and most included in their elaborate secret oaths and rituals a member's pledge to obey society's laws and forego any political uses of the brotherhood.

Other men's organizations also engaged in secret action. It was as if spying and meddling had become a male act of patriotism. In April 1918, for example, a secret society calling itself the "Vigilantes" reported on its operations, keeping persons of German background under close surveillance and "causing" the departure of residents whom the group suspected were not patriotic enough. In Birmingham and elsewhere, self-styled loyalty and preservation leagues functioned away from the public eye to protect communities from "unpatriotic" citizens.

In May 1918, the Ku Klux Klan marched in front of Hugo Black's old office building in downtown Birmingham. Waving a large silk American flag, a hooded Klansman led the silent march on horseback, followed by a burning cross, a symbol that "justice must once more be gained through their efforts." None of the 150 robed and masked Kluxers spoke a word as they slowly paraded through the city, although they handed out flyers to bystanders. The Klan no longer boasted of its members' ancestral links to old Confederate heroes nor did it merely mirror Reconstruction images of white supremacist redeemers, images still in replay at local theaters continuing to show *Birth of a Nation*. Keeping up with the temper of the times, Kluxers had joined their worship of the region's past with a watchful allegiance to national patriotism. Now, the Klan took up the battle cry of Americanism and the sacred duty of enforcing it.

Their leaflets warned: "No able-bodied man, rich or poor, has a right to consume without producing. Take heed and go to work. The eye of scrutiny is upon you! Be respectful to the flag . . . And *by every means* . . . the suppression of disloyalty by either speech or action . . .You are either for or against America's success at arms and the winning of its righteous war for peace and a world democracy. The Ku Klux Klan is pledged to the *enforcement* of the above tenets."

Elsewhere in Alabama, Mobile businessman Frank Boykin created his own Klan after organizers from the International Workers of the World arrived at the city's shipyards. Aided by his black chauffeur, Boykin claimed eight hundred members among dock workers, including Negroes, Catholics, Jews, and Protestants, and supplied them with green robes in which to prowl the night and fight the Wobblies' influence. Apparently, gunfire and violence became commonplace around the docks, and Boykin's Ku Klux was credited publicly with kidnapping and "deporting" at least one outside "negro agitator."

Birmingham's own labor disputes prompted similar, secret activities. In February, more than four thousand skilled, white steelworkers went on strike demanding an eight-hour work day. By early summer, realizing an interracial strike was the only way to shut down the plants, unions began organizing black workers in the mills' unskilled production jobs. In June, amid company claims that unions were spreading social equality, a secret "Vigilance Committee" kidnapped two labor organizers. They flogged, tarred, and feathered the black organizer and warned both union men to leave town.[7]

Meanwhile, the most elaborate and influential secret network for suppressing disloyalty and slackers of all sorts avoided public credit for its clandestine operations. Alabama's division of the American Protective League (APL) had state headquarters in Birmingham, and, like other affiliates across the nation, it acted in complete secrecy as an independent, private organization "organized with approval and operating under direction of United States Department of Justice, Bureau of Investigation."

Begun at war's outbreak in Chicago, where a businessman convinced an Alabama-born FBI agent that volunteers could help his office fight espionage and disloyalty, the League grew rapidly throughout the country since it gave businessmen and others at home a way to be wartime soldiers against the nation's menace. The group received the U.S. attorney general's blessings since the FBI in 1918 was only a tiny investigative unit that needed added manpower.

The League's work was always secret, but its activities and members aimed to locate and uproot any so-called unpatriotic menace behind any suspicious activity. APL agents spied on citizens suspected of disloyalty, blacklisted slackers, and helped FBI agents across the nation when the agency needed local dossiers. The League wiretapped private banks for financial transactions and secretly used the new "dictaphone" to tape private conversations and the sounds of illicit sex. They applied "social ostracism" and physical violence when the law or indirect methods of punishment were inadequate. A U.S. Attorney in the Midwest called the League "the Ku Klux Klan of the Prairies," and Klan Wizard William Simmons was a member of Atlanta's APL auxiliary.

Details of the Alabama Protective League's work remain shrouded, but surviving records depict an organization active in extra-legal and secret activities to protect their version of Americanism. APL members tracked down and "nabbed" Army deserters. They cooperated with military intelligence in identifying Negro agitators and silenced "doubtful" newspaper publicity about Negro patriotism.

At the War Department's request, the APL clandestinely investigated questionable groups, such as disciples of the Church of God in isolated, rural Red Bay, Alabama, whose "Members . . . are known to be 'conscientious objectors' to war," warned the state APL leader. "Judging from the "Funderbergs' and other 'Bergs' among their membership," he added, "they smell strongly of German." In the Black Belt, an APL county agent's report did not spell out the activities his unit was undertaking, but he plainly indicated that it was far more than secret intelligence and spying. "The thing that I am putting special stress upon and maintaining," he told APL's state chief, "is prudence on the part of our men,—no one to *move* without orders."

The Alabama League had chapters in all sixty-seven counties and operated through conservative, established businessmen. Its county "chief agents" included several presidents of local banks, industrialists, and corporate managers or lawyers. Alabama's "State Inspector" was president of Birmingham's Chamber of Commerce. By the time Captain Hugo Black returned to Birmingham on furlough in mid-1918, the Protective League and the state's Council of Defense, which Governor Charles Henderson had established to coordinate local measures for the war effort, were effectively meshed as one organization. Their local representatives often were in both organizations. For example, Jefferson County's APL chief was H. K. "Key" Milner, an investor-developer and descendant of one of Birmingham's founders. As local APL chief, Milner held a seat on the County Defense Council under the chairmanship of Forney Johnston.[8]

Johnston maintained a strong influence in both organizations, especially in matters of industrial labor and "Negro agitation." During the steelworkers strike, Johnston became alarmed that the "labor situation in this district is menacing." He charged that Negro workers were taking advantage of the war "by receiving such high compensation . . . that the majority of them are idle one or two days per week. Large numbers of them are idle three or four days in the week or more," Johnston fumed. As head of the local Defense Council, Johnston led a delegation of twenty-five industrialists who quickly convinced Birmingham's commissioners that it was their patriotic duty to adopt a new ordinance outlawing loitering. On the same day, Johnston wrote Governor Henderson: "As I came to town this morning, I saw at least three hundred darkies loafing around the streets." He asked Henderson to denounce "slackers . . . who fail to work to the limit" and to instruct sheriffs to arrest loafers under vagrancy laws.

Since the legislature did not meet until 1919, the state's Defense Council circulated Johnston's model ordinance to all local chapters and, by late summer, Alabama's three largest cities and at least twelve counties had adopted the new law. Johnston's model allowed local officials to arrest almost anyone they wanted. It provided that a person "guilty of wandering or strolling about, or remaining in idleness during any working day in any calendar week" was presumed to be a "vagrant" unless the accused could prove otherwise. By design, the law could keep white strikers off the streets and black workers on the job.

Following Johnston's lead, Alabama's Defense Council chairman Lloyd M. Hooper of Selma declared a "Registration Day," enlisting Alabama's "wartime workers" to work six full days each week for the good of their country. Created by the governor's executive order, the Defense Council was supported entirely by corporate gifts and possessed no legal authority to require work of anyone. Yet the Council's "labor cards" were enforced like a conscription law. In south Alabama, an African American leader complained that worker registration was "producing virtual slavery for the colored people." He described how town marshals required black workers to meet the work schedules on their cards and arrested some Negroes for not working hard enough. In one case, a marshal refused to allow a black man to quit his job since he "could not leave . . . without his employer's consent, *under the law"* of work registration.[9]

With Johnston's advice, the Alabama Protective League and Defense Council cooperated in late 1918 in surveying the state to determine how many African Americans were beginning to discuss "social equality" or the right to vote as rightful claims on American citizenship. The APL supplied their information to Governor Henderson and other Southern governors. Later, APL's findings helped to inform a meeting of six Southern Councils of Defense who met to discuss the problems of Negro "uppityness." At a second meeting, Lloyd Hooper and others of Alabama's Defense Council met with the state's Congressional delegation in Washington, where Hooper's friend, Senator Oscar W. Underwood, served as "understanding" spokesman.

The group's "understanding" considered both the past and future in plotting how to suppress democratic aspirations and preserve white supremacy. "No individual or group . . . should take independent action in counties," they decided. "Service rendered should be as sworn deputies," as they had been in all labor strikes in Birmingham. "The Reconstruction period . . . is not expected to repeat itself, as we are now in the citadel and being in control of the state shall proceed in lawful and authorized manner to meet any emergency," the white leaders agreed. They also agreed that the state government needed a secret intelligence department to keep tabs on labor and Yankee agitators and an all-white state militia to keep the peace after the war. Both were vital means to back up local law enforcement and prevent federal interference. "[I]t is the government alone that will be able to maintain supremacy . . . No two races living together can survive upon equal terms, one must control," they concluded.

These leaders of Alabama business and politics were concerned about more than African Americans. They also worried about the yearnings of Alabama's poor white population who had sacrificed at home and as soldiers. Poor whites would want their new democratic due, and it worried APL leaders. One League agent, a Talladega merchant, observed that while "the colored population . . . will respond to the best [citizens], poor white folks give more trouble along these lines, and cause more trouble with the negro." Assembled leaders agreed. After armistice, poor whites had to be controlled. State leaders would need, on one hand, to keep poor whites away from labor alliances with blacks and, on the other, check them against vigilante efforts that might prompt federal interference. "The conservative citizens of the respective communities," the Defense Council solemnly concluded, "must organize in such a way as to render it impossible for citizens of less stability to administer affairs in their own way."[10] White citizens of less stability may have fought to "make the world safe for democracy," but democracy in the Deep South was not safe in their hands.

UNDER NORMAL CIRCUMSTANCES, these conflicts and developments would have earned Black's attention and involvement, but for a soldier on his way to France they were merely shadows of the lingering war at home. Captain Black was in Birmingham to put his own worldly affairs in proper order, in the event he joined his three brothers on the other side of eternity. Black's finances were first among his affairs needing attention. Before the war, Black signed as a guarantor on a large promissory note to Birmingham's First National Bank in order to avoid the bankruptcy of a small bank where he sat on the board of directors with, among others, local department store owner Louis Pizitz. Now, First National demanded payment from Black and other directors for the small bank's bad loans. Several wanted to hire Forney Johnston to contest the liability, but, without an heir or certain future, Black settled his obligation by turning over all Birmingham property he had purchased with Albert Lee Smith in the last five years.

Black also revised his will, naming Herman Beck as sole executor of what was left of his estate. Beck placed the document in his office safe. If ever the two men had evaded the thought before, they now knew that a Jewish candy merchant from the Black Belt "stood . . . in the place of a father" for the ambitious Baptist lawyer who as a young man could never embrace his own. Whatever his fate in France, Black's name and position as judge was preserved for Birmingham's posterity. In May, the Masonic general commander presented a metal box for the cornerstone of the new federal post office building, where federal courts also were to be located. Inscribed on the inside of the box for discovery in a future century were the names of the local Masonic lodge's leaders, including "Judge Hugo L. Black."

Captain Black's grand farewell came on June 26 among friends of the Knights of Pythias. Spearheaded by Herman Beck and Judge William Fort, the celebration officially honored Black for his recent appointment as the Pythias' "grand inner guard of the grand domain of Alabama," a position arranged when Jefferson's last county solicitor was under attack. Lodge rules aside, the Pythians were actually saying goodbye to their friend who was going to guard America's democracy overseas. It was a soldier's farewell.

"We are going over to France with joy," Captain Black declared after listening to a long string of tributes. As he looked about the packed hall, Black spoke with an old warrior's pride and a young man's nervousness. "My own regiment, that is, the regiment to which I belong, is the most cheerful crowd of men I ever saw—singing continuously (we won first prize as songsters), and praying to be over there soon," Black said. "One thing we do hope for faithfully, is that we will have the chance to do most of our fighting 'out in the open' and not from the trenches . . . as all true, red-blooded, typical Americans love to fight on open ground, man to man."

Like his Uncle Merit Street thirty years earlier, Black sensed that war was reshaping himself and others into "typical Americans" whose immediate future would overwhelm past divisions and nostalgia. The "cheerful" white men with whom he had trained and would risk life and limb in France were not Yankees or Southerners. All were now Americans:

> When we meet on the fields of France;
> May the spirit of Grant be with us there;
> As the sons of the North advance . . .
> When we meet on the fields of France;
> May the spirit of Lee be with us there;
> As the sons of the South advance;

But here's to the Blue and Gray as one,
When we meet on the fields of France;
May the spirit of God be with us all
As the sons of Old Glory advance.

On the subject of patriotism at home, Captain Black fell into the strident cadence of the day. Black saw the prospects of death and injury for himself and others as too real, too near at hand to permit anything short of total dedication from every American, beggar, laborer, and industrialist. Like the American trade union movement, Black believed that, to win the war, the country had to conscript not only working men's labor but also wealthy men's riches. "Every penny, every nickel and dollar should be spent unstintingly by those at home until Old Glory waves from the highest peak of the biggest palace in Berlin," Black declared, ". . . and the man who does not give his every dollar, both profit and otherwise, to helping the boys 'over there,' the man who does not give every ounce of work and service that is in his power to give is a coward *and a traitor.*"[11]

As it turned out, Captain Black never left the American shore. Before departing Birmingham, he received an Army telegram ordering him back to Fort Sill into a new regiment. While the 81st Field Artillery was on its way to France, the Army had reassigned Colonel Littebrandt to train another brigade, and he needed his old adjutant. Black returned crestfallen to an office job. His impressive talent at outfoxing the Army's bureaucrats and second lieutenants had earned him a promotion to major and saved him and Albert Lee Smith from the chance to fight and die in Europe's trenches. Within three months, Armistice arrived and the war was over. Black "never fired a shot against the nation's enemy," as he remembered late in life, but he also never forgot the ultimate sacrifice which he faced and which many Americans, including new friends in the 81st, gave freely for their country in time of war.

Black declined Uncle Toland's offer to practice law in California and returned to Alabama. When he arrived at Birmingham's train depot, Black might have had second thoughts. He had a sinking feeling that his life had been put into reverse. "I found myself without a job, an office, or a client, without money or other property, and even without a boarding house," he remembered, ". . . very much as when I arrived in the City years before." Black took a room at the Molton Hotel, less than a half a block from Mrs. Crim's old boarding house.

Black went from despair to desperate illness. In the Army, where free medical care was available, Black had avoided becoming a victim of the deadly flu epidemic of 1918 that killed half the war's servicemen and almost seven hundred thousand Americans. Worldwide, the pandemic killed forty million people within a year. Now, Black contracted the deadly flu, struggled, and lapsed with pneumonia. There were no veterans benefits. Black was admitted to the local hospital where his fever broke after two weeks of frequent ice rubs. Afterwards, he swallowed his pride and borrowed money from brother Orlando's widow to pay his hospital bills.

After recuperating, Black, without money to pay his debt or rent, opened an office. "Captain Black has resumed practice and has opened his office on the ninth floor of the First National Bank Building," noted the local newspaper a week before Christmas.[12] Black certainly needed free publicity and the season's good will. After twelve years of law practice and public service as judge, prosecutor, and Army officer, Hugo Black was flat broke. Worse, he was in debt and penniless. At the end of 1918, after giving up all his worldly possessions, "his every nickel and dollar" in time of war, Black found himself poorer at age thirty-two than he had been at age twenty-two. Welcome home, soldier!

7

'Ego' and the Miniards

A Case of Southern Honor
and Northern Corporations

The divisive vocabulary of Americanism seeping into Birmingham's public life during the Great War ironically signaled a new sense of national belonging among Southerners. In the heart of Dixie, the American flag and patriotism had miraculously joined emblems of the old Confederacy as marketable, cultural symbols of assault harnessed chiefly by men pursuing ancient hatreds, selfish antagonisms, or base greed which they costumed as national self-preservation. The hoisting of Old Glory as a rallying cry in Birmingham indicated that many ordinary citizens to whom the peddlers of hate appealed were beginning to identify themselves as Americans as much as Southerners, for the first time since the early days of the Republic.

In Alabama alone, more than fifty thousand young white men had risked injury and death as American soldiers. One out of ten had died in their American uniforms. Twenty-five thousand Negroes from Alabama had been inducted in the U.S. Army, and many fought and died for their nation at a time when they had precious few rights as Southern citizens. Like Hugo Black, many veterans of both races returned home without jobs or reward. Though denied the vote, women on both sides of Alabama's color line had mastered new responsibilities as workers and citizens during wartime. Having done their patriotic duty, some Southerners now considered making new claims on the *American* democratic promise.

These emerging voices competed with the authoritarian language of Americanism, but, most of all, they had to survive the traditional vernacular of Southern race relations. Like granite memorials from another war, Southern racialism stood guard against meaningful changes, always facing Southward as constant markers across land and language of the central difference that held the white South together and apart from the nation.

In 1919, Birmingham residents, like other Southerners, were returning to life without a common, distant enemy, searching for ways to satisfy material needs and moral certainty. Daily routine revealed the complex competition between fragile American aspirations and overbearing Old South morality. The full meaning of Southern words and phrases was coded in a past—real and mythical—that jealously insisted on ruling the present.

This collective memory always measured friend and foe, neighbor and stranger, by certain words, phrases, accents, colors, and customs that served an unquestioning faith in one separate Southern civilization that never was, but always must be, in the rightness of one blundering, peculiar past that demonized black skin color to assure the triumph of aristocratic white control, in a South held captive by Northern riches and biracial poverty, and in a past that took profane, even morally obscene, human deeds and transfixed them into a holy cross of regionalism. All this was done each day, with words and phrases whose true meaning flashed back and forth from the present to the past amid everyday conversations in homes, on street corners, in shops and restaurants, at work, in schools, churches, parks, and courtrooms.

WEDNESDAY, OCTOBER 8, 1919, THE JEFFERSON COUNTY COURTHOUSE:
"What did the nigger woman do when she got in the car?"

"She came in, and the fellow with her sat her down."

"About how many seats was this nigger woman from you and your wife? Two or three?"

"Something like that," replied the witness.

"Were all the seats in the car taken?" the lawyer asked.

"No, sir."

"Were there any niggers in the car?" Hugo Black inquired further.

"Yes, sir, a bunch of them."

"Negro men? And negro women?"

"Yes, sir."

"Many white people in there?"

"Not as many as colored," replied the witness.

H. R. Miniard, a crane operator at U.S. Steel's Ensley plant, was on the witness stand, retelling his journey six months earlier with his wife and child on the Illinois Central Railroad in April 1919. Mrs. Miniard was carrying her eight-month-old baby when they boarded the train in Chicago shortly after dark, heading back to Birmingham. The Miniards could afford only coach tickets and were preparing to sleep the night sitting upright during the first leg of a long journey home.[1]

Near the witness sat twelve white men, the jury empanelled earlier in the day by Circuit Court Judge Romaine Boyd. Like Miniard, these men worked in Birmingham's mills, factories, offices, shops, and mines. They were assembled in the heart of Dixie to administer justice in the aftermath of war in a strange little case involving the intermingled issues of race, class, place, Southern womanhood, and Northern corporations. It was a case of how simple, common words defined Southern justice as much as uncommon, tortured deeds.

"Now, after the woman got on this car, did she curse any . . . ?" Black continued.

"Yes, sir, with the fellow trying to seat her."

"Did the conductor make any effort to pull her off?"

"I didn't see him make any effort . . ."

"Was she using vile language?" Black asked.

"Yes, sir. I would call it vile language," Miniard replied.

Black focused on the conductor who at times sat in the back of the rail car. "What was he doing back there?" the attorney asked.

"Just carrying on a conversation," Miniard replied.

"Did he seem to be tickled; was he laughing or was he sad?" Black asked.

"I object to leading the witness," interrupted LeRoy Percy representing the defendant railroad company and its employees. The son of attorney Walker Percy, Roy had been admitted to practice law in 1914 but, due to wartime service, he had less than three years of experience as a lawyer. He was the junior member of a law firm bearing the name of his father, who had killed himself a few months before the start of World War I.

"What was he doing?" persisted Black.

"We object to that," Percy repeated. "He is suggesting an answer."

The law firm of Percy, Benners, and Burr represented their clients, primarily U.S. Steel, mine owners, railroads, and banks, against the large and small claims of workers and citizens who charged that corporate negligence had put them in harm's way. Ordinarily, these cases involved broken bones, dislodged legs, or lost lives as the toll of industrial business. In this instance, the issue was quite different, one which LeRoy Percy's senior partners decided their youngest attorney should handle alone.

Mary Miniard alleged that, while a passenger on the Illinois Central Railroad, she was called "vile names" by a mentally disturbed Negro woman. The plaintiff was "greatly embarrassed, frightened, chagrined, and humiliated, and as a . . . result was caused to suffer great mental pain and anguish, was made sick, frightened, and nervous . . . ," according to the complaint written and filed by Hugo Black. Because the railroad's conductors did not stop this abuse "and immodest conduct," Black was asking a jury to award his client $2,999.99, an amount almost ten times larger than Mr. Miniard's yearly pay.

By a penny this peculiar sum was just low enough to prevent the railroad from removing Black's case to the federal courts. By Congressional act, when a dispute involved $3,000 or more, the federal district courts had original jurisdiction if the persons involved were from different states. Because Northern corporations, including railroads, were incorporated outside of Alabama and were considered "persons" under the federal Constitution, their attorneys often invoked this jurisdiction in personal injury cases.[2]

In most cases, Black avoided federal courts like a litigious plague. The cornerstone of Birmingham's federal court building bore Judge Black's name, but he practiced so rarely in federal courts that in 1919, thirteen years after graduating from law school, Black had never appeared before a federal appellate court. In Black's view, the federal bench was populated by Republicans (sometimes in the sheep's clothing of Democrats) and former corporation lawyers, often a threatening redundancy that disadvantaged poor and working people.

Appointed for life by the President, usually for political patronage, and confirmed by the U.S. Senate, Southern federal judges seemed much less sympathetic than elected state judges to the typical plight of Black's clients. For example, a week before the Miniard case began, Black's old friend U.S. Judge William I. Grubb sliced in half the jury award for a widow in a damage case simply because he decided the "amount was too large." Federal judges also were more restrictive of a plaintiff's lawyer's courtroom conduct, lines of inquiry, and interpretations of state law. In addition, federal juries convened in Birmingham were drawn from different, rural parts of northern Alabama, including a few Republican areas, whose residents had no visceral understanding of Birmingham's corporate and industrial practices.

Ten months after reopening his law office, Black was in state court trying the Miniard case because Percy and his partners had refused to settle. They considered Mary Miniard's compliant more a nuisance than a case of negligence. It probably was a case which few, if any, other Birmingham attorneys would have brought to court. Confident of his own talents and short of cash, Black could not afford to be too selective about cases. He started 1919 with no clients, no retainers, and in debt from medical bills. During the year, Colonel Crampton Harris had joined Black as a partner, but he, too, had nothing but his talents to bring to the new firm.

Black's circumstances were no longer desperate, but, as the Miniard case illustrated, his rebuilt reputation as a damage suit lawyer had not yet attracted the most lucrative cases involving personal injuries. In this instance, state circuit court judge Romaine Boyd, a former city attorney and an advocate for government ownership of utility industries, was perfectly willing to give Black ample opportunity to show how the railroad had injured his client. Over Percy's objections, Judge Boyd allowed Black to continue questioning his first witness.[3]

"How long was the negro woman in the car with you people in all?"

"From eight-fifteen at night until we crossed the Mason & Dixon line; that is where she got out," replied Mr. Miniard.

"About . . . what time?" Black asked further.

"Between four and five in the morning."

"She stayed in the car all that time?"

"Yes, sir."

Roy Percy took charge of the witness. With a word, he quickly indicated to jurors that his client and its agents had no more regard for the troublemaker in this case than did the plaintiff.

"When did this crazy nigger get on there, Mr. Miniard?" Percy asked.

"Eight-fifteen."

"Did she strike anybody while she was in the car?"

"No, sir."

"She was evidently crazy, and acting crazy,—bug-house, or something?" Percy inquired.

"Well, I am not much judge of that," Miniard replied.

"She wasn't much like you, was she?" Percy insisted. Apparently drawing laughter from the courtroom, the lawyer corrected himself. "I don't mean that;

you are no darky, but you can tell whether she was bug-house; she looked out-of-her head?" Percy asked.

In an answer suggesting careful rehearsal with his wife's lawyer, the witness replied, "She was mad at me and mad at her attendant . . . She seemed to be mad at the person she was with, and everybody."

"Did you undertake at all to protect your wife from this woman?" Percy asked the white man sitting in the witness box.

"No," replied the plaintiff's husband. "I did not take any hand. If she had started to hit her, or anything . . ." he muttered.

"Sir?" persisted Percy.

"I was with her all the time to be sure that she did not," Miniard blurted out.

Black interrupted. "Sure that she did not,—what?" he shouted from his seat. Black didn't like this exchange and wanted Mr. Miniard to state affirmatively to the jury that he had been prepared to protect his wife.

"Sure that she didn't hit her," Miniard continued.

Percy turned to another line of questioning. He asked if the conductor had apologized to Mrs. Miniard for any displeasure.

"Yes, sir; he said that he was very sorry that the thing happened."

"And as soon as they got to where they did have the Jim Crow car he put this woman in there?" Percy said.

"Yes, sir," the witness conceded.

"Jim Crow" cars—separate passenger train compartments for blacks—had been legalized by the U.S. Supreme Court's 1896 *Plessy v. Ferguson* decision that "separate but equal" public facilities did not violate the Fourteenth Amendment. The decision not only upheld Jim Crow laws across the South but removed the shield of the American Constitution. Thereafter, and for the next half-century, white Southern leaders used *Plessy* to impose second-class status on black citizens in almost every aspect of life.

Before and after *Plessy*, black leaders found Jim Crow cars one of the most offensive forms of segregation. African Americans had to pay the same fares as whites to travel in separate facilities that were almost always unequal and degrading. Often, a Jim Crow car was an ancient, filthy unit no longer considered suitable for use by whites, or a makeshift car, without working toilets and lavatories, located directly behind the soot-spewing coal car. Some railroad companies partitioned passenger cars, crowding blacks into standing room so that white men might sit and use the other half as a smoking room. A fledgling National Association for the Advancement of Colored People (NAACP) instigated a redoubled campaign in 1919 to push Washington to outlaw Jim Crow cars, but all three branches of the federal government were unsympathetic.

"Jim Crow laws applied to *all* Negroes—not merely the rowdy, drunken, or surly, or ignorant ones," explained C. Vann Woodward, dean of Southern history. "The new laws did not countenance the old conservative tendency to distinguish between classes of the race, to encourage the 'better' element" of African Americans with opportunities for better treatment. "Those laws backed up the Alabamian who told the disfranchising convention of his state that no Negro of the world was the equal of 'the least, poorest, lowest-down white man I ever knew.'"

After the adoption of the 1901 Alabama Constitution, Birmingham segregation often treated blacks as a single, lowly caste, but Jim Crow developed randomly. Passengers at Birmingham's rail terminal sat in racially divided waiting rooms and boarded trains with Jim Crow cars, but Birmingham citizens also crowded together on the same street corner to travel on the same local jitneys and street cars without strict, racial separation. The city mandated that picture houses, auditoriums, ball parks, or other indoor or outdoor places of entertainment had to have physical barriers separating the races. But segregation did not prevent black and white citizens from sharing the same sidewalks, entrances, services, or merchandise in stores and commercial buildings.

At times, segregation was adopted to preserve the peace. By custom, restaurants serving working men had seated whites on one side and blacks on the other. After a rash of interracial fighting and violence at lunch counters, however, it became "deleterious to the peace and happiness of the community," City Commissioner A. O. Lane suggested, to have "whites and negroes eat in the same room." In 1914, Lane introduced an ordinance forcing restaurants serving both races to build "a solid partition extending from the floor upward to a distance of seven feet."

At other times, Jim Crow practices endangered both black and white citizens. In a city where the races lived and interacted in close daily proximity, the Birmingham health department initially responded to a 1916 typhoid epidemic by offering free vaccinations only to whites. Also, despite one of the highest rates of active tuberculosis in America, Birmingham had no medical institution that admitted an African American with the infectious disease.[4]

Segregation in the workplace was rarely imposed by statute. In Birmingham, blacks and whites often worked in the same mines, steel mills, and factories, and in 1919 almost two out of three iron and steel workers were African Americans. Jobs—not the workplace—were separate. And the pay—not so much working conditions—was unequal. For example, in Birmingham's steel mills, including U.S. Steel's Ensley plant where H. R. Miniard worked, skilled jobs were reserved for whites and unskilled jobs for blacks. This Jim Crow custom was primarily the product of white labor unions. While United Mine Workers members shared jobs and pay, regardless of race, most Birmingham unions were all-white, and racial segregation was one of their basic objectives.

The city's industrialists considered complete control of African Americans—not racial segregation—as their essential tool for industrial growth. "The negro is a good laborer when his labor can be controlled and directed," observed Walker Percy, who had been the city's foremost spokesman on matters of race and the local economy. Reared in the Mississippi Delta, where his brother maintained the family plantation, Walker Percy (Roy Percy's father) believed Birmingham's Negro workers served the same economic role as their slave ancestors and possessed the same inferior characteristics. "Now, the ordinary Negro . . . works the least percentage of time," Percy once explained. "They want to squander their money. The chief use they have for it is for three purposes—craps, women, and whiskey."

Birmingham industrialists in general believed blacks were "good laborers," despite their assumed, innate deficiencies, because African Americans could be "controlled and directed" more like inexpensive, industrial tools than free human beings. Within a competitive, national economy, the unfettered control of black labor was Birmingham's fundamental industrial advantage, and it was possible so long as white supremacy—not really Jim Crow or segregation—defined Southern society.

In practice, Jim Crow was often unprofitable or unnecessary for industrialists. Railroad corporations had to add waiting rooms, cars, and facilities at most stops on every Southern route to comply with Jim Crow, even when the numbers of black and white passengers did not fill one compartment. Railroads generally preferred money, instead of race, as a means for dividing up customers into different classes: first class ("Pullman" cars with sleepers on overnight trips) for the "best" and "better" citizens and coach seats for the rest. With the South's biracial poverty, such "class" divisions confined practically all blacks and most plain white folk to coach cars. In effect, Jim Crow was for the white masses, not the upper classes. Accordingly, Alabama's Jim Crow law provided a penalty only for persons who rode in "a *coach* or a division of a *coach,* designated for a race to which he does not belong." Money usually kept first class separate.

Segregation also frustrated the workings of U.S. Steel and other Birmingham industrialists. Their control of black labor proved most advantageous when it created interracial competition in the workplace. Often, the white unions' efforts to segregate job categories frustrated the use of black labor to direct and lower the costs of white labor. As a result, Birmingham's white industrialists and white unions fought bitterly over moving African Americans into semi-skilled and skilled jobs. With this change, industrialists enlarged good-paying work for African Americans and diminished previous Jim Crow boundaries. The industrialists weren't reordering the South's racial rank. Instead, by reducing segregated work, industrial managers increased their advantageous control over all labor, so long as black and white workers remained divided and antagonistic.[5]

Birmingham's white labor leaders habitually obliged industrialists by using segregation as their preferred method for meeting the needs of white working families. "The negro is a parasite; he pays no taxes, no school taxes," charged J. B. Wood, a former president of the Birmingham Trades Council and past vice president of the state Federation of Labor. Many working whites felt they were overtaxed and their children undereducated. Birmingham already appropriated almost seven times more school money for a white child than a black child. Yet, Alabama's white per-pupil expenditure was far below the national average, and white union leaders proposed to segregate tax revenues as a strategy to increase financing for the education of poor white children.

Birmingham's white unions also had joined forces with others to oppose the use by blacks of public facilities built, they argued, primarily by white tax dollars. In earlier years, Birmingham had built seventeen playgrounds for white children and none for black children. In 1914, A. O. Lane and fellow commissioners opened a small Negro park which, afterwards, was maintained by African Americans' volunteer efforts. The city also excluded blacks from its new zoo and library.

Using segregation to redistribute scarce resources to working whites was, at best, a rearguard action. For years, labor unions had struggled to increase taxes paid by Birmingham industries, but this campaign routinely failed. Alabama's 1901 Constitution invested the power to tax exclusively in the state legislature, and it routinely opposed a more progressive tax system. In Montgomery, moneyed industrialists and Black Belt planters—whose political power was swollen by blacks who were counted in the census but were denied the vote—usually prevailed on economic issues. Left to live with what little they got, Birmingham's skilled and unskilled white men often turned to Jim Crow. At least he paid them a "psychological wage" every time segregation belittled a black person and occasionally redistributed thin slices of monetary privilege towards their own white families.[6]

Caught between competing interests of white managers and white workers, Birmingham's black community was in no position to appreciate the differing motives and means that animated Jim Crow. Whoever was "the class of white persons in control of legislation and finances," African Americans always faced manipulation to serve as someone else's tool. "Whether the control has been that by slave-owners, humanitarians, planters, financiers, or white farmers and workers," observed Horace Mann Bond, "it is obvious that each has wished to provide . . . its own concept of Negro status in the social and economic order." This predicament created for African Americans a "double-consciousness," as W. E. B. DuBois saw it at the turn of the century, "this sense of always looking at one's self through the eyes of others, of measuring one's soul by the tape of a world that looks on in amused contempt and pity."[7]

"YOU ARE THE PLAINTIFF IN THIS CASE, Mrs. Miniard . . . ?" Hugo Black asked.

"Yes, sir."

"Now, just tell the jury exactly what happened . . . when you got on that train."

"Well, I got on the train . . . and it didn't seem but just like a very few minutes and the negro woman commenced raving and cursing; I never heard such language in all my life, so I didn't know what to think, it excited me, and scared me. I thought at first the negro was drunk, or something, and would start some kind of a row, and shoot on the train, so I got kind of excited.

"In a short while a negro came by, a physician that was with her . . . and told me not to take any exceptions whatever; he said I seen she was crazy and didn't know what she was talking about, and not to pay any attention to it,—or I would have made a complaint at first. So I tried to stand it and put up with it all night. I got excited, and nervous, and worried; she started running once, and got loose; took part of her clothes off, kept herself half undressed, and got loose from the negro and run and jumped over the baby, and scared me nearly to death."

"Over your baby?" asked Black, as if hearing his client's story for the first time.

"Yes, sir; over my baby; I had her lying on one seat. And my husband, he stood up; he said that he hated to hit the woman if she was crazy. He said if she came back and started anything he would try to kill her. I got scared so my husband, or either one of us, couldn't even go to the lavatory; I wouldn't let him go, and I wouldn't pass her myself. Well, I suppose about three or four—about three o'clock in the morning, she directed a cursing to me . . . She cursed me in the presence of all of the negro men, and the white men too, and me the only white woman in the car; so I called the porter.

"In the meantime one of the conductors did sit back on the seat and carried on a conversation with the man; and he didn't seem to pay any attention to it whatever, to her cursing; he didn't seem to think it was anything at all. So one of the porters did sit and talk to some of the colored women and listened to it all the time; it seemed to be kind of a show. So I told the porter to go and tell the conductor to come in, I was bothered so. In I suppose an hour, or an hour and a half he came in; I told him just what had happened, that I wasn't used to any such as that. The negro doctor said that they might remove her to the baggage coach; he said that they had put crazy passengers in the baggage coach, but he hated to put her in there."

Roy Percy objected. "I move to exclude that, what the negro said." Black insisted, however, that the statement was a part of the *"res gestae"*—evidence so spontaneous that it captures the essential character of the event in question. The judge agreed. Percy remained dissatisfied. To note his objection, Percy had the court reporter read the disputed testimony so he could grace it with a litany of adjectives—"illegal, incompetent, irrelevant, and immaterial and hearsay."

Roy Percy had good reason to fret about this testimony. A key issue in cases of gross negligence, as the judge would explain later to the jury, is how the defendant took reasonable care in protecting its riders from disturbances. The confession of the black doctor that railroad agents had on other occasions removed insane passengers to the baggage car could be a damning item of evidence.

Now Black asked Mrs. Miniard to finish.

"So the conductor came in just before they got to the Mason & Dixon line, and said that he was awful sorry it happened; he said, though 'I am not the conductor that let her on the train; but,' he said 'I will get her out; so we won't have much longer until we get to Cairo,'—I think that is the name of the station; anyway, it divides the North from the South. So when he got there he made all of the colored passengers move, and that was the first action they taken."

"Did he ever say or do anything at all before that?" Black asked.

"No; nothing at all."

"When he was sitting back there talking, did he laugh, or was he serious?"

"Well, he was carrying on a conversation, and once in a while he would laugh; I noticed that he would laugh at the negro's action; she was dancing, and cutting up, and cursing and swearing."

"Did you sleep any that night?"

"Not a wink; no," Mrs. Miniard said.

"You say she cursed directly at you. Did you tell the conductor that?"

"Yes; I told the conductor that."

Black now revealed a weakness in his client's own case—a weak link that he hoped would appear understandable if he brought out the facts before the opposing counsel did. "Do you know which conductor it was; do you know whether this was the conductor?" Black asked as he pointed to a man in the courtroom audience.

"Well, really, I don't know," Mary Miniard said, "with their uniforms on . . . I didn't notice their faces."

Roy Percy's questioning of Mrs. Miniard was short. He realized that he could accomplish little by grilling a local white woman about the extent of her "frightened" experience with an "immodest" black woman on a train in the North. But, he did try to recast parts of her testimony.

"Who did you say the conductor was carrying on the conversation with in one of the seats . . . do you remember?" Percy inquired.

"Some man," said Mrs. Miniard.

"Not these negroes?"

"No, sir; not the negroes."

"You noticed from time to time that he laughed as he was talking?"

"Yes, sir."

"You don't know what he was laughing at, do you?" Percy insisted.

"No, sir; I couldn't say."

"He might have been telling funny stories to the next man to him?"

"I didn't hear the conversation."

"As soon as they got to the Mason & Dixon line they took the niggers right on off?" Percy stated.

"Yes, sir; as soon as they got there, which they had to do anyhow."

"They did it, anyhow?" Percy reiterated.

"Yes, sir; they done it then," Mary Miniard conceded.

WHEN MARY MINIARD STEPPED DOWN from the witness chair, Black rested his entire case on her words. No doctor testified about her distress and trauma. No family member, friend, or neighbor verified how she had suffered emotional or physical problems since the train ride. In October 1919, as suffragists fought for passage of a national constitutional amendment guaranteeing women a right to vote, Hugo Black depended on twelve white men on a Birmingham jury to understand completely the unspoken pain and suffering his client had endured—and to act upon the tradition that every "Southern woman has a protection and champion in every Southern man."

The protection of white women was, at bottom, the white South's explanation for much of the Negrophobia and racial violence that extended into the twentieth century. It remained a Southern white man's article of faith that a black man had an uncontrollable, primitive lust for a white woman. In public rhetoric, this racialized notion of sexual danger was dressed up with references to the evils of "social equality," but it structured Southern society on the permanent necessity for both the black man's captivity and the white woman's dependency.

At the 1901 Alabama Constitutional Convention disfranchising African Americans, a Black Belt delegate proclaimed that "not one of our fair women has ever been assaulted in this land but that the infamous act may be traced to the Fifteenth Amendment"—which gave former male slaves and their descendants the right to vote. From 1904 until 1919, there were eighty-two reported cases of blacks being lynched in Alabama. As if aroused by their own corrupt fascination with sex, race, and violence, white men insisted lynchings were a sacred, honorable act of revenge for blacks' alleged or merely feared bespoiling of white womanhood. On the eve of the Miniard trial, explaining recent lynchings in Alabama and elsewhere, the *Birmingham Ledger's* editor declared that Southern honor had become an American virtue. "The white man, wherever he is found, is going to protect his women from the negro," the editor concluded.

This white masculine honor was fortified through law. In 1915, the Alabama legislature made it a misdemeanor crime for a white female nurse to attend to a black man regardless of his medical condition. There were barely one hundred black physicians and not many more trained black nurses throughout Alabama, mainly because African Americans were barred from attending the state's professional schools. Yet, alarmed by reports that white women might be touching black war veterans in Tuskegee's federal hospital, state representatives were willing to imprison white women nurses to protect white womanhood.

Safeguarding white female purity went beyond the color line. At night, any male who, without legal cause, looked into a room occupied by a woman who was not his wife was guilty of being a "Peeping Tom" and faced imprisonment of up to six months. A similar punishment was meted out for using "abusive, insulting, or obscene language" in the hearing of a girl or woman. These statutes were not merely on the books. They were enforced in Alabama in the early part of the century.[8]

The historical, idolized image of the Southern lady on a pedestal—innocent, pure white, and naturally unsuited for worldly matters—rarely had portrayed real life, and in 1919 it cruelly ridiculed a majority of Alabama's white women. Most white females carried out grueling work in crude circumstances on small farms, where every member of the family worked from sunup to sunset. Women had to cook three large, daily meals, raise small children, keep house, maintain the livestock, grow and preserve household food, hand-wash clothes, and (often carrying a baby and a pallet with her) hoe or harvest the fields. If there was a pedestal for these women, it was near the backside of a cow at milking time. Della Black did these chores during her days in Harlan, and so did most rural Alabama white women in 1919.

Urban women were not necessarily better off. Birmingham's Avondale Mills was built as a convenient place for poor white women and children to work while husbands went to steel mills. The number of poor white women working in the South's textile mills increased during the world war, and afterwards almost one of five Alabama women was employed outside the household. Women "lint heads" in Alabama's textile mills worked ten to twelve hours each day, and, according to a later survey, had the lowest wages in the nation. As guardians of Southern womanhood, the all-male Alabama legislature never thought to regulate hours, wages, or conditions for workers, except to provide by law that, *whenever possible*, female workers should have a stool available—not exactly a pedestal.[9] Yet, as Nannie Cornelius, Black's client in an earlier railroad case, knew, Alabama's railroads and other industries offered a stool only to Southern ladies, not working white women.

Had it been his desire, any man on Mary Miniard's jury could have walked less than six blocks from the courthouse, across the rail tracks, to pay for sex with a Southern woman. The city no longer recognized a red light district, as it did when Black sat as police court judge, but white prostitution still flourished. At the same time, in Alabama's rural communities, county officials attempted to protect innocent young men from teenage white girls who "lay out in the woods and begile boys" for "imoral (sic) purposes." In Walker County, for example, a sixteen-year-old white girl was convicted of vagrancy. According to various local male officials, she was guilty of being a "very profane and vulgar" girl with a "bad nature common to prostitutes" who entrapped reputable young men. As punishment, the white girl was sentenced to labor in a *men's* convict camp.

The notion in Alabama that a woman's place was beneath a man extended beyond coital practices. By law, in 1919 married women could not dispose of their own properties without their husband's consent. A mother had no standing in court to sue for the wrongful death of her minor child, unless the father was dead. Upon marriage, a woman's will was automatically revoked. Women could not serve on juries and by custom were barred from courtrooms when sensitive or crude testimony was presented. And, women could not vote.

For decades, women had lobbied for their right to vote in Alabama. At the 1901 Constitutional Convention, Frances Griffin, a self-described "old maid," proclaimed: "The man without a vote is a subject, not a citizen; the woman without a vote is an inferior, not an equal." The convention wholeheartedly agreed. It disfranchised black men and many poor white men and left women below the man. On the convention floor, "Cotton Tom" Heflin referred to women suffragists as "a few cranks strolling over the state."

With the rise of an urban white middle class, a small segment of Alabama women were freed of constant child care, homemaking, and daily household duties. They used their freedom to stroll across the state organizing women's clubs and temperance unions. Leaders of their associations included wives and sisters of industrialists and planters, although after the war they often were women married to merchants, doctors, lawyers, and small businessmen. All were expected by husbands to assure a peaceful, domestic life, but in their own time the women became activists for prohibition, child welfare, and suffrage. Ironically, their freedom to be active citizens outside the home was enabled by the growing employment of black women as servants in white middle-class homes.[10]

By the time Mary Miniard went to court, the status and role of Alabama women were changing. Thousands had worked tirelessly for prohibition. They had organized speakers' bureaus and took to the streets in massive temperance parades at a time when a middle-class woman's world was supposed to be indoors. They successfully lobbied the Alabama legislature for ratification of federal prohibition. Others worked for passage of the state's first, modest child labor law. They assured by law that women would be appointed to local and state boards of the new child welfare department and women could serve on local boards of education, although none could vote in school elections.

In the summer of 1919, the Alabama legislature considered the Nineteenth Amendment, granting women the vote. Supporters included women activists and progressive, dry political leaders, men such as former Senator Frank White and Alabama's Chief Justice John Anderson. Opposed were U.S. Senator John Bankhead (and his large family of politicians), former Governor Emmett O'Neal, and Senator Oscar W. Underwood, among other anti-prohibitionists.

In July, led by former Alabama first lady Mrs. Charles Henderson, the Women's Anti-Ratification Committee sent the legislature a written message—an actual appearance before the legislature was considered unlady-like—"on behalf of 80 percent of the white women" in the state. These women asked "the men of Alabama" to continue "to stand between us and the rough things of life." They beseeched the legislature "to protect us against this device of Northern Abolitionists" who sought to "mongrelize" the South's "Anglo-Saxon civilization." A Black Belt legislator joined the women's chorus by condemning the Susan B. Anthony amendment as "Blood brother of the Fourteenth and Fifteenth Amendments" of the U.S. Constitution. All three federal provisions, he declared, were "conceived in inequity and born in sin, based on hatred and frenzied desire of carpetbag scalawaggery, dominated by the most depraved considerations for racial equality."

Working for corporate clients in Montgomery, Forney Johnston tried to be "neutral" on the women's amendment when discussing the matter with his own wife, a quiet "suffragette." Johnston had met a "pippin from the East" lobbying for state passage. He thought she was "forlorn, deserted," and "evidently waiting for a man." Johnston warned his wife that the "bobtailed legislature" would be "gun shy of Susie's Amendment" as soon as "the anti-bodies" stampeded. He was right. The amendment failed less than a month before the Miniard trial opened. Alabama women nevertheless gained the right to vote a year later after the amendment was ratified by states outside the Deep South.[11]

Hugo Black favored the women's vote. He thought it would continue political support for prohibition, and it fit his concepts of equal rights. Like most men of his generation, however, Black could not conceive of men and women having the same roles in society or at home. He thought a woman's role was to instruct and support a man's work through her examples of human goodness in child-rearing, family life, and society, as did his own mother and her friends of Ashland's Ladies Aid Society. Black "could idolize a woman to the point where he believed she was near perfect," especially if she evoked the memory of his mother, but he also could denounce a woman as "made for men" and their sexual desires if she flaunted her body. Yet, even a woman with a questionable appearance and reputation won Black's heart and help if her mistakes were attributable to the trials of living with an alcoholic, abusive husband. Also, Black was deeply outraged when men sexually abused women. As prosecutor, he had sought the death penalty in 1914 for an Italian who kidnapped and raped a woman. He was sorely disappointed when the jury sentenced the accused to twenty years in prison and he subsequently opposed the man's pardon, even after his victim later forgave and married her attacker.

In Black's view, gender divided human beings by character as well as physique. Men were generally complex, contradictory creatures. "A good man will sometimes hurt people and be selfish," Black once observed, but "a good woman will never hurt anybody." Women embodied human virtue or human vice, "all good or all bad."[12]

Nothing in the record of Mary Miniard's case reveals her physical appearance or personal characteristics, except for her race, class, recent motherhood, and her own words about an experience up North on the Illinois Central. In Black's opinion, this evidence was good enough.

A. M. Wakefield, a white conductor from the Illinois Central, was the defense's first witness. He had been the last conductor on Mary Miniard's ride from Chicago to Cairo Junction, where in accordance with Southern custom and Northern duplicity, the insane black woman and all other African Americans on the rails were removed to Jim Crow cars.

"When did you first see this crazy nigger?"

"Well, when I gotten at the train at Centralia."

"What was the nigger doing at the time that you saw her?"

"She wasn't doing anything particularly, only sitting there on the seat," replied the conductor.

"What did she do to act crazy in your presence?"

"The only thing I saw her do out of the way was to sit on the back of the seat, and hang from the hat rack, and sing a little."

"Where was the train approximately, when you got the message from Mrs. Miniard to come back?"

"I don't just remember, but I think it was thirty minutes before I got to Cairo Junction."

"When you got back there what did you do?" Percy asked.

"I went to this lady and she told me she was being disturbed by this crazy person . . ."

Mr. Black: "I can't quite understand you."

"She told me she was being disturbed by this crazy woman on the train, and she asked me how far it was before the niggers had to get out of that car. I told her the next stop was Cairo Junction; and she said she would be very glad, that she was afraid of niggers—afraid of crazy niggers," the conductor stated more loudly. "I told her that I was sorry, but we would transfer at Cairo Junction just as quick as the law permitted . . . At that time I was in the State of Illinois. It is a thirty minutes run to Cairo Junction."

"I believe in the State of Illinois they don't have Jim Crow cars?" Percy mused innocently.

"No, sir."

"Where did you first pick up the Jim Crow cars?"

"Cairo Junction."

"Where is that?"

"It is just on the north side of the Ohio River."

"You put this crazy nigger in the Jim Crow car as soon as you got there?" Percy repeated.

"Just as quick as we stopped at Cairo Junction; we always transfer."

RACE RELATIONS ON BOTH SIDES of the Ohio River were mean-spirited and violent in 1919. In the aftermath of World War I, many black soldiers were disappointed that they had fought overseas to make the world safe for democracy only to return to an anti-democratic South of segregation, white supremacy, and personal humiliation. North and South, many whites thought black ex-soldiers had become unruly, discourteous, and dangerous.

African Americans were organizing anew to improve themselves and to challenge racist practices. The NAACP had set up scores of new chapters across the South, and a large stream of black migration out of the South revealed a growing number of Negroes determined to escape a regime of outrageous racism. Thomas Parke, a white Birmingham physician, recorded the new mood of black defiance in the privacy of his diary: "It seems to me that evidence of fight in negroes against social injustice are cropping up all the while and that negroes more and more are proving a willingness to take the consequences of fighting for their rights. To my mind it means that the immediate future holds trouble."

The spring and summer of 1919 did bring trouble, the greatest period of interracial strife the nation had ever known. More than forty race riots took place, beginning in Charleston, S.C., and Longview, Texas, where white posses burned several Negro shops and houses as a warning against black retaliation for a recent lynching. In Washington, D.C., gangs of whites and blacks fought for several days and left four dead and more than a dozen seriously wounded. Two thousand federal troops and torrential rains were necessary to close violent streets.

Between April when the Miniards left Chicago and their October trial, the Windy City also endured a race riot. On July 3, a white saloonkeeper in Chicago died of heart trouble, although the press incorrectly reported that a black man killed him. That evening, gangs of white youth rode through one of Chicago's black sections shooting wildly at African Americans. On July 4, white gangs announced that they were going to "get all the niggers," and when a black accidentally entered a "white only" section of Chicago's lake beaches, he was stoned to death. Blacks retaliated. A week later, forty had been killed and more than five hundred injured.

A week before the Miniard trial, America's season of racial blood-letting reached a climax in the fields of the Arkansas Delta at Elaine. On October 1, reports of a "Negro Insurrection" were telegraphed across the nation. Black tenants had organized to oppose white landlords threatening to evict them. Violence erupted. "Race War Rages In Streets of Arkansas Mill Village," announced enormous headlines on the front page of Birmingham's morning paper on Thursday, October 2.

Racial hysteria was not distant news. Less than a week before the Miniard trial, three African Americans were lynched in Alabama's state capital within a span of twelve hours. The national NAACP declared that a "reign of terrorism" in Montgomery was forcing "colored people, among them professional men and property owners" to leave the city. By week's end, a state circuit judge dismissed a special Montgomery grand jury that could find "no information whatsoever to establish the identity of any of the parties engaged in these killings." From neighboring Georgia, wire dispatches reaching Birmingham on October 6 and 7 reported that two African Americans arrested for murder were burned on wooden stakes and a third was shot repeatedly at close range by a white mob.

In response to Alabama's lynchings, Governor Thomas E. Kilby publicly condemned "mob law" with a promise that anyone involved would be prosecuted. Kilby's words drew praise and attention from the nation's press, as the U.S. Congress considered federal legislation to deal with the Southern lynchings—a prospect of federal intervention worrying Kilby and other officials. Yet, no one was brought to court in Alabama for lynching a black man in 1919.

Birmingham's race relations also deteriorated. In March a near riot had erupted, as the city barely avoided what a seasoned black observer said "would have been one of the worst in the history of the nation." A Negro, later identified as a professional robber dressed in a soldier's uniform, killed a white policeman. African Americans then reacted angrily to "the rough methods of the police in combing the Negro districts" to find the murderer—the same methods used two weeks earlier when police searched for another black suspect. On the night of March 1, rumors spread throughout black and white neighborhoods that the other "race" was readying an attack. Many in both communities armed themselves. Several hundred revolvers and rifles and more than $6,000 worth of ammunition were purchased in a single day. Industrial plants reported that over two tons of dynamite had been stolen. It was one of the longest nights in the city's young history.

In early fall, Judge William Fort presided over a local race relations conference where for the first time local black and white men discussed race problems openly, but without firm promises of change. Afterwards, tensions continued to mount. Jefferson County Sheriff J. C. Hartsfield feared race riots involving "negro mobs of six hundred or eight hundred men." The sheriff reported that at all-black mining camps outside Birmingham "negroes are heavily armed and are well equipped with pistols, guns and ammunition." In response, white men "are arming themselves to protect their families."

As Hugo Black prepared for the Miniard trial, paperboys rushed to the streets below his office hawking the *Birmingham Age-Herald*, whose front-page banner headline screamed: "NEGROES PLAN SLAUGHTER OF WHITES." The secondary headline read, "Wholesale Murder of White People In Arkansas May Be Part of Plot Against South." Local and state officials, encouraged by an eager press, concluded that Bolshevists—agents of the recent Russian Revolution three continents away—were agitating among African Americans. White leaders were morally incapable of imagining any other explanation for blacks fighting back. The lesson was clear to Birmingham editors: "No one among the white residents of a community knows how far such agitation has gone until there is a reign of terror, such as Chicago had."

By Saturday, October 4, four days before Mary Miniard took the stand, tensions and antagonism between the city's races seemed explosive. At Twentieth Street and Fourth Avenue, a shopping area between the courthouse and city hall, four hundred African Americans gathered on Saturday afternoon. "With drawn knives and threats of violence," the crowd cheered madly as a black man made "an inflammatory speech against the white race." According to the *Birmingham Ledger* reporter, police ordered white women to seek safety in the stores, and shouts of "Kill him!" rang out when a white man challenged the black crowd. The gathering finally dispersed peacefully, but Birmingham's atmosphere "was never more filled with hysteria . . . than at this hour," according to black newspaper editor Oscar Adams.

Reactions in the white community to local racial tensions were more orderly, although no less threatening. Sheriff Hartsfield readied two machine guns on loan from the state militia. White men continued to arm themselves. Businessmen discussed reviving the American Protective League. The police arrested a white man in Ensley's Tuxedo Negro Theater for telling his black audience that they should stand up for their American rights. The speaker was sentenced to six months hard labor.

At the courthouse, newly appointed Circuit Judge Horace Wilkinson demonstrated the reactionary force of the criminal justice system. Wilkinson sentenced a Negro burglar to fifteen-to-twenty years, a long, possibly deadly tenure as convict laborer, for breaking into an empty house in a white neighborhood. "Why, judge," the black defendant vainly protested, "you could kill a nigger and only get ten years for it." The lament was true enough. But, in Birmingham in October 1919, white leaders used any wayward act to show the heavy power of the white man's law over a black man's transgression in order to restore good race relations. "Negro men of Alabama," beckoned black editor Oscar Adams, "these are perilous times for us."

When Hugo Black began his cross-examination of the Illinois Central Railway's conductor, the trainman who worked the route between Illinois and Birmingham, newsboys were on Birmingham's streets, within earshot of the courtroom, crying out, "Read All About Race Riot. Get your paper here. Read All About Race Riot."[13]

"MR. WAKEFIELD, didn't you hear that nigger woman say anything?" Black demanded.

"Sir?"

"Didn't you hear that nigger saying anything—any cursing?"

"I did not; no, sir," the conductor insisted.

"She was just singing, and hanging to the rack?" Black asked.

"That is all that I saw her do."

"How was she hanging to the racks?"

"Hanging up by her hands."

"What was she singing?"

"I don't know; humming a little song."

"Singing it in a loud voice?"

"Just kind of low."

"Kind of a soft, gentle voice?" Black inquired.

"Yes, sir."

"Had her hands up on the hat rack, and singing familiar songs in a soft, tender voice?" Black asked again.

"She seemed to be amusing the passengers rather than hurting them," Wakefield replied. Here was a real admission. The jury had heard the plaintiff state that most passengers were Negroes, and now the conductor testified that these passengers were amused by the situation. Black decided he had scored an important point. He moved slowly towards another.

"The first time you went through what was she doing? . . . Was she singing in the soft, gentle tone?" Black asked in his own rural, white Southern accent.

"Kind of a gentle tone of voice," the witness repeated.

"Singing in a soft, gentle tone," Black repeated.

"I don't know," the conductor replied nervously. "There wasn't any words to it, or any tune, very much."

"She was singing in that soft, gentle tone, sitting in the seat, and the next time you came through she was hanging on the hat racks?" Black continued.

"I saw her hang on the hat rack," the witness affirmed.

"Each time you came through she was singing in that soft, gentle tone," Black repeated.

Black had repeated the term "in a soft gentle tone" so often that the words now seemed to belong to the witness, although in truth Black originated the phrase and only he had used it—seven times. Now, Mary Miniard's lawyer was ready to turn the words he had grafted onto the conductor's testimony against the witness.

"Now when this lady called you back there did she tell you that she was scared of this woman because she was singing *in that soft, gentle tone*, or did she tell you that she was scared because she was *cursing and came over her*?" Black demanded.

"Because she was crazy," the conductor said.

"Did she tell you that this woman had been cursing her?" Black continued.

"No, sir."

"What?" Black asked, although he probably heard the response.

"No, sir; she did not."

"You swear positive she didn't tell you that."

"I certainly do, sir."

"Well, now, about what time was it the first time you went through when she was sitting up on the back of the seat singing *in that soft, gentle tone?*" mocked Black.

"I suppose two-thirty, or two-thirty-five, or forty."

"How many stations did you pass after that where your train stopped before you got to Cairo?"

"We only made one stop . . . Carbondale, Illinois."

"Any hotels there?" Black asked.

"Plenty of them."

Next, Black asked the conductor if the train had any drawing rooms on the first-class Pullman cars where the company could have relocated the Miniards or the crazy woman.

"Yes, sir; two."

"Did you investigate to see whether or not any of those were vacant?"

"I did not," Wakefield stated.

"You did not?" Black repeated for effect.

"I did not," the witness repeated.

"How many passenger coaches were there on the train?"

"Two."

"Was this a large woman, or small woman?" Black inquired.

"Which one?" the witness asked defiantly. This was a costly, insolent response. There were only two women in question, a white Southerner who was sitting in front of him and a "crazy nigger" woman from the North whom no juror had seen. By Southern linguistic standards, the witness insinuated he saw no difference—made no social distinction—between these two women. The conductor's earlier reference to Mary Miniard as a "lady" no longer counted for anything.

"This negro woman?" said Black, quite willing to explain the obvious.

"I don't remember much about her."

"Was she a black one?" the lawyer wanted to know.

"I don't think she was a very large woman. I don't think she was black."

"Yellow?" Black inquired.

"Yes, sir; I think so."

"You are absolutely sure, are you, that this *lady* [pointing to Mrs. Miniard] did not tell you that this nigger had been cursing?" Black asked.

"She told me she would be glad when we arrived at a point where they taken the niggers out of the car, on account of being afraid of the crazy nigger."

Black released the witness, but the conductor stayed in his chair. Roy Percy needed to make a couple of final points to recover the damage his witness had done to his own credibility. Percy asked: "Did *either* Mr. or Mrs. Miniard ask to put her into a different car or different seat?"

"No, sir."

Casually, very deliberately, Percy asked one more question: "Where were you born?"

"I was born . . ." the conductor said as simultaneously Hugo Black exploded, "We object to where he was born!"

Ambushed by Black's shouting, the witness was unable to verify that he was no Yankee conductor disputing and disparaging a Southern white woman. Percy maneuvered again. "We expect to show," he informed the judge for benefit of jurors' ears, ". . . that he was born in Tennessee."

"We object to where he was born!" Black shouted again, but this time the jury had heard. The conductor was by the grace of God a Southerner. Faced with a test of sectional loyalty, Black told judge and jury: "We offer to show that our client was born in Greensboro, Alabama," a small town in the Black Belt where the South's traditional race relations could easily have been born and certainly were well preserved.

Angered by Percy's tactics, Black decided to counter-attack. He asked the conductor: "Who was it told you that this woman was crazy?"

"I think it was Mr. Springer, the conductor that I relieved at Centralia."

"Is he out here," asked Black waving towards a door leading from the courtroom.

"Yes, sir."

Trapped by Black's inquiry, Percy now was obliged to call the other conductor—the Yankee conductor who worked the train from Chicago to Centralia, Illinois—on the wrong side of the Mason & Dixon.

By 1919, white Southerners had landscaped their region with innumerable Confederate monuments, erected in recent decades to memorialize an Old South of mythical proportions. Yet, as a cultural marker, the invisible "Mason & Dixon line" enshrined an equally expansive, historical distance between the North and South arising from the Civil War's aftermath as much as its outcome. More than forty years had passed since the end of Alabama's Reconstruction, but in the twilight "between living memory and written history," biracial Reconstruction had become the symbolic terms through which the white South understood itself, its own conditions, and the necessity for its distinct, segregated way of life.

Like almost every other white Southerner, Hugo Black considered Reconstruction the bleakest, most painful era of American and Southern history, even more devastating than the Civil War. When Black was growing up, no one in Clay county—Populist, conservative Democrat, male or female, black or white—defended Reconstruction. Textbooks from Black's days as a boy were unabashedly chauvinistic on the subject. "Alabama, like other Southern States, was simply turned upside down," declared one standard Alabama textbook. "For the first time in America, if not the world, the least intelligent were set to work governing States . . . It was not the fault of the negroes themselves that they were thrust into this false position," the textbook instructed students. "If they had been left to themselves, the result might have been merely comical, but they were not left to themselves. They were guided by irresponsible white men" primarily from the North.

Black saw no virtue in Alabama's shortlived episode of biracial Republican rule. Throughout his life, Black argued that Talladega's J. L. M. Curry (the educator named in Uncle Merit Street's will), not the "Reconstruction Regime," was responsible for "the real beginnings of the State school system" despite the findings of recent historians. This perspective was fortified after the turn of the century when historian Walter Fleming's book on Alabama Reconstruction quickly became one of Jim Crow's definitive works, a book that Black read and reread. "For the misgovernment of Reconstruction," Fleming wrote, "the negro, who was in no way to blame, has been made to suffer, since those who were really responsible could not be reached." They were on the other side of the Mason & Dixon.

One of his favorite historians, John William Draper, whom Black began reading in Birmingham, cast a similar outlook in *History of the American Civil War*. In explaining the outbreak of the war, Draper wrote that whites in both the North and South believed that the African American "will never be more than an overgrown child." Sectional conflicts, therefore, grew from other fundamental differences between the nation's white peoples. "The people of the North and those of the South have had a different origin," Draper wrote in passages which Black underscored in his own book, "they have lived in different climates; they are actuated by different ideas; they have had a different history; there is absolutely no hope of restoring equality between them."[14]

More than any other private institution, railroads were emblematic of this troubled history between the North and the South. The Civil War (called a "war of secession" in the South and a "war of rebellion" in the North in 1919) upended the South's early railroad construction and badly damaged Alabama rail lines. Yet, soon after Robert E. Lee surrendered, entrepreneurs resumed rail expansion in Alabama at a rate previously unimagined.

Under the leadership of a provisional governor, with his own favored Northern industrialists, the Alabama legislature guaranteed bonds for railroad construction in the extravagant amount of $12,000 per mile. Later, the Reconstruction legislature increased the rate to a scandalous $16,000 per railroad mile and approved additional state bonds. Reconstruction represented a morality play about power and human equality, but, as one careful historian has observed, "railroads became the most important single factor in Reconstruction politics." From 1867 to 1871, the state endorsed railroad bonds and loans of approximately $17 million and pumped up state debt to almost $30 million.

Despite bipartisan greed and misdeeds, conservative Democrats used Reconstruction's railroad debt and footloose financing to help win the 1874 election and "redeem" Alabama to white supremacy. White Democrats, however, did not dethrone railroads. They simply changed the form of favoritism. The state's 1875 Constitution prohibited underwriting of private "works of internal improvements" and provided for railroad regulation. But it also guaranteed light taxes for railroads and full payment to Northern financiers holding the state's outstanding railroad bonds. With less tax revenues and big bonds to pay off, the state had to cut expenses, and Northern financiers suggested two ways: cut school appropriations and prisoner costs. For more than fifty years, Alabama's state government followed exactly that course.

The railroads made sure the state kept its bargain. From 1875 until B. B. Comer took office, most Alabama governors were financially tied to a railroad company, usually the L&N. The state railroad commission was created in 1881 with very limited, conciliatory powers, and, despite their rhetoric, Populists made little impact in reducing railroad influence. As one Alabama historian succinctly stated: "The railroads were in control."[15]

Control of the railroads on both sides of the Mason & Dixon did change.

First, in 1902, J. P. Morgan, the premiere Northern empire builder, maneuvered on Wall Street to take control of the L&N railroad, less than ten years after he had taken ownership of more than four thousand miles of rail track consolidated as the Southern Railway. When stock trades were settled, Morgan had dominant influence in the three major railroads in Alabama and the South. In the words of one observer, Northern "giants divided the Southern colony, according to mutual interest." About the same time, railroad politics in Alabama was born again at the Constitutional Convention of 1901, where Frank White led the movement for real railroad regulation. The battle was lost there, but White formed a state association which included men as diverse as Herman Beck and Charles Henderson. This group agreed that railroads were the common enemy of small businessmen, merchants, farmers, and laborers.

They shared a simple grievance. Controlled by Northern interests, railroads charged more per mile for the transport of merchandise, farm products, and supplies originating in Alabama than for the shipment of goods into Alabama. The rates hiked the prices of Alabama products exported from the state but reduced the costs of imported Northern goods. An owner of grain and cotton mills, B. B. Comer charged "bossism in the railroads!" A swarm of railroad lawyers, including John H. Bankhead, Jr., attempted to derail reform in Montgomery, but charges of "bossism" frightened the legislature into creating a new, more powerful railroad commission. Within a year, B. B. Comer was elected its chairman, and in 1906 he became Alabama's anti-railroad governor.

Losing at politics, railroads resorted to federal courts and often to former governor Thomas Goode Jones. Republican President Theodore Roosevelt had appointed Jones, once the state's chief L&N attorney, to the federal bench. Every means Governor Comer used to bring railroads under his control, Judge Jones found unlawful. Exasperated, the Comer legislature passed an act, later struck down, that removed a railroad company's right to do business in Alabama if it went to federal court to challenge any state law.

Soon after he arrived at Birmingham's L&N station, Black began to learn first-hand about railroad issues. Both local merchants and laborers complained that Northern corporations, including the railroads, did not pay a fair share of taxes and ruled the city for their economic convenience. Until 1916 the L&N stubbornly blocked all civic efforts to build more than one street across rail tracks at Birmingham's core. The city's original deed provided that all streets except Twentieth should forever dead end at the edge of the rail tracks, and the L&N did not want to give up this "convenience" even after Birmingham had more than one hundred thousand people. For years, Twentieth Street was clogged with streetcars, carriages, automobiles, wagons, and pedestrians using the one passageway that connected north and south Birmingham.

Following 1907, when J. P. Morgan arranged U.S. Steel's takeover of T.C.I. (which should have included an "R" for Tennessee Coal, Iron, and *Railway* Co.), Birmingham's labor disputes were always a struggle between Alabama workers and Southern managers of Northern corporations. By 1919, this history hovered ominously. Jefferson County Sheriff J. C. Hartsfield warned, "The difference between capital and labor are soon to be settled," and, in September, the city endured sporadic hostilities during a national steel strike. Production at U.S. Steel's Ensley plant, where H. R. Miniard worked, was hardest hit after over a hundred workers walked off the job.

In October, Birmingham and the nation were bracing for an upcoming coal strike, and all of Alabama's basic industries—mining, iron, steel, and railroads—were rallying together in the single cause of Northern "capital." The state's chief railroad lawyer and Black's nemesis, Forney Johnston saw what loomed ahead. He warned that Alabama faced a "phenomenal cleavage between the working classes and the business interests."[16] To be accurate, *Northern* business interests.

Representing the Northern business interests, Roy Percy reluctantly called the Yankee conductor to testify. He was brief with Mr. Springer. "What was she doing when she got on the train," Percy asked concerning the Negro woman. ". . . Was she running a foot race, or dancing a jig, or what was she doing?"

"She sang a little," the conductor replied.

"Well, was she crazy, or singing?"

"Well, she was crazy, all right. She sang a little."

"Was she abusing anybody while you were present?" Percy asked.

"Not in my presence, no, sir," the conductor replied.

"Did she curse in your presence?" Percy asked.

"Well, a little; yes, sir," replied Springer.

Realizing the Northern conductor's admission of "a little" cursing differed from testimony of his Southern conductor, Percy sought a better answer. "Did she curse Mrs. Miniard in your presence?"

"Well, I don't think so; no," Springer answered, far too tentatively.

Uncertain of his own witness, Percy had no choice but to leave Springer to Black's interrogation. Black seem delighted to have the Northern witness. He focused immediately on the discrepancy in the defense's testimony. "She just cursed a little, did she?" Black asked.

"She was standing up looking out of the front door of the car. I don't think anybody positive could have heard her," the witness said.

"She never did talk loud enough so anybody could hear her but the conductor?" Black inquired.

"I don't think so," Springer said.

"She didn't sing loud enough for anybody to hear?"

"Oh, yes, sir."

"Didn't she sing in a *soft, gentle tone*?" Black asked, resurrecting his phrase from the last witness.

"Well—" the witness started.

"Pretty loud, or soft tone?"

"I don't know what you consider soft . . . ," the conductor hedged.

"Loud, do you mean?"

"Fairly loud."

"Did you see her when she was performing antics, standing up on the seat, and holding on the hat rack?"

"No, sir. I never went near her," the conductor replied.

Black liked the conductor's answer and repeated it, in his own words, for the jury's benefit. "You wouldn't go around her; you wouldn't go back where she was," Black emphasized. Giving the witness not a second to correct this interpretation, Black quickly pointed to his client and demanded of the Yankee conductor: "You knew *this lady* was in there?"

"Knew,—what?" replied Springer, startled by Black's abrupt shift in tone and pace.

"You knew that *this lady* was back there?" Black demanded again.

"I knew there was several people in the car," the conductor protested.

Black had asked twice about "this lady," and the witness had answered without direct reference to the plaintiff as a "lady." To attentive Southern men, the Northern conductor could appear unaccustomed—or unwilling—to referring to a Southern white woman, especially a working class white woman, as a "lady." To underscore this point to the jury, Mary Miniard's attorney added an adjective in his follow-up question, one that was unnecessary in the white South of 1919 when speaking to people who understood the Southern way of life. In a word, Hugo Black's discredited the defense witness.

"You knew there were several *white* ladies?" Black asked.

"Yes, sir," the Yankee admitted.

"You knew there were a lot of nigger men in there?" Black added.

"Well, really, I couldn't say," the conductor replied vaguely.

"You knew there was a lot of nigger men and women, and you knew this woman was crazy, and you had heard that she was crazy?"

"Just at one certain time, standing in the door."

"She was trying to undress?" Black suggested.

"No, sir."

"Who was she cussing so softly?"

"Nobody; of course, I guess everybody in general."

"How many more times did you go through there?" Black asked.

"I guess I was through the train once more after that."

"For fifty-three miles?" Black asked with quick math.

"Yes, sir."

"You knew the woman was crazy?"

"Yes, sir."

"You didn't stay long?" asked Black, matter-of-factly.

"No, sir," the conductor said.

Again, Black liked the conductor's curt reply. It gave Black a chance to make the answer "no" sound like "yes," and to ask a follow-up question making the witness sound as if he was contradicting himself. Black rephrased his question: "You got out as quickly as possible?"

"No; not quicker than any other time," the witness pleaded.

"Did you have any other passenger cars beside this one?"

"Yes, sir."

"Did you have any other passenger cars in which there was no *white ladies* riding?" inquired Black, as he whitened his noun again to highlight the witness' failure to understand the South's color code.

"Had a smoking car; never *white ladies* in there," the conductor replied. Now, in responding to Black's own language, the witness had referred to "white ladies," a damning redundancy for a Northern man testifying about a Southern woman and a "crazy nigger" woman.

"No *white ladies* in there?" Black repeated to underscore the language.

"No, sir."

"You had a number of Pullmans in there?"

"Four, I believe."

"They had a baggage car?"

"Half baggage."

"Didn't you tell Mr. Wakefield [the Southern-born conductor] when he got on . . . there was a crazy woman, he had better watch for her?"

"I told him a crazy woman was on the train."

"Better watch out for her?"

"No more than I would."

"Did you tell him that or not?" Black insisted.

"I don't know whether I did or not."

"You are absolutely sure there wasn't anything but *soft, gentle,* melodious singing going on?"

"I didn't say that; just an ordinary tone," the witness stated. "I don't know what you call it." The Yankee conductor was no longer sure of anything.

"Who was that nigger that stood up and was sworn as a witness?" Black asked.

"The porter. Not my porter," the conductor answered.

"What is his name?"

"I don't know. He is not with me at all," the witness concluded.

"THE RULE" APPARENTLY had been invoked in the Miniard case. It was not a principle of justice, but shorthand for the usual practice of trial lawyers to remove potential witnesses from a courtroom so that they cannot hear others' testimony. It was standard practice when attorneys believed that they might discover and show discrepancies of testimony among the other party's witnesses. At the beginning of the Miniard trial, "the rule" had been invoked for two defense witnesses, the Yankee conductor, Springer, and the unnamed black porter.

In 1919, Southern courtrooms also observed other customary rules reflecting the etiquette of race relations instead of principles of law, procedure, or justice. It was, for instance, ordinary procedure to consider a white person's testimony to be more truthful than any statement of an African American.

On the street and in the courtroom, a Negro was expected never to flatly contradict a white person's word, and the black person's manner and tone of voice should always be deferential. In all places, including the courtroom, Southern tradition demanded that an African American address white men with the title of "Mr.," "Sir," "Captain," or some other appropriate rank of respect and authority. In public, a polite "yes" without a deferential "Sir" approached racial blasphemy. The rules also commanded that a black person refer to any white woman of reputable character as a "lady." In return, white persons usually addressed black persons by their first name, no matter how well the African Americans were known. From birth to death, a black man could be called "boy" by a white person since the term was supposed to capture a Negro man's fixed level of maturity. A black female was at best a "woman" and, to Mr. Springer's ignorance, never a "lady." A reference to a "white lady" could suggest that a speaker thought a black woman could be a "lady"—and the social equal of a white woman.

In 1919, by Southern custom, "nigger" was a commonplace term used in and outside the presence of Negroes. "Coon" was another. Some whites thought "darkey" was a kinder expression for the African American, although it too was universally despised in the black community. Other forms of racial epithets were common, including mimicking black speech patterns. For instance, while staying at the Willard Hotel in Washington in late 1919, Forney Johnston was viscerally offended by a few black Republicans attending a conference at the ritzy hotel. Money usually segregated blacks, but not this time. "The colored brother has been in evidence most prominently," Johnston reported back home. "The three or four coons in the crowd have made the best of having Headquarters in a white man's hotel," Johnston complained, "and have stuck religiously to the lobby mingling with the white pussons."

If a Negro wanted to establish in a hotel, courtroom, or elsewhere that he knew and accepted his lowly place assigned by Southern white society he used a racial epithet in referring to himself or another black when talking with a white person. Any attempt, no matter how slight, by a black man to circumvent these general rules of etiquette, especially among white strangers, was often perceived by Southern whites as insolent and uppity.

When an American of African descent was called to the stand in an Alabama courtroom, he entered an all-white environment and, even if he was not accused of a crime, he knew he was at the precipice of mortal danger. In 1919, there were probably four black lawyers in the entire state. None of the judges, jurors, or law officers was African American. A Negro had good reason to believe that never would "absolute justice . . . be accorded me in the courts," and many leading activists and scholars saw the "courts as the means of reenslaving the blacks."[17]

Given these Southern rules and customs, if it was the defense counsel's decision to bring a distant black man to Birmingham and to swear him as a potential witness against a local white woman, it was a baffling, egregious error, even for a young attorney. Perhaps, realizing his strategic mistake, Roy Percy did not swallow Black's bait a second time. Percy rested the defense's case without calling the unnamed black porter.

Hugo Black, however, was not finished. In rebuttal, he called "Albert Lewis (c)" to the stand. What is your name?" Black inquired.

"Lewis—Albert Lewis."

"What do you do, Albert?" Black asked.

"Train porter . . . Illinois Central."

"Where do you work, Albert?"

"Between Cairo and Centralia," the porter replied.

"Cairo and Centralia?" Black repeated for emphasis with the jury. Here was a black man from the other side of the Mason & Dixon.

"Were you there the night that this crazy nigger woman was on there, Albert?" Black asked.

"Yes, sir."

"Did you stay on that car all the time, Albert?" Black continued.

"Yes, sir."

"This lady came and complained to you about that nigger woman?"

"No, sir," replied the porter, contradicting Mary Miniard's earlier testimony. It was a point Black repeated.

"Didn't mention it to you at all?" Black suggested.

"No, sir," Lewis restated.

"She didn't mention it to you; did she mention it to you and you go back and tell Mr. Wakefield?" Black asked.

"She told me that she—she asked me where was the conductor. I said, he is in the head car. She said, I would like to see him. I said, all right," Lewis remembered.

"Now, Albert, when you got on, did you see this negro woman in there? Was she cursing?"

"No, sir," Lewis stated. Another contradiction of Mrs. Miniard's testimony. Here, again, Black didn't try to move the porter off his conflicting testimony, as he had at times with white conductors. Instead, he encouraged Lewis to repeat it—and repeat it.

"She never did curse, did she?" Black continued.

"No, sir; not in my presence."

"And never cursed during the whole time on there?"

"Not in my presence."

"She didn't do anything extraordinary?" Black remarked as a question.

"Singing and talking," Lewis said.

"Singing *soft and gentle?*"

"Just singing, and talking," Lewis testified.

"Just laughing and talking like any other ordinary individual?" Black stated, as if testing how far Lewis would go in contradicting the testimony of all white witnesses.

"Oh, no," replied Lewis.

As Lewis's testimony progressed, almost any answer aided Black's client. If the porter, a Northern black man, gave statements which differed from the testimony of Mrs. Miniard, a Southern lady, the jury would have no problem deciding whose testimony to believe. When Black led Lewis to contradict testimony from one or both of the white conductors, Black's case also gained credibility.

"Did you see her get up and have a little dance in the aisle?" Black asked.

"No, sir."

"Did you see her try to take off her clothes?"

"No, sir."

"Were you there when the conductor came back where this lady was?" Black asked. With Lewis, Black had no need to whiten the "lady."

"No, sir."

"You didn't stay on this car much where that crazy woman was?" Black observed.

"I made several trips through there."

"You didn't stay long when you made those trips?" Black wondered.

"Yes; once and a while I would take a seat in there."

"Did you go to sleep?"

"No, sir," the porter protested.

"You were in there most of the time, wasn't you, while that nigger woman was in there, with the lady?"

"Pretty much back and forth in the train," Lewis replied evasively.

"How did you happen to speak to this lady; did she call you?"

"Yes, sir."

"Just before this lady called you what was the crazy nigger woman doing?"

"Not doing anything that I seen."

"She was entirely quiet then?"

"Yes, sir," Lewis replied.

"And the nigger woman wasn't doing anything?" Black persisted.

"No, sir."

"When you went back to see the conductor what did you tell him?"

"I told him the lady over in the car wanted to see him . . . He said, What did she want? I said, I don't know." Lewis knew the rules. "The lady" applied to a white woman.

"Albert, the conductor hadn't been back there much?"

"Yes, sir."

"Don't you know as a matter of fact he didn't care to go back there where the crazy woman was?" Black pointedly asked the black man.

"He had to work his train; after he worked it he had to get his sleeper tickets," the porter explained.

"He didn't do that all night?" Black protested.

"I don't know," Lewis said in retreat.

"Did you see him sit down in the car?"

"No, sir."

"Where did he sit down to work up his tickets?"

"He was in the smoking car, working his tickets."

"In the smoking car right ahead?" Black emphasized.

Black now confirmed the fact that, while the white conductor sat elsewhere tallying his tickets, the black porter was left to look after Mary Miniard, sitting among a large number of Negro men. The plaintiff could not have asked for better testimony.

"In the smoking car, yes, sir," Lewis repeated.

Roy Percy had no questions for the porter, but Black recalled Mary Miniard so that the Southern "lady" might have the very last word. "Mrs. Miniard, did you know at the time that the conductor came back there where the change was made as to the Mason and Dixon line?"

"No, I didn't. I knew there was a change made, but I didn't know exactly where at," his client stated.

"Did you know that Cairo was the place where the changes were made?"

"No, sir; I did not."

"Did you ask him when he came back how long before he got to Cairo?"

"No; I did not."

"Did you call the conductor back there and ask him what time you got there, and say you were afraid of niggers?" Black continued.

"No; I didn't say I was afraid of niggers at all."

"Did you tell him, or not, that the nigger woman had been cursing you and threatening you?"

"I certainly did. I told him the nigger woman had started to cursing at me directly."

"This other conductor that came in a while ago, you saw him take the stand? Do you know whether he was the one that sat down there?"

"No, I wouldn't say for sure. I know there was some white man with a conductor's uniform on, or railroad uniform on, that sat down and talked to some man about thirty minutes."

"And while he was there . . . she was doing the cursing," Black stated.

"Yes, sir," the witness concluded.

LeRoy Percy chose again not to cross question Mary Miniard. The evidence in the case was closed.

Next morning, Judge Boyd decided to exclude part of Mary Miniard's testimony, where she stated that the "nigger doctor said that they might remove her [the black woman] to the baggage car." "That part of the testimony is excluded," the judge instructed the jury, "and you are expressly charged that you must not consider that evidence for any purpose."

No exact record of final arguments in the case has survived, but, if usual procedure was followed, Roy Percy stood first before the jury to interpret and explain the evidence. In the cool of the October morning, the railroad lawyer probably underlined the basic facts of the case: a "crazy nigger woman" was the cause of this unfortunate incident, not agents of the Illinois Central. The defendant and its employees were not responsible for the problem and did all that the law allowed to remedy it. The conductors and porter had several cars to service and, when they were in the car with Mrs. Miniard, they saw no conduct that allowed them by law to remove the crazy woman from the train. Of course, they could not—and did not—see everything; however, after Mary Miniard complained to the railroad agents, they removed the "crazy nigger woman" within 30 minutes. At first opportunity, when the train crossed the Mason & Dixon line, the woman and all other African Americans were placed in a Jim Crow car.

Yet, Percy realized that the law governing common carriers was not really at issue in this case. The real issue—or how Hugo Black had manipulated the real issue—appears to have truly disturbed Roy Percy. The two opposing lawyers were contemporaries. Black was only three years older. Yet, they were different in most respects and experience. Black had practiced law for 13 years—three times longer than Percy. Black came from Alabama's poor backwoods and skipped over a high school diploma and a liberal arts education for a law degree from the state's university. Without money or connections, Black built a law practice from scratch. Black was Baptist, bone dry, a joiner, politically ambitious, disciplined in all habits, seldom inclined towards self analysis, and a consummate showman.

By contrast, Roy Percy's family came from a Mississippi Delta plantation. His father moved to Birmingham, married the daughter of the town's richest industrialist, Henry DeBardeleben, and set up a law practice representing his father-in-law's company and other industrialists. Roy pursued advanced studies in Europe at the University of Heidelberg after graduating from both Princeton and Harvard Law School. Roy had a good job, a girlfriend and future wife, an extended family, and assured wealth waiting for him when he returned to Birmingham. Most in his family were Catholic or Episcopalian. He extravagantly enjoyed hunting, drinking, and gambling, all the pastimes of the Delta gentleman. By nature, Roy was reflective and moody.

These differences may have been the chemistry of friction between the two men but were commonplace among many opposing lawyers. In this instance, Roy Percy was more likely distressed by the ways he saw Black deliberately manipulating and debasing Southern male honor in order to manufacture a case against his client. In a contest of ordinary words about proper language, conduct, and etiquette within the unspoken rules of Southern race relations, the case's real disagreement wasn't about the lawful duty of a common carrier or even the conduct of a "crazy nigger woman." It centered on whether

Mary Miniard was a Southern "lady" grievously left unprotected by Percy's Northern client under terms of Southern honor. Men of the Percy family had preserved a worshipful, belligerent regard for a Southern gentleman's honor, the self-enforced, individual code of conduct that once governed the South's old plantation life as the rule of law. Roy's beloved uncle in the Delta continued, in large measure, to live and rule his community in 1919 by this code despite encroachments from white rabble rousers and modern life. Roy's father Walker brought the code with him as a constant guide of his actions and the defining terms of his own identity when he moved from the plantation to the unsettling ways of emerging, industrial Birmingham.

According to biographers of the Percy family, Walker Percy probably committed suicide in 1917 because of deep feelings of moral inadequacy, despair, or confusion about whether he was upholding the honor of the Old South in a city where men of all ranks hungered for wealth and power, rarely in a chivalrous manner. After successfully defending the takeover of T.C.I. by U.S. Steel, Roy's father may have decided that he had betrayed the honor that defined him, that he had planted rapacious Northern capitalism as the South's future tree of plenty and foreclosed all possibilities that the Old South's order of right and honor would rule Birmingham and the South.

What drives a brilliant, talented, and wealthy man at mature age to take a shotgun and kill himself in his own attic reaches to questions beyond human understanding. Yet, Old South honor as an all-defining identity was as real as life and death for Percy men. The son who discovered his father's body amid a deep pool of blood and flesh could not have spoken a more fitting eulogy or described the character of all Percy men better than did the Birmingham editorial remembering Walker Percy: "He had the truest of pride, and was the embodiment of honor in all his relations."

In the Miniard case, Hugo Black was asking twelve white men on the basis of Southern honor to rebuke the Illinois Central Railroad for failing to protect a Southern white lady from the unbecoming conduct of a "crazy nigger" in the North. In effect, Black was using the code of conduct that defined life and death for Percy men in order to extract money from Percy's client because a white crane operator (who worked for another of Percy's clients) and his wife bought a coach ticket—instead of a first-class Pullman berth—in Chicago and rode to the Mason & Dixon line with a car full of black folk, including one "crazy nigger."

By aristocratic Percy standards, Black's case mimicked and manipulated Old South honor. In attempting to punish a Northern corporation in an Alabama court for events beyond the Mason & Dixon, Black was subverting the essential nature of a honor code, a gentleman's individual responsibility to enforce respectful conduct on his own. Had he been a true Southern gentleman, instead of a common white man, Mary Miniard's husband would have defended his wife on his honor during the train ride. To defend one's personal honor, a Southern gentleman did not rely upon other men to do their duty. He did not appeal to unknown Northern conductors to protect Southern womanhood or to twelve strangers in a jury box—and certainly not to a colored porter.

After his own father's suicide, Roy had demonstrated how Percy men defended their honor. When a Birmingham lawyer questioned his integrity, Percy demanded a private duel or, as he stated, "any satisfaction you now or hereafter desire in any manner, shape, or form."[18] Percy was dead serious. He was duty-bound to defend his honor. He did not go to court and file an action for defamation of character so that twelve white strangers could recover his honor.

Mary Miniard may have been born in Alabama's Black Belt, but she was not a Southern lady by Delta standards. She was the wife of a semi-skilled laborer, and her poor grammar on the witness stand amply evidenced her lack of education and refinement. In a telling pattern of speech, Percy never referred to Mary Miniard as a "lady" until and unless required to do so by Black or his own witnesses' choice of words. By the commonest terms of the region's race relations, a Negro might call Mary a "lady," but by the Old South's code this white woman was not a "Southern lady." Mary's fear of the "crazy nigger woman" was proof enough, since a lady of the Old South certainly knew how to handle her Negro women.

Confronted with Black's efforts to democratize Southern honor, Roy Percy attacked both the lawsuit and the lawyer. He apparently ridiculed Black as a hungry, over-confident plaintiff's lawyer searching for an easy buck in a merit-less case. "Ego" Black brought this matter to court, Percy informed the jury. The case involved no suffering of a widow, no bodily injury. No one lost a life or limb. The only reason for the lawsuit, Percy stated, was an attorney's ego and hunger for an unjustifiable fee. If Mary Miniard needed a Southern protector, her husband was sitting next to her during the entire trip. But, he did nothing. The train's agents saw no abusive behavior. They did their diligent duty. Only at the Ohio River did Illinois law allow Jim Crow to take over. The railroad did its lawful duty.

When Percy returned to his chair, Black faced the jury. Mary Miniard's own testimony was the heart of his case. Under oath, she had told the jury of her long, tiresome journey home and how the "nigger woman" bothered her from the Chicago depot to the Mason & Dixon line for more than eight hours. The Negro had directly cursed her with vile language. Mrs. Miniard said it "scared me nearly to death." A young, vulnerable mother was so frightened that she would not pass the "nigger woman" in order to go to the bathroom throughout the ordeal. As late as three o'clock in the morning—in the darkest hour of night—the Negro woman cursed Mrs. Miniard "in the presence of all of the negro men . . . and me the only white woman in the car." When the Negro porter was called to fetch the conductor, it was an hour later before the conductor arrived. He said that the crazy woman would be removed when the train reached Cairo.

Black's case was strengthened by key, undisputed testimony from the railroad's own witnesses. Other cars were available in which the "nigger woman" could have been isolated or in which Mrs. Miniard could have been comfortably relocated. There were several stations, at least one with a hotel, where the Negro woman could have been let off. Yet, nothing was done before the train reached the Mason & Dixon. Every defense witness admitted that none of the railroad's white men spent very much time in the car. One conductor said the "nigger woman" was just singing lullabies "in a soft gentle tone" and never cursed. The other admitted that her so-called singing was "fairly loud" and that she did curse at everybody. The only real contradiction of Mrs. Miniard's testimony came from Albert Lewis (c), the porter, whom the defense brought from Illinois to testify.

What Black told the jury can only be speculation, although his line for questioning and lawyer's style suggest that he asked the Southern white jurymen to do what two white men and one Negro of the Illinois Central Railroad would not: carry out their rightful duty to defend a young mother, a Southern lady. Mary Miniard was not rich. Her young husband was still building their future at the steel plant, and he could not afford a Pullman berth for his wife, nursing their first born to manhood. She was not the wife of an aristocrat or an industrialist. She was not a Northerner. But, is that any reason why she should have been exposed to vile and immodest conduct in the presence of a crowd of Negro men? Mary Miniard suffered a cruelty and indignity that a Southern lady should never have to endure. For eight hours, for their apparent amusement, agents of the Illinois Central Railroad needlessly permitted Negroes to torment Mary Miniard.

When Black finished, the judge charged the jury on the law. He told them that it is the duty of railroads to use the highest degree of skill and care to protect passengers from personal injury, insult or abuse. He noted that a common carrier has the right to eject a passenger who is abusive or vile, but the passenger should not be removed at a time and place which would unnecessarily expose her to great danger. It was a rather generous statement of the law for the plaintiff, and Roy Percy objected for purposes of a possible appeal.

When the jury retired, Percy returned to his law office and recounted for a senior partner his closing argument about "Ego" Black. "Has the jury come in?" Augustus Benners responded. Percy confessed that it had not and was admonished to hold his tongue until after the jurymen spoke. Before sunset, William E. Hargrove, a public accountant and jury foreman, informed Judge Boyd that, "a jury of good and lawful men" had found in favor of the plaintiff "in the amount of $2,999.99." Percy was stunned and silenced. A Birmingham jury had awarded an Ensley woman almost $3,000, five times the average yearly wages of a local white worker, for sitting in the same rail car with a mentally disturbed black woman from Chicago to the Mason & Dixon line.[19]

THE MINIARD CASE DID NOT END in October 1919. Roy Percy appealed the verdict to the Alabama Supreme Court since it was "against the great preponderance of evidence" and an "excessive amount." On June 3, 1920, the Court overturned the jury's verdict in an opinion written by Justice Anthony D. Sayre, the state's premiere lawgiver on matters of Old South ethics. Justice Sayre had little sympathy for Mary Miniard's claims. His virtual contempt for the character of Alabama's common white folks had not diminished since Black appeared before him on behalf of Nannie Cornelius, another poor, young white mother who sued the railroads for her pain and suffering. Justice Sayre's daughter Zelda captured his outlook on life at the time of his death several years after the Miniard case. She acknowledged her father's "brave, uncompromising effort to preserve conceptions" of an Old South, although he smothered her own sensual vitality, and she wondered "what ironic sequence, what stamina of spirit" had made Anthony Sayre "think so little of the world and so much of justice and integrity?" Old South justice and integrity, that is.

Two months before Justice Sayre sat in his office writing the Court's opinion describing Mary Miniard's train trip up North, Zelda Sayre had left her home traveling alone by rail from Montgomery to New York against her father's sternly expressed wishes. She was on her way to marry a young, extravagant writer, F. Scott Fitzgerald, who had pursued Zelda incessantly since he was stationed in Alabama during the war. Sayre's court opinion betrayed signs of a father's impatience with young Southern women who blithely venture above the Mason & Dixon to discover frightening, unpleasant ways of life. The "wrong of which plaintiff complains," Sayre wrote, "occurred in the state of Illinois, where . . . Jim Crow cars are prohibited and negro passengers on railroad trains are entitled to share accommodations with white passengers, without discrimination on account of race, color, or previous condition of servitude—a state of law and fact for which, of course, the defendant in this case can in no wise be held answerable." Beware, young Southern white women, you are on your own above the Mason & Dixon line.

Guided by a fixed devotion to Old South standards, Justice Sayre appeared as infuriated as Roy Percy by the case's claims and verdict. Amid his stilted, neutered words, Justice Sayre's sarcasm jumps off the page as he openly mocked Black's language asserting that Mary Miniard "was greatly embarrassed, frightened, chagrined, humiliated, and as a proximate result thereof was caused to suffer great mental pain and anguish, was made sick, frightened, and nervous, all to the plaintiff's damage" as she sat in a train car with a crazy Negro. In fact, Sayre stated, "We do not . . . find any evidence in the record which would warrant the conclusion that plaintiff was at any time in danger of physical harm. It is a matter of serious doubt that the evidence shows any cause of offense to plaintiff" and certainly no evidence of "wanton wrong" by the railroads, he added.

Sayre also dismissed Black's claim that the Illinois Central had a duty to remove the crazy Negro woman to another rail car to protect Miniard's sensibilities. Assuming, for sake of argument, the Negro woman was an "annoyance," Sayre stated, the railroad had "no *moral* or legal right to shift the annoyance . . . from plaintiff and other passengers in the coach with her to others equally entitled to protection." In plainer words, Justice Sayre proclaimed that the railroad as a legal "person" under the Constitution was not bound by Southern morality or man's law to provide Mary Miniard with any more consideration than it would extend to anyone else, including the Negro men in the same passenger car and the white men who had paid for Pullman berths. Neither law nor Sayre's Old South morality gave this poor white woman standing for privileges as a Southern lady.

The Court ordered the judgment reversed and found that Judge Boyd should have instructed jurors, in essence, that the verdict must be for the defendant if the railroad's agents exercise "judgement and discretion" in the good faith management of the crazy woman.

On February 10, 1921, amid a mining strike in the Birmingham area, Black returned to the Jefferson courthouse to try the case before another jury. The evidence was virtually the same, with two exceptions. H. R. Miniard's testimony from the first trial was read into the record because he was in Gary, Indiana. Apparently, the Miniards were no longer living together. They had separated or he had lost his job shortly after the 1919 steel mill strikes, perhaps due to union involvement. Either way, Black wanted to get before the jury the fact that Mary Miniard was now struggling with a child on her own. Also, "Albert Lewis (c)," the porter, was not called to testify. In keeping with Justice Sayre's ruling, the trial judge charged the jury with a more restrictive statement of the law. This time, on Roy Percy's request the judge instructed the jury: "You cannot give damages in this case for the purpose of punishing the Illinois Central Railroad Company." Despite this instruction, the jury found in favor of Mary Miniard, although this time they awarded her a bit less money, $2,500.

Again, the railroad lawyers appealed. Again, on May 11, 1922, the Alabama Supreme Court overturned the verdict. Again, it held that the trial judge had charged the jury improperly. Judge Boyd should have instructed the jury that it was the railroad's duty to carry the crazy Negro woman on the train "as long as she showed no evidence of becoming violent." It appears that in 1923 Hugo Black presented the case for Mary Miniard to a third jury in Birmingham, and his client was awarded a third judgment. At this point, amid the growing presence of Birmingham's Ku Klux Klan, Roy Percy gave up.[20]

The Miniard case has been forgotten over time for it holds no importance in Alabama law, although it remains another example of how the state's appellate courts found a basis to overturn an Alabama jury verdict that the judges particularly disliked. For Roy Percy, the cases were professionally disappointing and personally troubling. His lawyer's pride was not insubstantial, and losing "a case or performing poorly in court would send him into a spiral of despondency." Percy was defeated by "Ego" three times in this case of Southern honor. Tormented with severe bouts of rage and depression, doused in whiskey, Percy never thought he measured up to his own father's example in defending business interests, challenging demagoguery, and protecting his family's sacred, Old South traditions. Living in his father's old house, working at his father's desk in his father's old law firm, Roy walked every day in Walker Percy's larger-than-life shadow. Four years of the Miniard case could only exaggerate Roy's omnivorous self doubt and help stir up the same spiritual demons that heckled his father.

This case of Southern honor marked a deathly symmetry for the Percy family. The second Miniard trial began at the fourth anniversary of Walker Percy's funeral. The case concluded in 1923, six years after Roy's father shot himself, and, within six more years, in a very similar setting Roy Percy would shoot himself in the face with a gun of the same gauge and type his father had used. Southern honor of the old order seemed a deadly, self-inflicting wound for the true bearers of its creed in a city without traditions, in an era of warring white interests and raw racialism, and in a local economy paying homage to maximum profits. Roy was survived by a wife and three children, including his oldest son Walker, who were moved to the Mississippi Delta. After discovering the goodness of time, the second Walker Percy spent his own life pondering and writing evocatively of race, death, and privilege in the South, and he would die a natural death at a ripe old age.

For Hugo Black, the Miniard case signaled rapidly returning fortunes in the practice of law. Within a year of destitute circumstances, Black seems to have turned the corner with the first Miniard trial. He was on his way towards earning over $10,000 in the next year—a very handsome income at that time.

The Miniard award was quite remarkable. During the week when Black won his first verdict, juries rendered two other judgments at the county courthouse. One awarded $4,000 for a man killed by a reckless automobile, and another gave $5,000 to the family of an L&N line worker, killed when two trains negligently collided. In contrast, Black secured a verdict of $3,000 (minus that important penny) for Mary Miniard's eight-hour ordeal of words.

Black kept a copy of the transcript of the 1919 trial for the rest of his life, as if it was a keepsake of a momentous event. Several decades later, Black had no difficulty remembering for an old friend the specifics of the case. On the trial's forty-fifth anniversary, the exact day of October 8, Hugo's law partner

Crampton Harris delighted old cronies at a local barbershop with his recollections of Black's performance in the case.

Judge Black never spoke to anyone on the U.S. Supreme Court about Mary Miniard or Albert Lewis, but he may have remembered them when an Alabama case came before the Court during the 1960s civil rights era. The son of Birmingham's black newspaper editor, Oscar W. Adams, Jr., represented Mary Hamilton, a black woman found in contempt of court in Gadsden, Alabama, and sentenced to five days in jail and a fine of $50. When called to the stand in her trial about a civil rights demonstration, Hamilton had the following exchange with a local white prosecutor:

> "What is your name, please."
> "Miss Mary Hamilton."
> "Mary, I believe—you were arrested—who were you arrested by?"
> "My name is Miss Hamilton. Please address me correctly."
> "Who were you arrested by, Mary?"
> "I will not answer a question—"
> The Court: "Answer the question."
> "I will not answer them until I am addressed correctly."
> The Court: "You are in contempt of court."

When reviewed by the Alabama Supreme Court, the contempt punishment was upheld. "Many witnesses are addressed by various titles," the state court dryly observed, "but one's own name is acceptable appellation at law." When the case arrived in Washington, three members of the U.S. Supreme Court thought it was a rather "silly" case, but Justice Black joined Chief Justice Earl Warren and others in voting to take the case and reverse the contempt citation.

To Chief Justice Warren, the case involved a lack of respect for simple, human dignity, and his summary unsigned opinion for the Court cited a prior case outlawing courtroom segregation as a violation of equal protection of the laws. Writing briefly, Black concurred in the opinion's judgment, but not its reasoning. Black cited prior cases holding that a judge's summary actions in convicting a person without a trial to determine evidence of guilt was a violation of due process.

As the lawyer who called the "nigger" porter, "Albert Lewis (c)," to the stand and examined "Albert" in 1919, Justice Black's differing reasoning in the Hamilton case is another intrigue about how plain words take their true meaning from memory and experience as well as law. In 1964, Judge Black's Supreme Court colleagues held that the courtroom practice of using a first name only for black witnesses was a segregationist practice contrary to the U.S. Constitution. Black held differently: punishing someone on the spot for refusing to adhere to a segregationist practice was unlawful. The Court outlawed the segregationist practice. Judge Black outlawed summary punishment for a person refusing to go along with the practice. In this subtle, legalistic difference may lie the experience and recollections of the Alabama lawyer who brought the Miniard case.[21]

BEYOND ITS SIGNIFICANCE for those at the trial, the Miniard case remains an artifact of another Southern era, only a few generations passed. It speaks of everyday words and relationships too strange in their sensibilities and inbred morality, too stained by the recorded atrocities of that bloody, awful year of race riots, too much a study of how the South's coded language governed deeds to be left in a storage box as nothing more than a keepsake of a lawyer's recovered, prosperous career. Hugo Black took obvious pride in his performance as a lawyer at the Miniard trial. It was, in fact, astonishing—and, decades later, equally saddening.

Black represented his client amazingly well, but his choice of words and his courtroom techniques suggest the work of a bigot, at least by modern American standards. "Nigger" alone speaks volumes today. So does Black's treatment of "Albert Lewis (c)" as the fall guy who helped Black affirm Mary Miniard's testimony by leading him to contradict her. The whole notion of the case, rewarding a white woman for sitting in a train car with a disturbed, black woman, is deeply repugnant to American standards of justice at the twenty-first century.

The case's style and essence also seem frightfully at odds with the public record that Hugo Black had built by 1919. At odds with the man who sat paternalistically, but fairly, as Birmingham's police court judge eight years earlier. The trial doesn't appear to square with the man who represented Sam Bradford and other black workers against local corporations. It seems to contradict the ways of a county prosecutor whose Old Testament version of legal equality was usually at war with Old South racialism and its bastard by-products, the fee system, police brutality, and convict leasing. In thousands of reviewed pages of transcripts from grand jury testimony, where Solicitor Black asked innumerable questions of hundreds of black and white witnesses in all sorts of cases, not once did Black ever speak the word "nigger."

Of course, Black's life had changed immediately after the war. He was penniless and in debt four months before Mary Miniard retained him on a contingency fee. It was a humbling, uncertain status for a former celebrated, local judge and a talented attorney who gave up a rising income to become a public prosecutor, and Black wanted none of it.

What had not changed was Black's unswerving, total dedication to winning a case. He possessed this drive as a boy. He had it in Girard for prohibition. He had it in Bessemer for black suspects, and he had it for Sam Bradford, a black miner, and Nannie Cornelius, another poor, white woman. Black's total commitment to winning was necessary for survival and prosperity as a lawyer. He made his money only if he won his cases. He attracted additional cases only if he was known as a winning lawyer. His ability to win cases had won him the respect of his opponents, like Judge William Grubb and Walker Percy, and enhanced his public career. Winning was also his ethical duty. As lawyer, Black was duty-bound to give his client the best representation he could muster, not to uphold notions of truth or justice. To Black, "best" meant winning before juries within the rules of the courtroom and the South.

In the Miniard trial, Black said nothing of "race" to which anyone in the all-white courtroom objected. Nothing he said about "race" prompted Justice Sayre to object. By strategically, deliberately using common racial epithets—and, thereby, portraying black people as his client had seen them on that night leaving Chicago, Black aided the white jurymen in understanding his client's fears and predicament. In so doing, Black compromised no existing custom, law, or rule of a Southern courtroom, and he was joined in his language by most other whites who spoke for the record. In this case, Hugo Black was the plaintiff's lawyer, not a judge of fairness.

Yet, even these factors explain too little. More important than how he got this case and more significant than his proper lawyer's role was Black's own perspective. To Hugo Black, this case wasn't about race relations or black folk. It was about Southern plain white folk and, particularly, about the mistreatment a young mother because she was a white woman whose poor income put her in a coach car among Negroes outside the South. It was about how Northern-owned railroads and their white agents used Negroes to embarrass and abuse the South's poor, working white folk in a manner echoing the prevailing Southern understanding of the "Reconstruction Regime."

Nothing was said in Judge Boyd's courtroom about African Americans that wasn't repeated a thousand times daily across Birmingham and the Mason & Dixon. No individual black person was harmed or penalized by the Miniard verdict. No African American suffered a judgment from the lawsuit. The railroad, the Northern corporation, paid for *its* misconduct against one of Dixie's poor white women.

This was a peculiar, little case. In a virtually all-white courtroom, with one white woman sitting at the plaintiff's table and one black man making a brief appearance, white male protagonists were at war over the everyday social privileges of the white South. Roy Percy saw the honor of the South's old order under attack by "Ego" Black who tried to enrich himself in vulgarizing the essence of Old South honor. Hugo Black was defending common Southern white folk, in this case a young mother, against the abusive snobbery and mischief of Northern corporations, their Yankee agents, and their Southern protectors. Every white man involved in this case, from lawyer to juror to judge, understood the case was about whether a Southern white woman had suffered, in Justice Sayre's words, "abuse and epithets." None heard epithets against black people. All spoke and heard words about the experience of a white woman, not the depiction of black folks. Blacks were just there—on the train and in the courtroom to be used or abused, by whoever among white folks had opportunity, motive, and means.

Mary Miniard's cause surely was helped by racial hysteria and violence spreading through Chicago, Birmingham, and the nation in 1919. The fact that this timid, white woman sat with her baby in a coach car amid a crowd of Negro men from Chicago to Cairo was an essential imagery that Black created for the white jurymen. At that moment in history, in Birmingham, most white men believed that the presence of one unknown black man, much less a train car filled with them, could be a real and present danger for a white woman. But, when white men battled one another, Negroes were a part of the physical scenery, not the human equation. They were considered things in need of control, dangerous things that could cause offense and torment. They were *things* which white men on both sides of this case, often on both sides of the Mason & Dixon, always tried to control and manipulate to win battle with other white men. *Things.* Just *things.*

Here, in the blinding whiteness of this case, lies the profound sadness of Mary Miniard's cause. Amid yearnings of African Americans (and some Southern women) for a person's stake in America's democratic promise, almost every white Southerner man, aristocratic or democratic, Baptist or Catholic, dry or wet, Old South or New South, could not find the historical and moral imagination to see the horrible terms of their daily ways and language when fighting other whites for money, power, or position. It was true in 1901 and now in 1919. Virtually no white person could hear or see how their parasitic words piled up small stones of bigotry, reinforcing each individual's psychological wall of racism, often rabid racial egotism, which did more than separate people by skin color. It eliminated all but whiteness from their senses and their hearts.

For quite different reasons, with vastly different visions of a good society, warring factions of the South's white men could not see morally beyond each other. Word by word, they nurtured the ethics-devouring racialism that kept other human beings as physical property, whenever white greed or goodness needed to use black things as an advantage in their all-white struggles for political, religious, moral, or social triumph. The South and Birmingham were at that moment a white society where racial epitaphs did not exist because anything spoken—sometimes anything done—in keeping with white supremacy, no matter how trivial, profane, or vile, could be accepted in common usage as a symbol of the scared truth that held the white South together, apart from the nation. In aristocratic or democratic form, Southern honor was now little more than an idolized self image with the deadly power to blot out all words, ideals, and thoughts that did not conform to one's own version of white manhood.

Decades later, the Reverend Dr. Martin Luther King, Jr., would recognize the legacy of this crippled morality when he observed of one Southern state what was true of the Deep South. "Mississippi has treated the Negro as if he is a thing instead of a person," King said. In 1919, there was a slight opportunity to uproot the surging force of this legacy. The war for democracy had stirred new moral and practical possibilities for claiming full American personhood in the South for the first time in this century. But, most Southerners were slipping fast, back into the region's profound habits of thought and speech that gave allegiance to white supremacy and segregation of white persons from black things.

For African Americans after World War I, living in the South was a knowing act of self-sacrifice, submitting one's belittled fate to the will of a vengeful demigod that hungered for your humanity. For many whites, it was a daily ritual of spoken communion with the South's worst, mistaken past, through which all drank of the same corrupted blood and partook of the same spoiled flesh of past racialism, so that they would know its powers and it would possess them.

If a black Southerner in 1919 took flight seeking democratic deliverance on the other side of the Mason & Dixon, he often could not find America there, for the priests of American racialism long ago had mortgaged him as another, perishable tool of industry in the white North. If lucky, he might find "Up South" a new psychological space, a bit of money, and less overt racial violence, but not his citizenship or full personhood. If the Negro stayed South and fought sanely or savagely for personhood, he became a direct danger to Southern white womanhood. And the demigod's wrath would find him sooner or later.

When white Southerners of any rank insanely overindulged in the demonic taste of white supremacy, with its god-like power of transforming persons into things, they performed the deadly tragic, animalistic feast which public reports designated neutrally as a "lynching." But, the daily ways for communion sustaining the manly faith of Southern racialism were far more banal. A single word, a simple phrase, or even a question carefully, casually placed in conversation—or cross-examination—was often quite enough to uplift a white person's racial egotism and to enshrine the meaning, corruption, and rituals of the South's past.

Yet, the chilling echoes of this vernacular tradition as well as the personal significance of the Miniard case—each grew clearer only in time and with advances in democracy and justice, long after the fact. At the start of the 1920s, only this much could have been known. First, in the racially torn fall of 1919, second during Birmingham's labor strife of 1921, and, finally, in 1923, when Birmingham's Robert E. Lee chapter of the Ku Klux Klan was growing by leaps and bounds, "Ego" and the Miniards proved that Hugo Black knew the collective mind of the white, male South when facing questions of race and place, gender and Jim Crow, class and caste as they traveled together across time and the Mason & Dixon line.

8

'. . . For Better, for Worse . . .'

A Union of Opposites

Nine or ten miles beyond Jones Valley, northwest of the blazing pig iron furnaces in Birmingham's suburbs, scars of piled, blackened rocks often marked the timbered shafts that reached downward into catacombs where much of the city's industrial fortunes were unearthed by workers as dark as the coal they dug. In the infancy of Alabama coal mining after the Civil War, Jefferson County's African American population had been insignificant, but, as industrial hunger for raw materials and fuel grew, blacks migrated into the area—some by choice and some by force—to fill the jobs considered too dangerous or too dirty or too low-paying for whites. By 1920, 40 percent of the county's population was black, and of the twenty-three thousand miners working for private companies around Birmingham, almost seven of ten were black men. In the more hazardous, unproductive mines, another couple of thousand black convicts picked at coal because they had been leased to mine operators by the state.

For more than a generation, black men had brought their families and meager worldly possessions to these scars of cleared earth, hidden almost from the sight of God, seeking to emancipate themselves and their heirs from the doom of agricultural servitude. Many found simply a different form of bondage. Miners usually lived at the mine's lip in colonies owned, maintained, and supervised by the coal companies. Often only a rail track and primitive paths connected the villages to the nearest town, seldom closer than five or six miles. The color line divided company towns into white and black sections. Miners and their families occupied wood cabins or shanties unevenly placed in crowded, rows along the ravines where wagon ruts and machine tracks led underground. In some villages, such as those owned by U.S. Steel, houses were built on dirt streets with running water and electricity. Most mine operators, however, did not provide indoor plumbing or electrical wiring, and most cabins were heated in the winter by potbelly stoves of burning wood or coal that the company supplied—at a price.

Usually, the only place within miles to buy goods was the company-owned store, whose monopoly was usually reflected in higher prices. Mining companies paid their workers in "commissary checks" or scrip, a company-issued currency which could be redeemed at full value only at the company store. The company store also gave miners' families credit between checks, with the predictable result that many miners, in the words of a popular song, owed their "soul to the company store." Some scrip was accepted at Birmingham banks two weeks after payday or redeemed sooner at much less than face value by Birmingham speculators.

Mining families often grew small vegetable gardens although the hilly, rocky terrain was poor for crops, and several companies preferred their residents to "beautify" homes with flower gardens. In company towns where labor relations were tense, supervisors didn't permit crops such as corn, since high stalks obscured surveillance by company guards who served as village police and informants. Where there was no running water in the houses, women washed their husbands' filthy coveralls daily at communal spigots or in streams serving the whole town. Children too young to work were provided a school building, usually in poor or dilapidated condition in 1920, for no more than an elementary education. On Sunday, the whole family could attend the company-owned church to hear a company-paid preacher deliver the message of the company's own God.

The largest mining enterprises, owned by DeBardeleben, U.S. Steel, and Woodward, provided "social services" to their towns' occupants. To stabilize the workforce, U.S. Steel's local president George Crawford in 1909 had begun a major program of establishing new schools, kindergartens, home economics classes, and community gardens in the company towns, as well as "beautification competitions"—with prizes for the mining villages with the cleanest yards, best flower gardens, or finest quilting. Company doctors, dentists, and hygienists were also hired for miners and their families. Other companies imitated parts of U.S. Steel's welfare capitalism, including company-sponsored picnics on summer holidays, village ball games, and visits by welfare workers.

The cost of providing necessities and services was "divided between the company and the employees," Crawford explained, "which is fair, as both derive benefit from it." The compulsory costs were deducted from miners' commissary checks. Housing deductions were $7 to $15 a month (several companies increased the rent deduction whenever they had to increase workers' pay). Paychecks also were docked $2.50 to $6 for social welfare services and access to the company doctor. With average pay of $75 to $80 a month, miners often got only half their paycheck after all company deductions.[1]

Alabama miners worked in the nation's most dangerous mines. Beyond the deadly effects of what years later would be called "black-lung" disease, hundreds of men died and thousands were injured in mining accidents and explosions. During a fifteen-year period beginning in 1910, 542 men died in Alabama mines while only 380 died in Pennsylvania, although the Northern state employed eight times as many miners. For their hazardous duty, Alabama's non-convict workers were paid according to the amount of coal they dug. At the beginning of 1920, a miner received around eighty-five cents for each ton of coal he picked and loaded into the train hopper. White supervisors were paid according to the tonnage their crews produced.

Negroes had become the workers of choice for mining companies in the emerging industrial South. "The salvation of the South depends upon its industrial welfare," observed a DeBardeleben Coal Company's vice-president, "and the chief factor in our industrial welfare is the negro." His labor was inexpensive. His numbers were vast, and his ability to withhold his own work was severely limited. As the more manageable group, black workers also were a check on the demands and pay of more independent white workers. In mining and related industries, lower wages for blacks helped to assure low wages for whites since coal operators maintained the option of hiring additional blacks at lesser pay or of contracting for convict labor at minimal cost. If free miners made collective demands, operators also could bring black "scabs" from rural south Alabama to annul the effects of a strike. "We have a low grade of iron and . . . coal," explained a Birmingham businessman discussing Alabama's strategy for competing with Northern coalfields. "And one of the advantages that we have had is the immunity from these labor disturbances, our cheap docile negro labor."

In the harsh, complex realities of white supremacy, this exploitation had some relative advantages for free blacks. In trying to keep black workers cheap, loyal, and docile, Birmingham industrialists actually provided many African

Americans with better conditions than they had ever enjoyed in the South. Jim Crow did not lurk everywhere in the bowels of Alabama's earth, where eternal night and coal's soot blackened every face. By sweat and muscle, black miners could make as much or *more* money than whites since pay was based solely on a worker's production. And because there were white miners, the miners' pay scale was not outrageously cheap by historical standards.

By design, company towns resembled an industrial version of the Old South's plantation where masters could supervise black slaves' entire life, but mining methods for keeping blacks under control were better than many alternatives. Mining villages were segregated, but some companies like U.S. Steel provided equal housing regardless of race. Welfare programs were paternalistic, but some were useful. Because they were available to both races, the companies' services constituted a partial recognition that blacks had *human* needs just like whites. Also, to deliver their programs to town residents, mining companies employed a fair number of blacks, including preachers, nurses, and social workers who helped to sustain Birmingham's slight black middle class.

The industrialists' practices won the support of Birmingham's black ministers and black leaders, including newspaper editor Oscar Adams, who vocally opposed Negroes joining unions, and they received the excessive praise of Yankee visitors concerned with improving Southern race relations. After a visit to company towns in 1918, one Northern businessman proclaimed that U.S. Steel's handling of the "racial lines" was a "contribution to the so called race problem" that would prove more useful than Negro education.

These material and psychological benefits were considerable for black workers at a time and place where even small kindnesses from the other race were rare, but they were not the blessings of American freedom or the recognition of full personhood. They were fruits of semi-captivity or precarious byproducts of shifting industrial warfare between Southern white workers and white capitalists on both sides of the Mason & Dixon line. Black folks' bounty existed so long as neither white faction won the industrial war, so long as white unions couldn't eliminate black workers from the urban workplace and white capitalists couldn't yoke African Americans as industrial slaves.

In the final measure, the New South industrialist could be as much—and as little—of the Negro's ally and protector as was the Old South planter, a conclusion confirmed in the mining strike of 1908 when labor organizers tried to unite black and white miners. Mining executives unleashed the demigods of racialism, accusing miners of seeking social equality, a state of the Southern white mind apparently where black men could command, touch, and copulate white women.[2]

While Birmingham labor relations were usually unsettled, Alabama's coal-fields had been comparatively quiet since that bloody strike of 1908 when Hugo Black was tutored in the ways of Southern industrialism. In the strike's aftermath, the United Mine Workers (UMW) in Alabama fell into shambles and by 1914 had fewer than thirty dues-paying members. Within two years, however, Alabama miners were again beseeching the UMW to help combat the "company devil." A black operative for DeBardeleben Coal warned his white boss that "the Negro labor of the Alabama mining district is an incoherent mass, united in nothing save the conviction that Capital has the 'cards marked and stacked' against it." In the spring of 1917, the UMW began rebuilding an Alabama union. World War I vastly enlarged demand and prices for coal and placed the nation's mines under government regulation, including labor standards, to assure essential fuels for military production and support. At the insistence of the Woodrow Wilson administration, Alabama coal operators reluctantly signed an agreement with the UMW during the war. The accord included national pay rates recommended by the government, an eight-hour workday, workers' right to unionize without reprisal, a bar against "blacklist-ing" miners for union involvement, and possible UMW committees to address grievances and disputes.

Only the seduction of consistently high war profits and the threat of a hostile government wartime takeover had coerced Birmingham's industrialists into agreeing to terms they had never entertained before. This uneasy truce ended soon after the last shot was fired in France. Washington could no longer bully coal operators into conciliation. Three weeks after Hugo Black secured the first verdict in the Miniard trial, UMW president John L. Lewis called a national strike including Alabama mines. After a federal court's injunction, Lewis grudgingly halted the work stoppage and resumed negotiations. In the end, the UMW and the nation's large coal companies agreed to a 14 percent wage increase. The vast majority of Alabama coal operators, however, refused any agreement and, for good measure, discharged many union members who had walked off the job during Lewis's earlier strike. In vain, local UMW presi-dent Jacob R. Kennamer asked Washington to intervene.

Many Alabama politicians also abandoned all signs of tolerance and cooperation with organized labor. In September 1919, the prohibitionist legislature made it a criminal offense for workers to enter into "a combination or agreement to interfere" with Alabama industry for any purpose. Governor Thomas E. Kilby diplomatically pocket-vetoed the legislation since anti-picketing and anti-boycott statutes were already on the books. Lawyers and lobbyists for Birmingham's corporations, led by Forney Johnston and Borden Burr, packed the state capitol to convince the legislature to gut Kilby's bill improving workers' compensation for on-the-job injuries. Instead, the legislature passed a stingy pro-industrialist bill. In turn, Kilby estranged Alabama labor leaders during the UMW's short national strike by calling out the state militia to protect mine companies' property, although there were no indications of labor violence or unrest.[3]

In Washington, as soon as he was elected to the U.S. Senate in 1914, Alabama's Oscar W. Underwood deserted a pro-labor voting record earned as Birmingham's Congressman. Using Forney Johnston's massive intellect and his own statesmanship, Underwood began in late 1919 shaping legislation to reorganize the nation's postwar railroads with a key provision effectively banning rail strikes. Johnston said the bill protected railroads investors from "the direct assaults of Labor which knows very well what it wants and is willing to double its fists to get it." Underwood called his legislation morally "right." But the law was a double-fisted assault against labor unions, according to the Brotherhood of Railway Trainmen, whose Birmingham local retained Hugo Black for legal work in late 1919. Underwood proposed a national labor board to regulate rail workers' wages, working conditions, and right to strike. Birmingham's *Labor Advocate* said the law swung "a big stick at labor and a toy balloon at the railroads." As a result, president of the American Federation of Labor (AFL) Samuel Gompers declared Underwood was one of the six worst U.S. Senators.

To counter growing hostility, Alabama labor leaders rallied members into politics. In 1918, state AFL president Bill Harrison was elected as one of Jefferson County's state legislators. Around Birmingham and other centers of unionism—Jasper, Gadsden, and Anniston—labor leaders conducted voter registration drives and helped pay members' poll taxes. In Jefferson, labor officials estimated the number of union voters had quadrupled, helping to enlarge county voter rolls from eighteen thousand in 1918 to near thirty thousand in 1920. In February, as Senator Underwood prepared to launch his campaign for reelection, state labor leaders announced: "For the first time in Alabama, all branches of organized labor . . . have recommended to their people . . . one candidate for a high office." The unions, including the UMW, were supporting L. B. "Breck" Musgrove to defeat Underwood.

Musgrove was an unconventional candidate for labor's crucial test of political strength. A millionaire who owned or operated eight small mining companies (all recognizing the UMW) north of Jefferson, Musgrove was a lifelong bachelor who enjoyed lavish entertainment, good whiskey, and rough politics. Some years he kept a suite at New York's Waldorf-Astoria Hotel for business and pleasure and once he shipped ten possums, a treasure of Alabama fruits and vegetables, and his own Alabama cook to New York's Hotel Marlborough to expose prominent Yankees to a seven-course meal of Southern delicacies. Richer than most Birmingham managers and many local industrialists, Musgrove associated himself politically with prohibitionists, war heroes, Protestant ministers, and labor leaders. He helped to build most of the churches in his hometown, although he wasn't a member of any. He was probably the largest financial supporter of the Alabama Anti-Saloon League, but he rarely practiced prohibition.

Six years earlier, Musgrove had been Richmond Hobson's campaign manager when he matched frenzied invective with Forney Johnston who was running Underwood's campaign. Unaccustomed to defeat, Musgrove seemed hardly able to wait until 1920 to mount another challenge—this time as the candidate. All of Alabama, including Senator Underwood, knew Musgrove would use both his own wealth and wicked tongue to make the campaign a tough race.[4]

The strategy to defeat Underwood was simple. "There has been started in Alabama a union between farmers, union labor, and the prohibition forces," Musgrove declared, "that will drive into the ocean from the Atlantic to the Pacific all standpatters," including the "fossiliferous old asses of reaction" like Underwood. Because of a sharp decline in agricultural prices, Alabama farmers were restless. The state Farmers Union endorsed Musgrove, and during the past year "the union labor people have been working on the farmers," according to an Underwood supporter, "in an effort to get them to stand with union or organized labor in a political way."

The Anti-Saloon League also squarely backed Musgrove. In late 1919, the Eighteenth Amendment requiring national prohibition had become law, but Alabama League president Breck Lawrence wanted to unseat Underwood as "the leader of the liquor interest in the United States." Dry activists feared Underwood would frustrate national enforcement as vigorously as he opposed prohibition. Alabama's suffrage leaders also worked against Underwood. The senator had spoken against "Susie's Amendment" as an encroachment on the states' right to control suffrage, an elemental power for preserving white political supremacy, and he viscerally disliked "that horde of women" who crowded the capitol for suffrage.

Underwood's reelection plans were to run as a statesman. Shortly before the campaign, he became the Democratic leader of the U.S. Senate, the first person to lead a political party in both the U.S. House and Senate since Henry Clay. Alabama's business leaders, daily newspaper editors, and Black Belt planters were solidly behind the senator, and many of his political friends were already assembled in a ready-made organization. His campaign chairman was Lloyd Hooper, former head of the state's Council of Defense, and most of Underwood's county contacts were businessmen and corporate attorneys who had been local leaders in the Defense Council and its shadow, the Alabama Protective League (APL). In a show of loyalty, Birmingham's Chamber of Commerce president (formerly state APL chief) evicted the Farmers Union from its building after the group endorsed Musgrove.

During three intense months of what Forney Johnston planned as a "short and snappy" campaign, Underwood and Musgrove engaged in a bitter, scurrilous exchange that often appealed to the worst of human nature. Musgrove's stump speakers, like Anniston editor Harry Ayres and William Jennings Bryan, the eternal flame of agrarian Populism, took the high road by condemning Underwood as the stooge of "booze and business." On the low road, Musgrove and his weekly newspaper crowned Underwood as Pope "Leo Oscar . . . truckling to any foreign sinister element." Anonymous handbills, entitled "Shall the People or the Pope Rule America," alleged that Underwood had "stooped to kiss the ring of the Pope," a shameless distortion of an event in 1917 when the senator knelt publicly in homage to New York's Catholic Cardinal on St. Patrick's Day. These "dodgers" attempted to stir up word-of-mouth rumors that Underwood, an Episcopalian for more than thirty years, was really a closet Catholic. Birmingham's Society of True Americans may have believed it. The TAs endorsed Musgrove at a secret meeting.

In April, following Johnston's counsel, Senator Underwood launched his own barrage of words, aimed primarily at making the "assaults of Labor" the campaign's prime issue. After promising Alabama voters that he supported enforcing prohibition as long as it was law, Underwood charged he was the victim of a national labor conspiracy led by AFL president Samuel Gompers. "This is the issue," Underwood stated repeatedly. "A man not of this state, sitting in his office in Washington, gives orders to defeat me because I did not let him dictate to me how to vote . . . I am blacklisted because I represented you in the Senate and not this labor leader." In Mobile, Underwood warned that Bolshevists of the Russian Workers' Revolution were at work close to home. "Europe is afire," he exclaimed. "The sparks are flying here . . . Our government is in danger."

The *Birmingham News* plainly stated what Senator Underwood, a poor stump speaker, had only implied about Musgrove. "He boldly advocates the array of classes against classes. A rich man himself," the paper noted, Musgrove "adds fuel to the radical flames of the day in advocacy of the union of the farmers and of the mine and factory workers for crushing capital and establishing a government of part of the people . . . That is not only demogogy, but dangerous demogogy." Throughout rural Alabama, Underwood supporters echoed the attacks upon "bolshevists," "foreign agitators," and "Union Labor" who were conspiring against Underwood to take over the state.[5]

As the campaign developed, Underwood and his advisors received various reports on how "Musgrove's managers" were working "hand-in-glove" with UMW agitators around Birmingham. In one report, Jefferson County's former APL chief Key Milner supplied Underwood and Forney Johnston with confidential information that he considered vital to the campaign. Milner prepared the document as head of a new state intelligence unit that Governor Kilby had secretly authorized—in keeping with recommendations made by the Council of Defense when it met with Underwood at the end of the war. Immediately, the senator asked Johnston and Lloyd Hooper to devise the best way "to visualize this situation to the people of the State."

Ten days before the election, Johnston and Hooper had found the best way. Sparrow Advertising, a public relations firm used by Birmingham industrialists, was preparing a special political ad to be published in the state's newspapers near election day. Plates were being set at daily newspaper plants in Mobile, Montgomery, and Birmingham. The ad's content frightened Musgrove's managers and Alabama labor leaders after they learned of the material, apparently from a newspaper typesetter.

At eleven o'clock on a Saturday night, Jefferson County's Circuit Judge Horace Wilkinson awoke at home to loud, persistent knocking. On his doorstep stood Hugo Black with an apology and a bundle of papers. The hour was late and the courthouse was locked, but Black was there on behalf of Alabama's labor unions to ask the judge to issue an immediate court injunction, without hearing from anyone else, to prevent the Underwood campaign and three of the state's largest newspapers from distributing or publishing Sparrow's ads.

In the petition, Black represented state AFL president Bill Harrison, his "organization of laboring men . . . of approximately forty thousand," the Birmingham Trade Council, the Brotherhood of Railway Trainmen, the Farmers Union, and the United Mine Workers and its president Jacob R. Kennamer. These men and unions represented the "best and most cherished ideals of *Alabama citizenship*," Black claimed, but feared "incalculable damage and injury" if the advertisement was published. Defendants, Black alleged, "have conspired together to publish and distribute" this ad in all parts of the state "in order that there shall not be time and opportunity to reply to the insidious statements . . . until after the primary election."

According to Black, the advertisement was nothing more than "a cleverly concealed attempt . . . to attack and disrupt" Alabama's labor unions. It was "a secret attempt to undermine the trust and confidence of the public" in organized labor. The ad was a "malicious and libelous document" with "slanderous imputations." It alleged that Alabama labor unions and their leaders "were in favor of organizing negro miners into the same union with white members, and . . . believing in marriage between white people and negroes, and . . . in political and social familiarity between the white race and the negro race."

Black contended that the "whole effect and purpose of the publication . . . is to engender friction and discord between the white and black races in the state, to stir up race prejudice, and foment ill will and hatred on the part of one race for the other." His legal theory was less dramatic, although rather novel. Simply, the property rights of labor unions—their right to do business in Alabama—would be permanently damaged if the newspapers and others exercised their rights of free speech and free press as a part of this conspiracy to destroy Alabama's labor unions. In summary, Black charged that "the distribution of this document of defamatory matter . . . will destroy the prestige of said organizations in Alabama and will tear down the work and struggle of years, and its insidious poison could not be eradicated in all the years to come."

Governor Kilby had appointed Judge Wilkinson recently to the state circuit court as a reward for his service as a special attorney prosecuting corrupt local sheriffs and lynching cases involving white victims. Wilkinson was an ambitious, mercurial politician facing his own election. He was aware that unions now had a large bloc of Jefferson County's organized voters, although he had shown very little interest in labor's cause. Wilkinson also possessed the highest regard for his own wisdom and a fierce reputation as a menacing prosecutor among the state's sheriffs—just the kind of local judge who might use his authority without delay to enjoin defendants throughout the state. The judge, however, was unwilling to issue a midnight decree for Black's clients.

Throughout most of Sunday, Wilkinson studied Black's documents and consulted with the circuit's presiding judge to affirm the reach of his civil jurisdiction. Although he deliberated throughout the day, Wilkinson did not notify defendants to give them a chance to respond to Black's *ex parte* petition. By Sunday night, Judge Wilkinson summoned the court's register to a largely darkened courthouse and enrolled his decree and opinion in the official minutes, issuing to all Alabama sheriffs an injunction prohibiting the *Birmingham Age-Herald*, *Montgomery Advertiser*, *Mobile Register*, Lloyd Hooper, and other Underwood supporters from publishing or circulating any ad suggesting that Black's clients "employ, advocate, encourage, or recognize social equality between the white and black races in the State of Alabama, or racial amalgamation, intermarriage, or political and racial familiarity."

In a written opinion, taken at times word for word from Black's petition and brief, Wilkinson cited only two prior cases: an opinion by Judge Somerville, Black's old law professor, holding that the right to do business was an important "property right" which courts could protect by injunction, and another case stating that it was libelous in Alabama to charge falsely that someone advocated social equality between the races. "The constitutional right of an individual freely to express his sentiments upon any subject is as much entitled to the protections of the court as any other constitutional right," the opinion stated. "But . . . courts are not impairing or infringing this right of free speech by enjoining publications which are incidental to or in aid of an unlawful conspiracy to injure the business of another."

Judge Wilkinson also repeated Black's language on the issue of race. "The people of Alabama will not knowingly tolerate any body of men or organizations that advocate or seek to bring about social and business equality between the negro and the white man . . . But remaining socially separate, it is not contended . . . that the colored man, or any other man no matter what the color of his skin may be, is not entitled to equal rights before the law." [6]

By Monday morning, the Underwood ad had been stopped, and the state's newspapers contained no such material. In the afternoon issue of the *Birmingham News,* however, a front-page story reprinted the complete text of the ad that the court had enjoined. Complying with the court order, the newspaper did not run or circulate the ad, but, in covering the day's news, it published the ad's full text charging unions with promoting social equality, interracial marriage, and black political power. Carefully avoiding a breach of the court decree, the *News* and Alabama's wire services trumpeted the Underwood campaign's allegations as front-page news across the state a few days before election.

The Musgrove camp had intended to use the ad as a campaign issue within Birmingham and actually advertised in both the *Age-Herald* and the *News* on Sunday—before Judge Wilkinson had enrolled and issued his opinion – inviting supporters to a Capitol Park rally on Monday night to learn of the "Unbelievable Political Trickery" of "Underwood's Mud-Slingers." In Monday's papers, Musgrove managers promised to reveal the real details of the "unlawful conspiracy" at the rally, while their large ads on the *News'* second page responded to each allegation of the banned advertisement.

Underwood's Jefferson County campaign manager (Forney Johnston's law partner) told reporters he knew nothing about the ad which the court had enjoined him from circulating. In sworn statements, however, the Sparrow agency and the *Age-Herald* admitted that they were on the verge of publishing and circulating the material for Underwood. The *Mobile Register* publisher averred that he wasn't aware of unions promoting social equality but he did know that at a Mobile meeting in May 1919 the Alabama AFL convention entertained a resolution asking that "the negro be allowed the use of the ballot as in other states." The convention passed a resolution endorsing the goal of making "every man a legal voter in the State of Alabama." The *News* and others printed the publisher's statement.

In rural south Alabama, Underwood supporters were ecstatic. News coverage of Wilkinson's injunction was more useful than paid ads in spreading word about Alabama labor's interracialism. A Black Belt factory owner (a former local APL chief) informed Underwood that the injunction "has proven a very great asset to your campaign." In Birmingham, local candidates without union support played up the issue. A candidate for coroner, for instance, advertised that "the people of Jefferson County do not want their candidates . . . selected by persons who sit in convention halls with negro delegates." Explaining why he received no union endorsement, the candidate stated: "There were FIVE NEGRO DELEGATES who were suppose to EXAMINE ALL WHITE CANDIDATES" in the screening process.

In his last speeches, Breck Musgrove told Alabama that he would rather "wear the union label than that of the stock gamblers of New York." In a feeble effort, he tried to shift racial slander with a wornout allegation. Musgrove recalled that Underwood had voted for a bill to enfranchise Negroes in the District of Columbia. Yet, at this final rally, Musgrove seemed beset by the better spirits of the past. He recalled the great promise of the Populist movement of the 1890s when "the same alliance" of plain white people was attacked by the same giant forces he now called his enemies. In defiance, the millionaire proclaimed, "I will not be tied to their interests."

After votes were counted, the rural counties gave Underwood a statewide victory of 54 percent of the white electorate. The large industrial counties, including Underwood's own Jefferson, went for Musgrove. Forney Johnston saw the returns as a worrisome sign of the class cleavage, but his senator refused to fret. In Washington, Underwood portrayed himself as a principled statesman victimized by hate mongers. He wrote that "the effort made by the Musgrove crowd against me because I am not willing to condemn the Catholics of Alabama . . . is a contemptible piece of demagoguery."

From Mississippi's Delta, the elder LeRoy Percy told Underwood that his defeat would have required all "courageous, conservative men to retire from public office" since the "road to public office was only open to those who truckle to the labor vote and prohibition vote and all the other 'ism' of the day." Mobile businessman Frank Boykin, forever ingratiating himself with a winner, telegraphed his joyful obituary of the Musgrove alliance: "With all their money, their Bryans, Unions, and Breck Lawrences, they never had a chance."[7]

As in all elections, it was a victor's moment when one's own misadventures disappear and the words and deeds of the vanquished are retold self-righteously for their indecency or lame effect. Yet, Breck Musgrove seemed touched by the muse of history when at the campaign's last moment he recalled Alabama's earlier Populists who also never prevailed in a statewide election. In 1920, religious intolerance had become a sharp weapon in political warfare, but as in the days of Fayette Black and the Democratic and Conservative Party of Alabama, racialism's destructive powers remained the surest force to enable another's defeat.

The 1920 election was not one of Alabama's worst examples of racial demagoguery. Quite the contrary, it was fairly routine. Mindless, repetitive, and ordinary, racialism had become year after year the endowed character of white politics, defining a moral existence by the certainty that everyone would lose it. No one's credentials and credibility in Alabama politics protected him from becoming the victim—or the vessel—of racialism. Both Breck Musgove and Oscar Underwood had lived, led, and prospered in Alabama for decades by the color line. Both had always done his public service to sustain white supremacy. Musgrove had become rich from the toil of black miners, and the family wealth of Underwood's wife was built from Birmingham's Woodward mines where black men dug up white profits.

Yet, neither man felt really safe from racialism in politics. Nor were they. No matter how many times a man had sworn faith to white supremacy or praised its name, the next day he could discover that he had failed somehow to pay proper homage. Everyone knew how to summon this potentially annihilating force, how easy it was to win if only racialism would take hold and color the other's character. This constant temptation to victimize—and constant fear of becoming a victim—created a self-devouring cycle by which each political oblation to racialism strengthened its force and enlarged a candidate's tendency to beckon or fear its presence in the next election.

As leader of the Democratic party in the U.S. Senate, Oscar Underwood might have won his reelection without conjuring racialism as a last, unanswerable attack upon Musgrove. Obviously, the Underwood camp feared that he would not win, and a fairly narrow margin of victory—dependent on the rural counties where the Sparrow ad was aimed—suggests that the election could have gone the other way. But of course, Musgrove was the more vulnerable, for in 1920 he linked his political fortunes openly with organized labor whose extensive grassroots work at voter registration could not overcome the stain of too much "racial familiarity." Most unions in the Alabama AFL were racially segregated, and many union members in Birmingham and elsewhere had led "white only" efforts. Yet, in one of Alabama's most important industries, one union included both black and white workers who stood together at moments in common destiny.

"The United Mine Workers are not preaching social equality," Jacob R. Kennamer told white workers during the senatorial campaign, "but they are preaching industrial equality because of the fact that they know that unless the colored man is brought up to the standard of the white man he will carry the white man down to his standard." Speaking in the third person about his own union, Kennamer added: "So they say, 'Let us have an equal justice to all.'" As an interracial effort, the Alabama miners' union was by definition a creature of "racial familiarity" which the Southern white mind knew was one step away from Negro men marrying white women and other images of biracial Reconstruction rule.

Nothing could work its demonic effect better than Underwood's last min-ute tactics, and nothing could protect Musgrove from racialism's wrath. Even Musgrove's countering whispering campaign of anti-Catholicism, in an era of rabid, growing religious intolerance, could not trump Underwood's use of the color line, thus reaffirming in Alabama politics what Hugo Black had stated in his emergency complaint before the circuit court—an "appeal to the instincts of the people of Alabama for the preservation of the supremacy of the white race will work an irreparable injury."

This episode also may have been the earliest defining moment for the lawyer who would become the nation's most ardent advocate of an absolute right of a free press to publish. No other juncture in Black's life demonstrated earlier or more clearly the folly and futility of suppressing the right to publish and speak. At best, an injunction to stop the publication of the ad was an attempt to control damage, without any real hope that its message could be effectively banned from the public. At worst, it was a misguided ploy in which Black and the unions tried to use the industrialists' methods of suppression, which had strangled past labor strikes. By whatever design, labor's effort to gain politically by limiting the speech of others had failed miserably.

Forty-six years later, Judge Black of Alabama would tell the nation that the First Amendment meant that no law and no court could ban a newspaper from publishing opinions at the last moment of an election. He wrote in another Birmingham newspaper case (involving the *Post-Herald*, successor to the *Age-Herald*), one where litigants justified their attempts to bar eleventh hour "electioneering" as necessary to "protect the public from confusive last minute charges." In upholding the newspaper's right to publish, Judge Black would note as a matter of fact that even if such censorship efforts were constitutional, they would never succeed.[8] He knew. In the summer of 1920, however, Hugo Black and Alabama's labor leaders knew only that they had been fatally wounded with an "invidious poison." They were desperate men. After years of quietly rebuilding the unions and their white members' political strength, the all-consuming power of white supremacy threatened quickly to destroy labor's struggles in politics and the workplace. While gladly compromising the right of free speech in an attempt to control the devastation of racialism, these men now knew that, following their defeat at the polls, lingering problems in Birmingham's coal fields might soon turn Hugo Black's prophesy of doom into the obituary for all of Alabama's labor movement.

In the early fall of 1920, challenged by belligerent coal operators seeking to bust unionism, Birmingham's miners began a series of local wildcat strikes with demands for better pay and union recognition. At midnight on September 7, Alabama UMW president Jacob Kennamer led thousands of workers out of the mines to shut down the state's entire industry. Above all else, the UMW sought recognition as the workers' union, but coal companies wanted to destroy the "U.M.W. of America . . . an oligarchy of agitators" who they said had a history of violence and "of associating the black man on terms of perfect equality with the white man." Industrialists attributed the walkout to the fact that 80 percent of the union members were black, easily misled by "foreign" influences. As local operator Frank Nelson stated, "This will mean . . . enslaving of 23,000 loyal coal miners . . . dominated by a few whites and Yankeeized negro agitators."

Mine owners confidently predicted the strike would fail and began to ship into Birmingham several thousand new workers, mostly black field hands from south Alabama. "Scab" workers were less efficient, but mines could afford to operate less productively since owners had stored reserves and coal demand had declined after the war. In addition, mines operating with convict labor were unaffected by the strike.

Alabama law was clearly on the side of the owners. Sweeping anti-strike statutes made it a crime for anyone to loiter near a place of business with the intent of influencing another not to work. If two or more people did so, it was an illegal conspiracy. In effect, all picketing was outlawed. Also, Alabama law forbade the printing, publishing, or circulating of any notice of such a "boycott or ban." Using company-town guards, often sworn as deputy sheriffs, coal companies had the power to arrest UMW members who came onto company property.

Within two weeks, attorney John Bankhead, Jr., asked the federal courts to enjoin the UMW strike against the Pratt Consolidated Coal Company, alleging that union strikers were using "opprobrious words, threats, and intimidation" against new workers. On September 13, Judge W. I. Grubb ordered UMW officials to cease picketing or loitering around the mining company's properties.

Violence erupted on both sides. After a black scab aided a white deputy sheriff in arresting a black striker, a white union man intervened. Three died in an ensuing fight. Coal operators accused the union of dynamiting the homes of strikebreakers and shooting at scabs on the trains and at boarding houses. In turn, the union claimed that a gang of company guards had killed "an inoffensive old colored man" for sport. At Carona Coal Company, according to union officials, "company thugs" acting as sworn deputies created a reign of terror by violently removing strikers' families from company houses. In one case, three women and two children were evicted only after deputies fired 150 shots into the house.

Carona's manager was out for blood and vengeance. Declaring that strikers had no right to hold meetings anywhere, the coal operator bragged that his deputies "would disperse their meetings as fast as they assembled . . . even if it had to be done in blood." As one of deputies yelled, "Come on. I can run any damn miner off by the stomp of my foot," the armed gang raided a union hall miles away from company property; however, union members were waiting for them. The manager and one deputy were found dead, and three others seriously wounded. The company claimed murder by ambush, and the union charged that its members had defended themselves only after being fired upon.[9]

Governor Kilby responded by dispatching four companies of state troops to mining districts. Commanding General Robert E. Steiner, a Montgomery corporate attorney, revealed quickly his approach to law and order. "We are here as representatives of the state of Alabama," he informed both sides. "If everyone will cooperate *and have no assemblies or speaking that will tend to influence the public mind* the situation will be helped materially." Steiner outlawed all mass meetings in the coalfields and ordered unions to meet only to conduct regular business. As unions discovered, "regular business" meant no talk about the strike, and Steiner dispatched soldiers to each meeting "for the purpose of suppressing" such talk.

Earlier, UMW leaders had requested state troops because they wanted the militia to disarm everyone in the mining district. The soldiers, however, added gunpowder to the coal companies' growing arsenal in a concerted attempt to control every worker, every meeting, and every spoken word in every square foot of the mining areas. Across Walker and Jefferson counties, soldiers stopped strikers' meetings, arrested men who used "abusive language" in public speaking, and dismissed assemblies if discussions turned directly to the strike. Apparently only fraternal lodges such as Masons met undisturbed.

In the small mining communities of Adger and Warrior, Steiner's men prohibited all public meetings including Warrior's city council. In another location, soldiers barred AFL's Bill Harrison from speaking since he was not a member in that specific UMW chapter. When UMW organizer Van A. Bittner criticized Governor Kilby in a speech at a union hall, soldiers stopped him until he apologized and promised never to speak ill of the governor again. Soon, state soldiers were breaking up all UMW meetings in the coalfields. The militia arrested so many miners for illegal assembly and speech that they had to be housed at Rickwood Field, Birmingham's minor league baseball park owned by Oscar Underwood's brother-in-law. Most jailed miners stayed there until union lawyers or Breck Musgrove made their bond.

According to strikers, soldiers barred one hundred men from a meeting at a farm in Jefferson County on October 19 because a handbill included the words, "Labor Discussion In Interest of Organized Labor." A local public official protested that the U.S. Constitution gave citizens the right to assemble peacefully and to speak on private property. "To hell with the laws of the United States," responded the militia's lieutenant, "I am not going by the laws of the United States, I am getting my orders from General Steiner."[10]

Stationed at the new, elegant Tutwiler Hotel in downtown Birmingham, Steiner complained to Governor Kilby that "Union Agitators" persisted in trying to hold meetings in the mining districts. "These Mass Meetings always tend to provoke a breach of the peace," he insisted, and "as a rule the speeches are very inflammatory, and law and order are opposed to them." When former U.S. Senator Frank White, UMW's chief attorney, joined union leaders in pleading with Steiner to lift the total ban, the General threatened to order his soldiers "to shoot to kill." After a massive rally by miners and supporters in downtown's Capital Park, the UMW informed its local leaders that "General Steiner would not allow another one to be held," although the General had no legal authority within Birmingham's city limits.

With almost seven hundred soldiers patrolling the mining areas in concert with a larger number of company-paid deputies and guards, coal operators accelerated efforts to purge their company towns of all union workers and families. By November, UMW leaders had set up a thousand tents for the evicted. By the end of the year, the Cahaba Coal Company alone had evicted twelve hundred families.

Despite legal challenges, the numbers of homeless families increased weekly during a harsh Alabama winter that brought unusually cold weather and three deep snowfalls. Once evicted, miners were blacklisted as "agitators" and barred permanently from future employment at any Alabama company mine. The coal companies also circulated blacklists to other businesses, contrary to Alabama law, to purge unionism throughout the community.

Workers remaining on the job lived in armed camps. High fences stood around company towns, and gunmen were on constant duty to assure that workers went only into the mines and no one—no union organizer, relative, or farmer bearing food—came into the company town. Anyone leaving had to receive a rare permit from the company supervisor. According to local white citizens, Adger's company guards entered private homes to force black workers into the mines for overtime.

At Woodward Iron Company's mines, three hundred black miners gathered to protest the company's special strike rules, but state soldiers dispersed them since they met without General Steiner's approval. After his visit to a mining camp, Birmingham physician Thomas Parke observed that the strike "made out a good case against a typical law enforcement officer being in reality a law breaker of the worst sort."[11]

The ban on assembling and speaking apparently did not apply to Birmingham's best citizens. At a large meeting sponsored by the Kiwanis Club, businessmen castigated UMW members as outlaws, and an officer of Sloss-Sheffield Coal and Iron called upon vigilantes to attack unions. A Birmingham banker said he could enlist one hundred men to "shoulder a rifle." Businessmen also took out full-page ads in the *Age-Herald* charging that Van Bittner and other UMW organizers were solely responsible for stirring up local black workers to commit acts of violence. Robert Jemison, Sr., and other businessmen intimated that if Bittner didn't leave soon, someone in Birmingham would "act lawlessly in getting him out of the state."

The ads captured the city's fundamental problem. "It is but another exhibition of the narrowness and reaction of our better circumstanced people," Dr. Parke wrote within the seclusion of his diary. "It means more than its face value for it shows the essential lawlessness of our solid business men."

Union officials tried to explain their side to the public. After the Kiwanis meeting, the UMW issued a long statement in the *Labor Advocate*. "The coal operators of Alabama have since 1904 driven thousands of white miners from the state because they dared to belong to the United Mine Workers of America, and employed negro miners whom they hoped would lower standards . . . by working for starvation wages," the union stated. "The fight . . . is not a social fight. We dare not even dream that the time will ever come in the history of Alabama when these coal barons will ever consider that the white miners and their families are their social equals . . . The negro miners are a fine set of men for the coal operators as long as they are willing to work for starvation wages without complaint, but when they join the United Mine Workers of America and attempt to raise the standard of living for the white miner and his family as well as for themselves, then the coal operators attempt to prejudice the case of the miners by taking up the race question," the union continued.

In handbills, UMW leaders challenged the charge that they were "outside agitators"—men who did not hold dear the South's customs—by pointing out that several special deputies on the companies' payroll were brought from New York City and other Northern areas. Besides, most of Alabama's coal industry had "foreign" owners. "Very little of it is Alabama men and Alabama capital," the union observed. The UMW also reminded citizens that, if a government bans people from asking "others to enter their organization," the next step is to make it illegal for a citizen to "ask his friend and neighbor to join his church and go to heaven with him."

Governor Kilby dispatched the state's new law enforcement unit to Birmingham in December. He had created the agency two years earlier as a strike force against illegal liquor and appointed as chief Conrad Austin, Jefferson's former deputy sheriff. In addition, the governor continued to received reports from Key Milner of the state secret intelligence department, who kept Montgomery well informed of how the strike threatened social customs and business interests.[12]

Conditions quickly worsened. Three days before Christmas in Nauvoo, a small Walker County mining town, Willie Baird killed a soldier who earlier had fatally shot Baird's father-in-law. Baird, a white miner, later turned himself into the sheriff of nearby Winston County on Christmas Day. On the same day, a soldier shot and killed a miner imprisoned at Rickwood Field. Yet, it was the death of Steiner's soldier—not the jailed miner—that rapidly moved the strike to a new level of hostility.

The commanding general abandoned all pretenses of impartial law enforcement and declared unofficial war on strikers and their leaders. Throughout mining areas, soldiers enforced Steiner's law to stop lodge meetings, revivals, and church services. Merchants complained that soldiers dispersed men from their stores when two or more were seen talking. Steiner pressed Governor Kilby and Alabama Supreme Court Justice James Mayfield (Kilby's legal advisor on the strike) for a formal declaration of martial law allowing soldiers to take up arms against union leaders. "While the strike is broken in that coal production is normal and labor is plentiful," Steiner informed Kilby, "the strikers are not broken and it is this last situation we have to deal with." Steiner wanted an order establishing that "the duty of the troops will be to see that these men who are preaching this bolshevism are sent out of the State or punished."

In late December, Steiner and Conrad Austin met at the militia's field headquarters in Walker County where the grand jury was proceeding to indict Willie Baird. "Chief, . . . the Governor isn't satisfied with what you are doing in the mining district," Steiner told Austin, "he thinks that this thing ought to be brought to a close, and you ought to beat hell out of these fellows, and run them out of here."

"Well," replied Austin, "suppose I should give my men orders to beat hell out of these fellows . . . suppose they should get into trouble . . . and they have to kill or be killed?" Austin asked. "If they were tried for the beatings, there would be legal costs and possible fines."

"Oh, well," Steiner said, "we will take care of that . . . so far as the financial part of it is, we will look after that."

Austin's men moved quickly against Phil Painter, a local union newspaper editor who wrote harshly about Steiner, Austin, scabs, and company thugs. Austin suspected Painter had sent anonymous, threatening letters (one signed "KKK") to the governor in support of strikers. After the two men met on the Birmingham streets, Austin's deputies lingered and attacked Painter. With blood dripping off his face, as the lawmen hurried away, Painter screamed, "Mr. Austin, . . . Why is your crowd ganging me?"

Austin's men also tried to "gang" state AFL president Bill Harrison and Van Bittner, the chief UMW organizer from Pittsburgh. Wherever Harrison and Bittner went, Austin's plain-clothed police were sure to follow. Late one night, as Harrison left his office alone, the same two lawmen who had waylaid Phil Painter quickly followed. The union leader ran to his Model T Ford, parked several blocks away in a darkened alley, cranked it, and sped away just as the deputies turned the corner. "Go to hell, you son of a bitch!" yelled the lawmen as they raced after Harrison's car with the apparent intention of trying to hasten his journey there.[13]

A few days afterwards, in the predawn of January 13, two carloads of masked men entered the Walker County jail and overpowered a night watchman to kidnap miner Willie Baird, awaiting trial for the murder of Steiner's soldier. Next day, a mail carrier found Baird's bullet-riddled body on the roadside. Within five days, local investigators followed the lynching mob's conspicuous trail directly to the encampment of Steiner's soldiers. Apparently, with little fear of discovery, nine soldiers had hired two local taxis to pick them up at the military camp and to carry them throughout their mission. After they pushed Baird out of the taxi and shot him twelve times, the soldiers instructed the hired drivers to keep their mouths shut and return them to their barracks just in time to dress and answer reveille.

UMW officials requested President Wilson to send federal troops to the coalfields and Governor Kilby to withdraw state troops. The President demurred, and Kilby blanched in anger. "The trouble in the strike district has been handled admirably by the guardsmen," the governor snorted. A coroner's jury found that the soldiers of company M "constituted a mob that lynched" Willie Baird and called upon "the good citizenship of Alabama" to assure the guilty were punished. Kilby commissioned Horace Wilkinson to prosecute the accused soldiers, but the governor fully agreed with General Steiner's assessment. He desperately wanted to end the substantial costs of soldiering the strike and to rid the state of UMW outsiders. In frustration, Kilby complained that Van Bittner and strike leaders "are careful to avoid doing anything that will subject them to arrest and punishment."[14]

Union officials refused to be dragooned any longer. In a sweeping challenge of official lawlessness, Hugo Black filed suit in state court on behalf of

Bill Harrison, alleging that Kilby's state law enforcement bureau was violating Harrison's rights and civil liberties guaranteed by state and federal constitutions. Black complained that state lawmen "armed with deadly weapons" were shadowing Harrison, eavesdropping on his conversations, harassing him with threats of violence, and "picketing" constantly in front of his office building, although the labor leader was not suspected or accused of a crime. The chief defendant was Conrad Austin, who as a Jefferson deputy sheriff in 1915 had accused Solicitor Black of coddling black criminals and imprisoning innocent whites.

Black alleged that Austin and his men were violating his client's "Constitutional right to be let alone," had deprived him of liberty without due process of law, were violating Alabama's criminal statutes against picketing, for which hundreds of striking miners had been arrested, and were destroying Harrison's "right of privacy." Kilby's police force—a "constant intimidation to the miners"—came to the UMW offices, according to Black, and caused Harrison's wife to be "in constant terror and anxiety" about her husband's safety. In an affidavit, Harrison recounted his nighttime flight from Austin's deputies and another incident when Austin's men shoved him off the sidewalk.

These were not playful incidents, Black argued during an expedited hearing before Judge Hugh Locke, a former local law school dean. Black offered sworn statements about the beating of Phil Painter. Was the unprovoked, bloody attack on this friend of labor simply surveillance? Nothing in Alabama law, Black argued, gave gun-brandishing state lawmen the right to patrol around his client's business, home, and person, threatening him, and making him fear going out at night.

Conrad Austin responded. He argued that surveillance was necessary due to widespread lawlessness and the reign of terror against nonunion miners. He listed nine killings and dozens of acts of violence that had happened since the strike. Austin swore that the violence had increased in mid-December after UMW officials instructed members "to prevent men from going to work in the mines." He also blamed some violence on editor Phil Painter's "incendiary article" about scabs. Austin's lawyers claimed that state lawmen were only watching "for the purpose of preventing the execution of the threatened conspiracy to violate the penal laws of the State of Alabama."

General Steiner also filed an affidavit accusing UMW leaders of inciting violence. He claimed his troops had stopped union violence. "This condition continued until about the 10th day of December, 1920," he stated, when UMW officials ordered picketing to recommence. Afterwards, union leaders instigated "a renewal of disorders and violations of the law," Steiner asserted.

Yet, violence wasn't the union's only transgression claimed as justification for the state's actions. Austin and his deputies filed affidavits swearing that Joseph Sorsby, the African American serving as Alabama's UMW vice president, had been seen "giving orders and directing affairs generally" in the union's Birmingham headquarters, including giving "orders to a white lady stenographer." Sorsby "dictated to the white stenographers with his hat on his head, and with a cigar in his mouth," according to lawmen. Also, deputies swore that "white members at the organization address the negro as 'Mr. Sorsby.'"

In oral arguments before the chancery court—during the same week as the second Mary Miniard case—Black ignored Austin's attack on the union's racial practices and focused on restoring the union officials' civil liberties. He asked the court to reject the state's view that a history of violence by a relatively small number of union members *and* nonunion workers justified the actions of Austin's men. Judge Locke, however, refused to issue a restraining order. Black filed an immediate appeal.

Stopped in court, Black's lawsuit nonetheless raised public questions that prompted others to act. In a special charge to a local grand jury, Judge William Fort instructed jurors to use Black's suit as a "basis on which to make an investigation" into UMW officials' claims that union members "were being persecuted by law enforcement officers and their liberties trampled upon." Fort also asked the jury to investigate charges of miners' lawlessness, but he did not include an inquiry into Austin's racial charges.

A day later, after appearing before the grand jury, Sid Cowan—Austin's deputy in charge of Walker County—resigned and issued a public statement revealing Austin's December instructions to lawmen "to beat the hell out" of union leaders. In Washington, U.S. Senator Robert LaFollette of Wisconsin, labor's progressive friend, called Alabama coal operators to testify before his committee to explain their labor practices and coal prices. Birmingham Congressman George Huddleston condemned the coal operators as "arrogant, overbearing barons" who were gouging the public.

Kilby moved to forestall growing opposition. He recalled Chief Austin and his men to Montgomery to take up prohibition enforcement. "It is the best thing the governor has done for a long time," remarked the *Birmingham*

Post editor. "Law enforcement in Jefferson County will not suffer because of the loss of them."[15]

Austin's withdrawal was the only victory Black and the union could claim. The mines continued to produce sufficient quantities of coal. In late January, U.S. Steel's Borden Burr had returned from Montgomery with a state Supreme Court opinion allowing coal companies to evict strikers' families from company towns on one day's notice. Most contracts gave companies an exclusive right to cancel leases at any time, and the state court held that, fair or foul, a contract is a contract. Immediately, coal operators began evicting as many families as possible, and by mid-February the eight thousand homeless strikers were living in tents. Each week, the UMW fed more than forty thousand people. Most were striking miners' children. Many needed warm clothes and shoes. And none of the homeless miners had any prospects for local employment inside or outside mines.

Throughout the state, prominent businessmen and public officials rallied behind the soldiers accused of lynching Willie Baird. Former Governor B. B. Comer contributed $50 to their defense committee and publicly defended the soldiers' actions: "if proven guilty," Comer declared, "it is still evident that there was strong provocation and an element of self-defense in the conduct of these young men," nine of whom had shot unarmed Willie Baird twelve times with Winchester rifles at close range. "I never could appreciate," protested Comer, "how . . . a number of men . . . under carpetbag and scalawag leadership, named collective bargaining . . . could lawfully superinduce and indefinitely continue conditions which carry turmoil, lawlessness, murder." During a well-publicized trial in rural Hamilton, lawyers for Willie Baird's murderers followed Governor Comer's lead by spotlighting the white victim's membership in a predominantly black union with black leaders. Although he personally knew nothing of the case's facts, UMW Vice-President Joe Sorsby and another black miner were subpoenaed by defense lawyers and kept in the courtroom throughout the trial. The UMW charged that the soldiers were trying "to inject racial feelings into the trial and to point to Sorsby as a type of Alabama miner." The prosecution charged "friends of the accused" of stirring up "propaganda" about the black man as Willie Baird's union boss. Despite a vigorous prosecution, on February 7 six farmers on the jury would not vote to convict the soldiers of any crime—prompting a mistrial.

In Montgomery, with Austin's affidavits on UMW's "racial familiarity" in hand, Governor Kilby issued a statement declaring the strike was over—if labor leaders would only admit the facts and go home. He called upon UMW leaders and "agitators" to leave the state and asked the people of Alabama to address these men "in plain, positive and unmistakable terms" to accomplish what he could not do through his lawful powers. It was an open invitation for lawlessness from a governor celebrated by the national press a year earlier for his condemnation of lynchings.

The public response from Birmingham's "men of affairs" was immediate and vocal. A group appointed by Birmingham's "businessmen and other leading citizens," including Key Milner, issued their own findings on the strike. The problems began, they declared, when UMW's Van Bittner arrived from the North. "Accompanying him came a band of northern negroes and northern whites . . . negro organizers and white organizers speaking from the same platform, arousing passions, inflaming feelings." The report asked: "What was the result of this invasion of negro and white organizers of the United Mine Workers of America brought to Alabama. . .? *The Reign of Bloodshed and Terrorism Begins.*"

A federal labor mediator from Washington suggested that the governor and others were describing only one side of the dispute. Promptly, the official was returned to Washington at the insistence of Senator Underwood, who also received copies of Austin's affidavits. U.S. Steel's Borden Burr widely circulated the sworn statements as "undenied in the court proceedings in Jefferson County."

Austin's racial charges authenticated other similar rumors spread by operators and their agents. Coal owners accused the UMW of several sins, including discouraging workers from going to church, but the most consistent theme was "racial familiarity." Burr told Alabama businessmen that the UMW had Negroes presiding at meetings where white women and children were in the audience with "the negro man sitting next to the white woman." "One of those Yankee negroes married a white woman, too," exclaimed a Birmingham coal owner. "I have had several of our men tell me," he continued, "that the union promised them equal votes and equal marriage laws."[16]

At a defiant, enthusiastic rally on February 14 at Birmingham's Bijou Theater, union leaders condemned "narrow sectionalism and a restriction of free speech and free assembly." But labor's cause was lost. John L. Lewis and his international union could not support forty thousand people indefinitely.

As in 1908, union leaders realized that, without the right to assemble, picket, or speak freely, strikers were doomed when opposed by industrialists, paid deputies, the state militia, the governor, and the state's "men of affairs" who were summoning the powers of Southern racialism. If soldiers could lynch Willie Baird without certain punishment, all black and white miners were in jeopardy.

Hugo Black's failure to halt government attacks and reverse public opinion left the union with no recourse. The strike had to end. When *Birmingham News* publisher Victor Hanson suggested arbitration by a panel of uninvolved citizens chosen solely by the governor, UMW officials had no choice but to agree.

On February 22, with little real hope for a favorable settlement, UMW leaders announced publicly that the strike was over.[17] At the Farley Building, union officials and their lawyers hammered out terms and strategies for how the union could present its best case to the governor's arbitration panel. In truth, the UMW could sue only for merciful terms of surrender, but even that diminutive goal appeared unlikely.

It was a depressing, hopeless moment for Alabama's labor movement, one which Hugo Black had foreshadowed a year earlier in court pleadings during the Underwood campaign. And it was a moment when union officials had to persevere without Black's advice and assistance. As other UMW lawyers prepared briefs and developed testimony for upcoming arbitration, Black was readying himself to complete another extensive negotiation, one which he had finally completed by resolving conflicts between vastly differing parties that now were preparing to join together in a binding contract. Black was needed elsewhere immediately to perfect that contract. A marriage contract. His own.

The announcement of Hugo Black's marriage to Miss Josephine Foster, daughter of Dr. and Mrs. Sterling J. Foster of the city's fashionable Southside, was an item of special notice in Birmingham society. "Few wedding announcements have been read with greater interest than this one," remarked the society editor. "Miss Foster has been an acknowledged belle during her young womanhood. Her beauty and winsome personality have made her a favorite wherever she has gone. Miss Foster also possesses patriotism of the highest order. During the war she went to New York and . . . was made a yeo-woman . . . in naval intelligence . . . Mr. Black is a rising young lawyer, who has already made a success in his chosen profession. A wide circle of friends," the editor observed diplomatically, "is deeply interested in the future of these splendid young people."

Miss Foster's friends had good reason to be deeply interested and concerned. Josephine and Hugo were as different in personality and background as were the societal forces at conflict within Birmingham. Unlike her future husband from Alabama's backwoods, Josephine was born into the privileges of Southern tradition and culture. Her mother's father was a colonel in the Civil War serving with the Olympian Nathan Bedford Forrest. Later her uncle represented Memphis for several terms in the U.S. Congress until defeated by an ally of "The Great Commoner" William Jennings Bryan. Another uncle, Malcolm Patterson, was a successful lawyer and former governor of Tennessee.

Nicknamed "Sis" at an early age, Josephine was reared with the benefits of her father's rich Black Belt traditions. Dr. Foster's father met his future wife in a stockade in south Alabama when both were seeking refuge from warring Creek Indians. In time, the Fosters prospered at a plantation near Union Springs until the Civil War, which the first Sterling Foster opposed. Foster sent a substitute to fight in his place, a privilege that cost him more than $1,000, according to a family secret. His refusal to buy Confederate bonds and an astute decision to keep much of his money in a Liverpool bank enabled the Fosters to maintain their prosperity immediately after the war. Like Hugo's Uncle Merit Street, Foster was one of the few men in the Deep South who had hard cash during Reconstruction, and he used it to purchase more land and to plant more cotton.

Sis's parents met in Memphis, and the second Sterling Foster became the minister of a Presbyterian Church where his father-in-law was an elder. Dr. Foster had been sent to school at Southwestern in Memphis, Princeton Theological Seminary, and overseas to Edinburgh and the University of Berlin. In 1903, when Josephine was four, Dr. Foster accepted an invitation to pastor at Birmingham's South Highland Presbyterian Church where one of his wife's cousins, Judge Samuel Weakley, the great prohibitionist, served as elder. As one of the city's religious leaders, Dr. Foster belonged to the best clubs and socialized with Birmingham's best citizens. His wife's friends were women from the best families, including Forney Johnston's wife, Clara. Mrs. Foster occupied her time with social duties of the Cadmean Circle, an exclusive women's club, and her church.

Her children, Sterling III, Josephine, and the youngest child, Virginia, played in the shady, neatly clipped yards of southside Birmingham under the watchful eye of the family's black maid.

During summers and at Christmas, Dr. Foster's children stayed at their grandparents' plantation in Bullock County. For Virginia, it was "a perfect Eden" preserved in memory for decades:

> The Foster family still lived just exactly as they had lived before the War with large numbers of servants, plenty of money. Ex-slaves did not leave the plantation but remained on as tenants, and the "house slaves" stayed as servants who still lived in the back yard.
>
> It was a beautiful, old white house surrounded by great stretches of meadowland on all sides. Around the house was a large front yard, with gardens to the side, an enormous scuppernong arbor, and in the back were fruit trees, berries and a very large vegetable garden. The people on the plantation killed the hogs and lambs for meat, had cows for milk and cream and butter, killed some beef cattle, and, of course, had enormous numbers of chickens and eggs. In the winter, there were dove and quail shoots and rabbit shoots, and the table had every known kind of wild game that was in Alabama.
>
> Josephine was a favorite with all of her kin, Grandmother and Grandfather, Uncles and Aunts. She was a beautiful child, with deep blue eyes and brown hair, and was considered an angel—a real angel. All of her cousins adored her, too, and she was a great favorite with the black children on the place, as they all played together in the backyard. She had an instinctively gentle, sweet nature . . . Everybody used to worry because they thought she was so sweet she'd die young. Poor Sis, crying one day after she heard everybody say she was going to die young because she was such an angel.[18]

While the Foster children knew nothing of the misery and unending toil of other children who worked in factories and fields, their own lives were not entirely idyllic. Before Josephine was ten, her father lost his pulpit in a theological battle over the literal interpretation of the Bible. Dr. Foster's European education led him to believe that the Bible offered symbolic, not literal meaning. Although he was a deeply conservative man with traditional Black Belt politics, Foster was a liberal on Jonah and the Whale.

While often vague and flowery, Foster's sermons finally convinced a majority of his church elders, including his wife's cousin, Judge Weakley, that

Alabama locations involved in Hugo Black's early life and career.

ABOVE, *W. L. Black family, Clay County, 1892. From left, Orlando, Robert Lee, W. L. Black, Hugo, Della, Daisy, Lenora, Vernon Merit, and Pelham.* BELOW, *a teenage Hugo Black (top row, second from left), wearing "town cap," with Barney Whatley at his side (third from left), as the boys join some of Ashland's male residents for a photograph.*

Landmarks from Hugo Black's boyhood in Ashland: TOP, *the First Baptist Church;* BOTTOM, *the county jail.*

LEFT, *Hugo Black's law school class photograph, 1906.* BELOW, *the view that would have confronted Black on his arrival at the L&N train station in Birmingham in 1907, looking north along Twentieth Street, with the Brown-Marx Building "skyscraper" nearing completion.*

Young lawyer Black would have been familiar with (TOP) chain gangs on Birmingham streets, 1909; (RIGHT) miners in entrance to area coal shaft, ca. 1920; and (BELOW) Tennessee Coal and Iron Company's Ensley Steel Plant, ca. 1906.

Black's early legal work involved cases on behalf of poor whites and blacks, including convicts, against the coal and steel companies for injuries or deaths in the often dangerous mines.

TOP *and* CENTER, *area mines, ca. 1920;* LEFT, *company houses at the U.S. Steel plant, ca. 1930.*

The ardently prohibitionist Black made a statewide name for himself in 1916 when he helped break up extensive illegal liquor operations in Girard (present-day Phenix City). ABOVE, some of the contraband. BELOW, Black, second from right, with Attorney General Logan Martin.

In 1916, Birmingham's white community was caught up in a frenzied half-century commemoration of the Civil War, including the above parade down Twentieth Street. Two years later, World War I captured the attention of citizens, including Josephine Foster, RIGHT, yeomanette third-class, U.S. Navy women's division, 1919.

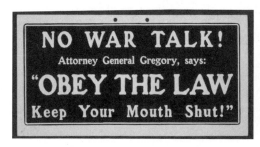

NO WAR TALK!
Attorney General Gregory, says:
"OBEY THE LAW
Keep Your Mouth Shut!"

ABOVE, *visiting Clay County in 1918, Captain Black in uniform jokes with his niece, Grace, Robert Lee Black's daughter.* LEFT, *John Bankhead, Sr., U. S. senator during World War I, began his public career as a prison warden expanding the convict leasing system which became the basis for his family's political and financial dynasty.*

ABOVE, *Josephine Foster and Hugo Black near the time of their wedding in February 1921.* **RIGHT,** *Josephine Black's Grandmother Foster sits on the porch of her mansion near Union Springs, Alabama.*

SOURCES OF PHOTOS:

Barney Whatley: 2-b.
Birmingham News: 9-a, 12-c, 13-a.
Birmingham Public Library: 5-a, 5-b, 6-a, 8-a, 10-a, 12-a, 12-b.
D. L. Vaughn: 3-a, 3-b.
Library of Congress: 4-b, 5-c, 6-b, 6-c, 8-c, 9-b, 10-b, 13-c, 14-a, 14-b, 15-a, 15-b, 16-a, 16-b.
Steve Franklin: 7-a, 7-b.
Virginia Durr: 2-a, 4-a, 8-b, 10-c, 11-a, 11-b, 15-c.

ABOVE, *Josephine
Black with her young
Alabama-born boys,
Sterling and Hugo Jr.,
in the late 1920s.* LEFT,
*Mary Marble, the Black
family's maid who cared
for the Black boys in
Alabama and later
in Washington, with
Sterling.*

ABOVE, *from the balcony of the Tutwiler Hotel, President Warren G. Harding reviews a Birmingham parade during the city's 50th anniversary in 1921.* BELOW LEFT, *St. Paul's Cathedral stands adjacent to the high towers of the old Jefferson County courthouse where lawyer Black defended the Rev. Edwin Stephenson for the murder of Father James Coyle.* BELOW RIGHT, *Klansman handing out literature on a Birmingham street in the 1920s.*

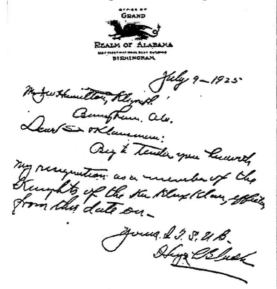

Top, *a 1926 meeting of the Robert E. Lee klavern of the KKK to which Black belonged for approximately 22 months.* Above left, *his July 9, 1925, letter resigning from the Klan.* Above right, *Imperial Wizard Hiram Evans parades along Pennsylvania Avenue in Washington in September 1926.*

ABOVE, *Senator "Cotton" Tom Heflin, whom Black joined in representing Alabama in the U.S. Senate, was known for his extravagant storytelling and rabid anti-Catholicism.* BELOW, *at his desk in Washington, Senator Oscar W. Underwood declined to seek reelection in 1926, a decision opening the way for Black's election.*

ABOVE, *U.S. Assistant Attorney General Mabel Willebrandt, here with seated President Calvin Coolidge, enforced national prohibition and supported Hugo Black's prosecution of Mobile business leaders in 1924.* BELOW LEFT, *Senator-elect Black, Governor Bibb Graves, and Senator Oscar W. Underwood, posing after a meeting on the Muscle Shoals dam, represented the new and old political leadership of Alabama in 1927.* BELOW RIGHT, *Black's campaign poster from his 1926 Senate race.*

Top, *Justice Black, (back row, far right) with his colleagues of the U.S. Supreme Court in 1938, including former U.S. Attorney General Harlan F. Stone (back row, second from left).* Bottom, *Justice Black's study in his home in Alexandria, Virginia.*

their minister was a Biblical heretic. Led by Weakley and industrialist James Bowron, two men who agreed on little more than a literal Bible and absolute prohibition, the church session gave Foster a week to decide if he believed every literal word of the story of Jonah and the Whale. For seven days, Sis's father walked up and down in his study. "Oh, God, Oh Lord," he shouted for guidance. "Well," Foster said, "I suppose Jonah had a little camp cot in the whale's belly and I suppose he ate the sardines that came down the Whale's gullet and had a little oil stove inside of him." The Foster house was in stark terror. The children huddled together, with their father marching and shouting across the study, and their mother crying, upset with her cousins and distressed by her husband's certain fate. The church removed Dr. Foster when he confessed that he could not believe that the Biblical story was literally true.

After a prolonged recuperation, Dr. Foster and his family resumed their social status in Birmingham where a good number of the best citizens thought that he had been shabbily treated. Relying principally on money from the Foster plantation, the former minister began selling insurance, a job which he considered beneath his station, and investing in business schemes usually offered by men as "crooked as a snake," according to his daughter. The Foster family had to watch costs closely, although they continued to belong to the country club and to live in a large, comfortable home carefully appointed with good books and fine furniture and maintained by black servants.

The children occasionally returned to Union Springs, where only their grandmother survived, for a visit into rural aristocracy. Grandmother Foster was a regal figure, assisted by "Mammy Easter," a black servant who slept at the end of her employer's bed. The old white woman rode to church in a buggy lined with red satin and driven by a black coachman with a high silk hat. Once a week, the driver steered his large matching team of red-coated horses to the local town where clerks brought cloth and goods out to Mrs. Foster as she sat in her shaded barouche.

When Josephine was nine years old, Grandmother Foster and Easter decided it was time to let the South's serpent into her Eden. Easter called the black and white children together. "Now look," she told the black kids, "you can't call Miss Josephine 'Sis' anymore. You've got to start calling her 'Miss Josephine.' She's too big for you to call her 'Sis' anymore." Sternly, Easter laid down the law. It was the children's first, direct instruction on the South's race relations. After Easter left, both black and white children were upset, sitting still and silent.

Josephine perked up. "I tell you," she said to the others, "instead of calling me 'Miss Josephine,' you can just call me 'Miss Sis.'" The children unanimously adopted the idea, and for the rest of her life, family members often called Josephine "Miss Sis," a private tribute to her enduring innocence.

At home, the girls' mother was not so concerned about their etiquette of race relations. Josephine and Virginia seldom played with black children, and none lived in the neighborhood. Mrs. Foster was much more preoccupied by her mother-in-law's extravagances. Often Grandmother Foster sent the girls home wearing panties of red Irish linen and lace. Upon their return from the Black Belt, after a loving hug, Miss Sis's mother turned the girls upside down to examine their undergarments. Mrs. Foster already had enough trouble maintaining good relations with local churchwomen and did not need a new scandal about her daughters' petticoats.

As an active teenager, Miss Sis was often desired as a club member and companion. She and her siblings played tennis at the country club, although they dared not order a cold lemonade since the family's credit was nil. Like others in the neighborhood, Sis was a Girl Scout and attended nearby public schools. After she graduated from Central High School with a host of eager young men following her every step, Dr. Foster sent his first daughter to Sweet Briar Academy in Virginia. Sweet Briar was considered one of the most appropriate places for a girl of society to learn the lessons of Southern ladyhood. But Josephine was stricken there with a mild rheumatic fever that weakened her heart and soured her memories of the school.

While away at school, Josephine visited a family friend living on New York's Madison Avenue when World War I was declared. Quickly, she joined the Navy's women's division as a third-class yeomanette and performed clerical duties in the intelligence department. Her parents were shocked by her unilateral action, although pleased by her patriotism. Mrs. Foster also worried that Josephine would be exposed to Northern men. There was little reason to fret. Even in New York, Southern boys on their way to Europe stopped regularly to visit Josephine. Her diary recorded three or four dates each night.

After the Great War, Josephine returned in uniform to Birmingham. The Foster home was now on Southside's Niazuma Street where a new Packard sat in the driveway. Grandmother Foster had died, and Dr. Foster's portion of the estate brought a new aura of security to his family's lives. Continuing to wear her military suit, dark blue with a matching cap and cape trimmed in red,

Miss Sis was inundated with male admirers. On Sundays, when the number of male visitors measured a young woman's popularity, the Foster parlor was overflowing. Bringing flowers, poems, and pounds of chocolates, young men came in what seemed to Josephine's sister as "droves, droves, and droves."[19]

On a clear day in late 1919, probably a few weeks after his spirited defense of the virtues of Southern womanhood in the Miniard case, Hugo Black was walking home to a Southside apartment, which he once again shared with other bachelors. Black had a big, expensive automobile, but he preferred to walk briskly for the exercise and perhaps to avoid the traffic jams near the one railroad crossing that divided north and south Birmingham. On this morning, Black passed near the Foster house and noticed ahead of him a young woman walking up a steep hill and "wearing, as was then the style, a long, very tight-fitting dress." It was Josephine in her military uniform. Black was star-struck by the woman's poise, grace, shape, beauty, and uniform. He was very interested. Later in the week, he found her again at the country club and asked for a dance.

Shortly afterwards, Black began acting as if he and Josephine were destined to be husband and wife. It was country club gossip that Black was "crazy" about a young Jewish woman. If so, that relationship ended abruptly. After growing up in a home with a loveless marriage, Black had patiently searched for the woman who captured his desires, his heart, and his ideals. Having now met her, Black's attention and affection had only one object.

For more than a year, Black pursued Josephine in a manner resembling an aggressive campaign as much as a loving courtship. He showered her with presents and flowers night and day and went after her affection as if no other beau existed in her life. Black cut a rather handsome figure. He dressed fashionably and now parted his hair on the right side—giving him a less severe, symmetrical face. Gone was the silly fellow who argued about Twiddle Dee. Appearing youthful, Black was a determined, totally adoring suitor who exposed Josephine to much more than playful chatter. He talked about ideas and books he was reading. He gave her sister Virginia books like Charles Beard's *American Government and Politics*. "I had never seen any man before with so much confidence. He assumed that I was fated to marry him," Josephine recalled years later, "and that everybody else was out of the picture. He was like an irresistible force; he just kept coming at me."

Unlike most of twenty-two-year-old Josephine's admirers, Black was a mature man of thirty-five. The spread of age and experience was remarkable. When in 1913 Hugo Black was a former police court judge and volunteer legal advisor to the Boys Club, Josephine was a child of fourteen attending Campfire Girl meetings. Black had seen most of Birmingham's poverty and despair, while Josephine knew little about social conditions outside Southside and Madison Avenue. Hugo held and expressed firm opinions about the day's most important economic and social issues, but Josephine knew little about those concerns from either observation or experience.[20]

Despite differences, each was attracted by the other. Black saw a young woman of striking beauty and innate goodness, traits he remembered and idealized in his own mother as virtues of Southern womanhood. He also saw an intellectual curiosity and capability in this former yeowoman that was very rare among women on Southside. The fact that Josephine was only twenty-two was also a decided attraction. Robbed of his parents and two beloved brothers before he was out of school, Black had decided to choose a woman who would outlive him. He wanted a wife for the rest of his life.

Josephine found Hugo vastly more mature and poised than other suitors. "I had never been exposed to a mind like his. And, of course," she remembered, "he had the charm of a much older man who still has his youthful appearance; he seemed so sophisticated yet somehow so youthful." Within a few months, Josephine decided she truly loved this man and accepted his proposal of marriage. But soon afterwards, she changed her mind. She was a little frightened, as well as attracted, by the power and strength of Hugo's personality. Gentle, sensitive, universally charitable, Josephine did not have a great deal of physical energy, and Hugo sometimes tired her with his endless supply and tireless self-discipline.

Few of Josephine's family or friends encouraged this unlikely romance. Without important family connections, the lawyer from Clay County was considered crude by some of her girl friends. Josephine's mother was partial to the rich son of a member of the Cadmean Circle, and Dr. Foster's associates considered Black nothing more than "a damage suit lawyer," or worse, "a bolshevik." Forney Johnston warned Sterling Foster of "Ego" Black and his views, and Hugo's recent legal work on behalf of the United Mine Workers, with Northern agitators and "nigger members," worsened Hugo's reputation among the Fosters' circle. Black, nevertheless, eventually charmed Josephine's mother, and Dr. Foster seemed satisfied that at least Black had money.

Only begrudgingly did Josephine's friends admit that Black was one of the best and most successful lawyers in town. It did not matter to them that he was a member of the country club or that he had a lucrative law practice in 1921. In Birmingham, the lines in white society had always been drawn between those who ran the factories, mines, and mills on one side and those who worked in them on the other. And, as always, members of the best families were expected to stay with their own kind.

Regardless of her friends' opinions, generously shared, Josephine decided for good that Hugo was the love of her life. Perhaps, the memory of Jonah and the Whale gave her the courage to reject the intolerance of some of Birmingham's best citizens. She may have succumbed to Hugo's ever present, absolute certainty as a compensation for her own occasional feelings of insecurity. Her maternal political heritage may have attracted her to Hugo's unquenched political ambitions. Whatever the source of her desire and courage, Josephine's decision remained a mystery, at best, to many friends and extended family.

"Some of the gossip concerning the doings of Dan Cupid is confirmed today," wrote the women's page columnist of the *Birmingham News*, "by the formal announcement of the engagement of Miss Josephine Foster and Mr. Hugo Black whose nuptial ceremonies is scheduled for Wednesday February 23. Miss Foster . . . one of the society girls who did a valuable amount of war work . . . has been universally popular. Mr. Black is . . . one of the popular young bachelors. The wedding is to be quietly celebrated at the home of the bride's parents."[21]

Bogged down in labor warfare, Black had little to do with preparing for the wedding, but he had one firm condition. He insisted it must be small with only members of the two families. Otherwise, Black declared, "I'll have to invite ten thousand people." As recently elected Grand Chancellor of Alabama's Knights of Phythias and an active member of every other local fraternal order that included middle- and working-class white men, Black had many friends and brethren. With lingering political ambitions, he could not afford to invite some friends and exclude others.

On Wednesday afternoon, February 23rd, as news of the end of the miners' strike spread across the state, Black arrived at Niazuma Street in his best black business suit for "the most important event of the season," as the local society editor blithely called it. In keeping with Black's wishes, the society page reported that a former governor and former congressman of Tennessee among others—all members of the family—attended this "event of conspicuous social interest in Birmingham and throughout the state." "Miss Virginia Foster, sister of the bride was her maid of honor and only attendant . . . The bride was given in marriage by her father . . . She was met at the altar by the groom with his best man, Mr. Sterling Foster, Jr., brother of the bride."

In truth, Josephine and Hugo invited a couple of friends. She asked a young woman from the wealthy mine-owning Woodward family, a relative by marriage of Senator Underwood, and he invited Albert Lee Smith who actually served as Hugo's best man (the society editor got it wrong). "He told me right at the last minute to come on out there," Smith recalled. This innocent deception about the wedding party may have saved Black both political friends and embarrassing grief. As bachelors, Albert Lee and Hugo had attended a large number of weddings and always enjoyed a chance to "give the groom hell." Now, it was Hugo's turn to be the groom and the victim, but Black wanted none of it, especially in the presence of the high-society Foster family.

In a house overflowing with roses, narcissi, and early spring flowers, the wedding was lovely, but not free of tension and embarrassment. The Fosters met the Blacks for the first time as Hugo's brother and sister came up from east Alabama. To the urbane, aristocratic Fosters and Pattersons, the Black clan appeared very common and countrified. "Good God, you should see what's come up from Clay County," snipped Josephine's cousin upstairs in the dressing rooms. Most of the Foster clan were hospitable and considerate, but "the terrible excitement" about Hugo's country relatives made the bride very nervous and insecure. To calm Josephine, her aunt Louise—the family's smart-talking renegade who smoked and drank—gave the bride a strong helping of whiskey. The bride had never tasted liquor, and the remedy worked exceedingly well. Under the influence of illegal whiskey, Josephine floated dreamily down the stairs, in step with the piano's wedding march, to marry one of the state's leading prohibitionists. When Hugo leaned over and kissed his new bride, he was astonished to taste liquor on her lips. In the most unexpected place, it was the closest he had ever come to consuming the demon whiskey.

"If I have accomplished anything in this world," Black later bragged to his sons, "it was talking your mother into marrying me." To some he would add, "I don't know how I did it." To a few others who knew that Josephine was a tiny bit intoxicated when the knot was tied, Hugo would confess in mock serenity that his bride "didn't know what she was doing."

After the service, conducted by the Reverend Henry Edmonds (another minister recently removed from the Southside Presbyterian pulpit for failing a test of literal Biblical meaning), Albert Lee drove the newlyweds to the train depot. For reasons Smith never knew, Black instructed him to drive across Red Mountain to the Gracies/Calera station. On this occasion, the L&N train at Gracies came to a complete stop to load the newlyweds' extensive luggage, and, perhaps for the first time at this depot, the conductor had to put down a stool. On his wedding day, Hugo Black had proved beyond all reasonable doubt that a Southern lady boarded the train at Gracies/Calera—in this case for a honeymoon trip to the Pacific Ocean.

On the way to the depot, Black had sat in the back seat like a stiff board next to his bride. Perhaps, he was recovering from the shock of his first taste of alcohol—or thinking about Nannie Cornelius of Gracies. Whatever occupied him, Black did not act like a new bridegroom, and his chauffeur wanted to get him going. "He sat back there so dammed dignified that I saw a big old tree ... and stopped by a little store," Smith recalled. "Hugo, there's some mistletoe over us," Albert Lee instructed. Black awoke, turned to his new bride, and took a huge kiss permitted by folklore and friend.

As the passengers merrily sped away, none realized that within minutes of their Christian ceremony the couple had performed an ancient Druidic rite of Black's ancestral Ireland. In ancient days, the parasitic mistletoe was thought to have power to transform sworn enemies into lifelong friends if they would embrace beneath it. Graced by both pagan and Christian rituals of union, Hugo and Josephine were safe in the bonds of marriage, despite vast personal differences and enlarging hostility between their past worlds. Theirs would become a "marriage of justice and mercy." Yet, they were leaving behind a Birmingham that continued to worship the region's demigods of human division and soon would reenact another ancient Druid ritual—that of human sacrifice.[22]

GOVERNOR THOMAS KILBY APPOINTED A COMMITTEE of three Montgomery businessmen in late February to arbitrate the mining strike. "We are here with unbiased minds," they stated. "We came to Birmingham with open minds to base our report on the evidence." In a meeting on the second floor of the Tutwiler Hotel, UMW chief organizer Van Bittner presented the union's arguments to the committee. He asked for the right of workers to organize and bargain collectively, increased wages, and an end to the practice of subcontracting with mining companies using convict miners. "Gentlemen," he added, "the strike cannot be ended practically until these striking miners are reemployed." Van Bittner also complained that coal operators were continuing to evict families from company homes and condemned the action as a violation "of the armistice now existing."

The committee received briefs from the union and traveled throughout the mining areas. "Coming from the agricultural section of the state, we are more or less unfamiliar with the actual operations and conditions in and about the mines," the committee chairman explained. The coal operators, however, were reluctant to meet the committee since owners did not want to recognize the right of any government authority to meddle in their business. When they finally did appear, operators and their lawyers were received like a long-lost wealthy relative. "We could not go back home," the chairman exuded, "without hearing the attitude of the operator."

The businessmen soon got to the heart of the matter. "Mr. Rodden," a committee member asked, "you draw the color line in your camp, do you not?"

"Yes, sir, we have always done that, we have to do it," replied Ben Roden, owner of Roden Coal and Coke Company.

"Does the Union draw the color line?"

"No," stated Rodden.

"Are there negroes who are officers of the Union?" a committee member asked.

"Yes, sir, a negro vice president at every place . . . Yes, the negro vice president presides, whenever the President is away. He has presided a good many times at our place," the coal owner stated.

DeBardeleben Coal's vice president told the committee that "it would be a fatal mistake to deliver our negroes into the hands of these men who come from the North."

"If they should instill into our negroes union ideas, would those negroes spread that through the balance of the state?" a committee member inquired.

"It would travel through the rest of the state," declared the coal operator. "If left alone we Southern white men can handle our destinies by treating the negro right . . . as we always have, since we got over the other experience in the South in 1870–75, when the same kind of folks came down here and misled them."

The Alabama Manufacturing Association's president was the last witness who lambasted "misleaders" of labor. He assured the south Alabama gentlemen that Negro miners were living in housing just as good as their own tenant farmers despite colder climates in the state's northern hills. "We have to consider the nature of the negro" in order to understand what he needs, explained the business promoter. For example, everyone has "seen negro houses on the side of the road with the front door open on the coldest night . . . They must have air. It is the nature of the animal, if you can apply the word 'animal' to that race."

The committee prepared to return to Montgomery to report to the governor. "At none of the mines did we hear complaints as to living conditions or wages," the chairman revealed, "but we have heard much with regard to recognition of the union from union mines." Committee member John W. Durr later told his family (including his son who became Virginia Foster's husband) that the "mine companies were the most benevolent, paternalistic, high-minded, splendid organizations in the world."[23]

In late March, the governor's decision reflected the committee's sentiments. He conceded nothing to the union. "This strike, being called without just cause . . . was illegal and immoral. It proves beyond cavil that the written contract . . . of the United Mine Workers of America cannot be relied on and that recognition would give no assurance of industrial peace," Kilby stated. The governor also echoed the coal operators' basic view of the strike. "The only explanation, perhaps, lies in the fact that from 70 percent to 80 percent of the miners are negroes. The Southern negro is easily misled, especially when given a prominent and official place in an organization in which both races are members . . .The colored miners were undoubtedly deceived." No reemployment. No union recognition. No wage increase. Nothing.

UMW leaders hadn't expected Kilby to be generous, but his decision left them stunned and embittered. "Alabama's two-by-four governor did not write the decision in the coal strike," Van Bittner bellowed at a union meeting in the coalfields. "Charley DeBardeleben . . . and the other coal operators wrote that decision." Scabs were now in the mines, Bittner told strikers. "They may have a right to work but by the eternal Gods, they haven't any right to your jobs. It has been entirely too healthy for scabs," he insisted. "What would you do with a rattlesnake if one of them would start coming into this meeting now?" "Kill him," voices shouted. "A rattlesnake never did you half as much harm as a scab did," Bittner declared.

Responses to Bittner's speech were almost as intemperate. Kilby asked if the union leader could be charged with an attempt to incite a riot. A minister at Birmingham's Episcopal Church of the Advent pleaded: "Surely there should be some means for bringing about his departure, forced if necessary." Developer Robert Jemison, Jr., was more succinct: "Outsiders or anyone inside the state will not be allowed to preach such doctrines."

Alabama AFL's Bill Harrison attempted to calm the rhetoric. "We stand for law and order, and are against violence," he assured the public, "and we do not approve of anything that tends to incite violence, whether in speeches or otherwise." Far from repentant, Bittner released a biting retraction, urging union members to abstain from violence and to turn the other cheek, even if he considered it humanly impossible. "Observance of laws is the first tenet of democracy. . . The laws may have been violated when . . . chief of the law enforcement squad ordered his men to beat hell out of the organizers. . . The law may have been violated when General Steiner took away your liberties by preventing the right of assemblage and free speech . . . The laws may have been violated when Governor Kilby told the coal operators they didn't have to give you back your jobs. . . and thus starve you and your wives and little children," Bittner observed. "But despite all this, abstain from using violence," he said. "Violate no laws."

UMW's International Secretary-Treasurer William Green assured the press that the union would abide by Kilby's decision. "The strike is over. It cannot and will not be renewed." Yet, Birmingham's "men of affairs" wanted a pound of flesh. A business group cited five recent incidents of violence and proclaimed that "these murders and law violations were caused by and resulted from the incendiary speeches of the union leaders." Circuit Solicitor Joseph Tate, always looking for a free ride in politics, jumped on the bandwagon after lawmen arrested three union members for the murder of a scab. "Van Bittner says he stands for law and order," Tate told reporters. "If the union attempts to get these men out on bond or if they furnish counsel, they will show where they stand."

If coal operators and their friends were oblivious to Bittner's charge that official lawlessness exceeded and prompted strikers' violence, Judge William Fort's grand jury saw the problems of law and order in a broader context. "We commend the greater body of the miners in their conduct and action during the strike," jurors stated. "While there were a few who violated the law and committed crimes, yet the great body of the miners who came out on strike have conducted themselves commensurate with the keeping of the peace and observance of the law."

In April, the United Mine Workers withdrew organizers and financial assistance from Alabama. The strike had cost them over a million dollars, and the results were disastrous. The union was right back where it was in late 1908. Soon after UMW organizers left, thousands of unemployed miners and their families began suffering extreme hardships. "The situation is alarming," remarked a local Salvation Army official. "I was in one home yesterday where eight persons had nothing to eat for twenty-four hours . . . It is such situations as this that create anarchy and breed the dangerous bolshevism."[24]

Operators and business groups said the misery was exaggerated, and, in any event, "these miners were not locked out by their employers. Months ago they . . . abandoned their positions and struck." The governor agreed: "the United Mine Workers of America is responsible for the present strikers being without employment, and . . . should support" them. In private, Kilby ridiculed pleas for help.

Alabama's union officials organized a relief committee, chaired by Judge Fort and Louis Pizitz, a local department store owner whose business depended on workers more than industrialists. Unions planned a series of fundraising events, including Sunday movies at local theaters, but the city commission denied them a permit since it had enforced an absolute ban on Sunday movies since 1918. By May, only $2,000 had been raised, largely from other union halls, and only one hundred pounds of flour, meal, and bread had been donated.

"There is widespread destitution, especially among women and children," a reporter discovered after touring tent colonies left by the UMW in mining areas. He told of a white family of eight children. Only a boy of sixteen had found work. "He gets $12 a week in a mattress factory. That's all they have." In both black and white camps, "people were clean—poorly dressed, but neat. There was no squander, no careless disregard for person or house." And they all wanted to work, although many had given up hope and were trying to migrate north. "I have had hundreds of men coming to my store asking me if I know where they could get some work of any kind," Pizitz told reporters. In all, ten thousand miners were jobless, according to an U.S. Labor official, and fifty thousand men, women, and children were in need of immediate help, particularly food. Former miners who found work were fortunate to get ten cents an hour. Scabs and nonunion miners also found themselves victims of the labor dispute. Freed of unionism, with tacit approval from Governor Kilby, many coal operators reduced wages by 20 to 40 percent.[25]

The Birmingham to which Hugo Black and his new wife returned in late April 1921 was riddled with more than the lingering hardship and recriminations of a violent labor dispute. Two years after armistice, Alabamians—a little later than most Americans—were afflicted with a postwar depression of finances and community spirit. It was as if people had hoped war's sacrifices would sustain both common prosperity and one civic faith, only to discover that victory helped to defuse the economy and divide communities. Now, groups insisted that America could be found only in their own image. The nation seemed unable to live with its differences and unwilling to agree on societal values and morality, as the growth of cities, industries, and technology reordered life. If anything, each conflicting group saw itself more threatened than before by what they perceived as lawlessness, immorality, and others' un-American attitudes.

The Russian Revolution, with rhetoric of the rising working classes on another continent, sent chills down the spines of Alabama coal operators, mill owners, and manufacturers who condemned the labor movement at home as the revolution's un-American agent. Senator Underwood voiced this sentiment, and many of Birmingham's most prominent citizens agreed. One warned his fellow citizens not to be "flim-flammed by communistic propagandists posing as honest labor leaders." Fear of spreading Bolshevism, the new polar opposite of Americanism, motivated coal operators and wealthy Birmingham businessmen to raise more than $50,000 in February 1921 for starving children in central Europe at the border of the new Russian Republic. Ironically, the same fear motivated the same businessmen to ignore pleas for helping hungry, wretched children in Alabama coalfields just miles away.

Unions in Alabama saw themselves as keepers of a new Americanism and their enemies as the same giants that tried to slay workers in the Haymarket Riots of 1886. "It is for labor . . . to uphold America . . . Powerful corporations . . . attempt to destroy government of the people, for the people, and by the people by buying those whose duty it is to make and administer the law," labor leaders declared. "We have no gunmen employed. We are fighting for the ideals and principles of America." In December 1920 Alabama's AFL secretary had informed citizens in Anniston that miners would continue striking "until the Alabama Coal Operators recognize the rights of miners, the wives and little children *as Americans* and give to them the same things that miners, wives, and little children enjoy in every other coal field in America."

The "most stupendous struggle between organized labor and organized industry that Alabama has ever known" ended with industry's complete conquest within twelve months. But the war of ideals over what America was and should be and how far south the new America could extend merely shifted ground, as other organizations and leaders reemerged more visibly after the strike, searching for tactics, strategies, and rhetoric that would signify the new white ruling order. Prohibitionists continued to fight for their civic righteousness. Most suburban Baptist and Methodist congregations still wanted to end public dancing, and women's clubs worked to censor all films with corrupting or foreign features. After the 1917 elections, a new city commission not only banned Sunday movies but also appointed a city movie inspector who, with the assistance of the middle-class women's clubs, previewed for good taste all films at local theaters. The film inspector also tried to drum up support to censor photographs in Birmingham newspapers.

Anti-Catholic sentiment bled in Birmingham like a deep, open wound. Members of the True Americans continued to judge the city by its likeness to their own Protestant Americanism. The Reverend James Coyle of Birmingham's prosperous St. Paul's Catholic Church was a special target for public and private threats after the war, perhaps because of the priest's visible interest in Irish Catholic causes and his untiring literary responses to inarticulate anti-Catholic tirades. In a public exchange early in 1921, for example, Father Coyle dismissed with condescending literary flourish a local Protestant minister who charged that the "Jesuit is a creeping damn snake and like a snake should be shot." In private letters, threats on Coyle's life were even more personal and graphic.[26]

Americanism was also now the staple of Birmingham's chapters of the Ku Klux Klan. "The boast of the Klan is that no one is eligible to membership unless he is a 100 percent American," proclaimed a Kluxer press release. "It excludes all who have allegiance to some foreign country either by birth, church, or state." The Klan no longer mirrored only Reconstruction's imagery. It now claimed sixteen hundred Birmingham members as "best" Americans. According to the Imperial Wizard, "That the best class of citizens in Birmingham are connected with the Klan can be seen from the fact that . . . of the members in

Birmingham, two hundred are automobile owners." In other words, one in eight Klansmen could afford to own America's newest badge of upward mobility.

On the fifty-fourth anniversary of the birth of the original Klan, modern Kluxers returned to the city's fairgrounds, where the group had made its Birmingham debut in 1915, and where now a gigantic iron statue of the mythological Vulcan, symbol of Birmingham's steel-hard nature, stood guard. Ten thousand shrouded Klansmen from across the South formed a human cross with torches in their hands. As searchlights blazed, "Klan kandidates"—four abreast—marched to the front where a high cross of red and white electrical lights stood behind the Imperial Wizard. "Men who spend their days behind desks, men who work in steel plants, men who are employed in the stores of Birmingham all stood shoulder to shoulder and swore to protect the homes and to maintain the supremacy of the white race forever," observed a local reporter.

The Imperial Wizard assured Birmingham's public that the Klan promoted law and order. During the miners' strike, "people who have infringed on the rights of both white and black have sought to cast the blame for their lawless conduct on the Klan," Simmons complained. "I have offered a reward of $100 for the . . . conviction of any person who uses the name of the Ku Klux Klan in an unlawful . . . purpose or moment." No one apparently secured the Wizard's reward.[27]

These differing claims on postwar America absorbed communities across the nation, but struggles for defining Americanism in Birmingham and Alabama were forged from a common, special character after the end of the UMW strike. For at least the next forty years no broad interracial movement would emerge ever again in the heart of Dixie. Few would ever dare again to try to convince Alabama's white citizens or white society's controlling leaders to accept an American citizenship that openly upheld an ideal where "colored" and "white" shared the same "standard" as workers, persons, or citizens. In fact, this generation of Alabamians would rarely hear again a friend or neighbor echo the thunderous proclamation spoken from the steps of Clay County's courthouse thirty years earlier, and repeated before defeat by UMW's Jacob Kennamer: "Let us have," he told black and white workers, "an *equal justice to all.*"

In late 1921, no group had yet named the new Southern age or formulated a new public creed, but no movement among Alabama whites dared try to bring America's civic ideals to the South. Each sought hegemony through negotiating a sectional treaty that allowed the white South to secede from some American standards and embrace others, to merge Old South codes with new American ambitions. In supporting constitutional prohibition, for example, Southern dry leaders had overridden the cherished principle of state's rights, the region's bulwark doctrine against racial progress, but many continued to justify prohibition as a cornerstone for white supremacy. Prohibitionists and censors promoted their community restraints as both American and Southern, but their call for moral limits failed to address the Southern hunger for America's material wealth and individual opportunities. Censors may have seen themselves as protecting America's Christian values, but they ignored both the American Constitution and Southern working people's needs for more in life than self-denial.

The organization True Americans tapped an ancient hatred that seemed virtuous by some regional and national standards of Protestantism, but the subjugation of Catholics did not create a new America. Recent Kluxers had broadened the appeal of exclusion to "birth, church, or state" and combined the rhetoric of Americanism with Old South icons in a fraternal order of secret codes and hand signs. Their tent was certainly large and vacuous enough, but Colonel Simmons's jumbled images failed to capture white Southerners' essential American aspirations and to sustain the shared emotions that bind men in ways that common rituals only acknowledge.

Since the days of Henry Grady, for almost two generations, the South's white business and political leaders had been trying to form the region into a "New South" that would merge the Old South into full commerce with the new, more prosperous America. Yet, during World War I, Birmingham's industrialists were reminded that to have America in the South meant paying higher wages and dealing with a union of Negro and white miners. This was not an American New South they would accept. "We can't take the standards used . . . in Illinois, and West Virginia, and Indiana," explained DeBardeleben Coal's vice president after the strike. ". . . we have got to settle it . . . according to the standards of southern white people."

Senator Underwood, Alabama's spokesman for the business of a New South, tried to use Americanism as a campaign tool when he attacked labor's foreign, un-American ways. Yet, his appeal seemed hollow and was ineffectual until his campaign symbolized the unions as dangerously un-Southern. Similarly, industrialist bombast about un-American "bolshevist" labor unions fell largely on deaf ears until appeals to the Old South's racialism rallied decisive support to end the strike. After Birmingham's miners' strike, anyone who "misused" Negro workers with ideas of equality or independence was guilty of, and punishable for, being un-Southern—not so much "bolshevist" or un-American.

The triumph of capital over labor in the coal mines kept Southern white supremacy serving industrial needs on both sides of the Mason & Dixon line. It upended the most threatening version of Americanism in Alabama. But it also cast Birmingham industrialists into a public role as high priests of a separate South and denied them an opportunity to define Alabama's growing national-ism in ways that served their national business interests. In essence, Alabama industrialists had become captives of their own sectional contradictions. Un-derwood and industrialists condemned Northern agitators as un-American, while in truth Northern capitalists owned Birmingham's large industries. In conjuring up the horrors of biracial Reconstruction and beckoning Old South racialism, industrialists had become the major guardians of a Southern past that assured them of nothing more than a sectional future.

Even on these terms, even with the complete destruction of organized labor, Birmingham's big businesses did not have an assured preeminence in Alabama's white politics. As stark proof, at the end of the miners' strike, Black Belt planters, industrialists, and wets campaigned across Alabama for the adoption of a new state constitutional amendment. The changes would have given voter registrars in each county complete "discretion and judgement"—operative Old South terms which Justice Sayre invoked in Hugo Black's Miniard case—to decide if a person was of "good character" and understood "the duties and obligations of citizenship under a republican form of government" to qualify to vote.

Its proponents claimed this amendment was necessary as a "safety value" against the U.S. Constitution's Nineteenth Amendment enfranchising women. America's new high law did not distinguish between white and black women, and in Birmingham black women had attempted to register to vote. There-fore, Alabama needed "a law which will back up her registrars in refusing the right to vote in any case where one of the *vicious element* [black women] try to vote," proclaimed Jelks Cabaniss, Underwood's 1920 local campaign manager. America's Constitution now "has introduced into the electorate a mass of voters, the negro women of the state," warned former Governor Emmet O'Neal. "It . . . has threatened our future with peril it would be folly to ignore."

Alabama and Birmingham voters embraced folly. They defeated the proposal.

Perhaps voters were suspicious of corporate lawyers and "wet" politicians. Like their ancestors of the 1890s, some voters may have believed the change would disfranchise working-class whites as much as black women. Labor leaders clearly thought that industrialists sought to nullify their intensive work in registering union members. By whatever coalition of white interests, in a light turnout, Alabama voters said "no" to changes that industrialists claimed were essential in preventing a return of biracial Reconstruction.

In 1920–21, whatever the coming age, both the South and nation heard a peculiar, new battle cry: "Back to Christ, the Bible, and the Constitution!"[28] In secret fraternal halls and from pulpits, men proclaimed faith in a society ruled by Christ the Son and the Founding Fathers. Men and women continued a crusade to make all of America the land of the "dry" and home of the Protestant, and some industrial workers still hoped against hope that Christian or American standards could harness the South's corporate managers and their control of the economy. Most men did not seek conversion or reconciliation. They issued a battle cry against those who were foreign-born, non-Protestant, and anything but bone-dry Anglo-Saxon. This new, aggressive moral movement in Alabama and America had not yet molded its own character nor chosen its leading prophets, but the vows of a tragic mixed marriage soon marked one of its earliest victims and one of its more unlikely, transient heroes.

"ARE YOU SURE THAT THIS is Brother Stevenson?" Hugo Black shouted into the receiver as he struggled to hear the distant, crackling voice. Crampton Harris's Shakespearean, modulated words, usually unmistakably clear in every slow syllable, were faint and distorted on the phone line that connected the office of Black and Harris in Birmingham to the Glenwood Springs Hotel in Colorado where Black was vacationing.

Black was astonished. His law partner told him that the Methodist preacher, Brother Stevenson, had killed Father James Coyle on the streets of Birmingham. Friends of the Protestant minister were now on their way to his law office to ask Black to represent the accused, and the priest's Catholic friends were asking him to be a special prosecutor. Black knew the Reverend Stevenson as a respected pastor of the West End Methodist Church. He had trouble imagining why the preacher, whom he had known for several years, would have murdered the dean of St. Paul's Catholic Church.

Harris said all he knew at that moment was that the Methodist preacher had shot Coyle and his partner needed to decide whom the firm would represent. Black informed Harris to take the case for Stevenson since he did not relish the thought of his Methodist friend going to the gallows.

The news from Birmingham was troubling, but Black did not interrupt his last two weeks in Colorado. Five months after marriage, Hugo had taken his new bride on a second honeymoon. He wanted Josephine to meet his old friend, Barney Whatley, and on this second wedding trip Albert Lee Smith joined the party. Apparently, it was Black's idea of romance and friendship. Despite being a foursome, the new couple had a delightful time as they spent half their visit at Barney's mountain cabin and the remainder at the hotel in Glenwood Springs. They enjoyed mountain breezes near Barney's favorite fishing spot and the clean, hot air at the grand hotel, which offered hot pools, tennis, and golf. The newlyweds also enjoyed the tenderness of their own company, for it was here that they conceived their first child.

Yet, Hugo remained the student of self-improvement. Both Smith and Black were underweight again, and each tried to put on ten pounds. They stuffed themselves at every meal, napped in the afternoon, and snacked on a quart of milk and two raw eggs. Hugo also tried to improve his golf game with lessons. The instructor was a slow, deliberate man, a decided mismatch for Black's boundless, constant motion. "Woo, woo, woo, there, steady, steady, now," the instructor pleaded as Hugo impatiently jerked back his club in a quick, choppy swing. Black canceled the golf lessons and confined himself to tennis.[29]

Nestled in the Rocky Mountains, enjoying their new relationships, Hugo and Josephine were unaware that most of Birmingham was reliving the tragedy of another marriage. Father Coyle's death was much more than it seemed from Black's brief conversation with his partner who may have said far less about what he knew or suspected. The man accused of murdering the priest was not the Reverend Henry M. Stevenson of the West End Methodist Church, but the Reverend Edwin R. Stephenson, who had no church. The case did not involve a personal dispute between men of God. It was a tragic act amid a crazed religious warfare, a bizarre case of hatred that began with the strange fruit of love.

The case started on the morning of August 11, 1921, when a middle-aged man, Pedro Gussman, did not show up for work as a paperhanger. A Puerto Rican by birth, Gussman arrived in America at age twenty and had lived in the South and Birmingham for the last twenty-two years. A small man usually dressed in coveralls with a white cap pushed to the back of his head, Gussman was a widower about to take a second bride.

He met his fiancée, Ruth Stephenson, at a prearranged location in north Birmingham. They took a taxi to the Bessemer annex where a licensing office issued a marriage permit and to the rectory of a nearby Catholic church. When the priest failed to appear, the couple went to Birmingham's St. Paul's. They carefully approached the Cathedral since it stood next to the county courthouse, separated only by the rectory and a well-kept green hedge. Quietly, Ruth and Pedro waited in the church until Father Coyle arrived.

A man of average weight and height with a soft tender face often bearing a mischievous Irish smile, the Reverend Coyle read the couple's marriage certificate. The priest recognized Ruth by name. Six years earlier, as a girl of twelve, she had sat on his front porch asking to join the Catholic Church until her father rushed her home. Coyle knew that Ruth had renounced her Protestant faith last April and joined Our Lady of Sorrow Catholic Church. Calling his sister and housekeeper from the rectory to serve as witnesses, Father Coyle married the forty-two-year-old Puerto Rican and the eighteen-year-old converted Catholic in a simple ceremony.

As the couple slipped away to a local boarding house for their wedding night, the courthouse clock struck five. Mrs. Stephenson, Ruth's mother, heard the clock from next door—inside the sheriff's office at the courthouse. Since noon, when Ruth was discovered missing, the Reverend and Mrs. Stephenson had searched the city. The preacher feared Catholics had kidnapped his daughter. He requested city police chief J. T. Shirley to dispatch his men to watch all departing trains. Later, the preacher insisted city detectives search the convent at West End and other Catholic institutions. The minister left empty-handed, but his wife also called to beg for help.

By five o'clock, Mrs. Stephenson was pleading with the county sheriff, and her husband was wandering up and down streets stopping automobiles, asking drivers if they had seen his Ruth. Shortly after six, the Methodist preacher walked down the south side of Third Avenue north, passed Lige Long's mortuary, and headed towards the courthouse.

On the rectory porch, as day descended into dark, Father Coyle recognized Stephenson. Miss Coyle and the housekeeper were in the rear. From a distance, Coyle and Stephenson would have appeared only as blurred images if anyone saw them together. Suddenly, three gunshots were fired. Foot patrolmen looked eastward into the blackening air, and workingmen strained to see outside the lighted windows of shops and stores.

With a revolver in his hand, the Reverend Stephenson stepped down from the porch and walked through an opening in the hedge towards the courthouse. Men ran towards the church, and on the porch the housekeeper screamed, "Father Coyle has been shot!" Stephenson walked straight to the courthouse where he met a policeman, dropped the pistol, and was escorted to the county jail. "I want to be locked up," Stephenson stated. "He shot a man out here just now," the policeman explained.[30]

Outside the church rectory, small pools of Father Coyle's blood stained the porch; his parish cap remained in the swing. The priest had been rushed to St. Vincent's Hospital. Unconscious and vomiting, he died within an hour of a bullet wound that fractured his skull. Amid the crowd outside the church, a few men (perhaps from the Knights of Columbus lodge a few doors away) talked about lynching Stephenson. Most spectators stood in silence or whispering disbelief.

By the next afternoon, Friday, August 12, most Birmingham residents knew about Stephenson's actions. From the jail yard he spoke to reporters and posed for photographers. "They are telling things that are not true," protested the minister. "I am an ordained minister and have been since 1905." He did not have a church, however. He made a living as the marrying parson at the Jefferson County courthouse, and, before the shooting, he usually was found near the probate judge's office where couples obtained marriage licenses. Stephenson often approached a young white couple in the hallway. The preacher assisted them in getting a license and, afterwards, in the corridor—on the second floor near the end of the hall, using anyone at hand as witnesses—he conducted a brief marriage ceremony for a modest fee. Habitually dressed in severe black, carrying a cane for an injured foot, the marrying parson proudly told reporters that he had conducted more than eleven hundred marriages in the last two years.

Stephenson confirmed that he had asked Hugo Black to represent him at trial but remained mute on circumstances surrounding the killing. Others were not so taciturn. Reporters learned that circuit solicitor Joseph Tate had questioned the preacher in his jail cell during the evening. "It was purely a case of self-defense," Stephenson reportedly said. "I did not shoot until Father Coyle had struck me on the head twice and knocked me to my knees."

The dead priest's friends challenged the story. They stated that Coyle was an even-tempered man who never carried a weapon. He would not have struck the preacher twice with or without provocation. Local newspaper editors were equally unimpressed by claims of self-defense. "All Birmingham deplores the tragic death of Father James E. Coyle," wrote the *Birmingham Post* editor. "It was a terrible deed, shameful and apparently unexcusable, and the fact that it was committed by an itinerant minister makes it even more deplored by everyone." The *Birmingham News* said Coyle was "the victim of the political religious prejudice prevalent in Birmingham the last few years."

On Saturday, as Father Coyle lay in an open casket at the foot of St. Paul's chancery rail, Alabama's presiding Catholic bishop blamed the death on the enemies of Catholicism. "This terrible tragedy is the direct result of a miserable policy of self-seeking politicians," proclaimed Bishop Edward Allen before a congregation standing in the aisles and overflowing onto the church's steps. "The awful tragedy is the outcome of a spirit encouraged by a few politicians" and "secret societies that do not invoke American principles." Four years ago, the bishop said, "there came into this town mountebanks to attack the Catholic Church . . . These miscreants have been allowed to misrepresent the Catholic Church."

At Father Coyle's funeral on Sunday, thousands paid their final tribute to the Ireland-born priest who had graced Birmingham since 1905. "Now your good pastor is still in death and he is here in the church for the last time. But would you have Father Coyle change places with his murderer?" asked Mobile's Rev. Michael Henry in a broken voice. "The Catholic Church does not call for vengeance," he stated. "It preaches Christ and remembering his words, prays, 'Father, forgive them, for they know not what they do.'"

Stephenson's friends were not so certain Catholics would settle for forgiveness. "Professor" G. W. Davis, who ran a barber's college, stayed at the minister's home guarding Mrs. Stephenson while her husband was in the county jail's safety. Davis and other men had performed the same duty earlier in the year when Stephenson suspected Catholics were going to kidnap Ruth. These old and new friends, thankful that the minister had done "his part to help make Birmingham a safe place to live," volunteered to help Crampton Harris locate witnesses.

At home, Mrs. Stephenson worried about her daughter as much her husband. Ruth had failed to call after father was arrested. "There is no excuse for what he did," Ruth told reporters. "I do not care to see him after the deed he has committed." Ruth Stephenson Gussman was expected to be the chief witness against her father in what the newspapers billed as "a struggle between church vows and blood ties as dramatic as those around which history's greatest tragedies have been written." As for her own marriage, Ruth declared, "we are wonderfully happy."

On Monday, August 21, Ruth appeared before the grand jury and Joseph Tate. The jurymen were considering an indictment against Stephenson. "Did you ever hear him express his feelings towards Father Coyle or any of these priests," Tate asked Ruth Gussman.

"Yes, sir, all my life . . . He said that he hated them, that Catholicism was rotten," Ruth replied, "and I have heard my mother say, many a time, that she would like to set a bomb under St. Paul Cathedral." Ruth told the grand jury that she spoke with Father Coyle only twice in her life—once when she was married and six years earlier. No, she had never been pressured by any Catholic to join the church. "No one can persuade me to do anything that I don't want to do," she asserted.

"Do you know of his ever taking part in the lynching of anybody?" a juror asked.

"Yes, sir, he was one—actively, in the lynching of a negro in Cedartown, Georgia, in 1902."

"What was the negro lynched for?" the foreman asked.

"For assaulting a white girl," Ruth replied.

"He was doing a noble deed then, wasn't he?" one juror suggested. "He certainly was," another added in an Old South amen.

A third juror wanted to know about Gussman. "What nationality is your husband?" he asked. "He is Spanish," she replied. "Is he a full-blooded Italian, belong to the Caucasian race?" the juror persisted. "Yes!" Ruth replied.[31]

The Stephensons finally saw their daughter, almost two weeks after their frantic, tragic search. She appeared in court to testify for the prosecution at a preliminary hearing. Crampton Harris had rushed to hold a hearing before the grand jury returned an indictment so that he could see the case Tate had against his client. Ruth was the prosecution's last witness. Dressed in fashionable blue, with a matching hat, the witness avoided her mother's eyes and her father's stern gaze. It was her testimony the state intended to use to prove the murder was premeditated and punishable with hanging. "Several times my father said that he wished the whole Catholic institution was in hell," Ruth declared in a courtroom where every seat was taken and ropes bordered the hallway doors. "You'll be the cause of the deaths of Coyle, and Burke," she testified quoting her father. Burke was Ruth's Catholic godfather in whose house she had spent a few nights after joining the church in fear that "my father would kill me."

Crampton Harris was more interested in Ruth's conduct than his own client's. He asked Ruth about several incidents when her parents desperately tried to keep her out of the Catholic church. Ruth admitted that her parents promised to send her to a girls school if she would forego joining the Catholic church after reaching eighteen. "But they just promised and never made any steps really to send me to school," Ruth retorted.

Harris pried into Ruth's courtship with Pedro Gussman. She testified they had met when she was thirteen and, at that time, he asked her to marry him. Her acceptance of his offer came five years later in a letter she wrote to him during the late summer. "How many times had you seen Gussman before you wrote that letter telling him you had decided to marry him?" Harris demanded.

"Oh, it was sometime in the winter before."

"You mean to say," Harris dramatized, "that you had not seen or talked to him in all that time?" Ripples of laughter emerged from the audience.

Harris asked Ruth if she had ever gone to a public house with Pedro Gussman before she married him, but Ruth indignantly denied any premarital sex. She did admit Gussman had never paid a "social visit to her home."

"Isn't Pedro Gussman a Puerto Rican with very dark complexion?" Harris asked.

"No," Ruth stated. "He is a Spaniard."

"Can he speak good English?"

"Of course, he can," Ruth replied.

"Did you find it difficult to understand him when he proposed to you when you were thirteen years old?" Harris inquired. Ruth turned to the judge. "What can my love affair have to do with the killing?" she pleaded. The judge did not answer but ordered the defendant bound over to the grand jury.[32]

Two days later, in another bizarre twist, Pedro Gussman was arrested for murder. He was charged as a fugitive from Peoria, Illinois, where he was wanted for the murder of his wife. Apparently, Peoria's police chief had read wire stories of the Coyle case and wrote local authorities that he held a warrant for "one Pedro Gussman (Mexican)." While measured for vital statistics at police headquarters, reporters swarmed Gussman. "Are you guilty?" a reporter asked.

"Of course not. I was never in Peoria in my life," Gussman replied.

Describing Gussman standing in the Bertillon room, another reporter wrote: "He speaks English readily but with an accent and at times reporters had difficulty in understanding him. His complexion is not unusually dark and his features are finely chiseled in a Caucasian mold."

After police transferred Gussman to the county jail, sitting down the hallway from his new father-in-law, his new wife employed a lawyer to release him. "I love him and I'm going to stick to him thru thick and thin," she insisted. "I know he is innocent." Yet, it was not merely her husband's jeopardy she feared. On Friday, August 26, Ruth's lawyer filed suit seeking to prevent her from being committed to an insane asylum. The petition alleged local officials were on verge of charging her with an unsound mind in a longstanding conspiracy between her father and law officers to punish her for her Catholicism.

Developments in the case moved like a three-ring circus. Ruth's attorney revealed anonymous letters he received warning, "Remember tar and feathers." The police denied that they had any intention of committing Ruth to an asylum. Pedro Gussman was released from jail in a case of mistaken identity, but as soon as he rejoined Ruth, his new wife left him. In early September, Ruth packed her bags and caught a train north.

In a letter delivered to the local press by a girl friend, Ruth said she spoke to "gratify the curiosity of the so-called murder fans." "I left my husband because . . . the anti-Catholic faction in Birmingham, the True Americans, have bought him out; he has given his honor as a man for money, and has betrayed me to the enemy." She added: "He is expecting to testify . . . as a witness for the defense. He is going to swear that his marriage to me was the result of a carefully laid plan of mine and my father's, in order to give my father an excuse to kill Father Coyle . . . Now this is the work of the anti-Catholic faction in Birmingham," Ruth continued. "Words simply will not express my Scathing contempt for his actions and the actions of the 'True Americans' who are sponsoring him."[33]

Ruth's sudden departure coincided with Hugo Black's return from vacation. In their first meeting, Black took good news to his prospective client. The grand jury returned a second-degree murder indictment. Apparently, the charge was a compromise between those who thought that no indictment was necessary and others who argued for first-degree murder. The maximum penalty was life imprisonment. "We do not know just what course we will follow," Black told reporters on his way to meet Stephenson.

A defense committee was established, and petitions of support circulated around the state. On September 7, the day after meeting Stephenson, Black formally agreed to represent the minister at trial. He received a $500 check for the case—one half the total retainer—from the defense committee. The remaining amount was to be paid before the start of trial on October 17. Backers of the Stephenson Defense Committee preferred to remain anonymous, although its chairman denied the group was an anti-Catholic organization. "It seems that since Bishop Allen made the unwarranted statement that a certain society was responsible for the death of Priest Coyle the press has sought to make true his words by connecting that society with the defense of the minister," the spokesman stated. "This committee, which is several hundred strong, is composed of friends of the minister, who may or may not belong to the unions, honored societies, and fraternal orders of the city." Stephenson, nonetheless, understood the genesis of his public support and granted his only full interview to the editor of the *Menace*, a national anti-Catholic newspaper and favorite reading for True Americans.

With Ruth Gussman in hiding and her father in jail, Birmingham's "murder fans" were starved for daily reports for an entire month, except for a few days when they could speculate over the long lists of prospective witnesses. Hundreds of Birmingham citizens did receive a ghoulish moment of entertainment earlier, when two black convicts were publicly hanged. It was by modern standards a surreal public ceremony symbolizing both a white community's macabre mood and the era's coarse racial insensibilities. Thirty-five white women were escorted to reserved seats on the jailhouse balcony where they had a privileged, bird's-eye view. Fifty African-American harmony singers filled the jail yard with religious hymns about "over yonder," as the executioner placed a large hood over the head of Willie Morton, an African American (and perhaps the same man Hugo Black represented as a convict miner a decade earlier). Now, Morton was sentenced to die for highway robbery. The other condemned man was convicted of murdering a white man.

Having breakfasted on chicken and biscuits, his last earthly pleasure, Morton stood silently as the iron cuffs were placed around his hands and feet and the noose circled his neck. St. Paul's Cathedral cast long shadows creating sharp-edged shapes of light and darkness. Then, along with his companion, Morton dropped from the scaffolding in the presence of three hundred crowded guests and hundreds more who craned their necks to see the event from windows in surrounding office buildings. Reporters noted in detail how the two limp black bodies slowly twisted to stillness and the fact that none of the white spectators, man or woman, turned their faces away until all signs of life had left the dead. Despite warring differences on religion, white Birmingham still seemed quite at one with itself on the matters of law, order, and race.

In a more secluded ceremony, just two days before his trial, the Reverend Stephenson welcomed a young white couple into his jail cell where he conducted their marriage ceremony as deputy sheriffs acted as witnesses.[34] The couple had secured a marriage license as the courthouse was closing on Saturday and were unable to locate a judge or Protestant minister until someone told them that the marrying parson was in temporary residence in the county jail.

MORE THAN AN HOUR BEFORE the opening gavel on the morning of Monday, October 17, all seats outside the rail were occupied in Judge William Fort's courtroom. Most of those present were potential witnesses; between them, the prosecution and defense had summoned a total of more than 185 people. Mrs. Stephenson appeared a few minutes before ten o'clock and sat directly behind the defense table where she ceaselessly pulled at her handkerchief. When her husband was brought into court, wearing his dark suit, a high stiff collar, and no handcuffs, Mrs. Stephenson moved to his side and offered a gentle kiss.

"Ruth Gussman," called the clerk, as the routine of organizing a trial began in earnest. Twice more her name was called without answer. Pedro Gussman, the estranged husband, answered his call as a witness for both sides. "As his name was shouted," one reporter observed, "Mrs. Stephenson perceptibly started from her seat." After lengthy procedures, twelve men were left in the jury box after the defense eliminated thirty-four potential jurors and the prosecution struck seventeen.

Hugo Black told the jurors that "the defense is going to plead 'not guilty.'" In fact, Stephenson pled "not guilty" twice. His lawyer filed a new plea—"not guilty by reason of temporary insanity"—to supplement the earlier plea of self-defense. According to press reports, this second line of defense "would throw the gates wide open for introduction of testimony of the most varied nature" including testimony about Stephenson's "views on Catholicism, his alleged troubles with his daughter, his opposition to her marriage and the other things which, the defense may claim, caused him to become temporarily insane."[35]

Circuit solicitor Joseph Tate and three assistants began the trial by calling Father Coyle's attending physician. Dr. J. A. Mason described how one bullet entered the priest's head in front of the left ear and emerged at the back. He stated that no powder burns—usually found on victims shot at very close range—were discovered on Coyle's clothing. Miss Marcella Coyle, the dead priest's sister, was dressed in black with a long veil which she raised when she sat down in the witness chair. Miss Coyle told the jury that she heard no signs of an argument or struggle before the shots were fired killing her brother and that, when she arrived on the porch, all she saw was a "man standing up and my brother on the floor."

"Do you see the man in this courtroom?" the prosecutor asked. "Yes," replied the sister looking into Stephenson's face; his jaws moved constantly chewing a piece of gum.

Black established that Miss Coyle was in the kitchen, at the back of the rectory when the shots were fired. "Could there have been a little scuffle and noise out on the front porch . . . and you not heard it?" he asked. "Yes, I suppose so," Miss Coyle admitted.

With every seat taken, an officer stood at the courtroom's double doors to permit one spectator to enter only in the rare event of someone else leaving. Because Judge Fort didn't permit standing in the aisles, the overflowing crowd stood in the hallway with an occasional spectator pushing his nose against the glass window of the door to get a peek. At the end of the hall, little groups of cigarette-puffing men congregated on the iron steps or near windows as whispers of news about each witness's testimony was relayed down the hall.

Moving speedily, solicitors called W. D. Childs, a former miner who now lived in Indiana. Childs was an eyewitness to the killing. He and his brother-in-law, Edward McGinty, were standing in front of the courthouse when the first shot was fired. Childs testified that he turned and saw Stephenson shoot twice more. Repeating grand jury testimony, Childs said it "didn't look like there was any tussling at all," and that Coyle "kind of fell on his feet and under the swing. There won't any chairs or nothing out of his place," he stated. "I didn't see anything in the world lying close to Father Coyle, but some newspapers"—certainly no weapon.

On cross-examination, Black asked Childs about his own activities during the morning of August 11th. When the witness proved vague and uncertain,

Black pressed the witness to remember where he was a few minutes before the shooting. The witness could not. "Were you asleep? Were you drunk?" Black demanded.

"I had an eye open, all right," the witness shot back.

"Well, what was that eye looking at?" Black asked without getting a response.

Black wanted to know who paid Childs's expenses to return to Birmingham for the trial. "I paid my own fare," Childs insisted.

"Do you swear that no person promised to pay your expenses?" Black demanded.

"No, sir." responded Childs.

"Well then, who did?" Black demanded.

"The state promised to pay," the witness asserted, but he couldn't remember the person who guaranteed his refund. Yes, Childs stated in response to Black's last question, both he and his brother-in-law were Catholics.

On reexamination, in a baffling inquiry, the prosecutors asked Childs who had promised to pay his expenses—only to confirm again that the witness could not—or would not—remember the person's name.

Edward McGinty followed his brother-in-law and collaborated Childs's direct testimony. But under cross-examination McGinty also suffered from a poor recollection about everything except the shooting. "His knowledge of what he and Childs did on the morning of the shooting was as vague as that of Childs'," reported one observer. "He said he was 'all over town' . . . in answer to the defense's tangling questions . . . He didn't remember where he was exactly or what he was doing the next morning after the shooting."

With more than an hour before noon, the state called its fifth witness, J. F. Greer, the first person to arrive on the rectory porch after Miss Coyle screamed. "I saw Father Coyle stretched on the porch with his head against the wall and his feet under the swing. In the swing was a pile of magazines and papers, arranged in orderly manner with the priest's hat on top," he testified. Under defense questioning, Greer proved to have a better memory than the two eye-witnesses. He denied picking up anything—a gun or any other object—from the porch floor. When asked, Greer testified he had been attending St. Paul's since he was eleven years old.

As the witness came down, an assistant solicitor announced to universal surprise that "the state rests." The large clock on the wall showed that the prosecution had presented its main case in less than two hours—and most of that time had been used by Black for the defense in cross-examination.[36]

At two o'clock, after a long recess to assemble witnesses, Black began by calling three people to vouch for the defendant's good character and reputation. The fourth witness was a real estate salesman, J. W. Sellman, whose offices faced St. Paul's rectory. "I was sitting at the back end of the office, and I heard the shots . . . I went up to the front immediately and I looked up and down the streets . . . I didn't see anyone," Sellman swore. "Of course, I looked across the street first." Retelling his grand jury testimony, Sellman contradicted the state's eyewitnesses who claimed that they were standing near the rectory on the courthouse lawn. The day's final witness testified that Stephenson, sobbing, had told him often of his fears that his daughter was "being carried into the Catholic Church." After a long lawyers' dispute, Judge Fort allowed the witness to state that he thought Stephenson was "abnormal" on the day of the shooting.

Birmingham's evening papers carried detailed accounts of the first day's trial. One reporter wrote that the state's eyewitness, W. D. Childs, "made a very poor witness." Another found the state's quick conclusion of its case very curious. "The state had done nothing but to establish the fact that Father Coyle was killed by the defendant," a reporter noted. None of these comments, however, reached the jury. Sequestered at the Hillman Hotel, jurors were given newspapers carefully clipped of all references to the trial—little more than the comics page was left unshredded.

On the second day, Black and his defense team marched a host of witnesses before the jury to prop up the defendant's questionable reputation. Men as diverse in their occupations as the jurors themselves testified about Stephenson's good character. A railroad engineer said the defendant was a fine Christian man who cherished his family. A dentist said that Stephenson was an honest citizen, and a clerk vouched for the defendant's professional reputation. All eleven men, including the owner of a local laundry company and a circuit judge, vouched for Stephenson's good character.

Nine other witnesses, including two city detectives and Birmingham's federal commissioner, testified about Stephenson's obsessive fear of his daughter's interest in Catholicism and his "abnormal" behavior on the day of the killing. A Baptist minister remembered sending several young Protestant men to see Ruth at the request of her father, who feared his daughter wasn't associating with upright men. A barber who saw the defendant before the shooting said the preacher was "incoherent." The manager of a Jewish-owned department store testified that Stephenson was greatly agitated that afternoon.

City police chief T. J. Shirley gave the most detailed account. The chief recalled that, after Ruth joined the Catholic Church, her "father got down on his knees and begged the girl to return to him and her mother and give up the Catholic faith. He offered to place $1,000 to her credit on a checking account and get another house for her and her mother." On the day of Father Coyle's death, Shirley remembered, "Rev. Stephenson seemed very much excited. He told me the Catholics had taken her away . . . Each time he called he talked about the Catholics and seemed very much upset."

Throughout Black's questioning, prosecutors objected to testimony about Stephenson's erratic behavior. "There hasn't been a single witness who said this defendant was insane at any time," objected assistant solicitor John Morrow. Judge Fort, however, ruled that all testimony tending to show the defendant's mental state was relevant in light of a plea of insanity. Morrow also attempted to show that all defense witnesses were anti-Catholic or unreliably vague. He charged that Chief Shirley had an undue interest in Stephenson's problems because of the chief's own prejudice against Catholics, and he challenged the chief's statements about the defendant's mental condition. Shirley admitted Stephenson did not appear so abnormal or so crazy that he should have been restrained by police.[37]

Several officials who saw Stephenson shortly after the shooting were called to establish self-defense. The arresting officer stated that Stephenson's "collar was turned up. I noticed his belt was hanging down." The county physician who saw Stephenson in jail an hour before the killing testified, "I found a small knot on top of his head . . . It was about as large as a good-sized bird egg." The defendant also complained of an injured side although no marks or bruises were visible. Under prosecutor's questioning, the doctor admitted he could not tell when the bump occurred. He also said Stephenson at the time of his visit "was very nervous and excited but . . . rational."

The assistant coroner also saw Stephenson the night of the killing in the company of a deputy sheriff and Joseph Tate. The coroner testified that both Tate and he felt the knot on the defendant's head. At this point, a news reporter noted, "Hugo Black . . . charged that the state was endeavoring to keep quiet about such information which it considered detrimental to the prosecution."

In a lawyers' argument, which concluded the day, John Morrow admitted that he had never heard his boss Joseph Tate tell the accused he had a legal right to remain silent.

Sizing up the day's witnesses, a local reporter observed that "the defense had made little advance in its plea of temporary insanity" since "all witnesses to the conduct of Rev. Stephenson on the fatal afternoon refused to say point-blank that the minister was insane." Black perhaps agreed since he called the accused minister to the stand on the following day. The Reverend Edwin Stephenson gave his age, fifty-one, and said he had been an ordained Methodist minister for twenty-five years. He described his family including his only child, Ruth, whom he had tried to raise in a "Christian" environment. "Do you love her, Mr. Stephenson?" Black asked.

"Yes I do," the defendant replied firmly.

Ruth, however, had not been a child of joy. She ran away from home five times. Stephenson led the jury through the entire day of her last escape and onto the porch of St. Paul's rectory at dusk. "I just came in to see if you could help find my daughter," the minister recalled saying.

"I don't know anything about it," the Catholic priest reportedly replied.

"Well, I'm very much concerned." Stephenson recounted.

"But, I'm not," Coyle supposedly said. "... Besides don't you know your daughter ... is not subject to your orders. She belongs to the Catholic church." Coyle stepped into the house and quickly returned, according to Stephenson.

"She's still my daughter," Stephenson continued, recreating the dialogue. "... I have a right ... a claim on my own daughter's religion. She is under age."

"Yes, but a girl married, no matter what her age is, is not subject to her father," the priest replied. "Ruth is married and a Catholic."

"My girl is not married. She was not married when she left home," Stephenson remembered saying.

"Well, she's married now because I married her myself—today!" Coyle supposedly declared.

"To whom?" Stephenson responded.

"To Pedro Gussman, a Catholic," Stephenson remembered the priest stating.

Stephenson's low voice choked into a half-sob as he sat in the witness stand.

His body visibly trembled as tears welled into his eyes, according to reporters. He waited for composure before ending his story.

"To Pedro Gussman, a Catholic," repeated the Protestant preacher. "You have married her to that nigger!" Stephenson charged. "You have treated me like a dirty dog." Stephenson testified that the preacher "told me not to repeat that, and when I did, he called me a heretical bastard—and struck me. He hit me on the head, kicked me in the side, caught me by the belt, and made a motion toward his pocket. While I was on my knees . . . I fired." Stephenson's voice collapsed into a loud sob that he muffled in a handkerchief. The only other noise throughout the courtroom was the hum of the ceiling fans attacking October's late fit of heat.

"Bring in Pedro Gussman!" Hugo Black suddenly commanded.

As a deputy went to the witness room, one reporter noted that Black adjusted the courtroom shades to deflect any direct sun light "so that Gussman's complexion would be accentuated."

Another reporter chronicled Gussman's entrance as he walked to the rail near the center of the courtroom. "The man whom Attorney Black had previously referred to as 'a negro, dago, or a Puerto Rican,' looked around in wide-eyed amazement. Evidently he didn't understand what was wanted of him but he seemed perfectly willing to do as told." "After a moment Gussman turned as if to walk out again," reported a third newsman. "One of the jury men on the back row asked that he be brought closer and the bailiff escorted him in front of the jury box. For a full moment he stood there without speaking, and with each jury man staring at him."

"I just wanted the jury to see the man," stated Black as he sat down.

Assistant prosecutor John Morrow had plenty of questions for Stephenson. When Morrow asked about his "feeling towards the Catholic church," Stephenson replied, "I have no ill will against the Catholic church."

"Any ill will against the Catholics in general?" Morrow persisted. Stephenson hesitated, and Black objected successfully to the question.

"Is Pedro Gussman a negro?" Morrow asked.

"He impresses me as a negro," the defendant replied.

"Do you know for sure that he is a negro?" Morrow inquired. The witness hesitated and admitted he did not. The assistant solicitor vainly tried to have Stephenson admit that he shot Father Coyle without provocation. Stephenson refused to reenact the shooting for the prosecutors, but Morrow established that the defendant was alone in his jail cell for an hour before the knot on his head was seen by anyone else.

On redirect, Black returned to Joseph Tate's visit on the night of the shooting. The minister testified that the circuit solicitor told him that he must make some kind of statement. "No," Stephenson answered, the prosecutor never told him that his statement might be used against him or that he had a lawful right to remain silent.

Black's questions prompted Morrow to reexamine the defendant. Didn't Tate actually state "it was necessary for me to make an *investigation*?" Morrow asked.

No, the witness replied. He said, "It is necessary for you to make a statement."

Stalled, Morrow asked why Stephenson hadn't mentioned to anyone before today the vile name—"heretical bastard"—that he claimed Coyle used. In a sweet moment of lawyerish triumph, Black objected to the question and reminded prosecutors that, although they had disregarded his client's constitutional rights to remain silent in the jail cell, they must observe such rights in open court. Judge Fort agreed that the question demanded an explanation for the defendant's silence and encroached upon his constitutional right.

Black's insinuations drew blood. Abandoning his advisory role, Joseph Tate took charge and called deputy sheriff Fred McDuff who had joined Tate in the cell with Stephenson as the state's first rebuttal witness. Tate asked the deputy if he had heard anyone tell Stephenson on the night of August 11 that he must make a statement. The deputy testified "yes." He heard Tate make just such a remark to the defendant.

When Tate asked the witness to recreate the jail cell conversation he overheard, Black blocked the answers by pointing out that Tate was the best source for his own statements, but the solicitor wasn't under oath to tell the truth. Immediately, Tate swore himself in as a witness—only to meet another objection. Black argued the prosecutor should not be allowed to testify about any statements made by his client since the evidence now showed that Tate had violated his client's constitutional rights in the jail cell. After consulting law books, Judge Fort agreed. Tate's testimony would be improper. Therefore, the jury was left to consider only the deputy's sworn testimony: Tate had violated Stephenson's constitutional rights in the jail cell—as the preacher had testified.

Two witnesses called by the state to challenge the defendant's character proved equally unhelpful. Both said they would not believe Stephenson under oath, but Black's cross-questioning revealed that they had personal grudges against Stephenson. The defendant had fired one from a barbering job.[38]

The state called Pedro Gussman to the stand. "I was born in Puerto Rico," the witness remarked in answer to Joseph Tate's question about his birth. "My father and mother were born in Spain."

When Black rose for questioning, he handed Gussman a newspaper clipping and asked if it was his picture. "I want the jury to see this picture, taken before the witness had his hair worked on," the defense counsel stated. "You've had the curls rubbed from your hair since you had that picture taken," Black insisted.

"I have had nothing done to my hair," Gussman countered.

"When have you been to the barber shop?" Black demanded.

"I had my hair cut Monday," the witness admitted. Gussman confirmed he had never been to the Stephenson home to see Ruth, but he denied that he had seen her only by accident over the past five years. "I was looking to meet her," he insisted.

"Who got you to marry her?" Black demanded.

"I got myself," Gussman shot back.

"She stayed with you but a week?" Black noted. The witness sadly agreed before coming out of the witness chair.

The state's next rebuttal witness, Douglas White, met vehement objections before he reached the courtroom rail. Black charged that White could not testify since he was not called to the stand before prosecutors closed their main case. After the jury retired, prosecutors told Judge Fort that they expected White to prove from his own eyewitness account that Stephenson opened fire on the priest without saying a word as he stepped onto the porch. They suggested they did not know the witness would testify until after their main case was closed.

To ascertain the facts, Assistant Solicitor Jim Davis was sworn as a witness. Davis admitted that he discovered White the previous Saturday, two days before the trial began, and immediately notified John Morrow who led the investigation. The witness did not appear at the courthouse on Monday, as requested, but did arrive on Tuesday. "It is the general rule of the law that the State should put on the stand all available witnesses to the facts" before it rests its case, Judge

Fort observed. "The State may then have the right to put on *strictly rebuttal* evidence. Evidence which constitutes part of the main case cannot be put on by the State after the Defendant has rested his case, because that would be starting the case over. . .," Fort stated. "In the opening part of the trial this rule was called to the attention of the Counsel for the State and Defendant by the Court, who cautioned Counsel that the rule would be strictly carried out, unless either side had witnesses which could not be reached by subpoena or other process of law before the main testimony was completed."

Judge Fort expressed his regret that solicitors had failed to inform him of this key witness *before* closing its case—within two hours of opening statements—since they knew about the witness two days before trial. "The Counsel for the State did not show any further reason for not having put this witness on the stand at the proper time, so the Court denied the request," Fort remembered. White did not testify.

The defense also met disappointment. "Judge Black," as Birmingham papers continued to call the chief defense lawyer, wanted Mrs. Stephenson to testify about her daughter's erratic courtship in rebuttal to Gussman's claims. Such testimony, Tate protested, was new evidence, not a rebuttal of prior testimony. "Well, why did you put Gussman on the stand . . . ?" Black inquired.

"I didn't put him up for that purpose," Tate responded. "I wanted to prove that he was not a negro."

Judge Fort agreed Mrs. Stephenson could not return to the stand, and in this anticlimax both sides rested. The wall clock's hand struck four, just about the time Pedro and Ruth had entered St. Paul's Cathedral two months earlier. By prior agreement, deputy sheriffs immediately escorted jurors out of the courtroom and down the courthouse steps. For fifteen minutes, twelve men stood about the porch of St. Paul's rectory, looking at the swing where Father Coyle sat, touching the two bullet holes in the window shutters, and reenacting in their own minds those shadowed moments of August 11. During the inspection, a black-robed priest opened the rectory door and watched in silence as the jurors stood around. High above, the Cathedral's melodious bells solemnly announced a funeral underway next door in the large sanctuary, where a gray casket was encircled by a double row of flickering candles.[39]

At that moment, the institutions of church and state stumbled together like strangers. In guarding the sanctity of life, in the name of God, religion was performing the rituals of death, pacifying the living with assurances that a loved one's passing was only a transition into everlasting life. In contrast, in the name of justice, guardians of man's civic ceremonies were examining the details of death as the price for life, like an accountant who would not reconcile life's books without balancing the sums of each person's actions and motives. One ceremony revered the mystery of life. The other insisted upon a plain accounting of death. At that awkward meeting on the porch of St. Paul's rectory, God's law and man's justice did not seem to know each other.

"The Protestants are in the great majority in this community," proclaimed assistant solicitor John Morrow, standing before the reassembled jury of twelve Protestant men, "and the Catholics are in the minority. It is now in the hands of Protestants as to whether they will give Catholics decent treatment." Each side had two-and-a-half hours to argue the meaning of the evidence as the last day of trial began. Ironically, the prosecutors would spend almost twice as long before the jury arguing about the meaning of the evidence than they had in presenting their main case. John Morrow had the first words, and the last was an assignment that Joseph Tate took for himself.

After reviewing the state's case, Morrow turned to the defendant. "Can you doubt that this man is a cold-blooded murderer and that if you acquit him you will have turned loose one of the guiltiest men ever tried? He says he has no prejudice against the Catholics, but who on the jury believes that statement? The eyes of the whole world are on this jury today, and . . . they are waiting to see whether Southern men will permit religious prejudice to free a cold-blooded murderer . . . When you render your verdict, gentlemen," Morrow pleaded, waving towards St. Paul's Cathedral outside the windows, "be fair and just to those people. Do not try to persecute them by crucifying one of their priests in this courtroom."

The courtroom was packed to the walls since Judge Fort had permitted men to stand in the aisles to hear final arguments. During lunch almost no one moved. Some people brought their own food, and others purchased sandwiches from enterprising vendors. Those who stayed were treated to a dramatic intermission after the jury departed. Ruth Gussman appeared in the courtroom for the first time and, after hesitating, rushed to embrace her mother.

"Kiss me darling if you want to," Mrs. Stephenson whispered. Although she had been scheduled as a prosecution witness, Ruth turned and kissed her father who lingered with tears in his eyes. "My little girl," he murmured affectionately as he stroked her hand.

When Hugo Black stood for his final statement, the jury was unaware of Stephenson's reconciliation, which proved to be another of Ruth's passing fancies. "Judge Black declared that there should be no halo of glory around the heads of the solicitors because they had prosecuted the case," one reporter wrote, "though they seemed to think so judging from what they said in their speeches." Black told jurors they should not be interested in the eyes of the world. "I admit that there are certain localities where a verdict of guilty from this jury would be looked upon with favor," Black continued, "but those eyes have nothing to do with the evidence in the case."

Black reminded the jury that the state held the burden of proving beyond all reasonable doubt that the defendant was guilty of killing Father Coyle with malice and forethought—and without provocation or the affliction of temporary insanity. Black ridiculed the state's eyewitnesses; he called them "Siamese twins" whose testimony was perjured simply because two Catholic brothers believed their priest was a better man than Stephenson. "Because a man becomes a priest does not mean that he is divine," Black asserted. "He has no more right to protection than a Protestant minister. Who believes Ruth Stephenson has not been proselyted? A child of a Methodist does not suddenly depart from her religion unless someone had planted in her mind the seeds of influence," Black proclaimed.

Black stressed evidence showing that his client put a pistol in his pocket early in the morning before any thought of Father Coyle. Stephenson had searched desperately all day for his daughter and suddenly on the rector's porch discovered that Coyle had married her in a Catholic ceremony to Pedro Gussman, "a negro." Of course, Black said, the state had attempted to show that his client had no reason to consider Gussman a Negro. He was a Spaniard from Puerto Rico, the state insisted. If Gussman was "of proud Castilian descent," Black proclaimed, "he's descended a long way. There are twenty mulattos to every Negro in Puerto Rico."

"If the eyes of the world are upon the verdict of this jury," Black said expansively, "I would write that verdict in words that cannot be misunderstood, that the homes of the people of Birmingham cannot be touched. If that brings disgrace, God hasten the disgrace."

In a last appeal, Joseph Tate reminded the jury that the priest's clothes had no powder burns, which should have been there if Coyle had held the defendant's suspenders when he was shot. The solicitor emphasized that three shots, not one, were fired. At one point, Tate told the jury that Stephenson was indicted for *first-degree* murder, only to be interrupted and corrected by defense lawyers. It was second-degree murder. "If you . . . render a verdict of not guilty," Tate told jurors in conclusion, "you will have all the narrow-minded, fuzzy-necked people come and pat you on the back, but for the remainder of your lives you will have your conscience to prick and sting you."

Judge Fort instructed the jury on the law for more than an hour. Afterwards, the men took supper at the hotel and retired to the jury room where they began by reading selected Bible verses from a pocket edition, which one of them had carried throughout the trial. On bent knees, twelve white jurymen were led in prayer by the foreman, a local arms company cashier, who asked for divine guidance during their sequestered deliberations. At 9:45 PM, the jury knocked on their locked door and informed the bailiff they had reached a decision. Judge Fort and defense lawyers rushed back to the courtroom from their homes, although no prosecutor could be found. Under the dim lights of the courtroom, half shadows occupied more space than a handful of spectators who accidentally learned of the impending verdict.

Stephenson wiped away a tear when he heard the foreman's words. Mrs. Stephenson sobbed. On the first ballot, the jury had found the minister not guilty by reason of self-defense. A spectator shouted a "rebel yell" of triumph as he ran from the courtroom to spread the news. Judge Fort instructed deputies to arrest him. Fort thanked the jury for their service in rendering an honest decision. The defendant approached the jury box where he grasped the hand of each member as he filed out. "God bless you, sir," he said. Mrs. Stephenson touched each juror's hand.

A small crowd of friends later surrounded the preacher, as he extended his hand to Hugo Black. "I'll never forget; I'll never forget," he told his lawyer. "As long as I live I shall live to show to the world that your fight was right." A deputy sheriff drove Stephenson and his wife home. Within weeks, the marrying parson returned to the hallway of the courthouse where he resumed his work of joining men and women in holy union.[40]

NEAR AND FAR, IN TIME AND GEOGRAPHY, many were never convinced that the trial and verdict were right. "After reading the verdict rendered on yesterday," former Governor Emmett O'Neal informed University of Alabama alumni at a luncheon, "no thoughtful citizen could but feel that human life had become cheaper and less secure in Alabama. We have not advanced far from savagery or barbarism if murder is to be justified on account of the religious creed of the victim." Roy Percy wrote his uncle in Mississippi that True Americans had made it "open season" for killing Catholics in Birmingham, and a few national publications indicted the Stephenson trial as another case of bigotry in Alabama courts.

In time, the Stephenson case became a symbol of bigoted justice, a rigged jury, and an appeal to prejudice. Birmingham's white liberal poet John Beecher, a young man at the time of the trial, never forgot or forgave. More than a half century later, Beecher roared with condemnation of the Stephenson jury and Hugo Black "for racist conduct in the Father Coyle trial!" In the centennial history of St. Paul's parish, the church remembers that "the jury composed of a majority of Klansmen reached a verdict of not guilty." Years afterwards, in a Pulitzer-prize winning series, a Pittsburgh *Post-Gazette* reporter called the trial a "struggle between the Ku Klux Klan and the Catholic Church" and later claimed that the "jury was packed with Klansmen." For inclusion in a book on Catholic martyrs, Coyle's biography calls Stephenson an "ignorant licensed preacher" who was "acquitted in a mock trial managed by the Ku Klux."[41]

Part of this perception was created by the generous recollections of James Esdale who had become the new cyclops of a growing local Klan klavern at the time of the trial. "Hugo didn't have much trouble winning that verdict," the Klan leader quipped to one historian, more than forty years after the fact. Esdale reminisced that the foreman of the Stephenson jury was a Klansman. Apparently, the same year he told another local historian that Klansmen were a majority of the jury. Later in 1971, the former KKK leader recalled that the foreman of the grand jury was a brother-in-secret but later corrected his story by saying the foreman of the trial jury was a Klansman.

Over the decades separating the Stephenson trial and his reminiscences, Esdale, after a few years of political influence in Alabama, had dropped from the public eye. He was disbarred as a practicing lawyer and reduced to operating a bail bond office for petty offenders. When historians caught up with him, beginning in the 1960s, Esdale had every temptation to rebuild his self-esteem by remembering a past larger than life.[42]

No real evidence of Klan control exists for this trial from sources other than Esdale. One of the twelve jurors became an Alabama Klan official five years after the trial and, a decade later, one of Stephenson's character witnesses was a Kluxer in Virginia. In addition, at the time of the trial, some of Stephenson's lawyers and the Jefferson County sheriff were Kluxers. Black and Judge William Fort later became Klansmen. But, these are Klan connections over a period of several years, not evidence of Klan control in a public trial in 1921.[43]

The circumstances surrounding the trial discount claims of Klan control. In 1921, Birmingham's phenomenal Ku Klux growth was just beginning, and, in late January, Wizard Simmons had placed Birmingham's Kluxer membership at only 1,600 in a county of 310,000 people. It was the True Americans, not the Klansmen, whom contemporary observers and participants of the Stephenson trial saw lurking in the shadows. The TAs were the established anti-Catholic group operating a secret underworld of influence, but even they were not an all-pervasive, secret society that could easily fix a jury verdict in Alabama's largest county. Although True Americans had helped to elect an anti-Catholic city government in 1917, anti-Catholicism suffered political defeat in 1921. On the day the Stephenson trial began, in fact, Birmingham voters rejected an incumbent city commissioner's plea that a "candidate for the City Commission must not trade and traffic with the Catholic political machine." The incumbent was defeated and replaced by a moderate slate, including the first woman to sit on the city's governing board. Also elected was Bill Harrison, Alabama's AFL president and recent UMW organizer.[44]

This message at the polls may have encouraged prosecutors to make a conspicuous, direct appeal for the jury to see the case as a choice between religious prejudice and tolerance in Birmingham. If so, it was one of a long string of errors, possibly deliberate errors, on their part. Tate and his assistants did far more damage to the case against Stephenson than anything or anyone else.

The prosecution failed miserably to prove guilt beyond a reasonable doubt. The state offered very little solid evidence to impeach Stephenson's reputation or character in the eyes of working and middle-class jurors and failed to rebut the defendant's host of character witnesses. The prosecutors failed to dislodge the truthfulness of Stephenson's version of the killing. They presented no testimony about Father Coyle's personality or habits to establish that the priest kept no gun or weapon in the rectory and was a man with a mild, nonviolent temperament. Despite dozens of persons summoned for possible testimony, only five witnesses were called to the stand by the state in their main case, and all except the attending doctor were Catholics. The state's only two eyewitnesses to the shooting seemed uncertain or unconvincing after cross-examination.

The state lost its best eyewitness, who was probably Protestant, by offering him after both sides had rested their main case. A student in the first year of law school would have known that an eyewitness to an alleged murder should be presented in the main case and can't be used as a rebuttal witness. Tate and his assistants, however, closed their case without calling the witness and without asking permission to call him later. This conspicuous, stupid blunder—so clear that it appears more sabotage than error—forced Judge Fort to exclude the best eyewitness to the killing.

Other missteps by Tate and his assistants were equally puzzling and damaging. Knowing they did not promise to refund expenses for their own eyewitnesses, the prosecutors pursued that line of questioning, only to add credence to the implication that unnamed Catholics were paying Catholic witnesses to testify. In addition, a defense witness testified that he saw neither of the state's eyewitnesses near the church grounds. The state also failed to discredit defense testimony about Stephenson's disheveled clothing and his egg-sized bump, prime evidence of the defendant's reputed scuffle with Coyle. Prosecutors put nothing into evidence on that issue, except the doctor's statement about the absence of powder burns on Coyle's clothes. At the same time, Tate showed himself to be a fool and a liar by calling two of his own witnesses to contradict his version of events in the jail cell.

With these incredible mistakes, the jury was left to decide the credibility of the only testimony before them about the actual movements on the rectory porch—the defendant's testimony. To at least one reporter at the trial, Stephenson's testimony evoked deep sympathy, if not honesty. "If the emotion is genuine," the reporter commented after the accused left the stand, "you say to yourself, here is a man whose heart is being torn apart by grief; one who has already suffered mental anguish far worse than any punishment that laws and courts can inflict."[45]

Whenever the Stephenson trial has been recalled in modern times, Hugo Black is remembered often as an accomplice in a rigged act of injustice. In accounts years after the trial, too often based on a few excerpts and remembrances, Black has been accused of helping to free a guilty man by appealing to the blind bigotry of a jury whose members ignored the evidence. But, the case is more complicated in its details and more instructive about Birmingham society.

Black devised a legal strategy that assumed, accurately, that an Alabama jury of white men in 1921 could easily believe that a fundamentalist white

Methodist minister would go "crazy" if he discovered suddenly that his only daughter, who had flirted with Catholicism, converted and married a Negro man. Accusing a white man falsely of favoring "social equality" was slanderous in Alabama. In such a society, what would happen to a person's state of mind when he learned that his daughter had just been married to a "nigger" by the Catholic priest before him? In this defense, Black attempted to establish Pedro Gussman as a black man in the eyes of Stephenson and Birmingham's white society. It was a part of a plausible, legitimate defense.

If Black's methods in pursuing this defense offend modern sensibilities and standards, they were not outside the bounds of courtroom tactics during the early 1920s nor were they questioned at any time by prosecutors who failed to object even when Black pulled the courtroom blinds to darken Gussman's appearance. Black's dramatic display of Gussman as an exhibit rather than a witness was designed to convince the jury that Stephenson had good reason to consider his daughter's new husband a Negro, based upon his appearance. Black wanted the jury to see Gussman as Stephenson saw him. In a society sustained by the fear of interracial marriage, the use of Gussman's physical appearance was relevant, plausible, and potentially explosive in pursuing a claim of temporarily insanity—and merging it with a claim of self-defense.

In truth, Birmingham's best citizens had made Black's defense plausible during the last year and a half. Beginning with Oscar Underwood's 1920 campaign, using "social equality" to stab at the heart of opposing unions, Birmingham industrial leaders had stoked fear of interracial marriage as the ultimate horror. It was the industrialists and their lawyers who recently brightened the color line in the white mind as the sacred divide, a separation that preserved Southern civilization against the horrors of interracial labor union and an unspeakable sexual union of black men and white women. Labor leaders had been damned for permitting UMW's black vice president to dictate letters to white female secretaries. Industrialists had told and retold explosive rumors about the UMW promising black men carnal access to white women.

Former Governor Emmet O'Neal had condemned black folk as the "vicious element" which had to be contained by white men. Former Governor B. B. Comer had carried the insane fear of interracialism to its ultimate conclusion when he proclaimed that a gang of white soldiers was acting in "self-defense" by shooting a defenseless white UMW miner a dozen times at close range. By Comer's logic, soldiers were defending themselves and their state from a union that would return Alabama to the horrors of interracial rule and inter-racial marriage.

Yet, Black's own racial histrionics did far more than present evidence, cleverly providing a way to build deep sympathy and overall credibility for the accused and distrust of the victim. This defense permitted wide-ranging testimony about Stephenson's troubles with his daughter, whose interest in Catholicism was woven inextricably to its devilish effect upon her parents. In Alabama in 1921 were there many members of a white Protestant jury who would not wonder what kind of holy man would marry Stephenson's daughter to Gussman, be he "black, mulatto, or a descendant of Castilian blood"? These sympathies and doubts redounded to Stephenson's benefit, perhaps illegitimately, and brought forward any anti-Catholic prejudice the jurors might share.

Judge Black held his own deep suspicions about the Catholic Church, although he had Catholic friends and at least two were members of St. Paul's. Black believed that the Church was an opponent of spiritual and political democracy and prohibition, and these suspicions were evident in Black's choice of words for Catholics testifying against his client. It was, nevertheless, appropriate for Black as defense lawyer to ask a witness about his church and religion, when the victim was the church's spiritual leader, just as it would be for a lawyer to ask a witness of his lodge memberships or friendships. All were relevant in establishing a witness's loyalty, motive, and credibility.

Black used another weapon in his defense, one that may have been as powerful as the techniques that historians and critics have questioned. At clos-ing arguments, Black realized that the prosecution had proceeded on a clear assumption—that St. Paul's urbane Catholic priest was a better human being than the courthouse's marrying Protestant parson. As Black said, "Because a man becomes a priest does not mean that he is divine. He has no more right to protection than a Protestant minister." This argument asked jurors to give Stephenson as a Protestant every benefit of the doubt, but it also hinted that a struggling preacher who married poor white kids in the courthouse halls deserved equal standing, in jurors' eyes, with the priest of Birmingham's Percys and DeBardelebens.

It did not matter if "the eyes of the world" saw Coyle as one of Birmingham's best citizens, Black told the jury, it was the eyes of jurors, working white men, that should focus on the evidence to do justice for a struggling preacher. Solicitor Tate did more than his part in helping Black with this undercurrent when the prosecutor stupidly ended the trial by referring to "narrow-minded" bigots as "fuzzy-necked people"—a term like "rednecks" and "lint heads" used occasionally to disparage poor white folk in northern Alabama.

Birmingham's industrialists who sat in Father Coyle's church may have gained almost complete control of labor relations, but they did not control social and class relations. Their triumph did not mean that working whites, like the clerks, stenographer, meat cutter, and mechanic on the Stephenson jury, accepted their social assumptions about "best citizens" and "fuzzy necked" white folk. UMW officials did not speak for themselves alone when they observed, "We dare not even dream that the time will even come in the history of Alabama when these coal barons [and their priest] will ever consider that the white miners and their families are their social equals."

In Birmingham in late 1921, Stephenson's jurors also could not easily shed years of deep fear or distrust of Catholicism that surely entered the jury room with them. Their Protestant institutions and their various secular visions of America were so different in form and structure from those of the Catholics, as it had been in the old countries. The antagonisms of centuries had not ended simply because families—some escaping religious persecution—had moved with their faiths to a new continent two or three generations earlier.

By an accident of local history, fortressed with huge, towering arches, St. Paul's Cathedral stood next door to the Jefferson County courthouse, casting large morning shadows over the seat of government. It was a menacing symbol for continuing the ancient struggles of church and state, for Protestant fears of a Catholic Church scheming to annex the state as a creature of their faith. This religious division appeared in the rhetoric and results of most Birmingham elections of this era. Irving Engel had been a young, struggling Jewish lawyer in Birmingham in 1921. Decades later he recalled vividly the "fear and hatred that I saw as a result of three hundred years of religious warfare." Dr. Thomas Parke, more an agnostic than a Christian, recorded much the same impression in his own diary during the controversy over Coyle's death. "It is not difficult to comprehend," Parke wrote of Birmingham, "what went on in Europe several hundred years ago when people generally took seriously their varying religions."[46]

As best as any trial can be reconstructed decades later, a verdict of freedom for Stephenson could have been based entirely on the evidence presented in the courtroom. On solely the testimony in court, there appears to be "reasonable doubt" about what happened on that porch. While both jurors and the Birmingham public knew who killed Father Coyle and why Stephenson was willing to pull the trigger—Coyle was a Catholic priest who had married the defendant's daughter to a "nigger"—the factual evidence presented at trial, all that can be considered legitimately in an American courtroom, did not command a jury's verdict of guilty. By God's law, Edwin Stephenson clearly was not innocent, but by man's justice he was not clearly guilty.

Hugo Black represented his client exceedingly well, as attorneys are sworn to do, and he accepted the incompetent prosecution by Tate and his assistants. As an advocate for Stephenson, Black created the opportunity for jurors to justify their religious, racial, or class prejudices as well as to render an honest verdict, whichever helped his client. Judge Fort and the prosecution allowed Black ample freedom to pursue his dual defense.

The jury, however, was assisted in their verdict more by Joseph Tate's poor prosecution than by Hugo Black's effective defense. The lawyers who spent over two hours appealing to the jury to ascend above their Protestant prejudices spent less than half that time presenting the main evidence to prove guilt. Perhaps poet Robert Frost was correct when he once observed that a "jury consists of twelve persons chosen to decide who has the better lawyer." Stephenson's prosecutors botched this case in disingenuous, stupid ways that may have been deliberate and were fatal.

Although they could have been a part of the jury, Kluxers and True Americans did not have to invade the jury room with secret oaths and illegal allegiances to rig the Stephenson trial. Nor was the jurors' decision a direct product of an appeal by Hugo Black to religious or racial hatred. Far more likely, the Stephenson verdict was the consequence of a white society profoundly injured by its own racialism and deeply divided by class and religious differences. It was a verdict brought about by a half-hearted, half-witted prosecution that offered far too little evidence for twelve sequestered white men in 1921 to transcend stereotypes and fears that—in themselves and in their community—were as old and sacred as the Protestant Bible on which they relied for guidance.

9

'The Bottom of the Evil'

KLANSMEN, CONVICTS, AND CONVICTIONS

As a community, Birmingham was too young in late 1921 to brood long about its own character and, as the third largest city in Dixie, too respectful of Southern tradition to forego worshiping its own past. Within a week of Edwin Stephenson's acquittal, the jury verdict was all but forgotten by townspeople who thronged to greet the President of the United States. A reserved, distinguished-looking man, Warren G. Harding was accompanied from Washington by Senator Oscar W. Underwood who had invited his "affectionate friend" from Ohio to help honor the city on its fiftieth anniversary. The President was welcomed with exuberant Southern hospitality, as if he were a rebel general coming home to a hero's welcome rather than the leader of the Republican party which Birmingham and the white South had rejected in every presidential election since the city's founding.

It was a massive, lavish occasion, planned by the local Chamber of Commerce with long parades, loud bands, military regiments, Ziegfeld girls, a fashion show with New York models, and beauty queens from each of Alabama's sixty-seven counties. "Some are honored for their beauty," observed a local businessman, explaining why each queen was invited, "others for their wit, and some are truly representative of the counties from which they come." More than one hundred thousand people crowded the streets as endless lines of floats and soldiers passed the dignitaries' balcony at the Tutwiler Hotel, where everyone wanted to see Birmingham's most prestigious guest. "Hope the president doesn't spring a charley horse in his arm," quipped a reporter watching the continuous exchange of salutes with America's commander-in-chief.

The event attempted to recreate a sense of oneness among Birmingham's white residents, a facile instance of togetherness evident in the city's recent history only during the first days of war against Germany and, earlier, at the 1916 Confederate Reunion. Yet, unity in Birmingham was virtually impossible in late 1921, even for a day, and in this case the guest of honor surprisingly spoiled it. Laureled with oversized bouquets, an occasional "rebel yell," and elaborate, chivalrous toasts, the President had come South not merely to praise Birmingham's past but to lecture white citizens about its future.

Before a huge segregated crowd in Woodrow Wilson Park (recently renamed from the original Capital Park), Harding urged white Southerners to improve the condition of their black neighbors. "It is a matter of the keenest national concern that the South shall not be encouraged to make its colored population a vast reservoir of ignorance," the President stated. Harding favored equal educational opportunities for blacks and whites. "This does not mean that both would become equally educated within a generation or two generation or ten generations," he explained. "But there must be such education among the colored people as would enable them to develop their own leaders . . . who will inspire the race with proper ideals."

The President was quick to assure Southerners that he stood uncompromisingly against any suggestion of "social equality," because of "fundamental, inescapable and eternal differences of race." These physiological differences would assure a "natural segregation" where Negroes performed the "manual work of a workaday world." Yet, adding shock to surprise for his white audience, President Harding proclaimed, "I would say, let the black man vote when he is fit. Prohibit the white man voting when he is unfit." Met by "loud and lusty cheers" from Negro sections and stone silence from whites, Harding also supported a similar economic equality: "In each case, I would mean equality proportionate to the honest capabilities and desserts of the individual." These "readjustments" were necessary if Birmingham's industries and the South's agriculture were to prosper, the President insisted, for a future South will have "to compete for the services of the colored man."

"The one thing we must sedulously avoid," Harding cautioned, "is the development of group and class organization." Warning white residents against "the demagogues who would array class against class," often with alliances across racial lines, the Republican chief executive proclaimed his faith in the "idea of our oneness as Americans."

Despite his audience's shock, the President chose an apt setting for a discussion of race relations. In 1921, Birmingham had the largest percentage of black population among major American cities. It had the seventh largest number of black residents in the country, second only to New Orleans in the South. Approximately one out of every four blacks in industrial America's mines, rolling mills, and metal-producing furnaces lived and worked in Birmingham. It was the urban center of black population and heavy industry for the South and the nation.

According to the black press, Harding's speech was the first time "any President of the United States has devoted a formal address" to race relations, and its message elated most of his black listeners and numbed white Southerners. In the days before microphones, perhaps one in fifty in attendance was close enough actually to hear the President's voice in Woodrow Wilson Park. But as Harding delivered his remarks, visible horror rolled across the sea of white faces. At one point, the President departed from his prepared remarks and awkwardly stabbed a forefinger towards the white sections. "Whether you like it or not," he said defiantly, "unless our democracy is a lie, you must stand for that equality." When Harding concluded, white folks stood up jilted and silent.

The *Birmingham News* tried to put the best face on the incident. "The South will have no quarrel with President Harding upon his address," the paper insisted. Birmingham's white citizens were too busy "thinking and reflecting" on the President's speech to applaud. "It was a matter not for cheering, but for study," the *News* concluded in an example of Southern courtesy.

The nation's black leaders and newspapers were more honest. Marcus Garvey, leader of a growing nationalist, back-to-Africa movement, telegraphed his congratulations on the President's "splendid interpretation" of the race problem. Many other African Americans applauded the President's remarks about political and educational equality, although W. E. B. DuBois, editor of the NAACP's *Crisis* magazine, called Harding's comments on social inequality "inconceivably dangerous and undemocratic." Howard University's Kelly Miller wrote an open letter to the President declaring that his assertion of eternal racial differences assured that "the Negro would be degraded into an inferior caste which would render any form of equality impossible."

The President spoke more for the ambitions of Republicans and Northern capitalists than from any moral imperative for racial progress. In a major triumph of American presidential politics, Harding had won election by the largest landslide in political history and had lost only eleven states—all Southern—in the 1920 election. Even in the South he carried over 45 percent of the total vote. If a significant number of Negroes, solidly faithful to the party of Lincoln, could vote and a large number of poor whites, uniformly Democratic, were disfranchised in the South, Republicans could have an unprecedented chance for winning the region and creating an indomitable political machine.

Harding also echoed Henry Grady's vision of a "New South," articulated before a New York audience thirty-five years earlier. In 1921 the nation was enduring the worst labor strife since 1886, and President Harding wanted to reclaim an industrialist version of "Americanism" as the controlling, unifying terms for future Southern development. As Grady had in his speech, which Harding had applauded as a young Ohio editor, the President spoke for a future South that used Negroes as the "laboring population," grateful and dependent on the "employing and land-owning class" for education and jobs. It was a New South that "put business above politics."

This was, of course, the New South that U.S. Steel and other Birmingham industrialists were attempting to create through company towns, welfare capitalism, and related employment practices that treated Negroes more humanely—so long as they stayed away from biracial unions. It was the outlook of DeBardeleben Coal's vice president who had stated in 1921: "The salvation of the South depends upon its industrial welfare, and the chief factor in our industrial welfare is the negro."

Yet Harding's version of New South Americanism was too little, too late in Alabama. Industrialists already had destroyed the possibilities for this vision by hardening the die of racialism among the white population to win the battle against biracial unions. In conjuring up the Old South's worst demons, business leaders had magnified the white fear and black fury of "social equality" so liberally that any notion of racial equality seemed now to lead directly to the end of Southern white civilization. Even a modest proposal for token black voting, which the *News* and black editor Oscar Adams had endorsed eighteen months earlier, was now beyond local white comprehension.

Harding's call for political and economic equality between the races, separated by "eternal differences" that would always preserve "natural segregation" and prevent social equality, made absolutely no sense to white Birmingham. By the time President Harding arrived, the city's industrialists had ravaged not only most of Alabama's unionism but also their own vision for a New South.

Amid the ruins, the Old South's ghosts and rituals materialized anew. On the same day as Harding's speech, another emerging national leader addressed the city. From Atlanta's Imperial Palace, Kluxer chief William Simmons published an open letter in the *Birmingham News* condemning nationwide attempts "to lynch the Ku Klux Klan before it had a chance to defend itself." Aided by two masterful public relations agents and his new, energetic Alabama lieutenant, James Esdale, Simmons was rapidly enlarging Klan ranks throughout the country and Birmingham.

As unique testimony to the Klan's growing influence and a President's expansive political ethics, rumors circulated throughout America that Wizard Simmons recently had stood in the White House's Green Room before a kneeling Warren Harding who secretly took the oath making him the nation's first Kluxer President. The chief executive privately dismissed such rumors but refused to deny them publicly. Harding also was reluctant to openly criticize the Klan.

In all likelihood, the President was trying to play everyone's political tune. As the White House let rumors of Harding's Klan affiliation ooze about the nation, U.S. Attorney General Harry Daugherty, Harding's former campaign manager, launched a Klan investigation in cooperation with Congressional Republicans in Northern districts where immigrant populations voted in large numbers. The Imperial Wizard played his part by mounting a public relations campaign to deny allegations of Klan violence and turning Washington's investigations into an ad blitz for Ku Kluxism.

On the day Harding arrived in Alabama, the state legislature reneged on a promise to end the state's convict leasing by 1922. More than any other aspect of the New South, convict leasing came closest to reinventing slavery. Since the Civil War's end, the South had used the criminal justice system as a primary means for controlling and profiting from black labor. The leasing of more than a thousand convicts—almost all African Americans—primarily to mine operators around Birmingham remained the worst daily example of the enduring Old South traditions. Governor Thomas Kilby and state legislators decided that convict leasing remained financially necessary to a modern Alabama and prolonged the system until 1924 or beyond.

Also, as President Harding traveled to Birmingham, the state government announced a decision more obscure but no less representative of Old South mores. The Alabama Supreme Court ruled that John Brown, a black convict injured in a local mining accident, was a nonperson in the eyes of the law. Brown was serving a life term and, like his slave ancestors, was now denied by law the right to appear in court to testify in a case concerning his own injuries and interests. The Supreme Court upheld an Alabama statute ordaining inmates under life sentences as "civilly dead."[1]

John Brown and many other convicts leased to Alabama coal operators were Hugo Black's clients. Brown had been convicted of robbery in 1909. He had lived largely underground as a convict miner for more than ten years until he was "severely burned and charred" over most of his body in a major accident at the Montevallo Mining Company's Aldrich mine, now worked exclusively by convict labor. After Black sued the company for gross negligence, the state refused to transfer Brown to Birmingham to testify in his own case.

Before Alabama's appellate courts, Black challenged the practice and law declaring Brown "civilly dead" since the Alabama Constitution guaranteed all persons access to the courts. "A sentence of life imprisonment was not intended to prevent a man receiving personal injuries from going into a court of justice to sue the wrongdoer," Black informed the court. "Although John Brown has been sentenced to the penitentiary for life, although he has been leased or hired by the State to the Montevallo Mining Company . . . he has not ceased to be a human being and a person."

The state responded that Black would "wreck the convict system" by giving prisoners a "vacation" from hard labor through tenuous or fabricated lawsuits. According to the state's attorneys, these "vacations" would disrupt mining operations and send the state's revenues into a free fall since the government received no money when prisoners were in court and not in the mines.

Black responded, "Shall there be no guarantee that the Montevallo Mining Company shall reasonably provide a safe place for John Brown and other convicts to work?" He warned that without equal access to courts, "lifer" convicts would be helpless to protect themselves against any horrible treatment or condition.

"It is conceded that the penitentiary or the coal mine is not a pleasure ground for convicts," Black stated, but "neither can it be conceded that they are revengeful hells . . . It was not the intentions of the makers of the constitution of Alabama, and it is not the crystallized opinion of the people of Alabama that such conditions exist." It was, however, the unanimous opinion of the Alabama Supreme Court. John Brown was civilly dead.

The court's opinion affected only prisoners with life terms, but it also returned Alabama law to the enslavement of human beings by permanently stripping them of the rights of legal existence, especially the right to speak and act on their own behalf. Black men in Alabama faced a real, daily danger of imprisonment for a wide range of offenses, including robbery, which could send them to prison for life—and now render them "civilly dead." "If the verdict of the court stands," Black worried, "no convict will be able to obtain a fair trial." Apparently, Black feared the opinion would spur the legislature or courts to widen the application of "civilly dead" to other prisoners.

State courts had often been blunt instruments of racial domination and were at best a deeply flawed institution, but they also were the last battered sanctuaries of democracy for black Alabamians. Since the turn of the century, black citizens had been denied the right to vote in a white-controlled government and the right to organize in the workplace. The U.S. Supreme Court had held that federal courts possessed little or no jurisdiction over most aspects of life and liberty in Alabama, except when corporate lawyers wanted to remove a case from state courts. Black citizens also could not hold positions of decision-making as judge or juror in Alabama's federal or state courts. In late 1921, however, Alabama's black citizens still had a *right* to be heard in state courts to protect their person, property, liberty, and interests. Racialism and Southern customs diminished this right, but, as a practical matter, it made Alabama's courts the sole, surviving democratic forum where African Americans could petition government for redress.

Making good on this right of access was a formidable challenge, mastered only by practitioners and plaintiffs who could convince a judge or jury of twelve ordinary white men to balance the scales of justice for black folk using the various weights of bigotry, history, expediency, self-interest, and high principle. With persistence and shrewdness, Hugo Black was one of these practitioners who proceeded—and often succeeded—in state court with the cases and causes of black clients. Black's lawsuit on behalf of Sam Bradford, a free black miner, was a case in point. Beginning in 1914, Black litigated the case through seven years, two trials, and two appeals. On the first appeal, the Alabama Supreme Court had reversed the award. The court said Bradford was partially at fault for his injury since he knowingly stayed in an unsafe mine. The opinion ignored the fact that Bradford continued to work only because his white supervisor threatened to fire him if he left.

In 1921, Black represented Bradford at a second jury trial against the Clinton Mining Company and its attorney Borden Burr. At the start, Black deftly identified a large, out-of-state insurance company as the practical defendant. Black announced to prospective jurors that he wanted to question them "as to whether they had any connection with Georgia Casualty Company, on the grounds that the defendant had a policy with them at the time of the accident." Afterwards, Black began his case with a white doctor who described himself as Bradford's "family physician," an indirect voucher for the plaintiff's good relations with the white community. The doctor described in detail Bradford's painful condition after the accident, including two months in the hospital on opiate, and he assured the white jury that such injuries, even among Negroes, were "much more of a shock to a man of the plaintiff's age than a younger man."

Black also used testimony from another black miner and a white former "timber boss," a former "company man" responsible for propping up ceiling rocks to prevent their fall. Both told jurors that Clinton Mining had skimped on safety. Bradford completed his own case by testifying about his accident and retelling how the company failed to heed his pleas for more timber to support the mine's ceiling.

In cross-examining Black's witnesses, Burr worked the color line. In contrast to Black, who always referred to his client as "the plaintiff," Burr called Bradford "Sam" while he alluded to white men by their last name with a customary title of "Mr." or "Dr." Burr tried to depict Bradford as a black man who didn't trust white people. He dwelled on the fact that Bradford insisted that he should be taken to "colored hospital" after his accident. In addition, Burr attempted to prove that the African American was lying about being as old as fifty-five to sixty. Bradford admitted that he "didn't know exactly how old he was" but "they" had told him that he was "born along slavery times."

Burr's affirmative defense involved the testimony of five white men. He called a mining inspector from U.S. Steel's T.C.I. mines (another of Burr's clients) who said Clinton's timber props were standard practice which his own company followed. In cross-examination, Black went for the jugular vein. "There are a few people that get killed down in the Tennessee Company's mines by not having those props closer?" Black suggested. Over Burr's objections, the engineer admitted people were killed in U.S. Steel's T.C.I. mines due to the same problems.

Burr's second witness, a white mining engineer, swore that Clinton Mining's practices were safe, but he, too, admitted under Black's questioning that men had been killed each year in local mines using industry standards. Next, Clinton's timber boss testified that the ceiling props around Bradford had been adequate, but admitted that he didn't "know anything about the money part" when Black later asked "if money was the reason" the company did not construct more props. Burr called Bradford's supervisor and the mine's superintendent who testified that Bradford's injury was due to his own mining mistakes, not improper timber props.

In arguments to the jury, Black indicted the entire mining industry which was willing for men—he need not say both black and white men—to die or be permanently disabled, unable to support their own families, because mining companies wanted to save money on timber props. It was an unnecessary sacrifice of life and livelihood by the American mining industry, Black contended. "The conditions in Germany are such," Black said, "that their loss from injuries have been reduced to one-half what they are in this country" because of German mining safeguards.

Originally, Clinton's insurance company offered to settle the case for $100. Later, they rejected an offer to settle for $750. After the first verdict, the company refused to settle for $1,500 but authorized Burr to offer $900. A jury "of lawful and good men," twelve white men, returned a verdict of $3,500 dollars for Sam Bradford in his second trial.

A few weeks after President Harding's speech, Black and Harris tried another case in state court on behalf of a black worker who had been injured at an ore mine. Woodruff Iron Company's lawyers also argued the plaintiff was guilty of contributory negligence by being at a dangerous place of work. This line of corporate defense was based on a legal fiction—that each worker had a right to contract for work wherever they wished (so long as there was no union contract). By choosing to stay in an unsafe mine, therefore, a worker shared responsibility for his own injury. Yet, Black's clients knew that they had no real freedom of choice. Thousands of unemployed whites and blacks from all over Alabama and elsewhere were ready to take their jobs. And more convict miners were also available for lease.

As in Sam Bradford's case, Black and Harris had to overcome white misconceptions to demonstrate the impact of an injury to a black man. "Doctor," Crampton Harris addressed a white physician on the stand, "which recovers more easily from an injury, an old negro man sixty years old or a young negro?" The answer was obvious to the doctor who said the sixty-two-year-old black man could not work again. However, the doctor had not seen his patient in two years, and his recollections of the black miner's injuries and recuperation were now vague.

Dan Thompson, the plaintiff, was the case's only other witness. By his own testimony, Thompson was not a miner, merely a handyman who made "the fires for the scale boss" and other white men in the "big office." Thompson had swept floors and picked up loose ore scraps that fell off the "dumps" coming out of the mines. The plaintiff was injured when a locomotive struck a rail car where he was perched, pitching in scraps. Thompson admitted in court that he never held a job for long and had worked at Woodward for only five months.

Thompson portrayed himself as an old, poor black man who accepted his place along the color line in Southern society. He suggested that his injury had been a deliberate act of the company engineer. In testimony, the plaintiff was always deferential to all whites, calling the defense lawyer "Colonel" and the company doctor who botched the stitching of his wounds a "white gentleman." Thompson's testimony was both artfully self-deprecating and truth-affirming. With pride, he volunteered that the mine's white folks had nicknamed him "Friday," and when a one-horse hearse with wooden stretchers arrived after the accident, Thompson testified, "They reported I was dead . . . came after a dead man they said." But, he added, "The court can see they were wrong about that." Thompson boasted to the jurors, "I could do anything before I got hurt . . . There wasn't no nigger as stout as I was before I got hurt."

Woodruff's lawyers decided not to put on a single witness after Black and Harris rested their case. Outside the jury's hearing, the trial judge scolded the plaintiff's lawyers for bringing the case to trial. Like the mining company attorneys, the judge saw the frivolous claim of a shiftless old black man who had no white man to vouch for his character or word.

When the jury retired, the only evidence about the accident was Thompson's own testimony that "there wasn't anything neither way to keep anybody up the track from seeing me," when the white engineer plowed his locomotive into the dump car where the black man was balanced. Accordingly, twelve white men whose own jobs ranged from laborer and shopkeeper to accountant returned a verdict of $2,500 for the black handyman.[2] In finding another instance of corporate negligence and arrogance, white jurors in state court decided to take the poor black man's testimony as a *person's* credible proof of wrongdoing, a consideration which both company lawyers and the trial judge found inconceivable.

In these and other cases, Black took the law and the jurymen where he found them. His methods of pursuing justice for black clients didn't involve confronting white men with the insanity of society's dwarfed morality or their own profoundly crude racialist views. In these cases, Black and his clients made no attempts to preach for "equal rights" or the rights of "a human being and a person," although those were the verdicts they sought. Self-righteous indignation or lofty appeals for racial justice by the plaintiff or his counsel did not win verdicts. Instead, lawyer Black and his black clients helped Southern white men to understand how injustices and injuries to African Americans jeopardized their own white community.

In the Bradford case, Black convinced the jury that the mining industry operated with dubious, cheap standards of safety that needlessly jeopardized all miners. Without saying as much, Black provided white jurors with an Alabama logic that removed any resistance to awarding a black man substantial damages against an Alabama corporation owned by Alabama-born white men: he revealed that the money would come from the coffers of an out-of-state insurance company.

In the Thompson case, white jurors probably developed sympathy for an old black man, an "Uncle" who knew his place and plight, and the plaintiff exhibited remarkable cunning in appealing to jurors' racist sympathies and better human nature. But, in this era of rigid white supremacy, white compassion for black misfortune rarely led to justice. Knowing this, the Woodward Iron lawyers in effect asked white jurors to ignore the rule of law that confined them to considering only the case's evidence. The defendants' failure to present witnesses was an act of corporate arrogance that assumed white jurors would violate their sworn duty in a "court of justice." The jurors refused to be treated in court like a black handyman and, as a result, rewarded just such a man with a fair verdict.

Hugo Black understood better than most lawyers that, when searching for justice, Birmingham's ordinary white men put themselves into the judgments they rendered. They could consider evidence and relationships beyond the color line if they saw how their verdict affirmed important standards touching the lives of friends, neighbors, and themselves. This formula was far from equal treatment under law, but it made access to the "courts of justice" vital to black folks' survival around Birmingham. This approach relied on white justice, but not Old South ethics. It reflected a parochial Alabama logic, which Black occasionally dressed up as "Alabama citizenship." But it kept alive traditions of common democracy, fairness, and individual worth that could ignore the color line as a matter of justice and self-interest, even as those values were under heavy assault by the revival of Old South morals and a New South's colonial economy.

None of Black's understanding or lawyering skills nor a chance to beguile white jurors with his own testimony was now available to John Brown and others who worked Birmingham's convict mines under life sentences. Yet, convicts not serving life terms also had been injured in the same accident at Aldrich mine. The Alabama Supreme Court had not blocked these men from filing suit or testifying on their own behalf, and several of their names appeared in Black's office files in cases against the Montevallo Mining Company.

Among the state's oldest, Montevallo's Aldrich mine had supplied raw materials for foundries in Selma where many of the Confederate cannons were manufactured. After the war, John Aldrich began Alabama's modern mining industry at Montevallo. In the early twentieth century, free blacks and whites worked the coal mine bearing Aldrich's name until a dispute arose over terms of a new contract. When the UMW threatened to strike, Montevallo fired free miners and leased more than one hundred and fifty state convicts, all African Americans. Union officials protested futilely that "whenever there are differences between miners and operators, convicts have been introduced." In 1917, Montevallo was the third-largest user of convict labor in the state. By 1920, Montevallo's caverns were the most dangerous in Alabama. Men crawled around on their stomachs and backs to mine the Aldrich coal, which was of rich quality despite its softness. Recently, influenza had killed twenty-three convicts at Aldrich before sufficient medical precautions were instituted. Aldrich's rate of death and injury was reportedly five times higher than the rate for free miners.

Henry Lewis, a leased convict, became an Aldrich accident statistic in September 1920, when the mine's roof collapsed, belching stones, explosive gases, and fire from the earth's private parts. Lewis's leg and foot were crushed, leaving him permanently crippled. Along with others, he sued the company in state court for negligence. It was, however, in federal court where Black prosecuted the case for Lewis and several other prisoners in November 1921. Each convict had sued for more than $3,000 in damages, and, while Montevallo Mining was owned and operated principally by men living in the Birmingham area, a parent corporation had been chartered in Delaware where it maintained a mailing address (probably along with a multitude of other corporations in a lawyer's office). On the basis of this legal residency in another state, company attorneys successfully argued that "the controversy in said suit is between *citizens* of different states" and should be transferred to federal court.

In other words, because the U.S. Supreme Court had decided in 1886 that a corporation was a "person" or citizen (actually the ruling meant white person) with individual rights under the Constitution, Montevallo's Delaware mailing address permitted it to escape state court for the federal court's more protective environment. This was a common legal maneuver in 1921, but its routine occurrence obscured an extraordinary irony about the complexity of race and class in Birmingham. At the end of 1921, virtually the only white group in Birmingham who applauded President Harding's call for greater political and economic equality for Southern Negroes was the city's best citizens, including leading industrialists. Yet, when their companies stood as persons in a courtroom, with both money and state law already in their favor, industrialists feared that ordinary white citizens on state court juries were overly generous or biased in favor of indigent black claimants.

Henry Lewis's case was presented before U.S. District Judge W. I. Grubb, who had been the lawyer opposing Black in Willie Morton's mining case in 1909. Black could have requested a federal jury, but he took his chances with Judge Grubb. Because Lewis was an illiterate pauper—able only to make his distinctive "X" as a signature on the affidavit—Judge Grubb permitted Hugo Black to summon witnesses without covering the usual court cost.

Absent a jury to persuade, Black presented his case in a straightforward, economical manner. Witnesses established the cause of the fallen rocks and the extent of Lewis's injury. Because Lewis had not been free to leave the mines, Black didn't have to rebut a defense of contributory negligence. He did put on evidence tending to show that the company had failed to place customary props in the mines to hold up the roof. On November 29, Judge Grubb awarded Henry Lewis $4,000.[3]

Judge Grubb's decision was unique. In 1921 only a trial judge in Alabama could hear a case involving a convict miner. All other states in the nation had outlawed the leasing of state prisoners to private companies. In Alabama the convict lease system had survived since the end of the Civil War when federal troops destroyed the state's prison (which Confederates had used as a munitions factory). In 1866, Alabama's Whig Governor Robert Patton leased convicts to a hidden subsidiary of the Alabama and Chattanooga Railroad for $5 and provided a state loan of $15,000 to feed and house them. Less than three years later, the governor became president of the same railroad that never repaid the state loan.

After Reconstruction, Alabama and other Southern states used convicts in lieu of slave labor for building new industries. Black men by the thousands were jailed for serious or petty offenses and sent from county and state prison into Southern marshes, swamps, and forests to lay railroad tracks and cut virgin lumber. Many were also sent into the mines. Alabama leased its entire prison population for a monthly fee of around five dollars per man.

"Most of these poor devils were from rural counties and didn't know the inside of a mine," observed one prison reformer. Yet they quickly adapted or died. Except on the Sabbath, convicts worked from before sunrise until after dark, and worked standing barefoot, summer and winter, in pools of chilly water inside the mines. "We would leave the cells at three o'clock AM and return at eight o'clock PM going the distance of three miles in rain and snow . . . we go to cell wet and arise wet," recalled one. "Day after day we looked death in the face & was afraid to speak." In 1873, 13 percent of Alabama's convicts died in mines while the state realized an income of a few thousand dollars.

In the face of extraordinary death rates, state officials blamed the prisoners. Alabama's prison warden explained that many convicts entered the mines with diseases and sickness and died from problems unrelated to a mine's hardships and conditions. "When a nigger gets down," explained a prison official, "he has no come-back" to survive illness. The state's own statistics told another story. Most causes of death among convicts were tuberculosis, pneumonia, diarrhea, and accidents—consequences of the mines' damp, dusty, and hazardous conditions. Other convict fatalities were attributed to "dirt eating" or "masturbation," reports that reflected not only a cover-up but also a corrupt imagination about sin and sex among poor whites and blacks.

In 1881, John H. Bankhead, Sr., became Alabama's prison warden. Trumpeting reform, Bankhead used lawsuits and threats of exposure to renegotiate state leases. Two years later, with Bankhead's blessing, Alabama largest mining operators met in a Birmingham hotel and divided convict laborers among themselves. The state's new contracts increased revenues and concentrated convicts in larger mines, primarily those owned by Pratt Mining Company. The prison warden promised that state inspectors would improve dangerous mines, but new leases were transacted only for added money and profits. The numbers of leased convicts rose from fifteen hundred to seven thousand, and Alabama's convict revenues enlarged tenfold within a decade. Working conditions and death rates remained much the same.

On a state salary of $2,000, Warden Bankhead began creating a political dynasty and family fortune. One former state official investigated the convict department and discovered obvious corruption. "How can the Governor fail to cause proceedings to be instituted at once [against Bankhead]?" he asked. "Are we all thieves?" Formal charges were never brought, but a Birmingham industrialist's diary survives to record that mining companies provided payoffs to John Bankhead even after he had left his position as prison warden and was serving in the U.S. Congress.

Whatever Bankhead's private sins and rewards, his public reforms did not improve prisoners' safety. The death rate for convict miners remained extraordinary, and state health officers declared their living conditions were unfit and unsanitary. Julia Tutwiler, daughter of a Black Belt educator and Alabama's premiere social crusader, declared that the leases "combine all the evils of slavery with none of its ameliorating features." Armed with a "Bible basket," Tutwiler often swung herself onto the last platform of the state's slow-moving trains as she traveled tirelessly for decades to implore legislators, industrialists, and the public to meet their Christian duty to abolish the lease system. Tutwiler almost single-handedly aroused support for better inmate conditions in mining stockades and prompted the state to become one of the first to build schoolrooms at convict camps. But she always fell short of her primary aim.

"We cannot do our work as efficiently or thoroughly . . . if we had a regular force of men," explained industrialist J. W. Sloss in the 1880s. The "unregular" convicts were also a guarantee of cheap labor. Leased convicts cost industrialists less than free miners, and the existence of inexpensive, forced workers, who labored every day except the Sabbath, suppressed free miners' wages. In 1886, the U.S. Bureau of Labor reported that labor costs of Alabama's free miners were reduced by 20 percent because of wage competition from convicts. Yet, the most critical advantage of convict labor was its "check on free labor, keeping down strikes" and union organizing. An official of the Knights of Labor defiantly declared: "Organized labor will line up in one brotherhood until no convict will compete with labor," but convict leasing survived far longer than the Knights' union.

At the end of the nineteenth century, Alabama's Populist and progressive politicians proclaimed opposition to convict leasing, but they were unable and, at times, unwilling to end the practice. Julia Tutwiler knew why. John Bankhead had arranged a Faustian bargain where both powerful whites and the state government could gain from the sale of black bodies. The state government had begun to receive substantial revenues from convict labor. In 1892, T. C. I. was paying the state almost $150,000 over two years for fifteen hundred miners at less than half the cost of free labor. "I am sorry to say that many citizens regard this fact as proof that our convict system is imminently successful," Tutwiler noted.

The convict death rate dropped to one of its lowest levels under T.C.I.'s leasing. Still, more than seventy black men died in the convict mines. Half of all convicts were imprisoned for misdemeanors or crimes involving less than a year's sentence. In 1893, a convict mine manager informed Governor Thomas Jones that among his fifteen hundred convicts the most "diseased and disabled are those who are likely to commit the petty offense for which they are sent here."

In the twentieth century, state officials increasingly relied upon selling convicts to mining companies, lumber camps, and cotton mills for tax revenues, which had been severely limited by the new 1901 constitution. By 1907, when B. B. Comer led Alabama as its first progressive governor, the state's yearly income from convict leases had swollen to $646,345—16 percent of state revenues and 27 percent of general funds (excluding ear-marked revenues for education and pensions). As a result, Comer and other politicians ignored the state inspectors' reports on the mining camps' terrifying problems, and a year later Birmingham industrialists relied on convicts to help break the 1908 miners' strike.

In 1913, UMW attorney Frank White spearheaded the Alabama Convict Improvement Association to abolish leasing. The association's members included a wide range of women civic leaders, labor officials, newspaper publishers, public officials like Judge William Fort, and advocates for better transportation who wanted convicts used for roadbuilding. White condemned leasing as worst than African slavery, and other reformers criticized the mining camps' use of the lash and the "dog house," a vertical hot-box large enough only for a man to stand erect as the Deep South's summer heat cooked his swollen body in the juices of his sweat and blood.[4]

Bedridden after years of activism, Julia Tutwiler endorsed the new initiative. "Alabama cannot afford to be ranked with Russia and Morocco," she pleaded. ". . . The law condemned these men to hard labor, the State put them to death." The *Mobile Register* said the "system stinks to the high heaven." A Birmingham reformer declared, "Alabama's lease system is her unholiest and most indefensible shame." After the 1908 strike, U.S. Steel's T.C.I. lost a bid for a new convict contract and, afterwards, declared that it did not care for the system.

In 1915, after months of study, a state legislative committee issued its findings: "the convict lease system of Alabama is a relic of barbarism, a species of human slavery, a crime against humanity." Committee members, including Will Welch (Black's assistant solicitor at the time), found that a convict's average life expectancy in the mines was only seven years, and that some convicts, like two farm boys convicted for taking a train ride without paying for it, died shortly after arriving from ignorance of mining procedures. DeBardeleben Coal Vice President Milton Fies testified against convict leasing before the committee, but the Alabama Coal Operators Association opposed reform. As the prime contractor for convicts, Pratt Coal dispatched officials and lawyer John H. Bankhead, Jr., to lobby against the committee's proposal. A bill passed the House, but Governor Charles Henderson reneged on a campaign promise to stop leasing. He explained that "the practical side of administering the convict system must not be lost."

The following year, despite charges that industrialists and politicians were "rolling up wealth by working convict labor to compete with free labor," Governor Henderson renewed contracts to Pratt Coal, Sloss-Sheffield Steel, Montevallo Mining, and a few other companies. Forty-eight convicts were killed that year in mining accidents in Alabama and many more died from the effects of the mines' deadly conditions.

Most of the dead were African Americans. Yet many state officials declared convict leasing a tremendous success. In 1916, for the first time in history, the state of Alabama generated higher gross revenues—more than $1.5 million—from convict leases than from general taxes. The leases accounted for 22 percent of state receipts and 38 percent of all revenues outside of earmarked funds.

During World War I, a Sloss-Sheffield official bitterly complained that the state wasn't supplying enough convicts in accordance with state contracts. Governor Henderson commiserated, assuring the mining manager that the state government also was "suffering" from a drop in the number of state prisoners.[5] It was a routine exchange between executives worrying about their bottom lines and nothing less than an open, brutal admission that both private profits and state revenues suffered because too many black men were fighting for their country and too few were available for arrest, conviction, and forced labor.

In 1919, another legislative committee investigated Alabama's unique "form of human slavery," and condemned the "policy of the state to brand the convict with the dollar mark" by leasing him to the "bidder who will pay the most for him, like so many slaves or cattle." The committee called leasing "legalized murder." Legislators had toured every convict camp and found numerous instances of senseless torture. In one case, a camp warden whipped a sick prisoner with a spiked rubber hose after other miners discovered him lying in a pool of underground water. The convict died in the washhouse. His cause of death was officially listed as "tuberculosis."

The committee discovered that 90 percent of all cripples in the prison department came from mistreatment or accidents in the mines and 80 percent of all state prisoners suffering from "tuberculosis" developed the illness in convict mines. According to a state physician, at least thirty convicts from the mines, including Montevallo's Aldrich, were in the prison infirmary because of severe lashings or whippings. The committee discovered five men at convict camps whose skins had been totally burned from their bodies. "They were lying on beds covered with oil cloth with secretions dripping from their burned bodies and scarcely breathing." Legislators concluded simply: the "system is wrong. It is indefensible."

Three Black Belt legislators authored a minority report dismissing complaints as unreliable stories about the past. They blessed the leasing system as a necessary evil serving a noble cause. "We must have money to educate the children of the State, to take care of the blind and helpless little ones," observed the dissenting members. While the people of Alabama were willing to pay taxes, these legislators declared, "We do not believe that they would be willing to pay more taxes to maintain in idleness and luxury the house-

breakers, highwaymen, and murderers." Black Belt politicians also opposed
moving convicts to work on public roads. In that case, black men would have
more chances to escape and menace society. The minority report cited recent
news from Georgia where "an escaped negro had been lynched . . . for raping
a delicate white woman."

Governor Thomas Kilby declared his support for abolishing the system, *if
and when* doing so became practical. Like other governors, Kilby concluded that
a "practical" time was always in the future—in someone else's administration.
In a show of duplicitous politics, Kilby and the legislature abolished the lease
system in 1919 with an effective date three years in the future, on December
31, 1922, the last days of Kilby's term. Now, as Birmingham concluded its
fiftieth anniversary, another legislature followed Governor Kilby's new recommendation to push back the deadline to 1924 or beyond.

Alabama's state government had become addicted to convict revenues. By
1920, the convict department generated almost $2.5 million—20 percent of
the state's total gross revenues. It was the largest source of state receipts and
almost a third of the state's entire, non-earmarked funds. The state's general
taxes produced only $1.76 million in 1920.[6]

Alabama's financial dependency on forced black labor now created as much
resistance to change as the coal companies' opposition. With the complete
collapse of Alabama's miners' union, most industrialists thought they could
manage a workforce of free black miners as well or better than one of convicts.
For state government, however, ending the convict lease system would have
required substantial new taxes, something the Kilby administration adamantly
opposed.

In late 1921, Governor Kilby was under strong criticism because he had
increased the taxable assessment of personal property by as much as 50 percent.
He had attempted earlier to revise Alabama's arcane tax system by proposing a
graduated income tax and small additional business taxes. Cheered on by the
conservative *Montgomery Advertiser,* corporate leaders and Black Belt planters successfully squashed the reform. Kilby's new taxes worsened an already
bizarre tax structure. In 1921, for example, the state's eighth largest source of
general revenues came from new registration licenses for dogs. The pet tax
produced one-third as much revenue as all taxes and licenses from the state's
private corporations. Alabama had the lowest per capita taxes and the lowest
corporate taxes in the nation. It also had the nation's only system of state fi-

nancing that depended on a "species of human slavery" to generate the state's largest source of revenue.

In the name of government efficiency, black convicts in the lease system in late 1921 were left to "look death in the face" within the darkness of three Alabama mines. According to federal reports, measured by deaths per worker, Alabama had the nation's most dangerous mines. The rate of death was even higher in the state's convict mines. An average of forty-four convicts died within mines each year from accidents. In addition, dozens of death certificates listing "pneumonia" and "tuberculosis"—today more accurately identified as black lung disease—confirm that the mines' everyday conditions were as deadly as falling rocks. In fact, based on the 1919 legislative committee's findings, more than eighty-five convicts, mostly African Americans, died from conditions and accidents in Alabama mines each year during the early 1920s.

Yet, death and illness were not the only daily horrors for convicts. Beyond the sight of legislative committees and reformers, beyond political duplicity, poor white men hired to guard the mining camps wore the "badge of cruelty and the inhumanity of the damnable convict lease system." These men took the Old South's mores at face value, not as a license to abuse people for profit, but as the inherent privileges of skin color in lives that had too few others tangible advantages. It was the same vile, exhilarating power for racial terror stained with the same insanity that fueled the South's lynching.

"They'd done told me never to take nothin' off them bastards," remembered Jim Saunders who had been hired to guard Alabama's convicts in one of the mines around Birmingham. Saunders recalled his first incident with a young black prisoner two weeks after he was given a lawman's oath and the power of life or death. "So I jes went over to him an' nearly beat his brains out with my club," the white man said. "That nigger wasn't able to dig no more coal for a long time."

Despite their brutal actions, guards like Saunders were not men living beyond society's own boundaries for sanity or decency. These men heard, understood, and echoed persisting sentiments. "They was a lot of people back then who was causin' trouble 'bout the convicts," the former guard continued. "They said it wasn't right fer th' State to hire 'em out to th' operators . . . But I don't know . . . A man wouldn't be so ready to rob or kill somebody if he knowed he was goin' to th' mines."

Following the larger white society's rationale, Saunders shrouded his behavior with reasonable, colorblind arguments of law and order. "I remember they told us to shoot quick as hell if anybody got rough, or tried runnin' off," continued Saunders like an actor hypnotized with the horror of his own monologue. "They said they was lots more whar these came from an' that when you knocked one of 'em off it was no worse'n killin' a hog or a cow. I never did have to kill nobody."

For decades the Alabama Convict Department's rules and regulations stated: "Each and every officer and guard is expected to deport himself as a gentleman"—Southern gentleman. In practice, it meant the opportunity to act on a white Southern gentleman's privilege, an unexamined, unaccountable liberty to do as a man pleases with other human beings on the other side of the color line. Yet, in industrial Birmingham a white man living on the margins and working with a gun and lash at his side did not have the same restraining self-interest as the Old South's gentleman who built his wealth by preserving as well as exploiting the slaves he owned and worked. At mining camps, places Hugo Black called "revengeful hells," there were no moments of shared humanity or human morality. The white man's Almighty became his skin color, without any other forceful moral or practical restraints. "We did some things that wasn't right, I know . . . ," the former guard confessed. "We useta keep a big barr'l out back of a shed at th' mines an' when I think back on it now, I know we whooped niggers jes' to have fun. We'd pull their britches off an' strop 'em across th' barr'l by their hands an' feet so they couldn't move, an' then we'd lay it on 'em with a leather strop," Saunders recalled. "I've seen niggers with their rumps lookin' like a piece of raw beef. Some of 'em would pass out like a light, but they'd all put up an awful howl, beggin' us to stop," he remembered.

"Th' company had lots of ways to make a bad convict work, but us guards didn't follow 'em much," Saunders admitted. "Didn't nobody want to put a convict in th' sweat box, or feed him on bread an' water, fer they wasn't no fun in watchin' that."[7]

WITHIN THREE MONTHS OF HIS DAY IN COURT, Henry Lewis discovered that judicial opinions about Alabama's convict miners could be circumvented as easily as legislative promises. In late January 1922, Montevallo Mining Company filed for voluntary bankruptcy in federal court and suspended all claims, contracts, and court awards against it. The company's lawyer was appointed temporary receiver to look after Montevallo's assets until a court hearing. Company president W. S. Lovell announced that a declining demand for coal and large unsold stockpiles dictated the decision. Before declaring bankruptcy, Lovell had asked Governor Kilby to revise the company's existing state contract so that Montevallo could lease fewer convicts. Kilby had refused.

The state offered to buy Montevallo for $85,000, the full-price difference between its assets and liabilities shown in a sworn statement filed in bankruptcy court. "Convict labor must be employed in some gainful occupations," Kilby said. ". . . If they cannot be used to obtain a financial return to the state it would be necessary to impose a tax burden of about $1,000,000 a year on the people to pay the cost of their upkeep." Lovell dismissed the proposal.

In close cooperation with Alabama Attorney General Harwell Davis, an old Baptist acquaintance and fellow Pythian, Hugo Black undertook to protect his clients' interests. He petitioned federal court to remove Montevallo from bankruptcy. Black charged that Montevallo was under no financial stress and was using bankruptcy as a subterfuge to escape its state contract and court awards for Henry Lewis and other injured convict miners.

Black's opportunity to prove his allegations came in Birmingham's federal court at a hearing to elect a trustee to run Montevallo during bankruptcy proceedings. Federal law gave the company's creditors and property owners the right to elect a trustee since they had the biggest stake in the company's future outcome. Usually, a trustee tries to put a company back on its feet or sell assets at the best price so creditors can get some of their money back. In this case, only one lawyer who was the law partner of Montevallo's own attorney represented all private creditors. Both Black and Harwell Davis's assistants objected to the sweetheart arrangement. They showed that Montevallo had offered the lawyer free of charge to all private creditors with assurances that each would get their bills paid in full. Despite Black's charges of sham, the commercial creditors unanimously elected David Roberts, Jr.

Coal ran in Roberts's blood. His father was an Englishman, one of Henry DeBardeleben's early business partners. Now Roberts Jr. had his own coal company on the city's outskirts. Under cross-questioning, Roberts Jr. admitted he had known Montevallo's president since he was a boy and had signed an order *before* the hearing agreeing to appoint the company's own lawyer as his trustee attorney.

Black called Montevallo's president to testify. W. S. Lovell explained that

Aldrich had mining expenses of $2,500 per workday and the company only had $15,000 in cash at the time of the bankruptcy filing. Yet Lovell admitted that no commercial creditor was pushing him for money and no one had denied him credit. At the same time, Lowell testified that Montevallo had lost court judgments totaling more than $22,000 during the last eighteen months and more than thirty additional lawsuits for personal injury of convict miners were pending in courts.

Line by line, Black led Lovell through his company's financial statements. Montevallo had a total debt of a little over half a million dollars. Assets, however, added up quite differently. Lovell testified to each category of company assets, and, in the end, reluctantly admitted his company had assets of more than $1.1 million. Montevallo's net worth was more than $600,000—not $85,000 as earlier claimed.

"You knew, didn't you, Mr. Lovell, at the time you filed your petition that you had practically twice as much assets as you had liabilities . . . ?" Black asked.

"Yes," the coal operator replied, "but I didn't have any money."

Finally, Black asked the crucial question, the kind he used before juries to go to the heart of an injustice. "Didn't you discuss the matter, and found out that by going into bankruptcy you could get the company released from the contract of the State, and get rid of the damage suits against you?" Without a jury to convince, Lovell denied the obvious, and the federal bankruptcy judge upheld both the company's filing and Roberts' election as trustee.[8]

Only two days passed before David Roberts terminated Montevallo's convict lease, while he continued its mining operations at a lower scale. "This procedure is just the beginning of a great fight," stated Attorney General Davis, who was helpless to stop the action. Around Birmingham, labor officials circulated a dodger Montevallo had distributed during the 1921 miners' strike. Entitled "The Sanctity of Contracts," the flyer read, "let us get back to the good old days of our fathers, whose word was as good their bond, and whose word was kept . . . regardless of its temporary effect on their fortunes."

In early March, Black asked the federal district court to overrule the bankruptcy judge's decision. Black insisted the mining company did not have clean hands. It was using bankruptcy solely to eliminate a state contract and lawful judgments due to its own negligence. If bankruptcy is so grossly misused, Black warned, no convict or person injured by a company's negligence could ever collect court-awarded damages. The court, nevertheless, held that federal law permitted Montevallo's actions. "The motive with which a lawful act is done is of no controlling importance," the court ruled, "for . . . a lawful act cannot be rendered unlawful . . . by an unworthy motive." According to the court, Montevallo "has the incontestable right to quit" even with a healthy balance sheet.

In fact, the company was far from quitting. Under David Roberts's guidance, the Aldrich mine continued to operate, and, by late April, had a new temporary lease for two-thirds its original number of convicts. Governor Kilby had agreed to a revised convict lease which six months earlier he found unacceptable. Kilby said he had no choice since the state could not do without convict revenues. Ironically, the United Mine Workers helped indirectly to put convicts back in the mines since the union was threatening to strike elsewhere in the country. As a result, the nation's heavy industries were stockpiling coal which Montevallo gladly helped supply.

Montevallo was doing a brisk business on the terms it wanted. It had eliminated the only disadvantage of convict leasing—contracts that limited "the capitalist's freedom to dismiss labor when it became superfluous"—and gained freedom from court awards for any mining negligence. The state retained a large part of its revenue from convict leasing, and Governor Kilby saved his future political fortunes by avoiding new taxes before leaving office in early 1923.

Returning to a dark existence, convict miners were the only ones who really had bankrupt fortunes. If the federal court's ruling stood, no convict could effectively turn to the courts, regardless of the company's misdeeds or negligence, if the company entered bankruptcy. With more than a dozen prisoners already dead in 1922 from mining accidents and poor conditions, convicts in Alabama's lease system were now entirely on their own, in a bondage outside of democratic redress and man's law.

Governor Kilby did banish the whip from all convict mines. The ban gave Kilby an appearance of compassion without changing black convicts' harsh reality, where they had no legal recourse for a negligent accident or a guard's abuse. Kilby made no mention in his ban of the "doghouse" or hosepipes, which were used to "work a man over pretty good . . . and never mark him." As one white guard stated, "I've worked on a thousand of 'em."[9]

Kilby's decision also came when his action would be least noticed, at least in and around Birmingham. At that moment, the city's white public was far more concerned about night-time floggings on public highways than in mining camps. Having cast aside celebration banners and self-congratulatory parading, Birmingham was up in arms about the problems of law, order, and morality on its own streets.

WITH A WIFE AND THREE SMALL CHILDREN in bed asleep, Dr. J. D. Dowling was in his nightshirt reading when someone came to his front door. The stranger informed the doctor that a man was injured and needed immediate care. As Jefferson County's health officer, Dowling had no recent medical experience or any equipment, not even an obligatory black bag, but he rushed to a waiting automobile. In the back seat, Dowling was met with a pistol pressed against his temple. The physician was pushed into the car, blindfolded, and instructed to keep his mouth shut. A gun poked at Dowling's ribs. The car drove away as a second automobile joined it during a ten-mile journey, at the end of which five unmasked men escorted a blindfolded Dowling into an isolated wooded area. With a pistol still stuck in his side, the physician was told to hug the tree. Four men took turns whipping Dowling's legs with a large harness strap. Each struck the doctor at least ten times. Between rounds, one man cursed the health officer for "acting too much like the damn Kaiser in Birmingham." After telling him to leave town, Dowling's captors abandoned him.

Citizens reacted with anger and disbelief as news of the flogging of their health officer spread across Birmingham on Sunday morning, May 21. Few saw Dowling's discolored, swollen legs, but they felt an injury to their community. The county board of health quickly called on "the righteous citizenship of its community to take whatever steps may be necessary to vindicate its good name." The sheriff called the incident the "most brutal crime that has been committed since I have been in office," and Governor Kilby posted a reward. A local businessman declared that "men should arm themselves and when approached by outlaws of such character they should shoot to kill."

The Baraca Men's Sunday school class of the city's First Baptist Church called for law and order in a fervent rebuke, condemning the incident as a "culmination of the recent attacks of a brutal and cowardly sort made upon citizens." With the markings of Judge Black's language, Baptists warned that "any citizen or person among us stands in great danger of being the next victim of these *enemies of society*." Black and his men's class called upon "all *good citizens* to cooperate in every way necessary to ferret out these despicable wretches in order that they should be punished by constituted authority in proportion to the enormity of their crime." Under Black's leadership, the local Civitan Club also condemned this act of "mob violence" with the hope that "every *good citizen* will unite in the effort to run down these vicious *enemies of society.*"

A few days later, Judge William Fort issued a special charge to the grand jury concerning Dowling's flogging. "If such attacks are countenanced in this great county," Fort stated, "it strikes at the very foundation of liberty and civilization . . . Our county will not long survive, if private vengeance is frequently wreaked without punishment in our midst."

Since December 1921, Birmingham had experienced a rash of floggings and whippings of both white and black victims. Only one, involving retaliation against a liquor informant, had resulted in an arrest. In separate incidents later in the summer, two black men were taken from work and flogged by unmasked men who made no efforts to hide their faces from the victims. In cases involving white victims, captors always hid their identity by blindfolding victims or masking themselves. Apparently, white men feared accountability only for violence only against other whites.

Dowling's flogging sparked the first concerted public outcry against group lawlessness. An association of prominent business leaders started the campaign by calling on Birmingham's masked, secret organizations to disband. They clearly were aiming at the Ku Klux Klan. At a public rally, U.S. Steel attorney Borden Burr condemned the Klan by name for recent floggings. At a meeting of the Birmingham Bar Association, UMW attorney Frank White joined Burr in proposing support for a city ban on parades by masked men. C. P. Beddow, an elderly damage suit lawyer, joined the effort, but most lawyers supporting the ban were attorneys representing corporate and business clients. The Junior Chamber of Commerce, a group of small, independent businessmen, voted to support the ban and to question all candidates in upcoming elections about their membership in secret orders.[10]

Within a week, the Klan controversy reached the Birmingham city commission. Frank White did not blame recent floggings on the Klan, but he insisted that the group's conduct encouraged lawless acts. In a heated, bitter discussion, amid a rancorous, packed crowd, one lawyer yelled from the audience, "To hell with the Ku Klux Klan!" A Klan spokesman from Atlanta responded with slurs on Jews, Catholics, and Negroes as he assured Birmingham that the Klan was a law-abiding group. In the end, seeing no direct link between orderly, masked parades and lawless violence, city commissioners refused to adopt a ban, although they did increase the penalty for floggings.

Frank White and Borden Burr returned to the bar association. Declaring Kluxers a menace to constitutional government, the two attorneys proposed that the association use its collective power to defeat Klan candidates. In a debate resembling a barroom brawl, one lawyer declared that if members "are as yellow as the city commission they had just as well give up the fight." Horace Wilkinson opposed putting the lawyers' group into politics. Crampton Harris, Black's law partner, suggested the proposal was aimed at damaging individual political careers rather than upholding principles. "Let's . . . not attempt to embarrass many of our members who are running for office," Harris boomed. Among those running were Walter Brower, Black's former roommate and now a Klan member. By a vote of 64 to 46, the Burr-White proposal passed.

On June 16, a Jefferson County grand jury initiated impeachment proceedings against three of the five city commissioners, including Police Commissioner Bill Cloe. The jury charged commissioners with illegally promising jobs in return for political support during the 1921 campaign and with failing to dismiss city employees who accepted bribes. Jurors also criticized the city government for failing to stem the city's rash of "whitecappings" and failing to ban masked parades. These proceedings ended a month-long investigation led by attorney Horace Wilkinson, who had launched a one-man campaign to discredit the commission after his legal retainer with the city had been canceled when the commissioners took office.

City commissioners hired Hugo Black, who immediately challenged the legality of the grand jury's work and Wilkinson's role. Black charged that "disappointed and disgruntled office seekers should not be allowed to prosecute in the name of the state of Alabama." Black announced that he would call the governor and the state's attorney general to an expedited hearing to prove that Wilkinson had not been commissioned to work with the Jefferson County grand jury. His role as a special prosecutor was an illegal fabrication.

In addition, remembering his own Bessemer investigations in 1915, Black filed demurrers noting that an Alabama grand jury had no power to impeach city officials. "If every word in these charges were sustained," Black told presiding Judge Harrington Heflin, "the state could not even then sustain an impeachment against these commissioners . . . The whole thing . . . is a prostitution of the judicial process." Judge Heflin reluctantly dismissed all charges. Wilkinson claimed illness prevented him from fully defending himself, but an assistant solicitor admitted the cases were "political prosecutions instituted by persons who have a grudge against the present commissioners."

Amid attacks upon city hall, one local leader proposed that the city expand—rather than restrict—public displays and discussions. One of Black's clients, the president of the local machinists' union, sought an ordinance to allow anyone to speak about public issues on Birmingham's street corners without a permit. Because a labor strike was fast approaching the city's rail yards, machinists were interested in finding ways to keep their union's own views before the public, especially if the governor summoned the militia to limit violence and public meetings. But the labor leader was proposing free speech for any citizen, not just his own members. "I would like to see anti-socialists and anti-union men and all others be allowed the privilege of speaking on the street corners . . . There can certainly be no harm in this," the union official pleaded. The embattled commission took the idea under advisement, where in the South's legislative chambers all ideas considered peculiar or unpopular quietly died.[11]

Absent from these public debates about law, liberty, and order was any effective proposal or action to redress floggings against African Americans. The latest two black victims were all but ignored, while the reward for Dowling's captors exceeded $1,000. "Men who had stood unconcerned by repeated whippings in our midst become excited and hysterical when Dowling is selected to lawless punishment," wrote physician Thomas Parke in his journal. In Birmingham's early days, "Parke the doctor" had been one of the three legendary, lonesome public leaders who worked to grow his city with American ideals of justice. Now tired and partially retired, Parke poured his views into a private diary to preserve his moral integrity and perhaps at times his own sanity.

From years of reflection and involvement, Parke understood the futility of Birmingham's selective outrage against violence: "Unless our people can see that it is useless to get excited over this affair alone and not to go to the bottom of the evil, it will amount to nothing. Here are two negroes recently whipped by unmasked men and yet they are so intimidated they will not tell who the whippers were. They should be protected and made to feel they are and will be protected, and then proceed after the men who whipped them."

Such moral action by a city saturated with Old South methods and mores was beyond its collective comprehension and sense of truth. According to Parke, the city's police commissioner seemed truly nonplussed when the physician privately suggested that the city should protect the black victims from retaliation in order to capture the floggers. When the victims' wives sought assistance from local officials, they were turned away brusquely, as if they had been asking for special privileges. Baseless rumors circulated among whites that one of the black men offered money to a white woman "to let him go to her room." The gossip sanctioned the beating by a Southern gentleman's code of honor and warned all others that "white folks *must* be careful how they stand on the affair," if they wished to maintain their own good social standing. According to the victims' physician, no police officer investigated the whippings, although the men knew their assailants.

In this instance, Birmingham's whites may have overtly harmed themselves with their own racialism. By pursuing the men who whipped the African Americans, the police might have caught Dowling's assailants since all three victims had been taken to the same wooded area and all were flogged with a large strap fitting the same description. Yet, bringing Dowling's captors to justice by enforcing law and order for black citizens was an alien notion. Deeply segregated in mind, body, and soul, white Birmingham and its officials could not bring themselves to look towards the bottom of the evil, perhaps because violent racialism had become too habitual—or, perhaps, because a surviving mote of morality kept them in mortal fear of the reflection they might see.

In an anguished moment, black editor Oscar Adams looked about his city and saw a problem larger than episodic night riding. When a community measures a violation of the law by the race and position of its victims, rather than by the misdeed, Adams warned, "the powers in our community are responsible for these acts" of lawlessness which will not soon end.[12]

In fact, city residents frequently turned to violence to settle private grudges, gripes, and grievances. Beginning in early August 1922, seven floggings were reported in the city over four weeks. Most were against Negroes, and in most instances assailants were unmasked. In one case, a boilermaker was whipped severely not far from his own shop, and in another case a young black was flogged close to downtown. In response, city businessmen set up a citizens' committee to protest the crime wave against the Negro, "helpless and dependent on the white man." The head of the law and order committee, a bank vice president, feared white citizens might misconstrue his motives. "It is not a matter of sentiment," T. O. Smith assured the public. "It is one of preserving for the South one of its fundamental industrial advantages."

The industrial advantages of "helpless and dependent" black workers were being realized at that moment in Birmingham. A national railroad strike had begun in July when more than eight thousand men in the city refused a 15 percent wage cut and walked off their jobs. A phalanx of lawyers, including Black and Harris representing the Brotherhood of Railway Trainmen, rushed to court to argue over a rash of lawsuits on the legality of the strike and strikers' picketing. Railroads also began hiring hundreds of scabs to replace union strikers. Most scabs were African Americans. As Birmingham's industrial "advantages" in times of labor disputes, black workers became enemies of striking white workers.

The rail strike's racial dynamics were decidedly different from others since World War I. Birmingham's recent union strikes usually included many African Americans who joined white members against the city's industrialists. In this strike, however, because most railroad unions were strictly segregated, only a small number of black workers joined the strike and a much larger number joined the railroad's scabs. When violence broke out, floggings became a tool of retaliation against black scabs. In fact, each of the seven reported floggings against blacks in August probably involved scabs.

Governor Kilby sent fifty-four armed state soldiers and an automatic machine gun to help local lawmen guard the L&N Railroad and other rail facilities. Jefferson's sheriff employed more than a hundred special deputies at railroad expense, and the company hired a larger number of armed guards. Railroads also secured federal court injunctions ordering local machinists back to work and barring strikers from picketing, congregating near railroad property, or speaking to scabs on the job. The L&N erected a twelve-foot fence around its shops, topped with three feet of barbed wire, while other railroads used boxcars as barricades against attack.

This show of strength did not prevent confrontation and violence. It only spread the tension and fighting away from the depot. Without a chance to picket, protest, or congregate near rail shops, some strikers attacked scabs at their homes. Other scabs were shot at in their own neighborhoods. In many scab households, someone sat by the front door with a loaded gun throughout the night. In the county's small, rural communities, the state militia reported a "reign of terror" with neighbors fighting neighbors. Dynamite blasts also ripped up portions of the rail lines. In Ensley, after a violent confrontation between striking machinists and scabs, one man was killed. Three machinists were charged with murder, and their union retained Hugo Black to defend them.

The railroad strike kept state troops in the Birmingham area throughout most of 1922, but the strike's violence mirrored larger social and economic forces. Outside the rail yards, Birmingham was beset with desperate economic conditions, disputed notions of social good, hysterical racial fears, and gang violence—conditions which had lingered or worsened since the 1920 miners' strike. Amid a national depression, in which unemployment had doubled, five thousand former miners and their families remained destitute in the Birmingham area. Local UMW leaders reported that, after two years of unemployment, many miners' families were living on roots and wild herbs. Twenty thousand men, women, and children were on the verge of starvation. After a brief spurt, output of coal in 1921 was the lowest in more than ten years. All local industries had cut workers, production, and wages, although capital investments in local corporations remained brisk. Factory workers' real earnings dropped by 25 percent to the lowest level in twenty-five years. During winter months, city hall had to keep its doors open around the clock to prevent hundreds of black and white homeless men from freezing. The local American Legion opened eleven soup kitchens to supplement insufficient private efforts to feed and shelter the hungry and homeless—many WWI veterans. School children outside Birmingham collected dry goods, peanuts, and potatoes for the city's poor.[13]

Even many families with jobs experienced hard times. An unusually high number of tax payments for homes were overdue at the courthouse. While railroad unions struck, other workers accepted lowered wages. Employed miners, for example, now made an average of 40 percent less than two years earlier. City workers also lived with reduced wages, and small businessmen and retailers declared Birmingham in the midst of a "depression."

It was a harsh, disappointing experience for a Birmingham that had expected a postwar boom—and especially for the city's veterans. Almost four thousand Alabamians had been wounded during the war and struggled without government care or assistance. Many veterans were without jobs in 1922. A few white ex-soldiers got odd jobs through an American Legion employment bureau and the Legion's makeshift car wash. Twelve hundred had attended special vocational training, although few had secured a job.

The U.S. Congress passed a veteran's bonus bill, but President Harding vetoed it. "The flagwaving patriots," responded an American Legion commander in north Alabama, ". . . can go where it is hotter than it is in Alabama before we will lift a hand again for J. P. Morgan, Standard Oil, and other big interests." Alabama did give white WWI veterans an exemption from unpaid poll taxes, but no pensions like those received by Confederate veterans. Charity chow lines were far more common than voting lines for ex-soldiers.

On a cold afternoon in early 1922, the plight of Birmingham's jobless veterans became a tragic public issue when a homeless ex-soldier died on the streets. He collapsed after the city's charity hospital had turned him away. The penniless, sick man was told that there were no available rooms. A few days afterwards, more than two thousand men in civilian and military clothes joined hands to accompany the body of this soldier to his gravesite. The long, silent procession, extending ten blocks, passed defiantly in front of Hillman Hospital (named for Pratt Mining Company's first president), where the veteran had been denied admission, and ended at Elmwood Cemetery, where another ten thousand people joined to pay last respects to a white man who served his country in war only to die four years later in poverty on Birmingham's streets.

The casket was draped with the American flag, and the veteran was given a full military funeral. After the firing party receded and as the bugler sounded "taps," five Klansmen in full regalia mysteriously appeared at the open grave. "The klansmen approached reverently, laid a beautiful floral tribute on the lowering casket," a local reporter wrote, "stood for a moment with hands outstretched over the grave, as if in pious consecration, then vanished into the crowd leaving no trace as to their identity."

The ceremony, preserved in newsreels, resembled consecration proceedings held four months earlier in Washington at the tomb for America's "unknown soldier." Yet, in Birmingham the largest funeral within memory was more than a replay of a national tribute to fallen servicemen. More than twelve thousand men and women also mourned the tragic actions of a local public institution, run for the poor by some of Birmingham's best citizens, which failed to treat a destitute, dying white veteran.[14]

STRUGGLING WITH POSTWAR POVERTY, Birmingham also grappled with the terms of peacetime morality. For a decade, whiskey had been the paramount moral issue in Alabama, and now, with the U.S. Constitution's Sixteenth

Amendment, abstinence was the highest law of the land. In Alabama, prohibition enjoyed support from both political parties, most Protestant groups, a majority of the state legislature, and the governor. It was, nonetheless, opposed bitterly and violently throughout the state. In both state and federal courts, liquor violations were the predominant crimes. In Birmingham, for example, thirty-five of the fifty-seven criminal cases on the federal docket in early 1922 were liquor cases. During the prior year, almost thirteen hundred stills and a million gallons of beer had been confiscated in Alabama.

Southerners who believed the government had no business interfering with their private enjoyment of liquor had resorted to violence—"whitecapping"—almost since the arrival of the first federal liquor agents in the nineteenth century. After national prohibition, they did so again. In late 1921, for example, federal agents arrested a Jefferson County gang for flogging a whiskey informant. A month before Dowling's whipping, Judge Fort attributed a large part of Jefferson County's violence to private vengeance against whiskey informants and prohibition officers. In another part of Alabama, officials discovered a dead man lashed with barbed-wire between two trees. The victim's assailants, mistaking him for a federal prohibition agent, had attempted to cremate him alive.

Another moral issue stirring deep disagreements in Birmingham was public dancing. Many local Protestant ministers, especially in the city's middle-class suburbs, believed devoutly that public dancing was a breeding place for unclean thoughts and illicit behavior—drinking, gambling, cursing, casual sex, and prostitution. Belief in Biblical authority for dancing as sin differed by congregation, but the nature of the opposition was captured by Alabama's federal prohibition officer when he asked the general public: "Did anyone ever dance in Heaven?" Apparently not in Alabama's heaven in 1922.

Fears about public dancing had as much to do with bedeviling changes in family life as with heaven and hell. In Alabama's new metropolitan areas white children were no longer under the constant, watchful influence of their parents, as they had been since the beginnings of Southern agricultural society when parents spent most of their farm day guiding their youngsters' chores and behavior with hardly any other influence outside of church and school. In Birmingham, middle-class adolescents were often free of parental supervision, able to explore many facets of an urban adult world. Poorer white children often worked as employees for mill owners—not as helpers to their fathers on the farm.

This unprecedented independence for children was leading to increased rebellion, juvenile delinquency, and an array of youthful fads that flowered across America as the "Roaring Twenties." Federal Judge W. I. Grubb warned that "lack of parental discipline" and "less discipline in the churches and schools" were "largely responsible for disrespect of restraint" among the young. Many Birmingham adults agreed and wanted to restrict the city's unsupervised, unwholesome public places, such as public dance halls and movie theaters, where young men and women might be tempted by immoral or dangerous influences which even many adults could not resist.

One city commissioner proposed to ban all public dancing, exempting churches and private country clubs. Bill Harrison wanted to permit dancing at East Lake's renovated public pavilion as inexpensive entertainment for local white mill workers, but suburban religious leaders who had stopped Harrison's earlier proposal for Sunday movies rallied their congregations again. After the issue was put on the ballot, city voters defeated Harrison's proposal by a margin of almost two to one.[15]

Amid these hardships and conflicts among white factions, Birmingham's black citizens could be convenient scapegoats for resentment and violence. In labor disputes, blacks were strikebreakers and often victims of floggings. African Americans were the vast majority of former miners whose starving families now paid dearly for having joined white workers to oppose local industrialists who now would not hire any former union member under any condition. Blacks also were denied opportunities for distant jobs as the city quickly arrested and jailed any Northern labor agent arriving in Birmingham. The city continued to enforce its vagrancy laws to assure that Birmingham's "industrial advantage" showed up for work regularly during times of strike or heavy demand.

In the moral wars, black men were arrested most often for violating the white Protestant social commandments against liquor, gambling, and dancing. And, despite Solicitor Black's efforts five years earlier, whites were still allowed to violate Moses's first commandment, almost with impunity, if the victim's skin color was darkened. "It is easy to shoot down and kill a human being in Birmingham," complained the city's black newspaper, whose despair seemed to grow daily, "if he happens to belong to a certain group or race."

The South's color line had always mapped exploitation, regardless of moral or economic conditions, but the predicament of Birmingham's black citizens in 1922 was extreme and was peculiarly aggravated by a city crime wave. The problem of violent crime by blacks *against* whites quickly became a paramount concern in the city's white mind.

In late January 1922, a black man attacked a white grocer and his wife with an ax. It was the fourth assault in three months against small grocery operators, and in two other instances an ax had been unsparingly used on white victims. Birmingham's white citizens suddenly realized that five white men and women had been killed by Negro attackers who remained at large, and reacted frantically in fear and anger about what they were sure was the work of one black maniac, nicknamed "Henry the Hacker."

Each bloody crime had been committed against neighborhood grocers in the city's black sections, but whites throughout greater Birmingham were alarmed about the safety of their neighborhoods and families. "Visualized in the minds of many citizens . . . is a picture of this cruel negro, who with hidden ax awaits the opportunity to kill," warned one local reporter. ". . .Though a negro mind, it has been conclusively shown that the shrewdness of the most keen criminal has been displayed."

In response, hooded Klansmen voluntarily patrolled Negro districts with a parade of automobiles that continued late into the night. White women and girls reportedly stopped walking in parts of the downtown commercial district after dark since African Americans were there. Several hundred white men sought new gun permits, and some storeowners considered hiring private guards. Police Commissioner Bill Cloe appealed "to the people of Birmingham not to give way to hysteria over recent ax murders. This is no time for hysteria," he pleaded. Responding angrily to Cloe's request, a white citizen replied: "Would buying guns and hiring guards be hysteria or 'safety first'?" Another resident advised: "Shoot to kill!"

The police made several arrests in 1922, but the "Hacker" cases proved difficult to crack as ax killings persisted. It became the city's largest murder spree in recent history. Bill Cloe told fellow commissioners that many killings arose from small immigrant merchants buying stolen property, and he recommended the city revoke the licenses of those engaged in such practices. The commission demurred, unwilling to shift blame from Henry the Hacker. For more than two years, many ax murders remained unsolved and occasionally reemerged as a public issue to alarm white citizens.

Throughout 1923 ax murders took on a different character. According to the local African American newspaper, Birmingham's casualty list involved seven "alley murders" in addition to fifteen dead shopkeepers and eighteen victims who survived an ax attack. The violence could have been the work of several copycat criminals, but the black paper speculated that some of the deaths were the work of a secret African American group "seeking to keep the race pure." The seven "alley murder" victims were white men and black women caught in the act of copulation; their heads were bloodily bashed by axes or hatchets. "There must be stricter adherence to the color line," black editor Oscar Adams warned readers, "especially as it regards the social intermingling of the races in Birmingham."

Following a well-honored approach for calming racial tensions, Birmingham adopted an ordinance segregating its streetcars by race—requiring separate entrances and partitions in the buses—although the practice of separate sitting was already customary. To avoid racial conflicts, Commissioner Cloe also proposed segregating store openings where customers of any race were known to push and shove to get a super sale. The ordinance failed, however, perhaps because no one could figure out how to segregate people who are walking around in the same store.[16]

If blacks lost often during white Birmingham's struggles with crime and unrest, the Ku Klux in 1922–23 was a primary beneficiary. Under the leadership of James Esdale, an attorney who had successfully led a local Elks club, the Ku Klux displayed an uncanny ability for timely public relations. The Klan had no hand in the ax murders, for example, but it quickly took advantage of the crisis. Riding in full costume at night, Kluxers exhibited the gallantry and courage of their Reconstruction forebearers as they rode through the town's black sections to challenge lawlessness at its source. "Let the Ku Klux Klan keep up its good work," shouted one white man on behalf of many.

After the homeless soldier died on Birmingham's streets, the Klan used its mysterious public pageantry to steal the most dramatic moment of tribute and protest—and to attract patriotic praise. "I'm might glad to know the klan has a soft spot in its heart for the ex-service man," one veteran stated. A few weeks later, Kluxers repeated the performance at the funeral of a local deputy sheriff, as the group continued to associate with heroic, unsung men protecting America. At a time when the city struggled with public morality, the Klan also presented cash awards and letters of commendation to Birmingham's Protestant evangelical ministers.

Rather than creating racial havoc or orchestrating a series of floggings, the

Klan in Birmingham at this time was more adroit at siphoning its strength from people's deep fears and anxieties already excited by other developments. The Klan "is a dangerous manifestation," Thomas Parke observed in his diary, "but even worst as showing the psychology of our people." Unlike any other group, Kluxers embodied a broad spectrum of white frustration and dissatisfaction in Birmingham because it acted often through symbols, not words. As odd as they seem decades afterwards, Klan insignia of flowing white robes and anonymous white righteousness were evocative and historically powerful for many white Southerners. The organization's endorsement of true Americanism was a gift from the Great War, and it remained undefined and malleable enough to fit any white person's moral or economic views.

The Klan belief in white supremacy was the standard faith of the white South, including all who voted or held office under the Democratic Party's banner of "White Supremacy." In Kluxers' public acts—usually silent, always ceremonial—anyone could pour his or her own interpretation into the organization's true message. When the Klansmen appeared at the ex-soldier's funeral, for example, some saw an act of protest against the treatment of a white pauper by the elite who ran the hospital. Others heralded it as a moving tribute to an unappreciated veteran. The Klan's ambiguity of symbols and rituals permitted it to foster "solidarity without consensus." The Klan had it both ways.

There also seems to have been a widespread, almost spontaneous, urge to join an organization uncontrolled by any leading faction that could unite a broad range of feelings and needs. Earlier, for example, Birmingham had witnessed a spontaneous rise of the Overalls Club, a group that any white man could join simply by hoisting a pair of galluses over his shoulders as if he were back on the farm in a simpler time. No one quite knew what the leaderless group stood for, although several politicians tried to interpret the movement to their own advantage. Breck Musgrove's supporters tried to ride its momentum by campaigning in overalls in 1920. Many other white men, including judges, lawyers, and merchants, donned for the first time a pair of overalls in fear that galluses were rallying whites together in a symbolic gesture that could lead somewhere.

In 1922, the Ku Klux served much the same function by giving people of Anglo-Saxon stock an organization to admire, join, or define for themselves through their own interpretations of the group's symbols and sensibilities—white robes and white supremacy, pagan pageantry and religious mystery, Americanism and exclusion, law-abiding order and night riding, Old South icons and New South anxieties. Efforts by the bar association and business groups to discredit the Klan proved largely ineffective because they failed to address developments that were spurring Klan growth. With James Esdale's knack for public relations, attacks on the Klan may have even helped it, especially among folk disgruntled with the city's corporate leaders who appeared indifferent to the community's moral and economic insecurity.

In the fall of 1922, the Klan held a "naturalization" ceremony for seven hundred "aliens" while more than two thousand Kluxers stood watch at the Dixie Flying Field. Reporters were allowed no closer than a hundred and fifty feet from the cyclops, who administered sacred oaths after the Boys' Industrial School Band performed several songs. Further in the background were spectators who could see little more than the fiery crosses and massive columns of white robes.[17] Only after a person of Anglo-Saxon heritage was invited to join the secret order would he have an opportunity to see more than the Klan's mystery and ceremony from afar.

Hugo Black was one of the Anglo Saxon men asked to join the Klan's interior world, but he begged off—citing commitments to other fraternal duties, his law practice, and family. In 1922, Black served as grand chancellor of Alabama's Knights of Pythias, a post requiring him to travel frequently throughout the state as he had done ten years earlier as assistant to leader Herman Beck. By mid-year, Black was also president of Birmingham's Civitan Club, an active chapter of a national civic organization. Each year the group orchestrated fundraising and charity events for college scholarships and the Mercy Home for Orphans.

Black's law practice was incredibly demanding. As lawyer for both trainmen's and machinists' unions, he had been involved in several skirmishes and courtroom battles during Birmingham's recent labor strikes, which he considered equivalent to "declarations of war" between labor and capital. The Montevallo Mining cases remained a messy travesty. Black feared the federal court would dismiss Henry Lewis's award against the company.

In another federal case, involving an old Clay County acquaintance, Black was preparing to argue for the first time—after seventeen years as a lawyer—before a federal appeals court. In state court, he was busy with both trials and appeals in a huge docket of seemingly unblemished victories before local juries. Since 1920, Black had been operating at full speed—"like a new Ford," recalled one of his courtroom adversaries: "He could go fast in forward or he could go fast in reverse. Either way, he'd just shift gears and kept coming out with a good case."

In one such case, Black convinced a jury to award his client, a "lady" from a white working-class neighborhood, $2,000 after she was briefly locked in the county jail on a false charge of larceny. Another client who was hit by a jitney bus won a verdict of $10,000 against a local transportation company. The Alabama Supreme Court in 1922 also affirmed a verdict of $5,000 dollars which Black won suing the Whistle Bottling Company. His client had taken a drink of the locally produced soda only to find a bug of the "thousand legs" variety in the bottle. No physical injury could be proven, but Black talked the jury into ordering the company to pay more than eight times the annual salary of an average Alabama industrial worker to compensate for his client's embarrassment and emotional trauma.

Black had become too successful with juries, according to the state's highest court. "One has only to read the record to see that the case presents a most favorable opportunity for a strong and passionate appeal to the jury in behalf of human rights and the condemnation of anything bordering upon oppression," the Alabama Supreme Court observed in the case of construction worker John Millonas, who had been fired at the insistence of his employer's insurance company which tried to coerce the worker into settling an injury claim. "Indeed, counsel for appellant [Hugo Black] demonstrated, upon the submission of this cause in oral argument, his ability to eloquently present the cause in the most forcible manner," the Court continued with damning praise. "The amount of the verdict—$25,000—is not only greatly disproportionate to the actual damages suffered," the Court stated in an unanimous opinion, "but . . . neither justice nor the public welfare call for the infliction of so heavy a penalty. We are of the opinion that passion and not reason dictated the amount of the verdict." The judges reduced the judgment to $6,000.

In another case, against the Southern Railway Company, Black persuaded a Birmingham jury to award his white client $50,000 compensation for a permanent leg injury. "No doubt the jury were overwhelmed with a feeling of horror and sympathy," the Supreme Court noted in dismay. "Courts, however, must deal with such cases in a practical rather than a sentimental and sympathetic way." The Court cut the award almost in half.

In a third case, a Birmingham jury brought back an award of $1,000 (twice a local worker's annual pay) because a fifteen-year-old white girl tripped over the rope of a towing truck. Black's client was not hospitalized but she had scratches on one side of her body and suffered "mental anguish" from the incident. The Alabama Supreme Court also seemed genuinely anguished by the case. "We cannot avoid the suspicion the jury in this case have been rather too liberal with the money of the defendant," wrote Justice Anthony D. Sayre, whose own daughter, Zelda, and her husband, F. Scott Fitzgerald, were blazing across America's literary skies as idols of free spending and hedonism in the Roaring Twenties. Caretaker of the old order, Justice Sayre did not approve of such liberalism by Alabama's most famous daughter or by working-class juries; however, he and the Court reluctantly allowed Black's verdict to stand, perhaps in fear that another jury in a retrial would return with an even higher verdict for the poor white girl.[18]

Unlike in earlier years, Black no longer embargoed himself at his law office six days a week, day and night, to handle a bulging workload, nor did he retreat freely after work to lodge halls or occasional evenings of solitude and serious reading. Now Black went home to a wife, an infant son, and a black housekeeper. The Blacks occupied a large, attractive French provincial, two-story house on the fashionable Southside, overlooking Birmingham's downtown, and located down the street from industrialists like developer Robert Jemison, Jr., and Donald Comer, the former governor's son and manager of Avondale Mills. It wasn't far from the Foster home or the country club where Josephine and Hugo periodically played golf and attended parties. The Blacks occasionally went out to the picture show or a lecture, but like most young couples with a small child their private lives centered on their own home.

The Blacks had a comfortable life, free of the financial hardships gripping the city, but Josephine had real difficulties adjusting to the different worlds in which her husband lived. She met her husband's extended family in Clay County only after their marriage vows. Miss Sis's initial exposure was a shock. Like many of Hugo's clients, the Blacks and Tolands were plain folk with patriarchal, country habits. At family gatherings, men congregated on the porch where they talked and smoked while the women fixed meals in the kitchen. The men ate first, served by the women, and only afterwards did women eat with the children at a second table.

These rural rituals were strange, uncomfortable experiences for Hugo's new wife. Josephine was no delicate belle who withered from contact with common people, nor a social snob. She admired Hugo's maturity, wide experience, and ability to cross society's social and economic boundaries. But she saw little of the qualities she admired most in Hugo—his wit, charm, and omnivorous intellect—at Black clan reunions. In addition, Josephine had been raised with social sensibilities more kin to those of the daughter of Anthony Sayre than the sisters of Hugo Black. The Fosters' daughter was used to being cared for by servants, not serving menfolk, and to being admired or even worshiped by others—certainly not shunned. As an attractive woman in her early twenties, with a kind, fragile personality and limited experience, Josephine was unable to adapt easily to the country customs of Alabama's plain white folk when they came too close to home.

Josephine also felt out of place at the First Baptist Church, where she began attending services with Hugo after their marriage. Although she was a minister's daughter, Dr. Foster was a Presbyterian and a Biblical liberal. Baptists, on the other hand, were usually literalists, akin theologically to the fundamentalist Presbyterians who had forced her daddy out of the pulpit. Josephine found it disconcerting to be called "Sister Black" by people whose religious doctrines had caused her family so much grief. Sis didn't quite know how to be a good Baptist. Under the circumstances, Hugo made adjustments. He continued teaching the city's largest Sunday school class, but—without the intellectual stimulation of Dr. Dickinson, who had resigned in a failed attempt to run for Congress on the backs of True Americans—Black gladly skipped the First Baptist's Sunday sermons. Like his mother, Black found his affirmation of faith primarily amid conversations with ordinary men and women—not from a pulpit. After Sunday school he often joined Josephine in attending the provocative sermons of Dr. Henry M. Edmonds, the exiled, independent Presbyterian minister who married the couple.

Black's adjustments were not difficult. He felt perfectly at home joining small merchants, white laborers, and union leaders early on Sundays at a Baptist church and later sitting with the families of industrialists who supported the Reverend Edmonds as the voice of privileged, Presbyterian reason. Black believed he belonged in any and all of Birmingham's different social, fraternal, and religious circles. Yet, he did not forsake his primary Baptist identity or obligations. Each year, Black tithed approximately 10 percent of his income largely to the Baptist Church.

Black also concurred with Josephine's distaste for many of Clay's country habits. Now married to an elegant, attractive Southern woman from an esteemed, if financially precarious family with ties to Birmingham's elite society, Black seemed determined to have a modern life style transcending past and present, old and new, rich and poor. It wasn't the life of Scott and Zelda Fitzgerald, but it also wasn't the life of Anthony Sayre or Lee Black. Hugo was evangelical in instructing younger relatives from Clay to shed old mannerisms and social customs. "I want you at all times to practice the cultured refined speech you would use in *any* social circle," Black informed his niece Hazel, Robert Lee's daughter who at age eighteen was on the way to her first job as a teacher in a small Alabama town. Uncle Hugo instructed her to stop saying "yes, sir" and "yes, ma'am"—forms of address he thought were left over from the Old South. "We have better ways today," he insisted.

"There is a predisposition on the part of many of our family to become moody, despondent, cynical, unduly critical of others and pessimistic," Uncle Hugo informed Hazel without offering any details of his own memory of Fayette Black's household. "That is an excellent thing to avoid," he instructed. "Optimism brings more happiness and makes more friends." Black saw in his niece the promise of a bright mind and a handsome woman, and as self-appointed patriarch of his extended family, Uncle Hugo set about to fashion Hazel in his own image of a Southern lady, with characteristics closely resembling those of his own wife.

Like a Polonius of the Roaring Twenties, quoting a gentleman's precedents from old books with learned looks, Black guided his niece with a string of homilies. "Remember that diplomacy mixed with persistence in work gets results," he advised. "Study people as well as books," he commanded. On another occasion, Uncle Hugo scolded Hazel not to neglect regular, moderate exercise—his prescription against sickness and lethargy—as she prepared to attend college, at his expense, at a normal school not far from Montevallo's mines.

When Hazel visited Birmingham, Black sent her off to the beauty shop under Josephine's care for a new hairdo and appearance. He reprimanded Hazel to stop sewing up her hose: "Save somewhere else, but wear perfect hose!" The man who once pressed his own britches under a mattress now schooled his niece on the fact that "looks certainly count in this world." And, of course, in Hugo Black's eyes, there was only one model for a woman's good looks. "Take all the advice Josephine will give you," he encouraged Hazel, "for she knows."[19]

If Black played Shakespeare's Polonius at times among his extended family, he remained Hamlet on the issue of joining the Ku Klux. In early 1923, friends and acquaintances pressed Black to join the Klan. Decades later, after leaving Alabama, he remembered privately that he resisted because he was troubled by the Klan exclusion of Jews and their possible involvement in lawlessness. Standing alone, this recollection was made at a time when the Klan's hooded image had become America's universal cultural symbol of racial hatred and violence, and it is a recollection that has always seemed self-serving. In fact, nothing survives to corroborate his memory about this rare moment of indecision.

Yet, bearing in mind the relationships and notions he held dear, Black probably was ruled by serious doubts. On a personal level, Black could not ignore the Klan's potential for "parting friends, sowing discord, dissension and hatred," as LeRoy Percy of Mississippi charged, "making man . . . wonder whether his neighbor is his friend or his secret enemy." In this respect, the Klan defied Black's small-town ideals of community and his "strong ties of personal loyalty" that framed his pursuit of an ethical life.

Outside the hooded order were two Birmingham men who had exerted early influences on Black: Herman Beck and Frank White. Beck had been more a father to Hugo than anyone else, but as a Jew was excluded from and ridiculed by the Klan. In considering the matter, Black may have remembered a Methodist minister who served with Beck as a Pythian officer in 1910. Black had reminded the minister that, according to many Protestants' beliefs, their grand chancellor could not go to heaven since he was a Jew who did not believe that Jesus Christ was his personal savior and the Son of God. Stunned for a moment by this possibility, the old minister looked Black in the eye and chose God's worldly grace over man's theology. "I would not want to go to a Heaven," the Methodist preacher declared, "that would not let Herman Beck in." In 1923, it was likely that Hugo Black would not want to join an organization, especially one ranking far below heaven on earth, if it would not let Herman Beck in.

In addition, Frank White's opposition to the Klan raised a related consideration. White had been law partner to Black's departed patron, A. O. Lane, whose own style of leadership would not have easily countenanced the Klan. Black was put off by White's bombastic style, but Black had often traveled along White's path in matters relating to the Baptist church, prohibition, labor unions, and opposition to convict leasing. White vocally opposed the

Klan because he saw no emergency conditions that justified the "law leagues" he had joined in the 1870s to end Reconstruction. Also, White's role in prosecuting "whitecapping" crimes in the late 1890s convinced him that people often misused secret groups to undertake violence for personal revenge—not public service.

Already inside the Klan, however, were Black's law partner Crampton Harris, his former roommate Walter Brower, and many other lawyers and friends—as well as a host of Protestant leaders and preachers with whom Black worked on moral and economic issues. Pompous and promiscuous, Harris was a brilliant man who helped Black get the only job he thought he never really earned—artillery captain. In 1915–16, Brower had worked tirelessly with Black to stop the law's abuse of African Americans. Judge William Fort, who helped Black draft his announcement to run for county prosecutor, and other local judges had probably joined the Klan by the middle of 1923. Black knew these friends and others did not tolerate or endorse group violence. Quite the opposite.

In a remembrance a half century after the fact, Black admitted that he also was concerned that if he failed to join the Klan he would hurt his chances in winning cases before juries. "I was trying a lot of cases against corporations, jury cases," he remembered, "and I found out that all the corporation lawyers were in the Klan. A lot of the jurors were, too, so I figured I'd better even up." Black had mentioned much the same concern earlier to his second son. "I wanted to know as many possible jurors as I could," he explained decades after the fact. Black didn't want to jeopardize his extravagant courtroom success, his family's very comfortable income, and the claims of his clients—black and white, Jew, Catholic, and Protestant.

Birmingham's lawyers and public figures were apparently joining the Klan at this time in large numbers. In March 1922, two months before Dowling's flogging, U.S. Steel's Roy Percy wrote to his uncle in the Mississippi Delta to congratulate him on a speech challenging the Klan and to lament that "such constructive leadership" could not be found in Birmingham even among its best citizens. Surveying the local growth of the True Americans and the Klan, Percy observed: "Every jack-legged politician that comes along has to join one of these things. I believe I am the only man in Jefferson County who does not belong to anything."

If they weren't signed up in early 1922, local attorneys had added incentive to join the Klan by June 1923, after the trial of Dowling's accused floggers.

Evidence in the case suggested that the public health officer's attempt to regulate dairies had angered several farmers who did not meet sanitary standards. The defendants were among those whose dairies were affected. Dowling identified one defendant as his assailant. According to Dr. Thomas Parke, the evidence seemed "plain and sharp" against the accused, although the prosecution had real problems. The jury quickly acquitted the defendant who was rumored to be a Kluxer. Away from public clamor, Parke concluded in his diary that the trial "looks very suspiciously like the Ku Klux methods."

Black had been asked, perhaps by the Klan, to represent the Dowling defendants. "So far, I have managed to successfully evade defending two or three of the defendants," Black informed Alabama's Attorney General Harwell Davis a couple of weeks before trial, although Black said he might still "get roped in on" one case. On behalf of Dowling's friends, Dr. B. L. Wyman of the Birmingham Medical Society wrote Davis and Alabama's new governor, W. W. "Bill" Brandon, asking for the "appointment of Hugo Black as special prosecuting attorney in these cases" to assure convictions.

On May 10, Davis wrote Black that "there is no lawyer at the Birmingham Bar that I would rather have represent the State in this matter" and asked about his fee for prosecuting the Dowling case. Black responded four days later. "I would want to be free as though I were acting as the duly selected solicitor," Black wrote, "or in identically the same position you would be, should you come to Birmingham to take charge (not of the prosecution of any particular individual) of an investigation into the entire situation." Black doubted if anyone could convict the defendants on existing evidence and believed it would be "a long hard struggle before any convictions are obtained in the cases." He wanted a fee of $5,000 since he would conduct an open-ended investigation, taking long hours for several months before he could assure conviction of the guilty.

Black knew his terms were unusual and prohibitive. It was less than two weeks before trial and Alabama's assistant attorneys general weren't paid $5,000 dollars in salary over two years, much less for one case. Yet, Black was adamant. He would accept nothing less. "I am heartily in favor of sending whoever did the floggings to the penitentiary," Black said, but he had "no yearning desire to be connected with the case on either side."

After the defendants were freed, Black joined other members of the Birmingham Bar's executive committee asking for an immediate state investigation into possible "criminal and unethical practices" by lawyers and others, although the group's resolution made no direct mention of the Dowling case or the defendants' lawyer. In the summer of 1923, Black was carefully navigating his independence and integrity as he struggled to reconcile competing calls for selfless, public duty and secret, self-serving alliances.

When his old friend Herman Beck urged him to join the Klan, Black made up his mind. "Hugo, if good men like you don't join the Klan," Beck advised, "it will be left to some of the rough necks." Beck counseled Harwell Davis to join, too. "We want some level-headed fellows on the inside," Beck reiterated, "to keep it from hurting Jews too much." Black also recalled department store owner Louis Pizitz echoing Beck's sentiments, and he got much the same advice from a well-to-do Protestant businessman down the street: "Join, if you want to do some good." Frank White's counsel on the matter was no longer available; he had died unexpectedly a few months earlier.

In the fall of 1923, Hugo Black gave the Ku Klux $10. According to Black, he arranged for Klan member John Anderson, chief justice of Alabama's Supreme Court, to sign him up.[20]

Despite confessions of reluctance and uncertainty, Black did not consider his Klan membership an ignoble or immoral compromise—or a personal endorsement of racial and religious hatred. For almost a half century, Black sporadically gave sketchy explanations about joining the Kluxers, often to young white Southerners trying to undo the Klan conundrum, trying to understand how one of America's foremost liberal democrats at the middle of the twentieth century could have been a member of the secret order of hate a few decades earlier.

Black never spoke fully on the subject to anyone. His silence was at times convenient, at other times embarrassing, even costly, and it forever veiled the topic with mystery, intrigue, and misunderstandings. The Klan connection was a very uncomfortable subject for a man who was ever vigilant about avoiding inconsistencies, one of his father's chief failings.

A full explanation from Black would have required more than simply an honest, soul-searching rendering of what was in his heart and head in 1923, a Hamlet-like introspection that was contrary to his outward-looking nature. It would have necessitated an exposition of that time and that place, of their puzzling prologue, of different factions, interests, motives, and beliefs at work in a story as complex and authentically strange as any Flannery O'Connor or

William Faulkner contributed to Southern literature—and as intermixed as the crazy quilt of social, economic, and political issues that stitched together the nature of the city Black adopted as home. Personally for Black, the Klan became a nagging subject without reward, always eluding conclusive proof. Years afterwards, discussions of his Klan connection opened up Judge Black to searching questions of character that never were and never would be settled de-finitively. It became the one case Black knew he could not argue successfully.

Under the circumstances, Black relied upon a series of one-liners and enig-matic remarks to friends, associates, young law clerks, and, finally, to posterity when asked about his ten-dollar Ku Klux membership. "If there'd been a B'nai B'rith," he once informed a young Jewish lawyer from the South, "I'd join that too." In another conversation with a young researcher, Judge Black said, "I would have joined the Knights of Columbus if they had let me!"

In discussing the Klan, Black repeatedly made the point that he was a joiner of almost every white fraternal group in Birmingham. "I was joining everything then," he reiterated decades later. In fact, he joined every large lodge except the Elks, who were known to serve liquor at their private functions. This was a simple fact, but one more complex and meaningful than what a person's membership cards ordinarily indicate today. Like many of Birmingham's salesmen, retailers, suppliers, politicians, and small business owners, Black had used lodges as much for promoting his business as enjoying fraternity. "I made friends in all these organizations," Black stated. They were the venues where he generated clients and income and where he made contact with the men most often serving on Birmingham's juries. Black once admitted that his fabulous success in the Birmingham courtroom was, in part, due to his ability to know the people sitting in the jury box. "I didn't draw a jury that I didn't know at least one person," Black observed. Fraternal lodges, men's associa-tions, churches, and labor unions—all afforded Black opportunities to know, understand, and win his juries.

In addition, lodges were where Black made and matured friends and as-sociations who helped him further his political ambitions. White men who forked over five or ten dollars for lodge dues were likely to pay poll taxes and vote. They also were often salesmen, union officers, and merchants who dealt regularly with a wider circle of potential voters. "I was running for office and looking for a position," Black explained to a friend (and a seasoned political operative), "and like every young man, I joined every organization that might help me in some way." At another time, Black admitted: "I would have joined any group if it helped me get votes."

In the middle of 1923, Black was only "looking for a position" in politics. He still held a lifelong ambition to run for a statewide office, but he didn't know which position or when to run. He knew fraternal memberships, like Jefferson's wildly growing Klan, were essential to future political success, but Black was not aiming or running for any specific office when he bought his Klan card. He was building a base of potential support for a future, undefined campaign, not preparing a real one.

In 1923, moreover, the Klan in Birmingham and Alabama had not yet proven significant political strength. Contrary to accepted wisdom, the Ku Klux had not yet become a powerful political force in any local or state election when Hugo Black joined. In late 1921, Birmingham voters had defeated rabidly anti-Catholic incumbents and replaced them with more moderate commissioners. An early Klan member, Bibb Graves lost Jefferson County to W. W. Brandon by a margin of six to one in the governor's race in August 1922. In local legislative races, Walter Brower, a Klansman, had won election to the state senate, but without winning a majority of the votes, and no Klan slate won Jefferson's legislative delegation. Press reports credited local labor unions in the middle of a railroad strike with a decisive role in local elections, and it was labor's political influence in Jefferson County that continued to worry Forney Johnston and other supporters of Senator Underwood.

The rapidly growing Klan's potential influence in Birmingham elections was apparent to all, including Black, in 1923 but its real impact wasn't proven until October 1925, when Klan-backed candidates won two of three posts on the city commission. Across the state, Kluxers had visible chapters in a dozen communities in the summer of 1923 but no extensive statewide organization. The Klan was still trying to sell itself across rural Alabama and meeting strong opposition in the state's other major cities. In May, Montgomery voters elected a slate of anti-Klan candidates to city offices, and the city enforced an anti-Klan parade law. In Mobile, Kluxers had no political influence.

For these reasons, looking back on his decision to join the Klan, Hugo Black could honestly tell newspaper editors decades later: "People think it was politics, but it wasn't politics." Certainly not just politics. Instead, it was a decision of an ambitious lawyer whose own poverty was only five years removed. It was the decision of a successful trial attorney who wanted to protect and promote *his own*—his own enormous, escalating income from jury verdicts, his own family's financial security, his own role as the generous, young patriarch in an extended family, and his own financial and practical means for gaining a future high office in Alabama.

It was equally the decision of a deeply self-confident man who saw himself as both an insider and an outsider, as both a part of and apart from the many groups and associations he maintained. During his sixteen years in Birmingham, Black had associated with all types of people, in all walks of life. He did so purposefully. "He knew Birmingham inside out and upside down—poor folks, rich folks, black folks, white folks, labor folks," recalled Virginia Foster Durr. In the courtroom, Black had represented and prosecuted Protestants, Jews, Catholics, immigrants, blacks, and whites. He appeared in court on behalf of a black convict or a poor white mother and, around home, he chatted with wealthy neighbors and the Fosters' friends from Birmingham's social elite. In fraternal orders, he joined laborers, merchants, clerks, professionals, farmers, and a few Republicans. On a typical day in 1922–23, Black might confer with an injured black convict or free miner, attend a Civitan luncheon with salesmen and small businessmen, meet with the Bar Association's executive committee of plaintiff's and corporate lawyers, visit Negro occupants in one of his three rental houses, join white Baptists at a church function, stop to chat with a Jewish friend, confer with union leaders, attend a lodge meeting of merchants, clerks, salesmen, and laborers, and go to dinner at the country club among the city's corporate managers.

Black's practice followed the patterns of his Clay County boyhood when he tried to navigate across conflicts of position, politics, and prayer dividing his mother and father, their families, and his community, but its inspiration came from his mentors, A. O. Lane and Herman Beck. As lawyer, judge, mayor, and city commissioner, Lane had interacted with all parts of Old Birmingham but was beholden to no group or faction. As a Jewish businessman, Herman Beck operated similarly in a Protestant world where he helped enliven Comerism and led several thousand of Alabama's largely Protestant Pythian members—at least one of whom was willing to take hell over heaven if Beck couldn't join him at the Pearly Gates.

In building a career along this style of leadership, Black possessed absolutely no doubt that he could always influence others while keeping himself free of undue influence, always maintain his individual core of fairness and independence when joining others of differing views. The same self-assurance led him to believe that he could win over almost any local jury in any case and prompted his detractors to refer to him as "Ego." Black believed that he kept free moral agency by being associated with many of Birmingham's different factions, by joining virtually all white organizations and lodges. He once explained that because he belonged to so many groups in Birmingham, he "never felt the slightest political debt to any one."[21]

However, the Ku Klux Klan was not, even in eyes of its own members, just another fraternal organization. It was not merely a lodge of white men conducting weird ceremonies or raising money for scholarships or charity. It was an organization accused of fostering violence and lawlessness across the nation, Alabama, and Birmingham. Often its representatives spewed the ugliest language of hate and exclusion, and many thought Kluxers acted in the dark of night with whips and guns to back up their vile words. In 1923, however, Hugo Black believed the Klan *as a group* was a law-abiding organization, even if all of its members were not. "The Klan in those days was not what it became later," Black explained. "There were a few extremists in it, but most of the people were the cream of Birmingham's middle class."

Surviving records of Klan activities and members for this specific period largely verify the gist of Black's recollections. Alabama and Birmingham Klans probably had a broad-based membership among tradesmen, craftsmen, skilled workers, and the middle class, as did many of the nation's growing klaverns. A Birmingham editor wrote in July 1922 that Kluxers included "some of the most prominent citizens." Nearly all surviving records of Klan officers in the Birmingham area for these years reveal professional men, small businessmen, skilled workers or craftsmen, and sole proprietors. Railroad men in the Alabama Black Belt were often Klan members, and in Talladega almost half the town's professionals and businessmen, including a bank president, were members.

Klan records elsewhere in the South vouch for a pattern of middle class and working class membership, including "nearly all the preachers," as Black once observed. A thoughtful, contemporary observer in Birmingham reached the same general conclusion. After a massive Klan rally in Tuskegee, Alabama, on July 4th, 1923—a protest against the hiring of black doctors instead of white physicians for a federal medical center there—Dr. Thomas Parke concluded that Kluxers were no longer a lower-class movement, if ever they were. Considering the hundreds of men from across Alabama who had traveled to Tuskegee for the Klan demonstration, Parke observed, "It means that the men with financial ability enough to permit going that far in train and auto are concerned in the movement. It means that the Ku Klux movement is not confined to the least financial classes of the community."[22] Wizard Simmons had made the same point several months earlier.

Far more important, no one mustered any real evidence, much less conclusive proof, that the Birmingham KKK was responsible for the city's clandestine gang violence in the years and months before Black joined the Klan. The rash of floggings and organized violence that plagued the city in 1922–23 occurred as the Klan swelled in numbers, but no one in Birmingham demonstrated that the Klan was responsible for any act of violence. Despite its modern image as the cultural synonym for lynchings and floggings, the Klan's documented history of terror was not evident or proven in Birmingham at this time.

The bulk of the city's reported incidents of organized violence was actually related to labor disputes and strikes around the rail yards. These violent attacks were most likely the work of striking union members fighting scabs and company informants—not Klan work. Other acts of group violence arose out of personal disputes over whiskey and sex. Dr. Dowling's own flogging appears from court testimony to have been a private act of personal revenge by a few disgruntled dairy farmers, although they may have used Kluxer membership as a passport to escape punishment.

In personal recollections of this particular period, Birmingham Jews and Catholics do not record a reign of subterranean violence and terror by the Klan against people of their faith. Life was tense and belittling, and possibilities of senseless danger were real for Birmingham's Jews and Catholics. Yet, Irving Engel, a young Jewish lawyer who moved to New York because of Birmingham's Klan domination in late 1924, did not remember a single incident in which a Birmingham Jew was targeted by Kluxers for physical harassment or harm before he left the city. Other Jews who lived through these years also could not recall "anything about mistreatment of Jewish people." In fact, "Cousin Joe" Denaburg's pawnshop was a favorite place for Klansmen to buy guns and white sheets for robes. Well aware that the proprietor was Jewish, Kluxers often yelled the brotherhood's secret greeting to "Cousin Joe" as they entered the store and offered him the secret Kluxer handshake. Always ready for a smile and a sale, Denaburg inevitably replied in kind.

In Birmingham's Little Italy, the Klan frequently marched or patrolled the streets during the city's crime waves, but their concern was not so much Catholics as it was illegal whiskey dealers. "The KKK was after the bootleggers," recalled one woman living with her family on the Italian community's main street. She and her children often hid under their beds as the Klan cars passed. "When they went out there at night," she recalled, "we'd hear them coming—the swish of all those cars going by late at night . . . We were scared."

These surviving remembrances may not tell the whole story. "We don't know how many men were run out of a shop . . . how many people suffered harm," observed a Birmingham Jewish leader. "Some were afraid to make a complaint."[23]

In 1922–23, many in Birmingham were gripped by fear, violent crime, joblessness, poverty, and utter deprivation. If the city had a "reign of terror," its targets were primarily economic, not ethnic. Since late 1920, Birmingham had endured three long, violent labor strikes with repeated conditions of martial law suspending civil liberties and spasmodic, deadly clashes between labor and capital. When the last strike ended in September 1922, labor disputes had left Birmingham with scores of workers dead or permanently injured and thousands of destitute workers with no jobs or prospects.

In 1923, Birmingham's Klan critics could only repeat Frank White's accusation: nighttime floggings started only after the Klan became viable in Birmingham and, therefore, Kluxers were responsible for committing or encouraging lawlessness. Yet, this charge presupposed that the Klan created a lawless climate by committing or sanctioning violence when, in large part, the Klan drew its strength and support from developments, fears, and violence that had other sources and a far longer lineage.

The origins and societal habits of Birmingham's violence and lawlessness were too deep, pervasive, and invidious in 1923 to be blamed on any one organization, no matter how evil or corrupt its general role in history. Birmingham had earned an early reputation as "Bad Birmingham." Crime was commonplace. It had been, perhaps, the most violent Southern town in the most violent region of a violent nation.

The city also had a frightful history of vigilantism and clandestine group violence. The ancestry of group violence belonged to a variety of white groups in Birmingham—primarily industrialists and unions, governors and special company guards, whiskey runners and fellow whitecappers. The toll was astonishingly large. In strikes from 1894 through 1922, more than twenty people were killed, and scores were wounded by black and white strikers, company guards, and state soldiers. Bridges and homes were blown up. Deputies became gunslingers on the payroll of mining companies. Thousands of children and their families were forced from their homes by company guards armed with guns and eviction notices. The state militia used rifles and bayonets to destroy the tents of unarmed families and to ban strikers' assemblies, pickets, boycotts, and speech. In one case, Alabama soldiers lynched a white union man.

In Birmingham's other labor disputes, group violence and intimidation were equally common. During most industrial strikes, state soldiers supplemented armed guards who surreptitiously patrolled the strike zones. In 1918, during labor efforts to organize Birmingham's steel workers, a vigilante group tarred and feathered a black union organizer. In the 1922 railroad strike, machine guns and armed state troops stood guard in Birmingham along rail tracks after a string of floggings, gunfire, and dynamite blasts.

For longer than Birmingham had been a city, the fight over liquor in the surrounding areas had been ruthless and violent. As a young attorney in the 1890s, Frank White prosecuted gangs of "whitecappers" who flogged and murdered to keep the government from interfering with their production and consumption of moonshine. When the 1894 miners' strike broke out, Governor Jones recalled the state soldiers who were on patrol across Alabama due to a rash of whiskey whitecappings. This tradition of violence escalated whenever the number of prohibition arrests increased, as they did in the 1920s after national prohibition.

Alabama's state and local governments also operated with statutory lawlessness and violence for more than fifty years. Long before Hugo Black's term as county solicitor, thousands of African Americans were arrested to enrich a local official and then convicted to provide mines, lumber camps, mills, and plantations with cheap forced labor. Languishing in places like the Bessemer jail and the Montevallo mine, thousands of convicts had been brutally mistreated. As Bessemer city fathers said in 1915, these practices were commonplace.

This institutional violence was cumulatively massive. During Birmingham's early years, death rates among convict miners were reported to range from 10 to 40 percent. As late as 1919, life expectancy in the convict mines was only seven years. In 1922-23, more than fifty convicts were killed annually from mining conditions and accidents in a system where one in four convicts were imprisoned for petty crimes or liquor violations. Another hundred convict miners, like Henry Lewis, were crippled for life each year. Therefore, over Birmingham's first half century, as many as eight thousand convict miners died and a much larger number was permanently crippled doing dangerous, forced labor, often for petty or victimless crimes.

These estimates of official, coerced death and violence amount to a governmental pogrom. And they do not calculate the innumerable brutal floggings that occurred in mining camps over the years (due to severe lashings or whippings, more than thirty convict miners were in the state prison infirmary on a single day in 1919 when a legislative committee visited). Such massive, routine human cruelty, primarily against African Americans, constitutes a toll far exceeding the numbers of recorded lynchings throughout the state's entire history. Convict leasing in Alabama was an official system of violence and terror that possessed, in the words of the state's white woman of conscience and the nation's foremost black historian/sociologist, the "worst evils of slavery."

Of course, the Ku Klux added to this violent tradition its own heritage of terrorism and death, remembered and repackaged with romantic nobility through the imagery of the popular film *Birth of a Nation,* which ends, lest we forget, with the triumphal castration of a black man. The original KKK's violence after the Civil War was real, brutal, and effective in several parts of the state, and its aftermath lingered in Alabama's Black Belt where former slaves were intimidated into voting against the insurgent farmers of Clay County and north Alabama. Yet, despite the resemblance, the Klan in the 1920s did not arise from the same conditions nor did it have the same Old South violence. The original Klan used intimidation and brute force, as well as bluff and banter, to overturn a social movement for black political and economic power during Reconstruction. In the early 1920s, the second Klan mimicked its forebears' racist heroics, but it did not arise to arrest a mass African American movement for protest or power in Alabama, Birmingham, or the South.

After the race riots in 1919, Southern whites often worried that "Yankeeized" labor organizers, labor agents, and rabble rousers might stir up trouble among local Negroes, and in Birmingham volatile white fear of black crime had escalated like a plague. But few if any whites in Birmingham in 1923 feared a rising tide of organized liberation among the South's own black population. Most whites, like Birmingham's bank officer, considered the city's Negro population to be "helpless and dependent on the white man."

This white perception of the race relations of the time is underscored by trends in lynchings, the common barometer of racial violence. Lynchings declined as the Klan rapidly emerged in Birmingham in 1922–23. In Alabama, lynchings reached their lowest levels between 1922 and 1924, a fact Kluxer leaders used later to defend the group's conduct and role. The Ku Klux deserved no credit for the decline, nor did the trend reflect an overall improvement in race relations. Yet, Klan violence in 1922–23 did not expand or sustain the number of lynchings in the state, including the Birmingham area.

There were mass migrations among African Americans in the South and Birmingham at this time. As agents of their own history, Southern blacks protested with their feet, their livelihoods, and their lives. More than six hundred thousand Negroes left the South during the first fifty years of Birmingham's history. More than half had moved since 1910. Yet, the overall number of blacks in the Magic City had grown steadily because of the attraction of industrial jobs and vigilant efforts to banish Northern labor agents.

In Birmingham's brief history, massive black protest arose in 1908 and 1920–21, when thousands of African Americans and their families refused to obey their white employers, and, joining with white union brothers, tried closing down the white man's mines and furnaces. It was the violence and intimidation of industrialists and their allies, not of Klansmen, that defeated those efforts for "equal justice to all." It was the industrialists' company guards, company-paid lawmen, and the governor's state militia—not Kluxers—who used a campaign of intimidation and brute force to prevent the return of Reconstruction and the horrors seen in the flickering surreality of D. W. Griffith's silent movie. By the middle of 1923, because of the acts of industrialists, prospects for another uprising among Birmingham's African Americans were beyond the immediate human horizon.

In the city's black community, more routine methods of survival and resistance followed the spirit of Booker T. Washington who had preached economic and moral self-help within accepted segregation. Birmingham's Penny Savings Bank, community supported schools, numerous black churches and black fraternal lodges (especially the black Knights of Pythias), and an active commercial district were black institutions quietly building for betterment and a better day.

There may have been occasional moments of violent group resistance from within the black community. One explanation for the unsolved "alley murders" was that a local African American group, possibly militant black nationalists, was reacting to the racial hypocrisy of self-righteous, sex-seeking white men. By whatever motive, these were unconventional, violent acts that notified the white community that, even in a rigid social order of white supremacy, the powerless are not always harmless.[24]

The Klan's extralegal activities—those falling short of actual violence but creating an intimidating presence—had many precedents in and around Birmingham. Night riding, anonymous secret patrols, and jury stacking were not new phenomena. Birmingham industrialists and corporate leaders had used quite similar methods for their own purposes in the past. Like the Klan, Birmingham's coal and iron operators preferred at moments to do their own work in secrecy. U.S. Steel kept secret informants within labor unions after the 1908 miners' strike. The Alabama Protective League, run by the president of Birmingham's Chamber of Commerce, did its work through anonymous actions to keep the war for democracy from agitating a black workforce. There was also the secret network which industrialist Key Milner and others spearheaded, with cooperation from at least two governors, to undertake clandestine activities to supplement law enforcement. In 1922, corporate leaders also created a semi-secret law enforcement committee to counter the Klan's own growth. While its members did not don robes and hoods, it proposed to operate with the same methods as the Klan, under the control of citizens who had the confidence of Birmingham's industrial and civic leaders.

Even Ku Klux methods with juries had a precedent. Jury rigging in Alabama had a long history, as Populists in Clay County and elsewhere knew decades before. According to the editor of the *Labor Advocate,* as late as 1920 Jefferson's jury commission had rigged the process by calling only those "men who were known to be favorable to the corporations" for jury duty. "No jury that returned a verdict for just damages would ever get the same chance again, and no man who was known to be fair was ever called upon to serve his county on a jury," charged the skilled unionists' paper. As a result, the *Advocate* believed that soon it could be "nearly impossible to win a damage suit against any of the large corporations."

At least one Klan opponent in the early 1920s saw basic parallels and precedents for Ku Klux methods. After listening to a lecture by Dr. Henry Edmonds, who condemned the Klan as a small band of anti-democratic men while praising the sons of Birmingham's "best citizens" as God-chosen leaders, Dr. Thomas Parke worried that both groups of self-deluded men were working to override "the capacity of democracy to function in progress." On another occasion, Parke concluded that Klan methods were similar to the past work of Black Belt planters "who held that false swearing and bulldozing at the polls were needed years ago" to stop the Populist movement.

Accurately assigning responsibility for specific, anonymous vigilantism and violence in 1923 was, in fact, a task beyond Birmingham's practical and moral capacity. Although local daily newspapers alertly reported such crimes, they ran no investigative stories on how and why they happened—because, in part, no one in 1923 was able or willing to pierce the veil of secrecy surrounding the Klan and other clandestine groups. In addition, Birmingham's white press, police, and public seldom saw good reason to pursue justice for an individual victim, "if he happens to belong to a certain group or race." In a racialized city chronically troubled by high levels of random crime, riotous labor disputes, murderous liquor fighting, systematic, legalized violence, and now Kluxers and other nativistic groups, the blame for violence was rarely based on a finding of fact.

The job of Klan exposé across the region was left to a few out-of-state Southern dailies and the Northern press which started running occasional series and features in 1921. These reports dug up frightful details and patterns, which Birmingham papers often reran, but the reports suffered from sensationalism and a blatant Yankee bias. These stories seemed to suggest that any shadowy violence came about as a directive of the Klan Empire, anything lawless or threatening in the night was a Klansman, any unlawful injury was a deadly Klan sign, and any white Protestant not allied with the region's industrialists was a demagogue or a vigilante. In 1923, for example, the *New York Times* looked South and declared in an editorial that "every Klansman, everywhere, is a potential lyncher and a public enemy." Of course, Southern reality begged for simplistic exaggeration and caricature, and Northern editors saw little else, especially as condemning Klan atrocities in the South became a beaten path to a coveted Pulitzer prize.

Hugo Black wouldn't buy it. He held his own exaggerated notion about the conspiring, biased tendencies of Yankee papers, industrialists, and the Republican party, and he was healthily skeptical of reports in Alabama's own dailies. Indeed, on the question of Klan violence, Black would have been among the last in Birmingham to blame local beatings on the Klan organization without real evidence. "There were a few extremists," he admitted, but the entire group could not be blamed for the independent acts of a few members. [25]

In every major labor strike in Birmingham, industrialists and their allies had accused unions of organizing violence and intimidation. In early 1921, for example, coal operators published a long list of beatings, armed attacks, and explosions (which exceeded all reports of violence in 1922–23) for which they blamed the United Mine Workers as an organization—not individual members. As a union attorney, Black had fought since 1908 against this industrialist strategy to create guilt by association, and in 1921 he went to court to show that the interracial UMW was the victim, not the perpetrator, of lawlessness and violence. In the 1922 rail strike, Black represented unions accused of organizing lawlessness and murder. In 1923, Black was unwilling to consider the Klan as an organization of violence simply because individual members might have committed acts of violence against people who were the object of the group's scorn.

Black's perspective was understandable, even reasonable at that moment in Birmingham's history, but it was a judgment made possible only by his money, standing, and white skin. Birmingham's black citizens had no such protection or privilege. They had no reason to care, much less wonder about how many different avenging angels of violence Birmingham's fractious whites could release into their midst. They knew the KKK's emergence as a societal force in the early 1920s was an undeniable symbol of how the region's worst nature and practices of hatred and violence lingered more than seventy years after emancipation. It did not, could not, matter to them in 1923 that the traditions of violence in the South's largest industrial city did not have their origins or even their primary malefactors in the Klan. It made life no more bearable, no less unjust even if the moment of original sin begetting Birmingham's lawlessness and brute force happened long before James Esdale adroitly masterminded the Klansmen's rise. And long before Hugo Black decided to give the Ku Klux his $10.

If this human evil had different white faces and different motives, it did not lessen its current horror nor remove its deadly yoke from the black bodies of the oppressed nor the souls of the white oppressor. In 1923 in Birmingham, the Klan stood as a self-evident symbol of a recurring cycle of pervasive racial bigotry and lawless violence within a racist social order. If Hugo Black did not knowingly, willingly join a band of masked, masquerading criminals, he nonetheless did help sustain an evil in the larger society by embracing the Klan's villainous purposes as his own, by helping the worst traditions of white society as it entered another chapter of insane behavior. Like all of his enemies and detractors and almost all of his white friends and neighbors, Hugo Black in 1923 could not bring himself to look carefully to the bottom of the evil.

IN REMEMBERING THE KLAN HE JOINED, Judge Black attempted later in his life to recast the Kluxers' mission beyond that of human hatred and white male superiority. "It was a fraternal organization, really," Black told the editors of the *New York Times* who agreed not to publish his words until after his death. "It wasn't anti-Catholic, anti-Jewish, or anti-Negro," he insisted.

Black must have forgotten that he was not before a jury of Southern white men in the segregated South. No one can support the proposition that Birmingham's Klan in the middle of 1923 was *not* "anti-Catholic, anti-Jewish, and anti-Negro" even if it also championed other moral principles, such as prohibition, and did not pursue its prejudice through organized, violent methods. On this point, Judge Black crudely misstated the facts.

The Klan's bias and ugly hatred permeated much of the public rhetoric and printed words of its leaders. It possessed the South's premiere, historical symbol of violent, white male supremacy, and its activities against Jews and Catholics were patterned after the Southern common man's view of race relations. An Alabama white man of this era often professed he knew and liked an individual "good" Negro, but he disliked the black race as potentially dangerous and inferior in mind and morals. A Birmingham Klan leader, for example, informed young Irving Engel in 1923 that he was not the kind of Jew against whom the Klan was preaching, at a time when the secret order was working to exclude Jews, Catholics, and African Americans from any influence or benefit in Birmingham society. As a group, Birmingham's Kluxers worked to have family, society, and government run by Protestant Anglo-Saxon men for Protestant Anglo-Saxon men.

In May 1923, the Klan ignited a large cross on the crest of Red Mountain, clearly visible from Hugo Black's neighborhood. With their fiery symbol ablaze and visible throughout Old Birmingham, a three-hundred car caravan of fully garbed Kluxers slowly and silently paraded through downtown. Klansmen on foot distributed handbills opposing the local school board's recent decision to spend a sizeable amount of their reduced budget on an industrial school for black children. Asking "Is the Birmingham News Fair?" Klan literature took issue with *News* publisher Victor Hanson and a Pratt Mining official who were leading efforts to upgrade Negro schooling. The Klan insisted that no additional public money be spent for Negro education until the school board had met the needs of *every* white child.

While trying to expand restrictions and phobias against Catholics and Jews that "True Americans" had set in motion, the Klan portrayed its own members as victims of religious and ethnic stereotypes. To drum up support among poor, uneducated whites in Protestant areas, a Klan newsletter, for instance, identified several Northern "Ku Klux Kleaners" who were accusing Kluxers of trading on "prejudice towards Catholics and Jews." The Alabama Klan editor turned the accusation on its head. Yankee critics, he wrote, were really saying, "Where there are no Kikes and Katholics there is no 'book learning.'"

When the "TWK [Trade With Klansmen] Monthly" hit Birmingham's streets in 1923, Hugo Black could read for himself the canned articles attacking all sorts of immoral Jewish cabals. "Violation and evasion of the prohibition laws has had a deep Jewish complexion from the very beginning," the newsletter proclaimed. It alleged "bootlegging is a 95 percent controlled Jewish business." Some Birmingham Jews had been in the liquor business before national prohibition, and this simple fact was ample proof for Klanish stereotypes and slurs.

Distrust of others may have been exceeded within the Anglo-Saxon Klan only by blind loyalty to its own. As the Dowling trial suggested, some Kluxers seemed willing to stand behind their brethren in court despite evidence of guilt. Black's own explanation for entering the Klan admits as much. He wanted to make certain that opposing lawyers did not get the upper hand with Klansmen on the juries simply because they were fraternal brothers.

Such Ku Klux influence could subvert the constitutional principles of America's jury system and often may have illegally affected verdicts, but seldom were situations clear-cut. Even in the Dowling case, the victim's identification of his attackers was contradicted by testimony from both defendants and others who gave them an alibi. The jury had to decide which sworn witnesses were more credible. If a juror believed a fellow Klansman more truthful than someone else, no specific law was violated by that act of personal judgment. It was like a coal operator deciding to put more stock in testimony of a fellow country club member than the words of an itinerant laborer, or, as in Black's Woodward case, a judge dismissing an old black man's story because he was an old black man. It constituted bias, but not a rigged jury.

If the Dowling case was an example of blind Klanish loyalty, it was a powerful, complicated one, in its own way stronger than religious prejudice. The case's background, which never came out at trial, reveals that Dowling had been appointed local health officer to succeed a Catholic physician whom True Americans pressured out of office. In 1917, Dowling took up his post as the candidate of anti-Catholic groups, but in 1923 those credentials may not have been enough for him to overcome the credibility of one of the Klan's own.[26]

Unfortunately, Black's gross overstatement about the Klan's loathsome nature has obscured a more realistic explanation. When compared with the majority of white Protestants in the South and Birmingham in 1923, Kluxers may not have been more bigoted than the vast majority. White supremacy was the fabric of Birmingham life. Reinforced over half a century, white racial superiority was, in the words of Oscar Underwood, the essential cornerstone of Southern civilization. The South's white leaders never questioned its wisdom or its sanctity. By 1920, as Black and Alabama's unions realized, a credible allegation that a group did not believe in white supremacy could be a death sentence. Amid this popular psychology, the Klan did little more than provide crude imagery for the South's central, inviolate principle, slightly expanded by adding Protestantism to the superior genes of the white male race. It was a small leap of faith, and one that many Alabamians had already made.

None of the Klan's stereotypes and bigotry, none of its moral imperatives for bone-dry, clean living introduced a single new thought into the currents of Alabama's consciousness, nor did the KKK broaden the range of human hatred in Birmingham by its elaborate doctrines and vile language. Yet the Klan's nature was different from its forebears and from all others who came before it. The Klan united the South's prevailing prejudices into one organization, one purpose—subordinating and vilifying black-skinned people and some nonconforming whites. In parading Protestantism, whiteness, and manhood as essential terms of virtue, the Ku Klux pushed Jews and Catholics partially across the South's color line so that heritage and religion became additional, indispensable terms of Old South Americanism.

Armed with this encompassing perspective, the Klan united several of Birmingham's longstanding factions within the white community into one loosely-knit organization that began taking on a life and force far greater than the past sum of its parts. By bonding white men through rituals of race, religion, and nationality, in active support of one another and a fundamentalist,

Protestant moral agenda, the Klan created a broad movement of middle-class and working-class men in Birmingham. Their intentions resurrected the basic ambitions of white craftsmen, proprietors, and civic leaders who poured into Birmingham in its first years, seeking to create a New South city where the region's white labor and white capital were equals in a good white society.

Amid one of Birmingham's worst economic depressions, the Klan rallied white men falling mostly near the middle ranks of society, men who were feeling the pressure of economic and social conditions. The hooded order gave them a common cause, common enemies, and the rituals of communion. These men came mostly from the ranks of shopkeepers, salesmen, and small proprietors whose livelihood depended on a local consumer economy (not national industrial markets); craftsmen and skilled workers whose jobs dwindled as the city's steel and metal industries harnessed new technologies and hired more semi-skilled, cheaper black labor; clerks, bookkeepers, and cashiers whose lives were controlled by the city's large corporations; suburban, fundamentalist Protestant ministers and church elders who feared a public decay of moral, patriarchal values; struggling WWI veterans who saw their own patriotism disgraced by the fate of the city's unknown soldier; farmers confronted by a ruinous agricultural market and increased local regulation; union men who lost wages, jobs, or bargaining power after unsuccessful strikes; and men of all occupations who saw themselves in the middle of a state of lawlessness or in a moral crusade for prohibition.

This confederation of white working- and middle-class Protestant men challenged Birmingham's established economic interests as much as the city's ethnic and racial communities. In effect, Birmingham's Klan in 1923 took up the articles of racialist faith which industrialists had trumpeted in destroying unionism in 1920–21. Now, the Klan insisted on creating the white society that a racialist faith promised every white Protestant. It was a movement to redistribute the control and benefits of racial domination from a relatively small number of whites of mixed religion and ethnicity to a wider range of Anglo-Saxon men.

Birmingham's Klan demanded that jobs and tax dollars go first and foremost to white men and their families who lived by the Protestant work ethic and worshiped a Protestant God. In so doing, the Klan confronted both the industrialists' New South vision (with black labor as the city's industrial advantage) and Birmingham's corporate control. In addition, by defining Klan membership and public virtue according to fundamental Protestantism and strict prohibition, the Klan excluded many industrialists and their allies from their confederation.

"The Klan was, in effect, . . . revived as a force to counter the corporations," Black once explained in confidence, as he remembered these days in Birmingham. Years later he also told a young, white Southerner: "The Klan was the liberal wing of the Democratic Party of Alabama. By that I mean anti-railroad and against the corporations." Black's sister-in-law Virginia Foster Durr recalled the Klan of 1923 as "an underground union." "The workers tried to form unions to make themselves politically effective and they were defeated," Durr recalled, "so they flocked to the Klan. They joined partly because they were determined to get more money and to be politically effective. They felt they could do this only through a secret organization."

Often when a KKK member attacked their enemies or the city's daily newspapers (which they saw as the voice of their elite enemies), he spoke in conspiratorial terms about almost every iniquity except economic injustice. "The enemies of the klan," remarked a citizen, "are . . . bootleggers, home destroyers, those who are against our government or the Protestant Christian religion, . . . or just common, ordinary fools."

Yet, the Kluxers' moral issues were solidly linked to economic interests in Birmingham and much of Alabama in 1923. The Klan's white moral movement became as threatening to Birmingham industrialists and Black Belt planters as an interracial labor movement. Both jeopardized the industrialists' settled economic advantages. When corporate leaders created a citizens committee in 1922 to counter Negro fears of floggings, harassment, and the Klan, industrialists acted to prevent losing cheap black workers. They did not want to rely on more costly white workers, and they feared, as the Reverend Henry Edmonds once jokingly observed, that the only response a Negro in Birmingham made to a Klan warning letter was to "read it on the train." Just as local industrialists needed to prevent Northern labor agents from luring African American workers away from the city, they had to oppose the Klan who could drive the city's black workers northward.

The Klan's moral agenda also presented industrialists with what Walker Percy would have called a "disorganization of labor." Kluxers wanted to deny cheap public amusements to poorer workers, including blacks and many immigrants. Their vigilante enforcement of prohibition and Protestant uprightness was aimed often at unskilled workers. The Klan's anti-Catholicism posed a direct challenge to Birmingham's immigrant workers, most of whom were Italian, and to the Catholic families of several prominent industrialists. Klan influence within juries and politics threatened to empower opponents of local industrialists. Altogether, the Klan's insurgent agenda imperiled industrialist control of labor and corporate clout within government. The Klan movement was "anti-corporation" because it challenged industrialists' control of Birmingham's white and black societies.

For this reason, the city's business representatives and corporate attorneys led the opposition to the KKK's growth. They did not—could not—attack Kluxers on economic terms. Because the Klan did not strike or picket workplaces, industrialists could not marshal special deputies, guards, and armed militia to fight them. Nor could industrialists attack the Klan by invoking the almighty demons of racialism that they themselves had elevated to new levels of worship. The Kluxers already had partaken of that wafer. Without other alternatives, Birmingham's elite and corporate spokesmen attacked the Klan for anti-democratic activities—violence, intimidation, secret spying, and vigilantism. Ironically, corporate leaders could not malign the Klan's madness, only its methods—methods which in the past had been the industrialists' stock in trade.

Roy Percy's uncle in the Mississippi Delta saw the challenge of the Klan in accurate, if romanticized terms. Four months after attacking the local Ku Klux, the elder Percy wrote that the Klan's arrival marked "the fading away of the old aristocracy of the South." In Birmingham, where Old South traditions had been amended with New South industries and Northern capitalism, the emergence of the Klan meant that the aristocratic rule of industrialists was in jeopardy.

From Talladega, a decidedly un-aristocratic Vern Scott saw the Klan's economic role. As a young man in the early 1920s, Scott sat near a stairway leading to a Talladega Klan hall where he sold peanuts in a night job. Over the years, Scott became a self-trained, local historian who in the 1960s asked Judge Black about the Klan. Scott wanted to know why the public voices of Alabama's industrialists and planters in the 1920s who "saw nothing wrong with beating a Convict to death in a coal mine (while distinguished people like Mrs. Tutwiler cried out against it) . . . go to the limit to uphold an old reprobate who had been whipped by the Klan?" After complimenting Scott for "a very good understanding of Alabama history," Black politely declined to address the question. No matter, Scott had his own answer. "I think in the first instance their set was property," he told Black. "But in the second instance their set was having their political and economic order deranged by the Klan."[27]

Scott's question might have equally been put to Birmingham's black newspaper editor who worried in print about local floggings and Klan rhetoric with not one word about convict leasing. Oscar Adams regularly commended coal companies for paternalistic care of black miners and their families and published the coal operators' speeches to their black workers amid industrialists' large paid ads. Adams was far outside the white property set, but he had hitched a ride with Birmingham's industrialists. During labor disputes, he loudly opposed interracial unionism as white trickery and recounted how local, all-white craft unions excluded qualified blacks from available jobs.

In the real life of Birmingham, Adams was trying to choose the lesser of evils. No group competing for white leadership in Birmingham in the early 1920s saw black folk as whole, free human beings. All sides attempted to use black workers for their own white group's gain. In this white competition, Adams sought the cooperation and favor of the city's elite whose growing welfare capitalism and recent endorsement of President Harding's "New South" outlook on race relations promised hopeful, humane features. In a candid, open letter in 1922 to "colored miners," Adams warned all of Birmingham's black citizens: "Our gains have come from the principles of right living, and our cause has been represented by men of power, of character, and no other has been a benefit."

For thousands of poor African Americans who went into the mines for petty and nonviolent crimes, Adams's conclusion must have lacked conviction. In raw human terms, the convict leasing system did far more damage to blacks in Birmingham in the early 1920s than the Klan, *even* assuming every nighttime whipping was by a Kluxer. While the KKK was a rough riding, visible symbol of racial bigotry and clandestine methods, no African American died at the hands of the Birmingham Ku Klux in the early 1920s. The number of reported floggings during the decade's first three years was less than fifteen. From available sources, there were about thirty night-time anonymous raids, although no one was reported physically injured from the events. Suppose that thrice as many floggings and raids went unreported. During the same years in the mines around Birmingham, nearly two hundred convicts—mostly African Americans, many convicted of small or victimless crimes—died. Scores more were crippled for life, and the incidents of severe, unprovoked whippings and "doghousing" of black convicts at the mines—even after Governor Kilby's ban—could not have been as small as thirty, sixty, or twenty times that number. "I can but think of our convict system," wrote Dr. Parke in his diary in 1923, "& of people singing 'How I Love Jesus' & yet holding out the collective hand to receive blood money from the profits of our terrible convict lease system."[28]

Of course, one more profoundly damaging wrong in Birmingham did not make the Klan right. But in 1923 in Birmingham, the Klan was not stained with the blood of deadly racial and religious injustice, as it would become in a few decades. In a deeply racialist society, where whites were in conflict over who would control and benefit from white supremacy, the Klan did less physical, tangible damage than others who in many instances were among the Klan's harshest critics.

The Klan's role, moreover, in furthering the worst aspects of a racialist society in the heart of Dixie may be comparatively less than modern history has assumed. In looking back over this period of history, W. E. B. DuBois concluded that after the defeat of Reconstruction the "instruments of group control—police, courts, government appropriations and the like" of the South's governments had laid the foundation for the region's legacy of lawlessness and violence. "Such evils led to widespread violence in the South, to murder and mobs," DuBois wrote. Over the years, the New South abandoned some of the more blunt instruments that ceased to treat an African American as "a human being and a person," but Alabama alone held onto a form of the Old South's "legalized slavery" for over a quarter of the twentieth century to sustain white greed, good government, and private profit.

In 1923, Black's decision to join the Klan was not advised by DuBois's sense of history. His home-grown sense of Biblical fairness was shaped honestly by his experience with corporate forces of group control and violence in Birmingham. Black had fought the oppression of Birmingham's industrialists who commonly used secret and open forces of violence and lawlessness. He had represented unions accused of fostering massive lawlessness and violence because of their individual members' action. He had represented the crippled bodies and widows of industrial negligence. He knew of the slavish use of African Americans for deadly profits in jails and convict mines.

Black's ambition would not allow him, as others did, to limit his beliefs to a private diary or to abandon a legal and political career in Alabama. His self-confidence and sense of duty led him to believe that he could persuade the Klan's white men of a right course, just as he had earlier won verdicts from Birmingham's all-white juries. He conducted himself by the ethics of responsibility as well as conviction. Faced with a rough choice, Hugo Black preferred a Klan town to a company town. On these terms, Black moved half-heartedly into the Klan after Herman Beck relieved him of the obligations of friendship. Like the rest of white Birmingham, Black had no African American friend whose approval was also necessary.

With limited choices in a profoundly immoral society, Black followed the Roman adage of Marcus Cicero, "Choose always the lesser of two evils," words Black once underlined and scribbled on the back flap of his book. Black knew in 1923 that he was not following exactly his own mother's precepts or Lizzie Patterson's instruction in childhood to "do right." But, he believed he was making the right choice. "I'm doing the right thing even though I don't like the Klan," Black reportedly told his sister Ora. In joining Birmingham's Kluxers, Black did not turn his back on human decency or on his own past. He did not abandon or reshape his moral principles in a devilish exchange for fortune, fame, or political gain. He did not stand silent in the face of growing evil. His hands were not stained by the blood of racial violence. Although, in retrospect, his decision was a hazardous moral judgment in a misbegotten society, Hugo Black did not suspend his moral compass when he decided, once and for all, to become a Klansman.

Practically no one outside his family, a few close friends, and local Kluxers knew that Black had joined the secret order. "We didn't know that he had joined," recalled Irving Engel who was one of several Jews keeping up with such developments in the early 1920s. In large part, they didn't know because they detected no change in Black's words and actions, public or private. "We never categorized Black as being a Klansman in spirit," explained Engel, who took a job offer in New York to escape the grip of Birmingham's growing Klan mentality.

At his first klavern meeting, Black may have felt obliged to establish his own belief in law and order. More than once, Black retold the story to relatives and friends. "I . . . told 'em I was against hate, I liked Negroes, I liked Jews, I liked Catholics," Black recalled, "and that if I saw any illegality goin' on I wouldn't worry about secrecy, I'd turn 'em in to the grand jury. Well when I finished, they cheered and said to me that's what you're obligated to do under our rules."

Black's memory of his own words stands as the only source for his terms of entrance into the Klan. Local reporters, however, were on hand September 11, 1923, to chronicle a gigantic induction ceremony, by far the largest in Birmingham's history. Throughout the warm day, cars filled up the dry lake bed at Edgewood Park as more than forty thousand whites crowded into the area to eat barbecue and watch their children swim. Local musicians played, and, contrary to law, supervised public dancing was permitted.

In the afternoon, several hundred Ku Kluxers, with and without masks, marched downtown behind the official Klan band from Chattanooga to drum up attendance for the later ceremonies. In a show of defiant strength, Kluxers paraded in front of the homes of some Birmingham's industrialists; none joined the procession. By nightfall, five thousand hooded Klansmen formed a human circle around some two thousand "unnaturalized" candidates. As fiery crosses hissed and crackled in the background, the new Kluxers marched solemnly in a circle, stopping at three different points to receive their vows. Somewhere among them was Hugo Black, unnoticed in the anonymity of hooded Klan dress.[29] Except, perhaps, for his excited hazel eyes, visible only at close range through the two slits in his white hood, Black would have looked like any other Klansman.

On this night, Black wasn't seeking truth or justice. There was no interrogation in his eyes. Instead, he was giving witness to a faith that was as confused in practice and principles as the history and conditions that had given the Klan new life. Although Black saw a lesser evil in joining, he must have seen no good in such massive, mystic demonstrations. With its pageantry of pagan ritual, this faceless ceremony was the first and last time Hugo Black would walk lockstep with Birmingham's hooded Klan.

Four weeks after that clear, dark night when he pledged his unfailing bond with all Klansmen, Black appeared before the U.S. Circuit Court of Appeals in New Orleans to plead for his client Henry Lewis and dozens of other black convicts who had been permanently injured in Montevallo's mine. As Black feared, the local federal courts had held in the summer of 1923 that judgments won by prisoners due to Montevallo Mining's negligence could not be recovered. The judges held that a court-ordered award for negligence under federal law was not a "debt" which a bankrupt company had to honor. Under this ruling, those who had loaned money or materials to Montevallo had a right to demand full payment. Those injured by Montevallo's negligence under forced labor did not.

In briefs and arguments before the appeals court, Black claimed that every other federal court was on his side. His problem was an earlier U.S. Supreme Court opinion that held that a court judgment for alimony to a wife was not a "debt" and could not be recovered in bankruptcy. In that case, the Court said that Congress intended to define "debts" only as monies owed by contracts, and alimony was not a "contractual" debt.

It proved a bothersome precedent that Black attempted to distinguish by arguing that Montevallo owed money to Henry Lewis because he was injured while, in effect, working as the employer's forced "servant" under contract with the state of Alabama. That contractual role of a "servant" differed from the relationship between husband and wife. Montevallo's lawyer derided Black's distinction. "Alimony is the outcome of the marriage contract and a servant's claim," the opposing lawyer stated. On this legal point in 1923, Black's client—and America's women—appeared stranded.

Developments in Montgomery were similarly dismal for Lewis and other convict miners. While proclaiming his opposition to the lease system, Alabama's Governor W. W. "Plain Bill" Brandon convinced the legislature to extend the system again, due to practical considerations, until March 1927—two months after Brandon would leave office. The governor defended his policy by asserting that new state inspectors would protect convict miners' safety and that mining was now a relatively safe occupation. In truth, the governor and legislature did not see how to end convict leasing without raising taxes. "The Alabama Convict Department," state reports crowed, "is now one of the largest business enterprises in the south"—and one of the more profitable ones. This corporate model of government continued to generate almost two million dollars in gross receipts from convict labor.

After Frank White's death, Birmingham's League of Women Voters recruited Judge William Fort (a Klansman) and Irving Engel to help renew public support to overturn the governor's decisions. Black's former roommate Walter Brower (a Klansman) was one of Jefferson's new state senators and became the chief legislative leader against convict leasing. To build support for Brower's proposed bill, a handful of League women worked daily to secure newspapers' endorsements and to string together local networks of men and women to buttonhole state legislators.

Judge Fort conducted a speaking tour around the state to rally opposition. Claiming support from thousands, including the Temperance Union and every other women's state organization, the new Statewide Campaign Committee for the Abolishment of the Convict Contract System made a special appeal to ministers. Many responded, including the minister of Montgomery's First Baptist Church who accused the state of slavery "as great as that in which the children of Israel found themselves in Egypt." Many legislators flinched at such harsh accusations, but, fortified by the governor, speaker of the house, *Montgomery Advertiser*, and Pratt Coal officials, the legislature did not budge. Instead, it passed a resolution without a recorded vote declaring that convicts were treated as good as they deserved and deploring "continued agitation of the convict question in this State by certain newspapers, public agitators, and ill-advised and misled citizens of the State."[30]

While resisting legislative changes, Governor Brandon couldn't prevent mining companies from manipulating the convict leases. In August, Montevallo's trustee decided again to abrogate its contract for convicts due to lowering coal demand. The company needed fewer miners in the foreseeable future, and the state had virtually no recourse but to accept Montevallo's decision. Now, Alabama faced the prospects of a substantial drop in convict revenues despite continuing the system.

In September, a week after Birmingham's massive Klan induction, convict miners sent Alabama their own message of distress and anger. Five hundred convicts at Pratt's Banner mines mutinied, claiming mistreatment. For several hours, convicts held mining supervisors and prison officials as hostages and wrecked machinery beneath the surface. With the legislature's swift consent, Governor Brandon reinstated official use of the whip, which the warden used liberally as soon as rebel leaders were in custody. Brandon also attempted to block a local grand jury inquiry on grounds that there was nothing to investigate.

In response, the Statewide Committee formed an ongoing organization that would make convict leasing a major issue in the 1926 elections and hoped to shape a better prison system. In late October, activists established the Alabama Prison Reform Association. Amelia Worthington Fisk, who had coordinated the group's past work, and two other women were elected working officers. To show a broad spectrum of support, the group elected an official of DeBardeleben Coal and a local UMW lawyer from Jasper as honorary vice-presidents. For president, the group elected Hugo Black, who accepted the position after learning of his choice in the newspapers. Less than two months after becoming a Kluxer, Black became Alabama's leading spokesman for the decent treatment of the state's African American convicts.

Bad news, however, continued traveling fast and frequently for convicts. On November 20, the federal Fifth Circuit Court of Appeals handed down a decision rejecting Black's arguments. Conceding that other federal courts differed, the judges held that the Supreme Court's alimony case governed. In bankruptcy Montevallo could eliminate all court awards for past negligence and, when David Roberts was ready, emerge from bankruptcy without those liabilities.[31] In effect, convicts in the Montevallo mine had no remedy of law, no matter how negligent or abusive the company became. Now, almost two hundred convicts at Montevallo were as doomed as Black's client John Brown. All stood outside the law. In effect, all were "civilly dead" in "revengeful hells."

Black considered going to the U.S. Supreme Court. A split among opinions of the federal circuits was a prime reason for the highest court to review a case, and a change in the Court's recent membership prompted Black to pursue an appeal. "In researching my case," Black remembered, "I turned up a federal district court decision made by Judge Sanford from Tennessee" that agreed with Black's position. The Tennessee judge was now Justice Edward Sanford who had been appointed by President Harding to the Supreme Court in February of 1923.

Less than two weeks after the Fifth Circuit's opinion, Crampton Harris wrote to the Supreme Court clerk asking "whether the Supreme Court make any exceptions to their rule, requiring thirty printed copies of the record in cases appealed *in forma pauperis?*" In the Fifth Circuit, Black and Harris had filed only one copy of the record and were allowed to borrow it from the court to prepare briefs in order to avoid costs. Now at the Supreme Court, Black's partner explained that their client was a convict with "no money and no opportunity for making money" and that the only way to print the record was for the lawyers to bear the cost. "I cannot afford to do this unless it is absolutely necessary," Harris insisted.

As was his wont, Harris exaggerated. Black and Harris probably grossed more than $50,000 during the previous year, and in 1923 the lawyers were on their way to even greater prosperity. The firm's out-of-pocket costs in the

Lewis case were relatively small, a little more than $90 by the time the case was ready for the Supreme Court. To his credit, Black had spent a great deal of time on the case with no prospect for a large fee, even if he won, and many lawyers would not have appealed. But, Black and Harris could easily "afford to do this."

Claims of hardship show more than Harris's penchant for embellishment. They sketch a self-portrait of the firm's partners. As plaintiff's lawyers, Black and Harris tended to see themselves like most of their clients, never far from the edge of hardship. Occasionally, despite his large income, Harris may have been on the edge due to bad luck as an addicted gambler. Free of such vices, Black might have been slightly cash-poor for brief moments in 1923. He had joined Albert Lee Smith again in investing in Birmingham real estate and sustained a very comfortable life style. Black also had to wait months or years before he collected on almost every big, favorable verdict that often had to be retried after appeal.

The simple truth is Black was stingy. Like many of his generation who achieved material success from modest beginnings, Black had a spendthrift nature and the self-image of a man always struggling to make ends meet. It was an outlook that persisted regardless of Black's level of comfort or wealth. Perhaps, he could never shake the feelings of unexpected poverty from the days after the world war. By all measures, he was a fantastically successful lawyer in 1923, but many years later Black remembered that he was a "struggling attorney" when he handled the Lewis case. Black could see himself no other way.

Apparently, the Supreme Court clerk was no less penny-wise. "There is practically no exception to the rule that thirty copies of a record shall be printed," he informed Harris. "If the case is one properly to be proceeded with *in forma pauperis*, of course, a motion to the court could be made," the clerk wrote. ". . . This, however, is rarely granted."

The clerk had good reason to discourage Henry Lewis's lawyers. For more than three decades the U.S. Supreme Court had construed narrowly a statute allowing federal courts to waive certain costs for poor litigants. In 1904, for instance, the Court held in a unanimous opinion that the pauper's law did not apply to appeals. Even after Congress expressly amended the statute in 1910 to state that poor litigants need not prepay "for the printing of the record in the appellate court," the Supreme Court ruled that such waivers depended solely on the Court's discretion. Judging from reported cases, the clerk's cool response truly reflected the Court's longstanding hostility to waiving its rules. Black, nevertheless, decided to try. He prepared a special motion for the Court and planned to make his plea in person to Justice Sanford before the end of the year.[32]

As Christmas approached, Black's case took on greater significance for Alabama's convicts. Governor Brandon announced a new plan for the lease system. Instead of leasing convicts to mining companies, the state was proposing to lease mines from companies. In turn, the state would supervise the convicts' work and sell coal back to the mining companies who would trade it in the free market. In this tortured arrangement, companies got their profit and the state got its revenues. Brandon proposed this conversion by 1925.

On the eve of his Washington trip, Black, as president of the Prison Reform Association, blasted the governor's proposal. "It does not take us one foot closer to the end. The last right of the convict is swept away" if this proposal is adopted, Black warned, and the "state has added burdens. A few mine owners alone receive the benefit." Black insisted that Alabama would not improve its revenues because the plan did not include "any effort to obtain the highest price for the coal."

Black's principal concern was how the proposal would devastate convict workers. The plan kept all the cruelties and indefensible characteristics of the existing system, Black charged, and took away "the last privilege of the convict"—the right to recover damages in court for injuries from coal operators' negligence. Access to the courts was the only countervailing force preventing mine operators—private or government—from treating convicts as animals, not humans. According to Alabama law, Black noted, the state could not be sued for its own wrongdoing and, therefore state operation of the mines would rob convicts of any means of redress.

In other words, Governor Brandon's proposal placed all the state's convict miners into the predicament of Henry Lewis, John Brown, and Montevallo miners. Regardless of how cruelly they might be treated, how dangerous the mines, how negligent or inhumane their supervisors, convicts would have no lawful remedy, no effective access to the courts. All of Alabama's convict miners—more than fifteen hundred—would effectively become civilly dead in 1925. Afterwards, Black feared many would be humanly dead.

At times like this, Black's enduring optimism had impressive rewards. After a long train ride to Washington, most men would have been fatigued and discouraged by the journey and events at home. Yet, Black must have been particularly energetic and persuasive when he walked up the Capitol steps to the Supreme Court offices near the old Senate chambers. After filing his motion with the clerk, Black went to see Justice Sanford, who luckily was available on New Year's Eve at his home, where justices then maintained their offices due to a lack of space in the Capitol. Black's motions and papers tell something of the meeting. "The litigation which Henry Lewis desires to bring before this Court involves one clear-cut question of Federal law," Black began. "There is no dispute about the facts. There is no disagreement as to the legal question raised." On his side of the question, Black noted, were all reported cases except the one decided by the Fifth Circuit against his client. "The decision creates a needless diversity of opinion on the construction of the Bankruptcy Act," he pleaded.

Black cited the 1910 Act of Congress authorizing an appeal by a poor person with a waiver of court costs. Black laid out Henry Lewis's affidavit, which Black had prepared:

> I am broken in body and health as a result of my injuries . . . I will never
> be able to work and earn a living. I have no money. I own no property. I
> have no way of earning money. I could not work and earn money even if
> any way were open to me . . . I have no relatives on whom I could call for
> help. Unless I am allowed to prosecute my petition . . . as a pauper, as pro-
> vided by the Acts of Congress . . . I will be unable to get my just and lawful
> compensation out of the estate of the bankrupt company that injured me so
> grievously. I am a negro, without education. I can figure out no way to get
> money for any purpose.

Black didn't know that Justice Sanford's father was a native of Connecticut who went to Tennessee shortly before the Civil War or that his mother was a Swiss uncomfortable with the Old South traditions. He did know that the judge had agreed with his position on the legal question while sitting in Knoxville on the federal bench. Both sets of facts must have helped. On the spot, Justice Sanford agreed to ask three of his colleagues to allow Lewis's case to be heard under the pauper statute.

Only three additional votes were needed because the Supreme Court accepted cases whenever four of nine justices agreed. Sanford probably began with

William Howard Taft, America's magisterial chief justice who had served as U.S. president until 1913. He was already Sanford's mentor who had navigated his Court appointment. The chief justice was also sympathetic. "Much remains to be done in cheapening litigation in the Federal Courts," Taft had told the American Bar Association a year earlier, "by reducing costs or transferring them to the public treasury." On January 7 of the New Year, Black received a *collect* telegram from the clerk of the U.S. Supreme Court. By order of the chief justice, the U.S. Supreme Court had granted Henry Lewis's motion.

Regardless of the final outcome, Black felt a lasting sense of achievement: "I was successful in convincing the Supreme Court through Justice Sanford that it should take indigent cases as the law provided."[33] It was an important, new practical precedent. No less, in retrospect, in measuring the meaning and motives of Black's early life and the place he called home, it was a telling moment. One of Alabama's newest Klansmen had won for Henry Lewis and other poor, black convicts their day of hope before the nation's highest court.

FIVE DAYS LATER, TELEGRAPH WIRES around Birmingham were jammed for an afternoon with news of a riot at Montevallo's mine. More than sixty-five convicts, including a half-dozen whites, had entombed themselves beneath the earth by blockading all mine entrances with heavy equipment, much of which they dynamited. In response, the mining supervisor shut off the air pumped into the shafts and prepared to wait out the convicts who had no food and only a limited supply of water. When armed guards attempted to rush the mine, prisoners hurled sticks of dynamite to deter them.

After a standoff of several hours, one of the convicts, Ed Duggar, agreed to speak by telephone to the state prison inspector in Montgomery. Duggar, who had been convicted of highway robbery in Jefferson County three years earlier, complained that the riot had been prompted by the warden's recent decision to place prisoners in the mining camp's "doghouse." The convicts wanted to meet with Governor Brandon and insisted that he dismiss the warden. After almost twenty-four hours, short on life's necessities, the prisoners agreed to come out so long as no one was flogged or "doghoused" for the mutiny until after a local grand jury investigation.

In early February, after Montevallo assessed its damage at $30,000, a local grand jury returned indictments for attempted murder against the reputed gang leaders. Duggar, Alonia Crusoe (a convicted murderer sentenced to life in prison in 1916), and five other black prisoners were indicted as prime accomplices. No white convict was charged, although earlier press reports claimed at least two whites were among the ringleaders. Running for reelection, the presiding judge of Shelby County declared that prisoners should not expect a "bed of flowers" in convict mines. The grand jury agreed and exonerated the warden's use of the doghouse and suggested that he use the whip more often.

State officials confessed lingering puzzlement about why the riot took place, but miners' recent conduct seemed a clear indication. After court decisions effectively denying them the right to challenge Montevallo's negligence and misconduct, a few prisoners had attempted to maim themselves so that they could no longer work as miners. The most common technique was to stuff half a stick of dynamite inside a shoe and blow off one foot. Apparently, smaller injuries had not been sufficient to remove convicts from the mine.

Alonia Crusoe had lost parts of both hands and permanently injured one arm in earlier mining accidents. Yet, as a life-term convict "civilly dead" for the last two years, Crusoe was denied the right to appear in court to testify against the company for their negligence in the accidents and, since November 20, had no right to recover damages from Montevallo, even if he could go to court, since the company was in bankruptcy. Despite his injuries, Crusoe had been returned to the mines since he still drew breath and on most days could walk and dig, if motivated by company guards.[34]

In late February, Crusoe was brought a few miles from the mining camp to the circuit court in Columbiana to stand trial. To everyone's surprise, the same man who sent Crusoe to prison in 1916 appeared in court in 1924 to volunteer as his lawyer. Former Jefferson County solicitor Hugo Black had rushed from a Pythian meeting in Birmingham to represent Crusoe. Against charges of attempted murder, Black was prepared to defend a convicted black murderer who everyone knew had helped to destroy $30,000 in mining machinery, thrown dynamite at the company's white guards, and endangered the lives of more than sixty other black and white miners.

In Black's view, Crusoe and other African American convicts had been driven to lawless violence by the government's decision to place them outside the law, to deny them any lawful protection or remedy against violence. Without effective access to courts, Crusoe had been removed from human grace and lawful society. The prisoners had been sentenced to death in a "revengeful hell" where the company could do anything to them without restraint. These black men had no choice but to fight official lawlessness with their own lawlessness. Before an all-white jury in a full trial, Black would defend this mob violence and lawlessness as entirely justifiable. It would be the single instance in his entire life when Hugo Black stood up to speak or to act in defense of group violence.

The presiding judge was in no mood for an unexpectedly long, acrimonious trial by a zealous attorney. He postponed Crusoe's case until the court's next term after upcoming elections. In the end, Black was never able to put Alabama's lawless convict lease system on trial through the Crusoe case. Another all-white jury refused to convict Crusoe's companion, Ed Duggar, and the prosecutor decided there was no reason to try Crusoe, who was already sentenced to forced labor for the rest of his life. Duggar also was not retried, although his reprieve was short-lived. Ten months after the riot, Ed Duggar was killed in the Montevallo mine by a "rock fall," at least according to official reports. [35]

10

The Golden Rule
of Good Citizenship

NATIONAL PROHIBITION POLITICS AND PROSECUTIONS

By 1924, the corroding metals of both the Old and New South—raw racialism, cheapened government, patriarchal rule, one hundred percent Americanism, Protestant-only fundamentalism, and industrialist greed—structured Alabama's "Steel City" with the dead load of a deeply repressive society and without the scaffolding of interracial cooperation or self-interested, aristocratic honor to repair outrageous abuses. But, like much of the South and the nation, many white citizens in Birmingham seemed to believe by the middle of the Roaring Twenties that their community was in grave, immediate danger of a collapse of traditional values and social order.

Five years after the passage of a federal constitutional amendment prohibiting the sale and consumption of alcoholic beverages, illegal beer and whiskey remained plentiful and profitable on both sides of the Mason & Dixon. Alabama's own Zelda Sayre Fitzgerald had become a poster child of an insolent, materialistic youth culture that spread across middle-class America as an early byproduct of the nation's emerging, consumer market. And, it remained a clamorous time with the continued growth of big cities, heavy industries, science and technology, and non-English immigration, as well as a wide range of progressive reformers demanding wholesale changes to reorder America into a more just, diverse society.

At this historical moment, in the mind's eye of many of the South's older white Christian men and women, a growing disregard for their traditional faith and values—and the laws enacted to uphold them—loomed far more dangerous than secret, extra-legal activities and occasional, random acts of intimidation undertaken to preserve that tradition and its social order. This amorphous fear of a breakdown in society's old values, old-time religion, and the current social order often exacerbated exploitation and coercion, but it also weld a new vocabulary of change and a reemerging definition of citizenship that sought to invoke old values as a mandate for addressing new challenges. This identity had existed for years and took ideals from both ancient and modern aspirations. It did not defy the South's cherished past but claimed a national character and origins from a source more holy and powerful than the Old South. This reform-minded, tradition-bound identity had a name, "good citizenship," and it came in large measure from the Good Book.

Speaking of the "Tasks of Good Citizenship" a few years earlier, the president of Baylor University, one of the South's premiere Baptist colleges, had informed Southerners that the good citizen "must know wrong when he see it, and correct errors as they arise . . . He caters to no class, but seeks the elevation of all men. He reveres the past, and uses it to throw light on the future." This "social-minded citizen" concerned himself with "what we drink" among other issues, Samuel Brooks declared. The good citizen "was American at heart" and no one, rich or poor, had "a right to throw off on good citizenship." Above all else, according to a state historian of neighboring Mississippi, "obedience" and "respect for law" were the essence of "good citizenship" which always led a person to examine the "moral side of every social, political, and economic problem."

This definition for one's self and the aims of one society resonated naturally with Hugo Black. Good citizenship digested the simple, most meaningful influences of his whole life and sculptured ancestral themes with materials of modern life and current agendas into an image where Black saw himself. In Hugo's childhood, Fayette Black's political idol, Grover Cleveland, had endorsed America's needs for "good citizenship," but it was William Jennings Bryan who brought together Populists and Democrats across America on these general terms. Fighting against Fayette Black and other "Gold Bugs" of 1896, Bryan spoke for "common citizenship" and for only one thing gold: "the golden rule to do unto others as you would have them do unto you." (And soon, in 1925, in the twilight of his long career, Bryan would rise again to defend laws banning teachings that were contrary to the literal words of the Good Book in the famous Scopes Trial.)

The only local man who transcended Clay County's divisions of politics, religion, and money was Merit Street. While Hugo could not see his uncle's feet of clay, he did hear family, friends, and neighbors speak of him as "a good citizen and staunch Democrat." As a boy, Black heard the language and meaning of everyday conversations—and almost every grand jury report—when Clay's men called "upon the *good citizens* of the county" to join them in doing whatever they thought was right.

The boy who never forgot Henry Grady's words, spoken on the year of his birth, carried forward Uncle Merit's outlook on the Old South: "The Confederacy was powerful, but the Union more powerful . . . the Bible was more mighty than either the Union or Confederacy." This Biblical version of a "New South" bound together a nation that the Old South had kept divided. It also took meaning from the innocent memories of Black's mother and female teachers who used the Good Book and the story of the Good Samaritan at home, school, and Sunday school as their children's guide to a world governed by the Golden Rule.

Yet, from Black's first days in Birmingham, it was not "good citizens" who ruled the city. It was the "best citizens," the old order's code that material wealth and mythic lineage to the Old Confederacy defined the natural aristocracy among white citizens even in the New South. When biracial unions formed, it was the city's best citizens or "leading citizens" who were called to prevent another "Reconstruction Rule." Walker Percy did not complain that "good citizens" weren't attracted to public office in Birmingham's council form of government. He sought a commission government run by the "best class of our citizens." The Alabama's Defense Council's corporate leaders and lawyers who met with Senator Oscar Underwood to plan the control of Alabama society after World War I did not issue a call for all "good citizens." No, they believed "*conservative citizens* of the respective communities must . . . render it impossible for *citizens of less stability* to administer affairs in their own way." As Justice Anthony D. Sayre knew, the "best" citizens in white society were "conservative" and the poor were unstable.

In his first ineffectual efforts to build the Klan in Birmingham in 1915, Wizard Simmons understood the assumptions of the old order and very little about why masses of working white folk did not flock to his call. "A Klan has been organized in Birmingham and they seek only the *best citizens*, who are closely affiliated with the Confederacy." Dr. Thomas Parke, the unheard voice of Birmingham's white egalitarian conscience, understood. Even in a diary only for his own eyes the doctor awkwardly refused to write the term, "best citizens," when condemning the "narrowness and reaction of our *better circumstanced people.*" Like Black, Parke refused to scale human worth by material wealth.

In 1916, when Black stood victorious as the new county prosecutor, he summoned "good citizens," not the "best citizens," to aid his new administration. When Black went to "courts of justice" for Sam Bradford or Mary Miniard, black men or white women, he preferred a judgment from "a jury of *good* and lawful men," not from Birmingham's "best men," including Federal Judge W. I. Grubb. In 1920, Black had invoked a different concept, "Alabama citizenship," when the state's interracial unions sued to stop the Underwood campaign's race-baiting tactics. There, Black and his clients stressed their allegiance to Alabama customs, logic, and traditions to rebut racial allegations by the state's "conservative citizens." Yet, after Willie Baird was lynched in the miners' strike, a coroner's jury appealed to the "*good citizenship* of Alabama" in seeking justice for a union member.

In 1922, after the Dowling floggings, Brother Black and other Baptists did not seek out Jefferson's "best citizens" to deal with the problems of law and order. They called upon all "*good citizens*," as did the Civitan Club where Black was president-elect. Although Black as a lawyer more than once interjected "nigger" into his public vocabulary, never did he represent or speak for "best citizens," only for "best friends" and "good citizens."

"In order to be a good citizen," Judge Black informed the Ensley Kiwanis Club in late March 1924, "one is *compelled* to observe the Golden Rule." While suffering from a painful, bad back, Black stood for forty minutes lecturing small businessmen on how to define and live as a good citizen. The "guarantees of the American Constitution" provided that "all citizens were free, equal, and permitted to enjoy unrestricted pursuit of happiness," Black declared, but a good citizen does not use these entitlements for his own personal pleasure or gain. A good citizen knows that "selfishness has no part in real American citizenship." Good citizenship requires service to others and "real education" through intellectual and spiritual self-improvement. In keeping with his evolving outlook, Black asserted that the "good citizen" had to "first of all protect his body which was the temple of the spirit and to protect and maintain one's home."

This version of the Golden Rule of good citizenship was no trite homily. In the context and language of 1924, it was a clarion call—first, to strictly obey laws and restraints, especially against illegal liquor which defiled each person's "temple of the spirit," and, second, to aggressively enforce the law against "home destroyers," including profiteering bootleggers. Judge Black was not rallying good citizens to dress the wounds of a stranger on the road to Samaria. Instead, he invoked the terms of an activist, militant Jesus challenging moneychangers who defiled the holy temple. "Destroy this temple," Jesus insisted, so that "the temple of the body" might become each person's sanctuary of true faith.[1]

In this era, "whatever you wish men might do to you, do so to them" did not translate into tolerance of others' shortcomings. The Golden Rule often meant a virtual intolerance of others' moral differences and a commandment to compel others to obey the same strict self-rule and the same abstinent virtues that Black required of himself—and gladly would have others demand of him. As the Good Samaritan, a Biblical "good citizen," Black was prepared to take care of the wounded stranger. But he would not nurse the afflicted victim to good health. His duty as a good citizen was to banish the source of affliction and punish the wrongdoers.

At the end of March 1924, Black had set his sights on one particular, blasphemous temple where he intended to put his version of the Golden Rule into action. Eight years after whirlwinds of a hurricane, earth tremor, and Alabama's equally treacherous prohibition politics had kept him away, Black returned to Mobile to close down a vast, illegal liquor traffic into Alabama. In 1915, Black had emptied the whiskey bottles found in the cellars and rabbit holes along the Chattahoochee River at the state line. Now, as a specially appointed assistant U.S. attorney general, he was preparing to drain the Gulf of Mexico of its illegal, Alabama-bound liquor.

By PREVAILING PROTESTANT STANDARDS, Mobile was truly Alabama's Sodom and Gomorrah. It was a coastal city where cultural influences from Spain and France lingered far beyond their past political rule when gilded saloons, extravagant gambling houses, and salons of both refined culture and pagan lechery shaped a city's social life. In more recent decades, the world's sailors and seamen came ashore at Mobile to enjoy and sustain the city's tolerant mores and brisk commerce. While it closely observed the South's terms for racial supremacy, Mobile was forever out of line with the state's prevailing moral agenda. It was the only city in Alabama to allow Sunday movies and Sunday baseball games. It refused to ban public dancing or to establish local censorship boards for regulating picture shows, and it tolerated prostitution. "I'd be a stockbroker in hell before I'd be a director of a Mardi gras," a revival preacher vainly warned Mobilians who were alone in Alabama in celebrating the annual debauched ritual even at the peril of damnation.

Mobile also fiercely opposed prohibition. Most local leaders, businessmen, and many residents believed that the port city could not financially subsist if liquor dried up. "Mobile has survived epidemics of Yellow Fever, overcome the devastation of storms, and depressions caused by financial panics," warned city leader Sid Lyons, "but I believe prohibition . . . would be the greatest blow." In 1907, with statewide prohibition before the legislature, a local banker warned: "Mobile is prepared to secede from the state of Alabama . . . and cease to be dominated by our country cousins."

When state and federal prohibition arrived, Mobile did not secede from Alabama—only from prohibition. In the years when Solicitor Black successfully prosecuted more than four hundred cases of liquor violations in Jefferson, Mobile registered only forty-four convictions and merely a hundred and seventy-seven indictments. Local dry leaders such as attorney Aubrey Boyles charged that the courthouse crowd rigged juries to assure bootleggers weren't indicted or convicted. Protestant preachers accused the city police and county sheriff of ignoring liquor traffic. During national prohibition, the prominent Lyons family openly operated a brewery in the city.

Many Protestant leaders believed that Mobile's large Catholic population was another reason for the city's open defiance. Catholics had long been the largest religious group in Mobile's white community. Their numbers were twice as large as Baptists and three times that of Methodists. The city had a noticeable number of prominent Catholic institutions: one of America's oldest Catholic colleges, several parochial schools (often outnumbering white public schools), hospitals, orphanages, convents, charities, and fraternal groups. It was also headquarters for the state's Catholic bishop and staff.

Complaints of illegal liquor in Mobile were often an indictment of Catholic influence. In 1907 a prominent Mobile churchwoman complained that liquor flowed openly because Mobile suffered from a Catholic mayor and the "tolerance" of a "Catholic city." In 1913, a Mobile Protestant informed Alabama's governor that "this County is controlled by the Catholic church, very much to the financial interests of that particular organization," and in 1919 Alabama's prohibitionist legislature feared Catholics were not only trafficking in illegal liquor but also stockpiling weapons for a papal insurrection. It ordered all Catholic convents in the state searched.[2]

In 1922, three years after national prohibition began, Mobile lawyer Aubrey Boyles was appointed U.S. Attorney for south Alabama with recommendations of both local Democratic and Republican politicians, including businessmen Bob Holcombe and Frank Boykin who were the "big men" in Mobile's illegal liquor. A graduate of Alabama's law school during Hugo Black's freshman year, Boyles was a handsome, energetic man considered more ambitious than prohibitionist, an essential qualification in Warren G. Harding's administration which maintained a profound reluctance to enforce prohibition. As a young attorney, Boyles helped lead local dry efforts and prosecute whiskey cases in state court, but in his private practice he seemed very accommodating to powerful businessmen and politicians who had made prohibition more lucrative than legalized liquor. In a demonstration of his flexibility, the new U.S. Attorney had converted to the Republican party only after the opportunity of his appointment arose.

U.S. Attorney General Harry Daugherty guided Boyles in enforcing federal dry laws. Daugherty's own familiarity with whiskey and liquor businesses led prohibitionist leaders to believe that, instead of searching for rum runners off the Gulf coast, the long arm of the federal government was often reaching for another illegal drink. In a national government overcrowded with Harding's cronies, Daugherty and roommate Jesse Smith maintained constant relations with the "Ohio Gang," including Daugherty's brother who openly flaunted prohibition laws in the nation's capitol. In an investigation of the Klan, the attorney general piously declared that government "will not be run or intimidated by men behind masks." Behind closed doors, however, Daugherty's cronies sold liquor-related permits, patents, government appointments, and presidential pardons to the highest bidders.

By the fall of 1923, after President Harding's unexpected death and the suicide of Daugherty's roommate, the attorney general's influence had plummeted. A straight-laced President Calvin Coolidge and an honest, determined U.S. assistant attorney general in charge of prohibition, Mabel Walker Willebrandt, encouraged strict law enforcement which Daugherty, with whispers of scandal sniping at him, was too busy and too weakened to obstruct. During this period, Aubrey Boyles initiated a series of undercover investigations after businessman Frank Boykin offered him bribes to shield Mobile's wholesale liquor business.

Boykin traded on the public power of his well-placed "friends," including the attorney general whose letters and personal photographs Boykin brandished as signs of political influence. In November, Boyles surprised Mobile by leading several liquor raids and later indicting more than one hundred Mobile citizens, including Boykin and many prominent politicians and businessmen.

More than $100,000 worth of liquor sat embargoed in a downtown alley, encased by electrified barbed wire and armed guards. Boyles's former associates and friends, now under indictment, were outraged. They accused Boyles of trying to destroy the local Democratic party, most of whose leaders were indicted, and they maneuvered to arrest the U.S. Attorney on state charges of attempting to bribe deputy sheriff William Holcombe, brother of local liquor magnate Bob Holcombe.

Estranged from old friends, Boyles was relieved of his official duties until the state charges were settled, and the U.S. Department of Justice eventually approved the appointment of Hugo L. Black as special assistant attorney general to handle the Mobile prohibition cases.[3] Like many opportunities and trials throughout his life, Black's new assignment came as a result of his proven sincerity of Protestant purpose, abundant ability, and the admiration of "good citizens" and good friends. And in this instance, his enemies were obliged by unique circumstances to do unto Black as they wished he would do unto them.

Black's selection probably originated with Mobile prohibitionists who admired his past courtroom work. The city's primary dry group, "The Citizens League," was composed of leading Baptist and Methodist clergy and elders. It was headed by state legislator Horace Turner, a Methodist dry and the wealthy owner of a local shipping company, who served as foreman of the grand jury issuing federal indictments after Boyles's raids.

Turner and the Citizens League were unwilling or unable to accept any prominent lawyer in Mobile since practically the entire local bar association was retained by the eight dozen defendants. Mobile prohibitionists had sought Black's services in 1916, and they still wanted Alabama's most aggressive dry prosecutor.

An enemy of the lawyers he knew best, Aubrey Boyles needed someone like Black who was from outside Mobile and capable of winning the cases—the U.S. Attorney's only hope for vindication. Boyles also needed a Democrat whose unquestionable party loyalty could dispel charges of partisan motives.

The Citizens League, moreover, was Boyles's only strong support, and by necessity their choice was his.

Alabama Attorney General Harwell G. Davis secured Black's appointment. Both men were politically and personally dry, active Baptists, and had been working for the same causes since 1909 when both assisted Herman Beck. After Boyles was indicted, Davis joined Mobile prohibitionists to have Black appointed as a federal prosecutor.

The Justice Department official in charge of prohibition, Mabel Walker Willebrandt was one of the few nonpolitical appointments under Attorney General Daugherty and was the only woman in a high government position. She was not a teetotaler, but Willebrandt was "straight as a string" and had supervised aggressive prohibition prosecutions. She had appointed an elderly Republican lawyer from Chattanooga, "a true Southern cavalier," to prosecute liquor cases recently against prominent citizens in Savannah, but the assignment exhausted the old attorney who took ill. As a result, Willebrandt turned to Black, whose record in prohibition outweighed his devotion to the Democratic party.

In an administration where the Golden Rule often meant those with the gold ruled, Daugherty was not so easily convinced. Frank Boykin had enjoyed steady access to the attorney general through his confidante Jesse Smith, and with political problems mounting, Daugherty did not want to commission a rabid Democratic prohibitionist who might connect him and his associates with Mobile's illegal liquor. Harwell Davis remembered Daugherty as a "big Irish crook" who "kept promising to give me the authority for Hugo, but wouldn't do it." Finally, Davis went to Washington and confronted the attorney general. "I'm not trying to embarrass you," Davis assured the nation's chief lawyer, but Daugherty persisted in refusing Black's commission.

Davis turned for assistance to the new Democratic leader of the U.S. Senate, Alabama's Oscar W. Underwood. The senator was not a prohibitionist, of course, and easily could have been warned by Forney Johnston about Black's involvement in the 1920 campaign. Underwood, however, had a few important prohibitionist supporters, including Mobile's Horace Turner, whom he wanted to please. The senator was seeking Alabama voters' endorsement in an upcoming campaign for President and at that moment did not need questions raised about his enthusiasm for prohibition.

According to Davis, Underwood picked up the telephone in his Senate office and called the U.S. attorney general. "I'm sending over one of my messengers down there to get the authority for Mr. Hugo Black to prosecute those cases in Mobile," the senator informed Daugherty. "The attorney general of Alabama has advised me as to what he has . . . We are not trying to embarrass you," Underwood reiterated. "But, of course, if I can't get that letter today, I'll have to . . . ah . . . take the floor of the Senate tomorrow to expose the situation." With great glee, Davis remembered, "I got the letter!"

Harry Daugherty resigned under pressure in March 1924 shortly before the Mobile cases went to trial. In authorizing Black as a special assistant U.S. attorney general, Daugherty made one last attempt to frustrate the appointment. He stipulated that Black could not be paid by the government for his services. Therefore, by appointment of a lame duck official who opposed prohibition, Hugo Black became a lawyer without pay for a Republican administration he despised, through the efforts of the Alabama senator known among prohibitionists as the stooge of "booze and business," to prosecute liquor cases which might expose the misdeeds of the man who appointed him. In the end, the tortured terms and circumstances of Daugherty's commission did not matter. They simply reaffirmed Black's real clients. The Citizen's League, Mobile's dry disciples, paid Black for his work as a government lawyer throughout most of the Mobile trials.[4]

By the end of March, Black had taken up temporary residence at Mobile's Cawthan Hotel where several months earlier, in rooms rigged with special mirrors and peep holes, undercover agents received protection money and liquor under the watchful eye of federal officials. As a result, the federal court docket at the Old Customs House a few blocks away was crowded with dozens of cases of buying, possessing, and selling liquor.

Black and two other special government lawyers saw no way to try these cases in their lifetimes, especially after a mistrial in their first case against lawyer Percy H. Kearns, Boyles's former partner, who acted as a bag man for ring leaders. Despite U.S. Attorney Boyles's direct testimony about Kearns's bribes, the jury had deadlocked.

Black convened a special grand jury. To set the stage, Black offered immunity to the city's mayor (a wise-cracking, one-eyed businessman), and to a local bank president (a member of the prominent Lyons family) if they would identify all the places they had purchased illegal liquor in the county during the last year. It was the mayor's habit during such difficult moments to remove his glass eye and roll it around on a tabletop to distract his questioner, but in this case Black persisted.

Both witnesses refused to talk. They claimed Black was attempting to entrap them for lying to a grand jury, since it was impossible for them to remember every Mobile location where they had purchased illegal liquor. In the end, Black discovered no new information, but he did maneuver city leaders into publicly confessing that they had violated prohibition laws so many times in one year that they could not reasonably remember every instance.

Black persuaded the grand jury to indict seventy-one citizens, including businessmen Frank Boykin and Bob Holcombe; William Holcombe (Bob's brother and deputy sheriff); Mobile's police chief; the county sheriff; and more than a dozen other businessmen. Almost all had been indicted earlier, but Black's new indictments charged a conspiracy to violate dry statutes. These charges permitted Black to try all defendants in one trial and to present overlapping evidence for one conspiracy instead of seventy-one separate cases.

The deadlocked jury in the Kearns case prompted Black to employ new strategies. He suspected that at least one juror in the prior case had been bought off and he asked undercover F.B.I. agents to investigate. Black also wanted to change juror selection. By local custom, juries had been drawn in cases arising in Mobile only from Mobile County and the small, adjoining Baldwin County, but Black now asked the court to require the clerk to draw names for a jury venire exclusively from the other eight Black Belt counties in the federal district.

Before Federal Judge Robert Ervin, Black observed that "attorneys for the defendants themselves had brought up the question of the difficulty in getting an entirely disinterested jury." Black agreed. If the jury was selected from Mobile, defendants would receive "a jury composed of friends" not peers, Black insisted. As a plaintiff's lawyer, Black always thought juries should be chosen only from Birmingham for Birmingham cases, but Black as federal prosecutor wanted a different method.

Black's proposal met a chorus of groans and objections from more than twenty defense attorneys who protested that he was underestimating local citizens. Defense lawyers agreed that local newspaper "headlines . . . make out a *prima facie* case of guilt" against their clients, but, in a novel twist, they argued that the pretrial publicity actually required the jury be chosen from Mobile. "People in the northern section of the district were forming their opinions on what they saw in the papers," the defense contended, while Mobile citizens could counter misinformation with informal sources of news. Judge Ervin sided with Black and ordered a jury drawn entirely from the district's upper division.

Next, Black looked toward Birmingham, down the hallway from the offices of Black and Harris on the fifth floor of the First National Bank Building. Although Black had contacts throughout south Alabama from Pythias lodges and other fraternal groups, he must not have recognized enough familiar names. He sent copies of the list of prospective jurors to James Esdale, now grand dragon of Alabama's Ku Klux. Esdale obliged his fellow Kluxer by indicating which men on the venire were brethren in "Klan citizenship." Because prohibition was a prime issue used in Klan organizing in south Alabama, Klansmen as jurors probably were as prosecution-oriented as Anti-Saloon League members. (Black couldn't cross-check his venires with membership rolls of the Women's Temperance Unions since women still did not sit on Alabama's juries even in federal courts.)

With prayers from the state's leading prohibitionists who called Mobile prosecutions "one of the outstanding campaigns instituted since the prohibition amendment," Black opened the government's case. He had carefully selected twelve jurors from outside of Mobile, including apparently some ex-servicemen and perhaps some Klansmen.

"Mobile citizenship stands for law enforcement," Black declared in his opening statement. "The only real soldier in times of peace is the man who walks in obedience to the law." According to Esdale, Black also recited lines from an obscure poem:

> God give us men! A time like this demands strong
> Men whom the lust of office does not kill
> Men whom the spoils of office can not buy . . .
> Tall men, sun-crowned, who live above the fog
> In public duty and in private thinking . . .
> Men who serve not for selfish booty,
> But real men, courageous, who flinch not at duty;
> Men of dependable character; men of sterling worth . . .
> God give us men!

Black may have spoken the poem by heart since he had repeated it, with slight alteration, in his KKK initiation ceremonies.[5]

Black explained his case against the defendants to the jury:

> Gentlemen . . . They are charged with conspiracy to violate the national prohibition law or whiskey law; they are charged with conspiracy to make Mobile a wet town by making it easy to sell liquor . . . they are charged with accepting money . . . those that paid were allowed to sell, and those that did not were pulled . . . Now, about Mr. Boykin, whom they tell us is the biggest businessman in Mobile . . . we expect to show . . . that in addition to his big business he was in constant communication with Jesse Smith and Mel Daugherty, brother of Attorney General Daugherty; that he would show these letters to the blind tiger operators and would tell him "I am a big man in Washington and here are letters and telegrams I have from Jesse Smith"—Jesse Smith being the late gentleman who was associated with Attorney General Daugherty . . . Mr. Boykin, as a part of his business, came to the district attorney and wanted to divide up the funds . . . We expect the evidence to show in regard to Mr. R. L. Holcombe that he was   boss of the ring . . . and it was he who pulled the strings . . . and that his pocket was one of the pockets that got the money that was paid by the protected boot-leggers.

During the next ten days, Black paraded a regiment of witnesses before the jury. Former police officers testified that their chief, Patrick O'Shaughnessy, maintained lists of bootleggers who were free from arrests and ordered policemen to pressure blind tigers to contribute to a local campaign fund. The police chief's assistant named defendants who split the surplus of the campaign fund as payments from the whiskey ring. Other witnesses who sold "shinny" on the streets told of payments to deputy sheriffs.

Overcrowded, the historic, elegant courtroom resembled a hare's warren with narrow passageways between mounds of people. The judge's bench was at the back wall, and directly below him, facing the audience, sat Black and his two assistants. To their right, next to an Italian Renaissance pillar vaulting thirty feet to the ceiling, was the witness stand which looked straight at the jury, boxed at the other side of the prosecution's work table. On the far side of the pillar, partially blocked from a direct view of the witness, were more than twenty defense lawyers. Within the four pillars at the middle of the room, defendants sat in a wide semi-circle directly confronting the judge and looking on a partial profile of witnesses. The three remaining walls of the enormous courtroom were filled by spectators in wooden pews.

This arrangement quickly led to discord. After calling his first witness, "Black was frequently interrupted by defense counsel H. C. Smith [representing Boykin], who insisted" that his client had a constitutional right to confront witnesses against him and "that as a matter of fact his client could only see the back of the head of the witness." Judge Ervin ruled that the right to confront witnesses didn't guarantee a right to be up front in the courtroom, although defense lawyers remained sullen.

Both defendants and spectators stirred when, pacing through passageways, Black examined the government's undercover agents. One explained a secret codebook used in cablegrams among shippers and runners at sea. "500 hurt" meant five hundred cases of Johnny Walker were on their way, and "500 dead" meant five hundred cases of White Horse whiskey would soon arrive. During prohibition, there had been countless "casualties" on the dangerous high seas of the Gulf of Mexico. One secret agent testified that whiskey dealers told him that Frank Boykin used part of the protection money to befriend Washington officials.

The most sensational witness was "Lone Wolf" Gonzaullas, a special agent who became a confidante of Mobile's wholesale bootleggers. Destined to become a famous Texas Ranger, Lone Wolf described how six big wholesale dealers rendezvoused with booze runners at sea and clandestinely shipped whiskey to customers across North America. He named attorney Percy Kearns as a bagman who paid him more than $2,000 for protection for the "Big Six." Gonzaullas also testified that wholesalers repeatedly identified Bob Holcombe and Frank Boykin as ringleaders.

Harry French, a "volunteer informant" and former Pinkerton agent, proved far less credible. He swore that Bob Holcombe gave him money in return for protection, but, while on the stand, French became mesmerized by Holcombe who sat across the room. The witness began staring only at the defendant and answering Black's questions as if he were in conversation with Holcombe—not testifying before a jury. "I laid my bank book on the table," French stated in response to Black's question, "and *you* [looking at Mr. Bob Holcombe] looked at it and *you* told me it was 'chicken feed.'"

Repeatedly, French answered Black's questions by addressing the answers to

Holcombe. "Designate the defendant by name!" Black harshly instructed his own witness in an effort to break the spell. Finally, as French began to awake from his trance-like state, Holcombe jumped up and shouted, "Keep looking at me and don't look down like that."

"I am telling *you* just what happened," the witness responded, "and I am looking at *you*."

"You *damned* liar," hissed William Holcombe, Bob's brother. Under cross-examination, French proved almost deserving of damnation. He admitted that as a U.S. undercover agent, he personally spent several thousand dollars received from bootleggers.

By the trial's seventh day, two other defendants had exchanged epithets and blows in open court after Black tricked one into believing that the other was turning state's evidence. Afterwards, Judge Ervin ordered all persons, except women and lawyers, searched for weapons before entering the courtroom.

On Thursday night, May 8, Black suspended nightly trial preparations to speak to the Men's Club of the St. Francis Street Methodist Church. He was introduced as a Christian gentleman whose private life was as exemplary as his public work, a teacher of men's Bible classes, and the man sent to "make Mobile a better city in which to live."

Judge Black stood to preach to the choir. He declared that a church that does not teach the "duty of citizenship" has failed its purpose. "If men of the church . . . sit supinely by and fail to rid their city of places where they would not like their young sons and daughters to go or of corrupt officials," Black proclaimed, "neither the church nor America will advance." Calling for a "militant and active church and Sunday school," Black invoked the parable of Jesus driving the moneychangers out of the temple of God as precedent for ridding the city of its whiskey ring.

By "militant," Black said, he did not mean people should commit violence in the name of Christ or that the church should get into politics by endorsing candidates. Yet, there were other ways to be a militant Christian. "Wrong cannot exist when men and women take up the banner of Christ," Black proclaimed. To illustrate, Black reviewed improvements in Birmingham since 1908 when prohibition emerged as a political issue. "If a candidate expects to get into office in Birmingham now," Black observed of a city increasingly subject to Klan activities and influence, "he at least must pretend to be a Christian gentleman," apparently now more than a Southern gentleman. The Bible is the foundation of the true American home, Black concluded, and he urged everyone to study it for themselves as active Christians and citizens.

In court the next morning, Black attacked the moneychangers. He attempted to introduce a stack of telegrams between Daugherty and Boykin that Black claimed were used to convince liquor dealers that Boykin's political connections would protect them. Daily headlines shouted news of congressional hearings on the former attorney general's corrupt practices, and Black was eager to publicize a connection between the local whiskey ring and national Republican leaders. Boykin's attorney argued that the telegrams were irrelevant to the conspiracy charge. In his chambers, Judge Ervin examined the documents. One telegram from Boykin to Daugherty in July 1923, implored, "Don't let anything happen to keep *it* from going over." Despite the message's conspiratorial tone, Black could not prove exactly what "it" was or how "it" was related to charges against Boykin.

According to Black, when he went back into the courtroom to retrieve another telegram, the document was missing. Judge Ervin questioned defendants to determine if they had it, and Frank Boykin admitted he did. Asked to produce the document, Boykin replied, "I can't. I ate it." In the end, Boykin's action did not matter. The judge ruled, in effect, that the telegrams might be edible but not admissible.

At this point, Black surprised everyone, including defense lawyers who jumped to their feet in unison when the special prosecutor announced that "the government rests." The defense had expected Aubrey Boyles's testimony as the centerpiece of the government's case. He was the only witness with direct evidence implicating Holcombe and Boykin as the two top ringleaders. Apparently, Black feared defense lawyers could effectively put Boyles on trial if he were called. As a result, Black had to dismiss indictments against Boykin and nine lesser defendants.[6]

Attorneys on the other side of the pillars developed a simple, extensive defense: their clients appeared on the stand and denied all testimony of all government witnesses. Many prominent Mobile citizens also testified to the defendants' good character or the government witnesses' unreliable and questionable character. Percy Kearns, the go-between lawyer, for instance, claimed that he was acting as an agent of U.S. Attorney Boyles and paid the "Lone Wolf" money to help catch crooked prohibition officers. City police commissioner George Crawford swore that no campaign fund existed and the police chief was diligent in enforcing liquor laws. He testified that both he and the chief had arrested four "big bootleggers," but most were very hard to catch.

In cross-examination, Black turned Crawford's denial into an admission. "You made a statement a while ago . . . describing how hard it is to catch the big bootleggers," Black said. "I assume from that that you have tried to catch some of them. Who were the big bootleggers . . . hard to catch . . . ?"

"I don't know who they are. I think the jury is trying to decide that now."

"I would like to ask you again . . . ," Black continued. The court reporter read Black's earlier question: "Who were the big bootleggers that . . . [you found] hard to catch . . . ?"

"My answer," Crawford pleaded, "is based on the result of what is brought up in court."

"Can you name us a single instance?" Black demanded.

"I don't know that."

"You are not an expert in catching bootleggers," Black told the police commissioner.

"No, sir," Crawford admitted, preferring to confess his shortcomings instead of naming the big men he had been unable to catch.

The police chief's denials of wrongdoing also sounded more like admissions of general guilt under Black's cross-examination. After denying all charges with a smile, the chief admitted he employed a deputy convicted of violating prohibition and allowed another deputy to live in a local "home brew emporium" that was raided several times. "I never drank in Mobile," the chief insisted. "I went out of town to do my drinking."

During the defense's main case, Black informed Judge Ervin that two defendants, Sheriff Cazalas and deputy sheriff William Holcombe, had given jurors a personal tour of the Mobile County jail. As a courtesy to the men deciding their guilt or innocence, the county's top lawmen had pointed out to jurors moonshine stills and photographs of seized liquor, although "it was not explained to them that the pictures were taken nine years ago," Black stated. The judge was aghast and scolded defendants for such gross impropriety, but at Black's request he did not declare a mistrial—Black did not want to restart the massive case.

Throughout the trial, each side appealed to the jurymen's racial and religious prejudices to discredit the opposition. The government had indicted a handful of African Americans who were deliverymen for wholesale whiskey dealers in an effort to force the black men to turn state's evidence. They were essential informants since, as one deputy sheriff explained at trial, "Negroes handle most of stuff for liquor dealers."

One federal agent also worked undercover with a black man, whom whiskey dealers jokingly dubbed "Cyclops"—a title ridiculing KKK leaders. Black had called one African American to testify, and others provided useful information to the prosecution.

At every opportunity, defense attorneys belittled the government's black informants and attempted to smear the prosecution with racial familiarity. After one black witness testified that he sold liquor to a defendant, the defense lawyer befuddled the Negro who, according to a local reporter, "became considerably confused and furnished much amusement for the court crowd by saying he was charged with 'sauspiracy.'" Another defense attorney accused a white government agent of being on friendly terms with Negroes, including drinking illegal liquor with them. (The lawyer also attacked the witness' credibility by mentioning the fact that he spoke six foreign languages.)

The defense also brought up "Cyclops." One lawyer asked a government undercover agent if he had been thrown out of a local blind tiger because the owner thought "you and Cyclops" were acting like social equals. Black objected to another question about "Cyclops," but the defense lawyer responded, "I submit that a man should be judged by his associates, and if he was going around with Cyclops, we want to know it." And he wanted the jury to know it.

Black attempted to neutralize the defense's racialized attacks by occasionally referring to Negro witnesses and defendants as "niggers." A young NAACP leader, John LeFlore, considered Black's epithet "scurrilous and insulting," but the prosecutor did not "inadvertently" mention the word. As he had done before, Black used the term in court deliberately—in this case to signal to white Black Belt jurors that he was not elevating African Americans beyond their given, Southern status.

For his part, Black underscored to jurors that several important defendants were Catholic. At one point, he interrupted his questioning of Percy Kearns to ask where the witness went to law school. When Kearns answered, "Georgetown," Black simply repeated the answer without further comment. He apparently felt certain that at least one Protestant juror would recognize the school as a Northern Catholic institution. In many instances, as with Police

Chief Patrick O'Shaughnessy, the defendant's ancestral and religious heritage was self-evident.

Years later, Boykin's lawyer accused Black of trying to convict his client by "attempting to prove he was a Catholic," although surviving transcripts fail to show any such strategy against Boykin and no direct, concerted appeals to anti-Catholicism. In a conspiracy case with seventy-one defendants, Black was attempting to connect everyone's vices and indirectly to nurture the popular connection between liquor and "Catholic influence." He tried to connect Boykin to the "big Irish crook" in Washington and to the Holcombe brothers who were well-known as "high Roman Catholic," according to Harwell Davis. But if any juror wanted to use "Catholic influence" as a basis for conviction, he didn't need Hugo Black's guidance in these Mobile cases.

After more than a hundred and fifty witnesses, prosecution and defense rested. The trial had lasted almost a month and produced more than two thousand pages of testimony. Yet, defense lawyers suggested that both sides waive closing arguments to permit jurors to return to their homes more quickly. Confusion was often a good defense, if jurors took seriously a presumption of innocence. "The suggestion in the presence of the jury," Black remarked, "was appreciated and we will consider it." Once the jury had retired, however, Black opposed the idea, and plans were made to give the defense thirteen hours for closing arguments and the prosecution six hours. Overnight, however, Black changed his mind and waived final arguments so that only the judge's instructions were left.

When Judge Ervin began his jury charge, the defense knew they had out-maneuvered themselves. Ervin decided to give jurors his own understanding of the evidence, although he told jurors that they did not have to accept his interpretation. "Now, the testimony tends to show that the following men were wholesalers," the judge bluntly declared, as he listed the men accused by the government. Judge Ervin said the evidence showed that the police chief and Percy Kearns were guilty. William Holcombe and other deputies also were guilty, the judge stated, but "they are guilty in a minor capacity" because they were only taking orders. The sheriff was merely a figurehead, weak and controlled by others. The judge told jurors he would find businessman Bob Holcombe innocent. "I could not . . .convict any man of a felony when the essential connection rested on the testimony of . . . French," the judge stated.

When the judge concluded a lecture lasting more than two hours, defense lawyers were on their feet noisily taking exception to every reference of guilt that touched their clients. After all objections were duly noted, jurors retired. They returned seventeen hours later and announced their verdicts, basically following Judge Ervin's findings. All whom he believed guilty were found guilty except the two men who had shown jurors around the county jail, Sheriff Cazalas and deputy William Holcombe. The jury did convict the city's chief of police. Only eleven of the original seventy-one defendants were convicted, but Percy Kearns and the "Big Six" wholesale dealers were among them.

Judge Ervin postponed sentencing for a month, although he suggested the guilty's fate after he was welcomed with deafening applause at the local Rotary Club. Rotarians sang, "They Say Old Judge Ervin, He Ain't Got No Style, But He's Style All The While," as the judge, an elderly, good-natured gentleman with half-shut eyes and a bushy, white mustache stood silent. Afterwards, Ervin provided a few impressions about the trial and, to uproarious laughter, speculated that his impressions would last two years for some people. The maximum sentence for conspiracy to violate prohibition laws was two years.

After departing for Birmingham to attend to his private law practice, a newly pregnant wife, and a one-year-old son, Black conferred with government lawyers about charges accusing U.S. Attorney Boyles of attempting to bribe William Holcombe. Because Mobile juries remained unreliable on prohibition, Black had used a special statute to remove the case to federal court. The case was set for trial in late June, but Will Holcombe could not be found. He had left the city surreptitiously to attend the Democratic National Convention in New York.[7] He was not alone. In late June 1924, many Alabamians were turning their attention to the Empire State where, for the first time, American radios would broadcast a national political convention and where Alabama's own Oscar W. Underwood would try to become the first Deep South politician since the Civil War to become President.

IN LATE JUNE, as Democratic delegates assembled in Madison Square Garden, Oscar Underwood, Forney Johnston, and a bevy of loyal operatives, politicians, and newspaper editors spoke confidently of the senator's chances. Yet the optimism that launched Underwood's national campaign in the late summer of 1923 when he spoke before an admiring, joint session of the Alabama legislature had died prematurely. Despite attempts to be "first"—the first candidate to announce, the first to win a state primary, the first to be nominated at the convention, and the first native Southerner to become president since the Civil War, Underwood did not arrive in New York in first place. In fact, except in Alabama, the senator had failed miserably in every Southern primary.

With Johnston as his alter ego and campaign manager, Senator Underwood had embarked on a speaking tour of the region amid August's deadening heat in 1923. The tour proved too demanding for an aging leader. "I can't go on in a general campaign," Underwood told Johnston, who maintained his Washington office while the senator recuperated at a summer home in Tate Springs, Tennessee. By late October, Johnston had arranged for Underwood to make a short tour of Texas since winning that state's large delegation "would mean his nomination and his election." Johnston wanted Underwood to make a few "short and informal" speeches without addressing issues, simply "for people to see you and come into contact with you."

When he arrived, Underwood entered a Texas-size political storm in which the Ku Klux Klan was both a primary force and a pivotal issue. The national Klan had a new Imperial Wizard, Hiram Evans, a Fort Worth dentist who was none other than the son of Clay County's former probate judge. Earlier, the younger Evans had joined the Texas Klan and as its grand dragon had built its political influence. Now, at the top of the national Klan, Evans led a rally of the Ku Kluxers at the Texas Fairgrounds where Underwood was scheduled to speak the following day. The Klan drew more than ten thousand spectators as Evans declared Catholics, Jews, and Negroes unfit to be American citizens. Underwood's subsequent speech on foreign affairs drew fewer than a thousand listeners. Afterwards, when Underwood spoke to a luncheon group, Evans publicly convened Klan leaders across the street at a hotel to plot the defeat of the presidential bid of the candidate of the "Jew, Jug, and Jesuit."

Two days later Underwood rose to speak in Houston, where Klan support had recently weakened. He was no longer willing to obey Forney Johnston's rules. Underwood had been cudgeled by Evans's Klanish taunts and now delivered a speech attacking the Kluxers. "When any group of men unites in a secret order to run the laws and the government, their action strikes at the very heart of government," Underwood declared. "No class or clan can assume control over a democracy."

"I did not take my position in my Houston speech captiously or without careful deliberation," Underwood later contended. "When I have once crossed the bridge where great principles are involved . . . I do not turn back." There was no turning back. In February 1924, Underwood spoke before the Mississippi legislature, some of whose members were Klansmen. "The intolerance that drove the Puritan to Massachusetts and the intolerance that drove the Catholic to Maryland were cemented in an instrument of faith and freedom in the Constitution of the United States," the senator proclaimed. "My friend of the Ku Klux Klan . . . the hour has come for you to stop. It is not fair . . . to try to conduct a government behind closed doors . . . if you think the laws of your state are being violated, stand up *on your hind legs* and go to the grand jury . . . Don't take a poor wretch, who is unable to defend himself, make him suffer at your hands, and deny the principles of the Constitution of your government."[8]

Underwood's attacks reflected his sincere belief that the Klan was a dangerous, secret political organization using extra-legal techniques. Yet the senator's opposition to the Klan was also an essential political strategy. The original campaign plan that Forney Johnston developed with "Oscar the Ingenuous" had two parts: first, win the delegates from the old Confederacy as a favorite son and, second, win the support of Northeastern Democratic states as a principled Southerner opposing the Klan.

Underwood understood that winning the South was not enough. The South comprised less than a third of the delegates to the Democratic convention. To win the nomination and general election, a Southerner had to attract support from Northern Democrats. "Who makes up the democracy of these northern states?" Underwood rhetorically asked. "Forty-eight percent of the doubtful states of this Union that you appeal to in a national election are foreign born, or the sons and daughters of foreign born. They are often captained by men of the Catholic faith; they are often sustained by men of the Jewish religion."

In Underwood's strategy, timing was everything. A favorite son candidacy in the South was always run best like a Confederate Reunion—appealing to collective white nostalgia and classless regional pride—while opposition to the Klan was deeply contentious and risky. For this reason, Forney Johnston had instructed Underwood to travel the South as the region's greatest living statesman. Yet, after Wizard Hiram Evans smoked the senator out of his statesman-like pose, Underwood had no choice but "to fight my way through on the principles I announced at Houston."

America's first presidential primary in 1924 was by design in Underwood's own Alabama where his chronic opponent Breck Musgrove, with campaign manager Bibb Graves, ran against him. Two weeks before the Alabama primary, one political observer predicted that Underwood could lose the state for ten reasons. The first five were Alabama's labor unions, unorganized labor groups, women's temperance unions, ex-servicemen, and the Anti-Saloon League. The "other five" he said, "are the Ku Klux Klan." Yet, Alabama voters rewarded Underwood with 62 percent of the vote. He received all the state's twenty-four convention delegates, thanks to a specially enacted law giving only an Alabama citizen the state's entire convention delegation if he won a simple plurality in the presidential primary.

Fearing this initial victory might mislead Underwood's new campaign managers, Forney Johnston warned against continuing to focus on the Klan or any other issue in remaining Southern primaries. "Unless we can get interest in UNDERWOOD, his personality and fitness and put anti-Klan and other 'issues' out of our councils of war in the Southern states," Johnston wrote, "we are candidates for disappointment and nothing else."

As usual, Johnston was correct. In every other Southern state, Underwood lost by significant margins. The senator's longtime opposition to prohibition, his anti-labor record in the Senate, his disdain for women suffrage, his vote against "bonus pay" for veterans, and his close association with corporate interests, including Johnston's own railroad clients, were political liabilities. Hiram Evans's Klan also orchestrated extensive efforts to defeat the senator, especially in Texas, Mississippi, and Georgia. With each Southern defeat, Underwood's campaign managers blamed it on the Kluxers, and, thereby, guaranteed that the Klan and related "issues" would be prominent in the next primary.

By the time Democratic delegates began arriving in New York for the national convention, Underwood had a disappointing seventy-four delegates—and only fifty came from outside of Alabama. More than seven hundred thirty votes, two-thirds of the convention, were needed to win. With such insignificant numbers, the Underwood camp hoped for a stalemate forced by the two-thirds rule and the countervailing strength of the two leading candidates, Woodrow Wilson's son-in-law, William McAdoo of California, and New York Governor Al Smith. Each had fewer than four hundred votes. Without the South's support, Underwood arrived in New York to make a last pitch for the "doubtful states" as the nation's opponent of Ku Kluxism. "It is either the Klan or the United States," Underwood proclaimed. "I choose my country." [9]

In New York City's summer heat, in the mammoth brick second location of Madison Square Garden, scheduled for demolition shortly afterwards, the Democratic National Convention was gaveled to order at midday on Tuesday, June 24. It did not adjourn for two and a half weeks, the longest convention in American history. On the first day, Mississippi Senator Pat Harrison gave a keynote speech with the aid of a new device, an amplifying microphone. Hampered by a strong Southern accent and an unreliable sound system, the senator intoned, "What America needs now is . . . a Paul Revere" as the galleries exploded wildly in applause. Later, it was discovered that New Yorkers in the convention bleachers had understood the prohibitionist senator to have said, "What America needs now is . . . real beer."

Nominations began by the second day. With the luck of the alphabet, Alabama was first. Forney Johnston stepped to a small speaker's rostrum, standing inconspicuously at the center of the arena. Almost as many guests and delegates were sitting and milling behind the platform as in front. Standing inside the white picket fence bordering the platform, above the clutter of four partially draped American flags, joined together behind an embossed American eagle, Johnston's head was not much higher than the four oversized microphones. Originally, Alabama's Governor Brandon, even shorter at barely five feet, was scheduled to make the Underwood nomination. The governor, however, declined the honor after learning of the campaign's new strategy.

"For decade after decade Alabama has yielded her first place in the roll of the States to permit the nomination of some great son by a sister commonwealth," Johnston informed an inattentive convention. "Upon this occasion we can not yield." Oscar Underwood was "one whose only employer for more than a quarter of a century past has been the people of the United States," declared Johnston. Senator Underwood was "the one outstanding figure in public life today" who had the "courage to lead the fight in this crisis in public morals and to restore to the people confidence in their public concerns."

Turning to the "greatest issues of our times," Johnston called Underwood the "chief living defender of the sanctity of the Constitution and of government by law." The speaker insisted that the party's nominee must go beyond vague platitudes and "condemn the mass action of secret political orders" that were "plainly contrary to the spirit of the Constitution . . . (Applause.)" Johnston continued: "The question before this party is whether secret organizations should be given powers immune from the Bill of Rights and superior to those delegated to the elected representatives of the people."

"No bare reference to the Constitution or the Bill of Rights actually mentioned in the oath of such organizations is adequate," Johnston boomed, as the vast audience fell quiet. " . . . The Bill of Rights are limitations only upon the State and Federal Governments and not upon private conspiracy," he stated. "I have . . . introduced a resolution concluding with this resolving clause. . .," Johnston continued. "'That we do . . . condemn as un-American and un-Democratic political action by secret or quasi-secret organizations . . . and in particular do we condemn such action . . . as is now proposed, practiced, and publicly acknowledged by the organization known as the *Ku . . . Klux . . . Klan* (Great applause)," shouted Johnston with bellowing indignation.

A sudden uproar consumed the convention hall. The galleries cheered wildly, and almost half the delegates began a spontaneous parade of support on the floor. Fistfights broke out on the convention floor, and, by day's end, the naturally pugnacious Johnston had exchanged a few punches with an Alabama delegate who felt betrayed. After fifteen minutes, the convention floor was brought back to order by the playing of the "Star Spangled Banner," which was then rapidly becoming the accepted national anthem. Johnston quickly placed the name of Oscar W. Underwood in nomination, and a brief, perfunctory display of support followed.

Both Johnston and the entire Underwood camp knew that the Klan was now the only issue that could make the senator the Democratic nominee. Without it, Underwood would drift into obscurity. If the convention endorsed the anti-Klan resolution, however, Underwood would be the candidate best able to uphold that banner. Since Al Smith had been openly anti-Klan in the primaries, his supporters could be the backbone of Underwood's reemergence as a victorious dark horse.

When the resolutions came to the convention floor, future U.S. Attorney General Homer Cumming of Connecticut presented the majority report which rejected Johnston's Klan resolution: "We insist at all times upon obedience to the orderly processes of law, and deplore and condemn any effort to arouse religious and racial dissensions." Johnston's resolution was presented as a minority report. William Jennings Bryan, the ageless Great Commoner who had been the party's nominee at three past conventions as far back as 1896, supported the majority resolution. "Note, my friends, . . . we offered to take every word of their report but three," Bryan announced as he remembered discussions with Johnston. "We said, 'Strike out three words [Ku Klux

Klan] and there will be no objection.' But three words were more important to them than the welfare of a party in a great campaign," Bryan charged. "It was Christ on the Cross who said, 'Father, forgive them, for they know not what they do.' And, my friends, we can exterminate Ku Kluxism better by recognizing their honesty and teaching them that they are wrong (Boos and hisses, followed by applause)."

Ensconced at a hotel a few blocks from the convention, Klan Imperial Wizard Hiram Evans and a handful of grand dragons, including Alabama's James Esdale, worked behind the scenes to block the Underwood-Johnston resolution. Esdale had organized a series of Klan induction ceremonies throughout Alabama on the eve of convention, as proof of its growing strength in the state. Although none knew for sure, several Northern reporters estimated that as many as eleven states across the nation had Klansmen occupying more than half their delegate seats and a total number approaching three hundred. Earlier in June, Evans had succeeded in keeping the Republican party from condemning the Klan by name. He expected to accomplish no less with the Democrats.

When the roll call began on the Klan resolution, near the stroke of midnight on Saturday June 29, Alabama supported the minority report. McAdoo's home state of California split its votes, but Al Smith delivered all ninety votes for the Underwood cause. North Carolina split hairs. It cast 3.85 votes for the Underwood resolution and 20.15 votes for the majority proposal. After an excruciatingly slow roll call, amended and revised amongst floor fights involving chairs, fists, and hammers, the presiding chair announced near two o'clock on Sunday morning that the Johnston-Underwood resolution had received 542 and 7/20 votes and the majority report 543 and 3/20 votes. After a motion by Al Smith's campaign manager, Franklin D. Roosevelt, the convention retired to observe the Sabbath, and Klan leaders went to bed with a victory of four-fifths of a vote.[10] The strategy to make Oscar W. Underwood the Democrat's dark horse had failed by a whisker.

Derailed, Johnston and Underwood strategists had ample time to consider options and developments. More than one hundred roll calls were taken over ten days of balloting. McAdoo and Smith were miserably deadlocked. Alabama Governor Bill Brandon, who had the voice of a bullfrog in the body of a tadpole, began each ballot with words that everyone in the convention could hear. "Alabama casts twenty-four votes for Oscar W. Underwood." Standing on a chair only sixty feet from the podium and the radio networks' stationary microphones, the governor's booming voice made him virtually the only person on the convention floor whom American listeners could hear during a roll call. After dozens of appearances, Brandon became momentarily a radio celebrity. Humorist Will Rogers suggested that the governor's words might replace the Lord's Prayer if the convention didn't end soon, and, by the fifth day, delegates and spectators throughout the Garden joined Brandon during each roll call in a rousing chorus of "Alabama casts twenty-four votes for Oscar W. Underwood." It was the only unity among delegates, as McAdoo and Al Smith moved back and forth by small margins without a winning majority.

Finally on July 9, after the convention had stayed in session until 4 AM the night before, leading candidates released their delegates, and the deadlock broke. On the one hundred and first ballot, John W. Davis, a Wall Street lawyer who had served the Wilson administration, took the lead with Underwood following. As a dry Democrat and an able speaker, Davis proved that it was more rewarding to come to a convention in 1924 with few votes and few enemies. On the one hundred and third roll call, Bill Brandon—and Oscar W. Underwood's lifelong ambitions—were recognized for the last time. The Democratic party, at long last, had its nominee. He was the favorite son of West Virginia.

Returning home short of money and rest, several Alabama delegates quickly separated themselves from the senator's convention strategy. Former Governor Thomas Kilby declared that Underwood lost the nomination because he insisted the Klan should be denounced by name. The publisher of the *Mobile Register* told his own reporters that he had advised strongly against the Klan resolution. After the fact, Alabamians also learned that a third of the state's delegates had voted against the Klan resolution. With a unit rule, however, the winner took all, and Forney Johnston's resolution carried all twenty-four Alabama votes.

Underwood was unrepentant. After resting, he traveled to Maine to boost the reelection of its Democratic senator who stood with him at the convention. "I come from a state where men and women shudder at night when a knock comes at the door, where men do not dare assert freedom of thought because an invisible hand may fall," Underwood told a Democratic gathering. At another event, he repeated his campaign line. "You can't be half Democrat and half Klan." Within a quagmired convention Underwood's direct public attack against the Klan was good strategy, but now his portrayal before Northern audiences of a frightened, Ku-Kluxed Alabama was politically reckless.

In Birmingham, Judge William Fort asked a grand jury to investigate Underwood's charges "against Jefferson County and Alabama." James Esdale appeared delighted since Underwood's indiscretion seemed good for business. In mid-October, the Klan staged a giant rally at Rickwood Field, Birmingham's baseball stadium named for Mrs. Underwood's brother. (It also was where an unarmed striking miner had been shot and killed after arrest by industrialists' special deputies.) Amid festivities, eighteen Kluxers acted as pallbearers in a mock funeral for the casket of Underwood's effigy before twenty-three thousand amused spectators. Alabama's grand dragon boasted that the Kluxers' victory in New York would be repeated in Alabama within two years when the senator faced reelection in his own home state.[11]

THREE DECADES AFTER THE 1924 CONVENTION, another U.S. senator, a Catholic Democrat from Massachusetts who would become President, remembered Oscar W. Underwood's campaign as one of America's significant *Profiles in Courage*. In 1955, as a third Klan emerged in the South, Senator John F. Kennedy wrote: "On the eve of the 1924 Democratic Convention, the advisors of *Senator Oscar W. Underwood of Alabama* . . . a leading presidential possibility—urged that he say nothing to offend the Ku Klux Klan . . . But Senator Underwood . . . denounced it in no uncertain terms . . . Southerners publicly repudiated him, and from that moment on his chances for the Presidency were nil."

Kennedy's Pulitzer prize-winning book preserved Underwood's reputation in obscure footnotes of political memory as a Southerner who valiantly sacrificed America's highest office for fidelity to high principle, a white Southerner who stood against the popular winds of bigotry at the cost of the Presidency. In truth, Kennedy's portrayal was a Yankee's stereotypical understanding of Southern politics. Oscar Underwood was not a Klan victim. He was a victim of his own making in a clash between his Old South leadership and his ambition to be a leader of a new America. As a presidential candidate, the senator was trapped between his past reliance on the worst regionalism and his current aspirations to lead a more diverse nation. In 1924, Underwood discovered that there was no way in popular politics to bridge the fundamental differences in heritage, experience, economy, politics or racial order symbolized by the Mason & Dixon line.

The Ku Klux's growth extended beyond the South in 1924 and demonstrated that many parts of America were attracted by Old South symbols of exclusion in combination with mystic rituals and plain Protestantism. Despite a cultural resemblance, the Klan was not a revival of an Old South. It was the underbelly of a new America. Oscar Underwood lost in 1924 because he was a representative of the aristocratic Old South.

As U.S. senator, Underwood earned the undying opposition of America's activist women and suffragists, World War I veterans, ardent prohibitionists, Protestant moralists, and labor unions on both sides of the Mason & Dixon. In combination with the Klan, this coalition endangered Underwood's prospects in the South. In the North, Underwood's public career in preserving Southern white supremacy and severely restricting immigration posed a tremendous political handicap. North and South, Underwood's Old South had no broad constituency. Groups as divergent as New York immigrants and Alabama Klansmen shared a political judgment: Oscar W. Underwood was not their candidate.

Gripped in such a political vise, Forney Johnston and his senator developed a two-headed strategy: appeal to a defeated region's longing to have a Southerner lead the nation and, afterwards, use attacks on the Klan as a dodge, so that the rest of America would see a man of high courage and conviction—not a senator with an Old South voting record. The strategy reflected both an honest self-portrait and, in Johnston's language, "a dodge for the parson." But, the strategy failed, and Underwood paid the political price for representing Old South values in an awakening New South and new America.

There was a noble vision in Underwood's campaign. In attacking the Klan, Underwood and Johnston prophesied the terms by which the North and South eventually would reunite as one nation. They invoked the U.S. Constitution and Bill of Rights as the basic measure of citizenship. Unlike leading prohibitionists, Klansmen, churchwomen, and even Alabama's specially appointed assistant U.S. attorney general, Underwood and Johnston rejected popular moral parables and religious precedents as standards for measuring citizenship. They proclaimed the federal Bill of Rights as universal terms for citizens on both sides of the Mason & Dixon.

In his nominating speech, Johnston seemed to go far beyond existing law by implying that the conduct of private citizens should be limited by standards of the federal Bill of Rights and by asserting that the "Bill of Rights are limitations only upon the *state* and federal governments." Since the founding of the Republic, the U.S. Supreme Court had held that the federal Bill of Rights did not control the actions of private individuals or states—only the federal government. Since Reconstruction, the South had insisted on this federalism of "states' rights" to keep the federal Constitution from interfering with Jim Crow. Yet, Johnston's resolution attempted to commit Democrats to opposing Kluxers or "any organization" that tried "to limit the civic rights of any citizen or body of citizens because of religion, birthplace, or racial origin."

Johnston's assertions were dramatic flourishes and a necessary misstatement of his views so that Underwood's attacks on the Klan would appear high-minded and appeal to Northerners. Both Johnston and Underwood had supported draconian actions by private industrialists and state officials violating the protections mentioned in state and federal bills of rights whenever necessary to end labor strikes. Johnston had opposed any and all attempts by the federal government to impose American constitutional standards on Alabama. The same was also Senator Underwood's philosophical stock in trade. Their posturing was merely another disingenuous moment in American politics—not a profile of one man's courage. Still, ironically, for the first time since the days of the early Republic, a Southern political leader spoke to the nation about the necessity for observing individual rights for all Americans.

In the decade when John F. Kennedy became President, this vision of a Constitutional America would begin to reunite a New South and a new nation.[12] In 1924, however, it was nothing more than a political "dodge for the parson" at a deadlocked convention—an ironic, fragile vision with no authentic prophet, no Southern spokesman, no voting constituency, and no legal force. Not until Forney Johnston's arch rival in Alabama's legal and political wars appeared on the nation's stage, not until an Alabama Klansman—the very person Johnston and Underwood attacked—became a member of the U.S. Supreme Court would America have a leading spokesman for the federal Constitution to become the nation's legal Bible and its Bill of Rights to become the Ten Commandments of a diverse, civic America.

ALONG WITH MANY OTHER WHITE ALABAMIANS, Hugo Black remained unconvinced and unmoved by the Johnston-Underwood campaign against the Klan. In the wake of the Democratic National Convention, Black increased his Ku Klux role by accepting the post of Klan Kladd, a ceremonial officer who led KKK oaths and initiation ceremonies. James Esdale may have insisted that any member who could repeat the Klan initiation prayer at a public trial should be willing to recite it with his new brothers in the hood. Among the oaths was a pledge to "preserve by any and all justifiable means and methods . . . white supremacy" as one of many terms for "the honor of citizenship in the Invisible Empire."

But the more Black participated in the closed Klan, the more he took pains to demonstrate his open independence of it. In 1924, when a local Klan klavern attempted to remove a Birmingham high school principal because he was a Jew, Black fought the effort inside the Klan and, when the klavern persisted, he defended the "best principal in the city" in a speech before fellow Civitans. Less than two months after the Democratic Convention, Black joined in a public tribute to Victor Hansen, publisher of the *Birmingham News*. Hanson was a loyal, vocal Underwood supporter who had opposed Klan meddling in local schools. In the "name of every man, woman, and child in this state that believes in the cause of education," Black lavishly praised Hansen for his work in preserving "educational freedom and progress."

A month later, in a parody of Klan loyalty, Black assisted William Simmons in efforts to build a new organization competing with the Klan. Inheriting his father's disregard for honesty among friends, Hiram Evans had become the Ku Klux Wizard by tricking, dethroning, and expelling old man Simmons from the Imperial Palace in Atlanta. As a result, the Klan founder tried to establish the "Knights of the Flaming Sword" as a new "white Protestant, gentile, eleemosynary institution." Under an assumed name, Black traveled to Toledo, Ohio, to join Simmons on September 22 at a church meeting where Black spoke favorably of the old man and his new brotherhood.[13]

The Klan wasn't Black's only personal affiliation that did not dictate his beliefs and actions. During the last days of the 1924 presidential campaign, despite his credentials as a special assistant U.S. attorney general in a Republican administration, Black campaigned against Calvin Coolidge. No one on earth doubted that John W. Davis would carry Alabama, but Black motored to the state's Appalachian foothills, a section "cursed" with Republican tendencies since the end of the Civil War, to speak for the Democratic ticket.

Sand Mountain was home to Alabama's Republican national committeeman, O. D. Street (no relation to Clay County's Merit Street), the state's most influential man on matters of Republican federal appointments. Street had emerged in Alabama politics as a Populist and migrated to the Republican party. An ardent prohibitionist and self-described "organization man," Street had held different appointive jobs, including that of U.S. Attorney, and over most of two decades he carefully husbanded federal patronage, while Alabama remained stubbornly Democratic at the polls.

On the Saturday before November's election, in a local trading center on Sand Mountain, Black debated Charles B. Kennamer, north Alabama's Republican U.S. Attorney, whose appointment Street had arranged. Starting around two o'clock in the afternoon in Boaz, so farmers might get home before dark, Judge Black was introduced as a former Birmingham judge and the current Republican administration's chief attorney in the Mobile whiskey cases. Black knew he was in a "good, peaceable law-abiding Republican community" but he did not attempt to trade on his Republican appointment. Quite the opposite. "I am a Democrat," Black proclaimed as he told farmers about the Democrat who once was confronted by Republican leaders in just such a community.

"This is a strange place for you to come," the Republican chairman declared, according to Black's story. ". . . Why are you a Democrat?"

"I don't know," Black said, "my father was a Democrat, his father was a Democrat, his father was a Democrat, and I am just a Democrat, too."

"Well, the chairman says: 'Suppose your father had been a fool, your grandfather had been a fool, and your great grandfather had been a fool, what would you have been then?'"

"Well," Black said, ". . . I reckon I would have been a Republican."

It was, however, foolish, evil "tariffs" that Black discussed. Echoing the old themes of William Jennings Bryan, Judge Black reminded farmers that Republican presidents had allowed Northern manufacturing firms to import raw materials from foreign lands with no tax while cotton and other produce of Southern farmers were burdened with high tariffs and suppressed prices. Like the subject of "budget deficits" decades later, tariffs were a national evil which Americans and Alabamians condemned and tolerated routinely. They were the standard text for appealing to small farmers.

The Republican U.S. Attorney preferred another topic. "In Charlie's reply, he made a rousing vote-getting speech," Black remembered a few years after the fact, "on the Catholic and negro question. He accused John W. Davis of having permitted some Catholic Priest in Boston to write his statement denouncing the Ku Klux Klan. He also referred to the Democratic party as being then the party of the negro and the Catholic. He referred to a negro candidate for Congress on the Democratic ticket" in a Northern state. "In my rebuttal," Black continued, "I naturally took up reconstruction and the negro Republican Committeeman in Georgia."

A Southerner whose father's generation served as Confederate soldiers and whose mother lost her true love at Gettysburg, Black raised the same themes about Reconstruction that were true of tariffs: the party of the North—*Republicans*—were manipulating the South on race in order to keep white Southerners subservient to Northern capitalism. Black "talked at length about corruption in the cabinet" of Republican presidents in a tale of Northern mendacity encompassing race, economics, politics, and prohibition. Black informed farmers that the Civil War, Reconstruction, economic depression, low cotton prices, persisting poverty, and the South's social tensions were the work of Northern Republicans who had controlled the White House and the Congress for most of the last sixty-five years.

In retrospect, Boaz appears to be the first campaign stage where Black confronted directly the volatile issues of religion and race, but the debate had no impact on the election or settled voting patterns. Calvin Coolidge was elected President. Sand Mountain voted Republican, and Alabama voted overwhelmingly for the defeated Democratic ticket. Reports of Black's speech, nonetheless, outraged O. D. Street. In a telegram to the U.S. attorney general's office, Street demanded to know why the Justice Department had this "demagogue in and out of court" on the Republican payroll while he openly condemned the administration that appointed him. Street insisted the Department rescind Black's commission.

Black was equally scandalized after learning of Street's telegram. He confronted the U.S. Attorney in his Birmingham office, but Kennamer denied knowing anything. Black was angered only by the telegram's use of one word— "demagogue." "Few people are more contemptible," Black said, "than those who are intellectually dishonest. A demagogue is an 'unprincipled politician,' who leads the people by appealing to unworthy passion and prejudice," Black continued in a letter to Street. "For such a man a gentleman has no respect."

After enduring years of harsh name-calling, everything from "Ego" to "bolshevik" to bigot to Catholic killer to "nigger lover," Black felt slandered by the one term he worked hardest to avoid—and often would meet in future years. Black had disciplined himself to live the life he preached, forever trying to keep a consistency of views and conduct which his father seldom accomplished. Hugo Black's guides in private practice and public service were one and the same—independence of thought and individual honesty. Unlike Fayette Black, the interests of no "ring," "clique" "clan," or even "klan" ruled Hugo Black.

Like A. O. Lane, Black saw himself as a good citizen and an honest public servant. Years earlier at Lane's last political rally, Black had declared, "So long as I believe my friend honest, I am for him." Yet, for Black the term "honest" went far deeper than merely defining someone who tells the truth. His meaning restored the Latin roots of the word *"honestus"*—"of *good* character" or "upright in principles, intentions, and actions." When Black appealed to a jury of ordinary Southern white men, he asked them to render a verdict within the meaning of the Latin legal term *"vivis legalibus et honestis,"* or as "lawful and *good* men."[14] For Black, an "honest" citizen was a "good citizen" who consistently followed his own conscience and upright principles. To be "dishonest" in public life was to be a demagogue.

In 1924, as a self-described "militant Christian" and "good citizen" following an Old Testament interpretation of both Christ in the Temple and the "Golden Rule," as a Klan Kladd who refused to give up his own democratic citizenship while he initiated others into secret "citizenship," as a "yellow-dog" Democrat serving in a corrupt Republican administration, as an assistant U.S. attorney general attacking the people who appointed him, as a Kluxer leading the attack on Alabama's convict lease system, Hugo Black saw himself as the antithesis of the demagogue.

In the widest range of associations, Black sought to be *"honestus"* in his own words and actions, public and private, and to lead as a good citizen, true democrat, loyal Democrat, and heir to the honest, political traditions of his father's community.

ALTHOUGH HIS COMMISSION as a special prosecutor was in jeopardy, Black returned to Mobile with one unaltered purpose, to imprison the whiskey trade's big men. After state charges against U.S. Attorney Aubrey Boyles were dismissed, Alabama Attorney General Harwell Davis appointed Black as a special state prosecutor to impeach Mobile County sheriff Paul G. Cazalas, but, on the eve of his trial before Alabama's Supreme Court, the sheriff resigned. He claimed he could not afford the cost of a trial proving his innocence, although he may have wanted to avoid family ghosts. Sixteen years earlier, Cazalas's father was impeached as Mobile's sheriff after he failed to take precautions to prevent a black man from being lynched.

Mobile was now free of both the chief of police and the sheriff who had profited from whiskey business. To keep the city dry, Davis quickly blocked the Holcombe brothers' efforts to bamboozle Governor Brandon into appointing one of their men as sheriff, while the Citizens League recommended a slate of "honest" candidates. The governor discovered on the League's list an old boyhood friend, Leon Schwarz, a Jewish leader of the local American Legion, and promptly appointed him.

At the same time, Black navigated a set of new indictments against the Holcombes, Frank Boykin, and other big men of Mobile's whiskey ring. They were indicted anew for violating an obscure federal Tariff Act, which had been amended to make it a crime to smuggle liquor into the United States or to bribe a federal officer. Responding to defense motions, Judge Ervin recused himself, since he had declared Will Holcombe guilty in his last trial, and U.S. District Judge W. I. Grubb of Birmingham agreed to preside at trial in February 1925.[15]

Less than two weeks before trial, Black traveled to Washington. He was scheduled to meet with U.S. Justice Department officials, who would decide if he was to continue as government attorney in Mobile, and to provide Henry Lewis and other poor black convicts their day before the nation's highest court. On January 29, Black stood for the first time before U.S. Supreme Court in a small decorative courtroom allotted to the third branch of government in the Capitol's west wing. Members of Congress had not reassembled since the November election, and it was a rare, quiet moment on Capitol Hill when the business of the Court took precedent.

Neither side had filed briefs, but Black argued that the case needed no extensive analysis. It was simple: the Birmingham District Court and the Fifth Circuit U.S. Court of Appeals had erred by ignoring decisions of several other federal courts when holding that Henry Lewis could not collect his court-ordered award against the bankrupt Montevallo Mining Company. At this stage, the case was no longer about the rights and welfare of black convict miners. It posed a narrow, legal question about what Congress intended when it passed the federal bankruptcy law. Black argued that the Southern federal circuit was wrong and all other circuits were correct in their interpretation.

When Black sat down, no one stood up for David Roberts and Montevallo.

Black's first case before the Supreme Court was heard without opposition. The company's lawyer had failed to appear since the issue was no longer of practical importance to his client. Montevallo no longer leased convicts from the state. The state now leased coal mines from Montevallo. Under this peculiar arrangement, private companies weren't liable for mining injuries since the state now worked convicts. The case raised an issue that affected only Montevallo's past liabilities—not future operations. The company's lawyer did file a written brief after Black's appearance, and Black countered with his own, which he paid a young attorney to draft while Black prepared for the Mobile trial.[16]

On the same trip, Black reported to the office of Assistant U.S. Attorney General Mabel Walker Willebrandt to settle O. D. Street's protests. Sitting in Willebrandt's office, as telephone calls from Republican politicians interrupted their meeting, Black listened to the nation's highest-ranking female official politely and firmly refuse to limit liquor prosecutions. In their meeting, Black defended his campaign speech as fair game for a devout Democrat and rehearsed the story about a Democrat in Republican Sand Mountain. Willebrandt laughed and promised to use the story herself (after reversing the order). She also agreed that Black's speech did not compromise his work. "But, you'll have to see the attorney general," she added.

Harlan Fisk Stone, the new U.S. attorney general, had divided most of his career between teaching in Columbia University Law School's classrooms and a New York corporate practice. President Coolidge chose Stone to demonstrate that the Justice Department would be administered honestly after Daugherty was forced out. A large man with a professional manner and mood, Stone was under consideration for an appointment to the U.S. Supreme Court at the time he met Black. His special attorney explained that when he was appointed "the authorities knew I was a Democrat, but I did not surrender my rights to uphold Democratic principles." Stone also learned that the federal government had not paid Black for his services.

Admitting a preference for a Republican lawyer, Stone was in no position to secure one with a major trial in Mobile beginning in less than two weeks. Black, moreover, had violated no canon of legal ethics and had done a splendid job. "You go back and do the job," Stone concluded. "I will make only one request, that you accept a salary for your services."[17]

Back in Alabama, Black took General Stone at his word. On February 10, the special assistant U.S. attorney general called his first witness in the case against Frank Boykin, both Holcombe brothers, and local businessman Alfred Staples on charges of smuggling illegal whiskey. Black used testimony and evidence from both the earlier conspiracy trial and the men whom he had convicted as "whiskey wholesalers." Three witnesses now serving time in the Atlanta penitentiary swore that Boykin recruited them to distribute illegal liquor and that William Holcombe set up the plan for protection money. After four days of testimony, the jury took only five hours to acquit everyone. They simply did not believe the government's prime witnesses, men already convicted of conspiring to violate prohibition laws.

Black was enraged. "We are ready to issue a statement," Black declared at a Sunday night meeting of federal officials, "that if the people of this community want such a government as the verdict of the jury on Saturday night showed, . . . we recommend that the convicts in the penitentiary at Atlanta be returned to this community and that the fight be ended." Aubrey Boyles disagreed. He said defense lawyers had "tricked" Black by keeping the U.S. Attorney off the witness stand in the last two trials. "You can never win this case without me," Boyles insisted. By telephone, Black reached Mabel Willebrandt to discuss the wisdom of using internal government documents to bolster Boyles as a witness. "Fight," she ordered.

On the following Monday morning, Black opened a new trial against the same defendants. In this case, Boykin, the Holcombes, and Staples were accused of attempting to bribe Aubrey Boyles and special agent "Lone Wolf" Gonzaullas. Black repeated many of the same witnesses he had called a week earlier before another jury, but this time his star witnesses were the "Lone Wolf" and Boyles. The U.S. Attorney testified that Boykin offered money in exchange for protection of the whiskey ring, and Black introduced letters sent to Willebrandt during that time relaying the details of each bribe. Boyles also swore that Will Holcombe offered him additional bribes.

The defendants denied all charges, but on Saturday afternoon, February 21, the jury's foreman announced two convictions and two mistrials. Frank Boykin and William Holcombe were guilty of attempted bribery. Judge Grubb sentenced both men to the maximum term, two years in federal jail. At last, in the last possible trial, Black had secured the convictions of two ring leaders.

When Black stepped from the Old Customs House onto Government Street after the jury verdict, crowds met him in jubilant celebration. Wild throngs of men and women, boys and girls rushed through the streets in utter delight over the arrival of a new day in Mobile. Masked men and women carried flaming torches as they paraded in front of the city's main buildings laboriously decked out with colorful streamers and bright bunting. The joyful, makeshift melodies of trumpets, saxophones, drums, and cymbals drifted from the waterfront where men and women danced.

Far from commemorating a new victorious day for prohibition, Mobile citizens were welcoming Mardi Gras, a decadent, all-consuming celebration of a vague, paganistic holiday which Mobilians observed with a gluttony and excess ranking second only to New Orleans. The presiding official for this year's days of paradise, King Felix III, was Francis H. Inge, a young lawyer and son of one of the chief defense attorneys whom Black had faced without majestic mask in each of the three major trials.

Mobile's festivities lasted beyond the weekend. On the following Monday, King Felix, Emperor of Joy, led a grand pageant of giant rainbow-feathered mechanical birds and perched on top of a royal yacht, from the Gulf into Mobile Bay where a fair queen awaited him. Later, the couple rode though the city in a chariot and presided over the pagan pageant of the Order of the Myths. Until the emperor arrived, however, Mobilians were ordered as his loyal subjects to stay masked, anonymously enjoying the city's liberating fruits of fellowship, flesh, and illegal whiskey.[18]

Amid the extravagant, drunken merriment, Hugo Black solemnly turned away towards the city's rail terminal, where snarling gargoyles of Spanish baroque architecture symbolically guarded the city's traditions and influences against all who trespassed. As his train departed northward, Black rightfully could appreciate his own professional and personal achievements. He had slowed the liquor traffic into Alabama and the nation. He had jailed several of Mobile's big men who exploited whiskey for big profits. For months, Black had been on the pages of virtually every state newspaper as prohibition's tireless warrior. For the first time in his adult life, Black had befriended a professional woman and, even more unusual for him, a high-ranking Republican outside the South. Black was not yet prepared to conclude as a general rule that "there are good Republicans," but, as an "honest public official" fighting for prohibition against the odds, Mabel Willebrandt had become one of Black's "best friends."

Despite this progress, Black had good reasons to doubt that a year's work in the federal courts had changed anything permanently in Mobile. It had taken him almost twelve months to get a conviction of only a few ringleaders—and only after he excluded all Mobile residents from the juries. Even on his day of triumph, Black could not ignore the truth that most of Mobile wanted to frolic in a cosmopolitan lifestyle that included many things he wanted to banish. Hugo Black had no choice but to turn his back on Mobile, to take heart from the rest of Alabama where his prohibitionist victory in Sunday's newspapers would appear as another decisive, righteous conquest to be celebrated by the state's good citizens with a communion of crackers and grape juice, a Protestant prayer, or a toast of thanksgiving no stronger than sweetened ice tea.

11

'The Humblest Son
of the Humblest Citizen'

The Dry-Protestant-Progressive Voters
Elect a U.S. Senator

The first part of 1925 was as an uncharacteristic time of political indecision and revision for Hugo Black. Long accustomed to sharpening his wits and improving his fortune amid the conflict of people, ideas, and ideals, Black seemed unable for once to reconcile the competing forces of personal ambition and family responsibility, of political risk and financial safety. A decade after the giants of Alabama's nineteenth-century politics had departed, Black was struggling to decide if being the son of a rural merchant, the state's most aggressive dry prosecutor, a card-carrying Klansman, an attorney for biracial unions, the Pythias' past grand chancellor, and the trial lawyer for poor black and white workers—any or all of these public personalities—gave him a chance to become one of the state's new political leaders.

Like many politicians, Black revealed his ambitions even before he knew his own mind. In early 1925, Black informed his sister Daisy that he was going to run for governor, "but you can't tell anybody." A few weeks afterwards, he amended his intentions. "I'm running for senator," he told her. Later, Black told a south Alabama cousin that he had decided *not* to run for the U.S. Senate. After reviewing possibilities with a small circle of friends, Black decided to forgo running for any office in 1926.

While his fame swelled momentarily after each publicized trial, Hugo Black was still not a household name in Alabama. In the last ten years, Black's courtroom advocacy of prohibition, organized labor, anti-convict leasing, and ordinary white folk—along with leadership in several statewide fraternities—had earned him publicity, friends, and admirers across Alabama. Yet, his record of public service looked puny in the eyes of many, including some friends, when compared with thirty years of Congressional service by the incumbent. "Senator Underwood is the 'biggest' man the South has in Congress," declared Horace Turner, Black's stalwart friend, who insisted the senator deserved reelection without opposition.

Similarly, Underwood's main opposition did not encourage Black. Organized labor and hard-shell prohibitionists, who narrowed Underwood's margin of victory in the last senatorial election, had weakened since 1920. Even with the fast-growing Ku Klux, anti-Underwood votes would splinter between Black and at least two other unofficial candidates, Governor Thomas E. Kilby and Breck Musgrove, Underwood's persistent antagonist. Kilby had a strong public record on prohibition, and, although Birmingham unions had not forgiven him for ending the 1921 miners' strike, some of Black's friends believed the former governor "had a pull with KK and labor forces" in south Alabama. Musgrove always seemed on friendly terms with labor unions, was a generous contributor to the Anti-Saloon League and temperance unions, and had run as the Klan candidate against Underwood in the state's presidential primary. Both businessmen were millionaire "free spenders in political races," observed one reporter, "and both have a very definite following in the state."

Because of Alabama's "no run-off" election law, passed ironically in 1916 to help prohibition candidates, Black and other challengers were destined to split opposition votes and leave Underwood, a local-optionist, with a plurality victory. Under all probable scenarios, Black's chances of winning a Senate race appeared marginal at best.

A campaign would be costly. Black's candidacy was sure to take him away from Josephine (and now two little boys) for several months and, without his law practice, Black would have to support his family on savings. If elected, Black's yearly income would drop from around $40,000 to $10,000. "It would be a great financial sacrifice!" confided Black.

Another personal consideration was Josephine, whom Hugo always tried to protect from life's rigors and unpleasantries. The common tools of Alabama politics were scandalous rumors and vicious, anonymous circulars, used often at the last minute in whispering campaigns to distort a person's character or inflame prejudices. Despite worldly radiance and Southern charm, Josephine was by nature the opposite of her husband. She suffered when facing friction, criticism, or personal attacks. Try as he might, Black knew he could not save his wife from the hostilities and harshness of real politics, especially in a contest that would be pitting James Esdale's Kluxers against Forney Johnston's senator.[1]

As events unfolded, Black's decision not to run for the U.S. Senate survived hardly a month. In early May, longstanding rumors of Senator Underwood's retirement were reborn when his office confirmed that the senator's family had purchased a country estate with a hundred and twenty acres and a Georgian house of twenty-two rooms near Mt. Vernon—in those days, sixteen long miles south of Washington.

Afflicted with lingering despair over his defeat at Madison Square Garden, Underwood's lack of commitment no longer sounded like a statesman's formalities. "There has been grave doubt in my mind for some time as to whether I will run for the Senate," Underwood stated. In private, he was more frank. "I am very much disposed not to be a candidate. Kilby and Musgrove intend to run. I think this would make the campaign less difficult for me," observed Underwood, fully aware that a divided opposition would permit his plurality victory, "but, on the other hand, both of them will probably spend a lot of money." Underwood said he didn't want to be forced to violate Alabama's 1916 law limiting campaign expenditures in order to assure victory. In truth, he had lost his political drive and dream. He had no energy for another campaign fighting Kluxers, or for another term amid what Forney Johnston condemned as the Senate's "pickpocket statesmanship." Underwood concluded that "it looks to me like it is a good time to quit."

Without waiting for Underwood's formal announcement, Kilby and Musgrove immediately confirmed their candidacies. Friends of attorney John Bankhead, who recently sold his Jasper mining company for $1 million, affirmed his intentions to follow his father's career. Former state supreme court justice James J. Mayfield of Tuscaloosa also was mentioned as a fitting successor. And, by the first of June, Hugo Black had changed his mind again. "Judge Black will announce his candidacy upon a progressive platform," his statement read, "that will appeal to the forward-thinking citizenship of Alabama and will be in line with the ideals exemplified by his private and public life."

"I am definitely and finally in the race," Black assured a friend. Black was now totally convinced he could win. His announcement, however, "came as somewhat of a surprise to political observers who were unaware that the former county solicitor entertained political aspirations," noted one reporter. Clay County's newspaper was more generous to a native son, whom the editor declared "an easy winner" who "would wear the senatorial toga with honor and distinction."

Black was confident, but not cocky. "I'm a novice in State politics," he admitted to Hugh Grant, an Auburn University professor volunteering to help a fellow Baptist, "and the only method I know how to use is to work and let people know what I stand for." The candidate who drew the largest plurality would win, and with Underwood out, no candidate began with a substantial lead. If Black divided up a coalition of anti-Underwood voters with Kilby and Musgrove, Bankhead and Mayfield also would split conservative, wet voters. As an Underwood loyalist later saw it: "John Bankhead or Judge Mayfield can be elected provided either one runs but not if both runs." The situation was right for a political novice.

Without a ready-made record or deep pockets, Black exhibited his instinct for turning a liability into an asset. "This office must not be purchased," Black warned his three millionaire opponents in a qualifying statement. "We will, therefore, conduct our campaign well within the expenditures allowed by law," he said. "This campaign will be conducted on our part entirely by volunteer workers and carried directly to the people."[2]

When Underwood announced his retirement on July 2, Black already was mailing dozens of letters to friends and family in every part of the state. Included were distant relatives; fellow members of the Knights of Pythias, American Legion, and Masons; boyhood friends; members of his University class of 1905; and, of course, Baptists and prohibitionists. Later, Black also made a special appeal to jurors in Mobile's whiskey trials. In Alabama, Black explained, "a man must depend upon his friends when he enters into a political campaign."

Both Kilby and Black assured reporters that they had no intention of commencing a campaign one year before the election, and both were the most active candidates from the beginning. Harry Ayers, editor of Kilby's hometown *Anniston Star,* made an early state tour to gather support from other editors. Even before Underwood's exit, Kilby had opened his purse. "I have understood," Black told a south Alabama publisher, "that one of my opponents is sending out letters to various weekly papers inferentially suggesting that it would be to their financial advantage to assist him."

Black turned most of his court cases over to a new law partner, William E. Fort, who had retired from the circuit court bench, and transformed his law office into campaign headquarters. Black bought a Whippet, an inexpensive car smaller and somewhat less reliable than Ford's Model T. Over the next five months, Black traveled the state, attending fraternal conventions, meeting friends and friends of friends, and visiting towns and crossroads where candidates for statewide office had seldom been seen. "He wouldn't make a political speech," recalled Clifford Durr, who in 1925 was engaged to Josephine's sister, Virginia. Mapping out the ground rules of Black's early nonpolitical campaigning, Durr recalled: "He might make a 'Mother's Day' speech at the Baptist church somewhere—he would do that—or a '4th of July' speech, but nothing on politics."

Before departing for his first tour to the state's American Legion convention, Black made a shorter trip four flights down from his new ninth-floor offices in Birmingham's First National Bank building. He went to see the Klan's James Esdale. Eight days after Underwood's announced retirement, Black wrote a very brief, handwritten letter of resignation to the local klavern secretary on the grand dragon's KKK stationary and signed it, "Yours ITSUB" (In The Sacred, Unfailing Bond). "Give me a letter of resignation," Esdale recalled telling Black, "and I'll keep it in my safe against the day when you'll need to say you're not a Klan member."

Without Underwood in the race, the Ku Klux was not likely to become a central, political issue, especially if no Klansman was a candidate. Apparently, Black and Esdale agreed that Black as a candidate would gain nothing by remaining a Kluxer. Yet, Black did not write the letter to prove in the future that he wasn't a Kluxer. To critics of Ku Kluxism, such proof of nonmembership would be like a burglar listing past crimes to prove his current innocence. These two men were too savvy in politics not to realize that such a letter on Esdale's own stationary, ending with the Klan pledge of loyalty, would be ridiculed as a shabby ploy by Black's opponents and anti-Klan editors like *Montgomery Advertiser's* Grover Hall.

If anything, the letter was designed only for Kluxers' eyes. Were Black as a candidate ever required to deny that he was Ku Klux, the letter could speak for itself in informing Klansmen that Black had resigned with Esdale's cooperation *after* the Underwood forces surrendered their fight against the Klan. In this way, Klansmen might understand Black's denial of membership not as abandonment, but merely as a strategy undertaken by the candidate and the grand dragon.[3] Ironically, while Black's decision to join the Klan was not an act of political expediency, his resignation from the Klan was.

After contriving with Esdale for the best of both worlds, Black seemed doubly determined to act independently of the Klan, to reaffirm that no group, affiliation, or grand dragon dictated his honest convictions. At Birmingham's Woodlawn klavern, Black confronted KKK leaders who claimed he was too friendly to "nigras and Jews." "I'm soft," admitted Black in his talk, "only to the extent that they are citizens . . . all citizens have rights. . .[and] rights are the glory of citizenship." The speech "kept them quiet," according to Black. In Alabama's second largest industrial center, Black also spoke out publicly against floggings and Klan raids only a week after armed Kluxers in Gadsden had captured a whiskey runner. This was only the latest incident over the past two years in a long series of floggings and nightriding resembling Birmingham's experience.

As featured speaker at a Pythian Convention, Black declared, "the need of the hour is observance of the laws of the country." Black went further. "He pleaded enforcement of the law," reported a Gadsden newsman, "by the constituted authorities only. He said that if people would only support the courts and their officers a much better condition would be brought about."

This plea for law enforcement "by constituted authorities only" was a public rebuke of anyone who had assumed the role of law officer or law breaker, even for the common good, but it was not an attack by name on the Klan as a group or its members. As in the past, Black followed William Jennings Bryan's course of recognizing the "honesty" of most Klansmen and "teaching them" the right when they were wrong. Black assailed misdeeds associated with the Klan, but not Klan members and not the Klan. To make clear that his own independence should not be mistaken for hostility, Judge Black also spoke in Gadsden at the induction ceremonies of a Junior Klan chapter. A new member, decades later, remembered Black's speech as an inspiring call to "do right." "It was almost like going to Sunday School . . . It wasn't one of those brimstone, hell-fire sermons," A. B. Stutts remembered. It wasn't about hate, race, or religion. "This was just a beautiful story . . . and a beautiful ceremony."[4]

Throughout the fall of 1925, Black spent most of his time driving across the state in his Whippet or negotiating train schedules to take him to Pythian meetings, KKK klaverns, Bible classes, Legionnaire conventions, or school functions. On several klavern visits, Esdale accompanied Black. Whatever the occasion, Black tried to stay in the local area for two or three days. "I not only expect to come to Camden for the purpose of making a speech," he told a supporter, "but I hope to be there . . . simply to meet the people . . . I expect so far as possible to carry my campaign directly to the people." At every stop, Black avoided the political custom of visiting only a few local influential leaders, men known thirty years earlier in Ashland as "Ring" leaders.

This new style of campaigning gave Black an enlarging circle of friends and neighbors and an opportunity to sound out people's views on public issues. "Hugo knew what he stood for and he'd throw out his idea and get an adverse reaction," Cliff Durr remembered. "But this was just a private conversation . . . Then he'd go down the road to the next crossroads and he'd throw out the same idea with a little different approach," Durr continued. "I would test myself," Black explained, "to see if I could honestly agree with them about their needs and their wants." By trial and error, Black said, "I schooled myself for the job."

Soon after beginning his speaking tours, Black organized his own political thoughts on paper. His initial efforts were surprisingly inarticulate, and his draft statements were vague and formalistic. In calling for increased federal revenues to address local needs, for instance, Black wrote of his "support of measures looking towards improvements in . . . public education, good roads, and rural free [mail] delivery." Having declared his candidacy on principles of Alabama citizenship—not good citizenship or American citizenship, Black's early draft proclaimed his "opposition to any abandonment of the cloture rule," the Senate rule enabling Southerners to filibuster national civil rights legislation to death. Horace Turner pointed out, however, that "the average voter does not even know what the 'Cloture rule' is," and Black dropped it.

Motoring across the state, Black learned first-hand about the need for improving roads. The entire state had less than fifteen thousand miles of surfaced roads, and on several trips Black lost his way on rough, unmarked roads, especially when trying to figure out detours that took him into cow paths. On one trip Black had to ditch his Whippet, only to be stranded later when a borrowed car's tires were punctured on sharp rocks. In other places, Black turned back because gravel roads, considered "surfaced" by government statistics, had been washed away by hard rains.

At home, Black faced unexpected roadblocks. On a swing through Birmingham to answer mail and pick up a fresh stack of pressed clothes, Black discovered that the Internal Revenue Service wanted several hundred dollars for back taxes and penalties. Black protested that he absolutely, positively did not owe one brown penny to the federal government. But, he agreed to pay. "I cannot spare the time from my campaign," he told the IRS agent. Since Black had never employed a bookkeeper, no one else could contest the government's claim on his behalf. In addition, Black stated, "I cannot afford, while making the race for the United States Senate, to give my opponents any talking point as to my income."

One of Black's opponents, Breck Musgrove, was very eager to talk privately to Black about his income. The Jasper businessman wanted to buy Black's withdrawal from the race and sent more than one emissary with offers. Musgrove knew that the two men drew from the same political well, and he probably realized early that Esdale was supporting Black. "I have no remote idea of withdrawing from this race," Black replied to each offer. Tell Musgrove, he informed one messenger, "There is not enough money in the United States to get me to do so."

Offers of money were the apples of Alabama political Eden, but they only motivated Black to work harder. He told students and old friends at opening day of Clay County schools that "Knowledge is power . . . when called into action by the heroic deeds of men with great souls and great passions for service" and "WORK is the key to knowledge." Using a Longfellow poem, Black projected his own strategy for using a "God-given opportunity" to succeed in the heart of Dixie:

> The heights by great men reached and kept,
> Were not attained by sudden flight,
> But they, while their companion slept,
> Were toiling upward in the night.

While employing hard work as the means, Black usually chose temperance and prohibition as his message during the last few months of 1925. "I am now, have always been, and always shall be in favor of the complete destruction of the liquor traffic," the candidate told a group of ministers. "I've taken an aggressive part in every fight for prohibition and its enforcement since I was a boy," Black proudly exclaimed. To distinguish himself from all the other candidates, Black declared throughout the campaign, "I have never in my life tasted whiskey." In Bible classes throughout the state, Black championed abstinence. In Albertville on World Temperance Sunday, Black reminded churchgoers that "the saloon is the deadly enemy of the home," and, with the help of the International Sunday School Lessons guide, Black miraculously discovered a text for the sins of whiskey in the poetic verses of love, hope, and charity from 1 Corinthians 13:13.

In early November, Black sent a special circular on his prohibition record to the state's Baptist ministers as prelude to his appearance at the Alabama Baptist Convention. Persisting on the theme of law and order, Judge Black spoke to several hundred delegates assembled in the Selma High School auditorium. America had become "the most lawless nation on the globe," Black proclaimed. He insisted that prohibition was the nation's true test of law and order and charged that "the question should not be should the Eighteenth Amendment be enforced, but how it can be enforced . . . Either a man is a patriot and obeys the laws or he is not a patriot and disobeys them."

"Americans have no right to complain of the Eighteenth Amendment and ignore its observance and turn to the Fifth Amendment [the right to remain silent] for protection," Black declared to loud applause. "The country's strength is embodied in her highest laws," he continued, "and Communism and Bolshevism present us no threat so long as the people appreciate that safety lies for America in the constitution as it stands *in its entirety* . . . Mothers should croon in their lullabies; schools should teach in their classrooms and churches from their pulpits the practice of obedience to law," proclaimed Black the Baptist.[5]

"Magnificent in its oratorial effects!" exclaimed the local editor. "Judge Hugo L. Black of Birmingham, and a candidate for the seat of Oscar Underwood . . . called forth a tremendous response from hundreds," he reported. The speech motivated several Baptist leaders and ministers to get busy on Black's behalf. Shortly after the state convention, a Baptist minister arranged for Black to speak before both Baptist and Methodist Bible classes in his town. "This will give you a chance to get before most of the people," the preacher told Brother Black. "Of course, . . . I think it best that there be no mention of politics. However, by these meetings we hope to foster your campaign in our city."

Editors in Birmingham's newsrooms did not share this Baptist enthusiasm for Black's candidacy. The *News* failed to mention Black's speech in Selma but gave excellent coverage to John Bankhead's address in neighboring Wilcox County. According to Black's information, the newspaper vastly exaggerated Bankhead's audience, and the article stated that only three candidates had announced for the Senate, Bankhead, Mayfield, and Kilby. As the first candidate to legally qualify, Black reacted with disgust to the news report "carefully prepared long before Mr. Bankhead delivered his speech 'to hundreds of Wilcox County citizens gathered to hear him.'" Black didn't expect the *Birmingham News* or any daily paper to endorse him, since he believed "they usually go with the man who has the most money." But he was disturbed that Victor Hanson's newspaper was so grossly unfair. "The method . . . ," he wrote the *News* publisher, "appears to be but a part of the plan of the old line politicians who have run Alabama politics for a long time, to attempt to ignore my candidacy." To keep an eye on such methods, Black subscribed to all state newspapers during the campaign's last six months.

By Christmas of 1925, Black had visited fifty of the state's sixty-seven counties and was planning to travel through eight more before February, if rain and snow didn't make country roads impassable. Robert Lee Black's son, Hollis, was now working in his uncle's office, writing letters and running them off on a mimeograph machine, the newest tool of direct campaigning. The letters were tailored to fit the specific concerns of Black's different friends, who took a stack and sent them out to their friends under their own signature. No printed campaign brochure had been prepared, but Black's secretary typed a constant stream of personal letters following up Black's visits and arranging others.

When Black assessed the first six months of unofficial campaigning, he was pleased. "My hopes . . . rest on the Dry-Protestant-Progressive Voters of the State," he informed a former Ashland teacher. Collecting his thoughts, Black foresaw the Senate race as a fight between money and morality. "The liquor forces and the big corporations will be almost solidly against me," he declared. On one side, he said, was the man who had represented several labor unions, fought liquor all his life, taught Alabama's largest Sunday school class, and had been a Baptist deacon for fifteen years. On the other side were three millionaires and a corporation lawyer, two of whom, Bankhead and Mayfield, represented an increasingly powerful private utility, the Alabama Power Company. "I am personally of the opinion," Black said, "that there has been so many millionaires and corporation lawyers in the United States Senate, that people rarely ever have a real representative."

Despite his Populist rhetoric, Black continued to see himself as a public servant standing for justice between society's warring factions. He stood in the middle ground between extremes, as "one who does not stand that labor has the right to use dynamite, and who is equally critical of the capitalistic Bolshevik who believes that the rich should be made richer and the poor should be made poorer." His opponents, Black admitted, were already calling him a "Bolshevik," only because "there is no corporation lawyer in all of Alabama who is supporting me." "I might also add," Black wrote, "that I am accused by *the opposition* of being a candidate of the Ku Klux Klan." The accusation pleased him. Breck Musgrove's stock in trade for campaigning was rumors and accusations about an opponent's papal tendencies, and public charges of a Klan connection, Black observed, "will further show that I am not amenable to Catholic influence."

As the campaign moved towards a new year and candidates began unwrapping their overtly political rhetoric for the August election, Black showed none of the uncertainty with which he began the political season. Now, he held no doubt about his future and the means to reach it. He was ready to rush forward with the same self confidence and same identity he had possessed since childhood, as a strong-willed person standing on his own terms between the clash of hostile factions, judging each issue on the basis of "justice for all, special favors for none." Yet, in the reality of politics, Black also had become a candidate whose values and abilities were being defined by the friends and the enemies he kept.[6] For the moment, at least, Black savored both identities as the marks of a victor.

AT THE START OF 1926, Black wasn't Alabama's only political renegade. Bibb Graves, former adjutant general of the state militia, was running for governor against the "railroad lawyers and wet politicians" and without support of any daily newspaper. Although he counted two of Alabama's early governors among his ancestors, Graves's grandfather reared him in Texas outside Montgomery's political and social circles. He also was educated outside the state with a degree in civil engineering and a law degree from Yale University, but his real interests led to the military where he associated with men from all ranks and walks of life.

Over the last ten years, Graves had emerged episodically in Alabama's political spotlight. In 1916, he became chairman of the state Democratic Executive Committee. He was a founding member of the state's American Legion after service in France during World War I. In 1922, he barely received a fifth of the votes in a two-man race for governor against "Plain Bill" Brandon, and in 1924 he managed Breck Musgrove's decisive loss against Senator Underwood in the presidential primary. By 1926, however, this short, slightly pudgy man had become a "master of three languages—Latin, the King's English, and the people's"—a politician able to move easily across groups and ranks in Alabama society in search of a new coalition.

Black and Graves were not good friends, but they shared common characteristics, concerns, and constituencies. Both were ex-soldiers and members of a dozen fraternal orders. Both were politically and personally dry. "I believe in prohibition so strongly that I practice it," Graves proclaimed. Like Black, Graves reached in his campaign beyond the courthouse ring directly to common folk. "I do not carry a railroad pass," declared Graves. He, too, offered a Populist platform, promising to increase public schools, health, and roads by enlarging taxes on profitable corporations, railroads, and public utilities. With a campaign slogan of "He puts man above the dollar," Graves actively opposed convict leasing, supported a seven-month school term for white kids, and favored reapportioning the state legislature to diminish the Black Belt's lopsided political power. At the beginning of 1926, Black and Graves were also alike in being virtually ignored by their opponents and the state's daily newspapers.

Both Black and Graves were "accused . . . of being a candidate of the Ku Klux Klan." Graves had pleased Klan leaders by running Musgrove's campaign against Underwood during the presidential primary, and, according to Klan records, Graves was a paid lecturer who toured the state's klaverns as early as 1923. In the fall of 1924, the *Associated Press* reported that Graves was already a candidate for governor "with the support of the Ku Klux Klan" and quoted one observer predicting that Klan support "will bring him the nomination, if the state's sentiment does not change within the next two years."

Despite such forecasts, the Klan had not shown commanding political strength across the state. In the March 1924 primary, Alabama's Ku Klux failed miserably in ambushing Underwood's presidential bid, and, later that summer, Birmingham Klan leader Walter Brower lost decisively to Underwood's chosen candidate in a statewide race for Alabama's elected post on the Democratic National Committee. In Birmingham's local elections in October 1925, the Klan successfully backed a majority of the new city commission, but the races were close. In Montgomery and Mobile, Klan influence in local politics remained limited. With strong Klan backing, but no proven Klan victory in statewide politics, Graves was initially dismissed by his opponents as a self-appointed "Crown Prince" with no serious chance of winning.

At the beginning of 1926, however, both Black and Graves appeared politically dangerous, and the state's "railroad lawyers and wet politicians," maneuvered in Montgomery to assure that the two political renegades did not win. "A great effort is being made by the opposition to put over a *double primary law*," Black telegraphed supporters during the second week of January. The "reactionary forces" were trying to convince the state legislature to require a run-off election, "a double primary law," in the event no candidate received a majority of votes in the upcoming primary election.

The current no-run-off law had passed in 1916 with the help of Bibb Graves and Rep. Will Welch, Solicitor Black's assistant, to aid prohibitionist candidates, but the law clearly would have helped reelect Oscar Underwood, prohibitionists' archenemy, if he had run against several opponents. Now, without the senator in the race, the current law promised to give Black and Graves a decisive advantage since the field of more conservative candidates would probably divide up the Underwood vote and allow Black and Graves to receive the largest numbers—all it would take to win. "The opposition to me," Black explained, "is hopelessly split up at the present time, and unless a double primary law [run-off] is enacted I do not see how they can overcome the handicap."[7]

After considerable wrangling, the run-off proposal failed. Many incumbents, including conservatives, joined Black and Graves in opposing the revision because they feared the uncertainty of changing a system on the eve of the next election. In yet another little twist of political irony, Alabama's renegades were saved as much by their opponents as by their supporters.

WITH THE DOUBLE PRIMARY DEFEATED, Black attacked the state's political tradition of double talk. Completing his state tour, *Anniston Star* editor Harry Ayers announced that Thomas Kilby was the certain victor over his three opponents—Bankhead, Mayfield, and Musgrove. Like the *Birmingham News*, Ayers's *Star* ignored Black as a candidate, and news reports of the editor's political analysis failed to point out Ayers's own partisan role in Kilby's campaign. Black called it another case of "newspaper propaganda."

"After completing a thorough canvas of fifty-seven counties in Alabama,"

Black informed reporters, ". . . I am not surprised that Governor Kilby wishes he could forget I am in the race." A handwritten draft of Black's unissued first response was more surly. "I have been reading with some . . . amusement the interviews given by Mr. Harry Ayers, the Campaign Manager of Mr. Kilby, to Mr. Harry Ayers, the newspaperman of Anniston," Black scribbled. "The day has passed in my humble judgment when 'money and key men' constitute an insurmountable political obstacle."

Amid constant traveling, Black prepared his campaign's kick-off speech for Ashland in late March. Black preferred to speak extemporaneously, as he did in the courtroom, and rarely prepared a written speech, but this one was an exception. It was "his first public profession of political faith," and Black intended to circulate it around the state as his primary campaign literature.

"Wealth is piling up in the hands of a few with ever increasing power," Black's manuscript begins, as he described a need for public servants who have not lost touch with "the common people" in times of great economic peril. "Great railroad systems are rolling under one control . . . Power systems spring up in one state and spread their wires over many states in a gigantic web that entangles the destiny of our children," he declared. Black's conversations with ordinary Alabamians over the last eight months had "schooled" him with a new boldness that abandoned the stilted, sectional language of his early campaign paper. "Hugo discovered that there was an awful lot of radical sentiment," among Alabama's plain white folk, Cliff Durr remembered, "when he talked to the people in their own language."

"I am not opposed to wealth honestly acquired and honestly used," Black's text continued. "Equality under the law to millionaire and pauper, factory owner and worker, is the test of a successful democracy. We must turn a deaf ear alike to the selfish appeals of those who attack property rights or human rights." Reviving the principle of good citizenship, Black wrote: "The golden rule of life should be the golden rule of politics and business," and, in keeping with his own self-image, Black declared that the true public servant's role in "the age-old struggle between those who have and those who want is to hold the scales of justice evenly."

When Clay County farmers and families crowded the Ashland town square on Saturday morning, March 20, Black had the text in hand as he stepped forward. Standing at the courthouse site of his boyhood dreams, Black drew a large, supportive crowd. "My Friends and Neighbors," he began. "The soil on which I stand is sacred to me . . . Only a few hundred yards away repose the ashes of my father who cherished hopes of my success, and the mother whose worn and wrinkled hand pointed every way to truth and light and faith," he said. "When I was on a farm in Clay County, Alabama, twenty miles from the nearest railroad, my father was struggling with the rocky soil and high-priced fertilizer, in an effort to grow enough cheap cotton to purchase the very necessities of life, made dear by unjust tariffs and unjust laws permitting organized manufacturers to exploit the unorganized farmer." Allowing political memory to conquer the truth, Black added, "I am indebted to the free Public Schools of Alabama for my education."

"I have held no great office . . . I am not now, and have never been a railroad, power company, or corporation lawyer," Black solemnly intoned. "They have never shaped my ideals, fashioned my political creed, nor helped me in my aspirations for public office. I am not a millionaire. I am not a Coal Operator. My father was not a United States senator and I am not running on his record. My father was a farmer. I have no hereditary claim to office; but is there any clause in our constitution which says the son of a senator shall be a senator, but the son of a farmer must always be a farmer?

"If the time has come when public office goes to the highest bidder," Black announced, "I lift my voice in vain. I could not compete with the millionaire opponents on an advertising or money-spending campaign. I would not, if I could . . . I do not believe that people want a United States senator who is willing to buy the help of political parasites and machine politicians."

Black assured the friendly crowd that he favored low tariffs, low personal taxes, and increased federal money for developing Alabama's roads and waterways, including the Muscle Shoals dam in north Alabama on the Tennessee River. "It was originally built to give the farmer cheap fertilizer in time of peace," Black reminded voters. "Selfish interests have succeeded in thwarting the people's will . . . If you want your great property at Muscle Shoals given away to the Alabama Power Company, or any other privately owned power company, do not vote for me."

Kluxers in Ashland had held a spirited rally at the courthouse the night before, and Black spoke to their issues of Americanism, on his own terms. About law and order, "the beginning and end of government," Black proclaimed, "Men may differ on opinions as to the wisdom of a law, but all *good citizens* stand for its enforcement when written. The people do not want, and must not have, officers who are politically dry and personally wet . . . I will obey the law and . . . do not believe in prosecuting only the weak and the helpless," trumpeted Black, repeating the language of fairness that had driven his solicitor's campaign.

Describing most immigrants as "ignorant, illiterate, and wholly incapable of ever appreciating the ideas and duties of *American* citizenship," Black declared that foreigners were being brought to American shores to lower American wages. "The melting-pot is dangerous," he insisted. "I oppose further immigration." Black's sentiment echoed the position of organized labor, but, in fact, less than 5 percent of Alabama's total population was foreign-born. Black also condemned as a "national disgrace" federal loans to foreign countries since money was going abroad while America's ex-soldiers suffered at home. "If I am your United States senator and it is in my power so to do," declared Black, "no Honorably Discharged soldier shall die a *pauper's death*" as did one in Birmingham in 1922. Black called for a "State where men truly worship the God of their fathers."

"The great goal of democracy is universal equity," Black proclaimed. Now, Black was seeking to reach good citizens by invoking the full claims of American citizenship, in effect, renouncing all plans for a campaign on "Alabama citizenship":

> The vision I see shines from justice to all and special favor to none . . . When freedom was wrestled from King George the Third by the homespun-clad soldiers of the Revolution, they sought to put a perpetual barrier against plutocracy and hereditary succession. The youth of America have been inspired to place their feet on the ladder of ambition . . . We have taxed the people to build schools, in order that the sons of the poor and obscure might have their chance in life struggles with the sons of the rich and more powerful. This is the boast of America . . . Whatever may be your verdict at the polls, I ask the fathers and mothers who love their children, the citizens of Alabama who prize the freedom of American opportunities, to strike at this idea that only the rich, the powerful, and the sons of the great can serve this state . . . It is true now . . . that the humblest son of the humblest citizen, born in the humblest surroundings, can lift his eyes toward the star of hope . . . Such is the spirit of *America*.[8]

The "subsidized press," as Black called major daily newspapers, covered Black's speech, but not well enough. Black wrote to the *Birmingham News* editor, disputing its report that he endorsed government ownership of the Muscle Shoals dam. "I am opposed to Government operation of any kind of industry on principle," Black insisted. "I did say in my speech that I am opposed to making the Alabama Power Company, or any other privately owned power company, a gift of Muscle Shoals."

To put his views directly before voters, Black traveled the state throughout April. He was slowed only by occasional bad weather, a single day of bed-ridden sickness, and the marriage of his sister-in-law, Virginia, to Cliff Durr (whose father had been on Kilby's 1922 miners' strike commission). Black took full advantage of large crowds during the spring opening of Alabama's criminal courts. He usually arranged to speak at lunchtime or during recess. Since murder cases always packed a courtroom, the former prosecutor and candidate of law and order often depended on Alabama's murderers to drum up his largest crowds.

"Alabama's seat in the Senate of the United States is not for sale," Black told many courtroom spectators, whom he treated like sitting jurors. "All over the United States our citizens are going to be proud of Alabama's loyalty to true Democracy. *Men will say . . . , 'down in Alabama money cannot buy the vote of the people.'* " Before the bar of justice, Black reminded his audience, "I have served the needs of the poor and unfortunate. In my practice I have represented the injured and broken, the widows and orphans of men killed beneath the wheels of trains or buried in the fallen rock down in the mines of coal and iron." As if pleading for a client, Black asked, "Is it wrong to help the helpless?"

Black accepted invitations to speak wherever he could generate them: a Sunday school lecture, a klavern speech, a commencement address, club parties, a stump speech off a wagon bed, or a graveside eulogy. On April 9th, for example, Judge Black spoke on "Law Enforcement" to the Auburn University students' Agricultural Club although few, if any students, could vote. "It is no longer the question whether the Eighteenth Amendment is right or wrong, but whether we will determine to enforce the great constitution of these United States." Black said that there were "not enough convictions in our courts, too many pardons for criminals, and too many technicalities standing between the criminal and punishment."

The speech was surprisingly well covered by the area's newspapers, because of Auburn political scientist Hugh Grant. The former newspaperman wrote a story about the speech and forwarded it to old acquaintances at several of the state's dailies and weeklies. To Black's delight, the papers ran Grant's story as their own reporting without a byline.[9]

This glimmer of good publicity was an exception, however, and Black continued to tussle with editors. He gingerly corrected a weekly newspaper editor who left him off a list of senatorial candidates but strongly challenged the Columbus (Georgia) editor who identified Kilby and Musgrove as the only dry candidates. "I was taking part in the fight against liquor," Black told the Klan-fighting, Pulitzer prize-winning editor Julian Harris, "when Mr. Kilby was not heard from." Ten years earlier, moreover, Black had been a celebrated hero cleaning up liquor in Girard and Phenix City across the state line from Columbus.

Black accused another paper of using canned editorials prepared by other candidates, and later he declined a request to write an article for the *Birmingham Age-Herald*. Apparently, Black imagined entrapment or deception lurking in the offer. He was certain he knew the methods and motives of the *Montgomery Times* poll that put him in last place among Jefferson County voters. In a letter to the editor, Black acknowledged the reporter's story "with interest and amusement"—terms in Black's lexicon that would have made any opposing lawyer shudder. Black demonstrated that the newspaper had interviewed fictional characters in its polling.

Black's combative style drew quick responses from two opponents. Kilby moved to take the lead as premier prohibitionist and businessman. In March, he placed newspaper ads across Alabama heralding the endorsement of former Governor B. B. Comer. In giant ads, Kilby also reminded voters that he had signed into law the first statewide dry statute. John Bankhead fashioned an image to fit his father's shadow. "It is generally admitted," Bankhead's advertising boasted, "that he has conducted a dignified and gentleman's campaign. He has refrained from engaging in campaign methods that are little and narrow . . . He has not sought to stir any prejudice or passion," the Bankhead Club boasted. "Keep your eye on Bankhead!"[10]

Kilby and Bankhead also adopted more vigorous campaigns in response to Black's direct-to-the-people style. "Governor Kilby was in town this morning," reported an amused Black volunteer, "shaking hands with all the people, going into garages, stores, and stopping those whom he met on the streets."

Bankhead, claiming his "heart beats with the struggles and aspirations and hopes of the plain people," visited practically every county in the state. Also, the other two opponents, Judge Mayfield the "constitutional candidate" and Breck Musgrove, traveled the state as never before.

Black's opponents could not match his energy and pace. By May, Black had returned to thirty-one counties, delivered more than seventy speeches, and offered handshakes and smiles to thousands. Black thrilled supporters when he listed depreciation of two Whippets as part of his campaign expenses in a preelection filing. "My car is not near worn out yet," volunteered a Black Belt friend who wanted no delay in scheduling Black for four more speeches. In another community, Black spoke to a large audience assembled for Friday night's silent film at a local theater. He appeared at an Opera House as prelude to live music, and in several communities he spoke to hundreds on monthly trade days when farmers and peddlers swapped goods and stories.

In tiny Vina, Black's appearance was a major event. "He stepped out dressed all in white—white linen suit, white necktie, white shoes," remembered a young Carl Elliott. "He just stood there by his car, completely at ease as an audience of about a hundred circled around him." Black was satisfied at other times with smaller crowds. "I am making speeches," he explained, "at places where no candidate ever spoke before." A Birmingham friend who occasionally traveled with Black remembered how the tiny Whippet bounced deep along rough roads and cow trails. "We met folks living so far in the backwoods that they considered a dirt crossroads as the den of iniquity," George Lewis Bailes recalled.

It was in Sheffield, near the Muscle Shoals dam, in late May where Black gathered his momentum. With the help of local friends, hundreds of circulars, and an old black man who walked around town inside a "sandwich sign," Black announced a rally at the town's airdrome to speak about the nearby dam. The candidate and the issue struck a responsive chord, and more than a thousand people stood inside the hangar, listening for more than two hours. Black told them that the dam which stood idle only five miles away at the Tennessee River should be put into operation for producing cheap fertilizer for farmers and electricity in their homes. He attacked Alabama Power Company's efforts to take over the dam as "greed" and pointed out that all of his opponents were Power Company lawyers, corporation lawyers, or millionaires who would not look after the common people's business.[11]

Within a week of the Sheffield speech, John Bankhead and Thomas Kilby agreed to a debate on the Muscle Shoals question in nearby Tuscumbia. The former governor had challenged Bankhead to such a debate weeks earlier, but now both men saw the necessity of drawing attention away from Black and his damn issue. Black, however, upstaged his opponents' event when he accused them of violating the Alabama Corrupt Practices Act by spending more than $10,000 on their campaigns. "The people of Alabama are getting tired of having men spend large sums of money to purchase public office," Black charged.

At the site of the Bankhead-Kilby debate, Black's volunteers were equally resourceful in deflating the debate. Two large signs were nailed onto a wagon that an old black man drove up and down Tuscumbia's streets prior to the event. Later, the wagon parked in front of the Palace Theater as the crowd left the debate. The wagon's signs read: "Bankhead says Kilby won't do. Kilby says Bankhead won't do. Both are right. Vote for Black." "The sign on the wagon was the best advertising stunt I could have pulled at that time," Black's volunteer wrote, "and it created quite a bit of comment throughout the district." Black never forgot the stunt, which he saw as a turning point in the campaign. It also vindicated his faith in the ingenuity and aid of friends, even if Black's stories years later gave himself complete credit for the coup.

Bankhead couldn't afford to disregard Black any longer. In a statement issued from his Birmingham headquarters, the Jasper lawyer accused Black of trying to "humbug the people" with pleas of poverty and accusations about millionaires' campaign chest. Bankhead accused Black of being a rich man who owned Birmingham real estate worth a quarter of a million dollars. "If Mr. Black lived in several Alabama counties, he would be the richest citizen in the county and would be known as the Duke," Bankhead charged.

Black appeared enchanted with the accusation. "Will Mr. Bankhead send me a check for one half of what he solemnly says my property in Birmingham is worth?" Black asked publicly. "If so, I just as solemnly agree to convey to him all my interest in real estate in Birmingham." "The issue in this race is not who has the money," Black stated, "but who is spending money behind the name of Clubs, and thus striking down the spirit of American Democracy." Black welcomed the attack as a concession by Bankhead: "I am the man he believes stands most in the way of what he evidently considers the Bankhead heritage."

Black's Whippets were in full gear throughout June as he crisscrossed the state to speak before large, enthusiastic audiences. In Opp, Black's friends pulled a wagon onto main street as a speaker's platform since no building in town had space for the more than one hundred and fifty people who gathered. At a speech in Wilcox County, according to his local campaign volunteer, Black won the entire audience—except for one person. "Upon further inquiry. . .," Black's friend wrote, "I found that he was deaf. I think that is the situation everywhere. *To hear you is to be convinced.*"

In a gigantic rally in Bessemer, where ten years earlier he had accused local officials of abusing poor African American prisoners, Black sized up the race: "If a cyclone doesn't strike this state between now and August 10 . . . the people are going to say that Alabama is surely the Blackest state in the whole category of American commonwealths (great applause)."[12]

The other four candidates reluctantly were coming to the same conclusion. Desperately they searched for a countervailing storm. Judge Mayfield condemned any man who would go to Washington to represent one "faction, class, or clan." It was Bolshevism, he said, when men got control of the government to take away the property of the minority for the benefit of the "numerical majority, called the mob." He decried "demagogues who seek to ride into office by fanning the flames . . . of passion and prejudice." Mayfield also asked his friends to take up a collection for "poor Mr. Black" since any man who paraded his poverty must surely be in bad shape. John Bankhead resurrected the language of class warfare, which in 1920 Oscar Underwood had used against Musgrove. He accused Black of awakening class strife. He also charged Black with improperly using the Baptist Church and "secret societies of which he is a member" to get votes. Kilby condemned Black's "appeal to prejudice" and political lies and attacked Black "as a damage suit lawyer," who enriched himself from the misfortune of people. "He has lived off the payrolls which I helped to create," the former governor declared.

Black's opponents employed other campaign methods. Bankhead hired a court reporter to follow Black around the state in an attempt to document Black's "prejudice"—his "bolshevik" appeals to the masses. Musgrove used his checkbook in early June to prevent Black from receiving the endorsement of the state's railroad brotherhoods, one of whom Black had represented for years. The state labor federation also failed to endorse anyone in the Senate race, probably for the same reason. Kilby pumped enormous sums of advertising dollars into the states' newspapers, and, according to Black's information, both Musgrove and Kilby persisted in attempts to buy the support of political rainmakers. James Esdale remembered Musgrove sitting in his office and offering thousands of dollars for the grand dragon's endorsement. "Colonel, everyone's got his price," Esdale confessed. But at that moment, the Klan leader was investing, not selling.

Perhaps at the Atlanta headquarters of the national Klan, Hiram Evans received Musgrove's generosity more warmly. On July 10, the candidate's campaign manager sent letters to local klaverns, heralding Wizard Evans's endorsement of Musgrove. "Dr. Evans regards this as a sacred promise, which the Klan should keep," the message insisted.

As Musgrove sought the Klan password at the polls, Judge Mayfield's friends pressed Black to confess that he was the Klan-connected candidate. "I have been told that Mr. Black was a Ku Klux, and that he was active in that organization," a lumberyard operator wrote to Bill Cloe, the Proctor & Gamble salesman and former Birmingham city commissioner who quietly promoted Black's candidacy as he traveled the state. "To me it would be a great calamity for the state," the businessman wrote, "to elect a man that would actively engage in furthering the cause of the Klan, as he would go as a group representative."

Black—not Cloe—responded. "I imagine that due to your close relationship with Judge Mayfield," Black replied, ". . . any answer I made to you with reference to the question asked, will not change your support of Judge Mayfield. So far as I am concerned," Black stated, "I do not expect the matter referred to in our letter today, made an issue by me." Like a schoolboy warned against certain utterances that would get him into trouble, Black awkwardly avoided mentioning the actual words "Ku Klux Klan." If other candidates persisted "in making any such extraneous matter an issue," Black charged, "it would be an unwise thing for the progress of the State."

While Black dodged the words "Ku Klux," Judge Mayfield stretched hard to mention them. Prior to the campaign, Mayfield had recompiled Alabama's new Code of Laws, including a new index referring for the first time to the "Ku Klux." As one reporter accurately noted, however, "there is no reference to Ku Klux in the code outside of the index, which contains the citation, 'Ku Klux prohibited,' referring students of the code to the sections prohibiting lynching and mobbing."

Now, Mayfield's supporters persisted in trying to index Black as "Ku Klux." Shortly after the Fourth of July, another lumber company owner asked Black for a direct statement about his Klan connections. After a few days, the candidate responded. "I've had a conference with a number of my friends in connection with the question of the Ku Klux Klan," reported Black, now ready to mention the forbidden words. "My judgment is, and that of my friends, among whom was my old friend, Herman Beck, that this is not, and should not be an issue. I have consistently taken the position that I would neither admit nor deny any connection with the Ku Klux Klan," Black stated.

Black offered to express his opinion on any issue "which you or anyone else think the Ku Klux Klan stands for." Yet, any statement about his "connection or non-connection" with the Klan would make the organization an issue. "To make the Ku Klux Klan an issue stirs up strife and antagonism, which should not exist in a political race. It is my information," Black concluded in a refrain he repeated for the rest of his life, "that every candidate for the senate is doing his best to get the Ku Klux Klan votes as well as other votes in Alabama."

No doubt Black honestly believed that the Klan as a political issue would stir up "strife and antagonism" from profligate racist impulses. As early as 1920 (probably much earlier), he considered race-based accusations to be deadly in an Alabama campaign. Over the years, Alabama politics had proven him woefully correct. Black's silence, however, was also the surest way to maintain Klan support without losing others for whom the Klan was a major issue.

Politically, Black could not move a millimeter on the Klan. On one side, Breck Musgrove was using every available dollar to get between Black and the local klaverns. If Black announced that he was not a Klansman, it could jeopardize a strategic block of Klan voters who might feel Black was distancing himself from them. On the other side was Mayfield who wanted to gain support by attacking Black and the Klan as one. If Black announced that he had been a Klansman until recently, Mayfield would have succeeded in making the Klan an issue, and Musgrove would have what he needed—evidence of Black's disloyalty to the group. In such an event, Black would have to use his resignation letter on Esdale's stationary to assure Kluxers that his departure was a sweetheart's parting, and Black would have to lean heavily on the Grand Dragon to help save the Klan vote—a development that would have made Black truly beholden to Esdale. With so little time left before the election, with so many different attacks against him as the front runner, and with his own independence at sake, Black's safest course was be a political "tar baby" and "don't say nothing."

Had Ku Klux votes turned simply on Esdale's endorsement, Black's predicament would not have been so tricky. The grand dragon's support was valuable, but Black knew that Alabama's secret order was not monolithic. Esdale sent out an official Klan sample ballot in June, endorsing Black and Bibb Graves, but at many klaverns there was no way to really know if Esdale's literature translated into votes contrary to Hiram Evans's endorsement of Musgrove. No Klansman was sworn to follow any leader's political endorsement.

Black also knew that Ku Klux support in different klaverns could not be left to Esdale's marked ballots. A Klan leader in Bullock County in early 1926 told Black that he had to work on his own to "get every Klan in the state lined up." In response, Black said he was doing his level best but welcomed any suggestions on how to actually do it. In the Birmingham area, some Klan groups opposed Black, but they worked for Bibb Graves, Esdale's other endorsed candidate. In Baldwin County, near Mobile, one of Graves's key Klan operatives handled Musgrove's local campaign. Musgrove also made inroads into other klaverns. From south Alabama, a local Klan volunteer sent Black urgent word: "Get Musgrove out of this race." At the same time, Bill Cloe, Black's loyal traveling salesmen, attended several klavern meetings to support Black and Bibb Graves's strongest opponent. If it was true the "public is on a secret hunt for Christian men to put in office," as one of Black's early correspondents suggested, not all those with a secret password agreed on who were the most Christian.[13]

While Black persisted in keeping secret his relationship with the Klan, his opponents met in secret to stop his advance. Black's plurality victory was becoming increasingly evident, so long as all remaining votes were split among the other four. Now belligerently opposed to Black, Selma's editor suggested that Mayfield, Bankhead, and Kilby confer to eliminate two candidates from the race. Black's own sources reported that old-line politicians and corporate leaders were pressuring John Bankhead in particular to quit. In early July, only a few weeks before the election, Bankhead and Musgrove apparently met at Birmingham's fashionable Tutwiler Hotel.

"Breck, they have got me beat in this race and there does not seem to be much use to remain any longer," a despondent Bankhead told his Jasper neighbor, "and they've got you beat and Kilby and Mayfield; Black is going to be the next senator." A pudgy-faced millionaire as dull as Musgrove was flamboyant, Bankhead suggested that someone had to exit the race. Musgrove agreed and told Bankhead to arrange a conference with other candidates. Soon afterwards,

Musgrove's operatives worked like madmen spreading word of Bankhead's confession in hopes that the lawyer's own words would eliminate him. The torchbearer of a self-made Bankhead legacy denied all, and a meeting of all candidates never took place. Stampeding to their own political destruction, none of Black's opponents would break from the pack.

Black had little to fear as the campaign entered its final weeks. A survey by school superintendents showed that he was leading in forty-nine counties. At a Birmingham meeting of the Alabama Bar Association, Black's friends overheard corporate lawyers discussing the pending tragedy. "If something isn't done, and done quickly, nothing short of an earthquake will keep Hugo Black out of the senate," a leading lawyer complained. "For God's sake," they muttered vainly to each other. Black was confident. "I have no earthly doubt about having them defeated at the present time," he assured a fellow ex-soldier. "I realize, of course, that they will spend a great deal of money and that is the only danger today outside of seeing that the votes are counted properly."

Black's foretaste of victory only enlarged his political appetite and energy. He distributed thousands of additional flyers and bumper stickers to his best volunteers, who were carefully listed in a little black book that Black always kept in his coat pocket. Black nudged friends to get free publicity about his opponents' millionaire spending by writing articles in local weekly papers and using his name as author. Black packed his schedule with even more speeches—four to eight a day—and traveled back and forth on the Pan American Railroad late into the early morning to keep nearly impossible schedules. He urged friends to send out a new batch of letters reminding their friends that he stood "not only for law enforcement, but for law observance and for equality before the law."

Others took a different line. "Black is the whitest man in the race," shouted supporters in rural, predominantly white Franklin County as they displayed "Hugo Black" windshield stickers and posters on their automobiles and drays. In Clay, Hugo's old friends lined up a hundred automobiles for a cavalcade of "Black" banners, pasted above the sideboards, announcing hometown support as they visited a half dozen towns in surrounding counties. Black's old law partner, David J. Davis, took three weeks from his own unsteady practice to coordinate, without pay, final campaign efforts.[14]

Black's opponents continued to believe that political money in large denominations could stem the Black tide. "Bankhead has passed out over a thousand dollars on this side of the county today," reported one of Black's workers in south Alabama. Another supporter saw "lots of money in all the counties in the wire grass" [lower Alabama] being spent by Kilby and Musgrove. B. B. Comer ordered his managers to induce mill hands to vote for Kilby. Near Clay, a lawyer warned: "Breck is flooding this county with literature this week, I suppose by hired men."

As political money gushed "like water" against Black, so did news coverage. The state's largest daily papers embargoed stories about Black's campaign and his large, receptive crowds. Despite heavy rains, a massive audience showed up at Birmingham's Jefferson Theater on July 31st to cheer wildly almost every sentence of Black's address, but Birmingham newspapers failed to devote a single column inch to the event. Instead, on the day of the rally, the *News* reported on page one that Black's momentum had been dampened by Bankhead's revelations concerning his income and Musgrove's aggressive campaigning. On its front page, the *Montgomery Advertiser* broadcast John Bankhead's warning that Black was "appealing to ignorance, prejudice, and superstition" while condemning to the back pages a small article on Black's speech in a nearby county.

It was John Bankhead, in a moment of political desperation, who broke the dam. With only ten days before the election, Bankhead knew the truth despite his own press coverage. He was drawing small crowds while Black was attracting hundreds if not a couple of thousand at a time. Bankhead ran full-page ads in the state's papers asking in bold, demanding terms, "Bankhead or Black?" Resurrecting Black's own earlier political tactics, Bankhead contended that "many patriotic men and women in Alabama are anxious to defeat a candidate who is undesirable" and claimed that only a Bankhead could do it. Kilby, of course, reacted a few days later in large ads insisting "Kilby's Strength Makes Bankhead for Black." Only a vote for the former governor, he insisted, would keep Black and his "prejudices" out of the Senate.

In his law office for a single day, dictating letters and designing ads, Black was ecstatic: "When the first of Mr. Bankhead's full page advertisements came out, a number of our friends called up," Black said, "and asked if we didn't play a trick on Mr. Bankhead and put that in ourselves as paid political advertisement, using his name." Black admitted that Bankhead had done his own campaign so much good that "we ought to at least pay half the cost." Black's own ad was simple. It declared, "Hugo Black is the Winner" and, using clippings from his opponents' ads, quoted all candidates as saying that he was the person to beat. Black seemed wickedly pleased for a chance to use his opponents' own admissions and hostile newspapers' own clippings to boost his race.

In an urgent effort a day before the election, the *Birmingham News* carried a front-page story proclaiming the Klan vote had shifted from Black to Musgrove due to a last minute endorsement from the Klan's Atlanta headquarters. Two days earlier, *News* editors had sent the same story by telegram to the state's other daily papers so they too could carry the "news"—news which the Birmingham paper had printed two weeks earlier with virtually the same details. In hindsight, the strategy was divide—and hope to conquer. Musgrove had the best chance of taking votes away from Black, and that political subtraction could only help Bankhead or Kilby.

The mischief was apparent to Black's supporters like Hugh Grant. Working the streets of Phenix City (which merged with Girard in 1923) shortly before the primary, Grant happened to go by the newsroom of the Klan-fighting Columbus paper "just in time to head off a telegram which had been sent there from the *Birmingham News*—propaganda against Black," he told David J. Davis, "to the effect that a certain vote friendly to Black had switched." In other locations, Black supporters didn't have to quell the story. The Associated Press circulated a competing report suggesting darkly that the Klan remained solidly behind Black, and some papers ran that wire story on election day.

For his own part, Black closed the campaign with a short, poignant statement: "Backed by no political machine, aided by no paid workers, my election will prove that the people of Alabama vote their *honest* convictions."[15]

NOT LONG INTO ELECTION NIGHT, voting returns flashing across the giant rolling ticker-tape screen outside the Birmingham Age-Herald Building showed that Hugo Black had an early, impressive lead. At his ninth-floor office, Black's friends gathered to analyze the numbers for themselves and to celebrate a great victory without, of course, Jack Daniel's intoxicating company. "We knew rather early in the evening that we had won," recalled Black's niece, Hazel. The candidate, however, was in a solitary, pensive mood. He drifted away from friends and family, virtually unrecognized amid a boisterous crowd lingering in front of the newspaper building. Black watched the electric screen cast dancing light onto the emotional faces of complete strangers, his chosen companions in time of victory. At his triumphant moment, realizing a lifelong ambition,

Black stood alone, as he had so often. "There are times that are so important in a man's life that he wants to be alone," Black explained afterwards in a rare moment of introspection. "I was asking the people of my state, the people I knew and loved, to give me the chance to play a part for them in one of the highest offices in the nation. It was a time—that night of the election—of tremendous import for me, and I wanted to be alone."

The inveterate joiner was, in truth, a loner. This second nature had developed out of a sense of forced separation in his early life, a detachment begun in childhood when a little boy distanced himself from his father, his name, and his ways, and when death left a young man of nineteen without parents and two beloved brothers.

It came from the solitary experiences of a young bachelor lawyer who never lived alone but who twice arrived penniless at Birmingham's rail station to build a new life on his own, by his own wits, words, and work. It was the natural state of mind of one who as a little boy navigated amid conflicts of class, church, politics, and liquor within his family and small community, a cocky kid who judged the claims and talents of adult lawyers in Ashland's courthouse, a city judge and county prosecutor who measured the scales of justice for all, special favors for none, a lawyer and "good citizen" who saw himself as both an insider and an outsider, and now the victorious senatorial candidate who saw that public duty in "the age-old struggle between those who have and those who want is to hold the scales of justice evenly."

Black's aloneness had become a primary source of personal strength and solace, although at times it appeared like arrogance or aloofness, adding to his reputation of "Ego." It nurtured sufficient willpower to observe a life of self-imposed abstinence and strict moderation. It uplifted self-restraint as a clear, guiding virtue—primary terms for his conduct and his expectations of others. On this night of all nights, Hugo Black could not join friends and family in wild revelry of his own sweet victory—unimagined by almost everyone else thirteen months earlier—because his inner strength came from a homegrown stoicism that habitually avoided the highest notes of joy and the lowest notes of despair. Having learned to survive and surmount life's worst and loneliest moments on his own, Black at the age of forty instinctively wanted to be alone in triumph.

An incredible self-discipline also meant that Black took nothing for granted, especially honesty in politics. Long after others had gone home certain of triumph, Black, William Fort, and David J. Davis sustained a marathon vigil to assure that Black's victory wasn't stolen. For two days and nights, Black monitored by telephone and telegram the official vote count as it inched along in distant counties. Particularly worrisome were the numerous late returns from Mobile where the liquor ring was attempting to return to political power in the aftermath of Black's federal prosecutions. In early March, a federal appeals court had reversed Black's major convictions, including those of businessman Frank Boykin and Will Holcombe. Also, President Coolidge had granted pardons to six other convicted defendants, after pleas of leniency from both national Republicans and Senator Underwood. Black was unable to prosecute the cases again, due to the campaign, and a few weeks before election day the government announced that Boykin and others would not be retried. Mobile's liquor leaders claimed righteous vindication and now were attempting to restore local political control, in part, by preventing the election of the man who had sent them to jail.

Solidly behind John Bankhead and a local slate, Mobile's wet politicians engaged in a slow-motion vote count. As Horace Turner reported to Black, "the counting stretched from twelve hours, ample time to have completed, into two days and two nights, in the effort to tire out the watchers and 'fix' the boxes." In the end, a fair count was forced by appointed Sheriff Leon Schwarz and a host of armed poll watchers hired by prohibitionists to stay with the ballots around the clock. Bankhead carried the county narrowly in the Senate race, but "the *good people* cleaned out the ring this time—for the first time in twenty-five years," exclaimed Turner. In benediction, he added, "We had hell."

Across the state, after the last votes were counted, it was heaven on earth for Black and his supporters. The good people's votes in both first and second choices on the ballot gave Black a lead of more than twenty-one thousand over his nearest opponent, Bankhead, who polled almost sixty-four thousand combined votes. Judge Mayfield was third with a few more than fifty thousand combined votes, and Musgrove followed. Kilby was last with fewer than forty thousand votes. Black received only one-third of the total votes, but he was the unquestioned victor and the next U.S. senator.

"Your election has brought joy to more homes in Alabama than any election since the Civil War," wrote the circuit clerk of upstate Madison County. Hugh Grant from Auburn declared a victory for progressive white democracy, the "finest thing that has occurred in Alabama politics since the days of secession." A south Alabama Baptist minister was also astonished. "We rejoice greatly over your victory," he wrote Brother Black, "which in face of the facts that big business, corporations, and very big newspapers was against you was marvelous."

The state's leading newspaper editors were conciliatory, although hardly enthusiastic or complimentary. The *Birmingham News* spoke of Black's "remarkable race" and his raw natural talent for hard work and organization, a sentiment which the Huntsville daily paper repeated. Grover Hall of the *Montgomery Advertiser* admitted that Underwood's successor had carried out a campaign of great energy and shrewdness but concluded: "Above all, he is the darling of the Ku Klux Klan." Several newspapers formally congratulated Black and Bibb Graves, who also prevailed in the governor's race, but they condemned the electoral system that allowed a minority of voters to elect the renegades. Birmingham's black editor Oscar Adams wrote: "while . . . victory was on the side of the best working machine, the cause of progress of all interests and purposes has won another notch." In the circumlocution of Southern race relations of the 1920s, Adams informed black readers that they might do as well with Klan-backed victors as other white candidates.[16]

Alabama's grand dragon was equally oblique in his public comments on the Alabama election, but his meaning was quite clear. Esdale bragged to a Yankee reporter that the Klan would halt their wet, Catholic New York Governor Al Smith in his tracks, if he dared run for president in 1928. "Mr. Esdale's statement," observed the *New York Times*, "was believed to had been prompted by the success of reputed Klan candidates," whom it named as Graves and Black. Within the Klan's sizable auditorium on Birmingham's Twentieth Street, three weeks after the election, Esdale purred with delight over the group's political accomplishments, as Klansmen across Alabama gathered for an annual business meeting. From a stage which he shared with Imperial Wizard Hiram Evans, Esdale looked across several hundred men and yelled, "Where is Klansman Graves? . . . Judge Black, you come up here too, please."

Crossed swords lay on an open Bible at the rear. In the front of the stage, the two Democratic nominees were instructed to join their right hands, forming a human cross, and receive gold-plated certificates as lifetime passports "which will admit you to the society of your fellow Klansmen where ever they are to be found." Esdale offered the cards as symbols of the unfailing bond between the nominees and the organization. "Since, we, your fellow Klansmen, have put you in such a position," Esdale bragged, the passports were just the ticket for their joint future. Graves, who served as the Montgomery County cyclops, pledged to take the passport with him to the grave. Pointing to the Klan's Christian cross in the background, Graves said, "The things that I swore about that altar, I want you to help me keep."

Black spoke afterwards. "My friends," the senator-elect began, "I know that without the support of members of this organization I would not have been called, even by my enemies, 'the junior senator from Alabama.' (Applause). I realize that I was elected by men who believe in the principles that I have sought to advocate and which are the principles of this organization," he assured the audience.

"My friends, I thank you," Black stated again. Thirteen times within the space of a ten-minute speech Black punctuated his remarks with a reference to "my friends" or "friends." "I thank the grand dragon. He has stood by me like a pillar of strength. Not only he, but many others who are here before me. There may be some who did not. That is all right. That is your privilege and prerogative as an American citizen. I would not take away from it in the slightest degree," Black declared.

In his introduction, Black had not been so forgiving of Hiram Evans, who came from Atlanta to mend fences with the senator-elect after having endorsed Breck Musgrove in the campaign. Without ever mentioning the imperial wizard by name, Black did remember Evans's father from his school days in Clay County as an inspirational teacher who taught Black and others that "if you can't say something good about a man, don't say it." Pointedly, Black had nothing to say about Wizard Evans.

"The great thing I like about this organization is not the burning of crosses, it is not attempting to regulate anybody—I don't know, some may do that—but my friends, I see a bigger vision." Returning to the metaphor of his opening campaign speech, Black declared, "I see a vision of America, honored by the nations of the world . . . with a smile of the great God of the universe, beaming down upon it, as it remains true to the principle of human liberty . . . May the time never come when there will be any power in this nation of ours that will shut the door of hope to the boy that comes up on the humble hillside, or in the lowly valley (Applause).

"My friends, I love you. I love the people of Alabama . . . The ideals of this great fraternity to which we belong are founded on the principles of that man who taught us to love our enemies . . . With my love, with my faith, with my trust, and with my undying prayer that this great organization will carry on sacredly, true to the real principles of American manhood and womanhood. . . true to the heaven-born principle of liberty which were written into the constitution of this country, and in the great historical documents straight from the heart of Anglo-Saxon patriots, I thank you . . . (Great applause)."

The Klansmen also heard from the imperial wizard. Abandoning Black's high tone, Evans delivered a stump speech for white supremacy ("The fact that we are native-born, white gentile-Protestants entitles us to supremacy and to lead.") and against social equality between the races and against efforts of a Northern group, the NAACP. "I mean to tell you," the former dentist proclaimed, "anytime they propose to produce equality between me and . . . a Negro, they're simply going to have to hold a funeral for the Negro."

Outside the klavern, Black was equally generous in appreciation and praise of others who supported him. Among more than a thousand letters of thanks, Black singled out the clergy for special note: "It is a matter of pride to me that the majority of the protestant ministers gave me their active support." He was especially grateful to ex-soldiers, members of the American Legion, and the unions and laboring men who supported him despite their leaders' ambivalence. Bill Cloe and "the traveling men of Alabama were of great assistance to me all over the State," Black observed. Another key group was Alabama's Knights of Pythias, many of whose local leaders and ten thousand members knew and supported their past grand chancellor. Black also believed that women active in temperance councils and church circles were significant to his victory. And, of course, he never tired of mentioning to old friends that "my opponent stated that wherever a man from Clay County had settled, it became a 'Black' community." All of these groups made up Black's "Dry-Protestant-Progressive" coalition.[17]

In 1926 and in future decades, questions persisted as to whether Black was, or should have been, beholden to Kluxers for his election. Some like the *Advertiser*'s Grover Hall believed at the time that the candidate was the Klan's "darling," although even Hall didn't think the Klan alone put Black into office. He wrote a decade afterwards that Black was elected "because he was a Baptist Bible school teacher, unorthodox prohibitionist, and had the support of thousands of Ku Klux Klansmen and union laborers."

Another newspaperman who opposed Black saw a similarly broad constituency. "Black is known as a prohibitionist, and very liberal in his political views," remarked the Opelika editor shortly after the election. "He received the backing of labor, the Klan, and a tremendous vote in the rural section."

The "tremendous vote" was evident in the overall turnout. More whites had voted in 1926 than in any other election in Alabama history. Turnout was almost two-thirds larger than in 1920 and more than double the voters in 1910. This enormous increase stemmed from several developments, including the addition of women voters in 1920, the right of WWI veterans to vote without paying poll taxes, and persistent efforts by the Anti-Saloon League, labor unions, and, more recently, the Kluxers to register their members.

Over the years, Black privately stated that the Klan as an organization never backed him although many of its members voted for him. With inquiring historians he usually was even less candid, reverting to the habit of avoiding any specific mentioning of the words "Ku Klux Klan." "I have no doubt myself but that many members of this organization supported each candidate for the Senate since each candidate did his best to get all the votes he could," Judge Black informed one historian in 1952. In all responses, Black understated the facts. Most candidates for the Senate wished they had Klan members' support, but the competition was largely between Black and Musgrove for KKK votes. Esdale did endorse Black, and Black's own records indicate that probably in eleven counties, perhaps a few more, local Klan leaders were his primary campaign workers. In most of these counties, Black led the ticket on election day. Most Senate candidates, moreover, were not invited to speak to klaverns around the state, as was Black, nor did anyone other than Black and Musgrove have Klansmen like traveling salesman Bill Cloe visiting Ku Klux chapters regularly on their behalf. John Bankhead, Thomas Kilby, and James Mayfield did not travel in Klan circles nor did they receive many votes from those who wore ceremonial white sheets.

Between Black and Musgrove, election returns suggest that Klan members usually voted for Black. He received more votes than the Jasper mine owner in all but four of Alabama's sixty-seven counties and received more than twice Musgrove's first-choice votes. In fact, Musgrove's support centered primarily among his friends and neighbors of Walker County. A third of all his first-place votes were cast in his home county and the handful of surrounding counties. If a large number of Alabama Klansmen (estimated between fifty thousand and eighty thousand strong in 1926) went to the polls, they did not vote often for Breck Musgrove. Of course, Klan connections lost Black some votes. Most Jews probably did not vote for Black. Even his "personal friend," Rabbi Morris Newfield of Birmingham did not. In addition, the Knights of Columbus circulated word among Alabama's fifty thousand Catholics in 1926 to oppose Black "on Klan grounds." This opposition was probably influential in Montgomery and Mobile.

The question remains: Did Klan votes constitute Black's largest or decisive segment of support? No one will ever know. Voting patterns do tell that Esdale's slate of Graves and Black did not create a uniform pattern across the state. In the Black Belt's Wilcox County, where Underwood's friends saw the rising political clout of the Klan, Black polled 637 votes—leading the Senate ticket, but Graves got only 193 votes. At the opposite end of the state, on the Tennessee River in Morgan County where Black relied primarily on Klan leaders, Black received more than twice the votes of Graves. In these communities and several others, wide differences between votes for Graves and Black suggest either that local Klan voters did not follow Esdale's slate or that slate-voting Klansmen were only a small part of the total votes. Only in eight counties in the extreme southern part of the state next to the Florida border did both Graves and Black receive total votes so close in number that there is any suggestion that Klan bloc voting dominated a county's returns. Overall, as an Alabama historian concluded after studying the 1926 voting returns: "The number of voters loyally supporting the Klan ticket was much smaller than we have been led to believe, or . . . Klansmen were deeply divided at the polls."

Even in Black's strongest Klan counties, it is impossible to ferret out if the Ku Klux affiliation was more decisive than other bonds of brotherhood. Most of the wiregrass counties had an unusually high percentage of Baptists in 1926. In Covington County, 61 percent of white church members were Baptist. Was it Black the Klansman or Black the Baptist who carried the county? Similarly, Black's primary supporter and "friend" in Covington was Tully Goodwin, a local Klan leader in Florala. He also was a local Baptist deacon and a member of the governing board of the Alabama Baptist Convention. In addition, he was chair of the county Democratic party, president of the local Kiwanis Club, owner of the local weekly newspaper, a high ranking Mason, and district leader of the Knights of Pythias. Goodwin rallied voters who carried the county for Black, but it is impossible to ascertain which affiliations influenced voters and which group's members turned out in largest numbers. In truth, Goodwin and most of

Black's Covington voters probably had overlapping affiliations—each qualifying them for membership in Black's "Dry-Protestant-Progressive" coalition.

Voting patterns in 1926 also evidence strong political forces outside the secret order. All candidates relied first and foremost on "friends and neighbors"—voters who lived near or personally knew the candidates. Black carried a majority of total votes in only Clay and its four surrounding counties. He also carried Bullock and DeKalb counties, where he and his wife had strong family ties. John Bankhead had to split the votes of his "friends and neighbors" with Breck Musgrove, a fellow Jasper resident. Had Bankhead been given the undivided votes in Walker County and surrounding counties, he would have come close to winning. Black's oldest son has suggested that the Klan, Prohibition, or other campaign issues in 1926 were secondary to the simple fact that his father won because "all of his opponents combined had not established one-half the 'best friendships' he enjoyed all over the state."

Across Alabama, one voting correlation stands out: Black usually prevailed where his brothers and sisters of the Baptist faith were a majority. Black carried twenty of the twenty-two Alabama counties in which Baptist members were more than 50 percent of white churchgoers. He lost only Winston County, which was the exception to almost every Alabama rule, and Shelby County, where Black had defended African American convicts who dynamited Montevallo mines.

Voting returns also suggest that Alabama's working men and women were an important part of Black's victory. He received more than a fifth of his total votes from three counties encompassing Birmingham, Gadsden, and Anniston, the state's industrial sites. In combined first- and second-place votes, Black also drew more votes in Anniston and its surrounding county than its hometown businessman, Thomas Kilby. As the candidate who had raised the economic issues of the Muscle Shoals dam, Black also received important support from farmers across the Tennessee Valley. He carried all eight counties bordering the Tennessee River.

Winning with only a third of the total votes, Black depended most of all on an electoral system that prevented a run-off. As the candidates of labor, Klan, and prohibitionists, Black and Musgrove together received ten thousand fewer first-choice votes than the combined totals of the other three candidates. Had a run-off been required, Black likely would have lost to Bankhead. Using Alabama's novel voting system, however, Black won a minority victory with the support of Klansmen, "friends and neighbors," Baptists, mill and factory workers, poor farmers, Pythians, Legionnaires, Masons, and temperance women. Without almost all of these groups, groomed as the "Dry-Protestant-Progressive" bloc, Black's narrow victory would have been lost.

The Klan did help Black uniquely in another, more significant way. Black's Klan connection ironically protected him from the deadly assaults of racialism—attacks like those Musgrove and Underwood had launched in the last two Senate campaigns. More than anyone else in Alabama's statewide politics since the end of Populism, Hugo Black had built a public record making him extremely vulnerable to accusations that he was far too friendly to Negro interests and was an advocate of "social equality." In 1926, no other candidate had represented a biracial labor union with Negro officers. None had clients whose black and white members committed acts of violence against local white citizens. No other candidate had represented the Alabama AFL at the time when it endorsed the right of *all* men to vote. No other Senate candidate had attempted to remove a city's police force and public officials because they mistreated black suspects and criminals. No one else represented African Americans in court against white industrialists. None but Hugo Black had defended the constitutional rights of convicted black murderers and robbers serving life terms in Alabama's prison system. And no one else had stood—much less volunteered—in open court to defend organized black lawlessness, to represent black criminals who rioted, dynamited, and destroyed several thousand dollars of equipment as they illegally seized control of the white man's mine.

This public record invited Black's opponents to have a field day of race-baiting. It led some Birmingham Kluxers to grouse about Black being "soft" on Negroes. Black's perceived Klan connections, however, rendered impotent any outside racialist attacks against him. His political opponents in 1926 could only accuse him of being a dangerously un-American "Bolshevik" who inflamed "prejudices"—at this time a word exclusively relating to appeals to "class" differences among whites. In a campaign where opponents desperately sought to derail his momentum, Black's Klan connection insulated him from racialist accusations that could certainly have crippled his candidacy.

Paradoxically, it is possible that Kluxers may have helped to loosen many white voters from racialism's obsessive grip, at least for one election. The Klan's presence—without the Klan rhetoric—may have freed Alabama's white voters from a preoccupation with racial rules. In effect, by helping to create a moment for an all-white democracy, the Klan may have immunized the 1926 elections with an assumption of white supremacy so that white voters momentarily could hear appeals to their economic self-interest and aspirations for "American principles." After all, voting in larger numbers than ever before, Alabama's whites broke precedent for the first time since Reconstruction by electing both a governor and U.S. senator who ran as "candidates of the masses" in campaigns ringing with Populist rhetoric and invoking "American dreams" and ideals at odds with idols of the Old South.

By historical terms, the 1926 campaign was exceptionally free of racial rhetoric, especially as a competition for an open seat in the U.S. Senate. Yet, it was but a moment. Nothing had drained racialism of its destructive potential. Its ominous capacity lingered near the surface of politics. "Oh, hell," exclaimed a north Alabamian writing to Birmingham's labor newspaper a few weeks before Black's election. He was quoting a local Democratic politician who reassured him that the surest tactic for winning at the polls remained what it had been—and would be—for decades in Alabama: "all you have to do is go out and yell nigger."[18]

IN THE AFTERMATH OF THE PRIMARY ELECTION, Black began to take stock. The election had cost him a little more than $9,000 and fifteen pounds off an already skeletal frame. Black believed his lost income and campaign expenses, well within legal limits, were a small price for the opportunity "to really *represent* the moral and progressive sentiment of the people of Alabama." His campaign costs were, in fact, a point of pride. "Barrels of money were spent," Black told his old buddy Barney Whatley, "and I waged a campaign without spending an unnecessary nickel."

Black could afford to swagger a little since his own financial status remained solidly upper-class, even after missing a year's income. In fact, Black would have suffered grievously if John Bankhead had called his bluff and written Black "a check for one half of what he says my property in Birmingham is worth." An insurance company's analysis of Black's estate, shortly after the election, shows that he owned property in Birmingham with a net market value of more than $270,000. Bankhead's campaign allegations underestimated Black's actual holdings by $20,000! In addition, Black had a cash value of $50,000 through fifteen insurance policies (written by his friend and real estate partner, Albert Lee Smith). Without considering future cash from cases on appeal, checking accounts, current cash, and passbook savings, Black had a net worth of more than $320,000 (equivalent to more than $3 million in 2000).

He was eager, nonetheless, to resume a law practice with his new partner, Judge William Fort. Black's salary as a U.S. senator would have to be supplemented if his family were to maintain two homes (in Washington and Birmingham) at their current, comfortable style of life. Black saw no reason why he couldn't represent clients occasionally in state courts, so long as they did not have an interest pending before Congress.

There had been, however, problems with continuing to practice with Crampton Harris. Before his campaign, Black separated from his old military commander on friendly terms, but for cause. Harris had become cyclops of the Klan's Robert E. Lee chapter, but he had not forsaken personal dealings with bootleggers and professional gamblers who satisfied his addictions. Black, running as a candidate whose moral and progressive agenda was "exemplified by his private and public life," wanted none of Harris's baggage.

The senator-elect also needed to organize his new public offices. Black offered his chief administrative position to Auburn professor Hugh Grant, who had impressed Black with his handling of the press. Another job went to the daughter of a south Alabama supporter, a merchant and local Klan leader. Black filled all positions with Alabamians loyal and active in his campaign.

The real business of solving constituent problems was more vexing. Unschooled in Washington's ways, Black deferred to the incumbents whenever citizens' problems arose before taking office. More than senatorial courtesy was involved. "To be perfectly frank with you (not for you to tell the people)," Black informed Hugh Grant, "I do not know, at the present time, how to proceed on these matters. After we go there, of course, we will understand all about it." Black did know how to campaign. Before the November general election, he traveled to Missouri and Kentucky, where he campaigned for Democratic candidates who were unfortunate enough to live in states where Republicans could win a general election.[19]

Black's election also took him seriously back to his family's past, a journey that, once revived, continued the rest of his life. Alabama's newest senator was asked to complete a questionnaire from the state archives for an official biographical statement. Ever careful, Black had good reason for caution in this case since the couple who served as state archivists were Judge Mayfield's nephew and John Bankhead's sister. "Masons, Odd Fellows, past Grand Chancellor Knights of Pythias, Moose," Black wrote in long-hand in answer to a question about "membership in any secret order." Also, he did not write the original order of his full name, "Lafayette Hugo." An ink blot at the crossing of the "H" hints that Black may have hesitated before writing "Hugo" first, but nothing else belies his decision as a teenager to put his father's name in the middle where it was always abbreviated with an "L."

At age forty, Black was at a loss for basic information about his family. Writing to older relatives, he asked for names, dates, and places from the families of both father and mother. He remembered little about his grandfather Black, except that the old man had been named "George Washington Black." In fact, he was "George Walker Black," although Hugo's grandfather did idolize the nation's first president. Perhaps both an absorbing ambition to succeed and a childhood longing to forget created mental blanks. "I have a vague recollection also that my grandfather Toland's family came from Ireland," he told Breck Toland, his mother's brother, "and that some member of the family had trouble over there on account of his religious belief." Uncle Breck may have added the spice of religious conflict to his stories about the Tolands in ancient Ireland's rebellions when he spellbound Hugo and other Black children in the late 1800s, but it was just as likely that Black's own battles with Catholics over whiskey had reinvented Robert Emmet's rebellion for Ireland's independence into a fight over "religious belief."

It was as if all the stories and relations of Black's childhood had faded from his mind like a neglected album. Hugo's memory, so vivid and accurate about other important matters, could produce only the incorrect names of his grandparents and the country of their origin. Having revised his own past during the campaign—having become the humblest son of the humblest farmer in the humblest surroundings—Black could not remember family facts. Indeed, the only real detail about family history that stayed within Black's easy recollection was the politically useful fact that his father had run away at the age of fifteen to join the Confederate Army.

Black had more than a year to wait before he assumed Oscar Underwood's seat in the nation's capital. During the interim, he crisscrossed the state meeting old and new friends. In January, he attended Bibb Graves's inauguration in Montgomery where he publicly endorsed the new governor as a fair-minded public servant. Speaking to a large crowd at the inaugural banquet, Black commended Graves for his pledge to remove all convicts from Alabama mines and urged him to go beyond his campaign promise to extend white children's school year to seven months. "They should be given not two or three, not four or five, not seven, but nine months school terms," Black proclaimed. Later, the new senator was a featured speaker in Anniston where he praised the valor and courage of aging Klansmen to whom he presented a cross of honor similar to those given to members of the original Ku Klux. Black's speech apparently impressed even the "conservative, long-headed folks" in the business community.

A proud father from Henry County announced the arrival of his newborn, "Hugo Black Bethune." In north Alabama, Black enjoyed a game of golf with campaign supporters and was guest of honor at an American Legion luncheon. Returning to Montgomery during the spring, Black attended receptions and banquets in his honor, played a few rounds of golf, and taught a men's Sunday school class. Afterwards, he was driven to the new state prison where friends advised him to "say the things that ought to be said to a bunch of convicts on Mother's Day."

To increase his income, Black tried a few cases during late 1926 and early 1927, and the jury verdicts were phenomenal—even higher than in the past. With an income approaching $40,000, Black wondered if he had reached a new plateau in the art of cross-examination and final argument. "Then it hit me," Black recalled. "I wondered if any of these jurors would feel I'm obligated to 'em and want favors from me." Black didn't have to wait long to find out. "There may have been a few who did not call on me later," the senator confessed, "but I can't remember who they were." Afterwards, Black decided to give up jury trials, the bulk of his law practice.[20]

Black had pressing concerns at home. A few weeks after the primary, Josephine became ill. During the campaign, Black had left his wife to suffer alone through a late, complicated miscarriage and now physical complications arose. Her condition didn't appear serious at first, but she kept a fever for more than a month while Birmingham doctors tried to diagnose the problem. Towards the end of 1926, Hugo accompanied Josephine to Baltimore where she was admitted for tests, and within a few days Johns Hopkins' physicians operated, apparently to correct botched surgery during her miscarriage. Her prognosis was now good, but Josephine recuperated slowly, with constant attention from Mary Marble, the Blacks' dedicated maid who also was raising two little white boys. By early summer, on doctor's advice, Black planned a family vacation to

Barney Whatley's mountain retreat. Josephine and the boys would go with him to Nashville where he was scheduled as keynote speaker at the International Civitans Convention. From there, the family would go to Colorado.

Black's address to the Civitans was more than a stopover. The convention attracted a large national audience of influential local leaders who helped shape their own communities' social agendas and understanding of public issues in an era before radio and television replaced them as opinion makers. It also was the first national forum for Alabama's new senator to acquit himself as one of the South's new thoughtful, dynamic leaders for a "moral and progressive" agenda.

Even with Josephine's condition, Black had ample time to review and reflect upon his own political philosophy before his speech in Nashville. During twenty years in Birmingham, Black had developed his own homespun notions about the role of law in society. He sharpened and articulated these principles in court briefs, closing arguments, Sunday school teachings, constant reading, and frequent public speaking. As a lawyer, he had been duty-bound to represent his client's interests foremost, but he deliberately avoided the practice of a "lawyer for revenue only." He was a public advocate who represented clients generally in keeping with his own principles.

After a childhood reared on the Baptist Bible and ancestral stories, Black combined his civic and religious faiths. "Religion is a vital part of . . . our national existence," Black once informed a Sunday school class. "Its sacred precepts established our home life; shaped our infant institutions and nourished a spirit of equality and democracy." To Black, of course, "religion" implied the Baptist tradition of independence in thought and local democratic control. "The voice of Roger Williams and his followers played no small part in impressing the principles and policies that molded our institutions and crystallized our sentiment into [a] written Constitution and laws." These Baptist "principles" included religious freedom and a wall of separation between church and state.

Also encompassed in Black's terms of "equality and democracy" in America's "written Constitution" were the claims of labor unions he represented over two decades. The United Mine Workers and other unions had insisted in every labor strike that members had constitutional rights to assemble, picket, and speak freely even during bitter, at times violent disputes. Black's clients lost every labor strike they initiated in Birmingham, in part because the government employed rifles and bayonets to protect property and to silence and separate union members. Black also had argued that his clients had a "Constitutional right to be let alone," to remain free of government agents who snooped about their homes or offices and shadowed them. And, he insisted, the Constitution provided for a right of association that did not allow the government to harass a union and its leaders simply because of violence undertaken independently by a few members.

As city judge and county prosecutor, Black had recognized the importance of rights held by persons accused of a crime. He believed the accused had a right to a speedy trial and should not be convicted by forced confession. He believed in the central role of the "good and lawful men" of a jury in deciding guilt and innocence. As a plaintiff's attorney, Black put the jury at the cornerstone of American jurisprudence, and he distrusted any judge's power to limit what a jury heard as evidence in deciding facts or verdicts. Access to the courts was in Black's estimation the fundamental safeguard of a lawful, democratic society. To eliminate a person's right to plead before an impartial court for individual justice, usually before a jury, was the most fundamental denial of the rights of citizenship and of society's best protection against lawlessness.

In virtually every role as lawyer and good citizen, Black had upheld a notion of "equal protection of the laws." He spoke of it in speeches and in pleadings. In civil actions, he routinely claimed his Negro clients were entitled to the same standing, standards and remedies in court as all citizens. Regardless of skin color, education, or income, Black the Prosecutor believed all people should be convicted of the crimes they commit. The law didn't allow people to be tortured because they are poor or black. "Equal protection" also meant to Black, as it had to A. O. Lane, that corporations should not have a "special favor" denied to real "persons" under the law. Mining companies should not be private employers at one moment and private governments with deputized guards at another. They should not be allowed to avoid paying their debts to workers by fictitiously claiming to be persons in "bankruptcy."

Finally, as a white Southerner, Hugo Black accepted racial segregation as a way of life and white supremacy as a fact of life. Yet, he did not enshrine them as permanent, indelible forces of life or law nor did he believe that white superiority meant that Negroes should be denied "equal rights" as citizens before the law. As Black stated in 1920, "remaining socially separate, the colored man, or any other man no matter what the color of his skin may be, is . . . entitled to equal rights before the law."

These were the major tenets of Black's views about society and law in 1927, but they were not the themes of his speech to the Civitans whose banner proclaimed their mission as "Builders of Good Citizenship." While he often had spoken of law and order in the last four years, Black mounted in Nashville his most forceful, uncompromising attack against constitutional protections that he believed were undermining good citizenship and American society.

Alabama's newest senator stood before several hundred Civitans as the voice of progress against a legal profession that was ultra-conservative and backward-thinking: "They look back to the dim and distant past . . . when liberty was first wrung from King John and Runnymede, and thinking of all those old dangers they say, 'Oh, let's leave all these safeguards about the citizen less he be punished when he is innocent.' But, my friends, the time has long since passed when there is much opportunity of convicting the innocent and the question which confronts the American people today is, can we protect the law abiding citizenship from the lawless . . . Is it possible . . . to make the criminal pay the price of his crime?"

Senator Black recalled that American safeguards came from England—"the old idea of a 'reasonable doubt,' the old idea of throwing around the defendant every possible advantage, the old idea of imposing the burden on the state because of its resources—tasks that are today practically impossible—those were borrowed from the English people," Black observed, "but along about 1876 England departed from the kind of criminal laws we borrowed from them. . . . But America . . . has clung to the safeguards provided for dangers which have ceased to exist for more than a century."

Black's impatience with ancient rights afforded America's criminal defendant arose from a lingering preoccupation with prohibition. Perhaps he was still smarting from the reversal of his federal prosecutions against the Mobile whiskey ring. He may have been deeply troubled by the growing popularity within his own national party of wet politicians like Al Smith of New York. Whatever his momentary displeasure, Black declared in the age of prohibition that the fight for law and order was a contest between lawless liquor owners and law abiding citizens. "The right of property is always secondary," he protested, "to the personal right to live and breathe and have our being in a country free." Senator Black called for amending the Constitution to limit the "property rights" of criminal defendants so that the nation could protect the "personal rights" of lawful citizens.

Black concluded with words that would be paraphrased unknowingly by his own harshest critics in future decades. "Those who occupy positions of trust and confidence . . . must realize the problem is not how we turn more criminals loose, but how can we obtain the convictions criminals so richly deserve. That is the problem in America today . . . ," he concluded to overwhelming applause.

Back in Birmingham, Black discovered a huge stack of mail from across the nation complimenting him on his Civitan remarks, entitled the "Majesty of the Law" when reprinted as the main article in the group's national newsletter. Amid this chorus of hallelujahs for law and order, Black decided he would try his last criminal case in Alabama. Despite the need to make final preparations for Washington, Senator Black yielded to pleas for his return to the circuit court where he began the practice of law twenty-two years earlier.[21] There was an urgent case of law and order on the docket, and it begged for nothing less than Black's special talents in upholding the majesty of law.

12

'. . . Not Near Free . . .'

The Last Smelley Case

Like a rotating cyclorama of Southern life, where symbols and land-scaped figures blur the boundaries between past and present, right and wrong, Hugo Black's last appeal to an Alabama jury about guilt and innocence began on the road to Ashland, where his own values and ambitions first emerged. After two decades of struggling amid warring factions in Birmingham's courtrooms, Black ended his career as a practicing lawyer face-to-face with the reenactment of a childhood tragedy. By the time the case unraveled, Hugo Black discovered amid the South's conflicted nature, along the crooked timbers of humanity, perhaps for the first time how fidelity to one virtue may defile another.

The case began on an ordinary holy day almost two years before the state's white citizens elected Black to the U.S. Senate. It was a chilly, cloudy Sunday morning in December 1924, when Will Smelley stuffed $30 in his trousers pocket and left his farmhouse outside Talladega. Smelley later joined his family in church where he quietly placed a ten-dollar bill, the congregation's largest donation, in the collection plate. As the biggest local farmer, Smelley had a reputation for generosity. Recently, he had furnished hired hands to build the local high school athletic field and was considered a fair man in dealing with white neighbors and black tenants.

After church, Smelley fetched Luke Ware, a gray-bearded black handyman from his farm. Smelley also met up with his brother-in-law, Will Farmer, and his son-in-law, Leland Haynes. All four men rode in a Model T over unpaved roads toward Clay County in a search for black tenants to farm Smelley's land in the coming spring. Ware had been reared in Clay, and Smelley trusted his houseman to help find the most reliable workers.

On the way back to Talladega, as nightfall approached, Smelley opened a jug of moonshine whiskey, and the four men emptied the bottle by the time they stopped a few miles from the Smelley farm. Once warm and friendly, the men's loud slurred voices were now sour with disagreement and anger.

Later, when Leland Haynes arrived alone in Talladega, news quickly spread that Will Smelley had been shot. The sheriff's men arrived an hour later at the scene, and they found Will Farmer standing like a nervous sentry. Smelley's body was crumpled under the Ford's steering wheel. He was dead from two bullets. Both Haynes and Farmer claimed they had heard gunshots and turned to see Luke Ware next to Smelley.

At dawn, deputies discovered Ware near his house on the Smelley farm, headed towards Leland Haynes's place. Ware drew a pistol and threatened to blow out his own brains if Smelley was dead. The sheriff informed Ware of the truth only after he had thrown down his gun. The pistol had three empty chambers. In jail, the African American remembered nothing, except that he was drunk. He pleaded that he would not have killed Mr. Smelley for anything in the world.[1]

The coroner convened a jury amid rumors and worried conversation. The facts, as discovered by the sheriff's office, did not square with the two white men's stories. If Ware had shot Smelley within the closeness of the front seat of the Ford, why were there no traces of gunpowder on Smelley's clothing? Why were bloodstains on the rear fender of the car? Why would Luke kill the man who had promoted him from field work to handyman? And why was Luke headed towards Haynes's house after his wife informed him he was wanted for shooting Smelley?

Talladega's "big man in body and heart" was laid to rest in the Oak Grove Methodist Church cemetery, as the coroner's jury visited the site of his killing and took statements from witnesses to his death. Will Farmer testified for almost an hour. He admitted that Haynes and his father-in-law argued but insisted he and Haynes were far beyond the automobile when shots were fired.

Haynes made two differing statements to the coroner's jury. At first, Haynes's testimony matched his earlier statement to the sheriff, but, when informed that the jury did not believe he had told the whole truth, Haynes offered a second version of events on December 7. He confessed that, after everyone started drinking, Smelley and he argued about the farm. But he insisted that the disagreement had passed before he left the car. Now, Haynes remembered a new, relevant fact: As the two white men were leaving the Model T, he heard Smelley say to Ware: "Give me that twenty dollars, you robber!" Shortly afterwards, gunshots were fired.

Ware's memory also improved once he was informed of Haynes's new testimony. Ware swore Haynes and Smelley quarreled, and, when Smelley stopped the car, his son-in-law was cursing. At that point, Haynes took a pistol from Ware's overalls pocket and told the Negro to get lost in the woods. Ware said that after going thirty to forty yards, he heard two or three shots. He wandered further into the woods until he fell asleep drunk. Later, awakened by rain, Ware returned to the roadside where he stumbled onto his gun. Before daybreak, Ware reached home on foot.

By late Wednesday afternoon, the coroner's jury charged all three men with the unlawful death of W. D. Smelley, and the sheriff placed the two white men in the county jail with Ware. "In fact since Monday morning when Luke Ware was arrested the question had been in many minds of the negro being the only one implicated in the crime," reported Talladega's newspaper editor.[2] Within twenty-four hours, Will Smelley's body was exhumed for an examination by Dr. E. B. Wren and a team of local physicians. Circuit solicitor J. B. Sanford wanted to determine the kind of weapon that killed Smelley. "The state has no other decision than to develop the truth in its investigation and to establish the guilt of the party or parties involved," the solicitor stated.[3]

The three men spent the Christmas holidays in jail. The next grand jury met on January 12 and examined more than twenty witnesses relating to Smelley's murder, including the three prisoners. Four days later, Leland Haynes and Will Farmer walked the streets of Talladega as free men while Luke Ware remained in jail now under indictment for murder in the first degree.

IN MARCH 1925, as temperatures oscillated too widely to confirm a change of seasons, Luke Ware stood trial for his life in a rural community that was neither hill country nor flat land, a small town at the crossroads of an Old South and its new aspirations. Since before the days of Hugo Black's youth, Talladega had been a commercial center with railroads bringing salesmen, passengers, and dry goods daily. Its name was taken from the Muskogee Indian word for "frontier town," but its local theater, opera house, and public library were monuments to the small town's appreciation of culture, learning, and reason as important guides in the life of a settled community. Alabama's most renowned educator,

J. L. M. Curry, had lived here. In addition, on the town's outskirts sat Tal-ladega College, one of the state's few private black schools of higher learning, started by white missionaries during Reconstruction. With the largest black population of any rural north Alabama county, white Talladega understood the practical advantages of peaceful, respectful race relations while it remained faithful to the region's longstanding social customs.

"Whatever Mr. Jake said, that was it," remembered an elderly black man who witnessed the events of 1925. "As long as that white man said that Luke was guilty, they were going to put him up for a lifetime." Or worse. By Southern custom, only one man could have protected Ware. He was the white man who could extend protection by assuring the white community that he knew *this* black man and *this* black man could not have done the killing. That white man was now dead, and Luke Ware faced life in prison or death on the gallows.

In early March, both black and white men crowded into the segregated seating of the second-floor courtroom. More than a hundred other people stood in the corridors on the first and second floors. Others milled about the lawn, following the sun's warmth from east to west as the day progressed. Inside the courtroom, a local Episcopal rector blessed the proceedings with a plea for God's help after Circuit Judge R. D. Carr gaveled for order. The black man who bowed his head amid a coterie of white men—lawyers, jurymen, deputy sheriffs, clerks, and judge—had every reason to believe that it would require divine intervention to extend his life beyond his current fifty years.

The state's case was presented by Solicitor J. B. Sanford, whose crippled leg and nurtured distemper earned him a reputation as a fearsome prosecutor who "could really take it off." He called several witnesses who established Smelley's death and Ware's arrest with possession of the gun that killed the white farmer. Other white witnesses stated that Ware was unreliable and dangerous. "This nigger had a bad reputation about getting drunk and mean when he got drunk," testified one white witness. The prosecutor's key witnesses were Haynes and Farmer, who repeated their last statements to the coroner's jury.

On cross-examination, Ware's court-appointed attorney from Anniston attempted to show that Haynes had given the coroner's jury two different stories. The solicitor protested, and the judge barred that line of questioning. Ware took the stand on his own behalf. He told his version of the killing. It contrasted sharply with the sworn testimony of the state's white witnesses. There was nothing more the defendant could do.

Shortly before supper on Tuesday, March 3, after closing arguments ended, Judge Carr charged the jury on the law. He told them that Luke Ware "is presumed to be innocent until he is proven guilty beyond a reasonable doubt by the evidence in this case." At the same time, the judge admonished the jury that the case's evidence tended "to impeach the defendant's character for veracity." After five hours of deliberation, the jury brought back a verdict to an almost empty courtroom. Luke Ware was guilty—but of first degree manslaughter, not murder. He was sentenced to ten years in prison, the maximum penalty, and his lawyers filed a routine notice of appeal.[4]

The verdict appears a compromise between conflicting views within the jury room and the community. In the minds of many white citizens, there was no doubt that Luke Ware had done the crime. "He told them that he had stumbled on the gun . . . You couldn't have found that gun that night with a flashlight," protested one of Talladega's lifelong white residents who remembered the case vividly sixty years later. "Somebody else did it and dropped the gun," continued the elderly man, parroting Luke Ware's basic story. "It just didn't make sense."

Others, both black and white, were not deaf to Leland Haynes's conflicting stories. Black folks knew that the worst evidence against Ware was that he was at the scene of the crime with the wrong skin color. No wonder he threatened to kill himself if Smelley was dead. A black man would pay for the crime regardless of the facts. They knew. Quietly, African American leaders discussed forming a local NAACP chapter to mount a new local "movement." In some of Talladega's handsome homes, white women took aside their trusted black maids to say confidentially, "I know he didn't kill Will Smelley." Others believed that demon whiskey was the real culprit. "The evidence in this case discloses that at the time of this homicide," an appeals court judge later wrote, "all of the parties present . . . were 'tanked up' on wild cat whiskey."

These untidy facts could not easily be hidden or denied under any racial code in a town like Talladega. They had spared Luke Ware's life. Had he been more prosperous, Ware also could have had his freedom for a time, since the judge set bail while the appeal was pending. But neither Ware nor his friends could post the cash bond, and he remained in the jailhouse.

A few nights after the verdict, on Friday, March 13, Ware was in his cell when the courthouse caught fire. Volunteer firefighters could not control the fire, and the courthouse burned leaving only the brick walls and the gray stone columns. The flames had brightened the sky for miles, and many circuit court records were destroyed. No one ever determined the cause of the fire, the worst in Talladega's history.[5]

AFTER MORE THAN A YEAR, the courthouse was renovated. The new building had no cupola clock. Gone, too, were the balconies once imitating those on which ancient Greeks stood to address their slaves. Talladega's revived house of justice was, nonetheless, an ambitious menagerie of symbols. The building's brick lines matched those on England's Buckingham Palace. The restored columns on the north and south sides were copied from the palace of Nepal. The new tapered bricks above the windows resembled heads of growing wheat, a motif taken from ancient Mesopotamia where the size of the wheat crop often determined life or death.[6]

Luke Ware also had new life. On May 25, 1926, the Alabama Court of Appeals overturned his conviction, holding that two substantial errors were made at trial. Judge Carr's refusal to let Ware's lawyer impeach Haynes's testimony was erroneous, as was the judge's charge to the jury discounting Ware's veracity.

Despite the legal victory, Ware remained in jail awaiting his new trial. And he waited. For reasons that no record can explain, Ware's case languished off the trial docket for almost thirteen months. It was as if white folks simply wanted the Ware case to disappear. During this time, Ware may have been consoled by the fact that he was closer to his wife and children than he would be as a state inmate. And, he did not face the darkness and dangers of Alabama's mines where he would be sent as a state convict. Also, in his second trial, Ware could not receive a punishment stiffer than his original sentence of ten years. Even so, when he finally returned to a remodeled courtroom for his new trial on Monday, May 30, 1927, Ware had served two and a half years in jail without a lawful conviction.

In Ware's second trial, Solicitor Sanford and his assistant Gordon Welch called Sheriff S. O. Wesley, who was the deputy arresting Ware in 1924. The Sheriff suggested the Negro threatened to kill himself because he was guilty of murder. As before, the main witnesses for the state were Will Farmer and Leland Haynes. Farmer kept to his earlier story, but Haynes's testimony was more specific. This time he testified that Ware shot Smelley when the farmer refused the Negro's demand for his pocket purse. From a distance, he said, he turned back and saw Luke Ware shoot Smelley.

In cross-examination, Anniston lawyer Hugh Merrill demonstrated that "Haynes deviated to a considerable extent from his testimony given at the former trial of the negro." Hammering away at the white men's multiple versions of truth, Merrill and his junior partner called the former sheriff who testified that both Farmer and Haynes told him a different story on the night of the murder. A member of the coroner's jury also testified that Haynes had given two different stories about the killing, both unlike his current testimony. Afterwards, under oath, Ware restated his version of the killing, a story that had not deviated since its first telling.

To counter defense attacks, Solicitor Sanford presented four white men who swore they knew Luke Ware was "bad." On that issue, the defense had no witness since the only white men who could have spoken for Ware were dead or accusing him of murder. Both sides rested their case by Tuesday afternoon.

In final arguments, the prosecution argued that "Ware shot Mr. Smelley when the latter refused the Negro a drink of liquor." In a conspicuous move, prosecutors abandoned their own eyewitness. Haynes had testified Ware killed for money, but Welch told the jury: "Evidence was given to show that the Negro had purchased one quarter of the half-gallon taken on the trip, and while in a drunken condition he fired the fatal shots when he was refused what he thought rightfully was due him."

"False in one, false in all!" bellowed defense attorney Hugh Merrill asking the jury to consider the conflicting testimony of Haynes and Farmer. Item by item, Merrill reviewed how both witnesses had contradicted themselves many times since Haynes arrived in Talladega with the news of Smelley's death.

Talladega's crusty old prosecutor had his own last words. "False in one, false in all, indeed!" he mocked. Sanford chided the defense for trying to hold out Ware "as an angel, to be believed in every statement, contrary to others." Sanford attacked Ware's credibility. He dismissed as "unbelievable" the defendant's testimony about how he came to possess the murder weapon as he stumbled in the dark of night.

Twelve jurors received instructions on the law from Judge Carr and began deliberations in a second-floor room shortly before noon on Wednesday. After less than two hours, the jury reached its verdict. Ware was "not guilty" of first degree manslaughter. At last—at long, long last—Luke Ware was a free man.[7]

As soon as the judge verified the verdict, Ware and his wife met other

African Americans who jubilantly led them outside so that, now unshackled, Ware could feel the fresh air of freedom once more. Down the hallway stairs, through the south doors, and onto the lawn, a spontaneous celebration of Ware's freedom broke into unrestrained jubilee. Black men and women yelled with innocent joy, as if the Promised Land had finally arrived, clapped, danced, or touched Ware and one another with excitement. In one of those very rare moments of Southern life in the early twentieth century, a black man had been freed by an all-white jury of the murder of a prominent white man in spite of damning accusations from two prominent white men. It truly was a remarkable, glorious moment for all black and white people of good will until two rapid shots killed Luke Ware.

Within four feet of a bleeding, slumped colored body, a white man lowered his gun and returned the smoking revolver to his holster. Ware looked up at his wife and friends surrounding him on the ground. "Mr. Chum Smelley shot me," Ware said as if the fact was as painful as the act. Other African Americans ran from the courthouse lawn in screams of disbelief and shock. "Lord, they shot Luke," men and women cried to a distant heaven.

Chum Smelley, Mr. Will's younger brother, walked slowly up the steps of the courthouse and directly to the sheriff's office on the first floor. He laid his pistol on the deputy's desk and said, "I just shot me a nigger."[8]

SMELLEY WAS TAKEN to the county jail where Luke Ware had languished for thirty months as the older black man was rushed to a local hospital. Dr. E. B. Wren arrived on the scene and accompanied Ware in the ambulance. In route, Wren told Ware he was probably dying. "While you can, Luke, this is the time to tell the truth," the white doctor instructed. "I've told the truth every time," Ware responded on the stretcher. He knew the unspoken question. "I didn't kill Mr. Smelley," he pleaded.

Dr. Wren operated immediately. On the surgery table, Luke continued to plead his case. As if believing that the judgment of whites around him would unlock St. Peter's Gates, Ware repeatedly muttered his innocence to nurses and doctors. "I've already told the truth," the etherized man said again and again. "I didn't shoot Mr. Smelley." Next morning, Ware died.

"A tragedy enacted in the shadows of the Talladega courthouse yesterday afternoon had a stunning effect upon the thoughtful people of our county," wrote the editor of the *Talladega Daily Home*. "It came right after a warning from the grand jury that neither life nor the integrity of the courts were safe when the spirit of mob violence prevailed." Two days before Luke's last trial, Judge Carr received reports from the local grand jury who had investigated the flogging of one man and the shooting of another's wife by unknown masked men.

"The *Home* feels that law and order have not been treated as the sacred things that they are in the minds of the public," the editor continued, "and hopes that this affair will quicken alike in the minds of officials and the general public that we are losing much as a community when we fail to regard with gravity all infringements made upon the good name of our county and its people."

However many times the newspaperman may have changed the typeset, worrying over exactly the right words, his ambiguous, impersonal prose could go no further than condemning those who had injured the county's "good name" by murdering Luke Ware. The reputation of the white community, not justice for a black man in 1927 in Alabama, was the commodity that had to be repaired.

African Americans in Talladega talked about the tragedy as a great deal more than a bespoiled reputation. Many considered the shooting as a staged event, planned with the cooperation of the sheriff's office. Ware's son "thought this thing was all cut and dry. He thought that they knew what was going to happen," remembered a black resident. Ware "came out of the courthouse in the yard and the police disappeared. People were congratulating him. Just shot him down," recalled an elderly black citizen who heard the stories. "He came out as a free man but he wasn't near free," another remembered.

Regardless of their opinions, Talladega's black folk were practically helpless to do anything about such injustice. Out of rightful fear for his life, and that of others, no African American dared organize a protest. Both students and faculty at the local black college remained mute. Earlier efforts to start an NAACP chapter withered. "Whatever Mr. Jake said, that was it." And now Mr. Jake and Talladega's other whites had to decide who was culpable for the death of Luke Ware.

Judge Carr convened a special grand jury on Friday, June 17, "to consider the killing of Luke Ware, negro, by G. S. (Chum) Smelley" who was a "street boss" in nearby Sylacauga. Chum was considered a likeable fellow by other white citizens and did a good job of supervising local jail inmates who cleaned and repaired the town's streets. "We do not know the circumstances of the tragedy which befell this county in December 1924, and probably never will know the truth of it," Judge Carr told jurors in explaining their duty, "but one thing is certain . . . liquor was at the root of the trouble." Within a few hours, the grand jury indicted Chum Smelley for first-degree murder.[9]

Because of a dispute over the election of a new circuit judge, Smelley's trial was delayed for five long months. During the postponement, a new wave of mob violence and acrimony peaked in Talladega County and across the state. Alabama Attorney General Charles McCall issued a report identifying as many as fifty whippings and floggings by masked nightriders in Talladega County during the past three years. The local grand jury complained, however, that the attorney general generated "so much publicity. . . before we had an opportunity to investigate" that they were unable to discover the facts.

One of Talladega's floggings involved Zemeriah Comer, whom Birmingham newspapers pictured as an honorable victim of a brutal, unwarranted attack. Metropolitan papers harshly attacked the Klan for the incident, but some local white residents saw a different reality. "I chopped cotton for Uncle Zim, and I saw part of what I will relate," remembered Talladega's respected, nonprofessional historian. "Uncle Zim lived alone, but he brought in three brothers and their families who pretended to farm and made whiskey. Then they brought in Lude [sic] women. Soon the quiet and respectable community was no longer safe," Vern Scott recalled. "People appealed to the sheriff who I saw ride by twice . . . But he came back and reported he found nothing. One night the Klan caught and whipped Uncle Zim and told the others to leave. During the next few days I saw reporters from the *Birmingham News* pass on their way three different times to interview Uncle Zim. What we saw in the papers shocked us," Scott said. "There was a picture of Uncle Zim leaning on his hoe handle. They described him as a scion of a highly respected old family and affectionately known throughout the community as Uncle Zim, etc., etc.," Scott stated. "I am sure the reporters knew better."

If the "Daily Press" exaggerated the innocent character of Klan victims, Ku Klux leaders were guilty of swaggering with gross self-aggrandizement. After the 1926 election, Grand Dragon James Esdale and many local Klan leaders abandoned all pretenses of selfless, civic impartiality and law-abiding self-restraint. Esdale publicly bragged that every statewide official and 90 percent of the state legislature were Klansmen he had elected. He privately arranged for

Attorney General McCall to pay him a salary as an assistant attorney general, but public protests squelched his plans when it became clear Esdale would have to work for his pay. The grand dragon also claimed he had handpicked most of the state's appointed officials and hinted that Governor Graves would arrange Klan control of every county's jury selection.

The "Daily Press" did not misunderstand the new rise in lawless floggings. After two Klansmen were elected to Birmingham's city commission, W. J. Worthington, a local cyclops, openly raided three Chinese restaurants, including Joy Young's. The Klansmen appeared puzzled and surprised when they were fined for assuming official duties, and Joy Young's owner hired another KKK cyclops, attorney Crampton Harris, to represent his interests. After the 1926 elections, floggings also escalated across the state. Four floggings (including one led by Worthington) occurred in early 1927 in Birmingham's outlying areas. In another incident, Worthington, a real estate agent, swindled a flogging victim out of his land while he helped coerce the black man to leave town. By late summer, masked men had attempted or carried out a series of whippings in seven other counties, including Talladega and Clay.

It was as if the taste of political influence had left several Kluxer leaders thirsting madly for the spoils of private vengeance and personal greed. Perhaps, in Herman Beck's language, "rough necks" had taken control in some locations. That certainly appears the case in Bessemer. The city's new Ku Klux cyclops was Ellis Houston, the former Bessemer police officer who lost his job in 1916 because of Solicitor Black's investigations. By whatever chain of events and motives, Alabama's Ku Klux now soured in greed and guttersnipe, publicly revealing the truth of Thomas Jefferson's observation that "Ignorance & bigotry, like other insanities, are incapable of self-government."

In response to Klan misdeeds, the "good and lawful men" of several local grand juries earnestly began investigating violence, and a few returned indictments against Klansmen. Citizens from all quarters who believed in self-government and self-restraint began speaking out. "No one believes the Ku Klux Klan responsible for all these outrages," the pastor of Birmingham's Southside Baptist Church proclaimed, but he blamed the Klan for allowing some "evil-minded persons" to join the group in order to use KKK regalia as a license to commit floggings. Merging high principle and good politics, state Republican leader O. D. Street called Kluxers a disgrace. One Birmingham resident credited the city's "best citizens" with shifting public sentiment against "mob rule," and the New York-based NAACP praised the state's "leading newspapers and the best citizens" as the prime opposition to "hooded gangs."

For the first time, all the state's big-city editors initiated a relentless investigation and editorial campaign against the Klan. Victor Hanson authorized editors at the *Birmingham News* and the new editor of the recently acquired *Montgomery Advertiser*, Grover Hall, to attack Klan activities, but Hanson cautioned them to go after Klan violence—not after the organization or its members. A new editor from William Randolph Hearst's national chain arrived in Birmingham in 1927 to run the *Age-Herald*. He quickly arranged secret payments to a deputy sheriff in return for reports on Klan meetings which he published. "A new day is dawning in Alabama," declared the *Age-Herald* in August 1927, "a day in which ignorance and intolerance will find themselves stripped of their capacity for evil."

The "Daily Press" challenged Governor Bibb Graves and Senators "Cotton Tom" Heflin and Hugo Black to speak out against Klan violence. Grover Hall ridiculed all three for remaining silent about the "drill-sergeants of hatred, the go-getters of intolerance, the high powered salesman of bigotry" who marched across the state flogging and night riding. Following the papers' lead, Attorney General Charles McCall publicly deserted the Klan. Graves condemned floggings, but not the Klan. Senator Black ignored the press.

Heflin fought back. He embarked on a speaking tour to attack the *Advertiser*, Hanson and the other "Daily Press." In early November, Senator Heflin appeared before more than a thousand citizens in Chum Smelley's Sylacauga, where Cotton Tom excited the crowd with extravagant condemnations of the evils of Catholicism and "Victor Hanson's newspapers."[10] A week later, Chum Smelley's jury assembled 20 miles down the road in Talladega to have its moment in defining good and evil, human guilt and innocence.

SMELLEY'S TRIAL BEGAN ON MONDAY, November 14, in a packed courtroom. He was surrounded by his family and his lawyers: E. M. Eubanks, a Klan lecturer and attorney from Rome, Georgia, and Marion H. Simms, a local attorney who gave up a judgeship earlier in life to return to the practice of law. At the state's table sat the grouchy Solicitor Sanford and Gordon Welch, who now were prosecuting the man accused of murdering the black man whom they had tried twice for murder. Judge Walter Merrill of Anniston presided.

As the judge gaveled the court to order, the audience gasped with surprise and excitement as spectators recognized Senator Hugo L. Black entering the rear of the courtroom. Jefferson County's former prosecutor went directly to the front and took his seat. In his last criminal case, Hugo Black appeared in court to represent the man who had killed Luke Ware.

Initially, Black had resisted involvement in the case. Two days before the defendant was indicted, an Alabama Klan operative told Black that he must help "our friend Chum Smelly . . . and without fail take charge of his case . . . As you already know this man is our friend and we all will have to stand together at this time. My friend W. F. Hurst of Talladega has in his possession a number of letters from friends" who wanted Black to help. The Klan official assured Black that there would be "no hitch in the financial."

"I'm retiring from the practice of law and have not taken any new business since March," Black replied. "I would like to do anything I can for my friends, but I do not see how I can take any new business," he concluded. By late September, after months of public attacks on the Klan by daily newspapers, Black had changed his mind—probably because of persistent pleas from pharmacist Bill Hurst and others who were Black's strongest political supporters in Talladega. Many, including Hurst, were members of the local klavern. In late 1926, Black had assured Talladega's Klan secretary that "I appreciate the good work of my friends in Talladega and want to show them that I do," but the senator had no idea that he would be implored to show his friendship in a courtroom. Beseeched by friends and neighbors close to home, Black belatedly agreed to represent Smelley.[11]

The trial moved quickly. Black and other defense lawyers struck only two people from the jury list. The state eliminated only one. Dr. E. B. Wren was the state's first witness, describing how two bullets entered Luke Ware's body in the back. As a former medical student, Black tried to shake Dr. Wren's unqualified statements, but the physician did not budge. Perhaps the doctor simply did his professional duty, or he may have remembered Luke Ware's dying words. Local black citizens speculated that Wren stuck to his guns because he felt Luke's pain. (The doctor had a dark-skinned son reportedly born from an affair with a local black woman.) In the end, the facts remained the same. The doctor told the plain truth to a community tempted to look the other way. He informed jurors that there could be no doubt: Chum Smelley killed Luke Ware by shooting him twice in the back at a distance of four to five feet.

A high school student told the jury how he had watched Smelley walk across the courthouse lawn, pull his gun, aim, and fire within four or five feet of the victim.

In cross-questioning, Black treated the young witness with a gentle hand, offering him a chance to exaggerate his own courage – and in so doing establish the existence of a large, hysterical crowd of black men and women surrounding Luke Ware.

"How many people were down there?" Black asked.

"I don't know. I didn't count them," replied young Corey Tucker.

"Well, you know approximately, don't you? Was it a hundred?"

"Sixteen or seventeen to the best of my knowledge," replied the boy, who stubbornly stuck to the facts.

Another young white witness was not so surefooted. Black enticed him to contradict part of Corey Tucker's testimony. Yet, this teenager also refused to overestimate the crowd's size. Afterwards, the state called the courthouse's assistant custodian, a black man who had been on the lawn with Luke.

"What was Luke Ware doing when Mr. Smelley shot him?" asked Solicitor Sanford.

"Shaking hands," the witness stated.

"Did Luke make a move as if to jump at Mr. Smelley?"

"No, he didn't jump."

"Did he make a move as if to draw a weapon?" the prosecutor asked.

"No, sir."

"Was Ware facing Mr. Smelley?" asked Sanford.

"No, sir. He was facing me, shaking hands," the witness said. The state rested.

For their case, defense lawyers called a local white man who contradicted the black custodian's testimony. According to this witness, the custodian was on the second floor of the courthouse—not on the lawn near Ware—at the time of the shooting.

Hugo Black's main witness was his client. After Chum Smelley settled comfortably into the witness chair, Senator Black immediately asked: "Did you shoot Luke Ware?"

"Yes, sir."

"Did you receive a letter a few days prior to the trial of Ware in May from an inmate of the Talladega County jail warning you of threats made upon your life by Ware?" asked Black.

"Yes, sir," Smelley replied. The defendant then read the letter to the jury. "Mr. Chum Smelley," he began, "I am writing to let you know what Mr. Luke Ware said he was going to do to you when he got out. He said he would kill you when he got out if he ever saw you, that you had worked so hard against him . . . You be on your watch out for him for he shure is mean to us boys hear. So you watch him. I think well of you and I don't want him to harm you, so I'm closing. From Roland Beck."

Smelley also testified that another inmate had called him to the jail to tell him that "Ware made threats against me."

"Now, Mr. Smelley, tell your actions preceding the shooting," Black instructed.

"I came up to the courthouse shortly before the verdict was rendered," the defendant stated. "I then walked into the clerk's office and when the verdict was rendered and the big demonstration made by the negroes in the court, I walked down the steps and stopped near the office of the sheriff. Ware came down a few minutes later and as he passed he pointed his finger at me and said something I didn't understand. He then walked out of the south entrance of the courthouse. I remained in the . . . courthouse only a few minutes and then walked out. A large crowd of negroes was standing on the west walk of the courthouse . . . when I heard someone say, 'there goes Chum Smelley.' I turned around and the negroes around Luke began to run and Ware came towards me like he was going to grab me. When he did, I pulled my gun and shot him."

"At that time did you have authority to carry a gun?" Black inquired.

"Yes, I was a street foreman in Sylacauga and had police authority."

The solicitor objected on grounds that a street foreman had no police authority and besides Smelley worked prisoners in Sylacauga—not in the town of Talladega. The judge sustained the objection.

"Did you bring prisoners with you the morning you came to Talladega?" asked Black in an attempt to offer an excuse for why Smelley brought a pistol to the trial.

"No, I brought two boys, not exactly prisoners," the defendant replied. The "boys" were black men indebted to Smelley, but not convicts who required the supervision of an armed officer.

Black diverted to another topic. "How was the negro facing when you shot him?" Black asked.

"He was facing me," Smelley declared in defiance of science and others' testimony.

The solicitor took the witness. Sanford established that Smelley had received the warning letter "two or three days before Luke Ware's trial."

"You had the letter with you throughout his trial and didn't tell any officer of this court then?" Sanford persisted.

"No sir."

Apparently, the letter's author had recently become unavailable for testimony since he had disappeared after being released from jail. At the solicitor's request, Smelley repeated his version of the shooting. This time, Smelley ended his monologue by concluding that when Ware "lunged at me I shot him."

"Did he say anything to you?" Sanford demanded.

"No, sir," replied the defendant.

"Did he make any demonstration like getting a gun?" Sanford asked.

"No, sir."

"When he lunged at you did he grab you?"

"No. I shot him," Smelley said.

"Was he coming towards you?"

"Yes."

"How is it then that he was shot in the back!" yelled the solicitor.

Like a simultaneous clap of lightning and thunder, Black and the other defense lawyers burst into loud objections, claiming that the evidence was inconclusive on whether the victim died from wounds in the back. The prosecutor scoffed and referred to Dr. Wren's direct testimony. Judge Merrill agreed that the evidence showed the victim was shot in the back and overruled defense objections. Smelley, however, had calmed down. He quietly retold his version of the killing—repeating that Ware was facing him when he started shooting.

Before the defense rested, Marion Simms called no less than fifteen white men to tell of the good character of Chum Smelley, and Klan attorney W. E. Eubanks called ten other white men to swear that Ware had a bad reputation as a "nigger" who was by nature "violent, dangerous, turbulent, and bloodthirsty."[12]

At the end of the day, defense lawyers proposed to waive all summary arguments but Sanford declined. On Tuesday morning, lawyers put the case in perspective for the jury. Smelley's out-of-state lawyer, provided by the national Klan, W. E. Eubanks, rehearsed the chorus of testimony about Smelley's good white character and Ware's bad black character. Luke, he repeated, was "dangerous, violent, and blood thirsty."

Senator Black concluded the defense's final argument with a studied, evocative portrayal of Chum's actions as tragic, but legally defensible and morally understandable. In earlier pleadings, Smelley's lawyers had pleaded "not guilty by reason of temporary insanity," but at arraignment they had claimed self-defense. Now, in light of Dr. Wren's testimony, Black blurred both lines of defense into one. He shrouded Chum's actions with both the sanction of ancient law and the forgiveness of a modern, progressive society.

The senator picked up books he had brought from his library at home. They were classic volumes on the origins of societal laws. Black paraphrased the French philosopher Rousseau's *Social Contract* concerning the importance of family obligations, especially the duties of the oldest living son to defend his family, as a cornerstone for man's early law and a basis for the maxim of an "eye-for-an-eye."

Black's second book, Henry Maine's 1883 *Ancient Law*, provided more specific points of authority. Black told jurors about Maine's doctrine of universal succession where from the oldest laws it was the duty of a surviving brother to protect a dead brother's family, reputation, and interests. Black claimed that the application of law was always subject to human understanding. As his underlined passages in *Ancient Law* contended, "social necessities and social opinions are always more or less an advance of law. Law is stable; society is progressive." Society—good citizens with mercy, understanding, and forgiveness—are the final arbiters of what is the law.

Looking up from his books, into the jurors' faces, Black said, "When Chum saw his brother's killer, . . . he just sort of exploded—his mind blew apart. This noble fella blew to pieces. Who knows what went on out there between Chum's brother and the dead man," Black asked. "They are both dead. In a scrap, who knows who is right? Chum lost his control. For that he is to blame."

"As for me, family loyalty is a great thing," Senator Black proclaimed. "I understand what Chum did. He loved his brother and he just blew apart. What would be served by convicting him? Nothing! All of us know Chum will never harm another soul if he is—if he is," Black paused. Perhaps remembering his own feelings of despair, anger, and confusion from the death of an older brother killed by whiskey, Black concluded with tears in his eyes, ". . . if he is not thrown in with a lot of bad people."

After less than twenty minutes of deliberation, the jury's foreman stood before a crowded courtroom and declared Chum Smelley "*not* guilty." He walked out of the courthouse, beyond the shadowed spot where he had killed Luke Ware, and returned safely home.

The local editor who insisted shortly after Ware's killing that "our people are in favor of law and order" sat silent in his office. In hotel lobbies and parlors, white folks discussed the case in hushed voices. Many saw perfect logic in the verdict. The jury "just felt like Luke was guilty and he got off free . . . so they let Chum Smelley go free." Perhaps they saw it as an eye for an eye. Yet, this reasoning must have been a curious human equation for black domestics to overhear. They knew Ware "came out a free man. But he wasn't near free." And now Ware was dead, and Chum Smelley was alive and free.

The verdict may have had a sinister side. "One of the best men I ever knew was a Ku Klux at the time," recounted the town's unofficial historian, "and he told me later that he didn't think it was an honest trial . . . This fellow who was being tried was a Ku Klux, he said, . . . and it was just a case of all of them looking out for their brother in the organization," Vern Scott recalled. "They all threw their influence back of it. Black had a good case all right but . . . it was cold-blooded murder."

The trial certainly had more than its share of conveniences to help Chum Smelley: the white man who conveniently recognized the black janitor inside the courthouse; the convenient letter verifying Ware's threats written from the jail by a presumably illiterate black man who spelled and wrote amazingly well, except for a few conspicuously stereotypical words; the convenient absence of any white adults who actually saw the shooting; and a convenient abundance of white men who knew before God and the law, for an absolute fact, that Chum was an angel and the fifty-year-old dead man was a dangerous, blood-thirsty devil. Chum Smelley also had the convenience of Klan brothers who helped to maintain a community's sentiment for countenancing or fixing the verdict of an all-white jury who took less than half an hour—after the pleadings of state's new U.S. senator – to find Smelley not guilty, despite the bullet holes in Ware's back.

Was it bigoted, Klanish loyalty? Was it the work of jurors who wanted a U.S. senator "obligated to 'em" in return for a favorable verdict? Was it the honest judgment of a jury moved by a lawyer's argument about ancient precepts of law and modern notions of mercy? Or, was it the verdict of twelve ordinary white men living in a community where no one spoke for a standard of justice that punished a white-skinned man for killing a black-skinned man after he had been freed of charges of killing the white man's brother? Surviving memories within Talladega's black community provide the most thoughtful answers. Stories among African Americans who lived with Luke Ware identify the killer as both "he" and "they" or simply abandon all nouns and pronouns. "Just shot him." It was an insane, evil act that came out of an insane, evil way of life. Either, both—all were stained. Only roles and degrees of guilt differed. The verdict was a travesty of justice because it came out of a rigged jury room or a rigged way of life.[13] The distinction was ultimately irrelevant, and the consequences were as common as the South's ever present devotion to white supremacy: a locally powerful white man was set free after he put two deadly bullets into the back of a powerless black man.

RETURNING TO BIRMINGHAM, Senator Black did not rejoice in his final victory as a trial lawyer in an Alabama courtroom. His financial records indicate that Black refused payment from the Klan or anyone else. Perhaps echoes of Black's own words gnawed his soul too much for him to accept compensation: words about the majesty of law ("the problem is not how we can turn more criminals loose, but how we can obtain the convictions criminals so richly deserve"); words about the duty of a public servant "who should be able to hold the scales of justice evenly"; words on behalf of another black man who had "not ceased to be a human being and a person"; words from the Bessemer grand jury report about a public official's solemn duty in "protecting the weak, unfortunate, and humble, as well as the rich and powerful"; and words from Clay County: "equal justice for all, special favor for none."

So near Ashland, Black stood in the memory of another painful time, another victim who like Luke Ware grew up black and poor in Clay County. While separated by thirty years, similarities of place and circumstances between the killing of Luke Ware and the murder of Eli Sims were memorable. Both were shot down in cold blood. Both killers were set free because they were white and their victims were black. Both were about ten years older than Hugo Black when they died. Both murders were examples of simple Southern injustice, tolerated in public silence by a white community out of respect for a white killer's family and ultimate disrespect for black lives.

Yet, one difference was profound. Flawed in character and deed, duplicitous with friends, family, and the truth, incapable of consistent self-discipline, Fayette Black had mustered in 1897 the integrity to stand against his community's acquittal of Eli Sims's murderer, although the killer was the son of Fayette's oldest living friend. In 1927, Fayette's own son, who had become a man of consummate self-control with a prodigious regard for personal consistency and fundamental fairness, helped to acquit a friend who murdered Luke Ware. After spending three decades distancing his life and motives from those of his own father, Hugo Black found himself unable to match his father's own integrity in a matter of life and death. But why? Why had Black participated in a defense that was a vicious attack on the memory of Luke Ware and quite possibly a rigged acquittal of Chum Smelley? Why did the upright Black fail where his flawed father had not?

Throughout his Alabama years, Black had negotiated imperfectly with the dangerous dilemmas of success and leadership in a region where structures and conditions were built on a ruling history of racial injustice and human exploitation. Because of his driving desire to succeed, Black occasionally had manipulated white society's racialism and bigotry to achieve a client's favorable verdict. He did as much for Mary Miniard and Edwin Stephenson—and for prohibition. Yet in those cases Black had not used racialism's direct force against black citizens or the "weak, unfortunate, and humble." In those cases, Black's victims were a powerful railroad corporation, whiskey's ring leaders, and one of Birmingham's leading white religious leaders who served Birmingham's most powerful families. As Willie Morton, Sam Bradford, and Henry Lewis knew, a significant portion of Black's professional work had been devoted to helping poor African Americans recover damages in an abusive economic system, escape unfair punishment in a racist judicial system, organize successfully with white workers in the mines, or enjoy the benefits of law and order in their own communities.

In Alabama in the first quarter of the twentieth century, Hugo Black had kept an amazing faith with his own Southern-born sense of fairness and justice within a broader society of virile white supremacy. In a region disfigured by extreme racialism, Black had acted in ways that put him within the rarest of rare company, a Southern white leader who believed in and worked to establish the basic notion of "justice for all" in law and custom—to enshrine the ideal of "equal" before the law within a separate South.

Despite such rank, Black faced the temptations of ambition and success every step of the way. Before a jury of white men or an electorate of white persons, success was surest if a man could invoke racialism's destructive force by accusing his opponent half-credibly of breaching the color line towards social equality. Every time Black stood before a jury on behalf of anyone other than a black person, every time he stood for election before Alabama's white people, he faced the temptation to win by the power of this evil. What is so surprising in Black's Alabama years was not a few instances of accommodation and even a Kluxer membership, but rather his consistent efforts to win the hearts and minds of Alabama's white folk *without* direct appeals to white supremacy and often against its force.

Looking as far back as the end of Reconstruction, Black stood virtually alone as a major political figure in Alabama politics who did not attack opponents with nor suffer from accusations of a breach of the color line. Perhaps the luck of the Irish saved him. In his solicitor's race, Black ran at an unusual moment, when local reforms combined the common interests of differing whites with many blacks. And in his Senate campaign, Black's past Kluxer connections ironically freed him of the dangers of becoming a victim—or a perpetuator—of appeals to racialism, despite a public career that left him extremely vulnerable.

Because of his achievements, Black's participation in the Smelley case seems all the more disconcerting. In a 1927 trial, six years away from the next election, there was no possibility for quick political gain. There was no fortune or fame in the case, and no evil chance tricked him into it. The Old South's racialism did not seduce him with claims of a white man's duty to barter right for wrong. No, Black defended Chum Smelley's act of cold-blooded murder by keeping faith with virtue, not vice. "So long as I believe my friend honest, I am for him," Black had declared. As the senator stated at Chum's trial, "loyalty is a great thing." Black's motives were clear and simple: loyalty to friends who had shown loyalty to him. Friendship. Within the South's tortured human relations this virtue—this murderous virtue—was the motive for Black's shameful involvement in the Smelley case.

After years of deliberately distancing himself from his own father and his father's friends, Black met the evil of others in himself. Perhaps for the first time, he came face-to-face with how fidelity to one virtue can compromise another. No matter how carefully he walked along the straight lines of self-discipline, old-time morality, and honest hard work, Black could not entirely avoid the wicked contradictions that were inevitable if he maintained both public leadership and personal loyalty in a society and government structured on injustice and bigotry.

As one of the South's emerging leaders, Black's principles about law and society were well-settled, as old as the Populists' rallying cry, and as rare and true as the experience of a Southern white liberal who often stood for the weak, helpless, and poor. In 1927, the question about Hugo Black was not whether he would locate a new philosophy in Washington to counter his own parochial views. Instead, it was whether and how he could pursue his parochial values and traditions, bred among the white people of his own Alabama, to win friends and neighbors away from the inherent evils of an overtly racialist society and a mostly white male electorate.

Hugo Black never forgot the Smelley case, although he discussed it with only a few people. He never forgot his own father's ominous prediction that had come true in the Eli Sims case: a murderer, once freed of responsibility for his crime, will murder again. Chum Smelley and Talladega friends knew Black was deeply troubled by his role in the case. For more than two decades, Chum Smelley periodically wrote Black, always as "your friend," often sending turkeys, fruits, or other small gifts of appreciation. Without explanation, Black once sent Smelley a citron—perhaps a symbolic warning that Ashland's erstwhile town boy now could tell the difference between the genuine article and a fake. Over the years, mutual friends reassured Black that his pledge to the jury and to himself had not been in vain. Chum Smelley never killed again nor did he seriously injure another human being. Smelley apparently struck only one person after 1927—a white man who in Smelley's presence condemned Hugo Black as a traitor to the South.

Throughout his life, Black was accused of many mistakes and several acts of gross injustice as a good citizen, lawyer, senator, and judge. In every instance, Judge Black of Alabama defended his actions, in private and public, as principled behavior. He made few excuses, no apologies. He backed away not one inch from the uprightness of his actions, based on an ethics of responsibility. Within the hazards of changing times and social forces in America's struggles for justice, nothing seemed more important to Black than to live a public and private life representing the consistency of high purpose and moral action, lessons his mother taught him first and his father abandoned earliest. Yet, that last case, that started on the road to his old home place, the case in which no one ever accused him of wrongdoing, burdened Black's conscience for the reminder of his years.

In the privacy of his own study, where the underlined copy of Henry Maine's *Ancient Law* stood on the shelf as a dutiful reminder of that day in Talladega's courthouse, Black confessed to his own son decades afterwards: "It was inexcusable. . . but Chum was my friend . . . I had to help him."[14]

Benediction

'Friends . . . My Friends'

Silhouetted by the white lights' glare, the old man stood alone, transfixed by the past. Poised amid Alabama's political landscape—past, present, and even future—Black stood like a solitary oak rising amid a flattened, infertile field, a near century-old tree shed of all greening, but shaped majestically by a body of broken and crooked branches stemming from one deep, authentic root still nurturing in the soil of an obscure, hallowed place. Now, as if it had been but a moment, the old man gently awoke from the past, as the admiring crowd at Birmingham's Parliament House sat anxiously awaiting Judge Black to speak again of his Alabama days.

Black, however, no longer wavered in the transit of prophesies, dreams, and reality that crisscross between birth and death. Too little and too much had passed away for him to convene a telling of his story and their history. Once, a few years earlier, he had attempted writing his autobiography and, inspired by his visit to Alabama, he would try again. But, his heart was not in it. He was a joiner of the here and now, a lover of people, and a lawgiver of enduring knowledge, not a poet or history teller. He would leave to others a full accounting of his past and theirs. They would have to take care of it by themselves.

Now, within two years of death, Justice Black offered a common prayer, a simple benediction on his story in Alabama. "I had some fine friends," he recalled, ". . . who remained *my friends* throughout their lives." And there he left it. On the riddled meaning of his forty years in the heart of Dixie, Black laid it down to the essence of simply "my friends." Like an Irish leprechaun's sentimental rhymes, his last words on the subject appear mischievous, banal, and ceremonial, signifying little and baring nothing. Yet, in the eye of the beholder of his life and times, Black's simple words are the shorthand of his own wisdom.

In the final weighting, balancing all, beyond all books of deeds and words, Black cast his own life as a story about friends and neighbors, good citizens, loyalty, and personal convictions—not so much a sweeping pageantry of the complex conflict of great ideas, terrible wrongs, and clamoring movements which took him from Clay County into America's twentieth century. No, it was more a parable of individual integrity and personal loyalty. A story of friends. It is left, perhaps, to the voice of Black's ancestral past to sing the final stanzas of his riddle. Poet William Butler Yeats, also reared on Robert Emmet's "magnificent" words, spoke for all Irish who brought everything down to that sole test, "Dream of the noble and beggarman" as equals before God, law, and humanity:

> You that would judge me do not judge alone
> This book or that, come to this hallowed place
> Where my friends' portraits hang and look thereon;
> . . . history in their lineaments trace;
> Think where man's glory most begins and ends
> And say my glory was I had such friends.[1]

Here, in his own Alabama, along the straight lines of abstinence, self improvement, careful consistency, historical Baptist morality, and learned moderation, Black had navigated the first half of his life amid economic, social, political, and moral conflicts that ultimately formed the character of both the New South and the new America. Yet, now near his own end, Black concluded, as he had after the Smelley trial, that reckoning friendship, loyalty, and personal integrity amid the crooked branches of humanity was the place on God's earth where man's glory most begins and ends.

Throughout his life, Hugo Black prized friendship as far more than a set of personal, pleasing relationships. Friendship defined much of his own identity and the means for pursuing his ambitions. As a teenager in Ashland, Black's friendship with Barney Whatley first helped to define his independence from his own father, and, after both of Black's parents died, friends began substituting for father and family. As a young Birmingham lawyer, Black shared with friends a precarious struggle for survival. These friendships, however, were built on more than a common, difficult experience. They grew from genuine bonds of solidarity and support among people who held mutual respect for one another's character and ambitions. Unlike more modern examples, Black's friendships rarely involved personal intimacy or shared emotional problems. As men who looked outward towards society far more than inward towards self, Black and his friends were bound together by the mutual regard and intense loyalty of good citizens struggling to build their own prosperity and a just world.

Over the years, Black decided that, more than anything else, wealth and power tempted people to corrupt democracy, citizenship, and friendship. As a boy, he watched it happen in Clay County where his father and others used public office for private gain. In Jefferson, he quickly recognized how the fee system and the convict lease system perverted public justice for private profit. He saw the petty, cruel misdeeds of corrupt JPs and the Bessemer police. He witnessed how the pursuit of private profit among Birmingham's "moneyed interests" crippled working men and destroyed a community's common good. These were age-old human failings that Black identified in his lifelong readings of the Greek and Roman classics. "Look not for disinterested friendship or for loyalty when a throne is in prospect," warned Cicero, the Roman philosopher, whose words Black later underlined and scribbled for easy reference.

Despite the ancient evils of money and power, Black's friendships were not confined strictly by class. He claimed a number of friends among Birmingham's "best citizens," men like George Ward and Walker Percy. So long as Black believed a man was selfless and upright (if not always right) in trying to promote Birmingham's greater good, he counted him among his friends.

The word "friend" always signified a special status in Black's language. In his attempted autobiography, abandoned three months after his 1970 homecoming, Judge Black wrote sixty pages about his Alabama days. They survive as interesting but usually unrevealing reminiscences, except in one major respect. On average, every other page of the manuscript refers to a "good friend," "friendship" or "loyal friend." The word "friend" appears more often in Judge Black's memoirs than almost any other noun.

During his Alabama years, Black often used a rhetorical style learned in the Populist era as a schoolboy, punctuating speeches with frequent references to "my friends." Black, nonetheless, did not use the term loosely. It always identified or beckoned people with whom Black thought he shared a sense of struggle for the "bigger vision," as he said before Klansmen in Birmingham in 1926. The word "friend" named those men and women, Kluxers, Pythians, Baptists, or industrialists who would join him in struggling to keep open "the door of hope to the boy that comes up on the humble hillside, or in the lowly valley."[2]

On these lifelong terms, friendship became the central, organizing principle for Black's moral code of behavior. According to Black, the only "ethical way" to build a law practice in Birmingham was for him to "make as many friends as possible." He did so by joining most local men's groups and building bonds of friendship on the basis of mutual esteem with other men within those groups. In this way, Black advanced himself by winning the respect of others. He gained the early, complete support of Herman Beck, "won the friendship of Judge Lane," attracted legal business and clients, and won verdicts for his black and white clients whose causes often depended on twelve "good and honest" male jurors.

Black also believed that he could seek public office in an ethical manner only if he relied solely on his own financial resources and on his friends' influence and volunteer work. In his race for county solicitor, Black often addressed his public statements and ads to "Friends," the men and women who knew and appreciated his character and notions of fairness. In both of Black's campaigns, his strategy was literally to befriend as many people as possible in hopes that they and their friends would elect him. As Black told a supporter in 1925, "a man must depend upon his friends when he enters into a political campaign." In 1926 Black's election was evidenced not merely in voting returns, which showed his highest levels of support among friends and neighbors in and surrounding Clay County, but equally in his little black campaign book which provided an accounting of each act of aid and kindness from hundreds of new friends throughout the state.[3] Black kept the book until the day he died.

This style of "friends and neighbors" politics was not "friends and favors"—a ruse for patronage and spoils. Black believed his friends elected him to perform public duties with independence, courage, honesty, and tolerance in keeping with his basic principles: to judge the competing claims between those who have and those who want in order to serve the greater good, not to enable a profit for a few. In using the powers of public office, Black felt obligated to help friends who helped him, but only when he thought their claims were legitimate or their advancement furthered justice for all. In fact, Black believed that a duty of friendship was to give special, undeserved favors to none.[4]

Shaped from an early age by the sins of a father who estranged his family, much of his community, and almost all his friends, Hugo Black held friendship as a sacred trust. It shaped the casing of his moral compass and, in many cases, the slippery slopes of his career. "When the time comes when I must repudiate friendship, such as existed between Judge Lane and myself . . . I am willing to resign every claim upon the friendship of any city or any community," Black declared in 1915. "So long as I believe my friend honest," he insisted, "I am for him." Months later, Black rushed across the continent to stand in the dock with Barney Whatley, his old friend charged with killing his own father. Black went without invitation and without knowing the facts because he knew an honest friend was in jeopardy.

Five years later, without knowing the facts, Black agreed to defend a Methodist minister who had killed a Catholic priest because Black mistakenly thought the defendant was one of his "friends." Two years later, Black joined the Klan after his friend Herman Beck encouraged him to do so. Less than two years afterwards, Black expediently resigned as a Kluxer with assurances that he would remain "I.T.S.U.B."—In The Sacred, Unfailing Bond of Brotherhood. So long as he lived, despite torrents of public criticism, Hugo Black never spoke a single word repudiating that pledge to "my friends" who were among Alabama's Klan members. And, two years after leaving the Klan, as the U.S. senator-elect, Black appeared in a Talladega courtroom for the defense.[5] Because the defendant was "my friend," not because he was a Klansman, Black joined in a blatant travesty of human justice which plagued his conscience for the rest of his life.

In reconciling loyalty to friends and fidelity to principles, Black probably never contemplated fully the ominous consequences of coming of age and influence in a society deeply flawed by oppressive racialism, color-coded democracy, and other damaging human stereotypes. Black did understand, as his Uncle Thomas Toland once wrote, that "your colored friends will be of little use to you" in all-white Southern politics. In elections, courtrooms, and even Klan halls, Black learned to make an honest, effective appeal to ordinary whites without abandoning his color-blind notions of justice for all. Yet, Black never foresaw how the cumulative effects of white supremacy could segregate his actions in Talladega from his heartfelt convictions. By reducing the human function of African Americans to that of things, not persons, Southern white society effectively disqualified Black's "colored friends" from the bonds of solidarity and mutual, equal obligation that formed the basis for Black's friendships and his code of conduct.[6]

Despite this flaw, Black's friendships took him into territory where few Southern white leaders ever ventured. Within a society controlled by a relatively small number of white men, Black deliberately associated with many men and women across factions, sectors, and the color line. Out of the turmoil of a divided family and community, Black became by choice a progressive democrat in a white male society of conservative Democrats. He cultivated his ideals and ideas for a "bigger vision" often from the seeds of Alabama's poor, working men and women—white men considered "rednecks" or "fuzzy necked" and white women not often deemed worthy of being called a "Southern lady."[7] These white folk helped Black grow a rooted vision of law, equality, and democracy amid the niggardly soil of Southern parochialism, lingering Old South's racialism, and the New South's anti-democratic tactics.

Black understood the moral shortcomings of Alabama's white poor and working class. He knew they could be dangerous and deadly. Along with Black Belt planters, industrialists, and managers of Northern capital, these plain white folk did their part at times to continue many of the South's profound evils. Yet, from the days of Populism through the era of Ku Kluxism, these were Alabama's white folk who crossed the color line in political alliances and union halls, who opposed disfranchisement and supported universal voting, who fought for interracial gains, and who sought to bring the American "glory of citizenship" to all who lived below the Mason & Dixon. From beginning to end, these common white folk's problems constituted the cases and causes that Black often represented, and their votes sent him to Washington to represent Alabama with his "honest convictions" about democracy and justice.

Now, after forty-five years in Washington and near his own twilight, Hugo Black looked back towards those days and those friends. With evident sadness, he told his audience, "I see practically none of those old friends tonight."

Between 1927 and 1970, Alabama had changed and almost all of Black's old friends had gone: David J. Davis, A.O. Lane, Herman Beck, William Fort, and many others including Chum Smelley. Yet, a few had survived, aged but alive: Barney Whatley, Albert Lee Smith, Crampton Harris, and even James Esdale, although the old grand dragon never really had been included in the judge's mental book of "old friends." Whatley was unable to attend the banquet since he was nursing an invalid wife in Colorado, but he remained always loyally Barney the "country boy" to his friend Hugo the "town boy." Smith and Harris were living in Birmingham only a few miles away from the hotel. Harris, however, had not been invited as a special guest and did not want to attend in any other role. Albert Lee's son was a conservative Republican actively aiming to run for the U.S. Congress, and he did not share his father's friendship or admiration for Justice Black. Both Smiths thought it best that the elder not attend.

These absences did not really matter. Black's remembrances of friends had become like faded snapshots treasured more for the feelings they invoke and the lessons they taught than for the actual scenes and people they depicted. "When I ask," Black continued at the podium, "'. . . Are you the son of Bill Smith that I knew so well?' I regret to say that the answer now is invariably, 'No, I'm his grandson.' This does not suit me altogether," Black confessed, "but age has a way of disappearing through the years."

Finally, reluctantly, leaving behind those disappearing years, Black took up his self-imposed duty of presenting Chief Justice Warren Burger to Alabama. Black spoke of his new Court colleague as a "new friend" – but a friend according to his old, guiding terms of friendship. "The worst thing I ever heard about him . . . is that he's a Republican," Black said of Burger. "But I found out through the years obviously that there are good Republicans, although it was hard for me to reach that conclusion." Black looked at Federal Judge Frank Johnson sitting in the audience. Yes, there were some good Republicans. "And there are good Democrats," added Black, unable to forsake old loyalties. "There could even be a good Populist in the old days."

Guided by his enduring terms of loyalty and friendship, grown from the nurturing soil of his roots, Justice Black proclaimed Warren Burger to be an "honest man" and a "good citizen," as were his other seven brethren on America's Supreme Court. All were men who measured up to the old man's enduring definition of good citizenship and public duty. His colleagues on the Supreme Court were "men of courage, stamina, honesty, tolerance who are not afraid, whatever the cost, to pronounce the judgment they have," Black proclaimed. "What more can be asked than for a man to have courage, express his views, and be ready to announce them without fear whichever side they happen to fall down on?"

At this final moment, back home, Black's praise of others in truth measured himself, and in this way he offered an explanation to his beloved Alabama, to white Southerners, to friends and neighbors as to why and how he had not really betrayed them. Yet, so long as they refused to find their own history in his story, to recognize how he had gathered his own individual integrity, independence, and rightness from their shared, historical soil, Black's words would echo outside the banquet room in George Wallace's Alabama and Richard Nixon's America like an old man's self-appeasing platitudes.

Through careful planning of old law clerks, Black stood publicly for the last time in Alabama, in the forum of his old enemies, as an insider and an outsider, a fellow Southerner introducing a colleague with whom he served the American people outside the South. "I present him to you," Black proclaimed proudly. "He is my chief justice. He's your chief justice. He is the chief justice of the United States . . . I present to you . . . not merely the chief justice . . . but *my friend.*"[8]

The audience stood up again, in a crescendo of heartening applause and loving sobs of tears, for they instinctively felt a deep sense of gratitude and sorrow. As the handsome, pompous chief justice rose like a guardian of a new order preparing to relieve a time-worn sentry of his last duties, Justice Black abruptly pulled himself back to the podium, and above the persisting noise he shouted a final amendment to his learned equation of truth.

"That does not mean," Black announced, "that I'm gonna vote with him every time he wants me to!" The crowd roared in concurrence. That much learned of friendship and integrity, past and present, Hugo Black of Alabama left the podium like a satisfied, truculent prophet long accustomed to speaking in the common tongue of a forgotten heritage and naturally finding virtue, wisdom, and glory in the unlikeliest places.

Notes

PREAMBLE

1. *Birmingham News*, 19 July 1970; transcript of Hugo L. Black speech, Alabama State Bar Association Annual Meeting, Birmingham, AL, 17 July 1970, in author's possession; Black's story of the "cemetery plot" is apocryphal, but the Alabama legislature did condemn the U.S. Supreme Court by resolution no less than a dozen times between 1955 and 1970; see, for example, *Alabama House Journal*, 2nd Extraordinary Sess., 1963, 104-105; *Acts of Alabama*, Special Sess., 1962, 73; *Alabama House Journal*, Reg. Sess., 1957, 546-47; *Alabama House Journal*, Reg. Sess., 1957, 40-42; anonymous person, interview by Charles Morgan, Jr., 4 August 1970; Virginia and Cliff Durr, interview by Charles Morgan, Jr., 18 July 1970; Daniel H. Thomas to Hugo L. Black, 30 January 1967, Hugo L. Black Papers, Manuscript Division, Library of Congress, Washington, DC (hereafter cited as Black Papers); C. J. Corley to Black, 23 July 1970, Black Papers; "Thomas, Daniel Holcombe," *The American Bench*, Minneapolis, 1977, 92; J. Mills Thornton, *Dividing Lines: Municipal Politics and the Struggle for Civil Rights in Montgomery, Birmingham, and Selma*, Tuscaloosa, 2002, 443-445.

2. Transcript, 17 July 1970; James North, interview by author, 1983; Daniel M. Berman, "Hugo Black, Southerner," *American University Law Review* 10, no. 1, January 1961, 40; HLB to Caffey Robertson, 2 February 1970, 27 May 1971, anonymous letters in correspondence file 29 and case files of *United States v. Barnett*, 6 April 1965, Black Papers.

(The latter letter ironically was prompted by a Supreme Court decision from which Black dissented; the correspondent could have been blinded to that fact by his hatred for Black or by the assumption that Black would join any opinion against any Southern segregationist leaders.) See also "Unknown Subject; Robert P. Cunningham–Complainant," Denver, 15 April 1969, *Hugo Black: Freedom of Information Act*, Part 1, Federal Bureau of Investigation, U.S. Justice Department; *Greensboro Watchman*, 27 May 1964; "SAC, Birmingham to Director, FBI," 17 July 1968, *Hugo Black: Freedom of Information Act*, Part 1; Black to Jerome A. Cooper, 22 June 1966, Black Papers; Jerome A. Cooper, *Sincerely your friend . . .: Letters of Mr. Justice Hugo L. Black to Jerome A. Cooper*, University of Alabama, 1973, section IV; Daniel J. Meador, "Justice Black And His Law Clerks," *Alabama Law Review* 15, 1962-63, 57; Hugo Black, Jr., *My Father*, New York, 1975, 209-216; David Vann, interview with author; Hugo L. Black and Elizabeth Black, *Mr. Justice and Mrs. Black*, New York, 1986, 74, 128; *New York Times*, 19 July 1970.

3. *New York Times*, 19 July 1970; Black and Black, 243, 245-6; Black to John Sparkman, 3 March 1970, Black Papers; Dan T. Carter, *The Politics of Rage: George Wallace, the Origins of Conservatism, and the Transformation of American Politics*, New York, 1995, 385, 392-395; Black to Patrick W. Richardson, 21 July 1970, Black Papers.

4. Transcript, 17 July 1970; Black and Black, 243-44; Paul L. Murphy, "The Early Social and

Political Philosophy of Hugo Black: Liquor as a Test Case," *Alabama Law Review*, 36, No. 3, Spring 1985, 879; Gerald T. Dunne, *Hugo Black And the Judicial Revolution*, New York, 1977, 24; "Salute to Justice Black," *The Nation*, 21 August 1937, 183-184; "The Education of Hugo Black," *The Nation*, 2 October 1937, 337-338; Max Lerner, "Hugo Black—A Personal History," *The Nation*, 9 October 1937, 367-369; Berman, 41; Virginia Van der Veer Hamilton, "Hugo Black: The Road to the Court," *Southwestern University Law Review*, 9, No. 4, 1977, 888.

5. *Birmingham News*, 19 July 1970; *New York Times*, 19 July 1970; transcript, 17 July 1970; HLB to Argosy Book Store, 21 May 1952.

6. Paul Avrich, *The Haymarket Tragedy*, Princeton, 1984, xi-xv, 412-431; Henry David, *The History of the Haymarket Affair*, New York, 1936, 3-24, 528-542; Risa Lieberwitz, "The Use of Criminal Conspiracy Prosecutions to Restrict Freedom of Speech," in Marianne Debouzy, ed., *In the Shadow of the Statue of Liberty: Immigrants, Workers, and Citizens in the American Republic, 1880-1920*, Urbana and Chicago, 1992, 275-288; John Higham, *Send These to Me: Jews and Other Immigrants in Urban America*, New York, 1995, 78-87; *Santa Clara County v. Southern Pacific Railroad*, 118 U.S. 394, 1886; Civil Rights Cases, 109 U.S. 3, 1883; Henry Grady, *The New South: Writings and Speeches of Henry Grady*, Savannah, 1971, 3-13. "The Resurrection of the Old South is threatening the New South," according to Rev. Jesse Jackson, *Atlanta Journal-Constitution*, 12 May 1996. "There has been an Old South, and there's been a New South . . . As we go into the next century, we have a choice about which direction we're going to go," stated presidential candidate Lamar Alexander, *New York Times*, 1 March 1996.

CHAPTER I

1. "Black Family Tree," Grace B. Smith to author, 6 September 1971; Albert James Pickett, *History of Alabama and incidentally of Georgia and Mississippi from the Earliest Period*, Birmingham, repr., 1962, 552-557; Joel W. Martin, *Sacred Revolt: The Muskogees' Struggle For A New World*, Boston, 1991, 158-159; Martin calls the battle in Hillabee "the most notorious Anglo-American massacre" of the war

against the Alabama Indians; *Ashland Standard*, 4 August 1905; Black, Jr., 3-4; Stephen B. Oates, *With Malice Towards None: The Life of Abraham Lincoln*, New York, 1977, 366; Black to James B. Rhoads, 17 July 1968 and Milo B. Howard to Black, 8 July 1968, Black Papers; Mitchell B. Garrett, *Horse and Buggy Days on Hatchet Creek*, Tuscaloosa, 1957, 35; Clement A. Evans, ed., *Confederate Military History*, vol. XII, Atlanta, 1899, 506, 511-512; Evans, vol. VII, 99-102; Shelby Foote, *The Civil War, a Narrative: Fort Sumter to Perryville*, New York, 1958, 505-508; Shelby Foote, *The Civil War, a Narrative: Fredericksburg to Meridian*, New York, 1963, 528-569; Black to Hazel Davis, 26 February 1971, Black Papers; Eddie B. Rozelle, *My Folks and Fields*, 1900, Talladega, 1960, 80, 87-90; "University of Iowa Survey," 29 February 1965, Black Papers; John P. Frank, *Mr. Justice Black, the Man and His Opinions*, New York, 1949, 3-4; Black to Irving Dillard, 13 July 1962, Black Papers; "G. W. Bluck" [*sic*], Manuscript Census, Alabama, Clay County, 1870; Black to C. J. Corley, 5, 10 September 1968, and Black to William Toland, 4 November 1968 and Black to Dick Littlejohn, 18 October 1970, 5 April 1971, Black Papers; Edna R. Joy and James P. Sloan, "Andrew Johnson: Seventeenth President of the U.S.," in *The Scrapbook: A Compilation of Historical Facts About Places and Events of Laurens County South Carolina*, Laurens, South Carolina, 1982, 248-250; Black and Black, 4; "Street, Thomas Hezekiah," card catalog index to *Civil Register of State Officials*, Reading Room, Alabama Department of Archives and History; "Street, Merit, Justice–Peace, Talladega County," card catalog index to *Civil Register of County Officials*, 1856, 1862, 1865, Reading Room, Alabama Department of Archives and History; R.G. Dun & Co., *Credit Reporting Ledgers of Mercantile Agency*, vol. 23, Alabama, Talladega County, Baker Library, Harvard University, 124, 145; "M. Street," Manuscript Census, 1870; "Mt. Ararat Cemetery," *Cemeteries of Clay County Alabama*, LaGrange, GA, 1987, 277; Black to Winnie Childre, 28 December 1970, Black Papers; Winnie Wright Childre, *Highlights And Shadows*, New York, 1970, 9. Childre's work uses assumed surnames in telling the story of the Merit Street family.

2. "LaFayette Black," "Julius Sims," "Sylvester Sims," and "G. W. Bluck" [*sic*], Manuscript Census, 1870; Albert B. Moore, *History of*

Alabama, Tuscaloosa, 1935, 456-459; Horace Mann Bond, *Negro Education in Alabama: A Study in Cotton and Steel*, New York, repr., 1969, 22-29; Walter L. Fleming, *Civil War and Reconstruction in Alabama*, Gloucester, MA., 1949, 503-515, 653-709; Black to Mildred Faucett, 14 June 1946, Black Papers; "W. L. Black," *Assessment of Taxes on Real Estate and Personal Property*, Clay County, Alabama, 1876.

3. William Warren Rogers, *The One-Gallused Rebellion: Agrarianism in Alabama, 1865-1896*, Baton Rouge, 1970, 41-49; William Warren Rogers, Robert David Ward, Leah Rawls Atkins, and Wayne Flynt, *Alabama: the History of a Deep South State*, Tuscaloosa, 1994, 261-264; *1876 Code of Alabama*, Title 6, chap. 2, 234-235; *1876 Code of Alabama*, Title 9, chap. 9, 343-345; "Black W. L., Clay, Co., Justice of Peace," card catalog index to *Civil Register of County Officials*, 1868-1882; *Official Bond Book A, 1876-1880*, Clay County, Alabama, 70; R. G. Dun & Co., vol. 23, 145; "W. L. Black," *Assessment of Taxes on Real Estate and Personal Property*, 1877 and 1878; "William L. Black," and "Joseph A. White," *Manuscript Census*, Alabama, Clay County, 1880; "Black Family Tree" (Note that the spelling of "Merit" in the Street family differed from "Merritt" in the Toland clan.); *1876 Code of Alabama*, 1038; also see occasional notations of duties by Black in *Clay County Alabama Marriage Book 'B', 1877-1882*; Marie B. Owen, *Our State—Alabama*, Montgomery, 1927, 639-640; Bond, 63-64; Pickett, 599-601; Albert B. Moore, 159-164; Gerald W. Johnson, *Andrew Jackson: An Epic in Homespun*, New York, 1927, 188-203; Malcolm Cook McMillan, *Constitutional Development in Alabama, 1798-1901: A Study in Politics, the Negro, and Sectionalism*, Spartanburg, S.C. repr., 1978, 93, 175-188.

4. *Ashland News*, 3, 31 May, 14, 21, 28 June, 26 July, 2, 9 August, 13 September, 11 October, 1, 8 November 1878; *Official Bond Book A, 1876-1880*, 29, 46, 47, 48, 70, and 107.

5. *Ashland Herald*, 26 September, 10 October 1879; *Ashland News*, 26 July 1878; Barney Whatley, interview of Charles Morgan, Jr., 4 March 1971; *Ashland News*, 20, 27 February, 16 April, 21 May, 4, 11, 18, 25 June, 2 July, 1 October 1880; *Mountain Picket*, 11 March 1881; John R. McCain, "Interesting Bits of Clay County History," *Clay County Historical Society Newsletter*, vol. VI, 9, 1995.

6. *Clay County Watchman*, 28 August 1885; Gaston, 85-90; *Ashland Banner*, 28 April, 5, 12 May, 16 June, 14, 28 July, 11 August, 8 September 1882.

7. *Ashland Banner*, 14 June 1878; "Postal Appointment for Harlan, Clay County, Alabama," vol. 25B and 44, National Archives; Whatley interview; Note for Files, 27 July 1964, Black Papers; Gerald Cullinan, *The Post Office Department*, New York, 1968, 90-93; *Ashland News*, 2 August 1878, 30 January 1880; *Acts of Alabama*, 1880-81, 203; "W. L. Black," *Assessment of Taxes on Real Estate and Personal Property, Clay County, Alabama, 1882, 1883, 1884*; "Black Family Tree"; Black and Black, 7-8.

8. Black to H. Pelham Martin, 14 July 1961, Black Papers; Frank, 4; Black to Irving Dilliard, 13 July 1962, Black Papers; *Clay County Watchman* 15 January, 23 April 1886; Hazel Black Davis, *Uncle Hugo: An Intimate Portrait of Mr. Justice Black*, Amarillo, 1965, 33; Black and Black, 4; Garrett, 131; "Black Family Tree."

9. *Ashland Standard*, 24 February, 4 August, 1907; Black, Jr., 4; *Assessment of Taxes, 1886*; *Clay County Watchman*, 14 May 1886.

10. *Clay County Watchman*, 2 April, 14 May, 11, 18, 25 June, 2, 23 July, 27 August 27 1886; Black to Gould Beech, 8 November 1937, Black Papers; Whatley interview.

11. See *Acts of Alabama, 1886-87*; *Clay County Advance*, 27 January, 2 March, 4, 11, 24 May, 15 June, 13 July, 10 August 1888; *Clay County Watchman*, 25 February 1887, 3, 17 February, 4 May, 3, 20 July 1888.

12. Black to Ralph Frohsin, 15 December 1967 with copy of 8 August 1888 bill of sale, Black Papers; Black and Black, 6-7; R. Herzfeld to Thomas G. Jones, 23 March 1891, Thomas G. Jones Papers, Alabama Department of Archives and History (hereafter Jones Papers); *Ashland Advance*, 2 March, 10 August 1888; *Clay County Watchman*, 2 January 1885, 26 February, 14 May, 16 July 1886, 11 November 1887, 3 February, 16 March, 24 July 1888; *Chicago Daily Times*, 18 August 1937; *Ashland Advance*, 2 March, 9 November 1888; Black, Jr., 10-12; Garrett, 170; *Clay County Watchman*, 16 January 1885.

13. Black, Jr., 12-13; "Black Family Tree"; Black to Irving Dilliard, 13 July 1962, Black

Papers; Helen Landreth, *The Pursuit of Robert Emmet*, New York, 1948, 338; Robert Emmet, "Protest Against Sentence As Traitor," in Lewis Copeland and Lawrence W. Lamm, eds., *The World's Great Speeches*, New York, 1973, 214-219; Garrett, 169-183; Rozelle, 19-26; *Clay County Watchman*, 12 March 1886, 25 March 1887; *Assessment of Taxes* 1888 and 1891; R. G. Dun & Co, vol. 23, 145; Childre, 51-63; *The Central Democrat*, 8 August 1889.

14. Whatley interview; C. M. Pruet, interview with author, 12 June 1970; Garrett, 102-108; *Clay County Watchman*, 24 June, 1 July 1887; *Acts of Alabama, 1871*, 228-229; *Clay County Advance*, 14 March 1890; *Alabama Official and Statistical Register, 1911*, Montgomery, 1912, 227.

15. *Clay County Advance*, 3 January, 18 April 1890; Rozelle, 11-13; *Acts of Alabama, 1870*, 19; *Acts of Alabama, 1878*, 167; *Acts of Alabama, 1886-87*, 164-65; *Acts of Alabama, 1888-89*, 45; Rogers, 12-25, 129-175.

16. *Clay County Advance*, 7 February, 4 July, 15 August 1890; *Advance*, 10 April 1891; Henry Pelham Martin, "A History of Politics in Clay County During the Period of Populism from 1886 to 1896," master's thesis, University of Alabama, Tuscaloosa, 1936, 14-44; *Advance*, 31 July, 4, 25 September 1891; Karl Rodabaugh, "Kolbites Versus Bourbons: The Alabama Gubernatorial Election of 1892," *Alabama Historical Quarterly*, Winter 1975, 275-321, including footnote 136, page 306; Black and Black, 8; A. S. Stockdale to Thomas G. Jones, 28 July 1892, Jones Papers.

17. Pruet interview; Whatley interview; Black and Black, 8-10; Black, Jr., 11-12; *Clay County Advance*, 9, 16 February, 23 March 1894; Black to Edna Street Barnes, 14 November 1962, Black Papers; "History of the First Baptist Church of Ashland, Alabama," mimeographed essay, First Baptist Church, Ashland, 10-11; Clarke Stallworth, "Hugo Black: The Boy and Man," *Birmingham News*, 22 February 1971; for more on the distinctive role of women in early Sunday schools, see Anne M. Boylan, *Sunday School: The Formation of An American Institution, 1790-1880*, New Haven, 1988, 101-118; Garrett, 154-160; *Mountain Picket*, 8 July 1881; *Noah Webster's American Spelling Book*, reprint, New York, 1958,18, 58; *McGuffey's Fourth Eclectic Reader*, New York, 1896, 115.

18. *People's Party Advocate*, 5, 26 January, 9, 16 February, 2, 23 March 1894; *Acts of Alabama, 1890-91*, 1210; Joyce Ann Patterson, "History of Clay County, Alabama," bachelor thesis, Jacksonville State University, 28 April 1970, 38-39; *Clay County Watchman*, 19 March 19 1886; *Ashland Advance*, 19 January, 8 June 1894.

19. *Acts of Alabama, 1892-93*, 837-851; Rodgers, *The One-Gallused Rebellion*, 236-248; David Ashley Bagwell, "The 'Magical Process': The Sayre Election Law of 1893," *Alabama Review*, April 1972, 83-104; *Clay County Advance*, 30 March, 19, 31 August, 9 November 1894; *People's Party Advocate*, 19 January, 9, 16 February, 4, 25 May, 13 July, 9 November 1894; *Minutes of County Commissioners Court*, Clay County, November 1894, 122; Henry Pelham Martin, 45-69; Sheldon Hackney, *Populism to Progressivism in Alabama*, Princeton, 1969, 67-69; Robert D. Ward and William W. Rogers, *Labor Revolt in Alabama: The Great Strike of 1894*, Tuscaloosa, 1965, 106-117.

20. "Sheriff's Sale" and "Stockholder Meeting," *Clay County Advance*, 29 May 1896; "Dividend Educational Fund," *Ashland News*, 17 January 1879; *Last Wills and Estates, 1890-1892*, Clay County, 90-101; the affidavits associated with Merit Street's reconstructed will suggests that his youngest son, an alcoholic, destroyed the will to prevent the stipulation that he stop drinking in order to receive his full share of the estate; Childre, 70-72, 88-89; see J. L. M. Curry Papers, Alabama Department of Archives and History; Black to Duncan Howlett, 10 March 1969, Black Papers; C.W. Ferguson to Thomas G. Jones, 20 March, 1891, Jones Papers; Whatley interview; *Advance*, 20 November 1891, 31 August 1894, 31 January 1896; *Assessment of Taxes, 1891,1892,1893,1 895,1896*, Clay County; *Abstract of Records of Mortgages or Articles to Pay Money 1896, 1897*, Clay County.

21. *Advance*, 25 January, 1 February, 19 July, 9 August, 1895, 20 March, 16 December, 1896; *People's Party Advocate*, 9 April, 21 May 1897; *Assessment of Taxes, 1895, 1896* Clay County; *People's Party Advocate*, 5 January 1894; *Clay County Advance*, 26 March 1897; *Acts of Alabama, 1888-89*, 466; *Birmingham News*, 14 January 1938; *Advance*, 4, 25 October, 22 November, 13, 25 December 1895, 14 May 1897; *Atlanta Journal Constitution* 31

December 1995, E-1; *Advocate,* 25 October, 22 November, 13 December 1895; Black and Black, 12; Black to Charles D. Butts, 18 January 1971; Black to Dick Littlejohn, 3 May 1971; Black to Robert V. Lott, 21 April 1965, Black Papers; Black, Jr., 5.

22. Whatley interview; Hugo L. Black, "Dedicatory Address," *Journal of Legal Education,* 5, no. 4, 1953, 417; most cases in Clay's circuit courtroom at this time involved illegally selling liquor, grand larceny, carrying a concealed weapon, and assault with a weapon according to the official records, *Biennial Report of the Attorney General of Alabama,* Montgomery, 1896, 52-53; Black, Jr., 7-8; *People's Party Advocate,* 25 January 1900; Black and Black, 15; *Clay County Advance,* 31 August 1894, 3, 19 July 1895; *Clay County Judgment Record 1895-1896.*

23. Black to Howard Muse, Jr., 8 September 1965, Black Papers; *People's Party Advocate,* 17 January, 6, 27 March, 10 April 1896; Hackney, *Populism to Progressivism in Alabama,* 13-14, 94-104; Henry Pelham Martin, 70-82; Black and Black, 7-8; Black to Irving Dillard, 13 July 1962, Black Papers; *Clay County Advance,* 20 March, 14 August, 6, 27 November, 4 December 1896.

24. *Clay County Advance,* 7, 14 May, 9 July 1897; *People's Party Advocate,* 9 July, 8 October 1897; *Birmingham Post,* 24 August 1935; J. G. Toland to Black, 21 May 1941, Black to Irving Dilliard, 13 July 1962, Black Papers; William Jennings Bryan, *The First Battle: A Story of the Campaign of 1896,* Chicago, 1896, 321; *Clay County Standard,* 2, 9, 23 June 1898; *Advocate,* 14, 22 April, 19 August 1898; Whatley interview.

25. Whatley interview; Black, Jr., 8-10, 17; Black and Black, 13-14; *Birmingham News,* 31 January 1937; *Clay County Standard,* 7 September 1898, 6 July 1899; *People's Party Advocate,* 3 May 1900.

26. Frank, 9-10; Virginia Van der Veer Hamilton, *Hugo Black: The Alabama Years,* Baton Rouge, 1972, 21-22; Whatley interview.

27. Black to A. Leo Oberdorfer, 16 December 1952, Black Papers; Black to Jenksie (Virginia Durr), 21 November 1956, Black Papers; "Eli Sims" and "James W. White," Manuscript Census, Clay County, 1880; *Clay County Standard,* 9 February, 4 May 1899; *Mountain Picket, 15 July 1881;* Michael An-

derson, "People in Cragford still talk about 1881 lynching," *Daily Home,* 20 May 1987; *Birmingham News,* 22 February 1976; Whatley interview.

28. McMillan, 14, 70-71, 104-105, 250-262; Contested Election Case, *Martin W. Whatley v. James E. Cobb,* from the Fifth Congressional District of Alabama, Washington, 1893; Hackney, 149-173; *Clay County Standard,* 9 March, 13 April, 4 May 1899, 19 April 1901. *Clay County Standard,* 20 January, 9 February, 13 July 1899, 25 January, 29 March, 19 April, 25 October 1900; *Clay County Advocate,* 29 March 1900; *Clay County Advance,* 9 November 1894, 21 May 1897; "Asa & Louisa Grey" *Mortgage Records,* Clay County, 1900 (listing as furnisher "W. L. Black or R. L. Black"); Black, Jr., 4; *Birmingham News,* 22 February 1976; "Ashland (Old) City Cemetery," *Cemeteries of Clay County Alabama,* 30; "Black, W. L., Deed, Est. of" *Administrators, Guardians, Executors Record, #1,* Clay County Probate Court, 29 October 1900; see first reference to "H. L. Black," *Standard,* 4 December 1904; Black, Jr., 4-5.

29. *Clay County Advocate,* 3 May, 22 November 1900; *Clay County Standard,* 10 January, 14 March, 6 September 1901, 13 June, 24 October 190 2, 12 June 1903; "R. L. Black, O. L. Black, G. P. Black," *Assessment of Taxes,* Clay County, 1900 "G. P. Black" *Attorneys' Receipts for Papers,* Clay County, 19 November 1900; Herbert Shelton, *The Deserter,* Talladega, 1900; Black, Jr., 5-6; Whatley interview; Black and Black, 11, 13; Frank, 8; *Birmingham News,* 22 February 1976; Hugo L. Black, "There is a South of Union And Freedom," 2 Ga. L. Rev. 10, 15, 1967; for an account of the original speeches (and their use by industrialists) which inspired the "New South" passage, see Gaston, especially 87-88, 258-259 endnote 20. Gaston's work sat on Black's library shelf later in life although it did not alter Black's love or interpretation of the New South passage. Daniel J. Meador, *Mr. Justice Black and His Books,* Charlottesville, 1974.

30. Black and Black, 11, 15-16; Whatley interview; Black, Jr., 15-16; Frank, 12; *Clay County Standard,* 12 June, 24 July, 9 October 1903; "To authorize the payment to Confederate pensioners of Clay County," *Acts of Alabama, 1903;* Whatley interview; Howard L. Holley, "Medical Education in Alabama," *Alabama*

Review, October 1954, 259-260; Transcript, 17 July 1970; Black to Mrs. Greer W. Smith, 15 November 1961, Black Papers; *Birmingham News,* 22 February 1976.

31. Hugo L. Black, "Reminiscences," 18 Ala. L. Rev. 3, 5-11, 1965; Black and Black, 16-19, 20-21; "Department of Law," *University of Alabama,* catalogue, 1905-1906, 90-95, 110; "LAW," *Corolla, 1905,* Tuscaloosa, 104-116; *Crimson White,* 4 October 1904; *Clay County Standard,* 17, 24 February, 31 March, 4 August 1905; "Petition to remove the disability of Hugo L. Black . . . ," County Court in Equity, Clay County, 19 May 1905; Black, Jr., 15-16.; *Corolla, 1905.*

32. *Clay County Standard,* 14, 28 April, 19 May, 23 June, 7, 14 July, 18 August 1905; Black to Kenneth Stewart, 6 March 1947, Black to Charles D. Butts, 18 January 1971, Black Papers; *Crimson White,* 25 October 1904, 24 January, 17 October, 14 November 1905; Black, "Reminiscences," 10-11; Black and Black, 16-19; *Corolla, 1906,* Tuscaloosa, 88-104.

33. Black and Black, 20-25; Hamilton, *Hugo Black: The Alabama Years,* 27; *Clay County Standard,* 17 August, 16 November 1907, 8, 15 March, 26 April, 17 May, 23 August, 6 September 1907; Black to Irving Dilliard, 13 July 1962, Black Papers; "H. L. Black, Ashland, Alabama," County Tax Commissioner, 14 May 1907, files of State Tax Commission, Alabama Department of Archives and History; *1907 Code of Alabama,* vol. 1, 914-919; G. T. McElderry to B. B. Comer, 22 February, 3 March 1905, Papers of B. B. Comer, Alabama Department of Archives and History (hereafter Comer Papers); Carl V. Harris, *Political Power in Birmingham, 1871-1921,* Knoxville, 1977, 114-118; Frank, 14.

CHAPTER 2

1. Malcolm C. McMillan, *Yesterday's Birmingham,* Miami, 1975, 73-102; Carl V. Harris, *Political Power in Birmingham, 1871-1921,* Knoxville, 1977, 12-38; Martha Mitchell Bigelow, "Birmingham's Carnival of Crime, 1871-1910," *Alabama Review,* April, 1950, 123-133; author's calculations from *Birmingham City Directory 1907.*

2. Harris, *Political Power in Birmingham,* 198-215; W. E. B. DuBois, *Black Reconstruc-*

tion in America, 1860-1880, New York, 1992, 698; Allen Johnston Going, *Bourbon Democracy in Alabama, 1874-1890,* Tuscaloosa, 1951, 187-190; George R. Leighton, *Five Cities: The Story of Their Youth and Old Age,* New York, 1939, 125; Henry M. McKiven Jr., *Iron and Steel: Class, Race, and Community in Birmingham, Alabama, 1875-1920,* Chapel Hill, 1995, 18-21, 27-30, 41-45; Daniel Letwin, *The Challenge of Interrracial Unionism: Alabama Coal Miners, 1878-1921,* Chapel Hill, 1998, 23-30, 57-87, 76; Leighton, 115.

3. Harris, *Political Power in Birmingham,* 34-38, 189-194; Wayne Flynt, "Religion in the Urban South: The Divided Religious Mind of Birmingham, 1900-1930," *Alabama Review,* April, 1977, 110-112; Terry Lawrence Jones, "Attitudes of Alabama Baptists Towards Negroes, 1890-1914," master's thesis, Samford University, 1968, 49.

4. Black and Black, 26, 33; "Debt-Free Celebration and Dedication," *First Baptist Church, Birmingham, Alabama,* June 23, 1946, 15, Birmingham Public Library Archives; Hackney, *Populism to Progressivism in Alabama,* 173, 237; John Howard Burrows, "The Social Philosophy and Theology of Alfred James Dickinson," master's thesis, Samford University, 1970, 51-91; *Alabama Baptist,* 20 November 1890 in Jones, 41; *Birmingham Age-Herald,* 14 July 1908, 15 March 1920.

5. Black and Black, 27-28; Hugo Black, Jr., *My Father,* New York, 1975, 17-18; Hamilton, *Hugo Black: The Alabama Years,* 32.

6. *Clay County Standard,* 1 November 1907; Harris, *Political Power in Birmingham,* 19, 192-193; C. Vann Woodward, *Origins of the New South, 1877-1913,* Baton Rouge, 1970, 292-296, 300-301; Davis, 47.

7. Black, Jr., 18-19; Black and Black, 29-32; James F. Doster, "Alabama's Political Revolution of 1904," *Alabama Review,* April, 1954, 87; Frances H. Hare, *A Historical Sketch of the Birmingham Bar, 1872-1907,* undated, University of Alabama Archives; "Lane, Alexander Oscar," *The Book of Birmingham and Alabama,* 1914, 109; Whatley interview.

8. Ward and Rogers, *Labor Revolt in Alabama,* 75-116; Letwin, *The Challenge of Interrracial Unionism,* 101-118; Philip Taft, *Organizing Dixie, Alabama Workers in the Industrial Era,* Westport, Conn., 1981, 19-27; Richard A. Straw, "The Collapse of Biracial

Unionism: The Alabama Coal Strike of 1908," *Alabama Historical Quarterly*, Summer 1975, 92-94; Daniel Letwin, "Interracial Unionism, Gender, and 'Social Equality' in the Alabama Coal Fields, 1878-1908," *Journal of Southern History*, August 1995, 550; *Birmingham Age-Herald*, 3 July 1908; *Labor Advocate*, 10 July 1908.

9. Straw, "The Collapse of Biracial Unionism," 95-101; *Birmingham Age-Herald*, 12, 17 July 1908; Durward Pruden, "The Opposition of the Press to the Ascension of Hugo Black to the Supreme Court of the United States," master's thesis, New York University, 1945, 31-32; *Woodruff v. State*, 54 So. 240, 1911. The case cites "H. H. Black" as lawyer for the miner; however, there was no other lawyer named Black practicing law in Birmingham at this time.

10. B. B. Comer to Wm. E. Fort, 22 July 1908, Frank S. White to B. B. Comer, 1 June 1908, Samuel D. Whatley to B. B. Comer, 15 February 1910, "Proclamation by Governor B. B. Comer," 10 August 1908, Comer Papers; Richard A. Straw, "Soldiers and Miners in a Strike Zone: Birmingham, 1908," *Alabama Review*, October, 1985, 287-297, 302; Straw, "The Collapse of Biracial Unionism," 100-104; *Birmingham Age-Herald*, 12 July, 3 August 1908.

11. Birmingham Age-Herald, 12, 13, 22, 23, 25, 26 August 1908; Straw, "The Collapse of Biracial Unionism," 104-107, 109-111; Letwin, *The Challenge of Interrracial Unionism*, 146-148, 151; *Birmingham Age-Herald*, 26 August 1908.

12. Ray Marshall, "The Negro in Southern Unions," in Julius Jacobson, ed., *The Negro and the American Labor Movement*, Garden City, 1968, 132-144; Taft, 27-28; Straw, "The Collapse of Biracial Unionism," 92-94, 107-114; Letwin, *The Challenge of Interrracial Unionism*, 148-152; *Labor Advocate*, 31 July, 28 August, 4 September, 1908; Taft, 28-29; Carter, *The Politics of Rage*, 32-33; Daniel Letwin, "Interracial Unionism, Gender, and 'Social Equality' in the Alabama Coal Fields, 1878-1908," 551, footnote 101; Brian Kelly, *Race, Class, and Power in the Alabama Coalfields, 1908-21*, Urbana, IL, 2001, 24; Frank V. Evans (compiler), "Coal Miners' Strike in the Alabama Coal District in the Year 1908: a compilation of facts which relates history," typed manuscript, Alabama

Coal Operators Association, undated, Comer Papers; Birmingham Age-Herald, 23 August 1908; "#88 Reports: Birmingham, Ala., Sunday, September, 27, 1908," (with handwritten notation from Geo. Crawford to Gov. B. B. Comer), Comer Papers.

13. Black and Black, 24, 32-34; Black Jr., 19-20; Whatley interview; *Alabama Journal* 22 March 1976; *Patterson v. State*, 54 So. 696, 1911; Davis, 4-7.

14. "Harry E. Yockey, Law Books," "Hugo L. Black," and "Black and Whatley," *Birmingham City Directory, 1909, 1911*; Black, Jr., 20-23; *Beecher v. Henderson*, 58 So. 805, 1912; *Beecher v. Henderson*, 6 Div. 143, *Appellate Court Records, 1911-1912*, Alabama Department of Archives and History; Black and Black, 35; *Birmingham News*, 31 January 1937; *Birmingham Age-Herald*, 11 June 1911, 19 September 1912; Whatley interview.

15. Black Jr., 21; Sellers, 130-148; Black to Lillian Dixon and Carrie F. Wilson, 27 September 1928, Black to Margaret P. Elliott, 4 March 1965, Black Papers; Whatley interview; Black and Black, 34.

16. Ginny Looney, "Black's Early Years As An Attorney," unpublished memorandum on published appellate cases, in possession of author, 1985; *Tennessee Coal, Iron, & R. Co. v. Cottrell*, 55 So.791, 1911; Hare, 13; Fred Larkins to Black, 20 November 1965, Black Papers; *Birmingham Age-Herald*, 9, 10, 26 April, 14, 28 May, 11 June 1911. Of course, there were frivolous lawsuits filed by Birmingham's plaintiff lawyers, but, as a pattern, it was probably the depth of injury, more than the legitimate causes of action, that were exaggerated. Governor LeRoy Collins of Florida, a plaintiff's lawyer during the first part of the 20th century, once recounted the folk wisdom of tort litigation in the South: ". . . used to be a saying that the way to produce a fine pure-bred, registered heifer was to take an old broke-down range cow and cross her with a Seaboard Coastline locomotive." See "The Leadership of LeRoy Collins," *Southern Changes*, January/February 1989, 18; Black and Black, 37; *The Book of Birmingham and Alabama*, 109.

17. Harris, *Political Power in Birmingham*, 81-84, 104-118, 227-228, quoting Percy on page 82 from *Birmingham Age-Herald*, 24 October 1907; Marlene Hunt Rikard, "George Gordon Crawford: Man of the New South,"

Alabama Review, July, 1978, 165-167, 171-172; Mollie Beck Jenkins, "The Social Work of the Tennessee, Coal, Iron, and Railroad Company, master's thesis, University of Alabama, 1929; Bond, 230, 232; Woodward, *Origins of the New South,* 364-365. After Gov. Comer's appointment of Frank White as county tax commissioner in 1907, White proposed to increase the taxable value of local industries, including U.S. Steel plants, by 17 million dollars. By 1910, corporations had cut the actual increase by two-thirds but opposed any additional taxes. At the same time, the "Greater Birmingham" movement, a vision for one great city with all suburbs within Birmingham's city limits, was strongly supported by many local public leaders and strongly opposed by industrialists. With most iron and steel plants sitting in the suburbs, Birmingham's corporate managers feared an increase in taxation if the surrounding communities were annexed. After an annex referendum passed in 1908, corporation lawyers voided the change in court on technical grounds. Later, Gov. Comer approved legislation for a selective, compromised annexation, allowing U.S. Steel's largest plant in Ensley to remain one block outside Birmingham's city limits while including a few other iron and steel mills assessed at less than half the value of the excluded, gigantic Ensley plant. See Carl V. Harris, "Annexation Struggles and Political Power in Birmingham, 1890-1910," *Alabama Review,* July 1974, 172-182; Mary-Helen Vick, "A Survey of the Governing Body of Birmingham, Alabama, 1910-1964," master's thesis, Alabama College, 1965, 9-10.

18. *Birmingham Age-Herald,* 12-14 April, 16-17 April 1911.

19. Vick, 11-12; *Birmingham Age-Herald,* 2, 12-13, 16, 27 April, 15, 29 July 2 August, 3 September, 25, 31 October 1911, 4 March, 2 April, 20 August, 15 September, 20 October 1912; *Birmingham News,* 31 January 1937; Black and Black, 36-37.

20. *Birmingham Age-Herald,* 21, 26 April, 10, 14 May, 14, 20, 21, 25, 27, 28 July, 10 August, 2 September 1911; Sellers, 169-171; Frank, 20; Black, Jr., 21.

21. Hamilton, *Hugo Black: The Alabama Years,* 41-43; Frank, 17-19; *Birmingham Age-Herald,* "A Study in Black," 26 November 1911; for domestic problems, see *Birmingham Age-Herald,* 19 July, 5 October, 3 November 1911, 27 June, 3, 6 July, 21, 29 August, 11, 24 September 1912; for shysters and folk doctors, see *Birmingham Age-Herald,* 17 June, 22 September, 8 December 1911, 7 February 1912; Frank, 19.

22. For vagrancy and jobless, see docket summaries and articles cited in footnote #19 above and in *Birmingham Age-Herald,* 23, 26, 30 July, 23, 29 November 1911, 25 January, 1 March, 9 September 1912; for prostitution and women's views, see docket summaries cited in footnote #19 and *Birmingham Age-Herald,* 26 January, 27 August, 25 September 1912; *Montgomery Journal,* 27 August 1937; Hamilton, *Hugo Black: The Alabama Years,* 42; Ellin Sterne, "Prostitution in Birmingham, Alabama, 1890-1925," master's thesis, Sanford University, 1977, 73-86; McMillan, 121.

23. *Birmingham Age-Herald,* 7 January, 21 February, 1 March, 23, 30 May, 25 June, 8 July, 19 September 1912; "Black, Hugo, 1911," *Country Club of Birmingham, 1930,* 40-41, Birmingham Public Library Archives; R. B. Clarke to Black, 30 June 1960, and Black to James J. Vickrey, Jr. 6 April 1965, Black Papers.

24. *Birmingham Age-Herald,* 18 April 1911, 14, 27 January, 2 February 1912 (grand jury report), 23 May, 19, 23 October 1912; Harris, *Political Power in Birmingham,* 207-215; Frank, 21; Black to Robert Bamburg, 14 October 1944, Black Papers; Hamilton, *Hugo Black: The Alabama Years,* 44-45.

CHAPTER 3

1. *Birmingham Age-Herald,* 4, 8 November, 14, 18 December 1913; Evans C. Johnson to Black, 1, 23 May 1952, Black Papers; *Birmingham Age-Herald,* 1, 2, 11 January, 8 February, 4 March 1914; *Birmingham News,* 21 January 1914; Ernest J. Sifford to Black, 29, September 1951, Black to L.L. Richter, Jr., 18 April 1935, Black to A. P. Johnson, 15 August 1949, Black Papers; Davis, 45-46; Albert Lee Smith, interview with author, 1971.

2. Albert Lee Smith interview with author, 1971; Albert Lee Smith to Black, 31 March 1941, Black to Albert Lee Smith, 18 February 1964, Black Papers; Davis, 6, 63; Newman, 50; Black and Black, 38-39; Hugo Black, Jr., 21; Frank, 21; *Chicago Daily Times* 19 August 1937; Jerome "Buddy" Cooper, interview with author, 1988.

3. "Black and Sadler . . . First National Bank Bldg.," *Birmingham City Directory, 1914;* Black and Black, 39; see illustrative cases: *Continental Casualty Co. v. Ogburn,* 64 So. 619, 1914, *Alabama Fuel & Iron Co. v. Benenate,* 66 So. 942, 1914, *Sloss-Sheffield S & I Co. v. Edwards,* 70 So. 285, 1915; *Louisville & N.R. Co. v. Cornelius,* 60 So. 740, 1912; *Louisville & N.R. Co. v. Cornelius,* 6 Div. 489, 1913, Records of the Alabama Supreme Court, Alabama Department of Archives and History (hereafter Alabama Supreme Court Records); *Louisville & N.R. Co. v. Cornelius,* 62 So. 710, 1913; Bagwell, *Alabama Review,* April 1972, 83-104; Nancy Milford, *Zelda, A Biography,* New York, 1970, 18-19, 21, 31, 210; Sarah Mayfield, *Exiles from Paradise: Zelda and Scott Fitzgerald,* New York, 1971, 5-18; Kendall Taylor, *Sometimes Madness is Wisdom: Zelda and Scott Fitzgerald: a Marriage,* New York, 2001, 16-17; *Clinton Mining Co. v. Bradford,* 69 So. 4,1915.

4. C. P. Beddow, interview with Charles Morgan, Jr., 1970; Newman, 62-63; for problems with train stops, see *Birmingham Age-Herald,* 10 December 1913, *Birmingham News,* 11 December 1913; Whatley Interview; Hamilton, *Hugo Black: The Alabama Years,* 46-47; *Acts of Alabama, 1886-7,* 710-711; *Local Acts of Alabama, 1907,* 586-87; "William Edwards Fort," *Alabama Official and Statistical Register, 1919,* Montgomery, 1920, 69; Black and Black, 39-40.

5. *Birmingham Age-Herald,* 3, 9, 13 November 1913; *Birmingham News,* 21, 29 December 1913, 11 January 1914; Harris, *Political Power in Birmingham,* 207-215; *Birmingham News,* 18 January 1914.

6. "Harrington Phillips Heflin," *Alabama Official and Statistical Register, 1931,* Montgomery, 1932, 123-24; *Birmingham News,* 21 November 1914; *Birmingham Age-Herald,* 21 January, 26 February, 8, 23 March 1914.

7. *Birmingham Age-Herald,* 12, 17, 18, 19, 22, 24, 26, 29 March, 2 April 1914; *Birmingham News,* 21 January 1914; Whatley interview; Black to James Saxon Childre, 13 January 1937, Black Papers; *Birmingham Age-Herald,* 8 January 1914; Black to Milton H. Fies, 19 March 1932, Black to George Ward, 26 August 1937, Black Papers.

8. *Birmingham Age-Herald,* 1 April 1914, 9-11; *Birmingham Age-Herald,* 2, 3, 4, 5, 6, 7, 8 April 1914; *Birmingham News,* 2 April 1914;

Birmingham Ledger, 4 April 1914; Black and Black, 41-42; Whatley interview; *Birmingham Age-Herald,* 9 April 1914.

9. *Birmingham Age-Herald,* 10, 12 November, 11, 22 December 1913, 1, 8 January, 4, 6 March, 9 April, 2 May 1914; *Birmingham News,* 4, 31 January 1914; Hamilton, *Hugo Black: The Alabama Years,* 53-57; Sellers, 176-180; Margaret Page Farmer, "Governor Charles Henderson," *Alabama Review,* October 1956, 244-246; Evans C. Johnson, *Oscar W. Underwood, A Political Biography,* Baton Rouge, 1980, 229-244; *Birmingham Age-Herald,* 4, 5 November 1913, 4 January, 25 March, 12 April, 3 May, 17 November 1914.

10. Pruden, 45; *Birmingham Age-Herald,* 8 January 1914; Meeting of 7 January 1914, Minutes of the State Democratic Executive Committee, Alabama Department of Archives and History; Black and Black, 41; Black to Evans Johnson, 7 May 1952, Black Papers.

11. *Birmingham Age-Herald,* 8, 25 March, 11 April, 4, 29, 30 November 1914; *Birmingham News,* 30 November 1914; *1886-7 Acts of Alabama,* 709-10, 996; *1888 Acts,* 17-18; *1890 Acts,* 1148-49; *1900 Acts,* 308-09; *1904 Acts,* 720-21; Black to W. L. Martin, 6 May 1916, Logan Martin Papers, Alabama Department of Archives and History (hereafter Martin Papers); Black and Black, 43-45; *Chicago Daily Times,* 19 August 1937; Pruden, 57; Black to Truman Hobbs, 3 December 1970, Black Papers; *Birmingham Age-Herald,* 12, 20, 30 December 1914, 6 January 1915.

12. *Birmingham Age-Herald,* 7, 27 January, 21, 22, 23 February, 3, 7, 9 March 1915.

13. *Birmingham Age-Herald,* 23 January, 3, 10, 11, 13, 14, 24, 27 March, 6, 7 April 1915.

14. *Birmingham Age-Herald,* 5 February, 21 March, 25 April, 15, 16 June 1915; *Birmingham Reporter,* 19 June 1915; Black and Black, 45-47; *Birmingham Age-Herald,* 25 April, 4, 5 May, 2 June 1915; Frank, 24; *State of Alabama v. Louis Walton,* Grand Jury Notes, Jefferson County, April Term, 1915, Birmingham Public Library Archives (hereafter Grand Jury Notes); *Birmingham Age-Herald,* 21 March, 16, 22 May, 19, 22, 25 June, 14 July 1915.

15. Ruth C. Burns to Black, 11 October 1963, Black Papers; Sellers, 184-85; 17 June 1914, Minutes of the Alabama State Demo-

cratic Executive Committee, Alabama Department of Archives and History, (hereafter State Democratic Executive Committee Papers); *1915 General Acts of Alabama*, 239-248, 250-257, 817-823; *Birmingham News, 29 November 1914,* extra edition; *Birmingham Age-Herald,* 12, 13, 23, 25 July, 6, 11 August, 21 September 1915; section 10, Act No. 720, *Acts of Alabama, 1915,* 823.

CHAPTER 4

1. Ethel Armes, *The Story of Coal and Iron in Alabama,* Leeds, Alabama, reprint, 1987, 334-35; W. David Lewis, *Sloss Furnaces and the Rise of the Birmingham District: An Industrial Epic,* Tuscaloosa, 1994, 141-142, 190-192; William Clayton Wright, "From Indians to Iron: A History of Bessemer, Alabama to 1917," master's thesis, University of Montevallo, 1970, 56-59, 69-70, 74; *Birmingham Age-Herald,* 14 October 1915.

2. 1910 U.S. Census; *Birmingham Age-Herald,* 6 September 1915; Untitled case, Grand Jury Notes, September Term, 1915, docket #187.

3. Black, Jr., 29; Frank, 27; *1907 Code of Alabama,* chapter 232, sec. 7124; *Birmingham Age-Herald,* 26 September 1915

4. Grand Jury Notes, September Term, 1915.

5. *Birmingham Age-Herald,* 17, 18, 20, 22, 26, 28, 29, 30 September, 1, 2, 3, 11, 12, 13, 14 October 1915; Black to Ralph Berry, 20 June 1966, Black Papers; *Birmingham Reporter,* 16 October 1915.

6. *Birmingham Age-Herald,* 12, 29 September, 7, 11, 17, 19 October 1915; *State of Alabama v. Shan Henry and Amos Smith and Arce Lee,* Grand Jury Notes, September Term, 1915, Jefferson County, Alabama, docket #329; *Birmingham News,* 15, 17 October 1915; Newman, 121; *Birmingham Age-Herald,* 16, 17 October 1915, 2 March 1916.

7. *Birmingham Age-Herald,* 20, 21 October, 3, 17 November 1915; as to suspicions of political engineering, Council president George Ross was reported in 1914 as a possible candidate against Will Welch, Black's assistant, for the legislature. *Birmingham Age-Herald,* 11 January 1914.

8. *State of Alabama v. W. C. Wingo,* Grand Jury Notes, September Term, 1915, docket

#139; *Birmingham Age-Herald,* 11, 19 November 1915; *State of Alabama v. Jim Daly and L. A. Grimes,* Grand Jury Notes, September Term, 1915, docket #112; *State v. T. J. Pierce,* Grand Jury Notes, April Term, 1913, docket #380; *Birmingham Age-Herald,* 17 October 1915.

9. *State of Alabama v. Albert Box,* Grand Jury Notes, April Term, 1915, docket #238; *Birmingham Age-Herald,* 19, 21, 22, 23 October 1915; Pruden, 55, 60, 68-69; *Birmingham Age-Herald,* 10 November, 12 December 1915. The grand jurors represented a wide range of white citizens, including a bank manager, machinist, clerk, miner, mechanic, and farmer. *Birmingham Age-Herald,* 7 September 1915.

10. *Chambers v Florida,* 309 U.S. 227, 1940, 235. A year after the grand jury's report, however, the president of Bessemer Coal, Iron, and Land Company complained: "The treatment that these unfortunate negroes are receiving from the police is enough to make them desire to depart for Kentucky or West Virginia." *Birmingham Age-Herald,* 22 September 1916.

CHAPTER 5

1. *Birmingham Age-Herald,* 2 January 1916. A few proposals to build a memorial to Lincoln in the South had been made and rejected earlier, elsewhere. See Michael G. Kammen, *Mystic Chords of Memory: the transformation of tradition in American culture,* New York, 1991, 109-110; *Birmingham Reporter,* 8 January 1916; *Birmingham Age-Herald,* 28 December 1915, 2, 17 January, 2, 5 March, 8 May 1916; *Birmingham Reporter,* 23 October 1915.

2. *Birmingham Age-Herald,* 30 October 1915, 20, 23, 25 February 1916; Sellers, 184; *1915 Acts of Alabama,* 1-8; *Birmingham Age-Herald,* 7, 23 November 1915, 31 January, 2, 12, 13, 25, 28, February, 5, 17, 23 March, 2, 6, April, 7, 9 May 1916; "Memoranda for Biographical Sketch of Borden Hughson Burr," 15 March 1917, Vertical Files, Alabama Department of Archives and History.

3. *Birmingham Age-Herald,* 23 February 1916; Hamilton, *Hugo Black: The Alabama Years,* 64; *Birmingham Age-Herald,* 13, 16 February 1916; *State ex re. Black v. Delaye,* 68 So. 993, 1915; Black's anti-ad litigation opened the way for enforcement in other Alabama cities; see *Biennial Report of the Attorney General of Alabama for 1914-16,* 23-24; *State of Alabama*

v. Monroe Parker, Grand Jury Notes, January Term, 1916, docket #275; *State of Alabama v. L&N R. R. Co,* Grand Jury Notes, January Term, 1916, docket #257; S*tate of Alabama v Louis Walton,* Grand Jury Notes, April Term, 1915, docket #128; Frank, 24-26; *Birmingham Age-Herald,* 9, 10, 11, 12, 14, March 1916; *State of Alabama v. Percy Fox,* Grand Jury Notes, January Term, 1916, docket #76; *Birmingham Age-Herald,* 29, 30 May, 2 June 1916.

4. *Birmingham Age-Herald,* 11-16, 19 May 1916.

5. *Columbus Ledger,* 17 May 1916; *Montgomery Advertiser,* 17, 18 May 1916; *Birmingham Age-Herald,* 18 May 1916.

6. Charles Henderson to W. L. Martin, 21 June 1916; telegram of Charles Henderson to N.E. Harris, governor of Georgia, 29 May 1916; R. Young Garrett to Charles Henderson, 19 July 1916, Charles Henderson Papers, Alabama Department of Archives and History (hereafter Henderson Papers); W. L. Martin to Charles Henderson, 21 August 1916, John H. Williams to W. L. Martin, 23 October 1915, Martin Papers; Farmer, 245; *Montgomery Advertiser,* 4 March 1907, 18, 19, 21 May 1916; "William Logan Martin," Vertical Files, Alabama Department of Archives and History; *Birmingham Age-Herald,* 19 May 1916; *1907 Code of Alabama,* chapter 254, 781-83; *1878-79 Acts of Alabama,* 180-186; *Columbus Ledger,* 19 May 1916.

7. *Columbus Ledger,* 18-22, 28, 29 May 1916; *Montgomery Advertiser,* 19-29 May 1916; CH to Pat Daniels, 3 May 1916, Henderson Papers.

8. *Montgomery Advertiser,* 19, 29 May, 1, 3, 10 June, 6-9 July 1916; *Columbus Ledger,* 31 May, 5-9 July 1916; *Birmingham Age-Herald,* 4 June, 6 July 1916; *Montgomery Advertiser,* 16 September 1916; "Impeachment No. 20 File," *State of Alabama ex. rel. R. B. Adams vs. Pal M. Daniel,* Sheriff of Russell County, Martin Papers.

9. W. L. Martin to B. A. Burt, 12 July 1916, W. L. Martin to T. M. Patterson, 8 August 1916, Martin Papers; letters of R.E. Lindsey to Charles Henderson, 19, 27 July, 3 August 1916, Henderson Papers; *Montgomery Advertiser,* 6, 16 June, 28 July, 5, 6 August 1916; *Columbus Ledger,* 20, 21, 23-27 July, 4, 6 August 1916; *Columbus Enquirer-Sun,* 26 July 1916; *1915 General Acts of Alabama,* 592-94,

719-721; *Biennial Report of the Attorney General of Alabama for 1914-16,* 141-145; interview of Harwell G. Davis, with F. W. Helenbold, by Arthur L. Walker, 21 April 1975, Samford University Library; *Birmingham Age-Herald,* 7 January, 14 March 1914.

10. *Rocky Mountain News,* 22-23, 25 June 1916; *Summit County Journal,* 24 June, 1, 8, 22 July, 5 August, 16 September, 4 November 1916; *Birmingham Age-Herald,* 22 June 1916; Newman, 45-46; *Columbus Ledger,* 7, 8 August 1916; *Columbus Enquirer-Sun,* 7, 8 August 1916.

11. *Columbus Ledger,* 9 August 1916; *Columbus Enquirer-Sun,* 9 August 1916.

12. *Columbus Ledger,* 10, 11, 13, August 1916; *Columbus Enquirer-Sun,* 10, 11 August 1916; draft motion "C" in State of Alabama v. ____, undated, Martin Papers.

13. *Columbus Ledger,* 10, 11, 13 August 1916; *1915 General Acts of Alabama,* 8-35, section 22; *Montgomery Advertiser,* 11 August 1916.

14. *Columbus Ledger,* 13 August 1916; Order of Chief Justice John Anderson (authorizing Hon. A. H. Alston to continue special term until criminal business of the grand jury is complete), 9 August 1916, Martin Papers; John A. Anderson to W. L. Martin, 11 August 1916, Martin Papers.

15. *Columbus Ledger,* 11, 13 August 1916; *Columbus Enquirer-Sun,* 11 August 1916; R.E. Lindsay to W. L. Martin, 18 August 1916, Martin Papers; *Montgomery Advertiser,* 11-13 August 1916; Sellers, 183; *Birmingham Age-Herald,* 30 September 1915, 11, 12 August 1916.

16. *Montgomery Advertiser,* 12, 13 August 1916; *Columbus Ledger,* 12-14 August 1916; *Columbus Enquirer-Sun,* 12-14 August 1916.

17. *Montgomery Advertiser,* 18 August 1916; *Columbus Enquirer-Sun,* 13 August 1916; excerpts from Grand Jury Minutes, testimony of J. W. Kelley, 15 August 1916, 147-161, Martin Papers; *Columbus Ledger,* 13-17 August 1916; W. L. Martin to M. E. Young, 13 October 1916, Martin Papers; *Columbus Ledger,* 23 August 1916.

18. *Birmingham Age-Herald,* 20, August 1916; see also *Columbus Ledger,* 28, 29 August 1916 and *Montgomery Advertiser, 31 August 1916.*

19. *Montgomery Advertiser*, 11 August 1916.

20. George Lewis Bailes, Sr., interview with author, 1971; *Birmingham Age-Herald*, 25 August 1912, 19 February 1916; see *Birmingham City Directory, 1916*, for locations of Black's work, home, church, and lodges; William Calhoun to Black, 9 August 1964, Black to Mrs. Eric C. Allen, 1 February 1927, Black Papers; Smith interview; Frank, 22; Black, Jr., 23; Black and Black, 48.

21. *Birmingham Age-Herald*, 30 October 1915, 7, 18, 20 July, 5 September 1916; *1915 General Acts of Alabama*, section 16, 7; on constitutionality of banning "innocent" beverages, see *Purity Extract and Tonic Company v. Lynch*, 226 U.S. 192, 1912, 204-05.

22. *Birmingham Age-Herald*, 6, 7, 11, 23, 24 September, 1, 3, 13 October 1916.

23. W. L. Martin to Frederick I. Thompson, 19 September 1916, Martin Papers; *Birmingham Age-Herald*, 18 October 1916.

24. *Birmingham Age-Herald*, 8 September, 2, 4 November 1916, 30 January 1917.

25. *Birmingham Age-Herald*, 27, 29 May, 23, 24 June, 11 July 1916; Harris, *Political Power in Birmingham*, 254, 260; Elizabeth Bonner Clark, "The Abolition of Convict Lease System in Alabama, 1913-1928," master's thesis, University of Alabama, 1949, 25-28; Harris, *Political Power in Birmingham*, 205-207; Wayne Flynt, "Religion in the Urban South: The Divided Religious Mind of Birmingham, 1900-1930," *Alabama Review*, April 1977, 127; *Birmingham Age-Herald*, 9 January 17 March, 9 April 1916; Harris, *Political Power in Birmingham*, 196-198.

26. *Birmingham Age-Herald*, 8, 9 March, 7 October, 6 December 1916; Harris, *Political Power in Birmingham*, 71-72, 78, 197.

27. *Birmingham Age-Herald*, 13 October, 12 December 1916, 2 January 1917; *State of Alabama v. J. B. Frost* alias Jonathan Frost, Grand Jury Notes, September Term, 1916.

28. *Birmingham Age-Herald*, 20 September 1916; on social uses of crime generally, see James W. Clarke, "Black-On-Black Violence," *Society*, July-August 1996; *Mobile Register*, 19 October 1916.

29. *Birmingham Age-Herald*, 19 October, 3 November 1916, 7 January 1917; *Montgomery Advertiser*, 26, 27 August, 8 September 1916;

Birmingham Age-Herald, 29 September, 18 October, 21 December 1916, W. L. Martin to Charles Henderson, 22 August 1916, Charles Henderson to W. L. Martin, 24 August 1916, Martin Papers; R. E. Lindsay to Charles Henderson, 27 July 1916, Charles Henderson to R. E. Lindsay, 27 July 1916, 8 January 1917, Henderson Papers; *Birmingham Age-Herald*, 8-10, 12 January 1917; Clifford Durr interview.

30. *Birmingham Age-Herald*, 9, 17, 20-24 January, 1 February 1917; "Johnston, Forney" *The Southerner, a Biographical Encyclopedia of Southern People*, Birmingham, 1944, 245; Johnson, *Oscar W. Underwood*, 133; *Birmingham Age-Herald*, 14, 15, 16 February 1917; *State ex rel. Gaston v. Black*, 74 So. 387, 393-94; *Birmingham Age-Herald*, 17, 22, 24, 27 February, 4, 8 March 1917.

31. *Birmingham Age-Herald*, 10 March, 1 April, 5 May 1917; surviving tombstone of Orlando Black, Wilsonville, Alabama; M. Claire to Black, undated, Black Papers; *Birmingham Age-Herald*, 6, 12, 13, 15-17 May 1917.

32. *Birmingham Age-Herald*, 14, 16-18 June 1917; *Hemmelweit v. State ex rel. Dedge*, 200 Ala. 203, 1917; 11 July 1917; *Henry v. State ex rel. Welch*, 70 So. 417, 1917, 418; *Birmingham Age-Herald*, 13, 14 July 1917; Black and Black, 50-51.

33. Frank, 22; review of Grand Jury Notes, 1915, 1916 and 1917 by author; *Biennial Report of the Attorney General for 1914-1916*, 430-434, 574-576; compare with Jefferson County statistics in *Biennial Report of the Attorney General, 1916-1918*, 71-74, and *Biennial Report of the Attorney General, 1910-1912*, 379-382; Black "personally, handled all cases before the Grand Jury" during his term, Black to S.H. Black, 9 September 1926, Black Papers; Francis H. Hare, *A Historical Sketch of the Birmingham Bar, 1872-1907*, Alabama Collection, Birmingham Public Library, undated, 23; *Birmingham Age-Herald*, 27 September 1931; *Chicago Daily Times*, 19 August 1937.

Chapter 6

1. *Birmingham Age-Herald*, 1, 11 July 1917; Albert B. Moore, 758; *Birmingham Age-Herald*, 13 May 1917.

2. *Birmingham Age-Herald*, 6-8, 11 April 1917; G. B. McCormack to Charles Henderson, 25 July 1917, Henderson Papers;

Birmingham Age-Herald, 25 July 1917; Michael A. Breedlove, "Progressivism and Nativism: The Race for the Presidency of the City Commission of Birmingham, Alabama in 1917," *Journal of the Birmingham Historical Society,* VI, no. 4, July 1980, 3-20.

3. Bailes interview; Paul Stevenson to Charles Henderson, 27 July 1917, Henderson Papers; Louis W. Koenig, *Bryan: A Political Biography of William Jennings Bryan,* New York, 1971, 555; Charles C. Combs to Black, 29 September 1949, Black Papers; Black and Black, 51-53; Daniel M. Berman, "The Political Philosophy of Hugo L. Black," doctoral dissertation, Rutgers University, 1957, footnote 12, 35; Black to Sterling Black, 13 May 1950, Black to Dexter M. Keezer, 12 October 1945, Black Papers; Black, Jr., 31-33.

4. Black to John V. Patrick, Jr., 27 September 1956, Black Papers; Black and Black, 53-55; Black to Wesley A. Sturges, 18 November 1947, George Walton to Black, circa. 4 March 1965, John H. Mitchell to Black, 20 March 1944, Black Papers.

5. Black to William Toland, 4 November 1968, Black to Eileen Donnan, 1 July 1969, Black to Martin Huff, 19 January 1971, Black Papers; Pruden, 86; John H. Mitchell to Black and reply, 20, 22 March 1944, Black Papers; John Milton Cooper, Jr., *Pivotal Decades: The United States, 1900-1920,* New York, 1990, 277-80; Smith interview.

6. Breedlove, 4-8.

7. Herbert Baughn, interview with author, 1972; *Birmingham Age-Herald,* 13 April, 7 May 1918; Frank W. Boykin to James F. Byrnes, 21 May 1956, Forney Johnston Papers, Alabama Department of Archives and History (hereafter Johnston Papers); Edward Boykin, *Everything's Made For Love in This Man's World: Vignettes from the Life of Frank W. Boykin,* Mobile, 1973, 49, 61; J. H. McCormick to A. C. Crowder, 7 November 1918, Henderson Papers; McKiven, 126; Letwin, *The Challenge of Interracial Unionism,* 181-82.

8. Joan M. Jensen, *The Price of Vigilance,* Chicago, 1968, 18-20, 57-59, 146-52, 288-89; J. B. Ellis to A. C. Crowder, 11 November 1918, Benjamin F. Elmore to A. C. Crowder, 23 November 1918; B. B. Hurst to John H. Drakeford, 31 October 1918, A. C. Crowder to Lloyd M. Hooper, 21 October 1918, Henderson Papers; various letters to A. C. Crowder

in files of Council of Defense indicate local business positions, Henderson Papers; "Bulletin No. 1. "Relations With American Protective League," 9 October 1918, Field Division, Council of National Defense, George W. Jones to Lloyd M. Hooper, 28 October 1918, Henderson Papers; "Jefferson County Council of Defense" stationary in A. R. Dearborn to Lloyd M. Hooper, 20 November 1918, Henderson Papers.

9. A. C. Crowder to Fred H. Gormley, 26 October 1918, Forney Johnston to Charles Henderson, 8 April 1918, Henderson Papers; Harris, *Political Power in Birmingham,* 200-201; draft ordinance, matching the Birmingham ordinance, attached to letter of Lloyd M. Hooper to "Several County Councils of Defense," 3 August 1918, Jon. Rich to Hooper, 27 August 1918, Henderson Papers; 13 September 1918, F. J. to "Girl," Johnston Papers; Chair of Lee County Council of Defense to Lloyd M. Hooper, 4 November 1918, Geo. G. Crawford to Hooper, 21 March 1918, Forney Johnston to Hooper, 23 March 1918; *General Laws of the Legislature of Alabama, Session of 1919,* xi-xii; H.S. Murphy to James W. Johnson, 9 November 1918, NAACP Papers, Library of Congress (hereafter NAACP Papers); H.S. Murphy to Monroe H. Work, 3 October 1918, Henderson Papers.

10. A. C. Crowder to Wm. C. Sanders (and all other APL county agents), 31 October 1918, Henderson Papers; A. C. Crowder to Charles Henderson, 8, 30 November 1918, Henderson Papers; Glenn Feldman, *From Demagogue to Dixiecrat: Horace Wilkinson and the Politics of Race,* Lanham, Maryland, 1995, 25-26; T. D. Boynton to A. C. Crowder, 1 November 1918, Henderson Papers; Feldman, *From Demagogue to Dixiecrat,* 27.

11. Black and Black, 32, 55-57; Hugh Ezelle to Black, 1 September 1952, Black Papers; *Birmingham Age-Herald,* 16 May 1918; Hugo L. Black, "The Lawyer and Individual Freedom," *Tennessee Law Review,* December, 1950, 470-471; on labor movement perspective, see Frank Morrison, "Labor's Challenge to Democracy," in James E. McCulloch, ed., *Democracy in Earnest,* Washington, 1918, 229-234; *Birmingham Age-Herald,* 26 June 1918.

12. Black and Black, 58-59; Newman, 49; Davis, 9; *New York Times,* 24 February 1998; *Atlanta Journal-Constitution,* 12 October 1997;

Black to R. R. Walker, 12 April 1926, Black Papers; *Birmingham Age-Herald*, 18 December 1918.

CHAPTER 7

1. *General Laws of the Legislature of Alabama, Session of 1919,* ix-x; all direct testimony in this chapter is taken from a transcript of the trial of *Mary Miniard v. Walker D. Hines* as Director General of Railroads, No. 11976, Circuit Court of Jefferson County, 8 October 1919, Birmingham Court Reporting Company, Black Papers. To reduce notations in the text, the author has refrained from noting continuous references to this transcript. In addition, the author has used ellipses to indicate only where a direct quotation is broken, but not where sections of testimony have been removed for clarity or brevity. All italicized words in the testimony are the author's emphasis. The Miniards apparently were "poor" or certainly on the margins of poverty despite H. R. Miniard's recent job as a semi-skilled crane operator. The Miniards are not listed in the city directories for 1918, 1919, or beyond. They probably rented a room with another working family in Ensley. See *Birmingham City Directory, 1918,* 1116; *Birmingham City Directory, 1919,* 1117.

2. Frances H. Hare, *A Historical Sketch of the Birmingham Bar 1872-1907,* undated, 13; *Martindale Listings,* "Biographical Section, Alabama," 1931, 2; Robert C. Brown "The Jurisdiction of the Federal Courts Based On Diversity of Citizenship," *University of Pennsylvania Law Review,* December 1929, 179-94. Apparently, plaintiff lawyers regularly limited their claims to less than 3,000 dollars in order to stay in state court (see *Louisville & Nashville R. R. Co. v. King,* 73 So. 456). Almost 20 years later, Justice Black helped to overturn a century-old precedent that gave federal courts the freedom to evade state laws in cases of diversity (*Erie Railroad Co. v. Tompkins,* 304 U.S. 64, 1938); see also Bernard Schwartz, *The Supreme Court: Constitutional Revolution in Retrospect,* New York, 1957, 152-160; *Hines v. Miniard,* 86 So. 23, 1920, 23-24; *Hines v. Miniard,* 6 Div. 51, 3 June 1920; *Hines v. Miniard,* 6 Div. 522, Alabama Supreme Court Records.

3. Black to Frank H. Mortimer, 6 October 1921, John Arthur Keefe to Black, 2 March 1969, Black Papers. Despite Woodrow Wilson's presidency, most federal judges in 1919 were Republicans. Presidents customarily appointed members of their own party to the federal bench, and Republicans had controlled the White House for most years since Grover Cleveland. See, Henry J. Abraham, *Justices and Presidents: A Political History of Appointments to the Supreme Court,* New York, 1974, 58-60; Black's perception of the federal courts' hostility to the poor was in line with current, national "Populist-progressive" thought. See Peter Graham Fish, *The Politics of Federal Judicial Administration,* Princeton, 1973, 17-19; (Judge Grubb's action) *Birmingham Age-Herald,* 2 October 1919; Crampton Harris, interview with Charles Morgan, Jr., 1971; (Judge Boyd) Harris, *Political Power in Birmingham,* 255; *Hines v. Miniard,* 86 So. 23, 1920.

4. The name "Jim Crow" has obscure, complex origins, although it probably began with black-faced minstrelsy in the early 1800s. The term also may have been used first in the North to refer to segregated facilities there. See Charles Reagan Wilson, "Jim Crow," in Charles Reagan Wilson and William Ferris, eds., *The Encyclopedia of Southern Culture,* Chapel Hill, 1989, 213-214. How the term drifted south to become a common name for segregation is another untold chapter in the stories about Southern language and history. Catherine A. Barnes, *Journey from Jim Crow: The Desegregation of Southern Transit,* New York, 1983, 5-19; J. L. LeFlore to James Weldon Johnson, 5 January 1927, NAACP Papers; James Weldon Johnson, *Along This Way: The Autobiography of James Weldon Johnson,* New York, 1933, 86-87; C. Vann Woodward, *The Strange Career of Jim Crow,* New York, 1966, 107, 100; Blaine A. Brownell, "Birmingham, Alabama: New South City in the 1920's," *Journal of Southern History,* 38, February, 1972, 28-31; August Meier and Elliott Rudwick, "The Boycott Against Jim Crow Streetcars in the South, 1900-1906," *Journal of American History,* March, 1969, 756-775; "To Stop Serving of Whites and Blacks in Same Restaurant," *Birmingham Age-Herald,* 15 December 1914; Thomas D. Parke Diary, entry for 25 September 1915, Birmingham Public Library Archives (hereafter *Parke Diary*) ; Pauli Murray, ed., *State Laws on Race and Color,* Washington, D.C., 1950, 615; Harris, *Political Power in Birmingham,* 187, 165-67.

5. Woodward, *The Strange Career of Jim*

Crow, 98; *Birmingham Age-Herald,* 16 August 1903; Harris, *Political Power in Birmingham,* 186, 198-201, 206-211; Lewis Baker, *The Percys of Mississippi: Politics and Literature in the New South,* Baton Rouge, 1983, 4-12; *Negroes in the United States, 1920-32,* Bureau of the Census, 1935, 55; William Archer, *Through Afro-America: an English Reading of the Race Problem,* London, 1910, 72-73; Murray, 34; even in *Plessy,* railroads did not want to observe Jim Crow due to the costs of enforcement (see A. Leon Higginbotham, Jr., *Shades of Freedom: Racial Politics and Presumptions of the American Legal Process,* New York, 1996, 111-12); McKiven, 28-30, 41-42, 121-25; Horace R. Clayton and George S. Mitchell, *Black Workers and the New Unions,* Chapel Hill, 1939, 314-320, 329-336; Bond, 144-145, 230-232.

6. Harris, *Political Power in Birmingham,* 165-174, 131-33; Bond, 180-183; McMillan, 322-324. The Black Belt's swollen political influence came from two facts: the 1901 Constitution gave the majority-black counties representation on the basis of both black and white people, although only whites could vote, and, afterwards, the legislature's refusal to reapportion. By 1919, one representative in the Alabama legislature from the Black Belt's Lowndes County represented less than 3,500 white persons while one Jefferson county legislator represented about 200,000 whites (See McMillan, 306-309; Hallie Farmer, *The Legislative Process in Alabama,* University of Alabama, 1949, 29, 35.); "psychological wage" is W. E. B. DuBois' term for working whites' sense of racial superiority in lieu of interracial solidarity in the workplace (DuBois, *Black Reconstruction in America,* 700); even Henry Grady, foremost spokesmen for the new, industrial South had resorted at times to arguing that Southern blacks were getting more than their fair share of tax monies. "The Negroes of Georgia," he wrote in 1890, "pay one-fortieth of the taxes, and yet they take forty nine per cent of the school fund." See Grady, 246.

7. Bond, 290; W. E. B. DuBois, *The Souls of Black Folk,* New York, 1989, 3, 132.

8. Ann Firor Scott, *The Southern Lady: From Pedestal to Politics, 1830-1930,* Chicago, 1970, 169; Jacquelyn Dowd Hall, *Revolt Against Chivalry: Jessie Daniel Ames and the Women's Campaign Against Lynching,* New York, 1979, 127-157; George M. Fredrickson, *The Black Image in the White Mind and the Debate on Afro-American Character and Destiny, 1817-1914,* New York, 1971, 271-282; McMillan, 292; Walter White, *Rape and Faggot: A Biography of Judge Lynch,* New York, 1929, 254; Robert L. Zangrande, *The NAACP Crusade Against Lynching, 1909-1950,* Philadelphia, 1980, 10-15; Virginia Foster Durr and Hollinger F. Barnard, ed., *Outside the Magic Circle: The Autobiography of Virginia Foster Durr,* Tuscaloosa, 1985, 44; *Birmingham Ledger,* 2 October 1919; *Parke Diary,* entry for 25 September 1915; *Negroes in the United States, 1920-1932,* 293, 303; Murray, 31; Marjorie Fine Knowles, "The Legal Status of Women in Alabama: A Crazy Quilt," 29 *Alabama Law Review* 427, 502; *Birmingham Age-Herald,* 17 April 1911; *Gadsden Times,* 1 August 1924.

9. Howard W. Odum, *Southern Regions of the United States,* Chapel Hill, 1936, 375-430; Wayne Flynt, *Poor But Proud: Alabama's Poor Whites,* Tuscaloosa, 1989, 81-82; Frank, 4; Gavin Wright, *Old South, New South: Renditions in the Southern Economy Since the Civil War,* New York, 1986, 55, 179-180; McKiven, 154-55; W. T. Couch, ed., *Culture in the South,* Chapel Hill, 1934, 665-671; Knowles, 506.

10. Sterne, 54-86; Ophelia L. Amigh of the Alabama Home of Refuge to Charles Henderson, 17 March 1915, J.D. Acuff to Charles Henderson, 14 August 1915, W. B. Bankhead to Charles Henderson, 14 August 1915, Henderson Papers; Knowles, 437-439, 445-446, 452, 481-485; *Birmingham Age-Herald,* 1 January 1914, 3, 4 April 1915; *Birmingham Post,* 1 March 1921; Scott, 172-73; *Official Proceedings of the Constitutional Convention of the State of Alabama, May 21st, 1901 to September 3rd, 1901,* Vol. 1, 466; McMillan, 279; Mary Martha Thomas, *The New Woman in Alabama: Social Reform and Suffrage, 1890-1920,* Tuscaloosa, 1992, 2-5, 10-11.

11. Thomas, 32-39, 93-117, 187-203; Gillian Goodrich, "Romance and Reality: The Birmingham Suffragists, 1982-1920," *Journal of the Birmingham Historical Society,* Vol. 5, No. 3, January, 1978, 5-21; Lee N. Allen, "The Woman Suffrage Movement, 1910-1920," *Alabama Review,* April 1958, 83-99; Michael McGerr, "Political Style and Women's Power, 1830-1930," *Journal of American History,* December 1990, 879; *Acts of Alabama, 1919,* 186; *Journal of the Alabama House of Represen-*

tatives, 1919, 846-47; Thomas, 197; Forney Johnston to "My Dearest," circa. September 1919, Johnston Papers.

12. Virginia Durr interview; Virginia Durr, 47; *Birmingham Age-Herald,* 12 April 1915; *Birmingham News,* 16 March 1920; Black, Jr., 123-25.

13. Allen D. Grimshaw, ed., *Racial Violence in the United States,* Chicago, 1969, 87-105; *Parke Diary,* entry for 5 October 1919; William M. Tuttle, Jr., *Race Riot, Chicago in the Red Summer of 1919,* New York, 1970, 228-229; Monroe Work, *Negro Year Book, 1919-1921,* Tuskegee, 1921, 73-83; *Birmingham Age-Herald,* 1-10 October 1919; J. C. Hartsfield to Thomas Kilby, 13 September 1919, Thomas Kilby Papers, Alabama Department of Archives and History (hereafter Kilby Papers); "Ku Klux Forces Wealthy Negroes to Flee Montgomery, Ala.," press release, 11 October 1919, NAACP Papers; *Birmingham Ledger,* 2-9 October 1919; Glenn Feldman, "Lynching in Alabama, 1889-1921," *Alabama Review,* April, 1995, 136-137; Glenn Feldman, "Conservative Progressivism: Antivigilantism in Post-World War I Alabama," *Alabama Review,* January, 1997, 19-20, 32; *Birmingham Reporter,* 27 September, 4, 11 October 1919; H. K. Milner to Thomas Kilby, 13 October 1919, Kilby Papers.

14. The "Mason & Dixon line" originated from a private land dispute and marked the common boundaries of Maryland and Pennsylvania. In 1820, the Missouri Compromise extended the line to include the 36th parallel as a division between slave and free American lands. Afterwards, it became "a symbolic division both politically and socially [and economically] between North and South," Elizabeth M. Makowski, "Mason-Dixon," in *The Encyclopedia of Southern Culture,* 573-74. Michael Kammer, *Mystic Chords of Memory: The Transformation of Tradition in American Culture,* New York, 1991, 112,115. Woodward's *The Strange Career of Jim Crow* was written in 1955 at another moment between "living memory and written history" (xii) in the long life of Jim Crow. William Garrott Brown, *A History of Alabama: for use in schools,* New York, 1903, 267-68; Black to Alfred A. Knopf, 2 October 1943, Black to Mrs. L. W. Waltem, 21 December 1931, Black to John Frank, 20 January 1948, Black Papers; Walter L. Fleming, *Civil War and Reconstruction in Alabama,* New York, 1905, 803; Fleming's

work reenforced Black's views about J. L. M. Curry's role in starting black education (pages 467-68, 625) and was a part of Jim Crow's scholarship. See I. A. Newby, *Jim Crow's Defense: Anti-Negro Thought in America,* Baton Rouge, 1965, 65; John William Draper, *History of the American Civil War,* vol. I, New York, 1868, 469. Black's notations are found in his copy of the book in the Hugo Black Room at the University of Alabama Law School Library (hereafter Black Book).

15. Bond, 32-62; Fleming, 580-605; Sarah Woolfolk Wiggins, *The Scalawags in Alabama Politics, 1865-1881,* University, Alabama, 1977, 72-76; Woodward, *Origins of the New South,* 8-11, 120-128, 291-298; McMillan, 208-209; James F. Doster, "Railroad Domination in Alabama, 1885-1905," *Alabama Review,* July, 1954, 186-198.

16. James F. Doster, "Alabama's Political Revolution of 1904," *Alabama Review,* April 1954, 85-98; James F. Doster, *Railroads in Alabama Politics, 1875-1914,* Tuscaloosa, 1957, 102-174; James F. Doster, "Comer, Smith, and Jones: Alabama's Railroad War of 1907-1914," *Alabama Review,* April 1957, 83-95; Hackney, *Populism to Progressivism in Alabama,* 12-16, 242-305; Sellers, 176-185; Wayne Flynt, "Organized Labor, Reform, and Alabama Politics," *Alabama Review,* July 1970, 164-165; Harris, *Political Power in Birmingham,* 114-118, 231-237; Forney Johnston to Underwood, 13 May 1920, Oscar W. Underwood Papers, Alabama Department of Archives and History (hereafter Underwood Papers).

17. Ralph I. Knowles, interview with author, 1981; Gunnar Myrdal, *An American Dilemma: The Negro Problem and Modern Democracy,* New York, 1944, 550-51, 611-612; John Dollard, *Caste and Class in a Southern Town,* New Haven, 1937, 178-179; Bertram W. Doyle, *The Etiquette of Race Relations in the South,* Chicago, 1937, 142-145; *Negro Year Book, 1919-1921,* 55-58; *Negroes in the United States, 1920-32,* 293; Forney Johnston to "Dearest Girl," undated, circa. 13 December 1919, Johnston Papers; DuBois, *The Souls of Black Folk,* 124-125; see also in general, Neil R. McMillen, *Dark Journey: Black Mississippians in the Age of Jim Crow,* Urbana, Illinois, 1989, 197-223.

18. Bertram Wyatt-Brown, *The House of Percy: Honor, Melancholy, and Imagination in*

a Southern Family, New York, 1994, 189, 251-253, 245-250; Baker, 49; Jay Tolson, *Pilgrim in the Ruins: A Life of Walker Percy,* New York, 1992, 31-37; Patrick H. Samway, *Walker Percy: A Life,* New York, 1997, 3-8, 14-17, 23-26; in 1922, Roy's Uncle LeRoy would make a nationally publicized speech against the Klan in his hometown, Greenville, Mississippi, and ask: "Since when has Southern womanhood needed to be defended by men in mask?," Wyatt-Brown, 231.

19. Abe Berkowitz to Black, 8 October 1964, and Black to Berkowitz, 13 October 1964, Black Papers; both Black's and Percy's final arguments are developed from the author's review of the transcript and of their lawyering styles; *Hines v. Miniard,* 6 Div. 51, 3 June 1920, Alabama Supreme Court Records.

20. *Hines v. Miniard,* 86 So. 23, 1920; *Hines v. Miniard,* 6 Div. 51, 3 June 1920, Alabama Supreme Court Records; Milford, 210; Mayfield, 15-16; *Hines v. Miniard,* 94 So. 302, 1922; *Hines v. Miniard,* 6 Div. 522, Alabama Supreme Court Records. Apparently, industrialists' fear of plaintiff lawyers and juries finding new ways "to punish" corporations was widespread. Roy Percy's senior partner, Augustus Benners, followed Walker Percy into the Alabama legislator as protector of corporate interests and in 1919 sponsored legislation effectively banning Northern labor agents from Alabama by making them liable for criminal penalties and civil actions if they failed to pay a license of up to $3,750 to do business in the state; however, the last section of Benner's act provides that railroads transporting passengers or workers "shall not be a labor agent within the meaning of that term." (*Acts of Alabama, 1919,* 187-88.). *Docket Book, 1923,* Circuit Court of Jefferson County, Birmingham Public Library Archives.

21. Wyatt-Brown, 253-255; 36-37, 41-45; *Hines v. Miniard,* 6 Div. 522, Alabama Supreme Court Records; *Birmingham Age-Herald,* 7-9 February 1917; *Birmingham Ledger,* 11 October 1919; Abe Berkowitz to Black, 8 October 1964, and Black to Berkowitz, 13 October 1964, Black Papers; perhaps because of his leadership as jury foreman, William E. Hargrove later became Black's friend and, in 1928, his accountant (Hargrove to Black, 3 August 1928, Black Papers). *Hamilton v. Alabama,* 156 So. 2d 926, 1963; *Hamilton v. Alabama,* 376

U.S. 650, 1964; Leon Friedman, ed., *Southern Justice,* New York, 1965, 138-140; Bernard Schwartz, *Super Chief: Earl Warren and His Supreme Court - A Judicial Biography,* New York, 1983, 529-530. The past continued to shape the meaning of Judge Black's words and decisions. Black believed that juries, not judges, should decide cases of courtroom contempt, and earlier in 1964 he dissented from the Court's opinion denying Mississippi's segregationist governor a right to trial for a federal court's contempt citation. Forty-five years after the *Miniard* case, Black's faith in a jury of "good and lawful men" remained undisturbed even in the most controversial circumstances (See *United States v. Barnett,* 376 U. S. 681, 700 1964.). On the day *Hamilton v. Alabama* was decided, moreover, Black joined other U.S. Supreme Court decisions reversing "evasive tactics" of the Alabama Supreme Court, which had denied civil rights leaders' appeals because they filed briefs either on the wrong-sized paper or not exactly in the prescribed form. Fifty-five years after losing his first circuit court trial for a Birmingham widow, due to senseless procedural, court-made rules, Black continued his fight to have litigation decided on a case's merits (*New York Times,* 29 June 1964).

CHAPTER 8

1. *Negroes in the United States, 1920-32,* 55; Lewis, 306; Wayne Flynt, *Poor But Proud,* 117-120; as legal entities, corporations operating in Alabama mining controlled 97.2 percent of the workers and 97.2 percent of production in 1919, while individual proprietors or partnership firms made up less than three percent (*Mines and Quarries, 1919,* Fourteenth Census of the United States, Vol. XI, 61-62); transcript of meeting of Governor's Coal Strike Commission, 4 March 1921, 16, 11-13, 16, 86, 104-105, and the following attachments: transcript of mass meeting under auspices of Birmingham Trade Council, 19 September 1920, 38-39, proceedings of mass meeting held at Anniston, Ala., 5 December 1920, 27, proceedings of speech of Mr. Van A. Bitner, 7 November 1920, 19-21, Governor's Coal Strike Commission, Birmingham Public Library Archives (hereafter Governor's Coal Strike Commission); "Tell the Governor what you think of this dodger," undated, Kilby Papers; *Birmingham Age-Herald,* 28 January 1921;

Journal of the Alabama House of Representatives, 1923, 73; Marlene Hunt Rikard, "Take Everything You Are . . .And Give it Away": Pioneer Industrial Social Workers at TCI," *Journal of the Birmingham Historical Society,* November, 1981, 30-32; Letwin, *The Challenge of Interracial Unionism,* 162-164; Mollie Beck Jenkins, "The Social Work of the Tennessee Coal Iron and Railroad Company," master's thesis, University of Alabama, 1929, 4-12; 17, 21-26. For later evidence, see "Remarkable Exhibits of Children's Work at Tennessee Co. Schools," *Birmingham Age-Herald,* 30 May 1923.

2. H. B. Humphrey, *Historical Summary of Coal-Mine Explosions in the United States, 1810-1958,* Bulletin 586, Bureau of Mines, U.S. Department of Interior, 1960, 45-93; Forrest T. Moyer, G. D. Jones, and V. E. Wrenn, *Injury Experience in Coal Mining, 1948,* Bulletin 509, Bureau of Mines, U.S. Department of Interior, 1948, 98-99; Flynt, *Poor But Proud,* 129-131; transcript of meeting of Governor's Coal Strike Commission, 4 March 1921, 91, 100; F. Ray Marshall, *Labor in the South,* Cambridge, 1967, 74; *Birmingham Reporter,* 26 February 1921; Letwin, *The Challenge of Interracial Unionism,* 166-172; Jenkins, 27-28.

3. Philip Taft, revised and edited by Gary M. Fink, *Organizing Dixie: Alabama Workers in the Industrial Era,* Westport, CN, 1981, 45-52, 59; Letwin, *The Challenge of Interracial Unionism,* 166, 158; Richard A. Straw "The United Mine Workers of America and the 1920 Coal Strike in Alabama" *Alabama Review,* April, 1975, 105-107; Jimmie Frank Gross, "Strikes in the Coal, Steel, and Railroad Industries in Birmingham," master's thesis, Auburn University, 1962, 55-56, 71-83; Forney Johnston to "Dearest," circa. September 1919, Johnston Papers; *Birmingham Age-Herald,* 2, 15 October 1919.

4. Johnson, *Oscar W. Underwood,* 297; Forney Johnston to "Dearest Girl," circa. 13 December 1919, Johnston Papers; Underwood to Charles Sumner, 23 March 1920, Underwood to E. W. Barrett, 27 February 1920, Underwood Papers; *Labor Advocate,* 10 January, 20 March, 1920; Wayne Flynt, "Organized Labor, Reform, and Alabama Politics, 1920" *Alabama Review,* 165-167; Robert H. Mangum to Underwood, 28 January 1920, Underwood Papers; *Mountain Eagle,* 18 February 1920; Winfred G. Sandlin, "Lycurgus Breckenridge Musgrove," *Alabama Review,* July, 1967, 208-09, 212-13; Johnson,

Oscar W. Underwood, 297.

5. Evans C. Johnson, "Oscar W. Underwood and the Senatorial Campaign of 1920," *Alabama Review,* January, 1968, 11-17; *Birmingham Age-Herald,* 26 March 1920; the author found various letters to and from A. C. Crowder in files of Council of Defense, Henderson Papers and compared them with letters from the same persons to and from Underwood, Underwood Papers; Johnson, *Oscar W. Underwood,* 288-89; Underwood to H.C. Pollard, 5 May 1920, telegram of Jelks H. Cabaniss to and letter from Oscar Underwood, 26, 28 April 1920, Underwood Papers; *Birmingham Age-Herald,* 2, 13, 16 April 1920; Flynt, "Organized Labor, Reform, and Alabama Politics, 1920," 169-76.

6. Underwood to Norman Gunn, 24 February 1920, H. K. Milner to and from Underwood, 23, 25 March 1920, telegrams between Hooper and Underwood, 2, 3 May 1920, Underwood Papers; *Harrison v. Hooper,* #6374, Original Bill and Proposed Writ of Injunction, 1 May 1920, Complainants' Brief, undated, Order and Opinion of Circuit Court, 2 May 1920, Chancery Minutes and Records, Jefferson County Courthouse (emphasis added); *Labor Advocate,* 8 May 1920; *Birmingham News,* 2 May 1920; *Birmingham Age-Herald,* 3 May 1920.

7. *Birmingham News,* 3-6 May 1920; *Birmingham Age-Herald,* 3-4 May 1920; *Harrison v. Hooper,* "Answer of Fredrick T. (sic) Thompson," undated, "Answer and Demurrer of Age-Herald Publishing Company," 4 June 1920, Chancery Minutes and Records, Jefferson County Courthouse; L. J. Bugg to Underwood, 15 May 1920, J. B. Ellis to Underwood, 10 May 1920, Underwood Papers; *Birmingham News,* 6, 7 May 1920; *Birmingham Age-Herald,* 4 May 1920; LeRoy Percy to Underwood, 15 May 1920, telegram of Frank Boykin to Underwood, 13 May 1920, Underwood Papers.

8. "Meetings of United Mine Workers," 28 March 1920, attached to transcript of meeting of Governor's Coal Strike Commission, 4 March 1921; *Mills v. Alabama,* 384 U.S. 214, 1966, 219-220. In announcing the U.S. Supreme Court's decision in *Mills,* Justice Black ad-libbed an acknowledgement of a friend from his past. While the official opinion states that the Alabama "trial court" originally held that the state's censorship violated the Constitu-

tion, Black declared from the bench that "Fritz Thompson held the statute abridged freedom of the press." In 1916, Hugo Black and Fritz Thompson had worked to clean up Girard for the cause of prohibition (*Mills v. Alabama,* "bench copy," No. 597, Oct. Term, 1965, Black Papers).

9. *Birmingham Age-Herald,* 10 February 1921 (emphasis added); Straw, "The United Mine Workers of America and the 1920 Coal Strike in Alabama," 109-116; Committee of Coal Operators Association to Kilby, 6 September 1920, Kilby Papers; transcript of meeting of Governor's Coal Strike Commission, 4 March 1921, 23-23; *1907 Code of Alabama,* chapter 176, 354-55, *Pratt Consolidated Coal Co. v. J. R. Kennamer,* #366, Complaint and Order of the Court, 13 September 1920, N. Dist. Al., National Archives, Atlanta Region; Taft, 54-55.

10. Straw, "The United Mine Workers of America and the 1920 Coal Strike in Alabama," 117-118; "Steiner, Robert Eugene," Thomas McAdory Owen, *History of Alabama and Dictionary of Alabama Biography,* Spartanburg, SC, repr., 1978, 1619; "Steiner, Crum, & Weil" (ad), *Hubbell's Legal Dictionary, 1917,* appendix, 9; George Beauchamp to Kilby, 9 October 1920, E. M. Bishop to Kilby, 12 November 1920, E. A. Terry to Kilby, 4 October 1920, Committee of Citizens of Beat 3, Adger to Kilby, 12 October 1920, "Reports of Troops . . .," 2, 8, 9 November 1920, Kilby Papers; Black to W. G. Lee, 2 June 1926, Black Papers; affidavits attached to Kilby letter to William Darden, 20 January 1921, Kilby Papers.

11. R. E. Steiner to Kilby, 26 September 1920, "memo," special meeting, publicity committee, United Mine Workers, 4 October 1920, Kilby Papers; transcript of meeting of Governor's Coal Strike Commission, 4 March 1921, 33; *Birmingham Age-Herald,* 6 February 1921; Straw, 120-122; Supplemental Report of Operators' Committee to Board of Investigation, undated, "Reports of Troops . . . ," 11/27-12/01, 12/0, 7; *Parke Diary,* entry of 21 September 1920.

12. Straw, "The United Mine Workers of America and the 1920 Coal Strike in Alabama," 118-119; *Parke Diary,* entry of 9 August 1920; *Birmingham Age-Herald,* 8-20 September, 1920; *Labor Advocate,* 12 October 1920; Taft, 56; "Tell the Governor what you

think of this dodger," undated, Kilby Papers; Straw, "The United Mine Workers of America and the 1920 Coal Strike in Alabama," 119; H. K. Milner to Underwood, 23 March 1920, Underwood Papers.

13. Straw, "The United Mine Workers of America and the 1920 Coal Strike in Alabama," 120; "Reports of Troops," 20, 26 December 1920, 10-23 January 1921, Kilby Papers; transcript of meeting of Governor's Coal Strike Commission, 4 March 1921, 92; R. E. Steiner to Kilby, 2 January 1921, "Testimony of Conrad W. Austin," before grand jury of Walker County, 25 January 1921, 10-12, Kilby Papers; State of Alabama v. W. H. Knox, #1170, 11, 15 (Austin recalled that he only reported to his men the Steiner's remarks.), 3-7, 21, 15-17 February 1921, Grand Jury Minutes; *Labor Advocate,* 8 January 1921; affidavit of William Harrison, 7 February 1921, *Harrison v. Austin,* #7782, Chancery Minutes and Records, Jefferson County Courthouse.

14. *Birmingham Age-Herald,* 17-19, 30 January 1921; R. E. Steiner to Kilby, 27 January 1921, Kilby to P. E. Day, 12 February 1921, Kilby to W. A. Burns, 14 February 1921, Kilby to J. B. Leath, 12 February 1921, Kilby Papers.

15. *Harrison v. Austin,* #7782, Original Bill and affidavits, 2 February 1921, Demurrer, Motion, Answer, and affidavits, 9 February 1921, Chancery Minutes and Records, Jefferson County Courthouse; *Birmingham Post,* 16 January, 1, 13, 19 February 1921; *Birmingham Age-Herald,* 10, 15, 16 February 1921; Straw, "The United Mine Workers of America and the 1920 Coal Strike in Alabama," 119-20; *Birmingham News,* 9-11 February 1921; affidavit of T. A. Boutwell, 12 February 1921, Kilby Papers; State of Alabama v. W. H. Knox, 1170/14, *Grand Jury Minutes,* 14, 11; transcript of meeting of Governor's Coal Strike Commission, 4 March 1921, 92; *Birmingham Post,* 13, 15, 16, 19 February 1921.

16. *Birmingham Age-Herald,* 28 January, 10, 18, 28 February 1921; Straw "The United Mine Workers of America and the 1920 Coal Strike in Alabama," 122; Glenn Feldman, "The Lynching of Willie Baird," *Alabama Heritage,* Winter, 1997, 250-26; *Birmingham Age-Herald,* 10, 15 February 1921; "The Facts" pamphlet, undated, Kilby Papers; transcript of meeting of Governor's Coal Strike Commission, 4 March

1921, 92-93.

17. *Advance,* 14 February 1921, Kilby Papers; *Birmingham Age-Herald,* 27, 30 January 1921, 1-8 February 1921; *Birmingham News,* 27 January 1921, 1-3 February 1921; Feldman, "The Lynching of Willie Baird," 24-30; *Birmingham Age-Herald,* 15 February 1921; *Advance,* 22 February 1921, Kilby Papers; Straw, 125; *Birmingham Post,* 23 February 1921.

18. *Birmingham Age-Herald,* 30 January 1921, 16 March 1918; Durr, *Outside the Magic Circle,* 3-4, 8-12; Virginia Durr to Charles Morgan, Jr., 12 April 1971, in author's possession; Virginia Durr interview.

19. Virginia Durr interview; *Birmingham Age-Herald,* 8 July 1908; Durr, *Outside the Magic Circle,* 5-7, 16, 19-20.

20. Virginia Durr interview; Black, Jr., 37-38; Durr, *Outside the Magic Circle,* 41, 42, 47; *Birmingham News,* 21 December 1913.

21. Virginia Durr interview; Black, Jr., 38, 179, 40; Virginia Durr to Charles Morgan, Jr., 12 April 1971, in author's possession; Durr, *Outside the Magic Circle,* 41, 43; *Birmingham News,* 30 January 1921.

22. Virginia Durr interview; Durr, *Outside the Magic Circle,* 44-45, *Birmingham News,* 23 February 1921; *Birmingham Age-Herald,* 24 February 1921; Black, Jr., 40; Smith interview; Virginia Durr interview.

23. *Birmingham Age-Herald,* 28 February, 2 March 1921; transcript of meeting of Governor's Coal Strike Commission, 4 March 1921, 2, 34-35, 91-92, 164-165; *Birmingham Age-Herald,* 4 March 1921; Virginia Durr interview.

24. *Birmingham Age-Herald,* 20, 31 March, 1 April 1921; extracts from Van Bittner's speech, 30 March 1921, Borden Burr to Kilby, 31 March 1921, Kilby Papers; *Birmingham Age-Herald,* 1, 3, 7 April 1921; "Representative Citizens Condemn Utterances of Van Bittner," attached to transcript of meeting of Governor's Coal Strike Commission, 4 March 1921; *Birmingham Age-Herald,* 5 April 1921; "Special Report" of the Grand Jury, March Term, 1921, Grand Jury Minutes, 1921; *Birmingham Age-Herald,* 10, 11 April 1921; *Birmingham Post,* 23 April 1921.

25. *Birmingham Age-Herald,* 4 May 1921; *Birmingham Post,* 25 April, 4 May 1921; Kilby to J. K. Brandon, 20 April 1921, Kilby Papers;

General and Local Laws of Alabama, 1921, 31-33; *Birmingham Age-Herald,* 7 April 1921; *Birmingham Post,* 29 April, 6 May 1921; *Birmingham Age-Herald,* 23 May, 24 June 1921.

26. See Alan Dawley, *Struggles for Justice: Social Responsibility and the Liberal State,* Cambridge, 1991, 228-250, 254-274; William E. Leuchtenburg, *The Perils of Prosperity, 1914-1932,* Chicago, 1958, 158-59, 204-224; *Birmingham Age-Herald,* 2, 5, 13 February, 1 April 1921; proceedings of mass meeting held at Anniston, Ala., 5 December 1920, 31, attached to transcript of meeting of Governor's Coal Strike Commission, 4 March 1921; *Birmingham Age-Herald,* 20 March 1921, *Birmingham Post,* 16 February 1921; "The Martyrs of the United States of America," unpublished, U.S. Catholic Conference, 1941, 40-41.

27. *Birmingham Age-Herald,* 27, 28 January, 17 June 1921.

28. Transcript of meeting of Governor's Coal Strike Commission, 4 March 1921, 93; *Birmingham Age-Herald,* 5, 6, 8, 10, 12 February 1921; see Kelly, 188; *Advance,* 22 February 1921, Kilby Papers; *Birmingham News,* 12 February 1921. A quarter of a century later, 53 percent of the white voters would adopt virtually the same proposed amendment to the Alabama Constitution in response to a U.S. Supreme Court opinion (*Smith v. Allwright,* 321 U.S. 649, 1944) in which Justice Hugo Black joined the Court in outlawing the all-white primary. See, V. O. Key, Jr., *Southern Politics,* New York, 1949, 632-635, as well as Norman F. Furniss, *The Fundamentalist Controversy, 1918-1931,* New York, 1963, 59.

29. Pruden, 100-101; Crampton Harris interview; *Birmingham Post,* 17, 31 August 1921; Smith interview; Whatley interview.

30. In addition to Crampton Harris' own vague, but corroborating recollection, circumstantial evidence vouches for Black's misunderstanding of the identity of the defendant. In the city directory, "Rev. H. M. Stevenson" is listed as minister of West End Methodist Church. There are, in fact, three listings for residents named "Rev. Stevenson." "Edwin R. Stephenson" is not listed as minister of any church in the directory, and his personal listing shows no occupation and does not provide him with a title of "Rev." (as it does for the three "Rev. Stevensons"), *Birmingham City Directory, 1920-21,* 161-165, 1509, 1511. Almost a week after the killing,

the editor of the *Labor Advocate* was unfamiliar with the accused, whom he identified as "R. E. Stevenson, a preacher of the Methodist Church and a barber by trade"—not as the courthouse's marrying parson. *Labor Advocate*, 20 February 1921. Black's "friendship" with "Brother Stevenson," is evident in later correspondence, Black to Henry M. Stevenson, 24 August 1937, Black Papers; *Birmingham Post*, 12, 13 August 1921; *Birmingham Age-Herald*, 12, 13 August 1921; *Birmingham News*, 12, 13 August 1921.

31. *Birmingham Post*, 13 August 1921; *Birmingham News*, 12, 14 August 1921; *Birmingham Post*, 14-18 August 1921; *Birmingham News*, 13-18 August 1921; G. W. Davis to Black, 1 July 1925, Black Papers; *State of Alabama v. Edwin R. Stephenson*, #1710, Grand Jury Minutes, Fall Term, 1923, 3-7.

32. *State of Alabama v. Edwin R. Stephenson*, #6860 (preliminary hearing), 23 August 1921, Black Papers; *Birmingham Post*, 22-24 August 1921 (carrier and final editions).

33. *Birmingham Post*, 25, 26 August 1921 (final and extra editions); *Birmingham Age-Herald*, 26 August 1921; *Birmingham Post*, 27, 30, 31 August, 2, 3 September 1921 (extra edition).

34. *Birmingham Post*, 7 September 1921; "Collections and Disbursements," Accounts Book, entry for 7 September 1921, Black Papers; *Birmingham Post*, 13 September 1921 (courier edition), 14 September 1921 (final edition), 26 August, 19 September 1921; *Birmingham Age-Herald*, 16 October 1921.

35. *Birmingham Post*, 17, 18 October 1921; *Birmingham News*, 17, 18 October 1921; *Birmingham Age-Herald*, 17, 18 October 1921.

36. *Birmingham Post*, 18 October 1921; *Birmingham Age-Herald*, 18 October 1921. *State of Alabama v. Edwin R. Stephenson*, #1710, Grand Jury Minutes, Fall Term, 1923, 35-36, 49-51; *Birmingham News*, 18 October 1921.

37. *Birmingham Post*, 18 October 1921; *Birmingham Age-Herald*, 18 October 1921; *Birmingham News*, 18 October 1921; *Birmingham Post*, 19 October 1921; *Birmingham Age-Herald*, 19 October 1921; *Birmingham News*, 19 October 1921.

38. *Birmingham Post*, 19 October 1921; *Birmingham Age-Herald*, 19 October 1921; *Birmingham News*, 19 October 1921; *Birmingham*

Age-Herald, 20 October 1921; Stephenson's testimony is composed from the accounts of all three newspapers.

39. *Birmingham Post*, 20, 21 October 1921; *Birmingham Age-Herald*, 20, 21 October 1921; *Birmingham News*, 20, 21 October 1921; William E. Fort to Joseph B. Keenan, 18 October 1937, Black Papers; *Birmingham Post*, 21 October 1921; *Birmingham Age-Herald*, 21 October 1921.

40. *Birmingham Post*, 20, 21 October 1921 (courier and extra editions); *Birmingham Age-Herald*, 20, 21 October 1921; Birmingham Reporter, 29 October 1921; *Birmingham Post*, 8 November 1921.

41. *Birmingham Age-Herald*, 12 October 1921; Tolson, 35; Charles P. Sweeney, "Bigotry Turns to Murder," *Nation*, 31 August 1921, 232; Rose Gibbons Lovett, "Centennial History of St. Paul's Parish, Birmingham, Alabama, 1872-1972," unpublished, 1972, 85, 88; "The Martyrs of the United States of America," 40-41; John Beecher, interview with author, 1976. Coyle's death struck close to home. At the time of Coyle's death, Beecher was a teenager in Birmingham, and his family members of St. Paul's. Beecher's mother wrote about the killing in the *Catholic Monthly*, September 1921, and compiled a book of Coyle's poetry in 1922 (Lovett, 78). John Beecher's poem, *Alter Christus*, is his version of Coyle's death and the community's cruel acceptance of it (John Beecher, *To Live and Die in Dixie*, Birmingham, 1966, 47-49.) *Pittsburgh Post-Gazette*, 29 September 1937, 6 August 1949. Ray Sprigle's 1937 article in the Pittsburgh paper documents that only one juror and one witness had Klan affiliations several years after the trial; however, by 1949 he translates these Klan connections into a "jury packed with Klansmen." These conclusions about a Klan-controlled trial have been accepted to differing degree by most of Black's biographers. See Hamilton, *Hugo Black: The Alabama Years*, 93; Dunne, 103-04; and Newman, 83, 86-87, who repeats almost every claim of Klan involvement as factual.

42. Hamilton, *Hugo Black: The Alabama Years*, 93, footnote 66; William Robert Snell, "The Ku Klux Klan in Jefferson County, Alabama, 1916-1930," master's thesis, Samford University, 1967, 28, footnote 15; James Esdale, interview with Charles Morgan, Jr., 1971; *Pittsburgh Post-Gazette*, 29 September 1937. In

Morgan's Esdale interview, the former cyclops claimed first that the grand jury foreman was a Kluxer but changed the story afterwards. Also Esdale claimed he "set up the trial" by allowing Black to compare the jury lists with Klan lists (Newman, 86) and in 1937 he was apparently the source for the rumor that Black repeated a Klan oath in his argument to the jury (*Alabama Magazine*, 13 October 1937). There is no circumstantial or corroborating evidence for these claims. The *Post Gazette* story, however, provides an opportunity to measure Esdale's veracity. The article quotes unnamed "Klan officials in 1921" (Esdale was the reporter's prime source) who stated that the Klan did not pay lawyers for defending Stephenson because Black volunteered his legal services to get free, valuable publicity. Others claim that the Klan raised the money to pay Black (Glenn Feldman, *Politics, Society, and the Klan in Alabama, 1915-1949*, Tuscaloosa, 1999, 67). In fact, Black was paid one thousand dollars ("Money Ledger" in accounts books, Box #502, Black Papers)—and not by the Klan but by an ad hoc "defense committee" that possessed no large treasury from growing Ku Klux membership dues. The committee had to go out of town collecting small contributions to pay Black's fee (*Birmingham Post*, 24 September 1921, carrier edition).

43. The counting of Kluxer connections is a misguided, misleading exercise for evidencing Klan involvement or control in a trial. For example, more Masons were probably connected to this trial than Kluxers, but it makes no sense to suggest that the Masons, who also were anti-Catholic, controlled the Stephenson trial. Similarly, despite a general history of Klan illegality, no evidence suggests that in 1921 most Kluxers in Birmingham were willing to ignore their lawful duty in a courtroom. Perhaps, in the minds of some citizens distressed by the Stephenson verdict, the coincidence of national exposes about Klan violence and misdeeds before and during the trial co-mingled with local developments to suggest a cause and an effect in the Stephenson trial. The *New York World* ran a syndicated series of exposes on the Klan in September 1921, and Congressional hearings on Kluxers were held in Washington during the time of the Stephenson trial. Birmingham newspapers covered extensively both events. The *World,* however, revealed no Klan violence in Alabama (Berman, 17, footnote #56) and

there were only three or four instances of floggings in Birmingham and Alabama attributed to Kluxers in 1921 (See Hamilton, *Hugo Black: The Alabama Years*, 84, Snell, "The Ku Klux Klan in Jefferson County, Alabama, 1916-1930," 19-25). In fact, on the day Stephenson shot Father Coyle, *Birmingham Age-Herald's* editor challenged allegations that the Klan was responsible for lawlessness, including Birmingham's spat of recent floggings (*Birmingham Age-Herald*, 11 August 1921).

44. See *Birmingham Age-Herald*, 26, 28 January 1921, for estimate of Klan membership, which Klan officials tended to exaggerate. Both Ruth Stephenson and Roy Percy named the True Americans, not the Klan, as the organization involved in the trial. The defeat of anti-Catholic incumbents at the polls when the trial began illustrates a lack of extensive influence by T. A.s and Kluxers in 1921 (*Birmingham Age-Herald,* 12, 18 October 1921; *Birmingham Post*, 18 October 1921; Harris, *Political Power in Birmingham*, 86). Another instructive indication of the Klan's lack of community strength is found in Thomas Parke's diary where he recounts the Klan's difficulties in getting its newspaper, "The Search Light," into the Birmingham Public Library in late 1921 (entry for 1 September 1921).

45. In recollections, a Birmingham reporter who covered the trial considered inept prosecution the most decisive factor (Hamilton, *Hugo Black: The Alabama Years*, 92-93). It was also Black's own opinion as to why he won the case (Frank, 36). In 1937, Judge Fort agreed, welcoming a careful scrutiny of the trial, especially "the case of the *State* against *Stephenson*" (Fort memorandum to Joseph B. Keenan, 19 October 1937, Black Papers). Certainly, at least one reporter thought Tate did very little to dislodge sympathy for Stephenson after his testimony (*Birmingham Post*, 20 October 1921). Tate's conduct six months later, after the county's health officer was kidnapped and flogged, raise questions about the prosecutor's motives and methods in the Stephenson trial. Before a grand jury in 1922, Dr. J. D. Dowling testified that he did not see his floggers. He only heard their voices. Solicitor Tate wanted to know if he smelled them. "These Italians always have an odor about them, Doctor," Tate said, "did you smell that?" The question arises: did Tate associate Father Coyle with smelly

Italians, most of whom were Catholics? At trial, Dowling testified that Solicitor Tate had instructed him prior to appearing before the grand jury not to "go into" his own suspicions about who flogged him. By following Tate's advice, Dowling's credibility was seriously weakened when he testified that he suspected soon after the incident that the accused had flogged him. The defense showed that he told the grand jury that he had no idea who committed the crime (*Birmingham News*, 30 May 1923; *Birmingham Age-Herald*, 30 May 1923). In both the Dowling case and Coyle case, it is difficult to determine whether prejudice or incompetence ruled Tate's conduct.

46. Paul M. Pruitt, Jr., "Private Tragedy, Public Shame," *Alabama Heritage*, Fall, 1993, 33-37. As to Black's suspicions of Catholicism (Black Jr., 176), they did not lessen admiration of individual friends like Judge William Grubb or Dr. Charles Whelan, members of St. Paul's ("Parishioners Rolls, 1908," St. Paul Cathedral, 43-53, Birmingham Public Library Archives); also see Black to Mrs. Charles Whelan, 17 February 1964, Black Papers. As to Black's use of Gussman's appearance in the courtroom, it was quite relevant to the factual and legal questions, unlike the use of Joseph Sorsby, the United Mine Worker's black vice-president at the trial of soldiers accused of killing Willie Baird in January 1921. The term "fuzzy-necked" married the sentiments of "redneck" and "lint head" to poor, working whites who weren't in the fields or mills. It was explained first to the author as a boy by his maternal grandfather who described it as a way of "throwing off on a man too poor to get a barber's cut" and considered too slovenly to care about clipping his neck hairs. Tate's use of the term was especially evocative for a defendant who as an itinerant worker continued to work as a barber on weekends. Perhaps, that fact recalled the term to the prosecutor. At bottom, most treatments of the Stephenson trial possess a basic assumption that the Klan must have been involved in the trial because their involvement is the best or only way deep religious or racial prejudice could have influenced the trial. Yet, if there was such decisive prejudice, it would have more likely come from deep, wide-ranging religious hostility that existed in Birmingham throughout the "ranks of citizenry" (*Birmingham News*, 12 August 1921; Irving Engel, interview by Charles Morgan, Jr., 1970; *Parke Diary*, entry for 12

August 1921; also, see generally, Wayne Flynt, "Religion in the Urban South: the Divided Mind of Birmingham, 1900-1930," *Alabama Review*, April 1977, 109-130).

CHAPTER 9

1. *Birmingham Age-Herald*, 22, 26, 27 October 1921; *Birmingham Post*, 26, 28 October 1921; *Birmingham News* 26 October 1921; *New York Times* 26-28 October 1921; Engel interview; Jacquelyn M. Diener, "President Warren G. Harding's Birmingham Address," *Journal of the Alabama Academy of Science*, no.1, 1972, 63-71; *Negroes in the United States, 1920-32*, 55, 291, 303, 517; Harris, *Political Power in Birmingham*, 33-34; Monroe N. Work, *Negro Yearbook, 1921-22*, 47-51; Cooper, Jr., 369-374; Bond, 242-243; *Atlanta Constitution*, 27, 28 October 1921 (After Birmingham, Harding spoke in downtown Atlanta in the shadow of the Henry Grady statue and invoked his 1886 speech as "the most famous oration" of his day which the President read with a "thrill" as a young man.); Wyn Craig Wade, *The Fiery Cross, the Ku Klux Klan in America*, New York, 1987, 165; Eugene P. Trani and David L. Wilson, *The Presidency of Warren G. Harding*, Topeka, Kansas, 1977, 104. Even after Harding's unexpected death in office, rumors of his Kluxer connections persisted among black leaders. See Kelly Miller to James Weldon Johnson, 26 August 1024, NAACP Papers; *Birmingham Age-Herald*, 29 October 1921; David Chalmers, *Hooded Americanism*, New York, 1981, 35-38; Elizabeth Boner Clark, "The Abolition of the Convict Lease System in Alabama, 1913-1928," master's thesis, University of Alabama, 1949, 82-84; Harris, *Political Power in Birmingham*, 204-205; *Ex parte Brown*, 91 So. 306, 1921.

2. "Money Ledger" in accounts books, Box #502, Black Papers; Ex parte Brown, 6 Div. 502, Alabama Supreme Court Records; *Clinton Mining Co. v. Bradford*, 69 So. 4, 1915, 76 So. 74, 1917; *Clinton Mining Co. v. Bradford*, Oct. Term, 1916-17, 6th Div., Alabama Supreme Court Records; *Woodward Iron Co. v. Thompson*, 88 So. 438, 1921, 95 So. 270, 1923; *Woodward Iron Co. v. Thompson*, 6th Div. 664, Alabama Supreme Court Records.

3. Jack Kytle, "I'm Allus Hongry," in James Seay Brown, ed., *Up Before Daylight: Life Histories from the Alabama Writers Project, 1938-1939*, Tuscaloosa, 1982, 126; Armes, 149-151,

270-71; letters of 1913 and 10 January 1914 to John P. White from J. R. Kennamer, *et. al.* as noted in Phillip Taft Papers, Birmingham Public Library Archives; Engel interview; "Cash Book Report, September, 1917," receipts from convict leasing, Henderson Papers; complaint in circuit court, Shelby County, 16 February 1921, Black to Frank H. Mortimer, 6 October 1921, Henry Lewis affidavit, 14 November 1921, Judgment, 29 November 1921, *Lewis v. Montevallo Mining Co.,* U.S.D.C., Northern District of Alabama, National Archives, Atlanta Region.

4. Milfred C. Fierce, *Slavery Revisited: Blacks and the Southern Convict Lease System, 1865-1933,* New York, 1994, 216-17, where the author notes that despite a 1917 state law banning convict leasing, North Carolina prison officials engaged in informal leasing of convicts until 1933; Edward L. Ayres, *Vengeance and Justice: Crime and Punishment in the 19th Century South,* Oxford, 1984, 185-222; Dan T. Carter, "Prisons, Politics and Business: The Convict Lease System in the Post-Civil War South," master's thesis, University of Wisconsin, 1964, 67-68, 78; Allen J. Going, *Bourbon Democrat in Alabama, 1874-1890,* University of Alabama, 1951, 1992, 170-190; Engel interview; *Proceedings of the National Prison Association, 1888,* Boston, 1888, 83-84; *Proceedings of the National Prison Association 1889,* Nashville, 1889, 115-116, 121-122; *Proceedings of the National Prison Association 1890,* Cincinnati, 1890, 108-116; C. Vann Woodward, *Origins of the New South,* 212-215; Robert J. Norrell, *James Bowron: The Autobiography of a New South Industrialist,* University of North Carolina, 1991, 101-03; Hackney, *Populism to Progressivism in Alabama,* 72-74, 144-145; Albert B. Moore, 810-815; H.W. Perry to Thomas G. Jones, 9 June 1893, Jones Papers; David M. Oshinsky, *Worst Than Slavery,* Free Press, 1996, 76-81; Candace Waid, "Julia Tutwiler: in the Vision of Her Time, 1841-1916," Women's Studies paper, University of Alabama, 1970, unpublished, 46-50, in possession of author; *Report of the State Auditor, 1907,* 58-59, 102-03; W. A. Burns to B. B. Comer, 29 August 1908, Comer Papers; Alex Lichtenstein, *Twice the Work of Free Labor,* New York, 1996, 90-104.

5. Clark, 25-70; "Movement to Take Convicts from Mines is Launched," *Birmingham News* clip, undated, Hugh D. Merrill to Frank S. White, 9 June 1913, Julia S. Tutwiler to Frank White, 13 June 1913, LWVP, Birmingham Public Library Archives; William F. Drummond, "Utilization of Convict Labor in the South," master's thesis, University of Alabama, 1933, 82; "Message of Gov. Emmet O'Neal," *General Laws of the Legislature of Alabama, 1915 Session,* ix-xi, xxxvi; "Message of Gov. Charles Henderson," *General Laws of the Legislature of Alabama, 1915 Session,* clxxvi; *Journal of the House of Representatives of Alabama, 1915 Session,* 1613-1660; *Journal of the Senate of Alabama, 1915 Session,* 3583-3584; *Quadrennial Report of the Board of Inspectors of Convicts, 1914-1918,* 32-41, 50-90; *Report of the State Auditor, 1916,* 21-23, 44-45; *Advance,* 15 March 1916; J. W. McQueen to and from Charles Henderson, 17, 19 October 1917, Henderson Papers.

6. *Journal of the House of Representatives of Alabama, 1919 Session,* 848-880; *Journal of the Senate of Alabama, 1919 Session,* 2060; *General and Local Laws of the Legislature of Alabama, Special 1919 Session,* 522-523; "Message of Gov. Thomas E. Kilby," Ibid., l-li, lxxxiv-lxxxvi; Clark, 71-84; *Report of the State Auditor, 1920,* 25-28; *Quadrennial Report of the Board of Control and Economy, Convict Department, 1919-1922,* 21-27; also see *Quadrennial Report of the Board of Administration, 1922-1926,* 16, 23-24, 46-73. The state's gross income from convicts was partially off-set by expenses for prisoners' upkeep and leasing. Statistics in the text are based on "gross receipts," not "net income" or profit, since every source of government revenue was lessened by disbursements for collection, generation, and maintenance. In fact, relative little money of the convict department's expenses was spent on prisoners. Between 1919-1922, for example, the Aldrich mine generated 952,000 dollars in state receipts and only 132,000 dollars were spent on prisoners' food, clothing, medical care, and "discharge money" (less than 3,000 dollars for this cost). Still, if calculated according to "net income," convict leasing generated in 1920 approximately one million dollars, the state's second largest source of revenue. As the "businessman governor," Thomas Kilby captured the role of the convict department when he renamed its supervisory agency the *Board of Control and Economy,* an enterprise whose *control* of black labor built Alabama's *economy* through generating salaries, jobs, and

revenues for the state and fueling private profits for the coal industry.

7. *Annual Report of the Coal Mines of Alabama, 1923,* 70-72; *Annual Report of Coal Mines, 1924,* 71-73; Emily Owen, "The Career of Thomas E. Kilby in Local and State Politics," master's thesis, University of Alabama, 1942, 38-54, 61-85; *Report of the State Auditor, 1920,* 25-28; tax calculations from Howard W. Odum, *Southern Regions of the United States,* Chapel Hill, 1936, 122, 124, 128; *Coal Mine Fatalities in the United States,* U.S. Bureau of Mines, 1920 and 1922; Forrest T. Moyer, G. D. Jones, and V. E. Wrenn, *Injury Experience in Coal Mining,1948,* 98-99; Flynt, *Poor but Proud,* 131, 267-268; Section 59 of *Rules and Regulations for Government of Convicts* (Board of Inspectors of Convicts, Montgomery, 1913), 17; Jack Kytle, "A Dead Convict Don't Cost Nothin'," in *Up Before Daylight,* 110-112. The WPA oral history incorrectly refers to "Red Diamond" as the mining company where the guard worked. That was the name of a popular coffee first sold in Alabama in 1906. "Red Feather Coal Co." is the mining company which began leasing convict labor in 1909 for approximately ten years. See Alabama's *State Auditor Reports,* beginning in 1909 and "Cash Box Report, September 1917," Henderson Papers.

8. *Birmingham Age-Herald,* 26, 27 January, 5-7, 10, 12, 15 February 1922; Justin Fuller, "Henry F. DeBardeleben, Industrialist of the New South," *Alabama Review,* January 1986, 9-12; Kilby to Nesbit, 2 January 1922, transcript of "Proceedings at the First Meeting of Creditors," In re: *Matter of Montevallo Mining Co,* No.18764, National Archives, Atlanta Region.

9. *Birmingham Age-Herald,* 3, 16 February, 4-5, 8 March, 25 April, 18 July 1922; *State of Alabama v. Montevallo Mining Co., 278 F. 989,* 1922, 990-91 (Black's petition was heard by U.S. District Judge Henry Clayton of Montgomery apparently because Judge W. I. Grubb was not in Birmingham at the time.); contract between David Roberts, Jr. and Thomas Kilby, 28 May 1922, Kilby Papers; *Annual Report of Coal Mines, 1923,* 70-72; Emily Owen, 65; Flynt, *Poor But Proud,* 268.

10. *Birmingham Age-Herald,* 29-31 December 1921, 24 February, 10, 21-31 May 1922; Hamilton, *Hugo Black: The Alabama Years,* 95-96; Snell, "The Ku Klux Klan in Jefferson

County, Alabama, 1916-1930," 31-35.

11. *Birmingham Age-Herald,* 18 May, 7, 8, 11, 17, 20-22, 29 June, 11 July 1922; Feldman, *From Demagogue to Dixiecrat,* 68-71. Historians have inadvertently misconstrued Black's defense of Birmingham's commissioners by portraying this work as a defense of their failure to take action against floggings, by characterizing the commission as beholding to the Klan for their prior election, or by referring to Black at this time as a "Ku Klux Klan attorney." The grand jury report and news coverage of the indictments show, however, that impeachment charges related only to corruption. The commissioners, moreover, were moderate candidates in the October 1921 election when they defeated anti-Catholic incumbents supported openly by True Americans. No available evidence shows that Black was retained by or associated with the Klan in 1922. Cf. Hamilton, *Hugo Black: The Alabama Years,* 96; Snell, "The Ku Klux Klan in Jefferson County, Alabama, 1916-1930," 40; Feldman, *From Demagogue to Dixiecrat,* 70-71.

12. *Parke Diary,* entries for 21, 23-27 May 1922; *Birmingham Age-Herald,* 7, 8, 11 June 1922; *Birmingham Reporter,* 27 May 1922.

13. *Birmingham Age-Herald,* 7, 13, 22, 30 August, 1, 3, 5 September 1922; Snell, "The Ku Klux Klan in Jefferson County, Alabama, 1916-1930," 43-44; *Birmingham Age-Herald,* 3 July, 8, 18, 29, 30 August, 8 September 1922, 15 September 1922; Gross, 149-165. In 1921, like others across America, Alabama factory workers saw real, yearly earnings decline from 555 dollars in 1919 to 416 dollars, the lowest recorded earnings since 1899 (Paul F. Brissenden, *Earnings of Factory Workers, 1899 to 1927,* Bureau of the Census, 1929, 150.); *Birmingham Age-Herald,* 10, 25 December 1921, 1, 13, 14 January, 3, 5, 16 February, 28 June 1922.

14. *Birmingham Age-Herald,* 1 February, 1 May 1920, 26 January, 2, 14, 16 February, 26 April, 8 June 1922; Emily Owen, 85-86; *Birmingham Age-Herald,* 16 January, 25, 26 April 1922; Armes, 490; Helen Bethea, *The Hillman Hospital: A Story of the Growth and Development of the First Hospital in Birmingham,* Birmingham, 1928, 22-24, 54-59; concern about Hillman as city's charity hospital persisted (*Birmingham News,* 29 March 1924).

15. Roy A. Haynes (Commissioner of Pro-

hibition) from O. D. Street, 6 July 1923, O. D. Street Papers, University of Alabama Library (hereafter Street Papers); Arthur F. Howington, "John Barley Corn Subdued: The Enforcement of Prohibition in Alabama," *Alabama Review,* July 1970, 212-218; Brownell, 38-39; Nancy MacLean, *Behind the Mask of Chivalry: The Making of the Second Ku Klux Klan,* New York, 1994, 40-41; McKiven, 141-145; *Birmingham News,* 10 January, 10 August 1922; *Birmingham Age-Herald,* 31 December 1921, 1, 13, 26 January, 3 February, 4 April, 19, 21 23 May 1922; Flynt, *Poor But Proud,* 269; Feldman, *From Demagogue to Dixiecrat,* 69-70; Birmingham's white voters also defeated a bond issue for building and renovating public schools; *Parke Diary,* entry for 28 January 1922.

16. *Birmingham Age-Herald,* 18 June, 7 July 1922; *Birmingham Reporter,* 25 February 1922; *Birmingham Age-Herald,* 26-29 January 8 March 1922, 30 May 1923, 29 February, 25 May 1924; *Birmingham News,* 2 March 1924; *Birmingham Reporter,* 4 February, 8 April 1922; Brownell, 29-30.

17. Esdale interview; *Birmingham Age-Herald,* 28 January, 4 April 1922; Snell, "The Ku Klux Klan in Jefferson County, Alabama, 1916-1930," 33; *Birmingham News,* 16 January 1922; *Birmingham Age-Herald* 18 April 1920, 15 January 1922; The Klan elsewhere arose from, rather than created, various problems of economic hard times, crime, social division, fears, and bigotry. See Shawn Lay, ed., *The Invisible Empire in the West: Towards a New Historical Appraisal of the Ku Klux Klan of the 1920s,* Chicago, 1992, 217-219; Kathleen M. Blee, *Women of the Klan: Racism and Gender in the 1920s,* Berkeley, 1991, 17-19; Robert A. Goldberg, *Hooded Empire,* Chicago, 1981, 164-168; William D. Jenkins, *Steel Valley Klan: The Ku Klux Klan in Ohio's Mahoning Valley,* Kent, Ohio, 1990, 162-165. David I. Kertzer, *Ritual, Politics, and* Power, New Haven, 1988, 69; Parke *Diary,* entry of 18 December 1920; McKiven, 164; Snell, "The Ku Klux Klan in Jefferson County, Alabama, 1916-1930," 45-46.

18. *Birmingham Age-Herald,* 23 February 1922; *Montgomery Advertiser,* 21 May 1924, Pythian supplement; Frank, 36; W.M. Franklin to and from Black, 30 September 1952, 28 October 1952, Black Papers; Max Lerner, "Hugo Black, a Personal History," 307-309;

Dunne, 113-14; Cliff Durr interview; Black to Frank H. Mortimer, 6 October 1921, Black Papers; *Riddle et al. v. U.S.* 279 F. 216, 1922; *Birmingham Age-Herald,* 22 March 1921, 13 November 1921; Roderick Beddow, Sr., interview with Charles Morgan, Jr., 1970; *Piggly-Wiggly Alabama Co. v. Rickles,* 103 So. 860, 1925; *Norwood Transportation Co. v. Crossett,* 92 So. 461, 1922; *Crosby v. Nunnally Co.,* 95 So. 343, 1923; *Whistle Bottling Co. v. Searson,* 92 So. 657, 1922; *United States Fidelity and Guaranty Co. v. Millonas,* 89 So. 732, 1921, 738; *Southern Railway Co. v. Dickson,* 100 So. 665, 1924, 672; *Whitman's Fifth Ave. Garage Co. v. Ricks,* 101 So. 53, 1924, 55.

19. Black, Jr., 41-43, 173; Newman, 67; *Birmingham City Directory, 1923,* 126, 409, 616; Virginia and Cliff Durr interview; financial records, account books, Black Papers; Davis, 11-12, 15-16, 47-48, 58.

20. *New York Times,* 26 September 1971; Black and Black, 33, 70; Newman, 98; John Moffatt Mecklin, *The Ku Klux Klan: A Study of the American Mind,* New York, 1924, 236; Jerome A. Cooper, "Mr. Justice Black of Alabama," *The Alabama Lawyer,* January, 1972, 18; William F. Holmes, "Moonshiners and Whitecaps in Alabama, 1893, "*Alabama Review,* January, 1981, 41; *Parke Diary,* entry for 1 June 1923; Pruden, 105-107; *Birmingham Age-Herald,* 28, 29, 30, 31 May 1922, 1, 2 June 1923; *Birmingham News,* 29, 30 May, 1 June 1923; see footnote #45 of chapter 8 for complications in the Dowling trial; B. L. Wyman to W. W. Brandon, 4 May 1923, Harwell Davis to B. L. Wyman, 10 May 1923, Harwell Davis to and from Black, 10, 14 May 1923, Harwell Davis Papers, Alabama Department of Archives and History (hereafter Davis papers); Birmingham Bar Association executive committee to Harwell Davis, 11 June 1923, Jim Davis to Harwell Davis, 11 June 1923, Davis Papers. Part of the difficulty in the Dowling case may have been the victim's reputation for "Kaiser-like" conduct. In February 1921, Dowling was found guilty of false imprisonment in city court because he had two women "suspected of social diseases" locked up in the city jail rather than confined in a hospital or detention home (*Birmingham Age-Herald,* 5 February 1921). About the same time, on another matter, Thomas Parke complained that Dowling did whatever he pleased and "was answerable" almost to no one (*Parke*

Diary, entry for 16 February 1921); Black and Black, 70; Anonymous Source #2, interview with author, 1974 (the interviewee lived near Black in 1923); Davis interview; *Birmingham Age-Herald*, 2 August 1922; Newman, 97-98.

21. Morris Abram, interview with Charles Morgan, Jr., 1971; Brandt Ayres, interview with author, 1987; Huff interview, Black Papers; Newman, 99; Black and Black, 70; *Birmingham Age-Herald*, 18-20 October 1921; *Birmingham Reporter*, 22 October 1921; *Birmingham Age-Herald*, 10-12 August 1922, 21, 22 May 1923; *Birmingham News*, 11 August 1922; William R. Snell, "Fiery Crosses in the Roaring Twenties: Activities of the Revised Klan in Alabama, 1915-1930," *Alabama Review*, October 1970, 263-64; *Montgomery Advertiser*, 21 May 1923, 28 June 1924; Jelks Cabaniss to Forney Johnston, 6 September 1923, Forney Johnston to R. B. Evins, undated, L. J. Buggs to R. B. Evins, 16 August 1924, Underwood Papers; *New York Times*, 16 November 1923; Walter White to and from W. G. Porter, 12, 16 March, 4 October 1922, "Ku Klux Klan" flyer (promising an induction of "5000 candidates" when in fact 700 were inducted in late 1922), undated, circa. 1922, NAACP Papers; *New York Times*, 26 September 1971; Berman, 16-17 including footnote 56; Newman, 97 including text footnote; Durr, *Outside the Magic Circle*, 43; Fred Rodell, "Justice Hugo Black," *American Mercury*, August 1944, 137-141.

22. *New York Times*, 26 September, 1971; see Sheldon Hackney, "The Clay County Origins of Mr. Justice Black: The Populist as Insider," *Alabama Law Review*, 839-840; *Birmingham Age-Herald*, 8 July 1922; Snell, "The Ku Klux Klan in Jefferson County, Alabama, 1916-1930," 20, 24, 42-43; Verner Max ("Vern") Scott, "Why the 1920's Ku Klux Klan?" *Talladega County Historical Association Newsletter*, January 1989, 16 of insert; Louis M. Spaulding to James Weldon Johnson, 25 September 1921, NAACP Papers; see more generally, Kenneth T. Jackson, *The Ku Klux Klan in the City*, 1915-1930, New York, 1967, 18-19; MacLean, 54-62; Leonard J. Moore, "Historical Interpretations of the 1920s Klan: The Traditional View and the Populist Revision," *Journal of Social History*, vol. 24, no. 2, 1990, 350-52; Lay, 219; *Parke Diary*, entry for 5 July 1923.

23. Identification of sources and circum-stances of violence is based on a comparative review and study of incidents reported by Birmingham newspapers during 1922 and 1923 (using primarily the *Birmingham Age Herald* and *Birmingham Reporter*), Snell, "The Ku Klux Klan in Jefferson County, Alabama, 1916-1930" (a primary source for previous scholarly assessments of Klan violence for these years in Birmingham), Gross, "Strikes in Coal, Steel, and Railroad Industries in Birmingham from 1918 to 1922," and Feldman, *Politics, Society, and the Klan in Alabama*. My assessment fits into the broader, mixed pattern of Klan violence during this era as measured by recent scholarship and the reevaluation of prior assumptions about the extent and attribution of Klan violence. See Leonard Moore, 346-52, and Shawn Lay, 219. Even Oscar Underwood admitted privately that "a great many good people belong to the Ku Klux Klan," Underwood to C. A. Beasley, 18 October 1923, Underwood Papers; Mark H. Elovitz, *A Century of Jewish Life in Dixie: The Birmingham Experience*, Tuscaloosa, 1974, 84-97; *The Italians: From Bisacquiro to Birmingham*, booklet, Birmingfind, undated; Mark Cowett, *Birmingham's Rabbi: Morris Newfield and Alabama, 1895-1940*, Tuscaloosa, 1986, 137.

24. Harold Joseph Goldstein, "Labor Unrest in the Birmingham District, 1871-1894," master's thesis, University of Alabama, 1951, 142-143; Ward and Rogers, 13-28; Gross, 63-84; Monroe W. Work, *Negro Year Book, 1921-22*, Tuskegee, 1922, 355-359; *Historical Statistics of the United States: Colonial Times to 1970, Part 1*, Bureau of the Census, 1975, 442; for a helpful, general perspective, see David Montgomery, "Violence and the Struggle for Unions in the South, 1880-1930," in Merle Black and J. S. Reed (eds.), *Perspectives on the American South: An Annual Review of Society, Politics and Culture*, vol. I, New York, 1981, 35-47. It is worthwhile to compare and ponder the numbers of lynching deaths and convict miners' deaths in Alabama over time. From 1889 to 1923, Alabama had roughly 340 reported lynching deaths. Thirty-seven of them took place from 1915-1923. Alabama, however, had no less than four hundred reported convict deaths from 1915 to 1923, more than all the state's lynchings since 1889. *Negroes in the United States, 1920-32*, 291, 303.

25. *Parke Diary*, entries for 23 May, 31

July 1923; A. W. Smith to Harwell Davis, 19 March 1923, Davis Papers; *Labor Advocate*, 29 May 1920; *New York Times*, 30 October 1923. In 1922-23, 1925-1926, and 1928, Pulitzer prizes went to newspapers, reporters, or editorial writers exposing or condemning the Klan (*The New York Times Almanac 2000*, New York, 1999, 848, 851); *New York Times*, 26 September 1971.

26. *New York Times*, 26 September 1971; Engel interview; Snell, "The Ku Klux Klan in Jefferson County, Alabama, 1916-1930," 53-55; *Parke Diary*, entry of 26 May 1923; "Semi-Monthly Bulletin, Province No.2" (KKK), Bibb Graves Vertical Files, Alabama Department of Archives and History; "TWK Monthly," February 1925, Birmingham Public Library Archives; *Parke Diary*, entry of 21 August 1917.

27. *New York Times*, 26 September 1971; Newman, 98; Ayres interview; Virginia Foster Durr, *Outside the Magic Circle*, 41; *Birmingham Post*, 9 April 1925; Henry M. Edmunds, *A Parson's Notebook*, Birmingham, 1961, 278; Wyatt-Brown, 236; Vern Scott to and from Black, 1, 4 March 1965, Black Papers.

28. *Birmingham Reporter*, 26 February 1921, 25 February, 1 April 1922, 6 January, 2 June 1923; *Quadrennial Report of the Board of Administration, 1922-1926*, 16, 23-24, 46-73; Snell, "The Ku Klux Klan in Jefferson County, Alabama, 1916-1930," 16-66; *Parke Diary*, entry of 15 April, 1923. For a careful understanding of the moral and practical roles of convict leasing in a society, see J. Mancini, *One Dies, Get Another: Convict Leasing in the American South, 1866-1928*, Columbia, SC, 1996, 32-38; *Parke Diary*, entry of 11 September 1923.

29. DuBois, *Black Reconstruction in America*, 669-700; Fierce, 239-241; Peter Lassman and Ronald Speirs, eds., *Weber: Political Writings*, Cambridge, 1994, 354-369; Newman, 96 (sister's quote); New York Times, 26 September 1971 (first KKK meeting); Marcus Tullius Cicero, Hubert M. Poteat (tr.), *Brutus. On the Nature of Gods. On Divination. On Duties*, Chicago, 1950, 602 and inside back-cover notations, Black Books; Cliff Durr interview; *Birmingham Age-Herald*, 12 September 1923; Snell, "The Ku Klux Klan in Jefferson County, Alabama, 1916-1930," 58-60.

30. *Henry Lewis v. David Roberts, Jr.*, Case No. 4174, transcript of record, motions, briefs, supplemental briefs, and miscellaneous papers of Hugo Black, Black and Harris, and W. H. Sadler, Jr., Files of the United States Circuit Court of Appeals for the Fifth Circuit, National Archives, Fort Worth Region; *State of Alabama v. Montevallo Mining Co.*, 278 F. 989, 1922, 990; Clark, 86-93; *Quadrennial Report of the Board of Inspectors of Convicts, 1922-1926*, 44; *Birmingham Age-Herald*, 26 July 1923; "Minutes, May 29,1923," Mary Black to Judge Fort, 8 July 1923, Roy L. Nolen to Irving M. Engel, 24 May 1923, William C. Davis to Amelia W. Fisk, 20 June 1923, Mrs. L. D. Mitchell to Mrs. Fisk, 19 July 1923, "Mass Meeting, Community Theatre, Thursday Evening, July 12th dodger ("When the Steamroller Rolled . . . ,"), undated, Mrs. Brenton K. Fisk to J. Sid Wood, 1 September 1923, League of Women Voters Papers, Birmingham Public Library Archives (hereafter League Papers); 1 July 1923, *Birmingham Post; Journal of the Senate, 1923*, 680; *Acts of Alabama, 1923*, 369-70.

31. David Roberts, Jr. to W. W. Brandon, 31 August 1923, W. W. Brandon Papers, Alabama Department of Archives and History (hereafter Brandon Papers); Clark, 94-96; *Birmingham Age-Herald*, 18 September 1923; *Birmingham News*, 20 September 1923; "Minutes," 31 October 1923, Mrs. Brenton K. Fisk to Milton Fies, 7 November 1923, Mrs. Brenton K. Fisk to Hugo Black, 7 November 1923, League Papers; *In re: Montevallo Mining Co.* 294 F. 171, 1923.

32. Huff interview, Black Papers (Note: Black does *not* cite any opinion by Judge Sanford as a district court judge in any of his briefs filed with the various federal courts in this case, and the author has been unable to locate any such reported opinion by Sanford about indigent access to the courts. It is possible that Black discovered an unpublished opinion by Sanford which another lawyer could have brought to his attention.); David Burner, "Edward Terry Sanford," in Leon Friedman and Fred L. Israel, eds., *The Justices of the United States Supreme Court 1789-1978*, vol. III, New York, 1980, 2203-2209; Crampton Harris to clerk of the Supreme Court of the United States, 7 December 1923, *Lewis v. Roberts*, No. 284, Supreme Court of the United States Case Files, National Archives (hereafter U.S. Supreme Court Case Files); "bill of costs,"

Lewis v. Montevallo Mining Co., U.S. District Court for North Alabama, National Archives, Atlanta Region; "bill of costs," Henry Lewis v. David Roberts, *Jr.,* Case No. 4174, United States Circuit Court of Appeals for the Fifth Circuit, National Archives, Fort Worth Region; "Montevallo Mine Cases," Account Books, Huff interview, Black Papers; Wm. R. Stansbury to Crampton Harris, 10 December 1923, *Lewis v. Roberts,* No. 284, U.S. Supreme Court Case Files; Ben C. Duniway, "The Poor Man in the Federal Courts," *Stanford Law Review,* June, 1966, 1271-1276, 1277-1280.

33. *Birmingham Age-Herald,* 28 December 1923; "Motion of Henry Lewis for an order allowing him to petition for a Writ of Certiorari in forma pauperis without a deposit for costs and without printed records," "Affidavit of Henry Lewis," Lewis v. Roberts, No. 284, U.S. Supreme Court Case Files; Huff interview, Black Papers; Irving Dilliard, "Introduction," in *One Man's Stand for Freedom: Mr. Justice Black and the Bill of Rights a Collection of His Supreme Court Opinions* New York, 1963, xxiv-xxv; A. C. Denison to William H. Taft, 11 January 1923, Edward Sanford to and from William Howard Taft, 11 January 1923 (two letters), 14 January 1923, William Howard Taft Papers, Library of Congress; Taft quoted in J. Maguire, "Poverty and Civil Litigation," *Harvard Law Review,* February 1923, 403; collect telegram from Wm. R. Stansbury to Hugo Black, 7 January 1924, U.S. Supreme Court Case Files; Huff interview, Black Papers.

34. *Mobile Register,* 12, 13, 29, 30 January, 7 February 1924; *Birmingham Age-Herald,* 13, 28, 30 January, 7 February 1924; *Birmingham News,* 11, 12, 29, 30 January, 7 February 1924; *Shelby County Reporter,* 7, 14 February 1924; also, see *Birmingham Post,* 23 March 1926.

35. *Birmingham Age-Herald,* 1 March 1924; *Birmingham News,* 26, 29 February, 1 March 1924; *Mobile Register,* 28 February, 1 March 1924; *Birmingham Post,* 1 March 1924; *People's Advocate* (Shelby County), 6 March 1924; "Death Records of State Convicts," *Quadrennial Report of the Board of Administration, 1922-1926,* 65. Black's clients, Adonia Cruseau and John Brown, apparently survived by wit or luck. According to prison records, "Adonia Cruseau" escaped on 26 June 1928, from the state Capitol where he was serving as a trusty for Governor Bibb Graves, who finally took convicts out of

the mines. John Brown also escaped from a road camp on 21 August 1929. Official reports list no date for both men under the column entitled "Recaptured" (*Quadrennial Report of the Board of Administration, 1926-1930,* State of Alabama, 58-59).

CHAPTER 10

1. Samuel P. Brooks, "The Tasks of Good Citizenship," *Democracy in Earnest,* Southern Sociological Congress, 1918, 15, 22; Dunbar Rowland, "Good Citizenship: The First Aim and Object of Education," commencement address, All Saints College, 2 June 1920, 11-13; William J. Bryan, *The First Battle,* Chicago, 1896, 190, 376-77; Grover Cleveland, *Good Citizenship,* Philadelphia, 1908; for other works illuminating the moral character of "good citizenship," see Rev. J.E. Hand, ed., *Good Citizenship,* London, 1899; xii-xx, Walter R. and Francis K. Hepner, *The Good Citizen: A Textbook in Social and Vocational Civics,* Boston, 1924; Hamilton, *Hugo Black: The Alabama Years,* 108 (emphasis added); *Birmingham Age-Herald,* 28 March 1924; *Birmingham News,* 28 March 1924; Matthew 7:12; John 2:14-21. There are only two instances in which the author has discovered Black's use of "best" to describe citizens or people. One is his reference to people who lived in Birmingham during his years there and who were considered at the time to be among its "best citizens." (e.g. Black to Mervyn H. Sterne, 16 March 1971, Black Papers, where Black recalls George Ward as "one of Alabama's *best* and courageous citizens.") Ward's background would fit him as one of the city's "best citizens." The other is a quotation from an unrecorded interview of biographer Roger Newman with Black late in his life (Newman, 98). While the author does not question the essential meaning of Newman's cited quotation, Black's use of the term "best people" to describe Birmingham's Klan members as a group would have been entirely foreign to his hard-earned, meaningful habits of speech and his own particular values.

2. Carl Cramer, *Stars Fell On Alabama,* New York, 1934, 233-235; Writers' Program of the Works Projects Administration; *Alabama: A Guide to the Deep South,* New York, 1941, 206-207; Michael Kenny, *Catholic Culture in Alabama,* New York, 1931, 1-24, 350-359; David Ernest Alsobrook, "Alabama's Port

City: Mobile During the Progressive Era, 1896-1917," Ph.D. dissertation, Auburn University, 1983, 34-38, 72-79, 315-321, 334-336; *Biennial Report of the Attorney General to the Governor of Alabama, 1914-16,* 430-434, 443-445; Sellers, 111, 121.

3. *Register of the Department of Justice,* 1 February 1922, Washington, 1922, 20, 48; Boykin, 61; Wm. H. Armbrecht to Oliver D. Street, 14 October 1925, Street Papers; *Crimson White,* 26 October 1905; Alsobrook, 335; *Nomination of Aubrey Boyles: Hearings before a Subcommittee of the Committee of the Judiciary,* United States Senate, Sixty-Ninth Congress, First Sess., 26, 27, 28 April 1926, Washington, 1926, 112-114, 142; *Birmingham Post,* 31 August, 21, 23 September 1921; Leuchtenburg, 91-94; Boykin to Oliver D. Street, 6 August 1923, Street Papers; Boyles to Willebrandt, 9 December 1922, 7 May 1923, Boykin to Boyles, 10 May 1923, Box 100, Case #6179, Mobile Criminal Cases, RG/21, National Archives, Atlanta Region (hereafter Mobile Criminal Cases) ; Hamilton, *Hugo Black: The Alabama Years,* 108-109; *Mobile Register,* 23 November 1923, 7-9 August 1924; Bob Holcombe to Kilby, 27 September 1920, Kilby Papers.

4. *Birmingham Age-Herald,* 20 December 1923; *Mobile Register,* 27 October 1928; *Nomination of Aubrey Boyles,* 144, 160; Davis interview; Case papers, Case #6180, Mobile Criminal Cases; Dorothy M. Brown, *Mabel Walker Willebrandt: A Study of Power, Loyalty, and Law,* Knoxville, 1984, 49-50, 56-62; *Mobile Register,* 10 August 1924; Sellers, 193-95; Lee N. Allen, "The 1924 Underwood Campaign in Alabama," *Alabama Review,* July 1956, 184; Underwood to Turner, 3 May 1920, Underwood Papers; *Birmingham Age-Herald,* 21, 23 December 1923; *Mobile Register,* 21 December 1923, 7 January 1924; Leuchtenburg, 94; Nicholas Stallworth to Black, 11 June 1926, Black to O. D. Street, 17 July 1929, Horace Turner to Black, 13 June 1925, Black Papers; *Mobile Register,* 6 December 1924.

5. *Mobile Register,* 4-8 April 1924; Tennant S. McWilliams, "The City of Mobile, the South, and Richard V. Taylor," *Alabama Review,* July 1993, 169; Alsobrook, 47, 72, 78-79; *Mobile Register,* 10, 13, 16, 20, 26-29 April 1924; Esdale interview. Esdale remembered that on the Mobile jury "all were in the Klan," a boastful, exaggerated error, as were many of

his memories. Generally, the author relies upon Esdale's memory for information about events that took place—such as this one—when he remembered it without prompting and when circumstantial evidence supports his claims. His recollections are usually considered unreliable in their details whenever Esdale puts himself and the Klan as omnipotent, all-powerful, or at time omniscient, especially when contrary to circumstantial or direct evidence. Newman, 65; indications of Klan status and issues in south Alabama found in *Mobile Register,* 31 December 1923, *Wilcox Progressive Era,* 14 May 1925, L. J. Bugg to R. B. Evins, 16 August 1924, State Democratic Executive Committee Papers; Hamilton, *Hugo Black: The Alabama Years,* 109; *Birmingham News,* 29 April 1924; *The Ku Klux Klan*: Hearings Before the Committee on Rules, House of Representatives, Sixty-Seventh Congress, First Session, Washington, 1921, 96.

6. *Mobile Register,* 29 April, 1-8 May 1924; *Alabama: A Guide to the Deep South,* 213; *Birmingham News,* 29 April 1924; Hamilton, *Hugo Black: The Alabama Years,* 109; *Mobile Register,* 27, 28 April, 2, 4, 9, 10, 11 May 1924 (emphasis added in French exchange); See Brownson Malsch, *"Lone Wolf" Gonzaullas, Texas Ranger,* Norman, OK, 1998; Mark 11:15-27; telegram of Boykin to Daugherty, 19 July 1923, Case #6180, Mobile Criminal Cases; Vernon Patrick, interview with author, 1983; *Montgomery Advertiser,* 10 May 1924.

7. *Mobile Register,* 13-15 May 1924; affidavit of Fred Hudoff, Case #5886, Mobile Criminal Cases; *Mobile Register,* 6 April, 3, 4, 8, 15-17, 20 May 1924; Newman, 64-65; J.L. LeFlore to Roy Wilkins, 12 August 1937, NAACP Papers; "Justice Black" (letter to the editor), American Mercury, April, 1945, 508; Boykin, 62; also see John Bester Robertson, Jr. to Black, 8 August 1926, Black Papers, where Boykin's attorney is described as "frantic" in his fight against Black's election to the U.S. Senate; Davis interview; *Mobile Register,* 22, 23 May, 7, 8, 12 June 1924; see *Ex parte* Young, 209 U.S. 123, 1908; *Mobile Register,* 18, 19, 27 June 1924.

8. *Montgomery Advertiser,* 1 August 1923; Lee N. Allen, "The Underwood Presidential Movement of 1924," doctoral dissertation, University of Pennsylvania, 1955, 37-39, 86-87; James Frank Vickrey, Jr., "A Rhetorical

Analysis of the Issues of the Ku Klux Klan in the Speeches of Senator Oscar W. Underwood in the 1924 Presidential Campaign," master's thesis, Auburn University, 1965, 33-34, 39-43; *Birmingham News,* 29 October 1923; Johnston to Underwood, 10 October 1923, Underwood to J.E. Jeffries, 11 January 1923, Underwood Papers; Johnson, *Oscar W. Underwood,* 386-387; D.K. Springen, "A Rhetorical Analysis of the Speaking of Oscar Underwood in His 1924 Campaign for the Democratic Presidential Nomination," doctoral dissertation, State University of Iowa, 1962, 388-389.

9. Underwood to L.E. Jeffries, 11 October 1923, Underwood Papers; *Birmingham News,* 28 February 1923, 12 October 1923; Springen, 47-49, 385-386; Allen, "The 1924 Underwood Campaign in Alabama," 180-184; (on Klan strength) *New York Times,* 16 November 1923, *Wilcox Progressive Era,* 14 May 1925, *Troy Messenger,* 13 February 1924, L. J. Bugg to R. B. Evins, 16 August 1924, State Democratic Executive Committee Papers; *Mobile Register,* 31 December 1923, 6 May, 15 June 1924; Johnston to Charles Corlin, 26 March 1924, Underwood Papers; Johnson, *Oscar W. Underwood,* 393-399.

10. Lee N. Allen, "The Underwood Presidential Movement of 1924," 250-252, 259-262; *Official Report of the Proceedings of the National Democratic Convention,* 24 June to 9 July 1924, Indianapolis, 1924, 19, 95-102; *Mobile Register,* 26 June 1924; Johnson, *Oscar W. Underwood,* 399-401; Lee N. Allen, "Twenty Four Votes for Oscar W. Underwood," 245, 254-266; *Proceedings of the National Democratic Convention,* 245, 247-248, 304-310; Arnold S. Rice, "The Southern Wing of the Ku Klux Klan in American Politics," doctoral dissertation, Indiana University, 1959, 152- 58; *New York Times,* 22 June 1924.

11. *Mobile Register,* 10, 24 July 1924; Johnson, *Oscar W. Underwood,* 405-06; *Birmingham Post,* 5, 7-9, 16 October 1924; Rice, 118; Esdale interview.

12. John F. Kennedy, *Profiles in Courage,* New York, 1955, 226-227; Johnson, *Oscar W. Underwood,* 407-408; George Fort Milton, a Southern white liberal, described Underwood's base of support in 1924 as "machine politicians, ultra-conservatives, and reactionaries, aided by what remains of the Southern 'wets.'" (George F. Milton, "The South—and 1924," *Outlook,*

2 January 1924, 29-30. Also, in December 1924, Milton wrote to Senator Thomas J. Walsh that the "big trouble with the Klan politically is that its mere existence allows a vicious band of reactionaries to shelter behind the anti-Klan charge . . ." Milton to Walsh, 15 December 1924, quoted in Rice, 14); "dodge for the parson" in Johnston to "Dearest Girl," circa. September 1919, Johnston Papers; *Proceedings of the National Democratic Convention,* 95-102. Johnston's official text uses the phrase *"Bills* of Rights" in describing limitations on state and federal governments, and, therefore, leaves open the possibility for interpreting his remarks to mean that only the states' bills of rights should limit state's actions and the federal Bill of Rights should limit only federal actions; however, releases to the press at the convention apparently used a singular term, where Johnston said, *"The Bill of Rights* (emphasis supplied) are limitations only upon the State and Federal Governments . . ." (*Mobile Register,* 26 June 1924). Whatever his words' motive and meaning, Johnston's basic message was that the nation's constitutional guarantees of individual rights should protect citizens from the activities of a private organization—ironically, a legal precedent found only in Reconstruction laws struck down by the U.S. Supreme Court. *Slaughter-House Cases,* 83 U.S. 36, 1873; *U.S. v. Cruikshank,* 92 U.S. 542, 1875; *Twining v. New Jersey,* 211 U.S. 78, 1908; for Black's views on the application of the federal Bill of Rights, see *Adamson v. California,* 332 U.S. 46, 1947, and CBS News Special, "Mr. Justice and the Bill of Rights," *Southwestern University Law Review,* 1977, no.4, 937-951 (transcript of broadcast on CBS Television Network of 3 December 1968).

13. Newman, 93-96; Snell, "The Ku Klux Klan in Jefferson County, Alabama, 1916-1930," 95-97; Rice, 16-20; Newman 94.

14. Hackney, *Populism to Progressivism in Alabama,* 114-115, 203; Samuel L. Webb, *Two-Party Politics in the One-Party South: Alabama's Hill Country, 1874-1920,* Tuscaloosa, 1997, 24-28; *Birmingham Age-Herald,* 2 February 1914, 16, 28 September 1921; O. D. Street to B. Mills, 24 April 1923, O. D. Street to Aubrey Boyles, 30 December 1925, Street Papers; Black to O.P. Bentley, 21 January 1928, Black Papers; *Sand Mountain Banner,* 30 October 1924; Black, "The Lawyer and

Individual Freedom," 464-465; Black to Mary C. Pittman, 18 January 1926, Black Papers; on tariffs, see Martin Torodash, "Underwood and the Tariff," *Alabama Review,* April 1967, 121-126; *Birmingham Reporter,* 5 February 1921; Black to and from O. D. Street, 10, 13, 17 July 1929, Black Papers; telegram from O. D. Street to Holland, 2 November 1924, "Appt. Clk. Fls." Appointment Files, U.S. Justice Department, National Archives; Black to O. D. Street, 17 July 1929, Black Papers; "honest" in Jesse Stein, ed., *The Random House Dictionary of English Language,* New York, 1966, 681; "honestus" in Henry Campbell Black, *Black's Law Dictionary,* St. Paul, Minn., 1951, 869.

15. *Mobile Register,* 17 July, 2, 7-9 August, 1 November 1924; H.G. Davis to and from W. W. Brandon, 10, 11 September 1924, Brandon Papers; Alsobrook, 175-184; *Mobile Register,* 23, 29 November, 6, 7, 9, 10 December 1924, 10, 18 January 1925.

16. *Lewis v. Roberts,* 267 U.S. 467, 1925; telegram to Crampton Harris from Wm. R. Stansbury, 27 July 1924, William H. Sadler, Jr. to Stansbury, 11 February 1925, Lewis v. Roberts case file, 284, U.S. Supreme Court Case Files. Huff interview, Black Papers.

17. Frank, 37; Black, "The Lawyer and Individual Freedom," 465; *Birmingham News,* 10 August 1924; Black to Mary C. Pittman, 18 January 1926, Black Papers; Alpheus Thomas Mason, "Harlan Fisk Stone," in Leon Friedman and Fred L. Israel, ed., *The Justices of the United States Supreme Court, 1789-1977,* vol. III, New York, 1980, 2221-2222; Black to O. D. Street, 17 July 1929, Black Papers.

18. *Mobile Register,* 10-15 February 1925; *Nomination of Aubrey Boyles,* 158-159; Boyles to Willebrandt, 9 December 1922, 7 May 1923, Box 100, Case #6179, RG/21, Mobile Criminal Cases; *Mobile Item,* 23, 25 February 1925; "Francis Harrison Inge," *Martindale-Hubbell Law Directory, 1931,* vol. 1, New York, 1931, 12; *Mobile Register,* 17-22 February 1925.

CHAPTER II

1. Newman, 101; *Southern Labor Review,* Christmas Edition, 1924; Black to Ulay W. Black, 5 June 1925, Black to John Frank, 20 January 1948, Black Papers; Horace Turner to Oscar W. Underwood, 2 July, 1925, Underwood Papers; *Birmingham Post,* 3, 7 April, 16

May 1925; J. M. Donnelly to Black, 4 June 1925, S. J. Gay to Black, 25 June 1925, Black Papers; Elizabeth S. Black, "Hugo Black, the Magnificent Rebel," *Southwestern University Law Review,* vol. 9, 1977, 890; Cliff Durr interview.

2. Oscar W. Underwood to Alfred M. Trunstall, 22 May 1925, Charles, Guimer to Underwood, 2 July 1925; Underwood Papers; Johnson, *Oscar W. Underwood,* 416-19; Forney Johnston to "Dearest Girl," circa. December 13.1919, Johnston Papers; Black to J. B. White, 26 June 1925, Black to S. J. Gay, 26 June 1925, S.H. Blan, Secretary of State, to Black, 1 July 1925, Black Papers; *Birmingham Post,* 27 December 1924, 3, 21 April, 16 May, 6, 8, 9 June 1925; *Montgomery Advertiser,* 22 June 1924; Davis, 18; Black to Hugh Grant, 12 June 1925, Black Papers; *Birmingham Post,* 30 June 1925.

3. *New York Times,* 2 July 1925; Black to Reuben Foshee, 4 July 1925, Black to Bays D. Catner, editor of *Leeds Enterprise,* 13 July 1925, Black to Ed Wise, 25 June 1925, T. A. Goodwin to Black, 21 June 1925, Black to T. H. Somerville, 17 June 1925, W. R. Kimbrough to Black, 4 August 1925, various Black letters in Box #87, "Mobile #3" file, Black to Herman Beck, 24 August 1925, Black Papers; *Ashland Progress,* quoting *Birmingham Age Herald,* 18 June 1925; Black to Ulay W. Black, 31 October 1925, Black to O. J. Stocks, 31 October 1925, Black Papers; *Sand Mountain Banner,* 10 September 1925; Cliff Durr interview; Hamilton, *Hugo Black: The Alabama Years,* 119-20; *New York Times,* 13 September 1937.

4. Newman, 104, footnote; *Gadsden Times,* 8, 16 July 1924, 8, 10 June, 14, 21 August 1925; A. B. Stutts, interview with author, 1976.

5. L. B. Riddle to Black, 22 September 1925, Black to P. D. Meadows, 21 September 1925, Black to Jim Ballew, 30 September 1925, Black to Thomas A. Dix, 12 October 1925, Black to Bruce Smith, 27 October 1925, F. M. Holton to Black, 12 November 1925, Black to Felix Tait, 24 August 1925, W. R. Kimbrough to Black, 4 August 1925, Black Papers; *Phenix-Girard Journal,* 2 November 1925; *Birmingham Post,* 13 August 1937; Cliff Durr interview; *Birmingham Age-Herald,* 31 July 1937; Black to and from Horace Turner, 25, 26 August 1925, Black Papers; Rupert B. Vance, *Human Geography of the South,* Chapel Hill, 1935, 459;

Black to John M. Roberts, Internal Revenue Service, 30 October 1925, Black to J. B. Long, 8 September 1925, David J. Davis to Black, 5 January 1932, Black Papers; *Ashland Progress*, 27 August 1925; Black to H. R. Arnold, 2 November 1925, Black to M.L. Mont, 4 November 1925, Black Papers; *Marion Times-Standard*, 5 August 1926; Bailes interview; *Select Notes on the International Sunday School Lessons, 1925*, Boston, 1924, 130-36, 230-35, 289-96, 305-13; Black's letters of 12 November 1925 to Baptist ministers, Black Papers; *Selma Times-Journal*, 19 November 1925.

6. *Selma Times-Journal*, 19 November 1925; *Alabama Baptist*, 26 November 1925; Rev. J. Powell Tucker to Black, 1 December 1925, H. B. Malone to Black, 16 November 1926, Rev. Hamilton Reid to Black, 23 November 1925, Black to Felix Tait, 24 August 1925, Black to "Publisher of *Birmingham News*," 30 November 1925, Black to Ulay Black, 22 December 1925, Black to E.H. Payne, 30 December 1925, Black to T. A. Goodwin, 30 December 1925, Black letters to Mary C. Pittman, 30 December 1925, 18 January 1926, Black Papers.

7. William E. Gilbert, "The First Administration of Governor Bibb Graves, 1927-1930," master's thesis, University of Alabama, 2-20; "Biographical Memoranda in Reference to Bibb Graves," Alabama Department of Archives and History; John Kohn, interview with Charles Morgan, Jr., 1970; *Pittsburgh Post-Gazette*, 18, 20 September 1937; *Mobile Register*, 11, 14 May, 31 August 1924; *Montgomery Advertiser*, 11 May 1924; Daniel W. Hollis, *An Alabama Newspaper Tradition: Grover C. Hall And the Hall Family*, Tuscaloosa, 1983, 33; *Alabama Official and Statistical Register, 1923*, 331-32; Black to R. W. West, 12 January 1926, Black to John J. Thornton, 12 January 1926, Black Papers.

8. Statement of 26 February 1926, Box #90, Black Papers; "Opening Speech of the Hon. Hugo L. Black, March 20, 1926," emphasis supplied in all cases except in reference to "pauper's death," box #105, Black Papers; Davis, 65-66; *Ashland Progress*, 18, 25 March 1926. Black's political faith closely resembles the agenda that the Southern white liberal, George Fort Milton, had outlined for "Southern Democracy" in 1924, including prohibition, economic liberalism, aid to farmers, and Muscle Shoals. See George F. Milton, "The South—and 1924," *Outlook*, 2 January 1924, 29.

9. Black's "Letter to Editor," 22 March 1926, Black to O. R. Stumpf, 30 March 1926, Black's "Letter to Editor," 7 April 1926, Black to Millard I. Jackson, 31 March 1926, Black to Marvin Vickers, 15 March 1926, Black to J. A. Coleman, 3 April 1926, Black to Jeff Barland, 22 March 1926, Black to John Robinson, 17 March 1926, Black to O. Mason, 22 April 1926, Ester G. Wood to J.D. Griffin, 25 March 1926, "Hugo Black—Candidate For the United States Senate" statement, undated, Box #476, Black to D.C. Mathews, 1 April 1926, R.S. New to Black, 11 March 1926, E. W. Campbell to Black, 16 March 1926, Ben Ray to Jack Sellars, 9 April 1926, Black to W. H. Merrill, 16 April 1926, Black to O. Mason, 22 April 1926, Black Papers; Hamilton, *Hugo Black: The Alabama Years*, 126; *Auburn Plainsman*, 9 April 1926; *Ashland Progress*, 15 April 1926; Hugh Grant to Black, 12 April 1926, Black Papers.

10. Black to Editor of *DeKalb County Herald*, 3 May 1926, Black to Julian Harris, 14 April 1926, Black to J. T. Mitchell, 30 April 1926, Black to C. M. Stanley, 12 April 1926, Black to *Montgomery Times*, 3 May 1926, Black Papers; *Wilcox Progressive Era*, 18 March, 8 April, 6 May 1926; *Sumter Journal*, 16 April 1926; *Mountain Eagle*, 21 April 1926; *Marion Times-Standard*, 18 March, 8 April, 6 May 1926; *Florence Times-News*, 4 May 1926; *Blocton Enterprise*, 26 March, 8 April 1926; *Phenix-Girard Journal*, 12 March, 9 April, 7 May 1926.

11. Roy Kimbrough to Black, 17 March 1926, Black Papers; *Ashland Progress*, 26 May 1926; Black to J. F. Clements, 25 May 1926, O. Mason to Black, 17 May 1926, Jeff Berland to Black, 4 April 1926, Black to W. T. Harris, 18 May 1926, Black Papers; Henry H. Mix, "The Life of James J. Mayfield," master's thesis, University of Alabama, 1935, 99-100; *Ashland Progress*, quoting the *Birmingham Age Herald*, 3 June 1926; Carl Elliott, Sr. and Michael D'orso, *The Cost of Courage*, New York, 1992, 33-34; Bailes interview; *Florence Times-News*, 21 May 1926; "Hugo Black—Candidate For the United States Senate" statement, undated, Box #476, O. R. Stumpf to Black, 14 June 1926, Hollis Black to Roy W. Kimbrough, 22 May 1926, Black Papers.

12. *Florence Times-News*, 17, 27 May, 10

June 1926; O. Mason to Black, 12 June 1926; Black to R. B. Evins, 17 May 1926, statement "To the People of Limestone County," 4 June 1926, Black to H. A. Darby, 5 June 1926, O. R. Stumpf to Black, 14 June 1926, Black Papers; Elizabeth Black, 891-92; *Gadsden Times*, 10 June 1926; *Birmingham News*, 8 July 1926; Hamilton, *Hugo Black: The Alabama Years*, 129-130; "Statement on Bankhead charges," undated, Box #105, Black Papers; B.W. Simmers to Black, 18 June 1926, J. Bruce Henderson to Black, 30 June 1926, "Speech of July 7, 1926 to Bessemer by Hugo L. Black," transcript, Box #90, Black Papers.

13. Untitled speech of James J. Mayfield, 1926, James J. Mayfield Papers, University of Alabama Library; *Birmingham News*, 4 August 1926; Thomas E. Kilby to Black, 6 July 1926, Black to W. G. Lee, 2 June 1926, Wm. E. Fort to O. C. McRae, 29 June 1926, Black to J. H. Church, 29 April 1926, Black to Roy Kimbrough, 8 July 1926, Black Papers; *Sumter Co. Journal*, 11 June 1926; *Mountain Eagle*, 9 June 1926; *Troy Messenger*, 26 July 1926; *Dothan Eagle*, 5 July 1926; *Birmingham News*, 8, 16 July 1926; "Bessemer Speech," 7 July 1926, Box #83, Ben G. Perry (Musgrove campaign manager) to J. C. Leavell, 10 July 1926, J. C. McGowin to W. B. Coe, 18 May 1926, Black to McGowin, 24 May 1926, Black Papers; *Mobile Register*, 13 August 1924; J. M. Dannelly, Jr. to and from Black, 6, 9 July 1926, T. R. Long to W. B. Coe, 8 May 1926, Black to Jeff Berland, 30 January 1926, J. A. Thornhill to and from Black, 16, 17 June 1926, Black Papers; Johnston Moore to Bibb Graves, Graves Vertical Files; R. H. Goldin to Black, 18 May 1926, R. W. West to and from Black, 8, 12 January 1926, R. W. West to Black, 31 May 1926, J. V. Stubbs, 1 October 1925, Black Papers.

14. Black to C. H. Andrews, 9 July 1926, Black to O. R. Stumpf, 8 July 1926, Roy Kimbrough to Black, 29 July 1926, Black Papers; *Birmingham News*, 26 July 1926; Hollis Black to D. M. Maxwell, 13 July 1926, John B. Robertson, Jr., to Black, 13 July 1926, Black to Robert M. Mitchell, 17 July 1926, Grady Marshall to Black, 17 July 1926, Black to J. C. Leach, 8 July 1926, "Schedule of Mr. Black," 21 July-3 August 1926, Box #89, R.G. Rowland to Black, 30 July 1926, Ernest Jones to Cary Phillips, 10 June 1926, W. H. Ozbirn to Black, 13 August 1926, Black Papers; *Ashland Progress*,

5 August 1926; W. C. Lumpkin to David J. Davis, 30 July 1926, David J. Davis to James Oakley, 31 July 1926, Black Papers.

15. C. H. Adams to Black, 7 August 1926, Tully Goodwin to Black, 15 August 1926, J. Hester to Black, 22 July 1926, David J. Davis to J. C. Burns, 2 August 1926, Black Papers; letter from manager of the Avondale Mill to Tom Heflin, undated, circa. 1937, folder 101, political correspondence, Thomas Heflin Papers, University of Alabama Library; *Birmingham News*, 30 July 1926; *Birmingham Age-Herald*, 30 July 1926; *Montgomery Advertiser*, 1, 4 August 1926; *Gadsden Times*, 10 August 1926; Roy Kimbrough to Black, 16 July 1926, Black Papers; *Birmingham News*, 4, 7 9 August 1926; *Birmingham Age-Herald*, 5-7 August 1926; Black to Felix L. Smith, 4 August 1926, Hugh Grant's letters to David J. Davis, 7, 27 August 1926, "Closing statement to the Press," 1926 Campaign, undated, Box #89, Black Papers.

16. Davis, 20; *Birmingham News*, 31 January 1937; Horace Turner to Black, 12, 13 August 1926, (emphasis supplied), 16 August 1926, Black papers; Case files in Box #80, 90, 100, Criminal Cases, U.S. District Court, Southern District of Alabama, 1924-1926, National Archives, Atlanta Region; *Boykin v. U.S.*, 11 Fed. (2d.) 484; Black to Nicholas Stallworth, 14 June 1926, Aubry Boyles to Black, 25 June 1926, Black to Leon Schwartz, 11 September 1926, Black Papers; *Official and Statistical Register of Alabama, 1927*, 358-59; Carter Rice to Black, 16 August 1926, Hugh Grant to Black, 12 August 1926, W.M. Olive to Black, 23 September 1926, Black Papers; *Birmingham News*, 15 August 1926; *Huntsville Daily News*, 16 August 1926; *Montgomery Advertiser*, 13 August 1926; *Birmingham Reporter*, 21 August 1926.

17. *New York Times*, 15 August 1927, 15, 16 September 1937; *Pittsburgh Post-Gazette*, 13-16 September 1937; Black to W. F. Price, 38 September 1926, Black to John H. Hill, 28 September 1926, Black to Roger P. Wilkins, 28 August 1926, Black Papers; "Program, Past Grand Chancellor Hugo l. Black, One Thousand Page Class," Knights of Pythias, 14 December 1926, Birmingham Public Library; Black to Shep Sheppard, 8 September 1926, Black to J. R. Baldwin, 26 August 1926, Black Papers.

18. Hollis, 56-57; *Opelika Daily News*, 13 August 1926, Black Papers; Black and Black, 70; Black to Evans C. Johnson, 29 April 1952, Black Papers; J. Morgan Kousser, *The Shaping of Southern Politics*, New Haven, 1974, 226-227, 240-45; voting turnout statistics in *Alabama Official and Statistical Register, 1903, 1911, 1927*; for levels of Black's active support between Klan and non-Klan local leaders, see correspondence in Black Papers, Boxes #82-89, including James Esdale to Black, 19 August 1926, J. A. Thornhill to Black, 7 June 1926, Black to and from R. R. Martin, 26 March, 7 April 1926, D. M. Maxwell to Black, 5 May 1926, T. A. Goodwin to Black, 25 July 1925, E. W. Campbell, Klan No. 24, to Black, 6 March 1926; on the basis of these files, the counties where Klan members appear to have been among Black's primary contacts were Bibb, Bullock, Calhoun, Cherokee, Connecuh, Covington, Escambia, Houston, Morgan, Monroe, Sumter, and Talladega—twelve of sixty-seven counties; indications of Klan strength in some of these and other counties are found in *Dothan Weekly Eagle*, 30 October 1925; *Wilcox Progressive Era*, 15 May 1925; *Sylacauga Advance*, 17 March 1925, J. M. Bonner to Oscar W. Underwood, 23 June 1925, Underwood Papers; Scott interview. Samuel L. Webb, "Hugo Black, Bibb Graves, and the Ku Klux Klan: A Revisionist View of the 1926 Alabama Democratic Primary," *Alabama Review*, October 2004, 243-273. There is also information suggesting a lack of James Esdale's local political influence in 1926 in Black files. One of Black's supporters, not a Klan member, lost a race for city commissioner despite the support and endorsement of the grand dragon (See letters of O. R. Stumpf to Black, 23 August, 13 October 1926, Black Papers); *Pittsburgh Post-Gazette*, 28 July 1937; Horace Turner to Black, 12 August 1926, Black Papers; analysis of voting patterns developed from *Alabama Official and Statistical Register, 1927*, 358-359, 362-363, and *Religious Bodies: 1926*, Vol. I, U.S. Bureau of the Census, 1930, 577-579. In 1926, Baptists comprised 41 percent of Alabama's membership in white religious bodies. The relationship between Black's political strength and a county's Baptist strength is also suggested by the fact that, outside the Tennessee Valley, Black lost six of the seven counties where Baptists were less than 30 percent of all white church members. A later analysis of Alabama's "friends and neighbors" is found in V. O. Key,

Southern Politics in State and Nation, New York, 1949, 37-41; Black, Jr., 58-59; *Southern Labor Review*, 30 June 1926.

19. Black to Mr. and Mrs. J. W. Porter, 8 September 1926, Black to Barney Whatley, 12 November 1926, Black to Mrs. T. B. Gaines, 9 September 1926, Black to C.G. Cote, 8 September 1926, Stanley S. Simpson, Mass. Mutual Life Insurance Co. to Black, 1 November 1927, Black Papers; Newman, 117; Hugh Grant to and from Black, 5 October 1926 and 22 January 1927, J.L. Thornton to Black, 16 November 1926, Black to J. A. Kykendall, 18 October 1926, Black Papers.

20. "Biographical Memoranda, Hugo Lafayette Black," undated, vertical files, Alabama Department of Archives and History; Black to M. H. Toland, 16 December 1926, Black to Hilliard Black, 12 December 1926, Black Papers; *Montgomery Advertiser*, 18 January 1927; Earle Parkhurst to Black, 18 December 1926, Steve ___ to Black, 11 January 1927, J. F. Mitchell to Black, 27 April 1927, Black to W. C. Bethune, Jr., 27 January 1927, letters of O. R. Stumpf to Black, 22 March 1927, 13 May 1927, Mrs. Mary Haskins to Black 15 May 1927, James Rice to Black, 29 April 1927, Black Papers; Black, Jr., 79.

21. Black to James C. Pegues, 22 March 1927, Black to Wayne Wheeler, 14 June 1927, letters of Black to Horace Turner, 7 October 1927, 17 October 1927, Black to W. E. James, 2 October 1926, Ester G. Wood to William S. Swanson, 1 December 1926, Black Papers; Newman, 118; Black to J. H. Henderson, 4 June 1927, Black to S. L. Johnson, 11 June 1927, Black Papers; Newman, 68; "The Majesty of Law," *Civitan*, August 1927, Box #476, Black Papers.

Chapter 12

1. *Talladega Daily Home*, 8-9 December 1924; Albert Radney, interview with author 1986; William "Bill" Rozelle, interview with author, 1986.

2. *Talladega Daily Home*, 11 December 1924; *Ware v. State*, 108 So. 645, 1926.

3. *Talladega Daily Home*, 18, 19 December 1925.

4. *Talladega Daily Home*, 13-16 January, 2, 4 March 1925; Rozelle interview; U. S. Moore, interview with author, 1986; Corey Tucker,

interview with author, 1986; *Ware v. State,* 108 So. 645,1926.

5. *Talladega Daily Home,* 3 March 1925; Aaron Brown Jr. to James Weldon Johnson, 16 March 1926, Director of Branches to Rev. S. S. Seay, 1 July 1926, NAACP Papers; Rozelle interview; Radney interview; Moore interview.

6. *Talladega Daily Home,* 14 March 1925; Rozelle interview; Scott interview; *Anniston Star,* 20 April 1975; Betty R. Lessley and Vern Scott, "150th Anniversary of the Founding of Talladega County, featuring the Talladega County Courthouse," pamphlet, Talladega, 1982; *Talladega County Historical Association Newsletter,* April 1985, 17.

7. *Ware v. State,* 108 So. 645, 1926, *Talladega Daily Home,* 30 May, 1 June 1927.

8. *Talladega Daily Home,* 1, 2 June 1927; *Sylacauga Advance,* 1 June 1927; Corey Tucker interview.

9. *Talladega Daily Home,* 2 June 1927; *Sylacauga Advance,* 8 June 1927; Mrs. Corey Tucker, interview with author, 1986; Corey Tucker interview; Scott interview; Moore interview; Radney interview; Leon P. Spencer, archivist of Talladega College to author, 6 May 1985; *Talladega Daily Home,* 11, 18 June 1927; Carelton Chapman to author, undated.

10. *Sylacauga Advance,* 8 June 1927; *Talladega Daily Home,* 11 November 1927; Vern Scott to Black, 1 March 1965, Black Papers; Snell, "The Ku Klux Klan in Jefferson County, Alabama, 1916-1930," 112, 133-135, 148, 153, 159-60, 167; *Anniston Star,* 31 October, 1, 2, 8, November, 7 December 1927; "Alabama Rallies Against the Klan," Press Service of the National Association for the Advancement of Colored People," 2 September 1927, James Weldon Johnson, letter to the editor, 23 September 1927, NAACP Papers; Feldman, *Politics. Society, and the Klan in Alabama,* 93-113, 139-155; Gilbert, 115-125; Hollis, 34-38, Baughn interview; *Sylacauga Advance,* 9 November 1927.

11. *Talladega Daily Home,* 14 November 1927; *Fayette Banner,* 1 January 1925; Sam W. Donaldson to and from Black, 15 June 1927, 7 June 1927, Black to M. H. Sims, 19 September 1927; Black to John R. Jones, 7 October 1926, W.S. Hurst to Black, 10 June 1936, Black Papers; Scott interview.

12. *Talladega Daily Home,* 15 November 1927; Corey Tucker interview; *Our Mountain Home,* 15 November 1927.

13. *Talladega Daily Home,* 15 November 1927; Black, Jr., 53-54; Henry Sumner Maine, *Ancient Law,* New York, 1883, xxvi-lxvii, 7; *Our Mountain Home,* 16 November 1927. Among several problems with the authenticity of Beck's letter is its reference to "Mr. Luke Ware" in addressing a warning to "Mr. Chum Smelley." "Mr.," as a title of address for both men represented a linguistic equality that no one in Talladega would naturally use in interracial conversations or letters. Certainly, a poor, jailed black man would not have dared such a reference in a letter to a white man, unless prompted to do so by white men clumsily attempting to dictate a useful document for trial.

14. "Fees & Payments" book, Box #502, Black Papers; W.S. Hurst to Black, 10 June 1936, Chum Smelley to Black, 11 June 1936, Black to Tom Hagan, 26 August 1937, telegram of "Chum and Tom" to Black, circa. 1 October 1937, W.S. Hurst to Black, 10 October 1942, G. S. "Chum" Smelley to Black, 21 November 1942, Black Papers; Newman, 657, endnote 13; Maine, *Ancient Law,* Black Books; Daniel J. Meador, *Mr. Justice and His Books,* Charlottesville, 1974, 114; Black, Jr., 54.

BENEDICTION

1. Transcript, 17 July 1970; see Wayne Flynt, *Alabama in the Twentieth Century,* Tuscaloosa, 2004, 29-106; W. B. Yeats, "September 1913," and "The Municipal Gallery Revisited," in Richard J. Finneran, ed., *The Collected Poems of W. B. Yeats,* New York, 1996, 108-09, 319-21; see also R.F. Foster, *W. B. Yeats: A Life I: The Apprentice Mage, 1865-1914,* Oxford University Press, 1997, 312-14, 529. Of course, it is almost certain that Hugo Black never read many, if any, Yeats poetry. Black's primary exposure to poetry was the memorized doggerel of his youth and the classic, narrative English and Greek poems that he read as instructive history. Black fully agreed with the Greek philosopher whom Diogenes quoted as saying that it is "not wide reading, but useful reading that lends to excellence." See handwritten notes inside the back cover of Diogenes Laertius, with R. D. Hicks (tr.), *Lives of Eminent Philosophers,* New York, 1925, 201, Black Books; Black and Black, 235-36, 240, and Black, Jr., 157-58.

2. For examples of Black's terms for friendship, see Black's letters to Mrs. Charles Whelan, 17 February 1964, to William M. Williamson (concerning Ben Ray), 24 April 1970, to David W. Thorton (concerning David M. White), 14 October 1957, Black Papers; Black, Jr., 140-145; Clifford Durr interview; Marcus Tullius Cicero, 474, and inside back-cover, Black Books; Black's choice of text for his own eulogy was Virgil's Song, where the Greek poet says, among other things, "Let me live free of solicitude, a stranger to the art of promising legacies in order to buy the friendship of the great." Black and Black, 80-81; Black to George Ward, 26 April 1937 and to Mervyn H. Sterne, 16 March 1971 (concerning George Ward), Black Papers; Black and Black, 3-63; the use of "friends" as a distinctive appellation in public speaking has a long tradition (David Konstan, *Friendship in the Classical World,* Cambridge University Press, 1997, 65), but it was especially popular in the Populist era among great orators such as William Jennings Bryan. See, for example, Bryan, *The First Battle,* 260-275, for speeches to "my friends" at the 1896 Populist Convention. While Black's concept of friendship was not the same as fraternal brotherhood, his many lodge memberships were primary means for developing friends across class lines. Also, for Black and other men, fraternal lodges served several practical functions, many of which, however, effectively segregated women from both leadership and friendships among men. See Mary Ann Clawson, *Constructing Brotherhood: Class, Gender, and Fraternalism,* Princeton, 1989, 22-23, 47-49, 211-217, 259-264.

3. Black to James Saxon Childres, 13 January 1937, Black Papers; Birmingham *Age-Herald,* 4 April, 14 May 1914; contents of "campaign book," box #90, Black to J. H. Sentell, 10 October 1925 and to J. F. Brown, 27 September 1926, Black Papers; Black was also fond of using the analogy of "friend" to describe his honest interest in someone's welfare. See promises to be the "best friend of the Port Development" (Black to Leon Schwartz, 11 September 1926, Black Papers) and his claim in campaign ads to be "the only friend of the working man who can win" (*Labor Advocate,* 7 August 1926).

4. In his race for solicitor, in "Hugo Black's Message to His Friends," Black concluded, "I can never repay you for your support except by my earnest, honest effort to serve you faithfully." Upon winning, he declared, "I shall go into office free from the embarrassment of any trade, combination, or promise, except the promise to do my duty." *Birmingham Age-Herald,* 5, 9 April 1914. In his unsuccessful campaign for circuit judge, David J. Davis had a similar message to "His Friends" where he declared that he was "under no obligation to any person or persons except to do my full duty, as I see it, guided only by my conscience." *Birmingham Age-Herald,* 8 May 1916. Black proclaimed in 1926 that his victory for the Senate showed that his friends voted their "honest convictions." ("Closing Statement to press, 1926 Campaign," undated, box #89, Black Papers). For Black's private statements illustrating his sense of obligation between friends while one is in public office, see Black to Truman Hobbs, 3 December 1970 (story about his relationship with his "old friend," Herman Beck), Black Papers. Black's reliance on friendship as a foundation for public ethics may have come from the mores of rural north Alabama, Baptist notions of "brotherhood," and even classical Greek literature that he read from boyhood. One of Plato's *Republic's* earliest dialogues discounts defining justice as helping friends and harming enemies. In the dialogue, however, a "friend" is defined as "one who really is honest [and good] as well as seeming so." Francis MacDonald Cornford (tr.), *The Republic of Plato,* New York, 1945, 13. "Friendship" holds a central place in one of Aristotle's treatises on public ethics, and, Black's own notions of friendship reflects many of the Greek philosopher's ideas. See W. D. Ross (tr.), *The Pocket Aristotle,* New York, 1968, 234-250, and David Konstan, 15-16, 56-64, 78.

5. John P. Frank, "Hugo Black: Little Man's Lawyer," Progressive, April 1946, 4; Cooper, "Mr. Justice Hugo Lafayette Black, of Alabama," 18-19; in 1964, Black paid his highest tribute to Jerome Cooper, his first Supreme Court law clerk, when he assured him that "You stick to your principles and your friends." Black believed that faith in one led to service to the other. Black to Jerome A. Cooper, 14 October 1964. In correspondence over the decades, Black used several phrases as a complimentary close, but he reserved "Sincerely your friend" for only a relatively few men whom Black felt had personally supported him during a difficult time in his struggle for advancing their shared,

"honest convictions." See, Cooper, *Sincerely your friend;* Black letters to Tom Hagan, 26 August 1938, John Temple Graves, 28 June 1927, Constantinos Lontos, 26 October 1926, Black Papers. See J. Mills Thornton, "Hugo Black and the Golden Age," in *Justice Hugo Black and Modern America,* Tuscaloosa, 1990, 144-147. In the 1926 campaign, Black's correspondence with roughly a dozen local Klan leaders and members usually referred to them as "friends," instead of fraternal brothers (Black to J. F. Brown, 27 September 1926, Black Papers). Equally telling, after the election, Klan operatives appealed to Black's duty to his "friend"—not to his secret brotherhood obligation—in order to get Black to represent Chum Smelley. See Sam W. Donaldson to Black, 15 June 1927, Black Papers. After his trial, realizing why Black helped acquit him, Chum Smelley adopted Black's own, special closing in correspondence with him. See G. S. "Chum" Smelley to Black, 21 November 1942, Black Papers.

6. Thomas O. Toland to Black, 16 July 1925, Black Papers; the South's caste system, which kept blacks economically dependent on white "friendliness" for favors as a substitute for justice, compounded the exclusion of African Americans from ranks of both good citizenship and friendship in Black's life. As an example, despite a lifelong relationship that included her role as the Foster family's washwoman and the Black family's cook, housekeeper, and nanny, Mary Marble never received a letter from Black closing "Sincerely your friend . . ." (See Black to Mary Marble, 25 March 1966, Black Papers.) Virginia Durr could not recall a single African American "friend" for her brother-in-law—or any other white person in Birmingham (Vir-

ginia Durr interview) before Black went to Washington. Of course, during these times, white Southerners habitually claimed friendships with and "friendliness" toward Negroes. In turn, dependent on industrialists for financial support, leading African American spokesman Booker T. Washington often claimed that the "best people of the South" were "friends of the race." See Charles T. Acker to Black, 6 October 1954, Black Papers, and Myrdal, 592-593, 1356-1357. The interracial "friendship fantasy" has had both a persisting, complex history and a continuing role in white understanding of race relations. See Gerald Early, "Whatever Happened to Integration," *Atlantic Monthly,* February 1997, 106-108; Benjamin DeMott, *Why Americans Can't Think Straight About Race,* New York, 1995, 7-42.

7. The term, "plain folk" has had differing meanings for historians inquiring into the Southern white population, but in this era I use it simply to identify those economically poor white men and women working on farms, in mills and factories, and behind store counters in Birmingham and Alabama. They became, in effect, the bulk of the "progressive" constituency in Black's "moral-dry-progressive" political coalition. Newby, *Plain Folk in the New South,* 1-19; Flynt, *Dixie's Forgotten People,* 1-14; Flynt, *Poor But Proud,* 255-277.

8. In his partial memoirs, Black did not mention James Esdale or identify Crampton Harris with his ever-present term of "friend," only as his "partner" (Black and Black, 51, 59); Whatley interview; Harris interview; "Albert Lee Smith," *Congressional Quarterly Weekly,* 3 January 1981; Smith interview; transcript, 17 July 1970.

Bibliography

Primary Sources

Manuscript Collections

Birmingham Public Library Archives, Birmingham Alabama

Governor's Coal Strike Commission Papers (1921)

Jefferson County Grand Jury Minutes and Notes

Jefferson County Circuit Court Docket Books

League of Women Voters Papers

Thomas D. Parke Diary and Papers

Alabama Department of Archives and History, Montgomery, Alabama

Alabama State Democratic Executive Committee Papers

Alabama Supreme Court Records

Alabama Tax Commission Records

B. B. Comer Papers

Charles Henderson Papers

Forney Johnston Papers

Harwell Davis Papers

J. L. M. Curry Papers

Oscar W. Underwood Papers

Thomas G. Jones Papers

Thomas Kilby Papers

W. Logan Martin Papers

W. W. Brandon Papers

Harvard University, Baker Library, Cambridge, Massachusetts

R.G. Dun & Co. Credit Reporting Ledgers

Library of Congress, Manuscript Division, Washington, DC

Hugo L. Black Papers

National Association for the Advancement of Colored People (NAACP) Papers

William Howard Taft Papers

National Archives, Washington, DC

Supreme Court of the United States Case Files

U.S. Justice Department Appointment Files

U.S. Postal Service Appointment Files

National Archives, Atlanta Region, East Point, Georgia

U.S. District Court, Northern District of Alabama Files

U.S. District Court, Southern District of Alabama Files

National Archives, Fort Worth Region, Fort Worth, Texas

United States Circuit Court of Appeals for the Fifth Circuit Files

University of Alabama Law School Library

Hugo Black Book Collection

University of Alabama Library Special Collections

James J. Mayfield Papers

O. D. Street Papers

Thomas Heflin Papers

Official Records

Alabama. *Annual Report of the Coal Mines of Alabama.* Montgomery: Brown Printing Company, 1921-1924.

Alabama. *Biennial Report of the Attorney General of Alabama.* Montgomery: Brown Printing Co., 1896-1918.

Alabama. Board of Administration. *Quadrennial Report of the Board of Administration,* Montgomery: Brown Printing Co., 1922-1930.

Alabama. Board of Control and Economy. *Quadrennial Report of the Board of Control and Economy, Convict Department.* Montgomery: Brown Printing Co., 1919-1922.

Alabama. Board of Inspectors. *Quadrennial Report of the Board of Inspectors of Convicts.* Montgomery: Brown Printing Co. 1914-1926.

Alabama. Board of Inspectors of Convicts. *Rules and Regulations for Government of Convicts.* Montgomery: Brown Printing Co., 1913.

Alabama. *Code of Alabama.* Montgomery. 1876, 1907.

Alabama. House of Representatives. *Alabama House of Representatives Journal.* Montgomery: Brown Printing Co., 1915-1971.

Alabama. *General Acts and Laws of the Legislature of Alabama.* Montgomery: Brown Printing Co., 1868-1971.

Alabama. *Local Acts and Laws of the Legislature of Alabama.* Montgomery: Brown Printing Co., 1871-1971.

Alabama. *Official Proceedings of the Constitutional Convention of the State of Alabama, May 21st, 1901 to September 3rd, 1901.* Vol. 1. Montgomery: Brown Printing Co., 1901.

Alabama. Senate. *Alabama Senate Journal.* Montgomery: Brown Printing Co., 1914-1925, 1954-1971.

Clay County. *Abstract of Records of Mortgages or Articles to Pay Money.* Clay County Courthouse, Ashland, AL. 1896 and 1897.

Clay County. *Administrators, Guardians, Executors Record, #1.* Clay County Probate Court, Clay County Courthouse, Ashland, AL, 1900.

Clay County. *Assessment of Taxes on Real Estate and Personal Property,* Clay County Courthouse, Ashland, AL, 1876-1901.

Clay County. *Attorneys' Receipts for Papers.* Clay County Courthouse, Ashland, AL, 1891-1900.

Clay County. *Clay County Alabama Marriage Book 'B'.* Clay County Courthouse, Ashland, AL, 1877-1882.

Clay County. *Clay County Judgment Record.* Clay County Courthouse, Ashland, AL, 1891-1896.

Clay County. *Last Wills and Estates.* Clay County Courthouse, Ashland, AL. 1890-1892.

Clay County. *Minutes of County Commissioners Court.* Clay County Courthouse, Ashland, AL. 1894.

Clay County. *Mortgage Records.* Clay County Courthouse, Ashland, AL, 1892-1897.

Clay County. *Official Bond Book A.* Clay County Courthouse, Ashland, AL, 1876-1882.

Clay County. "Petition to remove the disability of Hugo L. Black," County Court in Equity, Clay County Courthouse, Ashland, AL, 19 May 1905.

Jefferson County. *William L. Harrison v. Lloyd Hooper,* case files no. 6374, Tenth Judicial Circuit of Alabama, Office of the Circuit Clerk, Jefferson County Courthouse, Birmingham, AL, 1920.

Jefferson County. *W. L. Harrison v. Conrad W. Austin et al.,* case files no. 7782, Chancery Court Minutes and Records, Jefferson County Courthouse, Birmingham, AL, 1921.

U.S. Congress. Contested Election Case, *Martin W. Whatley v. James E. Cobb,* from the Fifth Congressional District of Alabama. National Archives, Washington, DC, 1893.

U.S. Congress. *The Ku Klux Klan.* Hearings Before the Committee on Rules, House of Representatives, Sixty-Seventh Congress, First Session, Washington, DC, 1921.

U.S. Congress. *Nomination of Aubrey Boyles: Hearings before a Subcommittee of the Committee of the Judiciary.* United States Senate, Sixty-Ninth Congress, First Sess., 26, 27, 28 April 1926. Washington, DC: U.S. Government Printing Office, 1926.

Other Works

Alabama Department of Archives and History. *Alabama Official and Statistical Register.* Montgomery: Brown Printing Co., 1903-27.

Alabama Department of Archives and History, "Biographical Memoranda in Reference to Bibb Graves." N.d. Vertical Files. Montgomery, AL.

Alabama Department of Archives and History. Biographical Memoranda in Reference to Borden Hughson Burr." N.d. Vertical Files. Montgomery, AL.

Alabama Department of Archives and History. Biographical Memoranda in Reference to Hugo Lafayette Black." N.d. Vertical files. Montgomery, AL.

Alabama Department of Archives and History. Index to *Civil Register of State Officials,* Reading Room, Alabama Department of Archives and History, Montgomery, AL, 1856-1882.

Alabama Historical Society. *Cemeteries of Clay County Alabama.* LaGrange, Ga.: Alabama Historical Society, 1987.

Birmingham City Directory. 1907-1921. Atlanta, GA: Mutual Publishing Company.

Black, Henry Campbell. *Black's Law Dictionary.* St. Paul, MN: West Publishing Company, 1951

Black, Hugo L. Speech delivered at the Alabama State Bar Association Annual Meeting, Birmingham, AL, 17 July 1970. Transcript, author's collection.

CBS. CBS News Special. "Mr. Justice and the Bill of Rights," 3 December 1968. Transcript published in *Southwestern University Law Review* no.4 (1977) 937-951.

Country Club of Birmingham, 1930. Birmingham Public Library Archives, Birmingham, AL.

Diogenes, Laertius. *The Lives of Eminent Philosophers / Diogenes Laertius.* Trans. R. D. Hicks. New York: Leob, 1925. Copy with handwritten notes in University of Alabama Law School Library, Tuscaloosa, AL.

Durr, Virginia. Letter to Charles Morgan, Jr., 12 April 1971, author's collection.

First Baptist Church. "Debt-Free Celebration and Dedication." First Baptist Church, Birmingham, Alabama, 23 June 1946. Birmingham Public Library Archives. Birmingham AL.

Hubbell, J. H. *Hubbell's Legal Dictionary, 1917.* New York: Hubbell Legal Directory Company, 1917.

Humphrey, H. B. *Historical Summary of Coal-Mine Explosions in the United States, 1810-1958.* Bulletin 586. Bureau of Mines, U.S. Department of Interior. Washington, DC: U.S. Government Printing Office, 1960.

Knights of Pythias. "Program, Past Grand Chancellor Hugo l. Black, One Thousand Page Class," 14 December 1926. Birmingham Public Library, Birmingham, AL, 1926.

Ku Klux Klan. "Semi-Monthly Bulletin, Province No. 2." Bibb Graves Vertical Files, Alabama Department of Archives and History, Montgomery, AL.

Martindale-Hubbell Law Directory, 1931. Vol. 1. New York: Martindale-Hubbell, 1931.

Moyer, Forrest T., G. D. Jones, and V. E. Wrenn. *Injury Experience in Coal Mining, 1948.* Bulletin 509. Bureau of Mines, U.S. Department of Interior. Washington, DC: U.S. Government Printing Office, 1948.

National Democratic Committee. *Official Report of the Proceedings of the National Democratic Convention, 24 June to 9 July 1924.* Indianapolis: Bookwalter-Ball-Greathouse Printing Co., 1924.

National Prison Association. *Proceedings of the National Prison Association 1888.* Boston, 1888.

National Prison Association. *Proceedings of the National Prison Association 1889.* Nashville, 1889.

National Prison Association. *Proceedings of the National Prison Association 1890.* Cincinnati, 1890.

St. Paul Cathedral. "Parishioners Rolls, 1908." Birmingham Public Library Archives. Birmingham, AL, 1908.

Smith, Grace B. Letter to author, 6 September 1971.

Stein, Jesse, ed. *The Random House Dictionary of English Language.* New York: Random House, 1966.

The Book of Birmingham and Alabama. Birmingham Public Library Archives. Birmingham, AL, 1914.

"TWK Monthly." February 1925. Birmingham Public Library Archives. Birmingham, AL.

University of Alabama. *Corolla.* Student Yearbook. University of Alabama Library, Special Collections, Tuscaloosa, AL, 1904-1905.

University of Alabama. "Department of Law." Catalogue. University of Alabama Library, Special Collections, Tuscaloosa, AL, 1905-1906.

U.S. Bureau of Census. Federal Manuscript Census, Clay County. Bureau of the Census, Washington, DC, 1970, 1880, 1910.

U.S. Bureau of the Census. *Historical Statistics of the United States: Colonial Times to 1970.* Part 1. Washington, DC, 1975.

U.S Bureau of the Census. *Mines and Quarries, 1919.* Fourteenth Census of the United States. Vol. 11. Washington, DC, 1919.

U.S Bureau of the Census. *Negroes in the United States, 1920-32.* U.S. Doc. 164. U.S. Government Printing Office. 1935.

U.S. Bureau of the Census. *Religious Bodies: 1926.* Vol. 1. Washington, DC, 1930.

U.S. Bureau of Mines. *Coal Mine Fatalities in the United States.* 1920 and 1922. Washington, DC: 1920-1922.

U.S. Department of Justice. Federal Bureau of Investigation. *Hugo Black: Freedom of Information Act,* Part 1. FBI Headquarters, FOIA Reading Room, Washington, DC.

U.S. Department of Justice. *Register of the Department of Justice,* 1 February 1922. Washington, DC.

Interviews (in author's collection unless otherwise noted)

Abram, Morris. Interview by Charles Morgan, Jr., 1971.

Anonymous. Interview by Charles Morgan, Jr., 1970.

Anonymous #2. Interview by author, 1974.

Ayres, Brandt. Interview by author, 1987.

Bailes, George Lewis, Sr. Interview by author, 1971.

Baughn, Herbert. Interview by author, 1972.

Beddow, C. P. Interview by Charles Morgan, Jr., 1970.

Beddow, Roderick, Sr. Interview by Charles Morgan, Jr., 1970.

Beecher, John. Interview by author, 1976.

Cooper, Jerome "Buddy." Interviews by author, 1982, 1983, 1986, 1988.

Davis, Harwell G. Interview, with F. W. Helenbold, by Arthur L. Walker, 1975, Samford University Library.

Durr, Virginia, and Cliff Durr. Interview by Charles Morgan, Jr., 1970.

Esdale, James. Interview by Charles Morgan, Jr., 1971.

Engel, Irving. Interview by Charles Morgan, Jr., 1970.

Harris, Crampton. Interview by Charles Morgan, Jr., 1971.

Kohn, John. Interview by Charles Morgan, Jr., 1970.

Knowles, Ralph I. Interview with author, 1981.

Moore, U. S. Interview by author, 1986.

North, James. Interview by author, 1983.

Patrick, Vernon. Interview by author, 1983.

Pruet, C. M. Interview by author, 12 June 1970;

Radney, Albert. Interview by author, 1986.

Rozelle, William. Interview by author, 1986.

Scott, Vern. Interview by author, 1986.

Smith, Albert Lee. Interview by author, 1971.

Stutts, A. B. Interview by author, 1976.

Tucker, Corey. Interview by author, 1986.

Tucker, Mrs. Corey. Interview by author, 1986.

Vann, David. Interview by author, 1983.

Whatley, Barney. Interview by Charles Morgan, Jr., 1971.

Memoirs

Black, Elizabeth S. "Hugo Black: The Magnificent Rebel" *Southwestern University Law Review* 9 (1977) 890.

Black, Hugo L, and Elizabeth Black. *Mr. Justice and Mrs. Black: The Memoirs of Hugo L. Black and Elizabeth Black*. New York: Random House, 1986.

Black, Hugo L. "Reminiscences," *Alabama Law Review* 18 (Fall 1965) 5-11.

Black, Hugo, Jr. *My Father, A Remembrance*. New York: Random House, 1975.

Cooper, Jerome A. *Sincerely Your Friend . . . : Letters of Mr. Justice Hugo L. Black to Jerome A. Cooper*. Birmingham: University of Alabama Press, 1973.

Durr, Virginia Foster. *Outside the Magic Circle: The Autobiography of Virginia Foster Durr*. Edited by Hollinger F. Barnard. Tuscaloosa: University of Alabama Press, 1985.

Elliot, Carl, Sr., and Michael D'orso. *The Cost of Courage: The Journey of an American Congressman*. New York: Doubleday, 1992.

Garrett, Mitchell B. *Horse and Buggy Days on Hatchet Creek*. Tuscaloosa: University of Alabama Press, 1957.

Rozelle, Eddie B. *My Folks and Fields, 1900: Recollections*. Talladega, AL: E. B. Rozelle, 1960.

Newspapers

Advance. July 1891-February 1921.

Advocate. October 1895-August 1898.

Alabama Baptist. November 1890-November 1925.

Alabama Journal. March 1976.

Anniston Star. October 1927-December 1927.

Ashland Advance. March 1888-June 1894

Ashland Banner. April 1882-September 1882.

Ashland Herald. September 1879-October 1879.

Ashland News. May 1878-October 1880.

Ashland Progress. June 1925-August 1926.

Ashland Standard. August 1905-August 1907.

Atlanta Constitution. October 1921.

Atlanta Journal-Constitution. December 1995-October 1997.

Auburn Plainsman. April 1926.

Birmingham Age-Herald. August 1903-July 1937.

Birmingham Ledger. April 1914-October 1919.

Birmingham News. December 1913-February 1976.

Birmingham Post. January 1921-August 1937.

Birmingham Reporter. June 1915-August 1926.

Blocton Enterprise. March 1926-April 1926.

Chicago Daily Times. August 1937.

Clay County Advance. January 1888-July 1897.

Clay County Advocate. March 1900.

Clay County Standard. June 1898-November 1907.

Clay County Watchman. January 1885-July 1888.

Columbus Enquirer-Sun. July 1916-August 1916.

Columbus Ledger. May 1916-August 1916.

Congressional Quarterly Weekly. January 1981.

Crimson White. October 1904.

Daily Home. May 1987.

DeKalb County Herald. May 1926.

Dothan Weekly Eagle. October 1925-July 1926.

Fayette Banner. January 1925.

Florence Times-News. May 1926-June 1926.

Gadsden Times. July 1924-August 1926.

Greensboro Watchman. May 1964.

Huntsville Daily News. August 1926.

Labor Advocate. July 1908-August 1926.

Leeds Enterprise. July 1925.

Marion Times-Standard. March 1926-August 1926.

Mobile Item. February 1925.

Mobile Register. October 1916-October 1928.

Montgomery Advertiser. March 1907-January 1927.

Montgomery Times. May 1926.

Mountain Eagle. February 1920-June 1926.

Mountain Picket. March 1881-July 1881.

New York Times. October 1921-February 1998.

Opelika Daily News. August 1926.

Our Mountain Home. November 1927.

People's Party Advocate. February 1894-May 1900.

People's Advocate. March, 1924.

Phenix-Girard Journal. November 1925-April 1926.

Pittsburgh Post-Gazette. July 1937-August 1949.

Rocky Mountain News. June 1916.

Sand Mountain Banner. September 1925.

Selma Times-Journal. November 1925.

Shelby County Reporter. February 1924.

Southern Labor Review. December 1924-June 1926.

Standard. December 1904.

Summit County Journal. June 1916-November 1916.

Sumter County Journal. April 1926-June 1926.

Sylacauga Advance. March 1925-November 1927.

Talladega Daily Home. December 1924-November 1927.

The Central Democrat. August 1889.

Troy Messenger. February 1924-July 1926.

Secondary Sources

Abraham, Henry J. *Justices and Presidents: A Political History of Appointments to the Supreme Court.* New York: Oxford University Press, 1974.

Allen, Lee N. "The 1924 Underwood Campaign in Alabama." *Alabama Review* 9, no. 3 (July 1956) 176-187.

Allen, Lee N. "The Underwood Presidential Movement of 1924." Ph.D. diss., University of Pennsylvania, 1955.

Allen, Lee N. "The Woman Suffrage Movement, 1910-1920." *Alabama Review* 11, no. 2 (April 1958) 83-99.

Allen, Lee N. "Twenty Four Votes for Oscar W. Underwood." *Alabama Review* 48 (October 1995) 243-268.

Alsobrook, David Ernest. "Alabama's Port City: Mobile during the Progressive Era, 1896-1917." Ph.D. diss., Auburn University, 1983.

Anderson, Michael. "People in Cragford Still Talk about 1881 Lynching." *Daily Home,* 20 May 1987.

Archer, William. *Through Afro-America: An English Reading of the Race Problem.* London: Chapman & Hall, 1910.

Armes, Ethel. *The Story of Coal and Iron in Alabama.* 1910. Reprint. Leeds, AL: Beechwood Books, 1987.

Avrich, Paul. *The Haymarket Tragedy.* Princeton: Princeton University Press, 1984.

Ayres, Edward L. *Vengeance and Justice: Crime and Punishment in the 19th Century South.* New York: Oxford University Press, 1984.

Bagwell, David Ashley. "The 'Magical Process': The Sayre Election Law of 1893." *Alabama Review* (April 1972) 83-104.

Baker, Lewis. *The Percys of Mississippi: Politics and Literature in the New South.* Baton Rouge: Louisiana State University, 1983.

Barnes, Catherine A. *Journey from Jim Crow: The Desegregation of Southern Transit.* New York: Columbia University Press, 1983.

Beecher, John. *To Live and Die in Dixie.* Birmingham: Red Mountain Editions, 1966.

Berman, Daniel M. "Hugo Black, Southerner." *American University Law Review* 10, no. 1 (January 1961) 35-42.

Berman, Daniel M. "The Political Philosophy of Hugo L. Black." Ph.D. diss., Rutgers University, 1957

Bethea, Helen. *The Hillman Hospital: A Story of the Growth and Development of the First Hospital in Birmingham.* Birmingham: private press, 1928.

Bigelow, Martha Mitchell. "Birmingham's Carnival of Crime, 1871-1910." *Alabama Review* 3, no. 2 (April 1950) 123-33.

Black, Hugo L. "Dedicatory Address." *Journal of Legal Education* 5, no. 4 (1953) 417.

Black, Hugo L. "The Lawyer and Individual Freedom." *Tennessee Law Review* 21 (December 1950) 461-71.

Black, Hugo L. "There is a South of Union and Freedom." *Georgia Law Review* 2 (1967-68) 10-15.

Blee, Kathleen M. *Women of the Klan: Racism and Gender in the 1920s.* Berkeley: University of California Press, 1991.

Bond, Horace Mann. *Negro Education in Alabama: A Study in Cotton and Steel.* Reprint. New York: Antheneum, 1969.

Boykin, Edward. *Everything's Made for Love in This Man's World: Vignettes from the Life of Frank W. Boykin.* Mobile, AL: privately printed, 1973.

Boylan, Anne M. *Sunday School: The Formation of an American Institution, 1790-1880.* New Haven: Yale University Press, 1988.

Breedlove, Michael A. "Progressivism and Nativism: The Race for the Presidency of the City Commission of Birmingham, Alabama in 1917." *Journal of the Birmingham Historical Society* 6, no. 4 (July 1980) 3-20.

Brissenden, Paul F. *Earnings of Factory Workers, 1899 to 1927: An Analysis of Pay-roll Statistics.* Bureau of the Census. Census Monograph 10. Washington, DC: Government Printing Office, 1929.

Brooks, Samuel P. "The Tasks of Good Citizenship." In *Democracy in Earnest,* ed. James E. McCulloch. Washington: Southern Sociological Congress, 1918.

Brown, Dorothy M. *Mabel Walker Willebrandt: A Study of Power, Loyalty, and Law.* Knoxville: University of Tennessee, 1984.

Brown, Robert. "The Jurisdiction of the Federal Courts based on Diversity of Citizenship," *University of Pennsylvania Law Review* (December 1929) 179-94.

Brown. William Garrott. *A History of Alabama: For Use in Schools.* New York: University Publishing Company, 1903.

Brownell, Blaine A. "Birmingham, Alabama: New South City in the 1920's." *Journal of Southern History* 38 (February 1972) 21-48.

Bryan, William J. *The First Battle: A Story of the Campaign of 1896.* Chicago: W. B. Conkey Company, 1896.

Bryan, William Jennings. *The First Battle: A Story of the Campaign of 1896.* Chicago: W. B. Conkey Company 1896.

Burrows, John Howard. "The Social Philosophy and Theology of Alfred James Dickinson." Master's thesis, Samford University, 1970.

Carter, Dan T. "Prisons, Politics and Business: The Convict Lease System in the Post-Civil War South." Master's thesis, University of Wisconsin, 1964.

Carter, Dan T. *The Politics of Rage: George Wallace, the Origins of Conservatism, and the Transformation of American Politics.* New York: Simon & Schuster, 1995.

Chalmers, David. *Hooded Americanism: The History of the Ku Klux Klan.* New York: Franklin Watts, 1981.

Chapman, Carelton. Letter to author, U.d.

Childre, Winnie Wright. *Highlights and Shadows.* New York: Carlton Press, 1970.

Cicero, Marcus Tullius. *Brutus. On the Nature of Gods. On Divination. On Duties.* Translated by Hubert M. Poteat. Chicago: University of Chicago Press, 1950. Copy with notation on page 602 and inside back-cover, University of Alabama Law Library.

Clark, Elizabeth Boner. "The Abolition of the Convict Lease System in Alabama, 1913-1928." Master's thesis, University of Alabama, 1949.

Clark, Elizabeth Bonner. "The Abolition of Convict Lease System in Alabama, 1913-1928." Master's thesis, University of Alabama, 1949.

Clarke, James W. "Black-on-Black Violence." *Society* (July-August 1996) 46-50.

Clawson, Mary Ann. *Constructing Brotherhood: Class, Gender, and Fraternalism.* Princeton, Princeton University Press, 1989.

Clayton, Horace R., and George S. Mitchell. *Black Workers and the New Unions.* Chapel Hill: University of North Carolina, 1939.

Cleveland, Grover. *Good Citizenship.* Philadelphia: H. Altemus, 1908.

Cooper, Jerome A. "Mr. Justice Black of Alabama," *The Alabama Lawyer* (January 1972) 18.

Cooper, John Milton, Jr. *Pivotal Decades: The United States, 1900-1920.* New York: Norton, 1990.

Cornford, Francis MacDonald, trans. *The Republic of Plato.* New York: Oxford, 1945.

Couch, W. T., ed. *Culture in the South.* Chapel Hill: University of North Carolina Press, 1934.

Cowett, Mark. *Birmingham's Rabbi: Morris Newfield and Alabama, 1895-1940.* Tuscaloosa: University of Alabama Press, 1986.

Cramer, Carl. *Stars Fell on Alabama.* New York: Literary Guild, 1934.

Cullinan, Gerald. *The Post Office Department:* New York: F. A. Praeger, 1968.

David Burner, "Edward Terry Sanford," in Leon Friedman and Fred L. Israel, eds. *The Justices of the United States Supreme Court 1789-1978,* vol. III, New York, 1980, 2203-2209;

David, Henry. *The History of the Haymarket Affair: A Study in the American Social-Revolutionary and Labor Movements.* New York: Farrar & Rinehart, 1936.

Davis, Hazel Black. *Uncle Hugo: An Intimate Portrait of Mr. Justice Black.* Amarillo, TX: 1965.

Dawley, Alan. *Struggles for Justice: Social Responsibility and the Liberal State.* Cambridge: Harvard University Press, 1991.

DeMott, Benjamin. *The Trouble with Friendships: Why Americans Can't Think Straight about Race.* New York: Yale University Press, 1995.

Diener, Jacquelyn M. "President Warren G. Harding's Birmingham Address." *Journal of the Alabama Academy of Science,* no. 1 (1972) 63-77.

Dilliard, Irving. "Introduction." In *One Man's Stand for Freedom: Mr. Justice Black and the Bill of Rights: A Collection of His Supreme Court Opinions.* Edited by Dillard Irving. New York: Knopf, 1963.

Dollard, John. *Caste and Class in a Southern Town.* New Haven: Yale University Press, 1937.

Doster, James F. "Alabama's Political Revolution of 1904." *Alabama Review* 7, no. 2 (April 1954) 85-98.

Doster, James F. "Comer, Smith, and Jones: Alabama's Railroad War of 1907-1914," *Alabama Review* 10, no. 2 (April 1957) 83-95.

Doster, James F. *Railroads in Alabama Politics, 1875-1914.* Tuscaloosa: University of Alabama Press, 1957.

Doster, James F. "Railroad Domination in Alabama, 1885-1905." *Alabama Review* 7, no. 3 (July 1954) 186-198.

Doyle, Bertram W. *The Etiquette of Race Relations in the South.* Chicago: University of Chicago Press, 1937.

Draper, John William. *History of the American Civil War.* Volume 1. New York: Harper & Brothers, 1868.

Drummond, William F. "Utilization of Convict Labor in the South." Master's thesis, University of Alabama, 1933.

DuBois, W. E. B. *Black Reconstruction in America, 1860-1880.* New York: Atheneum, 1992.

DuBois, W. E. B. *The Souls of Black Folk.* New York: Bantam Books, 1989.

Duniway, Ben C. "The Poor Man in the Federal Courts" *Stanford Law Review* (June 1966) 1271-1280.

Dunne, Gerald T. *Hugo Black and the Judicial Revolution.* New York: Simon & Schuster, 1977.

Early, Gerald. "Whatever Happened to Integration." *Atlantic Monthly* (February 1997) 106-108.

Edmonds, Henry M. *A Parson's Notebook.* Birmingham: Elizabeth Agee's Bookshelf, 1961.

Elovitz, Mark H. *A Century of Jewish Life in Dixie: The Birmingham Experience.* Tuscaloosa: University of Alabama Press, 1974.

Emmet, Robert. "Protest Against Sentence As Traitor." In *The World's Great Speeches,* edited by Lewis Copeland and Lawrence W. Lamm. New York: Dover, 1973.

Evans, Clement A., ed. *Confederate Military History.* Volumes 7 and 12. Atlanta: Confederate Publishing Company, 1899.

Evans, Frank V., comp. "Coal Miners' Strike in the Alabama Coal District in the Year 1908: a compilation of facts which relates history." N.d. Alabama Coal Operators Association, B. B. Comer Papers. Typed manuscript.

Farmer, Hallie. *The Legislative Process in Alabama.* Tuscaloosa: University of Alabama Press, 1949.

Farmer, Margaret Page. "Governor Charles Henderson." *Alabama Review* 9, no. 4 (October 1956) 243-50.

Federal Writers Program (Alabama). *Alabama: A Guide to the Deep South.* Compiled by workers of the Writers' Program of the Works Projects Administration in the State of Alabama. New York: R. R. Smith, 1941.

Feldman, Glenn. "Conservative Progressivism: Antivigilantism in Post-World War I Alabama." *Alabama Review* 50, no. 1 (January 1997) 18-36.

Feldman, Glenn. *From Demagogue to Dixiecrat: Horace Wilkinson and the Politics of Race.* Lanham, MD: University Press of America, 1995.

Feldman, Glenn. "Lynching in Alabama, 1889-1921." *Alabama Review* 48, no. 2 (April 1995) 114-141.

Feldman, Glenn. "The Lynching of Willie Baird." *Alabama Heritage* 43 (Winter 1997) 22-33.

Feldman, Glenn. *Politics, Society, and the Klan in Alabama, 1915-1949.* Tuscaloosa: University of Alabama Press, 1999.

Fierce, Milfred C. *Slavery Revisited: Blacks and the Southern Convict Lease System, 1865-1933.* New York: CUNY Press, 1994.

Fish, Peter Graham. *The Politics of Federal Judicial Administration.* Princeton: Princeton University Press, 1973.

Fleming, Walter L. *Civil War and Reconstruction in Alabama.* Gloucester, Mass.: Peter Smith, 1949.

Fleming, Walter L. *Civil War and Reconstruction in Alabama.* New York: MacMillan, 1905.

Flynt, J. Wayne. *Dixie's Forgotten People.* Bloomington, IN: University of Indiana Press, 1979.

Flynt, Wayne. *Alabama in the Twentieth Century.* Tuscaloosa: University of Alabama Press, 2004.

Flynt, Wayne. "Organized Labor, Reform, and Alabama Politics." *Alabama Review* 23, no. 3 (July 1970) 163-180.

Flynt, Wayne. "Religion in the Urban South: The Divided Religious Mind of Birmingham, 1900-1930." *Alabama Review* 30, no. 2 (April 1977) 108-134.

Flynt, Wayne. *Poor But Proud: Alabama's Poor Whites.* Tuscaloosa, NC: University of North Carolina Press, 1989.

Foote, Shelby. *The Civil War, a Narrative: Fort Sumter to Perryville.* New York: Random House, 1958.

Foote, Shelby. *The Civil War, a Narrative: Fredericksburg to Meridian,* New York: Random House, 1963.

Foster, R. F. *W. B. Yeats: A Life I: The Apprentice Mage, 1865-1914.* New York: Oxford University Press, 1997.

Frank, John P. "Hugo Black: Little Man's Lawyer" *Progressive* (April 1946) 4.

Frank, John P. *Mr. Justice Black, the Man and His Opinions.* New York: Alfred A. Knopf, 1949.

Fredrickson, George M. *The Black Image in the White Mind and the Debate on Afro-American Character and Destiny, 1817-1914.* New York: Harper & Row, 1971.

Friedman, Leon, ed. *Southern Justice.* New York: Pantheon, 1965.

Fuller, Justin. "Henry F. DeBardeleben, Industrialist of the New South." *Alabama Review* 39, no. 1 (January 1986) 3-18.

Furniss, Norman F. *The Fundamentalist Controversy, 1918-1931.* New York: Harper & Row, 1963.

Gaston, Paul. *New South Creed: A Study in Southern Mythmaking.* New York: Knopf, 1970.

Gilbert, William E. "The First Administration of Governor Bibb Graves, 1927-1930." Master's thesis, University of Alabama.

Going, Allen J. *Bourbon Democrat in Alabama, 1874-1890.* Tuscaloosa: University of Alabama Press, 1951.

Goldberg, Robert A. *Hooded Empire: The Ku Klux Klan in Colorado.* Urbana: University of Illinois Press, 1981.

Goldstein, Harold Joseph. "Labor Unrest in the Birmingham District, 1871-1894." Master's thesis, University of Alabama.

Goodrich, Gillian. "Romance and Reality: The Birmingham Suffragists, 1982-1920." *Journal of the Birmingham Historical Society* 5, no. 3 (January 1978) 5-21.

Grady, Henry. *The New South: Writings and Speeches of Henry Grady.* Savannah: Beehive Press, 1971.

Griffin, John. "The Leadership of LeRoy Collins." *Southern Changes* 2, no. 1 (1989) 17-23.

Grimshaw, Allen D., ed. *Racial Violence in the United States.* Chicago: Aldine, 1969.

Gross, Jimmie Frank. "Strikes in the Coal, Steel, and Railroad Industries in Birmingham." Master's thesis, Auburn University, 1962.

Hackney, Sheldon. "The Clay County Origins of Mr. Justice Black: The Populist as Insider" *Alabama Law Review* 36, no. 3, 835-843.

Hackney, Sheldon. *Populism to Progressivism in Alabama.* Princeton: University of Princeton Press, 1969.

Hall, Jacquelyn Dowd. *Revolt Against Chivalry: Jessie Daniel Ames and the Women's Campaign Against Lynching.* New York: Columbia University Press, 1979.

Hamilton, Virginia Van der Veer. *Hugo Black: The Alabama Years.* Baton Rouge: Louisiana State University Press, 1972.

Hamilton, Virginia, Van der Veer. "Hugo Black: The Road to the Court." *Southwestern University Law Review* 9, no. 4, (1977), 859-888.

Hand, Rev. J. E., ed. *Good Citizenship.* London: George Allen, 1899.

Hare, Frances H. *A Historical Sketch of the Birmingham Bar, 1872-1907.* N.d. University of Alabama Library, Special Collections, Tuscaloosa.

Harris, Carl V. "Annexation Struggles and Political Power in Birmingham, 1890-1910." *Alabama Review* 27, no. 3 (July 1974) 163-184.

Harris, Carl V. *Political Power in Birmingham, 1871-1921.* Knoxville: University of Tennessee Press, 1977.

Hepner, Walter R., and Francis K. Hepner. *The Good Citizen: A Textbook in Social and Vocational Civics.* Boston: Houghton Mifflin, 1924.

Higginbotham, A. Leon, Jr. *Shades of Freedom: Racial Politics and Presumptions of the American Legal Process.* New York: Oxford University Press, 1996.

Higham, John. *Send These to Me: Jews and Other Immigrants in Urban America.* New York: Atheneum, 1995.

"History of the First Baptist Church of Ashland, Alabama." N.d. First Baptist Church, Ashland, AL. Mimeographed.

Hollis, Daniel W. *An Alabama Newspaper Tradition: Grover C. Hall and the Hall Family.* Tuscaloosa: University of Alabama Press, 1983.

Holmes, William F. "Moonshiners and Whitecaps in Alabama, 1893. *Alabama Review* 34, no. 1 (January 1981) 31-49.

Howard L. Holley, "Medical Education in Alabama," *Alabama Review* 7, no.4 (October 1954) 245-264.

Howington, Arthur F. "John Barley Corn Subdued: The Enforcement of Prohibition in Alabama," *Alabama Review* 23, no. 3 (July 1970) 212-225.

Jackson, Kenneth T. *The Ku Klux Klan in the City, 1915-1930.* New York: Oxford University Press, 1967.

Jenkins, Mollie Beck. "The Social Work of the Tennessee Coal Iron and Railroad Company." Master's thesis, University of Alabama, 1929.

Jenkins, William D. *Steel Valley Klan: The Ku Klux Klan in Ohio's Mahoning Valley.* Kent, Ohio: Kent State University Press, 1990.

Jensen, Joan M. *The Price of Vigilance.* Chicago: Rand McNally & Company, 1968.

Johnson, Evans C. "Oscar, W. Underwood and the Senatorial Campaign of 1920." *Alabama Review* 21, no. 1 (January 1968) 3-20.

Johnson, Evans C. *Oscar Underwood: A Political Biography.* Baton Rouge: Louisiana State University, 1980.

Johnson, Gerald W. *Andrew Jackson: An Epic in Homespun.* New York: Minton, Balch & Company, 1927.

Johnson, James Weldon. *Along This Way: The Autobiography of James Weldon Johnson.* New York: Viking, 1933.

Jones, Terry Lawrence. "Attitudes of Alabama Baptists towards Negroes, 1890-1914." Master's thesis, Samford University, 1968.

Joy, Edna R., and James P. Sloan, "Andrew Johnson: Seventeenth President of the U.S." In *The Scrapbook: A Compilation of Historical Facts about Places and Events of Laurens County, South Carolina.* Laurens, SC: Laurens County Historical Society, 1982.

Kammen, Michael G. *Mystic Chords of Memory: The Transformation of Tradition in American Culture.* New York: Knopf, 1991.

Kelly, Brian. *Race, Class, and Power in the Alabama Coalfields, 1908-21.* Urbana, IL: University of Illinois, 2001.

Kennedy, John F. *Profiles in Courage.* New York: Harper, 1955.

Kenny, Michael. *Catholic Culture in Alabama: Centenary Story of Spring Hill College.* New York: America Press, 1931.

Kertzer, David I. *Ritual, Politics, and Power.* New Haven: Yale University Press, 1988.

Key, V. O., Jr. *Southern Politics in State and Nation.* New York: Vintage Books, 1949.

Knowles, Marjorie Fine. "The Legal Status of Women in Alabama: A Crazy Quilt," 29 *Alabama Law Review* 427-502.

Koenig, Louis W. *Bryan: A Political Biography of William Jennings Bryan.* New York: Putnam, 1971.

Konstan, David. *Friendship in the Classical World.* New York: Cambridge University Press, 1997.

Kousser, J. Morgan. *The Shaping of Southern Politics: Suffrage Restriction and the Establishment of the One-Party South, 1880-1910.* New Haven: Yale University Press, 1974.

Kytle, Jack. "A Dead Convict Don't Cost Nothin'." In James Seay Brown, Jr., ed., *Up Before Daylight: Life Histories from the Alabama Writers Project, 1938-1939.* Tuscaloosa: University of Alabama Press, 1982.

Kytle, Jack. "I'm Allus Hongry." In *Up Before Daylight: Life Histories from the Alabama Writers Project, 1938-1939.* Tuscaloosa: University of Alabama Press, 1982.

Landreth, Helen. *The Pursuit of Robert Emmet.* New York: McGraw Hill, 1948.

Lassman, Peter, and Ronald Speirs, eds. *Max Weber: Political Writings.* Cambridge: Cambridge University Press, 1994.

Lay, Shawn. ed. *The Invisible Empire in the West: Towards a New Historical Appraisal of the Ku Klux Klan of the 1920s.* Chicago: University of Illinois Press, 1992.

Leighton, George R. *Five Cities: The Story of Their Youth and Old Age.* New York: Harper & Brothers, 1939.

Lerner, Max. "Hugo Black—A Personal History." *The Nation* (October 9, 1937) 367-369.

Lessley, Betty R., and Vern Scott. "150th Anniversary of the Founding of Talladega County, featuring the Talladega County Courthouse." Talladega, 1982. Pamphlet.

Letwin, Daniel. *The Challenge of Interracial Unionism: Alabama Coal Miners, 1878-1921.* Chapel Hill: University of North Carolina, 1998.

Letwin, Daniel. "Interracial Unionism, Gender, and 'Social Equality' in the Alabama Coal Fields, 1878-1908." *Journal of Southern History* 61, no. 3 (August 1995) 519-554.

Leuchtenburg, William E. *The Perils of Prosperity, 1914-1932.* Chicago: University of Chicago Press, 1958.

Lewis, W. David. *Sloss Furnaces and the Rise of the Birmingham District: An Industrial Epic.* Tuscaloosa: University of Alabama Press, 1994.

Lichtenstein, Alex. *Twice the Work of Free Labor: The Political Economy of Convict Labor in the South.* New York: Verso, 1996.

Lieberwitz, Risa. "The Use of Criminal Conspiracy Prosecutions to Restrict Freedom of Speech." In *In the Shadow of the Statue of Liberty: Immigrants, Workers, and Citizens in the American Republic, 1880-1920,* edited by Marianne Debouzy. Urbana and Chicago, University of Illinois, 1992.

Looney, Ginny. "Black's Early Years as an Attorney." Unpublished memorandum on Hugo Black's published appellate cases, 1985. Photocopy.

Lovett, Rose Gibbons. "Centennial History of St. Paul's Parish, Birmingham, Alabama, 1872-1972." N.p., 1972.

MacLean, Nancy, *Behind the Mask of Chivalry: The Making of the Second Ku Klux Klan.* New York, Oxford University Press, 1994.

Maguire, J. "Poverty and Civil Litigation," *Harvard Law Review* 36 no. 4 (February 1923) 361-404.

Maine, Henry Sumner. *Ancient Law.* New York: MacMillan, 1883.

Malsch, Brownson. *"Lone Wolf" Gonzaullas, Texas Ranger.* Norman, OK: University of Oklahoma, 1998.

Mancini, Matthew J. *One Dies, Get Another: Convict Leasing in the American South, 1866-1928.* Columbia, SC: University of South Carolina Press, 1996.

Marshall, F. Ray. *Labor in the South.* Cambridge: Harvard University Press, 1967.

Marshall, Ray. "The Negro in Southern Unions." In *The Negro and the American Labor Movement,* ed. Julius Jacobson. Garden City: Doubleday, 1968.

Martin, Henry Pelham. "A History of Politics in Clay County during the Period of Populism from 1886 to 1896." Master's thesis, University of Alabama, 1936.

Martin, Joel W. *Sacred Revolt: The Muskogees' Struggle for a New World.* Boston: Beacon Press, 1991.

Mayfield, Sarah. *Exiles from Paradise: Zelda and Scott Fitzgerald.* New York: Delacorte Press, 1971.

McCain, John R. "Interesting Bits of Clay County History." *Clay County Historical Society Newsletter* 6, no. 9 (1995).

McGerr, Michael. "Political Style and Women's Power, 1830-1930." *Journal of American History* 77, no. 4 (December 1990) 864-885.

McGuffey, William H. *McGuffey's Fourth Eclectic Reader.* New York: Antwerp, Bragg & Co., 1879.

McKiven, Henry M., Jr. *Iron and Steel: Class, Race, and Community in Birmingham, Alabama, 1875-1920.* Chapel Hill: University of North Carolina, 1995.

McMillan, Malcolm C. *Yesterday's Birmingham.* Miami: Seamann, 1975.

McMillan, Malcolm. *Constitutional Development in Alabama, 1798-1901: A Study in Politics, the Negro, and Sectionalism.* Spartanburg, S.C.: Reprint Company, 1978.

McMillen, Neil R. *Dark Journey: Black Mississippians in the Age of Jim Crow.* Urbana: University of Illinois, 1989.

McWilliams, Tennant S. "The City of Mobile, the South, and Richard V. Taylor." *Alabama Review* 46, no. 3 (July 1993) 163-179.

Meador, Daniel J. "Justice Black and His Law Clerks." *Alabama Law Review* 15 (1962-63) 57-63.

Meador, Daniel J. *Mr. Justice Black and His Books.* Charlottesville: University of Virginia, 1974.

Mecklin, John Moffatt. *The Ku Klux Klan: A Study of the American Mind.* New York: Harcourt Brace, 1924.

Meier, August, and Elliott Rudwick. "The Boycott Movement against Jim Crow Streetcars in the South, 1900-1906," *Journal of American History* 55, no. 4 (March 1969) 756-775.

Milford, Nancy. *Zelda: A Biography.* New York: Harper & Row, 1970.

Milton, George F. "The South—and 1924." *Outlook* (2 January 1924) 29-30.

Mix, Henry H. "The Life of James J. Mayfield." Master's thesis, University of Alabama, 1935.

Montgomery, David. "Violence and the Struggle for Unions in the South, 1880-1930." In *Perspectives on the American South: An Annual Review of Society, Politics and Culture.* Vol. I, Edited by Merle Black and J. S. Reed. New York: Gordon & Breach, 1981.

Moore, Albert B. *History of Alabama.* Tuscaloosa: Alabama Book Store, 1935.

Moore, Leonard J. "Historical Interpretations of the 1920s Klan: The Traditional View and the Populist Revision." *Journal of Social History* 24, no. 2 (1990) 341-358.

Morrison, Frank. "Labor's Challenge to Democracy." In *Democracy in Earnest,* ed. James E. McCulloch. Washington: Southern Sociological Congress, 1918.

Moyer, Forrest T. et al. "Injury Experience in Coal Mining, 1948." Bulletin 509. Bureau of Mines, U.S. Department of Interior. Washington: U.S Government Printing Office, 1948.

Murphy, Paul L. "The Early Social and Political Philosophy of Hugo Black: Liquor As a Test Case." *Alabama Law Review* 36, no. 3 (Spring 1985) 861-879.

Murray, Pauli, ed. *State Laws on Race and Color.* Washington, DC, 1950.

Myrdal, Gunnar. *An American Dilemma: The Negro Problem and Modern Democracy.* New York: Harper & Row, 1944.

Newby, I. A. *Jim Crow's Defense: Anti-Negro Thought in America, 1900-1930.* Baton Rouge: University of Louisiana Press, 1965.

Newby, I. A. *Plain Folk in the New South.* Baton Rouge: Louisiana State University Press, 1989.

Newman, Roger K. *Hugo Black.* New York: Pantheon Books, 1994.

Noah Webster's American Spelling Book. Reprint. New York: Teachers College, 1958.

Norrell, Robert J. *The Italians: From Bisacquino to Birmingham* (booklet). Birmingham: Birmingfind, 1981.

Norrell, Robert J. *James Bowron: The Autobiography of a New South Industrialist.* Chapel Hill: University of North Carolina, 1991.

Oates, Stephen B. *With Malice Towards None: The Life of Abraham Lincoln*. New York: Harper & Row, 1977.

Odum, Howard W. *Southern Regions of the United States*. Chapel Hill, NC: University of North Carolina Press, 1936.

Oshinsky, David M. *"Worse Than Slavery": Parchman Farm and the Ordeal of Jim Crow Justice*. New York: Free Press, 1996.

Owen, Emily. "The Career of Thomas E. Kilby in Local and State Politics." Master's thesis, University of Alabama, 1942.

Owen, Marie B. *Our State—Alabama*. Montgomery: Birmingham Printing Co., 1927.

Owen, Thomas McAdory. *History of Alabama and Dictionary of Alabama Biography*. Spartanburg, SC: Reprint Company, 1978.

Patterson, Joyce Ann. "History of Clay County, Alabama." Bachelor's thesis, Jacksonville State University, 1970.

Peloubet, F. N., and Amos R. Wells. *Select Notes on the International Sunday School Lessons, 1925*. Boston: W. A. Wilde Company, 1924.

Pickett, Albert James. *History of Alabama and incidentally of Georgia and Mississippi from the Earliest Period*, Birmingham. Reprint. Tuscaloosa: Willo Publishing Company, 1962.

Pruden, Durward. "The Opposition of the Press to the Ascension of Hugo Black to the Supreme Court of the United States." Master's thesis, New York University, 1946.

Pruitt, Paul M., Jr. "The Killing of Father Coyle: Private Tragedy, Public Shame." *Alabama Heritage* (Fall 1993) 24-37.

Rice, Arnold S. "The Southern Wing of the Ku Klux Klan in American Politics." Ph.D. diss., Indiana University, 1959.

Rikard, Marlene Hunt, "George Gordon Crawford: Man of the New South." *Alabama Review* 31, no. 3, (July 1978) 163-181.

Rikard, Marlene Hunt. "Take Everything You Are . . . And Give it Away": Pioneer Industrial Social Workers at TCI." *Journal of the Birmingham Historical Society* 7, no. 2 (November 1981) 30-32.

Rodabaugh, Karl. "Kolbites versus Bourbons: The Alabama Gubernatorial Election of 1892." *Alabama Historical Quarterly* 37, no. 4 (Winter 1975) 275-321.

Rodell, Fred. "Justice Hugo Black." *American Mercury* 59, no. 248 (August 1944) 135-143.

Rogers, William Warren, et al. *Alabama: The History of a Deep South State*. Tuscaloosa: University of Alabama Press, 1994.

Rogers, William Warren. *The One-Gallused Rebellion: Agrarianism in Alabama, 1865-1896*. Baton Rouge: Louisiana State University Press, 1970.

Ross, W. D., trans. *The Pocket Aristotle*. New York: Pocket Books, 1968.

Rowland, Dunbar. "Good Citizenship: The First Aim and Object of Education." Commencement address, All Saints College, 2 June 1920. Vicksburg, Miss.

"Salute to Justice Black." *The Nation* (21 August 1937) 183-184.

Samway, Patrick H. *Walker Percy: A Life*. New York: Farrar, Strauss & Giroux, 1997.

Sandlin, Winfred G. "Lycurgus Breckenridge Musgrove." *Alabama Review* 20, no. 3 (July 1967), 205-215.

Schwartz, Bernard. *Super Chief: Earl Warren and His Supreme Court: A Judicial Biography*. New York, New York University Press, 1983.

Schwartz, Bernard. *The Supreme Court: Constitutional Revolution in Retrospect*. New York: Roland Press, 1957.

Scott, Ann Firor Scott. *The Southern Lady: From Pedestal to Politics, 1830-1930*. Chicago: University of Chicago Press, 1970.

Scott, Verner Max (Vern). "Why the 1920's Ku Klux Klan?" *Talladega County Historical Association Newsletter* (January 1989).

Sellers, James B. *The Prohibition Movement in Alabama, 1702-1943*. Chapel Hill: University of North Carolina Press, 1943.

Shelton, Herbert (Robert Lee Black). *The Deserter,* Talladega: Press of Our Mountain Home, 1900.

Snell, William R. "Fiery Crosses in the Roaring Twenties: Activities of the Revised Klan in Alabama, 1915-1930." *Alabama Review* 23, no. 4 (October 1970) 256-276.

Snell, William Robert. "The Ku Klux Klan in Jefferson County, Alabama, 1916-1930." Master's thesis, Samford University, 1967.

Spencer, Leon P. Letter to author, 6 May 1985.

Springen, D. K. "A Rhetorical Analysis of the Speaking of Oscar Underwood in His 1924 Campaign for the Democratic Presidential Nomination." Ph.D. diss., State University of Iowa, 1962.

Stallworth, Clarke. "Hugo Black: The Boy and Man." *Birmingham News,* 22 February 1971.

Sterne, Ellin. "Prostitution in Birmingham, Alabama, 1890-1925." Master's thesis, Samford University, 1977.

Straw, Richard A. "Soldiers and Miners in a Strike Zone: Birmingham, 1908." *Alabama Review* 39, no. 1 (October 1985) 287-308.

Straw, Richard A. "The United Mine Workers of America and the 1920 Coal Strike in Alabama." *Alabama Review* 28, no. 2 (April 1975) 104-128.

Straw, Richard A. "The Collapse of Biracial Unionism: The Alabama Coal Strike of 1908." *Alabama Historical Quarterly* 37, no. 2 (Summer 1975) 92-114.

Sweeney, Charles P. "Bigotry Turns to Murder." *Nation* (31 August 1921) 232.

Taft, Philip. *Organizing Dixie: Alabama Workers in the Industrial Era.* Revised and edited by Gary M. Fink. (Westport, CN: Greenwood Press, 1981.

Taft, Philip. *Organizing Dixie: Alabama Workers in the Industrial Era.* Westport, CT: Greenwood Press, 1981.

Talladega County Historical Association Newsletter. April 1985.

Tani, Eugene P., and David L. Wilson. *The Presidency of Warren G. Harding.* Topeka: University of Kansas Press, 1977.

Taylor, Kendall. *Sometimes Madness is Wisdom: Zelda and Scott Fitzgerald: A Marriage.* New York: Ballantine Books, 2001.

The American Bench: Judges of the Nation. Minneapolis: Reginald Bishop Forster & Associates, 1977.

"The Education of Hugo Black." *The Nation* (2 October 1937) 337-338.

The Southerner, a Biographical Encyclopedia of Southern People. Vol. 1. New Orleans: Southern Editors Association, 1944-1945.

Thomas, Mary Martha. *The New Woman in Alabama: Social Reform and Suffrage, 1890-1920.* Tuscaloosa: University of Alabama Press, 1992.

Thornton, J. Mills. *Dividing Lines: Municipal Politics and the Struggle for Civil Rights in Montgomery, Birmingham, and Selma.* Tuscaloosa: University of Alabama Press, 2002.

Thornton, J. Mills. "Hugo Black and the Golden Age." In *Justice Hugo Black and Modern America.* Edited by Tony Freyer. Tuscaloosa: University of Alabama Press, 1990.

Tolson, Jay. *Pilgrim in the Ruins: A Life of Walker Percy.* New York: Simon & Schuster, 1992.

Torodash, Martin. "Underwood and the Tariff." *Alabama Review* 20, no. 2 (April 1967) 115-130.

Tuttle, William M., Jr. *Race Riot, Chicago in the Red Summer of 1919.* New York: Atheneum, 1970.

U.S. Catholic Conference. "The Martyrs of the United States of America." 1941. U.S. Catholic Conference, Washington, DC.

Vance, Rupert B. *Human Geography of the South: A Study in Regional Resources and Human Adequacy.* Chapel Hill: University of North Carolina Press, 1935.

Vick, Mary-Helen. "A Survey of the Governing Body of Birmingham, Alabama, 1910-1964." Master's thesis, Alabama College, 1965.

Vickrey, James Frank, Jr. "A Rhetorical Analysis of the Issues of the Ku Klux Klan in the Speeches of Senator Oscar W. Underwood in the 1924 Presidential Campaign." Master's thesis, Auburn University, 1965.

Wade, Wyn Craig. *The Fiery Cross: The Ku Klux Klan in America.* New York: Simon & Schuster, 1987.

Waid, Candace. "Julia Tutwiler: In the Vision of Her Time, 1841-1916." 1970. Women's Studies paper, University of Alabama. Photocopy.

Ward, Robert D., and William W. Rogers. *Labor Revolt in Alabama: The Great Strike of 1894.* Tuscaloosa: University of Alabama Press, 1965.

Webb, Samuel L. "Hugo Black, Bibb Graves, and the Ku Klux Klan: A Revisionist View of the 1926 Alabama Democratic Primary." *Alabama Review* 57, no.4 (October 2004) 243-273.

Webb, Samuel L. *Two-Party Politics in the One-Party South: Alabama's Hill Country, 1874-1920.* Tuscaloosa: University of Alabama, 1997.

White, Walter. *Rape and Faggot: A Biography of Judge Lynch.* New York: Knopf, 1929.

Wiggins, Sarah Woolfolk. *The Scalawags in Alabama Politics, 1865-1881.* Tuscaloosa: University of Alabama Press, 1977.

Wilson, Charles Reagan. "Jim Crow." In *The Encyclopedia of Southern Culture,* edited by Charles Reagan Wilson and William Ferris. Chapel Hill, NC: University of North Carolina Press, 1989.

Woodward, C. Vann. *Origins of the New South, 1877-1913.* Baton Rouge: Louisiana State University Press, 1971.

Woodward, C. Vann. *The Strange Career of Jim Crow.* New York: Oxford University Press, 1966.

Work, Monroe. *The Negro Yearbook: An Annual Encyclopedia of the Negro, 1919-1921.* Tuskegee: Negro Year Book Publishing Company, Tuskegee Institute, 1921.

Wright, Gavin. *Old South, New South: Revolutions in the Southern Economy since the Civil War.* New York: Basic Books, 1986.

Wright, William Clayton. "From Indians to Iron: A History of Bessemer, Alabama to 1917." Master's thesis, University of Montevallo, 1970.

Wyatt-Brown, Bertram. *The House of Percy: Honor, Melancholy, and Imagination in a Southern Family.* New York: Oxford University Press, 1994.

Yeats, W. B. "September 1913." In *The Collected Poems of W. B. Yeats,* edited by Richard J. Finneran. New York: Simon & Schuster, 1996.

Yeats, W. B. "The Municipal Gallery Revisited." In *The Collected Poems of W. B. Yeats.* New York: Simon & Schuster, 1996.

Zangrande, Robert L. *The NAACP Crusade against Lynching, 1909-1950.* Philadelphia: Temple University Press, 1980.

Court Cases

Adamson v. California, 332 U.S. 46 (1947).

Alabama Fuel & Iron Co. v. Benenate, 66 So. 942 (1914).

Beecher v. Henderson, 58 So. 805 (1912).

Chambers v Florida, 309 U.S. 227 (1940).

Clinton Mining Co. v. Bradford, 69 So. 4 (1915).

Clinton Mining Co. v. Bradford, 76 So. 74 (1917).

Continental Casualty Co. v. Ogburn, 64 So. 619 (1914).

Crosby v. Nunnally Co., 95 So. 343 (1923).

Erie Railroad Co. v. Tompkins, 304 U.S. 64 (1938).

Ex parte Brown, 91 So. 306 (1921).

Ex parte Young, 209 U.S. 123 (1908).

Hamilton v. Alabama, 156 So. 2d 926 (1963).

Hamilton v. Alabama, 376 U.S. 650 (1964).

Hemmelweit v. State ex rel. Dedge, 200 Ala. 203 (1917).

Hines v. Miniard, 86 So. 23 (1920).

Hines v. Miniard, 94 So. 302 (1922).

In re: Montevallo Mining Co. 294 F. 171 (1923).

Louisville & Nashville R. R. Co. v. King, 73 So. 456 (1916).

Lewis v. Roberts, 267 U.S. 467 (1925).

Louisville & N.R. Co. v. Cornelius, 60 So. 740 (1912).

Louisville & N.R. R. Co. v. Cornelius, 62 So. 710 (1913).

Mills v. Alabama, 384 U.S. 214 (1966).

Norwood Transportation Co. v. Crossett, 92 So. 461 (1922).

Piggly-Wiggly Alabama Co. v. Rickles, 103 So. 860 (1925).

Purity Extract and Tonic Company v. Lynch, 226 U.S. 192 (1912).

Riddle et al. v. U.S, 279 F. 216 (1922).

Santa Clara County v. Southern Pacific Railroad Company, 118 U.S. 394 (1886).

Slaughter-House Cases, 83 U.S. 36 (1873).

Sloss-Sheffield S & I Co. v. Edwards, 70 So. 285 (1915).

Southern Railway Co. v. Dickson, 100 So. 665 (1924).

State ex re. Black v. Delaye, 68 So. 993 (1915).

State ex rel. Gaston v. Black, 74 So. 387 (1917).

State of Alabama v. Montevallo Mining Co., 278 F. 989 (1922).

Tennessee Coal, Iron, & R. Co. v. Cottrell, 55 So. 791 (1911);

Twining v. New Jersey, 211 U.S. 78 (1908).

U.S. v. Cruikshank, 92 U.S. 542 (1875).

United States Fidelity and Guaranty Co. v. Millonas, 89 So. 732 (1921).

United States v. Barnett, 376 U.S. 681 (1964).

United States v. Stanley et al. (Civil Rights Cases), 109 U.S. 3 (1883).

Ware v. State, 108 So. 645 (1926).

Whistle Bottling Co. v. Searson, 92 So. 657 (1922).

Whitman's Fifth Ave. Garage Co. v. Ricks, 101 So. 53 (1924).

Woodruff v. State, 54 So. 240 (1911).

Woodward Iron Co. v. Thompson, 88 So. 438 (1921).

Woodward Iron Co. v. Thompson, 95 So. 270 (1923).

Index